ENCYCLOPEDIA OF THE AMERICAN ARMED FORCES

ENCYCLOPEDIA OF THE AMERICAN ARMED FORCES

VOLUME I

Alan Axelrod

☑® Facts On File, Inc.

Encyclopedia of the American Armed Forces

Copyright © 2005 by Alan Axelrod

Facts On File, Inc.
132 West 31st Street
New York NY 10001

Library of Congress Cataloging-in-Publication Data

Axelrod, Alan, 1952–
Encyclopedia of the American armed forces / Alan Axelrod.
      p. cm.
Includes bibliographical references and index.
ISBN 0-8160-4700-6 (hardcover set : alk. paper) —ISBN 0-8160-6604-3 (v. 1: alk. paper)—
ISBN 0-8160-6605-1 (v. 2: alk. paper)
1. United States—Armed Forces—
Encyclopedias. 2. United States—Armed Forces—Biography—Encyclopedias. I. Title.

UA23.A875 2005
355'.00973'03—dc22   2004020549

You can find Facts On File on the World Wide Web at http://www.factsonfile.com

Text design by Joan M. Toro
Text design adapted by Erika K. Arroyo
Cover design by Ana Alekseyeva

Printed in the United States of America

VB FOF 10 9 8 7 6 5 4 3 2 1

This book is printed on acid-free paper.

Contents

FLO

List of Entries
UNITED STATES ARMY

List of Entries
UNITED STATES AIR FORCE

Acknowledgments

I wish to acknowledge the authors (many of whom are anonymous) of the books, articles, and online documents listed in the bibliography. I wish also to thank my Facts On File editor, Owen Lancer, for his contributions to this long and demanding work.

Deserving of far more acknowledgment and thanks than can be rendered here are, of course, the men and women of the United States Armed Forces, who, as I believe this encyclopedia attests, combine consummate professionalism with undaunted courage.

—Alan Axelrod
Atlanta, Georgia

Introduction

Bookstores and libraries are amply stocked with works devoted to American military history, including a wide variety of handbooks and biographical dictionaries. Narrative histories of the service branches are also available in some abundance, most of them quite specialized, a few more general and comprehensive. *Encyclopedia of the American Armed Forces,* however, is the only A-to-Z reference work devoted to each of the service branches, the United States Army, Air Force, Navy, and Marine Corps, and written from both historical and current points of view. Moreover, the encyclopedia provides comprehensive information on the institutional aspects of the services—organization, specialized offices and bureaus, relevant legislation—that is unavailable in other works intended for the nonmilitary professional and general reader. In addition to articles on the history of each service; on command organization, ranks, grades, and rates; on leaders and heroes; missions and roles; and special nomenclature and terminology, there is also extensive treatment of the weapons and equipment of each service—from small arms, to fighting vehicles, to aircraft, to the major types and classes of U.S. Navy ships—and every major fort, base, and installation.

Encyclopedia of the American Armed Forces is intended for use by researchers and students, as well as military professionals, military buffs, and the general reference reader. Most subjects of sufficient importance and relevance to merit inclusion in the encyclopedia are treated in separate, individual entries; however, four subject categories are treated more comprehensively.

Acronyms, for better or worse, have long been pervasive elements of U.S. military vocabulary. The most common acronyms used in each service are gathered and defined in an appendix. Entries on military bases, camps, forts, stations, and other major installations are grouped together in the following entries: FORTS AND OTHER INSTALLATIONS (U.S. ARMY), AIR FORCE BASES (U.S. AIR FORCE), bases, camps, and other installations (U.S. Marine Corps), and bases, stations, and other installations (U.S. Navy).

Discussions of individual decorations and medals (including badges and ribbons) are grouped together in the DECORATIONS AND MEDALS entry for each of the service volumes.

Ranks and grades are treated together in a RANKS AND GRADES entry for each of the services.

A work such as this draws on many sources for its information. The most important are listed in the bibliography. Because the *Encyclopedia of the American Armed Forces* is so largely focused on the modern army, air force, marines, and navy, including their current organization and equipment, many references are to official Web sites and other online sources, which generally present the most up-to-date information. Every effort has been made to list online sources that are most likely to remain readily available over the years.

United States Army

Entries A–Z

A

AAWS-M Javelin See ANTIARMOR WEAPONS.

Aberdeen Proving Ground See FORTS AND OTHER INSTALLATIONS.

Abrams, Creighton Williams, Jr. (1914–1974) *U.S. Army general*

Best known for his service in the VIETNAM WAR, Abrams was born in Springfield, Massachusetts, and graduated from the UNITED STATES MILITARY ACADEMY in 1936. Commissioned a second lieutenant of cavalry, he was promoted to captain in 1940 and transferred to armor. During WORLD WAR II in the European theater, he commanded the 37th Tank Battalion and, at the Battle of the Bulge, led the 4th Armored Division into Bastogne on December 6, 1944, successfully rescuing the surrounded 101ST AIRBORNE DIVISION.

After the war, Abrams was promoted to temporary colonel and was named director of the Armor School at Fort Knox, Kentucky. He served in this post from 1946 to 1948, then graduated from the COMMAND AND GENERAL STAFF COLLEGE in 1949 and saw service in the KOREAN WAR, as CHIEF OF STAFF, successively, for the I, X, and IX Corps during June 1950 through July 1953. After the cease-fire in 1953, Abrams attended the prestigious U.S. ARMY WAR COLLEGE and in 1956 was promoted to brigadier general. Appointed deputy assistant chief of staff for RESERVE COMPONENTS on the ARMY GENERAL STAFF, he was promoted to major general in May 1960 and was commander of the 3rd Armored Division from 1960 to 1962. In 1963, Abrams was promoted to lieutenant general and assigned to command V Corps in Germany. A year later, promoted to general, he was named army vice chief of staff.

As the Vietnam War escalated, Abrams was appointed deputy commander of the U.S. Military Assistance Command Vietnam (MACV) in May 1967. He directed the successful defense against the massive Tet Offensive (January 30–February 29, 1968) and was subsequently named to succeed General WILLIAM CHILDS WESTMORELAND as commander of U.S. MACV. Abrams abandoned Westmoreland's search and destroy approach, adopting instead a plan of patrol and ambush that was better suited to the guerrilla nature of the conflict. Abrams oversaw the "Vietnamization" phase (the transfer of the burden of the war from U.S. to South Vietnamese forces) of the war until July 1972, when he was appointed chief of staff of the army. He held this post until his death.

Acquisition Support Center (ASC)

The ASC is a field-operating agency under the assistant secretary of the army for acquisition, logistics and technology. Its mission is to support the readiness of warfighters by developing a world-class professional acquisition workforce, effectively acquiring and stewarding resources, and providing the best possible products and services.

The ASC is composed of the following divisions designed to support Army Acquisition Corps members in furthering their professional development and education:

Career Management Division: Develops career policies and programs, and provides career management support to the workforce. This support serves to ensure that the warfighter receives quality service. It also provides a career guide that enables and enriches the workforce both professionally and personally, contributing to improved retention of acquisition expertise in the army.

Contracting Career Program Office (CP-14): Manages the Army Contracting and Acquisition Career Program (CP-14), which provides a comprehensive career management framework for over 5,000 contracting and acquisition professionals.

Human Resources Management Division: Performs Major Army Command (MAJCOM) functions related to agency civilian and military personnel management.

Logistics Management Proponency Office (CP-13/17): Recruits, trains, and educates civilians in supply management and materiel maintenance management to support all army logistics operations.

Operations Division: Ensures the ASC's administrative requirements are carried out.

Program Structure and Information Analysis Division: Supports the senior army acquisition leadership and the acquisition community by developing policy and communicating real-time information; analyzing and providing manpower and force structure requirements; and managing and overseeing the process that ensures the army selects expert acquisition leaders.

Resource Management Division: Plans, programs, formulates, allocates, administers, and reviews the utilization of ASC resources to include both financial and manpower programs.

Strategic Communications: Provides direction and oversight for establishing, implementing, executing, maintaining, and measuring an effective, efficient, consistent, and comprehensive approach to communicating the vision and mission of the Army Acquisition Corps (AAC) within the acquisition community and across the entire army.

active army

The "active army" is that part of the army in full-time service. The REGULAR ARMY is always part of the active army. Members of the RESERVE COMPONENTS—ARMY NATIONAL GUARD (ARNG) and U.S. ARMY RESERVE (USAR)—are considered part of the active army whenever they are called to serve on a full-time basis, as in time of war or national emergency.

adjutant general (AG)

The AG is an administrative assistant to a command with a general staff. The AG's primary responsibility is administration and personnel matters.

See also ADJUTANT GENERAL CORPS.

Adjutant General Corps

A combat service support branch of the army, the Adjutant General Corps has as its mission the training of leaders and soldiers to provide personnel service support for the army through excellence in doctrine, leadership development, organization, materiel, and soldiers. The corps creates and administers systems to manage readiness, morale, and soldier career satisfaction, and to cover the life-cycle management of all army personnel in peacetime and war, from accession of new soldiers to discharge and retirement.

Adjutant General School

The Adjutant General School trains leaders and soldiers in providing personnel service support for the army. The school includes an Officer Training Division, Advanced Individual Training Division, and Interservice Postal Training Activity. The school is headquartered at Fort Jackson, South Carolina, and operates under the command of the ADJUTANT GENERAL CORPS.

African Americans in the U.S. Army

Except for some 40 years during the 19th century, when federal policy barred their enlistment, African Americans have served in the army and its antecedents since colonial times. In the North, pre–Revolutionary War militia companies enlisted black troops, and even militia companies in the South enlisted slaves in times of extreme emergency; however, after the Stono (South Carolina) slave revolt of 1739, most southern jurisdictions barred the arming of slaves under any circumstances.

Although African Americans served extensively in northern militia companies during the AMERICAN REVOLUTION, they were initially barred from the CONTINENTAL ARMY by resolution of the Continental Congress. This was in response to southern fears concerning the arming of slaves or, indeed, any African Americans, free or slave. The British army had no such qualms, however, and recruited local blacks. In 1776, GEORGE WASHINGTON, a slave-owning southerner himself, defied the congressional resolution and began to recruit African Americans. Such was Washington's stature that the Continental Congress made no challenge, and, by the end of the war, some 5,000 African Americans had served in the Continental forces. Many more served in the various militias.

African Americans have made important contributions to all U.S. wars. This photograph shows members of an African-American regiment on leave in France during World War I.   *(National Archives)*

After the Revolution, both the army and navy were almost completely demobilized; however, they were soon reestablished. Black troops were not only recruited but fully integrated with white soldiers. They served in various wars and skirmishes against the Indians and in the WAR OF 1812, but, in 1820, were once again banned from service. In that year, Secretary of War John C. Calhoun, a native of South Carolina, officially brought an end to African-American enlistments. As the then-current black terms of service expired, the army became an all-white force. This situation prevailed until the CIVIL WAR.

From the beginning of the Civil War, northern abolitionists and black activists such as Frederick Douglass called for recruitment of "colored troops" in the Union army. President Lincoln and Congress resisted, but some generals acted on their own initiative. Occupying New Orleans, Major General Benjamin Butler organized the Louisiana Native Guard, or Corps d'Afrique, which took to the field in November 1862. On the Union-held Sea Islands of Georgia and South Carolina, Major General David Hunter raised a black regiment. When the War Department objected, he disbanded all but a single company. In Kansas, a militia commander, Major General James H. Lane, recruited two black regiments consisting of fugitive slaves and free blacks, units that were, in 1863, finally approved by the War Department.

Congress and the president more or less backed into a policy of recruiting African Americans. A Confiscation Act of July 17, 1862, authorized the president to employ persons of African descent for the purpose of suppressing the rebellion, and on August 25, 1862, the War Department authorized the military governor of the Sea Islands to raise five black regiments. After the Emancipation Proclamation of January 1, 1863, President Lincoln finally—and personally—called for the raising of four black regiments. This grew rapidly, and by the end of the Civil War, some 178,985 African-American troops had served in 166 segregated regiments. This constituted about 10 percent of the army.

In the Civil War army blacks served mainly as laborers, although black units did fight in 449 engagements, including 39 major battles. Seventeen African-American soldiers received the Medal of Honor. Wholly segregated, black troops were nevertheless led by white officers; however, a handful (fewer than 100) of black soldiers were commissioned during the war. The highest rank held by African Americans was major; eight black majors served as army surgeons.

After the Civil War, Congress authorized four black regiments for the tiny postwar army: the 9th and 10th Cavalry and the 24th and 25th Infantry. Most of these troops were assigned to the West, where they earned a reputation as effective Indian fighters and where they gained the respect of their Native American adversaries, who called them "BUFFALO SOLDIERS," a term of admiration. The Buffalo Soldiers also saw action in the SPANISH-AMERICAN WAR and in the punitive expedition against Pancho Villa in Mexico. As in the Civil War, black officers were a rarity, although by 1898 three African Americans had graduated from the UNITED STATES MILITARY ACADEMY.

By the beginning of the 20th century, racial tensions in the United States ran high, especially in the South. The demands of WORLD WAR I spurred the enlistment or conscription of some 380,000 African Americans; however, 89 percent of these men were assigned to labor units, and only 11 percent were committed to combat. It was the clear policy of the army that black troops were to serve primarily as laborers or in other support roles. After the war, African-American membership in the army dwindled to 5,000 troops (2 percent of the service) and a mere five officers. WORLD WAR II saw a spectacular rise: 900,000 African Americans by the end of the war. Again, policy restricted African Americans to segregated units, and most were relegated to support roles; however, more opportunities were opened up, including positions for fighter pilots in all-black units. During the war, Colonel BENJAMIN O. DAVIS, SR. became the army's first African-American brigadier general. Moreover, General GEORGE SMITH PATTON, JR., one of few top commanders who voiced support for integration, authorized the partial integration of his THIRD U.S. ARMY during the Battle of the Bulge (December 16, 1944–January 25, 1945), when infantrymen were desperately needed to blunt a massive surprise German offensive. Some 4,500 African-American infantrymen, all assigned to segregated service units, volunteered for frontline combat in all-black platoons, which were integrated into larger white units. This small degree of integration remained in effect through the end of the war.

In 1948, President Harry S. Truman issued Executive Order 9981, which mandated equal opportunity and an end to segregation in all the services. Except for the newly formed U.S. Air Force, the services, including the army, were slow to comply; however, the exigencies of the KOREAN WAR forced recruitment of African Americans and integration into white units. The Korean War was the first modern American war fought with a fully integrated force. Nevertheless, by the cease-fire, only 3 percent of army officers were black—still, a better record than in the navy, marines, and air force, in which African Americans represented 1 percent or less of the officer corps.

The VIETNAM WAR saw the highest proportion of African Americans in army service, as high as 12.6 percent. Some activists in the antiwar movement of the period claimed that blacks served (and died) in Vietnam in disproportionate numbers. This was somewhat of an exaggeration; during 1965–69 blacks made up about 11 percent of the population of the United States, which makes the 12.6 percent figure not significantly disproportionate. At the worst, however, African-American soldiers did suffer a devastating 14.9 percent fatality rate in Vietnam, although this quickly declined to levels identical with those of non–African-American troops.

The end of conscription in 1973 and the introduction of the all-volunteer army sparked enlistment by a large number of African Americans. By the 1980s, blacks made up about a third of the army, a proportion that holds today. Most significantly, opportunities expanded within the service.

Today, about a third of the army's NCOs are black, and 17 percent of the officer corps is African American. Two prominent African Americans have held top army positions. In 1977, Clifford Alexander became the first black SECRETARY OF THE ARMY, and in 1988, COLIN LUTHER POWELL became chairman of the JOINT CHIEFS OF STAFF.

As of the opening decade of the 21st century, vocational and executive opportunities for African Americans significantly exceed what the civilian sector offers. This is both a testament to social and moral progress in the army and, regrettably, evidence of continued racial inequalities in American society at large.

AGM-114 Hellfire   See ANTIARMOR WEAPONS.

AH-1 Cobra   See AIRCRAFT.

AH-64 Apache   See AIRCRAFT.

aircraft

Currently (2005), the army operates the following major aircraft:

AH-1 Cobra

The AH-1 Cobra and variants are two-place, twin-engine attack helicopters designed for close air support (CAS), antiarmor/antihelicopter missions, armed escort, reconnaissance, and supporting arms coordination (SAC) during day or night and in adverse weather conditions. The aircraft was introduced during the VIETNAM WAR in 1967 and, continuously modernized, is still in active service with the army. The Cobra series was developed from the UH-1 Huey.

The Cobra has a crew of two, a rear-seat pilot primarily responsible for maneuvering the aircraft and a front-seat pilot who controls weapons systems (but also has a full set of aircraft controls). Variants include:

AH-1G: initial production model (1966)

AH-1S: upgraded during the late 1980s to fire the TOW missile

AH-1P: fitted with composite rotors, flat plate glass cockpits, and NVG capabilities.

AH-1E: fitted with Enhanced Cobra Armament System, incorporating the universal turret, 20-mm gun, automatic compensation for off-axis gun firing, and weapon management system.

AH-1F: current standard Cobra, also called the "Modernized Cobra"

General characteristics of the AH-1 Cobra include:

Primary contractor: Bell Helicopter Textron, Inc.

Power plant: 2 General Electric T700-GE-401 Turboshaft engines, each delivering 1,690 horsepower

Crew: 2 seats, in tandem—pilot in rear, copilot/gunner in front

Climb rate: 1,925 ft per min

Maximum altitude: 14,750 ft

Maximum speed: 196 mph

Cruising speed: 175 mph

Countermeasures: AN/ALE-39 Chaff system and SUU-4/1 Flare dispensers

Armament: 1 M-197 3-barrel 20-mm gun (mounted under the nose with 750 round ammo container); underwing attachments for 4 TOW missiles, 8 Hellfire missiles, or 1 AIM-9L Sidewinder missile; can also be equipped with Zuni rocket launchers

Main rotor diameter: 44 ft

Length (overall, rotors turning): 44 ft, 7 in

Height: 13 ft 6 in

Maximum takeoff and landing weight: 9,500 lb

Range at S/L with standard fuel, no reserves: 365 mi

AH-64 Apache

The AH-64 Apache is the army's primary attack helicopter, used as a quick-reacting, airborne weapons system for fighting close and deep to

The AH-1 Cobra in action   *(U.S. Army)*

destroy, disrupt, or delay enemy forces. Designed for survivability, the Apache fights by day or night and in adverse weather conditions. Its primary armament is the AGM-114 Hellfire, but it can also deploy a 30-mm M-230 chain gun and Hydra 70 (2.75-inch) rockets.

The AH-64A is a twin-engine, four-bladed attack helicopter. The crew includes a pilot, located in the rear cockpit position, and the copilot gunner (CPG), located in the front position. The powerplant consists of two General Electric gas turbine engines rated at 1890 shaft horsepower each, yielding a maximum gross takeoff weight of 17,650 pounds. Cruising airspeed is 145 miles per hour over three hours. Attack range can be extended with an external fuel tank. The aircraft is equipped with a suite of sensors, including forward-looking infrared (FLIR) and full GPS capability.

Apache production began in 1982, with the first aircraft deployed by the army in 1986. In addition to the AH-64A model, there is a newer Longbow Apache (LBA), designated AH-64D, capable of launching the Longbow Hellfire missile. Tests indicate that the Longbow model is 400 percent more lethal (hits more targets) than the AH-64A and is 720 percent more survivable.

General characteristics of the AH-64A and AH-64D include:

Contractors: Boeing McDonnell Douglas Helicopter Systems; General Electric; Martin Marietta
Power plant: 2 T700-GE-701Cs
Crew: 2
Length: 58.17 ft (64A); 58.17 ft (64D)
Height: 15.24 ft (64A); 13.30 ft (64D)
Wing span: 17.15 ft (64A); 17.15 ft (64D)
Gross weight: 15,075 lb (64A); 16,027 lb (64D)
Maximum rate of climb (IRP): 2,915 fpm (64A); 2,635 fpm (64D)
Cruise speed: 173 mph (64A); 168 mph (64D)
Range (both models): 250 mi (internal fuel); 1,180 mi (internal and external fuel)
Armament (both models): M-230 33-mm Gun; 70-mm (2.75-in) Hydra-70 Folding-Fin Aer-

An AH-64 Apache in full attack mode   *(U.S. Army)*

ial Rockets; AGM-114 Hellfire antitank missiles; AGM-122 Sidearm antiradar missile; AIM-9 Sidewinder Air-to-Air missiles

C-20 Gulfstream

The U.S. Air Force, U.S. Navy, and army operate the C-20, which is a military modification of the commercial Gulfstream aircraft, manufactured by Gulfstream Aerospace Corporation (GAC) of Savannah, Georgia. The principal C-20 mission is to provide distinguished visitor airlift for military and government officials.

General characteristics of the C-20 Gulfstream include:

Power plant: C-20A/B, 2 Rolls-Royce Spey Mark 511-8 turbofan engines; C-20H, 2 Rolls-Royce Tay Mark 611-8 turbofan engines
Length: C-20A/B, 83 ft, 2 in (25.4 m); C-20H, 88 ft, 4 in (26.9 m)
Height: 24 ft, 6 in
Wingspan: 77 ft, 10 in
Speed: 576 mph maximum
Maximum takeoff weight: C-20A/B, 69,700 lb; C-20H, 74,600 lb
Range: C-20A/B, 4,250 mi; C-20H, 4,850 mi
Ceiling: 45,000 ft

Load: 12 to 14 passengers
Crew: 5 (pilot, copilot, flight mechanic, communication system operator, flight attendant)
Date deployed: C-20A, 1983; C-20B, 1988; C-20H, 1992

C-23 Sherpa

The U.S. Air Force, Army, and ARMY NATIONAL GUARD operate this military freight version of the Shorts 330 regional airliner. The aircraft is used for missions requiring an aircraft capable of faster, higher-altitude, and longer-range coverage than helicopters. Through-loading is provided by means of a large forward freight door as well as by a hydraulic rear ramp. The C-23 is the only fixed-wing cargo aircraft flown by the army. It can also be configured for troop transport, medical evacuation, or for mixed-use troop transport and cargo.

General characteristics of the C-23 include:

Contractor: Short Brothers PLC
Power plant: 2 Pratt-Whitney PT6A-45R turboprops; Super Sherpa configuration, 2 Pratt-Whitney PT6A-65AR turboprops
Speed: 218 mph at 10,000 feet
Range: 770 mi with 5,000 lb payload
Wingspan: 74 ft 8 in
Length: 58 ft
Height: 16 ft 3 in
Gross weight: 25,500 lb maximum
Accommodations: crew of 3; up to 7,000 lb of freight
Date deployed: 1984

C-47 Dakota

Although long out of army service, the C-47 Dakota, military version of the Douglas DC-3 commercial airliner, played such a central role in army cargo transport and paratroop deployment in WORLD WAR II that it must be included here. It was also used in the KOREAN WAR and the Vietnam War.

The DC-3 first flew in 1935 and was first deployed with the army in 1941. The USAF flew the aircraft into the late 1960s, and, today, more than 40 nations still fly it. During World War II, the army used it for cargo as well as paratroop deployment. General of the Army DWIGHT DAVID EISENHOWER declared that, with the Jeep and the M-1 rifle, the C-47 was one of the three weapons without which the Allies could not have won World War II.

General characteristics of the C-47 include:

Manufacturer: Douglas Aircraft Company
Powerplant: 2 Pratt & Whitney R-1830-92 radial piston engines
Maximum takeoff weight: 26,000 lb
Maximum payload: 7,500 lb
Length: 64 ft 6 in
Height: 16 ft 9 in
Cargo volume: 1,245 cu ft
Speed: 229 mph maximum
Ceiling: 24,100 ft
Range: 2,700 mi maximum

CH-47 Chinook

The CH-47 Chinook is a twin-engine, tandem-rotor helicopter used to transport cargo, troops, and weapons in daylight and nighttime conditions, under visual as well as instrument flying rules. The aircraft has a top airspeed of 170 knots and a cruising speed of 130 knots. The minimum crew requirement is four: two pilots, one flight engineer, and one crew chief. The aircraft can accommodate two additional crew members, if the mission requires them.

The Chinook dates to the mid-1950s, but the basic design has proved so durable that the helicopter has been kept in active service through continual modernization and upgrade programs through the CH-47A, CH-47B, CH-47C, and CH-47D models. The CH-47A was first delivered for use in the Vietnam War in 1962. Its primary mission was moving artillery, ammunition, personnel, and supplies on the battlefield, but it additionally performed rescue, aeromedical, parachuting, aircraft recovery, and special operations missions.

The current model, CH-47D, was contracted for in 1976. Improvements include upgraded power plants and rotor transmissions, and the introduction

The U.S. Army workhorse: the twin-rotor CH-47 Chinook in action *(U.S. Army)*

of fiberglass rotor blades. Additionally, cockpit ergonomics were improved, as were the electrical systems, hydraulic systems, flight control system, and avionics. The Chinook can accommodate vehicles, artillery, 33 to 44 troops, or 24 litters plus two medical personnel. The aircraft can be armed with two door-mounting M-60D 7.62-mm machine guns.

The Improved Cargo Helicopter (ICH) is a remanufactured CH-47D, with new engines and other improvements intended to extend the service life of the helicopter well into the future.

General characteristics of the Chinook include:

Contractors: Boeing Helicopters; Elicotteri Meridionali, Italy; Kawasaki Heavy Industries, Japan
Power plant: 2 Textron Lycoming T55-L712 engines, 3,750 shp each
Rotor system: 3 fiberglass blades per hub (2 hubs)
Maximum takeoff weight: 50,000 lb

Rotor diameter: 60 ft
Length: 51 ft
Height: 18 ft 8 in
Cargo hold volume: 1,474 cu ft
Maximum speed: 146 mph
Ceiling: 8,500 ft
Mission radius: 115 mi
Ferry range: 1,265 mi
Crew: up to 6
Passengers: 33 seats or 24 litters

E-8C Joint STARS

The E-8C Joint Surveillance Target Attack Radar System (Joint STARS) is a joint USAF-army platform for airborne battle management and command and control. Joint STARS is an E-8C aircraft, a military modification of the Boeing 707-300 commercial airliner, equipped with a special suite of radar, communications, operations, and control subsystems designed to develop an understanding of the enemy situation in support of attack operations and targeting.

The E-8C is equipped with a large radome under the forward fuselage that houses a side-looking phased-array radar antenna, the heart of the surveillance system. The E-8C can fly a mission profile for nine hours without refueling, and it is capable of in flight refueling. All information gathered is relayed in near-real time to the army's common ground stations via a secure jam-resistant surveillance and control data link.

King Air 90

The USAF and army use the King Air 90, a military version of general aviation aircraft built by Beechcraft, for light utility, liaison, and VIP transport. The army variant is designated U-21A. Introduced in 1964, the King Air 90 has the following general characteristics:

Manufacturer: Beechcraft
Powerplant: 2 Pratt & Whitney PT61-20 turboprops
Maximum takeoff weight: 9,300 lb
Wingspan: 45 ft 10.5 in

Length: 35 ft 6 in
Height: 14 ft 8 in
Speed: 278 mph
Ceiling: 31,600 ft
Range: 1,580 mi

MH-60K Blackhawk SOF

The MH-60K is the special operations forces (SOF) variant of the Sikorsky UH-60 Blackhawk used by the army. It features the advanced avionics package also used on the SOF variant of the MH-47 Chinook, an advanced communications suite, a state-of-the-art navigation suite, and extensive self-defense capabilities, which include a Honeywell AN/AAR-47 missile-warning receiver, an ITT AN/ALQ-144(V)1 pulsed IR jammer, a General Instruments AN/APR-39(V)1 pulse radar-warning receiver, AEL AN/APR-44(V)3 CW radar-warning receiver, a Hughes-Danbury Optical Division AN/AVR-2 laser-warning receiver, and CM-130 chaff and flare dispensers. The helicopter is rigged with a cargo hook to carry up to 8,000 pounds.

The MH-60K was first deployed in 1991. Note that the USAF flies a variant, the MH-60G Pave Hawk.

General characteristics of the MH-60K include:

Contractor: Sikorsky Aircraft
Power plant: 2 General Electric T700-GE-701C turboshafts
Maximum takeoff weight: 24,034 lb
Rotor diameter: 53 ft 8 in
Length: 50 ft
Height: 12 ft 4 in
Maximum speed: 225 mph
Armament: 2 12.7-mm machine guns
Crew: 3 (pilot, copilot, crew chief)
Passengers: 7 to 12 troops

OH-6 Cayuse

The OH-6 is the military version of the Hughes (now McDonnell Douglas) 269 commercial helicopter and was first deployed in the Vietnam War in 1966 for light observation. The helicopter incorporates the NOTAR concept. There is no tail rotor; instead, compressed air is used to offset torque.

General characteristics of the Cayuse include:

Contractor: Hughes Helicopter (later McDonnell-Douglas Helicopter)
Power plant: 317-shaft-horsepower Allison T63
Rotor diameter: 26 ft 5 in
Length: 23 ft
Height: 8 ft 2 in
Maximum takeoff weight: 2,700 lb
Maximum speed: 147 mph
Range: 380 mi
Crew: 2 (pilot and copilot), plus 2 troops

OH-58 Kiowa

The OH-58A was introduced by the army in 1968 during the Vietnam War as a liaison, observation, fire direction, and, with modifications, antitank helicopter. A training version, the TH-67 New Training Helicopter, has also been produced. The current version is the OH-58D(R) Kiowa Warrior, which includes safety, electronic, and power plant improvements reflecting the state of the art.

The OH-58 helicopter is small, allowing a great range of maneuverability while presenting a small signature. These qualities are invaluable for real-time battlefield intelligence. The Kiowa Warrior is equipped with a Mast Mounted Sight (MMS) with a Television System, Thermal Imaging System, and Laser Rangefinder/Designator; Embedded Global Positioning System Inertial Navigation System; airborne Target Handover System or Improved Data Modem for digital communication, as well as highly advanced radios. A pair of Universal Weapons Pylons can accommodate two of the following: Hellfire missiles, Air-to-Air Stinger missiles, 2.75-inch Hydra 70 rockets, and/or a 50-caliber fixed machine gun.

General characteristics of the Kiowa include:

Primary contractor: Bell Helicopter
Power plant: 1 Allison T63-A-720 turboshaft
Maximum takeoff weight: 3,200 lb
Rotor diameter: 35 ft 4 in
Length: 40 ft 12 in
Height: 9 ft 6.5 in
Maximum speed: 138 mph

Range: 304 mi
Crew: 2 (pilot and copilot), plus 2 troops

RC-12/RU-21 Guardrail

The Guardrail aircraft is based on the Beechcraft King Air and Super King Air civilian general aviation aircraft and was first delivered to the army in 1974 as the RU-21J electronic surveillance aircraft. The aircraft carries the Guardrail Electronic Intelligence and Signals Intelligence systems designed to monitor enemy battlefield communications and relay these in real time to army forces.

General characteristics of the aircraft include:

Manufacturer: Beechcraft
Power plant: 2 Pratt & Whitney Canada PT6A-42 turboprops
Length: 43 ft 9 in
Height: 15 ft
Wingspan: 57 ft 10 in
Maximum weight: 4,570 lb
Range: 2,334 mi
Maximum speed: 326 mph
Ceiling: 35,000 ft

TH-67 New Training Helicopter

The TH-67 NTH, or Creek, is a version of the army's OH-58 Kiowa and is used to train Initial Entry Rotary Wing students. The aircraft was ordered in March 1993 to succeed the Bell UH-1 Huey. Unique to the aircraft is an advanced cockpit display system installed for the back-seat student. The aircraft is also fitted with heavy-duty skid shoes for touchdown autorotation training.

General characteristics include:

Primary contractor: Bell Helicopter
Power plant: 1 Allison T63-A-720 turboshaft
Maximum takeoff weight: 3,200 lb
Rotor diameter: 35 ft 4 in
Length: 40 ft 12 in
Height: 9 ft 6.5 in
Maximum speed: 138 mph
Range: 304 mi
Crew: 2 (pilot and copilot), plus 2 troops

UH-1 Huey/Iroquois

Universally dubbed the "Huey," the UH-1 is perhaps the most durable and ubiquitous military helicopter ever produced. Introduced in 1958, the Huey saw extensive Vietnam War service and has been produced in many variant versions.

General characteristics of the Huey include:

Contractor: Bell Helicopter Textron
Power plant: 1 Lycoming T53—L-13 turboshaft
Maximum takeoff load: 9,500 lb
Rotor diameter: 48 ft
Length: 41 ft 10 3/4 in
Height: 13 ft 5 in
Maximum speed: 127 mph
Service ceiling: 12,700 ft
Range: 777 mi
Crew: 2 (pilot, copilot)
Passengers: up to 14 troops

See also UH-1N Huey/Iroquois.

UH-1N Huey/Iroquois

The UH-1N is the twin-engine variant of the enormously successful UH-1 Huey/Iroquois. A Twin-Pac turboshaft consists of two turbines that drive a single output shaft, providing backup if one of the turbines fail. Except for this feature, the UH-1N is identical to the UH-1. The engines are Pratt & Whitney PT6T-3Bs or variants of this model.

UH-60 Blackhawk

The UH-60 Blackhawk provides air assault, general support, aeromedical evacuation, command and control, and special operations support to combat operations, stability operations, and support operations.

Entering army service in 1979 as a utility tactical transport helicopter to replace the UH-1 "Huey," the Blackhawk has proved highly versatile, greatly enhancing army mobility and providing major improvements over the Huey in troop capacity and cargo lift capability. On the asymmetric battlefield—antiguerrilla and anti-insurgent operations—the Blackhawk is sufficiently agile to get to the fight faster and to bring a mass response throughout the entire battle space.

A single Blackhawk can carry an entire 11-person, fully equipped infantry squad. The helicopter is also capable of repositioning a 105-mm HOW-ITZER, together with its crew of six and up to 30 rounds of ammunition. The Blackhawk is designed for survivability. Its critical components and systems are armored or redundant, and its airframe is designed to progressively crush on impact to protect the crew and passengers.

There are two principal versions: the UH-60A and UH-60L. The following general characteristics list specifications for the A version followed by the L version.

> **Manufacturer:** United Technologies (Stratford, Conn.) and General Electric (Lynn, Mass.)
> **Mass gross weight:** 20,250 lb, 22,000 lb
> **Cruise speed:** 160 mph, 173 mph
> **Endurance:** 2.3 hours, 2.1 hours
> **Maximum range:** 368 mi, 352 mi

A Florida National Guard UH-60 Blackhawk helicopter soars over the palm forest of Iraq on July 20, 2004.   *(Department of Defense)*

External load: 8,000 lb, 9,000 lb
Internal load: 2,640 lb or 11 combat-equipped troops
Crew: 4 (2 pilots; 2 crew chiefs)
Armament: 2 7.62-mm machine guns

air defense artillery

Currently (2004), the army inventory includes the following air defense artillery:

Avenger

The Avenger is an air-defense system consisting of an AM General High-Mobility Multipurpose Wheeled Vehicle (Humvee) mounting a Boeing Aerospace/General Electric pedestal-mounted Stinger. The Stinger is operated by one man and consists of an electrically driven gyro-stabilized turret with two four-round Stinger surface-to-air missile launchers supplemented by an FN M3P .50-caliber machine gun. The system includes forward-looking infrared (FLIR) and a laser rangefinder.

General characteristics include:

> **Weight:** 8,600 lb
> **Hull length:** 16 ft 3 in
> **Width:** 7 ft 2 in
> **Tactical height:** 8 ft 8 in
> **Power plant:** Detroit Diesel 135-hp V-8
> **Maximum speed:** 60 mph
> **Crew:** 3

M-42A1 Skysweeper

Familiarly called the Duster, this twin 40-mm self-propelled gun was intended as an antiaircraft vehicle. It is now obsolete for that purpose, but it is still used against ground targets. It shares its chassis with the M-41 Light Tank and is armed with a pair of 40-mm cannon, which fire high-explosive tracers and armor-piercing tracers. The Skysweeper came into operation in 1953.

General characteristics include:

> **Weight:** 49,498 lb
> **Hull length:** 19 ft 1 in

Width: 10 ft 7 in
Height: 9 ft 4 in
Power plant: 500-hp gasoline engine
Maximum speed: 45 mph
Crew: 6

M-48 Chaparral

This short-range surface-to-air missile (SAM) system consists of the M-54 launcher with four modified AIM-9 Sidewinder infrared-homing missiles mounted on the rear deck of a specially configured M-548 Tracked Cargo Carrier (modification designated M-730 or M-730A1). The system was developed in 1969. Its general characteristics include:

Weight: 25,353 lb
Hull length: 19 ft 11 in
Width: 8 ft 11 in
Height: 8 ft 10 in
Power plant: Detroit Diesel 6V-53T 275-hp V-6 diesel
Maximum speed: 38 mph
Crew: 4 to 5

M167 20-mm Vulcan Gatling Antiaircraft Mount

VADS, the Vulcan Air Defense System, is a towed AAA system consisting of the six-barrel M-167 Gatling gun, complete with an integral fire-control system. The original version of the gun started production in 1967 and an improved version entered service in 1987. The weapon's general characteristics include:

Weight: 3,450 lb
Barrel length: 5 ft
Muzzle velocity: 3,379 ft/min
Rate of fire in antiair mode: 3,000 rounds/min
Range in antiair mode: 3,937 ft
Crew: 1 gunner

MIM-23 Hawk

Achieving operational capability in 1960, the MIM-23 Hawk is the first mobile medium-range guided antiaircraft missile deployed by the army. The name is an acronym signifying "Homing All the Way Killer." The missiles are transported on and launched from M-192 triple-missile towed launchers and are deployed in batteries consisting of two platoons, each with three missile launchers. The Hawk system has been continuously improved and upgraded. General characteristics of the MIM-23A and MIM-23B configurations include:

Weight: 1290 lb (A), 1400 lb (B)
Length: 16 ft 8 in (A), 16 ft 6 in (B)
Finspan: 3 ft 11 in (AB)
Diameter: 14.5 in(AB)
Speed: Mach 2.5 (AB)
Ceiling: 45,000 ft (A), 58,000 ft (B)
Range: 15 mi (A), 25 mi (B)
Propulsion: Aerojet M22E8 dual-thrust solid-fueled rocket (A), Aerojet M-112 dual-thrust solid-fueled rocket (B)
Warhead: 119 lb blast-fragmentation (A), 163 lb blast-fragmentation (B)

MIM-104 Patriot

This medium-to-high-altitude surface-to-air missile system, which entered army service in 1985, provides defense against enemy aircraft, cruise missiles, and tactical ballistic missiles.

PATRIOT is an acronym—Phased Array Tracking Intercept of Target—and describes the heart of the missile system's fire unit, which consists of a phased-array radar set (RS), engagement control station (ECS), an electric power plant, an antenna mast group (AMG), a communications relay group (CRG), and up to eight launching stations (LS). The RS provides airspace surveillance and target detection, identification, classification, and tracking, as well as missile guidance and engagement support. The ECS is the human interface for command and control of operations. Each LS contains four PAC-2, guidance-enhanced missiles, which are sealed in canisters that serve as both shipping containers and launch tubes.

The latest upgrade to the system is the Patriot Advanced Capability-3 (PAC-3) upgrade program, which adds the new PAC-3 missile. It incorporates hit-to-kill technology for greater lethality against

A Patriot missile is launched by soldiers of the 11th Brigade, 43rd Air Defense Artillery, at MacGregor Range near El Paso, Texas on April 30, 1997. *(Department of Defense)*

tactical ballistic missiles armed with weapons of mass destruction. Also, as many as 16 PAC-3 missiles can be loaded per launcher, thereby greatly increasing firepower.

General characteristics of the MIM-104 Patriot include:

Contractors: Raytheon and Siemens
Weight, missile: 1,534 lb
Weight, warhead: 198 lb
Length, missile: 17 ft 5 in
Diameter: 16 in
Fin span: 3 ft
Propulsion: Thiokol TX-486 single-stage solid-fuel rocket
Speed: 1,983 mph
Range: 50+ mi
Warhead: blast fragmentation type

Air Defense Artillery Detachment   See JOINT TACTICAL GROUND STATION.

airfields, U.S. Army   See FORTS AND OTHER INSTALLATIONS.

American Campaign Medal   See DECORATIONS AND MEDALS.

American Defense Service Medal   See DECORATIONS AND MEDALS.

American Revolution

During the 1760s and 1770s, the government of King George III (r. 1760–1820) imposed a series of taxes on its North American colonies, which a growing number of colonists believed unjust and unjustifiable because the interests of the colonies were not (and could not properly be) represented in Parliament. The colonial tax protest evolved first into a movement to secure from the Crown greater autonomy and then became a militant movement for outright independence from the British Empire.

In 1773, the Crown attempted to give the British East India Company a monopoly on the colonial tea trade by imposing ruinous taxes on noncompany imports of tea into the colonies. This precipitated the act of civil disobedience and vandalism known as the Boston Tea Party on December 16, to which George and Parliament reacted with unprecedented severity. Parliament passed a series of Coercive Acts, which colonial activists dubbed the Intolerable Acts. The acts closed the port of Boston, greatly curtailed Massachusetts colonial government, and extended the much-hated Quartering Act, authorizing the permanent quartering of British troops in Boston at public expense. British general Thomas Gage was named both commander in chief of British forces in America and royal governor of Massachusetts in April 1774.

In response to the Boston crisis, 56 delegates from 12 colonies (Georgia abstained) heeded the call of the Massachusetts Assembly (banned by Gage) for a Continental Congress, which convened at Carpenter's Hall, Philadelphia, on September 5, 1774. The congress pronounced the Intolerable Acts unconstitutional, urged Massachusetts to form an independent government and to withhold taxes from the Crown until the acts were repealed, advised colonists to arm themselves, and recommended a general boycott of English-export goods. In the meantime, Gage consolidated his forces and, on September 1, 1774, seized cannon and powder from arsenals in nearby Cambridge and Charles Town. Reacting to this, the Continental Congress appropriated funds to buy new military supplies and authorized John Hancock to head a Committee of Safety and call out the militia, whose members were dubbed "Minutemen," because these citizen-soldiers pledged themselves to be armed, assembled, and prepared for battle on a minute's notice. A guerrilla war commenced against the British troops, and on April 18, Gage quietly assembled 600 to 800 troops on Boston Common under the command of Lieutenant Colonel Francis Smith and Major John Pitcairn. They set out for Lexington, where they were met by 70 or so Minutemen on April 19. Fire was exchanged, and the outnumbered militiamen scattered.

From Lexington, the British marched to Concord, where they met much more effective resistance and were forced to retreat to Boston, harried all the way by militia snipers.

The next month, the Second Continental Congress convened in Philadelphia and voted to mobilize 13,600 troops. It also called on local militia forces throughout New England to march to Boston, with the object of laying under siege the British forces headquartered there.

In the meantime, Benedict Arnold, a prosperous New Haven, Connecticut, merchant and captain of militia, was united with Vermont's Ethan Allen in leading an assault against Fort Ticonderoga in New York. The fort fell on May 10, enabling Allen to take the nearby fort at Crown Point as well. Together, the forts yielded 78 precious artillery pieces, six mortars, three HOWITZERS, a cache of cannonballs, flints for flintlock muskets, and other materiel. This artillery would be transported by HENRY KNOX to Boston and put to use in laying siege against the British troops there.

On the very day that Allen and Arnold took Fort Ticonderoga, the Second Continental Congress created the CONTINENTAL ARMY under the command of GEORGE WASHINGTON, provincial hero of the French and Indian War (1754–63). This body was the direct predecessor of the U.S. Army. Appointed as Washington's lieutenants were Artemas Ward (already commanding the Boston militia), Israel Putnam of Connecticut, Philip Schuyler of New York, and two recently retired officers of the British army, Charles Lee and Horatio Gates. By the end of 1775, Congress had 27,500 Continental army troops on its payroll, from all the colonies.

During spring 1775 New Englanders poured into Cambridge and adjacent towns to lay siege against Boston. By the end of May, some 10,000 colonial troops surrounded the city. On May 25, HMS *Cerberus* sailed into Boston harbor, bearing three major generals to assist Thomas Gage in crushing the rebellion: William Howe, the senior officer, John Burgoyne, and Henry Clinton. Howe proposed an amphibious attack to secure the high ground at Charles Town, a place called Bunker's Hill or Bunker Hill. Covering these operations would be the big guns of the British warships riding at anchor in Boston harbor. With Bunker Hill secured, Howe and Clinton would be in a position to attack the American flanks in a pincers movement converging on Cambridge.

Thanks to a network of colonial spies, however, the British lost the element of surprise, and General Ward was ordered to seize, occupy, and fortify Bunker Hill preemptively. He decided instead to concentrate his forces on Breed's Hill, which, although easier to fortify was tactically the inferior position. Despite this lapse in judgment, on June 17, 1,200 Americans repelled two assaults by about twice as many redcoats, inflicting heavy casualties.

Battle of Bunker Hill/Breed's Hill, June 17, 1775. Painting by John Trumbull   *(National Archives)*

A third assault broke through the Patriot lines and took Bunker Hill, but at such cost that the battle seemed (to the Patriots, at least) an American victory.

During the early period of the Revolution, Congress tried to entice Canada into joining the rebellion against the mother country. Rebuffed, Congress, on June 27, 1775, ordered an invasion of its northern neighbor. The expedition was repeatedly delayed and suffered from poor planning, inadequate numbers of troops, and generally poor execution—despite the genuine daring and heroism of General Benedict Arnold. By fall 1776, the invasion had collapsed, and the Patriots abandoned the Canadian campaign.

Back in Boston, by June 1775, some 15,000 provincial troops were now laying siege to Gage and his forces of about 11,000. On January 24, 1776, Henry Knox returned from Fort Ticonderoga

and Crown Point with the artillery that had been captured there, and Washington's army used them to fortify Dorchester Heights. Clearly surrounded and outnumbered, General Howe abandoned Boston, evacuating by ship from March 7 to March 17. The force reestablished itself at Halifax, Nova Scotia. The siege of Boston had consumed eight months, during which only 20 Patriot soldiers had been killed. In a contest with the army of the most powerful nation in the world, the Patriots had prevailed.

After evacuating Boston, the British command decided to avoid the New England strongholds of the independence movement and instead attack—and "liberate"—two places where Tories (loyalists to the Crown) were known to be abundant: South Carolina and New York.

New York City was strategically critical. Whoever controlled the city and its harbor also controlled the Hudson River, principal avenue into the American interior. Howe sailed from Halifax with a large army to take and occupy New York City. His plan was to extend British control of the Hudson River north to Albany, thereby isolating New England from the other colonies. From Canada, another British force led by General Guy Carleton would join Howe at Albany, and, from there, the two would be able to defeat decisively the remnants of the rebellion.

By the last week of August 1776, Howe had mustered 31,625 troops, of whom 24,464 were fit for duty. The land force was supported by 30 combat ships, mounting a total of 1,200 guns. Against these enormous forces, Washington had 20,000 troops deployed on Long Island on Governor's Island in New York harbor and elsewhere in and around New York City. This constituted the bulk of America's military strength. If these forces were lost, the Revolution would be over.

While it is generally conceded that Washington was a great leader of men, his grasp of military tactics was flawed. By splitting his forces between Manhattan and Long Island, with the East River and Long Island Sound between them, Washington had exposed his army to the British fleet. The British landings began on the night of August 26 and the main attack came the next day. By noon, American survivors were falling back on the defensive works at Brooklyn Heights.

To be sure, Washington's forces had been defeated on Long Island, but, considering the overwhelmingly superior number of the British, the Americans had actually performed remarkably well. Diminished, the Continental army was still intact, and, during the stormy and foggy night of August 29–30, Washington directed a masterful retreat to Manhattan.

General Nathanael Greene advised Washington to burn and abandon New York, but Congress barred this, and Washington resolved to defend the city as best he could. However, on September 7, he made the mistake of deploying his troops thinly over 16 miles of ground, leaving the weakest position in the middle of the island of Manhattan. On September 15, the British fleet sailed up the Hud

son and the East rivers, flanking Manhattan. Transport barges landed at Kip's Bay (where 34th Street today ends at FDR Drive) and unloaded troops who swept the handful of militiamen before them. Washington personally attempted to rally the troops, but without success, then retreated north to Harlem Heights and Fort Washington. The British lost the initiative by failing to pursue and, instead, settling in for a slow operation.

By nightfall on September 15, Howe had established forward posts from McGowan's Pass (at the northeast corner of present-day Central Park) southwest to the Hudson River (at about the location of 105th Street). Before dawn of the 16th, Lieutenant Colonel Thomas Knowlton led 100 elite Connecticut Rangers down the so-called Hollow Way, a steep descent from Harlem Heights to the Hudson. He ran into elements of the famed Black Watch Highland troops and engaged them fiercely, but he was forced to retreat as more Highlanders arrived. The British misinterpreted the retreat as the beginning of a general flight, and the advance elements of Howe's invading force now attacked in anticipation of triggering a rout. Instead, they got a full-scale fight that sent the Highlanders running in retreat across a buckwheat field that fronted the Hudson (on the site of today's Barnard College). To the American defenders, this small victory was greatly heartening. To Howe, it was discouraging out of all proportion. With thousands of well-equipped troops and a mighty naval fleet at his disposal, he could have struck Washington's position from the flanks or the rear. Instead, he did nothing, and by the middle of October, he had still failed to move against Fort Washington and Harlem Heights.

Washington observed that Howe's barges were probing for Hudson landings in Westchester County, above his own position. Believing that Howe was preparing an encirclement, Washington decided on October 16 that the time had come to evacuate Manhattan. He began slowly to withdraw northward to White Plains. Yet again, the American commander deployed his troops poorly, neglecting to fortify Chatterton Hill—the highest and, therefore, most important of the three hills on which he stationed soldiers. It was on precisely this position that Howe focused his attack, sending the Americans into retreat farther north. Taking a position at North Castle, Washington resupplied his force.

When he evacuated Manhattan, Washington left a garrison to hold Fort Washington at the northern end of the island. With reinforcements, the garrison numbered almost 3,000. Howe took the fort on November 16, making prisoners of 2,818 American officers and enlisted men. Fort Lee, across the Hudson, fell soon afterward. The American army was now split into three pieces: Charles Lee was up in North Castle, Westchester County; General William Heath was at Peekskill, farther up the Hudson from Manhattan; and Washington took the main body of troops on a long retreat through New Jersey.

Washington understood that he could not defeat the overwhelming military might of the British Empire, but he believed that if he could keep his army intact and fighting, the liberal wing of the British government might well prevail and America would win its independence. Keeping the army intact was no easy task, however. Casualties, the expiration of enlistments, and capture had reduced Washington's command to about 16,400 troops. He consolidated this number for operations in New Jersey, but by December he had retreated across the Delaware River and into Pennsylvania. Lord Cornwallis secured permission from Howe to halt at the Delaware and to wait for spring, when he and Howe planned to finish off the American army.

By Christmastime, Washington found that he had no more than 6,000 troops fit for duty. Fearing that he would soon lose most of these when current enlistments expired, he boldly decided on a counteroffensive. On Christmas night, Washington loaded 2,400 veteran troops and 18 cannon into Durham boats and crossed the Delaware in a vicious winter storm. He marched his men to Trenton, where Hessians, the Crown's much-feared German mercenaries, were camped, and there, at 7:30 on the morning of December 26, Washington secured a surprise and won a splendid victory. This was followed on January 3 by the Battle of Prince-

ton, another American victory. From here, Washington rode west to Morristown to make winter camp. For the present, the American Revolution had been saved.

Early spring 1777 brought the Americans fresh troops and a willingness among many veterans to extend their enlistments. In Paris, two congressional emissaries, Benjamin Franklin and Silas Deane, were gradually persuading the French government to conclude a formal alliance with the United States. Before this became a reality, Marie Joseph Paul Yves Roch Gilbert du Motier, Marquis de Lafayette, arrived in June with a party of other idealistic European adventurers (including the Baron de Kalb), all eager to impart European military expertise to the officers and men of the Continental army.

As for the British, General John Burgoyne now proposed a three-pronged attack through New York State: A principal force would advance south from Canada and proceeding down Lake Champlain and the upper Hudson; simultaneously, a smaller force would operate in the New York frontier country, from Oswego east through the Mohawk Valley. These two operations would be coordinated with Howe, who would send another major force up the Hudson, meeting Burgoyne's principal force at Albany, thereby effecting a pincers movement that would amputate New England from the rest of the colonies.

Burgoyne began his move south from St. Johns, Newfoundland, to Lake Champlain on June 17, 1777. In July, a British unit under General Simon Fraser recaptured Fort Ticonderoga. Burgoyne completed a wilderness road approaching Albany, intending to meet up with General Barry St. Leger from the Mohawk Valley and Howe from the south to deliver a crushing blow to the rebels and return to England in triumph. But on August 3, while camped near Fort Edward, waiting for his full forces to assemble, he received word from Howe that he, Howe, would attack Philadelphia and therefore would be unable to join Burgoyne's operation. As for St. Leger, falsely informed by POWs that the American stronghold at Fort Stanwix was formidably garrisoned, he delayed his planned attack on the fort, giving time for Patriot militia general Nicholas Herkimer to coordinate an attack on him and his mixed force of British regulars, Tory units, and Indians at Oriskany, New York. The August 6 battle was especially brutal. Most of the American officers were killed in the opening minutes of the battle, and Herkimer himself was severely wounded, his leg shattered by a musket ball. Nevertheless, the British-allied Indians were so disheartened by their heavy losses that they suddenly retreated, leaving the British no choice but to withdraw as well. This enabled the Americans to continue holding Fort Stanwix, and St. Leger broke off his attack on the fort, leaving behind equipment and losing face with his few remaining Indian allies.

Burgoyne detailed Hessian troops under Lieutenant Colonel Frederick Baum to take Bennington, Vermont. Opposing Baum were 200 militiamen under General John Stark and 400 men of the Vermont militia, led by Seth Warner. On August 16, Stark and Warner made a preemptive attack and defeated the Hessian and British forces, depriving Burgoyne of supplies he badly needed and thereby ending any possibility of his executing a grand strategy of splitting the American colonies in two.

Farther south, the Americans did not fare as well. After many delays, Howe transported 15,000 troops from New York to Philadelphia via Cape Charles and thence up the Chesapeake. To counter the threat against what was the capital of revolutionary America, Washington and his Continental army—at this point numbering about 11,000 men—paraded through Philadelphia on August 24, 1777, and, on September 11, engaged the British at the Brandywine Creek near Chadd's Ford, Pennsylvania. Washington suffered a severe defeat here, compounded, on September 20–21, by the "massacre" of some 150 American troops under General Anthony Wayne at Paoli, Pennsylvania. After this, Washington moved his troops to Pott's Grove (present-day Pottstown), Pennsylvania, whereupon the British advanced into Philadelphia, on September 23, unopposed. Washington mounted a daring counterattack from Germantown, a village adjacent to Philadelphia, on October 4. He suffered yet another defeat, but his leadership in pressing such a

daring offensive left French observers sufficiently impressed to recommend that their government at long last enter into a formal alliance with the Patriots. America was about to acquire a powerful ally.

And more hopeful news followed. Horatio Gates and Benedict Arnold defeated Burgoyne at two battles near Saratoga, New York. On October 13, Burgoyne surrendered an entire British army to Gates—a feat that validated the revolution not only for many in America but also for much of the international community.

Despite the triumph at Saratoga and the new French alliance, Washington faced insubordination from a clique of his officers; even worse, he faced a winter of great privation at Valley Forge, Pennsylvania. His troops were driven to the verge of mutiny by a Continental Congress that was unable to fund necessary food, clothing, and shelter. Nevertheless, whatever Washington's shortcomings as a tactician, he was a great leader, and the army remained intact. On June 28 he fought an inconclusive battle at Monmouth Courthouse, New Jersey, and troops under General John Sullivan campaigned against Indians and loyalists in upstate New York. By this time, however, the action began to take place increasingly in the South.

In 1776, the British had tried but failed to capture Charleston, South Carolina; however, two years later they did succeed in taking Savannah, Georgia. An attempt by Continental Army forces to retake Savannah failed miserably in 1779, and, during that year as well, Charleston fell to a second British assault. It was in the back country of the South that irregular American units, not part of the Continental army, had more success against British forces. Although it is also true that irregular units of Loyalists also took a brutal toll on the Patriots.

General Horatio Gates's defeat at Camden, South Carolina, on August 16, 1780, was a humiliating loss, somewhat compensated for by an American militia victory at King's Mountain on the border of North and South Carolina days later.

After the failure of Gates, Washington succeeded in replacing him with the far abler General Nathanael Greene as overall commander of Continental army forces in the South. Greene worked especially well with the skilled guerrilla leader Daniel Morgan, who, on January 16, 1781, won an important victory at Cowpens, little more than a backwoods South Carolina cattle pasturage.

After Cowpens, Cornwallis stripped his remaining troops of all the baggage that had for so long encumbered British armies in the American wilderness and, with his streamlined force, he pursued Greene's army northward, all the way to the Dan River, near the Virginia border. Once across that river, Greene took all the boats with him, and Cornwallis found himself on the near shore of the Dan, desperately low on supplies (having sacrificed them to gain speed) and forced to return to Hillsboro for resupply. In the meantime, Greene took the initiative. He recrossed the Dan into North Carolina to attack Cornwallis's lines of communication. Greene was careful, however, to avoid an all-out action until he had assembled enough men to outnumber Cornwallis. In the meantime, operations against local Tories—including a massacre of 400 of them at the hands of General Andrew Pickens—largely deprived the British general of his base of Loyalist support. At last, on March 14, 1781, Greene chose his battlefield: Guilford Courthouse, North Carolina. He did not achieve a decisive victory there, but he did force Cornwallis from the field.

After Guilford Courthouse, Cornwallis made the fateful decision to take and hold Yorktown, a sleepy tobacco port on the York River in Virginia. Washington joined forces with a large French army commanded by Jean Baptiste Rochambeau and began an advance against Cornwallis, intending to bottle him up on the Yorktown Peninsula. Coordination with French admiral de Grasse effectively cut off Cornwallis from escape or supply by sea, and Washington and Rochambeau patiently laid siege to the British position. On October 17, 1781, Cornwallis agreed to unconditional surrender, with the formal ceremony taking place on October 19.

By no means did Yorktown end the British presence in the United States, but it did end Britain's national resolve to continue resisting the Revolution. The pro-independence faction in Parliament steadily gained ground, and, on September

3, 1783, the Treaty of Paris was signed, ending the American Revolution and recognizing the United States as an independent and sovereign nation.

Anniston Army Depot (ANAD)   See FORTS AND OTHER INSTALLATIONS.

Antarctica Service Medal   See DECORATIONS AND MEDALS.

antiarmor weapons

Currently (2005), the army fields the following weapons systems specifically designed for use against tanks and other armored targets.

AAWS-M Javelin

The Advanced Antitank Weapons System-Medium, known as Javelin, is a man-portable antitank missile, which will entirely replace the M-47 Dragon. Whereas the M-47 is an optically sighted line-of-sight weapon, the AAWS-M uses an infrared fire-and-forget system. The M-47 requires sighting a target in the weapon's crosshairs and holding it there. With AAWS-M fire-and-forget system, a soldier can fire the weapon and then leave, relying on the missile's guidance system to find the target, thereby avoiding the risk of return fire on his position. The Javelin consists of an expendable tube (which serves as launcher as well as storage and carrying case), the missile, and a reusable Command Launch Unit, or CLU.

As an antitank weapon, the Javelin is designed to exploit armor where it is most vulnerable. When fired, the missile climbs from 330 to 660 feet, then approaches the target from a 45-degree dive in order to penetrate through the typically vulnerable top. The missile homes in on the target using a complex set of Long-Wave IR sensors.

General characteristics of the AAWS-M include:

Contractor: Texas Instruments/Martin Marietta

Weight, tube with missile: 41.9 lb

Propulsion: Atlantic Research 2-stage motor system
Range: 2,871 yd

AGM-114 Hellfire

This air-to-ground missile system provides heavy antiarmor capability for attack helicopters. The first three generations of Hellfire missiles use a laser seeker, while the latest, fourth-generation missile, Longbow Hellfire, uses a radar frequency seeker. The first-generation missiles constitute the main armament of the army's AH-64 Apache and USMC's AH-1 Cobra and AH-1W Super Cobra helicopters. The missiles, introduced in 1982, are produced by Lockheed Martin and Rockwell International.

The AGM-114K Hellfire II missile incorporates dual warheads for defeating reactive armor, electro-optical countermeasures hardening, semiactive laser seeker, and a programmable autopilot for trajectory shaping. The planned Longbow Hellfire missile will provide an adverse-weather, fire-and-forget, heavy antiarmor capability for attack helicopters.

General characteristics include:

Contractors: Rockwell International and Lockheed Martin
Weight: 100.9 lb (laser variant)
Length: 5 ft 4 in (laser variant)
Diameter: 7 in
Wingspan: 1 ft 0.8 in
Propulsion: Thiokol TX-657 solid-fuel rocket
Speed: Mach 1.1
Range: about 5 mi

BGM-71 TOW

TOW stands for Tube-launched, Optically tracked, Wire-guided. TOW is the most widely used antitank guided missile in the world. Extremely versatile, it may be fired from tripods, from vehicles, and from helicopters.

The Basic TOW, introduced in 1970, features a warhead five inches in diameter, an analog computer, and a range of 3,281 yards. Subsequently, five variants have been produced. The ITOW, or Improved TOW, added a telescoping standoff detonation probe, which ensures detonation at an optimum distance from the armor of a target. The ITOW carries a High-Explosive-Armor-Piercing (HEAP) warhead. The TOW 2 introduced a more sophisticated three-section probe, a more powerful motor, and a more powerful six-inch warhead. The TOW 2A uses tandem warheads to increase effectiveness against reactive armor. The first warhead detonates the reactive armor so that the second warhead can effectively penetrate it. Another variant, the TOW 2B, is especially designed for top attack.

General characteristics of the Basic TOW include:

Original contractors: Hughes Aircraft and McDonnell Douglas
Weight, on tripod: 173 lb
Length: 3 ft 10 in prelaunch
Diameter: 6 in
Propulsion: 2 Hercules solid fuel rocket motors
Speed: Mach 0.8–0.9
Crew: 4

M-47 Dragon

This shoulder-fired antitank guided missile system consists of a launcher, tracker, and missile. The expendable fiberglass launch tube also serves as the storage and carrying case for the missile. The Dragon is a wire-guided line-of-sight weapon intended for use against armored vehicles, fortified bunkers, concrete gun emplacements, and other hard targets. The system is designed to be carried and fired by an individual gunner.

Developed for the army in 1970, the Dragon is to be replaced by the AAWS-M Javelin.

General characteristics include:

Original contractor: McDonnell Douglas Aerospace
Weight, round: 25 lb
Weight, warhead: 6 lb
Length, tube: 3 ft 8 in
Length, rocket: 2 ft 5 in
Propulsion: Hercules motor
Speed: 328 fps in flight
Range: 1,094 yd

M-712 Copperhead

The M-712 Copperhead Cannon-Launched Guided Projectile is a 155-mm high-explosive artillery projectile that guides itself with great accuracy to a laser-designated target. Each projectile consists of three main sections, including a guidance section (forward), warhead section (center), and control section (rear). The guidance section contains the seeker head and the electronics assembly, and the nose of the projectile contains a laser seeker. The warhead section is packed with an HE antitank warhead in the form of 14.75 pounds of composition B. The control section has fins and wings that deploy in flight to allow a limited range of maneuverability. The Copperhead trajectory resembles that of a conventional artillery round until the projectile reaches a certain point in its descent. At this point, guidance and control systems are activated, enabling the projectile to alter the remainder of its trajectory. At 20 seconds from impact, the laser designator operator begins designating the target. The projectile acquires the reflected laser energy and initiates internal guidance and control.

General characteristics of the M712 include:

Contractor: Lockheed Martin
Weight: 137 lb
Length: 4 ft 6 in
Width: 6 in
Propulsion: launched by a 155-mm HOWITZER
Maximum range: 17,498 yd
Warhead: 49.6 lb high explosive

Armed Forces Expeditionary Medal   See DECORATIONS AND MEDALS.

Armed Forces Reserve Medal   See DECORATIONS AND MEDALS.

Armed Forces Service Medal   See DECORATIONS AND MEDALS.

armor

Armor is a combat branch of the army, which employs tanks and other armored vehicles to conduct highly mobile, highly effective warfare. The branch is headquartered at Fort Knox, Kentucky, and major army armored divisions, brigades, and armored CAVALRY regiments include 1ST ARMORED DIVISION (Old Ironsides), 49TH ARMORED DIVISION, 155th Separate Armored Brigade, 2nd Armored Cavalry Regiment, 3rd Armored Cavalry Regiment, and 278th Armored Cavalry Regiment.

Army armor has its origin in the American Expeditionary Force of WORLD WAR I, which established a Tank Corps to operate the newly developed tracked armored vehicles that, because they could traverse trench lines, promised to break the trench warfare stalemate of the western front. Army tankers in WORLD WAR I used British and French vehicles because the Tank Corps had yet to develop its own. Among the earliest pioneers of American armor tactics and warfare was GEORGE SMITH PATTON, who had the distinction of commanding the first army armored force to see combat.

The fledgling Tank Corps was abolished after World War I by the National Defense Act of 1920, which incorporated armor into the INFANTRY. This significantly retarded the development of armor in U.S. forces because American tanks were developed strictly as infantry support vehicles. In addition to tanks, which are tracked armored vehicles, the United States also developed armored cars, wheeled vehicles used mainly for reconnaissance and of limited utility in battle.

In 1928, the Department of War established within the army the Experimental Mechanized Force, which began testing the design and employment of tanks beyond the infantry support role. Two years later, Congress authorized establishment of the Army Mechanized Force, which essentially adapted cavalry tactics to the deployment of the Mechanized Force. This proved the undoing of the Mechanized Force, which was disbanded in 1931 because it was seen as duplicating the mission of the cavalry. Each combat arm was now instructed

A U.S. armored column rolls through the streets of Palermo, Sicily, on July 22, 1943.   *(National Archives)*

to develop its own mechanized program, and this led to the creation of the Mechanized Cavalry, which established itself at Fort Knox on January 1, 1932. From this point on, Fort Knox became the center of army armor.

The 1st Cavalry Regiment (Mechanized) was joined in 1936 by the 13th Cavalry Regiment, which discarded horses and adopted tanks. Together, the regiments formed the 7th Cavalry Brigade (Mechanized), and the officers and soldiers of the brigade set about developing army armor doctrine and tactics.

The pace of development sharply quickened after the German army invaded Poland in September 1939, thereby starting WORLD WAR II in Europe. The Polish blitzkrieg and the blitzkrieg invasion of France that followed the next year were propelled in large measure by Germany's highly advanced Panzer tanks and other armored vehicles. Army military planners concluded that armor could not be used effectively when subordinated to infantry or cavalry, and, on July 10, 1940, the Armored Force was created as an independent arm headquartered, along with the newly established I Armored Corps, at Fort Knox. On July 15, 1940, the 7th Cavalry Brigade (Mechanized) became the 1st Armored Division. Additionally, the 7th Provisional Tank Brigade, an infantry tank unit at Fort Benning, Georgia, became the 2nd Armored Division. The Tank Battalion was established at Fort Meade, Maryland.

The army also established the Armored Force School at Fort Knox on October 1, 1940, to train a generation of armored force soldiers in tank gunnery, armor tactics, communications, and maintenance. With U.S. entry into World War II, both the school and the Armored Force expanded rapidly. By the end of the war, the Armored Force consisted of 16 armored divisions and more than 100 separate tank battalions and mechanized cavalry squadrons.

The role of armor decreased in the postwar years, and tanks saw only limited deployment in the KOREAN WAR and in the VIETNAM WAR; however, after Vietnam, new vehicles were designed and deployed, and the importance of armor reasserted itself spectacularly in the PERSIAN GULF WAR. Today, armor tactics and doctrine are intensely focused on communication and coordination of forces and the integration of armor into the electronic battlefield.

army, size and composition

The U.S. Army is a vast organization. As of 2004, the army consisted of 499,000 soldiers on active duty and 205,000 in the Army Reserves (see UNITED STATES ARMY RESERVE COMMAND). In addition, 335,000 soldiers served in the ARMY NATIONAL GUARD. In 2004, therefore, total strength of the army was 1,039,000, plus 222,000 Department of the Army civilian employees.

The army consists of 23 combat division equivalents consisting of 10 active-duty divisions, 8 National Guard divisions, and 15 National Guard enhanced combat brigades (which are the equivalent of 5 divisions). In addition, hundreds of combat, combat support, and combat service support units are available to corps commands and higher-level support commands.

Army Air and Missile Defense Command

The mission of this command is, on order, strategically to deploy combat-ready air defense units and perform air and missile defense planning, coordination, integration, and execution in support of the commander in chief's priorities. The command is always assigned to the theater army and is charged with planning, coordinating, and executing army joint air and missile defense (AMD) operations, integrating battle information, and synchronizing and directing the conduct of AMD operations.

Army Aviation School

In 1973, all army aviation flight training was consolidated at the Army Aviation School, at Fort Rucker, Alabama and, since then, this facility has served as the training and upgrade training center for all army aviators. It is considered the "Home of Army Aviation."

The school teaches everything from initial rotary-wing courses to advanced courses in aviation safety. Students train to fly the AH-64A Apache, the UH-60A Blackhawk, the CH-47D Chinook, the OH-58D Kiowa Warrior, and the AH-60D Longbow Apache. Additionally, since 1971, the Fort Rucker facility has offered training to USAF helicopter pilots.

Army Chaplain Corps

The Army Chaplain Corps is a special branch of the army with a home station at Fort Jackson, South Carolina. The corps provides religious support to soldiers and their families. All major faiths are represented.

The history of the corps may be traced to the AMERICAN REVOLUTION, in which clergymen not only served to minister to the spiritual needs of militiamen as well as members of the CONTINENTAL ARMY but often, as community leaders, personally raised and organized military units from their own congregations. Many of the early clergymen served not only as chaplains but also as combat soldiers. William Emerson served at the Battle of Concord (April 19, 1775) exclusively in the capacity of chaplain and, therefore, is generally considered the first U.S. military chaplain. However, by the time GEORGE WASHINGTON assumed command of the Continental army at Cambridge, Massachusetts, at least 15 chaplains were serving with the 23 regiments gathered around Boston. The Continental Congress officially recognized the office of chaplain on July 29, 1775, when it voted pay for these clergymen and various other officers and enlisted personnel not previously covered by the July 16 resolution, which created the Continental army.

After the close of the American Revolution, the Continental army was almost immediately dis-

An army chaplain comforts the spouse of one of the victims of the September 11, 2001, terrorist attack on the Pentagon. *(Department of Defense)*

banded, and in 1789, when the new U.S. Constitution entered into force, the army consisted of a single regiment of 595 men—too small, Congress deemed, to warrant a chaplain. When, on March 3, 1791, Congress authorized the creation of a second regiment, it also authorized the president to appoint a chaplain. Consequently, on March 4, the Reverend John Hurt of Virginia, an Episcopalian, was appointed chaplain of the army's only brigade.

Hurt's appointment did not establish a chaplain corps and, in fact, the status of army chaplains remained highly uncertain throughout the early 19th century. On July 5, 1838, the army established a system of post chaplains, authorizing 15, which was later increased to 20; however, the actual number of chaplains rarely reached half these authorized numbers. At the start of the UNITED STATES–MEXICAN WAR in 1846, 13 chaplains served on army posts. Early the following year, Congress authorized the appointment of brigade chaplains and also permitted post chaplains to serve with units in the field. The fact that all the army chap

lains were Protestant created a problem as Mexican propagandists accused the United States of conducting a Protestant crusade against Roman Catholic Mexico. Mexican officials encouraged Catholic soldiers to desert and even take up arms against the United States. To counter this, President James K. Polk met with Catholic religious leaders, who sent two Jesuit priests to join the army as its first Catholic chaplains.

In the years between the war with Mexico and the CIVIL WAR, during 1850, 1853, and 1856, critics of the chaplaincy charged that the institution was an unconstitutional violation of the separation of church and state. The Judiciary Committee of the House of Representatives successfully answered these objections, and the chaplaincy continued.

During the Civil War, the army chaplaincy grew greatly in size, with the appointment of an estimated 3,000 chaplains during the war (as many as 1,079 served on active duty at any one time). It is not known how many chaplains served with Confederate forces, but historians estimate between 600 and 1,000. An act of August 3, 1861, provided regimental chaplains for the Union army, specifying that these were to be "regularly ordained ministers of some Christian denomination." This was changed on July 17, 1862, to permit the appointment of ordained ministers "of some religious denomination," which permitted the appointment of Jewish chaplains as well as the first Black and Indian chaplains.

After the Civil War, chaplains continued to serve, often doubling as instructors on army posts. In 1899, as part of a general reorganization and reform of the army, the chaplaincy was professionalized and standardized. Distinctive new insignia were introduced, a rationale for selection and screening candidates was formulated and standardized, and, in 1909, a Board of Chaplains was created to collect and tabulate suggestions from chaplains and commanders and, based on these, to make recommendations to the War Department for a more effective chaplaincy. Also in 1909, the army officially recognized the position of chaplain assistant, an enlisted soldier detailed for the purpose of assisting the chaplain in the performance of his official duties.

As in the Civil War, the entry of the United States into WORLD WAR I in 1917 was accompanied by a massive increase in the number of chaplains. From 74 REGULAR ARMY chaplains and 72 ARMY NATIONAL GUARD chaplains, the chaplaincy grew to 2,217 before the armistice. Eleven chaplains would be killed in action, and 27 earned the Purple Heart. Another 27 were awarded the Distinguished Service Cross and 18 the Silver Star. Chaplains now ministered to troops wherever they were stationed, including on the front lines. After battle, chaplains were required to collect the dead, see to their burial, and perform all grave registration duties. They were responsible for ensuring that each grave was marked with the deceased's full name, unit, and date of death, so that the information corresponded with unit records, and that the grave location was reported with the map coordinates, name, and scale. Chaplains also regularly visited the wounded in hospitals and wrote sympathy letters to the next of kin. Additionally, World War I–era chaplains served as the unit postal officer and censor. Informally, they often served as unit historians, librarians, post exchange officers, mess officers, defense counsels, regimental statistical officers, bond sales officers, band directors, athletic officers, morale officers, venereal disease control officers, education officers, couriers, and scorers on the rifle range. Even as the army called on chaplains to perform a wide range of miscellaneous duties, the service established at this time the ARMY CHAPLAIN SCHOOL, on February 9, 1918, originally based at Fort Monroe, Virginia.

Demobilization came rapidly and deeply after the war, reducing the number of chaplains to 125 on active duty in 1920. The National Defense Act of June 4, 1920, reorganized the army and, for the first time ever, organized the chaplaincy as a unique branch, the Army Chaplain Corps, commanded by an officer with the title of chief of chaplains.

The corps grew to its greatest extent during WORLD WAR II. On the day of Japan's surrender in September 1945, 8,191 chaplains were on active duty, including 2,278 Catholics, 243 Jews, and 5,620 Protestants. In addition to ministering to the needs of soldiers, chaplains also saw to the spiritual needs of enemy prisoners of war. In the immediate aftermath of the war, Jewish chaplains were assigned to aid displaced persons freed from concentration camps and to help reunite them with their families. The Jewish chaplains also helped to establish synagogues and to assist orphans. Chaplains of all denominations aided civilian populations, especially youth groups and relief programs throughout Europe. Although chaplains no longer held primary responsibility for burial and graves registration, they worked closely with the American Graves Registration Command to account for and to pray for soldiers whose bodies were recovered from various battlefields and reinterred in American military cemeteries.

Chaplains served in the KOREAN WAR. In the VIETNAM WAR they faced some of their most demanding and diverse challenges. The intense antiwar movement during the Vietnam years created an upsurge in the numbers of soldiers seeking separation from the army as conscientious objectors. Chaplains were assigned to conduct counseling interviews with these soldiers and to assess and rule on their sincerity as well as the validity of the religious basis of their application. Widespread drug abuse by demoralized soldiers marked another crisis brought by the Vietnam War. Chaplains were assigned specifically to counsel drug abusers and to establish antidrug educational programs in their units. Finally, the Vietnam War brought many army leaders to a greater awareness of issues of race relations in the service, and chaplains were in the forefront of creating and conducting programs to improve race relations among American soldiers. The end of the Vietnam era saw another milestone in the Army Chaplain Corps, namely, the commissioning of Reverend Alice M. Henderson in 1974 as the first woman to officially serve with the corps.

Since the end of the Vietnam era, members of the Army Chaplain Corps have devised the Unit Ministry Team (UMT) concept, which provides religious support to soldiers in combat by nurturing the living, caring for the casualties, and honoring the dead. The UMT moves continuously among the forward combat elements, ministering to soldiers before, during, and after contact with the enemy. In so doing, the UMT has completed the integration of the chaplain into the daily functioning of the army in every environment, task, and context.

Army Chaplain School

Located at Fort Jackson, South Carolina, the Army Chaplain School trains religious leaders for the army. The school offers three general course tracks. The chaplain officer basic course (CHOBC) is an intensive 12-week and four-day course that is battle-focused and intended to ensure combat survivability through intense physical fitness training and acquisition of basic military skills and knowledge. Courses include Military Acculturation, Individual Tactical Training, Day and Night Infiltration, Day and Night Land Navigation, the Confidence Course, Victory Tower rappelling, Nuclear-Biological-Chemical (NBC) training, First Aid, and the Team Work Development course. In Phase 1 of training, students learn how to serve as Special Staff Officers. Courses are offered in Military History, the Profession of Arms, Leadership Communication Skills (written and oral), Spiritual Fitness, Pluralism, and the Duties and Responsibilities of Officers and NCOs.

Phase 2 begins training in the 41 chaplain-specific critical tasks, including pastoral care specialist training, marriage counseling skills, critical incident stress management, worship leadership training, chaplain fund management, leadership and supervision, and unit ministry team philosophy.

Phase 3 completes training in the chaplain-specific critical tasks as conducted in the combat environment. This phase prepares the student for immediate deployment.

The Army Chaplain School also offers a course on Advanced Individual Training (AIT) for enlisted soldiers. This seven-week, three-day course is designed to train soldiers to function as effective members of the Unit Ministry Team. Training phases include religious support activities, pastoral care and counseling, religious support planning/operations, and management and administration. The emphasis is on acquiring the skills necessary to provide comprehensive religious support on the battlefield.

Finally, the school also provides a Chaplain Resource Manager course and a Funds Clerk course. These are two-week courses designed to teach chaplains and chaplain assistants the regulations, laws, and doctrine that govern the receipt of funds and property and their expenditure.

The Army Chaplain School was approved on February 9, 1918, and the school's first session commenced on March 3, 1918, at Fort Monroe, Virginia. The school was relocated a year later to Camp Zachary Taylor, Kentucky, and, during WORLD WAR I, a subsidiary chaplain school was established in France near the headquarters of the American Expeditionary Force at Chaumont.

After the war, the school was briefly suspended, then was reactivated on a permanent basis at Camp Grant, Illinois, in April 1920. It moved several times until 1996, when it was permanently established at Fort Jackson.

Army Chemical School

Located at Fort Leonard Wood, Missouri, the Army Chemical School has as its mission the protection of the force in such a way that the army can fight and win against a nuclear-biological-chemical (NBC) threat. The school develops doctrine, equipment, and training for NBC defense, which is intended to serve as a deterrent to any adversary possessing weapons of mass destruction. Additionally, the school provides the army with the combat multipliers of smoke, obscurant, and flame capabilities.

Offerings include courses in Biological Defense, which teaches battle-focused biological defense, including the use of detection equipment; a Chemical Captain's course; an NBC Defense course; a Tactical Radiation course; an NBC Reconnaissance course; and a special "Joint Senior Leaders'" course: "A Focus on Chemical, Biological, Radiological and Nuclear (CBRN) Defense and Response."

Army Dental Corps

The Army Dental Corps, a special branch of the army with a home station at Fort Sam Houston, Texas, is among the largest and most sophisticated dental providers in the world. In addition to providing routine maintenance of dental health for soldiers and their families, the corps specializes in treating the kinds of dental trauma that result from battle wounds and other injuries.

During the earliest period of the army, soldiers secured dental care from whatever civilian dental surgeons they could find. In emergency conditions, army physicians and hospital stewards (including a few who had rudimentary training in dentistry) provided care. Shortly before the commencement of the CIVIL WAR, on July 31, 1860, the American Dental Association held its first convention in Washington, D.C., and adopted a resolution to support the appointment of dental officers for the army and navy. The services did not respond; however, the provisional army of the Confederate States began conscripting dentists to provide dental care because it was apparent that most soldiers could not afford to pay civilian dentists. It was not until April 4, 1872, that William Saunders, a hospital steward at the UNITED STATES MILITARY ACADEMY at West Point, was officially recognized as a military dentist and was charged with providing dental service to cadets and staff. During the SPANISH-AMERICAN WAR, in 1898, individual army units appointed dental surgeons from among enlisted hospital corpsmen in locations where dental services were not available from civilian sources.

On February 2, 1901, Congress passed legislation directing the Army Surgeon General to employ 30 civilian contract dentists to provide dental care for officers and enlisted men. These individuals were attached to the Medical Department and were to be graduates of a medical or dental school who passed a qualifying dental examination. Dr. John Sayre Marshall, M.D., considered the father of the Army Dental Corps, was appointed the first contract dentist, senior supervising contract dental surgeon, and president of the first Army Board of Dental Examiners. On April 13, 1911, he became the army's first commissioned dental officer after the U.S. Army Dental Corps (DC) had been established by law on March 3, 1911.

Interestingly, dentists began preparing for WORLD WAR I a year before the United States entered the war. In March 1916, the Preparedness League of American Dentists, 1,700 civilian dentists, organized to provide free dental service for men preparing to enlist. The league also created a course for the military training of dentists, and some 4,000 to 5,000 individuals completed the training. The National Defense Act of June 1916 included reorganization of the Army Dental Corps and authorized creation of the Army Dental Reserve Corps. On April 6, 1917, when the United States declared war on Germany, the Army Dental Corps consisted of 86 regular officers. By the armistice, on November 11, 1918, the number of active duty dental officers peaked at 4,620. On November 15, 1917, basic training and combat casualty care courses were established for dental officers at the new Dental Section, Sanitary School, in Langres, France. On March 15, 1918, basic and technical training for dental officers and enlisted dental assistants was begun at Camp Greenleaf, Fort Oglethorpe, Georgia.

After the war, the National Defense Act of 1920 authorized 298 officers for the Army Dental Corps and established the Medical Department ROTC, which, in turn, allowed establishment of dental ROTC programs at eight dental schools in 1921 and 1922. In January 1922, the Army Dental School was established at Washington, D.C.

The United States entered WORLD WAR II on December 8, 1941, with an active duty dental corps of 316 REGULAR ARMY and 2,589 reserve DC officers. The Army Dental Corps active duty strength would reach its wartime peak in May 1945, with 15,292 officers.

The KOREAN WAR brought the Army Dental Corps to a strength of 2,641 officers, with 370 serving in Korea. A dental officer, Lieutenant Colonel Jack P. Pollock, was among the first army personnel to serve in an advisory capacity in Vietnam. At the peak of involvement, 2,817 dental personnel served in the VIETNAM WAR.

During the 1970s, the Army Dental Corps focused much effort on creating preventive dentistry programs and programs in dental hygiene, and, on November 8, 1983, the Surgeon General directed that combat casualty and surgical training be provided to dental officers to prepare them for alternate medical roles during wartime. Dental officers would be trained to provide general casualty care during periods of overwhelming casualties. During the post-Vietnam period, too, increasing emphasis was given to the development of forensic dentistry capability for the purpose of identifying human remains by means of dental examination and comparison with dental records.

Army General Staff

Part of the ARMY STAFF, the Army General Staff assists the CHIEF OF STAFF by addressing specific staff functions. The principal executives of the Army General Staff are general officers and they include: the Deputy Chief of Staff for Operations and Plans (DCSOPS), the Deputy Chief of Staff for Personnel (DCSPER), the Deputy Chief of Staff for Logistics (DCSLOG), the Deputy Chief of Staff for Intelligence (DCSI), the Deputy Chief of Staff for Programs, and the Deputy Chief of Staff for Installation Management.

Army Management Staff College

Located at Fort Belvoir, Virginia, the Army Management Staff College has as its mission the education and preparation of army civilian and military leaders for leadership and management responsibilities throughout the sustaining base of the army. Additionally, the college provides consulting services and conducts research in support of the sustaining base.

In 1985, the CHIEF OF STAFF of the army approved the establishment of the Army Management Staff College to educate and prepare civilian and military leaders for leadership and management operations. The college served to remedy the widely held belief that civilians entering into or already serving in army leadership positions were not well prepared for the special challenges they faced, while their military counterparts received leadership training in military staff and senior service colleges and lacked special management training. Moreover, there was a need for a comprehensive program to train military and civilian leaders in army-specific subjects. Accordingly, the Army Management Staff College opened its doors at the Maritime Institute of Technology and Graduate Studies in Linthicum, Maryland, in 1987. Later, the facility moved to the Radisson Mark Plaza Hotel in Alexandria, Virginia, and then, in 1993, to Fort Belvoir.

Key innovative courses include the Garrison Precommand course, the General Officer Installation Command course, the Garrison Sergeants Major course, Personnel Management for Executives, and the Chiefs of Staff course.

Army Medical Corps   See ARMY MEDICAL DEPARTMENT.

Army Medical Department

The Army Medical Department (AMEDD) is an army special branch tasked with providing medical care for army service members and their families. AMEDD includes the army's fixed hospitals and dental facilities; preventive health, medical research, development and training institutions; and a veterinary command, which provides food inspection and animal care services for the entire Department of Defense. On any given day, AMEDD administers or manages 1,295 occupied patient beds, 37,217 clinic visits, 6,400 dental visits, 359 patient admissions, 5,462 immunizations, 63 births, 49,226 laboratory procedures, 1,507 veterinary outpatient visits, 69,524 pharmacy procedures, and $15 million worth of food inspected. Whenever army field hospitals deploy, most clinical professional and support personnel come from AMEDD's fixed facilities. AMEDD provides trained medical specialists to combat medical units, which are assigned directly to combatant commanders.

Medics unload a casualty from a UH-1 helicopter in Vietnam.   *(AMEDD Medical Museum Foundation)*

On July 27, 1775, during the AMERICAN REVOLUTION, the Continental Congress created a medical service for the CONTINENTAL ARMY under the direction of Dr. Benjamin Church of Boston. In the general demobilization following the Revolution, army medical services were reduced to a single surgeon and four "surgeon's mates," and the army entered the WAR OF 1812 with no medical department at all—until Congress created one in 1813. In its military reorganization legislation of 1818, Congress created a permanent army medical service, and Dr. Joseph Lovell became the service's first Surgeon General. From virtually its earliest days, the Army Medical Department engaged in important research, including that of army surgeon William Beaumont, who, beginning in 1822 and for the next 10 years, observed the unclosed stomach wound of a Canadian trapper named Alexis St. Martin and made a pioneering study of human digestion.

In 1847, during the UNITED STATES–MEXICAN WAR, Congress authorized medical officers to receive military ranks. However, neither the fields of military medicine nor medicine in general were prepared for the CIVIL WAR. Emerging weapons technology created wounds of unprecedented devastation, and disease ravaged both Union and Confederate forces. Hospital facilities were woefully inadequate, and the care available to the sick and the wounded often served only to hasten death.

Early in 1862, Congress expanded and reorganized AMEDD, giving the army Surgeon General general-officer rank, which, in turn, gave him the authority to introduce many reforms, including the keeping of accurate records, the reorganization of medical field supplies, the establishment of forward hospitals, and the creation of an ambulance corps. After the war, in 1887, Congress created the Hospital Corps for specially trained enlisted men and, in 1893, established America's first school of public health and preventive medicine, the Army Medical School, which later evolved into the Walter Reed Army Institute of Research.

The SPANISH-AMERICAN WAR brought the grave challenges of typhoid, malaria, and especially yellow fever, all of which AMEDD vigorously attacked through research, proving, among other things, that yellow fever was mosquito-borne and could thus be controlled by controlling the mosquito population.

Early in the 20th century, the ARMY NURSE CORPS was created within AMEDD, and WORLD WAR I placed new and extensive demands on the department. AMEDD's strides in preventive medicine ensured that this would be the first U.S. war in which mortality from communicable disease was lower than that from battle wounds. The department also focused on the rapid evacuation of the wounded from the battlefield, developing a motor ambulance service.

After the war, in 1920, AMEDD established the Medical Field Service School at Carlisle Barracks, Pennsylvania, to train medical officers and enlisted medics in field medicine. Transferred to Fort Sam Houston, Texas, in 1947, the school evolved into today's AMEDD Center and School. The Medical Field Service School and its successor have been responsible for great advancements in the treatment of battlefield injury.

WORLD WAR II exposed soldiers to injury from new weapons and to the diseases endemic to every climate in the world. Vaccine research became an important AMEDD mission, as did the prevention and treatment of battle-related psychological disorders, including "battle fatigue." AMEDD was responsible for researching and promoting developments in the mass production of penicillin and the use of blood plasma as a substitute for the more fragile and perishable whole blood. In 1945, Captain Edwin Pulaski established a medical research unit at Halloran General Hospital, Staten Island, New York, which, after moving to Fort Sam Houston, Texas, evolved into the Institute of Surgical Research, a world-renowned burn center and pioneer of burn treatments. At its peak, the World War II strength of AMEDD topped 600,000 personnel.

After the war, AMEDD launched programs to develop its own medical and surgical specialists, and, in 1947, under AMEDD, Congress created the Medical Service Corps to absorb the Medical Administrative Corps, Sanitary Corps, and Pharmacy Corps, providing medical administrators, scientists, and staff trained in certain health-care specialties. The outbreak of the KOREAN WAR prompted extensive AMEDD research into the effects of cold weather and how to prevent cold weather injuries with protective clothing. AMEDD researchers also collaborated on the development of lightweight body armor to reduce wound severity for ground troops. In addition, the Korean War saw great advances in field hospital technology, in vascular surgery to reduce amputations, and in helicopter evacuation of the wounded. By war's end in 1953, over 17,000 casualties had been airlifted, and AMEDD experts helped to improve and refine helicopter medical evacuation, which played an even more important role in the VIETNAM WAR and subsequent operations and conflicts.

AMEDD research has increased and expanded since the Korean and Vietnam wars and is recognized as world class. Also, beginning in the 1960s, the number of army medical facilities has steadily and significantly increased. In 1973, all stateside army hospitals were unified under a new command, the U.S. Army Health Services Command (HSC), which later became the U.S. Army Medical Command (MEDCOM), headquartered at Fort Sam Houston, Texas. Operating under AMEDD, MEDCOM provides a single manager for the army's entire stateside health-care delivery and education system. HSC initially comprised seven Army Medical Centers (MEDCENs); Valley Forge General Hospital, Pennsylvania; and the Academy of Health Sciences. It soon took control of 37 Medical Department Activities (MEDDACs) or installation medical units (usually one hospital plus other medical elements), which previously had been commanded by post commanders. As the Vietnam conflict drew to a close, HSC organized the new medical system and closed several hospitals, including historic Valley Forge. But HSC's geographic spread expanded with the addition of Tripler Army Medical Center, Hawaii, and MEDDACs in Alaska and Panama. In mid-1974, HSC launched a regional system to control subordinate hospitals through MEDCENs.

AMEDD has not been immune to the rising cost of health care and the necessity for controlling costs. AMEDD has been more efficiently integrated with USN/USMC and USAF medical operations for greater efficiency, and, under MEDCOM, army health care has been effectively regionalized in ways that allow it to continue to provide services that ensure the health of soldiers.

Army Mountain Warfare School

Located at the Ethan Allen Firing Range in Jericho, Vermont, the Army Mountain Warfare School provides qualifying training for military mountaineer rating to members of the ARMY NATIONAL GUARD, U.S. ARMY RESERVE, and ACTIVE ARMY. Courses are given in basic and advanced mountain warfare and cold weather skills and tactics. In addition, the school trains, equips, and maintains a high-angle mountain search and rescue team.

Because approximately 38 percent of the world's landmass is classified as mountains, the army is concerned to prepare its soldiers to deter conflicts, resist coercion, and defeat aggression in rugged regions. The Army Mountain Warfare School teaches soldiers how to use adverse terrain and weather conditions to their advantage as a combat multiplier. The major objective is to teach mobility.

Coursework consists of two levels, summer and winter. The Level 1 summer course consists of 14 days of continuous training, with an average of 14 hours of training every day. The emphasis is on practical, realistic, and strenuous hands-on skills so that the student becomes increasingly proficient in the fundamentals, principles, and techniques of conducting small unit operations in mountainous terrain. The Level 1 winter course also consists of 14 days of continuous training, with an average of 12 hours of training every day. In addition to learning the skills and knowledge required to operate in mountainous terrain, the student's physical and mental endurance, stamina, and confidence are challenged by frigid temperatures and deep snow.

The Level 2 summer course consists of 10 days of continuous training, with an average of 14 hours of training every day. The course is given to selected soldiers and is intended to provide the knowledge and skills required to lead small units or teams over technically difficult, hazardous, or exposed mountainous terrain during summer months. The Level 2 winter course, 10 days of continuous training, with an average of 14 hours of training every day, is also a leadership course, designed to impart the knowledge and skills required to lead small units or teams over technically difficult, hazardous, or exposed mountainous terrain during winter months.

Army National Guard (ARNG)

The ARNG is part of the RESERVE COMPONENTS of the army and consists mainly of traditional guardsmen: civilians who serve on a part-time basis, typically one weekend each month and two weeks during the summer. The ARNG has a dual mission consisting of federal as well as state roles. Every state and territory as well as the District of Columbia has its own National Guard. For state missions, the governor, acting through the state adjutant general, commands ARNG forces. It is the governor's prerogative to call up the Guard during local or statewide emergencies, including natural disasters and civil disturbances. In the case of federal missions, the call to activation comes from the president of the United States. When federalized, ARNG units become part of the ACTIVE ARMY and are under the command of the combatant commander of the theater in which they are operating. Even when not federalized for a specific purpose, the ARNG fulfills the federal obligation of maintaining properly trained and equipped units, available for prompt mobilization for war, national emergency, or as otherwise needed.

The National Guard Bureau (NGB) assists the states, territories, and District of Columbia in procuring funding for the ARNG and in administer-

North Carolina National Guard members from Fayetteville and Baldenboro, North Carolina, help an unidentified woman from a Guard five-ton military truck near Tick Bite, North Carolina, on September 18, 1999. The woman was rescued by members of the National Guard from floodwaters caused by Hurricane Floyd. *(Department of Defense)*

ing policies; the NGB also serves as a liaison between the Department of the Army and the Department of the Air Force and the states. The NGB functions as a joint bureau of the two departments. The ARNG strength (2004) stands at about 335,000 soldiers.

Army Nurse Corps

Members of this combat service support branch are army nurses. The mission of the corps is "to provide nursing leadership and quality nursing care, both in peacetime and during contingency operations, within a professional military system and in support of the mission of the ARMY MEDICAL DEPARTMENT." Home station is Fort Sam Houston, Texas.

In July 1775, at the start of the AMERICAN REVOLUTION, the Second Continental Congress authorized medical support for a projected 20,000-man CONTINENTAL ARMY, to include a hospital (that is, Medical Department) with one female nurse for every 10 patients and a supervisory "matron" for every hundred sick or wounded. When the standing army was virtually disbanded following the Revolution, medical service was provided at regimental level, by assigned soldiers, and it was not until the Army Reorganization Act of August 14, 1818, that the Medical Department was reestablished by Congress, under a Surgeon General. There was no provision for nurses at this time, but in August 1856 the secretary of war was authorized to appoint enlisted men as hospital stewards.

The outbreak of the CIVIL WAR motivated the recruitment of women nurses for the army. On June 10, 1861, the secretary of war appointed Dorothea Lynde Dix, a public health reformer famous for her work on behalf of prisoners and the mentally ill, as superintendent of women nurses for the Union army. Under Dix's leadership, some 6,000 women eventually served the federal forces. Many were unskilled, but some received a short course in nursing under Dr. Elizabeth Blackwell, the first woman to receive a medical degree in the United States. The nurses were more closely integrated into the army on August 3, 1861, when Congress authorized the Surgeon General to employ women as nurses for

Army nurses checking blood shipment in Korea, 1951 (*AMEDD Medical Museum Foundation*)

army hospitals. Throughout the war, however, the army-affiliated nurses were supplemented by private citizens, including Catholic sisters of several orders and volunteers sponsored by the United States Sanitary Commission and other agencies. The nursing work was rarely medical in nature; rather, it involved mainly food preparation, housekeeping, and overseeing the distribution of supplies furnished by volunteer groups.

After the Civil War, soldiers resumed responsibility for patient care duties in army hospitals, and, on March 1, 1887, Congress established a Hospital Corps consisting of enlisted hospital stewards and privates as a part of the Army Medical Department. In 1891, the first company of instruction for members of the Hospital Corps was organized at Fort Riley, Kansas. The SPANISH-AMERICAN WAR in 1898 brought a request from the army Surgeon General for authority to appoint women nurses under contract. This revived military nursing in the army, which had virtually ceased to exist after the Civil War. The contract nurses were now certified professionals, about 1,500 in all, and included nuns in nursing orders. The end of the war brought a rapid demobilization of women nurses, down to 210 serving under contract in 1900. However, the war led to the establishment of an army organization officially called the Nurse Corps Division. On February 2, 1901, Congress passed legislation authorizing the establishment of the Nurse Corps (Female) as a permanent corps of the Army Medical Department. Nurses were now appointed in the REGULAR ARMY for a three-year renewable period. The Surgeon General also was directed to maintain a list of qualified nurses willing to serve in emergencies, thereby creating the first Reserve Corps authorized in the Army Medical Department.

In 1902, the authorized strength of the Nurse Corps was fixed at 100 nurses and the numbers increased modestly over the next several years. When the United States entered WORLD WAR I on April 6, 1917, 403 army nurses were on active duty, including 170 reserve nurses activated for the war. By June 1918, 12,186 nurses would serve on active duty in 198 stations worldwide. Also in 1918, the Army School of Nursing was authorized by the secretary of war, and, on July 9, 1918, the Nurse Corps (Female) was redesignated the Army Nurse Corps (ANC). On November 11, 1918, Armistice Day, the strength of the corps peaked at 21,480.

The Army Reorganization Act of June 4, 1920, authorized relative rank for army nurses from second lieutenant through major, but, by the following year, demobilization reduced the Army Nurse Corps to 851 nurses. When the United States entered WORLD WAR II, fewer than 7,000 army nurses were on duty. Within six months, the number rose to more than 12,000. During the war, African-American nurses were first accepted into the ANC, although, like African-American soldiers, they served exclusively in segregated units. World War II nurses also shared the dangers of combat to an unprecedented degree. In May 1942, 66 became prisoners of the Japanese after the fall of Corregidor. The peak strength of the ANC at the end of the war was more than 57,000.

The Army-Navy Nurse Act of 1947 established the Army Nurse Corps in the Medical Department of the regular army and authorized a strength of not less than 2,558 nurses and provided permanent commissioned officer status for members of the Army Nurse Corps in the grades of second lieutenant through lieutenant colonel. The postwar corps emphasized specialized education for nurses on a par with the best in civilian nursing education. In addition to courses in medical specialties, courses in hospital administration were also offered. Beginning in 1949, with the establishment of the first Army Health Nurse Program, emphasis was also placed on providing public health nursing services to the military community.

During the KOREAN WAR, the ANC peaked at 5,397 nurses, of which 540 Army Nurse Corps officers served throughout the Korean peninsula in 25 medical treatment facilities, including mobile army surgical hospitals; evacuation, field, and station hospitals; and hospital trains. Nurses were also among the first Americans to serve in the VIETNAM WAR, three army nurses accompanying the States Military Assistance Advisory Group (MAAG) in April 1956. The first full contingent of nurses arrived in Vietnam in March 1962, assigned to the 8th Field Hospital, Nha Trang. In April 1966, Special Call Number 38 was issued for the draft of 900 male nurses, 700 for the army and 200 for the USN, and on September 30, 1966, Congress authorized commissions in the regular army for male nurses. In all, more than 5,000 nurses, male and female, served in Vietnam, although the peak presence was just over 900 at any one time.

Army of Occupation Medal   See DECORATIONS AND MEDALS.

Army Physical Fitness Test (APFT)

The APFT is a three-event physical performance test the army uses to assess endurance. The intent of the test is to provide a baseline assessment regardless of MILITARY OCCUPATIONAL SPECIALTY or duty. Personnel are evaluated on their performance in completing push-ups, sit-ups, and a two-mile run. Scoring is keyed to age group and to gender.

Army Regulation 95-5 (AR 95-5)

Issued on June 20, 1941, AR 95-5 created the U.S. Army Air Forces (USAAF). AR 95-5 significantly enhanced the autonomy of the air arm over its former status as the U.S. Army Air Corps. The USAAF commander reported directly to the army chief of staff, and the Air Force Combat Command replaced the cumbersome General Headquarters Air Force. The effect of AR 95-5 and subsequent directives was to make the USAAF the functional equivalent of the army and navy.

Army Research Laboratory (ARL)

Headquartered at the Adelphi Laboratory Center in Adelphi, Maryland, and with facilities at the Aberdeen Proving Ground, the NASA Glenn Research Center in Ohio, the Army Research Office in North Carolina, the NASA Langley Research Center in Virginia, and the White Sands Missile Range in New Mexico, the ARL is the army's leading research facility in science as it relates to the army's missions. The ARL is administered by the U.S. ARMY MATERIEL COMMAND (AMC).

Army Reserve   See UNITED STATES ARMY RESERVE COMMAND.

Army Staff

The Army Staff reports to the SECRETARY OF THE ARMY and consists of the CHIEF OF STAFF, the ARMY GENERAL STAFF, the SPECIAL STAFF, and the PERSONAL STAFF.

Army Tactical Missile System (ATACMS)

The ATACMS Blocks I and IA are long-range ground-launched missile systems comprising a surface-to-surface guided missile with an antipersonnel/antimateriel (APAM) warhead consisting of M-74 fragmentation bomblets. Both Block I and IA are used to attack soft targets at ranges beyond the capabilities of existing cannons and rockets. They are launched from a modified M270 MLRS Self-Propelled Loader/Launcher (SPLL) at targets such as surface-to-surface missile sites, air defense systems, logistics elements, and command, control, and communication complexes.

Block I missiles carry about 950 bomblets, whereas Block IA incorporates a Global Positioning System (GPS) receiver in the missile for greater accuracy. Although it delivers fewer bomblets—about 300—its enhanced accuracy allows it to maintain the same level of lethality as the Block I version.

General characteristics of the ATACMS include:

Contractor: Lockheed Martin Vought Systems
Weight: (Block I) 3,661 lb
Length: 13 ft, 5 in
Diameter: 23.9 in
Speed: Supersonic
Warhead: 950 bomblets (I), 300 bomblets (IA)
Guidance: Inertial (I), Inertial + GPS (IA)
Range: 102.3 mi (I), 186 mi (IA)

Army Training Support Center (ATSC)

An element of U.S. ARMY TRAINING AND DOCTRINE COMMAND (TRADOC), ATSC is the army's principal training support planner, researcher, integrator, and service provider. Located at Fort Eustis, Virginia, the center manages the armywide Training Support System, which provides an operationally relevant training environment whenever and wherever needed.

The Army Training Support System is a system of systems, which provides the networked, integrated, interoperable training support necessary to enable an operationally relevant training environment for warfighters. It integrates a wide variety of training products, architectures, standards, and management, evaluation, and resource processes that enhance training effectiveness.

Army Veterinary Corps

This special branch of the army is charged with providing complete medical and surgical care to government-owned patrol dogs, laboratory animals, and ceremonial horses. The corps is also a research organization, active in disease control, biomedical research, microbiology, toxicology, animal-transmitted diseases, and epidemiological programs. The corps provides not only for army veterinary needs but also supports air force, navy, and marine corps units. Home station is Fort Sam Houston, Texas.

arsenals   See FORTS AND OTHER INSTALLATIONS.

Asiatic-Pacific Campaign Medal   See
DECORATIONS AND MEDALS.

assistant secretaries of the army

At present the SECRETARY OF THE ARMY oversees five assistant secretaries: for acquisition, logistics, and technology; for civil works; for financial management and comptroller; for installations and environment; and for manpower and reserve affairs.

Association of the United States Army (AUSA)

AUSA is a private, nonprofit educational organization that supports the army, including active components and RESERVE COMPONENTS as well as veterans, concerned civilians, and army family members.

The association was founded in 1950 with the purpose of "representing every American Soldier" by serving as the voice for all army components, fostering public support of the army role in national security, and providing professional education and information programs. Membership is open to all ranks and all components as well as to concerned citizens and family members. Community businesses and defense industry companies are also represented by AUSA. The organization may be contacted at its headquarters, 2425 Wilson Blvd., Arlington, VA 22201 (800) 336-4570.

Avenger   See AIR DEFENSE ARTILLERY.

aviation

Aviation is a combat branch of the army and operates rotary and fixed-wing AIRCRAFT in a very wide range of missions. The branch inventory holds more aircraft than either the U.S. Navy or U.S. Air Force. Branch headquarters is at Fort Rucker, Alabama.

Before the creation of an independent USAF in 1947, military aviation was the province of the army and navy.

Even before the creation of the USAF from the U.S. Army Air Forces in 1947, a rift was developing between aviation officers and others in the army. By the 1930s, most U.S. Army Air Corps leaders focused on the development of strategic air operations, carving out a role for the air arm that was essentially independent of ground forces. The emphasis on using aircraft to destroy enemy targets behind the lines of combat came at the expense of coordinating air and ground operations, the tactical use of aircraft in close air support roles. The absence of adequate air support was most immediately felt by artillery officers, who need observation aircraft and pilots for fire support and artillery spotting. The army therefore began experimenting with air support units "organic to" (that is, attached to and integral with) artillery units, and in the early 1940s, on the eve of United States entry into WORLD WAR II, the army began testing light single-engine aircraft dubbed Grasshoppers. Although the USAAC and, later, the USAAF were branches of the army, the emergence of the Grasshoppers marked the true birth of modern army aviation organic to the principal ground operations of the service.

The artillery spotter aircraft units constituted the foundation of the modern army aviation branch, and the first organic army aviators were trained by the Department of Air Training within the Field Artillery School at Fort Sill, Oklahoma. It was during the KOREAN WAR that army aviation began to come most fully into its own, as the service fielded its first combat helicopters. Army fixed-wing pilots still flew observation aircraft in Korea (chiefly the 0-1 Bird Dog), but a growing cadre of helicopter pilots flew H-13 Sioux rotary-wing craft on medical evacuation, command, and control, and light cargo transport missions. In 1951, the army organized five helicopter transport companies and began training warrant officers, not commissioned officers, as pilots. At this point, a certain degree of friction developed between the army and the still-youthful USAF over which service should assume responsibility for the aerial support of ground forces. Despite this, Department of Air Training operations and facilities at Fort Sill expanded to become, early in 1953, the ARMY AVIATION SCHOOL. When the school—and army aviation generally—outgrew Fort Sill, the school was moved to Camp (later Fort) Rucker, Alabama, in 1954. The Army Aviation Center was established there the following year, and in 1956 the army assumed from the USAF control over all of its own training.

In 1956, the Army Aviation Center began assembling and testing weapons on helicopters,

A soldier performs maintenance on an Apache Longbow helicopter on an airfield in Iraq. Army aviation assets are playing a key role in Operation Iraqi Freedom and the global war on terror. *(Department of Defense)*

and the first armed helicopter company was activated in Okinawa in 1962. This company was deployed to Thailand and then to Vietnam early in the VIETNAM WAR. Company crews and craft flew escort for lift (cargo and personnel) helicopters. It was 1966 before the Department of Defense *formally* authorized the army to arm helicopters; prior to this, only the USAF and USN were authorized to operate armed aircraft.

In 1962, the army formed the Tactical Mobility Requirements Board (also called the Howze Board) to develop and test the concept of air mobility. Based on the board's recommendations, the army began to develop organic air mobility, the doctrine now also called air assault. Air assault quickly came to encompass the use of helicopters to transport infantry troops, artillery, and supplies, as well as to provide aerial fire support. In 1963, the 1st Air Assault Division (Test) was created. In 1965, this unit became the 1st Cavalry Division (Airmobile) and received its baptism of fire in Vietnam. It was in the Vietnam War that the air assault concept was validated under exceedingly difficult and demanding combat conditions. Indeed, many commentators have characterized the conflict in Vietnam as America's "Helicopter War."

The mainstay of army air operations in Vietnam was the UH-1 Iroquois, better known as the Huey, which first began to arrive in country during 1964. By the time of American withdrawal from Vietnam, more than 5,000 Hueys had served in the theater. Army pilots operated Hueys for medical evacuation, command and control, air assault, personnel and materiel transport, and as gun ships to provide intensive ground fire. The bigger and more powerful AH-1 Cobra arrived in 1967, replacing many of the Hueys in the gun ship role. In addition to the Huey and Huey Cobra, army aviators flew the big CH-47 Chinook transport and the diminutive OH-6 Cayuse and the OH-58 Kiowa, which were used mainly for reconnaissance and artillery spotting.

Vietnam was a low-intensity war. After that conflict, army aviation planners began to develop doctrine and aircraft to fight in heavy combat environments as well as low-intensity environments.

The 1980s, therefore, brought much larger, faster, and more heavily armed helicopters, including the AH-64 Apache and the UH-60 Black Hawk, as well as a beefed-up version of the small Kiowa, the OH-58D. It was also during the 1980s that debate within the army and the Department of Defense raged over whether to create a full and formal army aviation branch. After intensive study, the branch was created on April 12, 1983. Aviation officer basic and advanced courses were initiated at Fort Rucker in 1984, and all army aviation-related activities were gradually consolidated there. From this time forward, army aviation has seen its role as providing the army warfighter with a vertical dimension to the battlefield, and aviation has participated in most major army operations ever since, including, most notably, the PERSIAN GULF WAR (1990–91) and Operation Iraqi Freedom (2003–   ).

Aviation and Missile Command (AMCOM)

Headquartered at Redstone Arsenal, Alabama, and administered under the U.S. ARMY MATERIEL COMMAND, AMCOM conducts, performs, and manages basic and applied research and engineering, acquisition, integrated logistics materiel readiness management, and advanced development and maintenance support functions for all assigned aviation and missile weapons systems and subsystems. Support missions include procurement, production, engineering, system engineering, product assurance, materiel management, system safety engineering, maintenance engineering, integrated logistics, configuration management, security assistance management activities, resource management, and staff and base support activities as required in such areas as legal, financial, personnel, and installation management.

B

barracks See FORTS AND OTHER INSTALLATIONS.

basic training

All army recruits undergo nine weeks of basic training—"boot camp"—at either Fort Jackson, South Carolina; Fort Knox, Kentucky; Fort Leonard Wood, Missouri; Fort McClellan, Alabama; Fort Sill, Oklahoma, Fort Benning, Georgia; or Fort Knox, Kentucky.

Basic Training is divided into three phases: Phase I (Red Phase), Phase II (White Phase), and Phase III (Blue Phase). However, preceding Phase I is the Reception Battalion, familiarly called Purgatory. In Reception Battalion, soldiers undergo necessary processing and also take the Initial PT [Physical Training] Test, which, for men, consists of 13 push-ups, 17 sit-ups, and a one-mile run in under eight and one-half minutes, and, for women, three push-ups, 17 sit-ups, and a one-mile run in under 10 and one-half minutes. Those who fail the test are consigned to a "Fat Camp" for physical conditioning. While in Reception Battalion, soldiers are given immunizations, issued uniforms, and receive a GI haircut.

Phase I ("Red Phase" or "Patriot Phase") occupies Weeks 1 to 3 of basic training. Another PT test is administered, and instruction in the basics of military drill and discipline is begun. The principal object of this early phase of training is to create "total control" over the recruit. Week 2 adds

courses in Army Core Values (including classes on sexual harassment and race relations) and other military-related subjects, including the rudiments of bayonet fighting and first aid training. Recruits are also exposed to tear gas training by week 2 and are introduced to the M-16A2 rifle.

Phase II ("White Phase" or "Gunfighter Phase") introduces weapons training, including use of the M-16, hand grenade, and bayonet. Antitank and other heavy weapons are also introduced during

Trainees high crawl through the mud on an obstacle course during Army Basic Combat Training at Fort Jackson, South Carolina. The nine-week course is designed to transform young American volunteers into soldiers. *(Department of Defense)*

this phase. PT continues, with the addition of an obstacle course.

Phase III ("Blue Phase" or "Warrior Phase") begins with a final PT test, which consists of the standard ARMY PHYSICAL FITNESS TEST. After this is passed, recruits are given field experience, including setting up tents, going on night patrols, and performing various night operations. The second week of Phase III (Week 8 of Basic) culminates in a special extended tactical field exercise, known as the Final Event. After successfully completing this, recruits spend a week preparing for the graduation ceremony.

Basic Training is followed by Advanced Individual Training (AIT) in a particular branch or specialty.

battalion   See ORGANIZATION BY UNITS.

Battle Command Battle Laboratory—Fort Leavenworth (BCBL)

One of three army battle command laboratories under the U.S. ARMY TRAINING AND DOCTRINE COMMAND (TRADOC), Battle Command Battle Laboratory—Fort Leavenworth is dedicated to innovating and systematizing the elements of leadership and decision making to enable effective battle command. Traditionally, "battle command" was defined as "the exercise of command in operations against a hostile, thinking enemy. Command is lawful authority exercised over subordinates by virtue of rank and assignment. Command remains a very personal function and is more an art than a science, although it exhibits characteristics of both." The battle command laboratories work to revise this definition and redefine battle command as "the art and science of applying leadership and decision making to achieve mission success." The laboratories create studies and other tools to help enable commanders to realize this new definition and put it to practical use in the field.

bayonet

The bayonet, a straight knife affixed to the end of a rifle or machine gun, is a weapon almost as old as the military musket. Its traditional mission was to defeat the enemy in hand-to-hand combat. This continues to hold true, but the advent of accurate, rapid-fire weapons has caused the bayonet to fall into disuse in modern combat situations; therefore, the modern bayonet is also designed to be used as a general field knife and a utility knife.

Modern bayonets are 10–12 inches long, overall, with a blade length that varies from six to nine inches. The blade is sharpened on both edges to facilitate slashing. Combat knives usually have "blood grooves" etched or embossed into the blade. These indentations on both sides of a blade make it easier to withdraw the knife after stabbing. Bayonets, in contrast, almost never feature blood grooves. Without these indentations, stabbing a victim tends to create a vacuum as the weapon is withdrawn, thereby increasing the amount of trauma created by the attack. Because the bayonet is affixed to the end of a long rifle, an attacker has sufficient leverage to withdraw the bayonet from a victim despite the vacuum created by the blade. If necessary, the attacker can push against the victim with his foot.

The word *bayonet* comes from Bayonne, the town in southwestern France where the weapon was first made, apparently in the 17th century. The first recorded use of the word in English occurred in 1704, suggesting that bayonets were in common use by the late 17th century. Certainly, they were extensively used in 18th-century warfare, when muzzle-loading flintlock muskets were both time consuming and awkward to load and reload (making rapid fire impossible), when the weapons were inaccurate at distances greater than 50 yards, and when they were notoriously unreliable, prone to frequent misfires and almost totally useless in the rain, which dampened gunpowder. Despite popular mythology, which depicts Patriot soldiers of the AMERICAN REVOLUTION firing at redcoats from behind trees, most battles were ultimately decided by combat with bayonets. At Yorktown, GEORGE WASHINGTON famously exhorted his troops to place their main faith in the bayonet, and such a command was typically heard not only throughout the 18th century but also well into the 19th.

Even as the bayonet has faded into the background, bayonet practice remains an important part of infantry training. Practice is typically on stuffed dummies, although the use of pugil sticks, six-foot poles with padded ends, also helps hone bayonet technique using a live opponent.

The M-6 bayonet entered army service in 1957 for use on the M-14 series rifle and as a hand weapon. The M-7 bayonet-knife was introduced in 1967 and is used as a bayonet on the M-16 rifle, the M-4 carbine, and as a hand weapon. The M-9, introduced in 1987, is an advanced multipurpose bayonet system, which is used as a bayonet on the M-16 series rifle, on the M-4 carbine, as a hand weapon, as a general field and utility knife, and, in conjunction with its scabbard, also as a wire cutter. The knife can also be used as a saw.

Blade length of the M-6 is 6.75 inches; M-7, 6.5 inches; and M-9, seven inches. Total length of each weapon is 11.5 inches, 11.75 inches, and 12 inches, respectively.

bazooka

The bazooka has not been a part of the army weapons inventory since the end of the KOREAN WAR era, when it was replaced by other man-portable antitank weapons (see ANTIARMOR WEAPONS); however, the army used the bazooka so extensively in WORLD WAR II that it merits inclusion in this encyclopedia.

Even before World War II, during the 1930s, the army was experimenting with various close-range antitank weapons for use by the infantry. Attempts to develop an antitank rifle did not get very far, but there was great interest in shaped-charge warheads, an interest that developed well before there was a weapon to fire them. As late as the end of 1941, the

Private Seiju Nakandakarc and Private Ralph Saul operate a new 3.5 bazooka on the front lines somewhere in Korea, 1950.   *(Library of Congress)*

army had accumulated a stockpile of shaped-charge warheads without the means to use them. By 1942, however, conventional mortar tubes were being modified to fire the shaped-charge projectile. The modification was refined as Rocket Launcher M-1, which went into production in 1942 and was soon dubbed the bazooka because it resembled a folk musical instrument—a kind of primitive trombone—that was popularized by 1930s radio comedian Bob Burns.

Although the bazooka can be fired by a single man, it is preferably served by two: a gunner (who aims and fires) and a loader (who prepares and loads the ammunition). All bazookas consist of a steel tube, 60 millimeters in diameter and open at both ends. The ammunition is a small, fin-stabilized rocket-propelled grenade, which the loader inserts into the rear of the tube while the gunner rests the weapon on his shoulder. The trigger is actually an electric switch, which closes a circuit, passing an electric current that ignites the ammunition's rocket stage.

The M-1 Bazooka had a one-piece tube and a battery-powered trigger mechanism powered by two batteries located inside the wooden shoulder rest. A small lamp on the left side of the shoulder rest indicated the on/off status of the weapon. The weapon was fitted with a two-piece iron sight. The weapon fired a projectile that was 55 centimeters in length and could penetrate 100 millimeters of armor. In addition, smoke and incendiary warheads were also available.

Beginning in 1943, Bazooka M-1A1 replaced the M-1 model and, most important, incorporated an improved sight and a funnel-shaped muzzle to protect the gunner from the backblast of the exiting projectile.

In 1944, Bazooka M-9 replaced M-1A1. The new weapon consisted of a two-piece tube manufactured out of light metal. Because it could be broken into its two constituent pieces, it was highly portable. The batteries, which had proven to be somewhat unreliable, were replaced by a small generator, and the gunsight was greatly improved. The wooden shoulder stock was replaced by a metal one.

After the end of World War II, the M-20 was developed. The new weapon fired a heavier two-pound, 3.5-inch round and had double, even triple, the penetration performance of the M-9; however, by this time, more effective portable antiarmor weapons were being developed, and the bazooka's days were numbered.

Benét Labs

Located at Watervliet Arsenal, Watervliet, New York, and headquartered at Picatinny Arsenal, Dover, New Jersey, Benét Laboratories is the army's center of expertise for technology, design, development, engineering, and production as well as field support for large-caliber armament systems, including cannons, mortars, and recoilless rifles, tank gun mounts and recoil mechanisms, munition handling systems, and tank turret components.

BGM-71 TOW   See ANTIARMOR WEAPONS.

Biggs Army Airfield, Texas   See FORTS AND OTHER INSTALLATIONS.

Bradley, Omar Nelson (1893–1981) U.S.
Army general

Popularly known as "The GI general" because of his high regard for and rapport with the enlisted soldier in WORLD WAR II, Bradley was born in Clark, Missouri, and graduated from the UNITED STATES MILITARY ACADEMY in 1915 with a commission as second lieutenant in the infantry. From 1915 to 1918, he served on posts in the American West and was promoted to major in 1918, but he did not serve overseas during WORLD WAR I.

In 1919, Bradley served as military instructor at South Dakota State College, then as an instructor at West Point from 1920 to 1924. After attending Infantry School at Fort Benning in 1925, he was posted to Hawaii from 1925 to 1928. In 1929, Bradley graduated from the COMMAND AND GENERAL STAFF COLLEGE at Fort Leavenworth and was assigned as an instructor at the Infantry School from 1929 to 1933. Bradley graduated from the U.S. ARMY WAR COLLEGE in 1934, then returned to West Point as a tactical officer, serving there from 1934 to 1938. He was promoted to lieutenant colonel in 1936.

Appointed to the ARMY GENERAL STAFF in 1938 and promoted to brigadier general in February 1941, Bradley became commandant of the Infantry School, serving there until February 1942, when he was assigned to command the 82nd Division and then the 28th Division. After serving briefly as deputy to General DWIGHT D. EISENHOWER from January to March 1943, Bradley was assigned to replace General GEORGE S. PATTON as commander of II Corps, which he led through the final stages of the Tunisian campaign and into the Sicilian campaign. In August 1943, Bradley was transferred to England to participate in planning the invasion of France.

At the start of 1944, Bradley was named commander of First Army and assigned the right-wing position in the D-day landing. After the initial assault, Bradley planned and led the Saint-Lô breakout at Normandy in July. In August, he became commander of the Twelfth Army Group, consisting of the First Army (under Courtney L. Hodges) and the Third (under George S. Patton). This put him in command of the southern wing of the massive Allied advance across France. With 1.3 million men, the Twelfth Army Group was the largest force ever commanded by an American general.

Promoted to general in March 1945, Bradley continued to command Twelfth Army Group through final operations in Germany. After the war, Bradley headed the Veterans Administration, then, in February 1948, succeeded Eisenhower as CHIEF OF STAFF. In 1949, he was named the first chairman of the Joint Chiefs of Staff and, in 1950, was promoted to general of the army. Bradley retired in 1953.

branches, army   See ORGANIZATION BY BRANCH.

brigade   See ORGANIZATION BY UNITS.

brigadier general   See RANKS AND GRADES.

Bronze Star   See DECORATIONS AND MEDALS.

Buffalo Soldiers

African-American troops serving mainly in the American West after the CIVIL WAR were commonly called "Buffalo Soldiers," a term respectfully conferred on them by the Native Americans they fought. The troops served in four segregated regiments, the 9th and 10th Cavalry and the 24th and 25th Infantry.

See also AFRICAN AMERICANS IN THE U.S. ARMY.

C

C-20 Gulfstream   See AIRCRAFT.

C-23 Sherpa   See AIRCRAFT.

C-47 Dakota   See AIRCRAFT.

"Caissons Go Rolling Along, The"

Officially titled "The U.S. Field Artillery March,"
this song is the universal but unofficial anthem of
the U.S. Army.

Over hill, over dale
As we hit the dusty trail,
And the Caissons go rolling along.
In and out, hear them shout,
Counter march and right about,
And the Caissons go rolling along.

Refrain: Then it's hi! hi! hee!
In the field artillery,
Shout out your numbers loud and strong,
For where'er you go,
You will always know
That the Caissons go rolling along.

In the storm, in the night,
Action left or action right
See those Caissons go rolling along.

Limber front, limber rear,
Prepare to mount your cannoneer
And those Caissons go rolling along.
Refrain: Then it's hi! hi! hee!
In the field artillery,
Shout out your numbers loud and strong,
For where'er you go,
You will always know
That the Caissons go rolling along.

Was it high, was it low,
Where the hell did that one go?
As those Caissons go rolling along.
Was it left, was it right?
Now we won't get home tonight
And those Caissons go rolling along.

Refrain: Then it's hi! hi! hee!
In the field artillery,
Shout out your numbers loud and strong,
For where'er you go,
You will always know
That the Caissons go rolling along.
That the Caissons go rolling along.
That the Caissons go rolling along

The song was written by Lieutenant Edmund L.
Gruber and was subsequently popularized by com-
poser and bandleader John Philip Sousa. In April
1908, while he was serving in the 2nd Battalion of
the 5th Field Artillery in the Philippines, Gruber

was asked to write a song for the regiment as they waited for the arrival of relief from the 1st Battalion. With the aid of six other lieutenants, Gruber composed the song. During the closing days of WORLD WAR I, at the request of the army, Sousa modified it somewhat and it became the official marching song of the field artillery. Sousa subsequently shared royalties with Gruber. According to Gruber, the song had been inspired by a difficult march across the Zambales Mountains in the Philippines.

camps   See FORTS AND OTHER INSTALLATIONS.

captain   See RANKS AND GRADES.

Carlisle Barracks, Pennsylvania   See FORTS AND OTHER INSTALLATIONS.

cavalry

Traditionally, the cavalry has enjoyed elite status in military organizations, including the army. This is due in part to the fact that the cavalryman can trace his lineage back to the noble knight of feudal times and also because of the sheer expense involved in equipping and maintaining cavalry units. Yet despite the prestige of the cavalry, in the army it has historically played a role secondary to the infantry and artillery branches—except during the INDIAN WARS (1866–91) when cavalry units were extensively employed against the mounted warriors of the Plains Indians.

By the early 20th century, machine guns and the advent of tanks and other armored vehicles were rapidly rendering the cavalry obsolete. However, cavalry organizations continue to exist in today's army. Units such as the 1ST CAVALRY DIVISION, originally established in the 19th century as a conventional cavalry outfit, retained the "cavalry" designation long after the horses were gone. The 1st Cavalry became the army's first "Airmobile" division, achieving cavalry-like mobility in the

VIETNAM WAR not on horseback but by means of helicopters. The term "air cavalry" is sometimes still used to describe various airborne (that is, helicopter-transported) units. A few other modern units, such as the 2nd Armored Cavalry Regiment, use tanks and other armored vehicles not in heavy assault roles but for reconnaissance and security—the functions that army horse soldiers excelled at.

During the AMERICAN REVOLUTION, GEORGE WASHINGTON, commanding the CONTINENTAL ARMY, made little use of cavalry—and was sometimes criticized for this. Doubtless, Washington's neglect of this branch was due in part to his experience as a soldier during the French and Indian War, which was largely a wilderness conflict unsuited to cavalry operations. Washington, commanding a financially hard-pressed army, was also keenly aware of the expense involved in organizing and maintaining cavalry units. He did make somewhat more extensive use of dragoons, troops who ride to battle, but fight dismounted rather than from horseback.

After the Revolution, army dragoon units continued to operate and were used throughout the period preceding the CIVIL WAR, but straight cavalry was rarely employed either in the WAR OF 1812 or in the UNITED STATES–MEXICAN WAR. During the Civil War, the cavalry was used chiefly for reconnaissance and raiding, not for heavy assault, and the Confederacy developed its cavalry assets earlier in the war and to a higher degree of skill than did the Union. Both the Confederacy and the Union favored light cavalry over heavy cavalry. The development of the rifled musket increased the accuracy of fire and, therefore, made heavy cavalry, suitable for massed assault, highly vulnerable. Indeed, the full-scale offensive cavalry charge was a great rarity in the Civil War.

The light cavalry techniques developed during the Civil War were used extensively in combat against the Plains Indians until nearly the end of the 19th century. But this was the last major use of traditional horse cavalry by the army. No American cavalry was used during WORLD WAR I, and, while many cavalry officers resisted mechanization during the period between World War I and

WORLD WAR II, some others embraced the new technology as an alternative means of mobility. Most notable among these officers was a veteran cavalry man, GEORGE SMITH PATTON, JR., who pioneered army armor during World War I and the interwar years.

The National Security Act of 1947 formally abolished the horse cavalry in the army, although the 1st Cavalry Division (and other, smaller units) retained its historical insignia even as it adopted armor and then helicopters for mobility.

Center for Army Lessons Learned (CALL)

The Center for Army Lessons Learned collects and analyzes data from a variety of current and historical sources, including army operations and training events, and uses these to produce lessons for military commanders, staff, and students. The center disseminates these lessons and other related research materials through a variety of print and electronic media, including its Web site.

centers

The army operates numerous facilities designated as centers for the conduct and administration of specific missions and functions. As of 2004, these included:

Army Center for Substance Abuse Programs (ACSAP)

Army Education Center

Armament Research, Development and Engineering Center (ARDEC)

ARMY TRAINING SUPPORT CENTER (ATSC)

CENTER FOR ARMY LESSONS LEARNED (CALL)

Charles E. Kelley Support Center

Cold Regions Test Center (CRTC)

COMBINED ARMS CENTER (CAC)

DEFENSE LANGUAGE INSTITUTE FOREIGN LANGUAGE CENTER

Environmental Awareness Resource Center (EARC)

FORSCOM Material Management Center (FMMC)

Information Technology Business Center (ITBC)

INTEGRATED MATERIEL MANAGEMENT CENTER (IMMC)

Maneuver Support Center (MANCEN)

Natick Soldier Center (NSC)

National Simulation Center (NSC)

Northeast Telecommunications Switching Center (NETSC)

NORTHERN WARFARE TRAINING CENTER (NWTC)

Parks Reserve Training Center

Pohukuloa Training Center

Redstone Scientific Information Center (RISC)

Safety Center

SBBCOM Integrated Materiel Management Center (IMMC)

Software Engineering Center—Lee

Soldier Systems Center

Tank Automotive Research, Development, and Engineering Center (TARDEC)

Tom Bevill Center for Professional Development

Topographic Engineering Center (TEC)

CH-47 Chinook   See AIRCRAFT.

Chaffee, Adna Romanza, Jr. (1884–1941)
U.S. Army general

Chaffee is widely recognized as the father of army armor. He was the only son of the legendary U.S. Army general Adna Chaffee, Sr., and graduated from the UNITED STATES MILITARY ACADEMY in 1906. As part of the 1st Cavalry, he served in the so-called Army of Cuban Pacification (1906–07), then attended the Mounted Services School at Fort Riley, Kansas, from 1907 to 1909. Chaffee, a champion equestrian, earned the honor of attendance at Saumur, the French cavalry school, during 1911–12. He returned to Fort Riley in 1912 as an instructor at the Mounted Services School, then shipped out with the 7th Cavalry to the Philippines in 1914, returning to West Point in 1916 as senior cavalry instructor. After promotion to captain, Chaffee was assigned in August 1917 as adjutant to the 81St Division at Camp Jackson, South Carolina. He served briefly as acting chief of staff for the division, then sailed with it to France in February 1918 for service on the western front in WORLD WAR I. In France, Chaffee attended the General Staff College (March–May 1918) then served there as an instructor. In August 1918, he was appointed assistant G-3 (operations officer) for IV Corps and, soon afterward, G-3 of the 81st Division and of VII Corps (August–October) during offensives at Saint-Mihiel (September 12–17, 1918) and Meuse-Argonne (September 26–November 11). During the last days of the war, Chaffee served with the temporary rank of colonel and was G-3 of III Corps. He remained in Europe with III Corps as part of the army of occupation in the Rhineland.

In 1919, Chaffee returned to the United States as an instructor at the Line and Staff School (now the COMMAND AND GENERAL STAFF College) at Fort Leavenworth, Kansas. After brief service with the 3rd Cavalry during May–August 1920, he was reassigned as G-2 (intelligence officer) of the IV Corps area in Atlanta from August 1920 until 1921, and then as G-3 of the 1ST CAVALRY DIVISION at Fort Bliss, Texas, serving there until July 1924. He graduated from the U.S. ARMY WAR COLLEGE in 1925 and was assigned command of a squadron of the 3rd Cavalry at Fort Myer, Virginia, serving until June 1927, when he was posted to the Operations and Training Division of the War Department General Staff.

Chaffee, now a lieutenant colonel, was assigned in 1931 to command the newly formed 1st Cavalry (Mechanized) Regiment at Fort Knox, Kentucky. He subsequently served as overall commander of the 1st Cavalry (1934), doing much to establish, train, and organize the army's first dedicated armored unit. Of even more enduring significance, it was Chaffee was developed the basic doctrine of mechanized warfare. When he headed up the Budget and Legislative Planning Branch of the War Department General Staff during 1934–38, Chaffee used his influence to fund increased mechanization. Returning to Fort Knox, he again served as commander of 1st Cavalry (Mechanized) (June–

November 1938) and, promoted to brigadier general on November 3, was made commander of the 7th Mechanized Brigade (1st and 13th Mechanized Cavalry Regiments).

As the United States moved toward entry into WORLD WAR II, Chaffee directed the 7th Brigade in large-scale maneuvers at Plattsburgh, New York (1939) and in Louisiana (summer 1940). For the army and for Chaffee, these were highly significant events that allowed him to refine and further develop American armor doctrine, including the crucial concept of combining armored, infantry, and artillery operations. This combined arms approach would prove extraordinarily valuable in the coming war.

Chaffee was named commander of the Armored Force on June 10, 1940, with responsibility for all infantry tank and mechanized cavalry units, as well as supporting artillery, motorized infantry, and engineer units. He created the 1st and 2nd Armored Divisions and was promoted to major general on October 2, 1940. However, at the height of his career and on the eve of war, Chaffee succumbed to cancer, dying the summer before Pearl Harbor.

Chemical Corps

A combat support branch of the army, the Chemical Corps protects the force and allows the army to fight and win against a nuclear-biological-chemical (NBC) threat. Branch members develop doctrine, equipment, and training for NBC defense, which are intended to deter potential adversaries possessing weapons of mass destruction. The branch home station is Fort Leonard Wood, Missouri.

Chemical Detachments   See CHEMICAL SERVICE ORGANIZATION.

Chemical Service Organization

Chemical Service Organizations are designated Chemical Detachments, Nuclear-Biological-Chemical (NBC) Element Teams, and NBC Elements. Their mission is to provide nuclear-biological-chemical (NBC) staff support and to operate NBC Warning and Reporting Systems (NBCWRS) and monitor the status of the command's NBC defense procedures and chemical assets. An NBC team may be attached or assigned to headquarters of a CORPS, a unified command, or an army.

Chief of Staff

The most senior officer in the army, the Chief of Staff reports to, assists, and advises the SECRETARY OF THE ARMY and serves on the JOINT CHIEFS OF STAFF (JCS). The Chief of Staff is responsible for the overall army mission as well as training, administration, and supply. The Chief of Staff is assisted by the ARMY GENERAL STAFF, the SPECIAL STAFF, and the PERSONAL STAFF. Chief of staff is also the title accorded any principal assistant to a commander at brigade level or higher.

Civil War (1861–1865)

Intense sectional tensions, present since colonial times and revolving ultimately around the issue of slavery, progressively increased during the 19th century. A series of unsatisfactory compromises and half measures staved off civil war until the 1860 election of Abraham Lincoln to the presidency. Although Lincoln was by no means a radical abolitionist, he had made clear his intention to stop the extension of slavery to new states and territories, and he was widely perceived in the South as very much inclined toward the abolitionist point of view. Upon his election, most of the slaveholding states of the South seceded from the Union. Deeming this a violation of the Constitution and federal sovereignty, the Lincoln administration prepared to wage war. For their part, the seceded states called themselves the Confederate States of America and likewise prepared for battle. Little more than a month after Lincoln's inauguration, at 4:30 on the morning of April 12, 1861, Pierre Gustave Toutant Beauregard, formerly of the U.S. Army and now a general in the provisional army of the Confederate States of America, ordered his artillery to open fire

on Fort Sumter, in Charleston Harbor. After prolonged bombardment, the fort was surrendered on April 13. This was the formal beginning of the Civil War.

The most senior army commander at this time was the aging and corpulent WINFIELD SCOTT. He realistically understood that the army was a small force made even smaller by the defection of significant numbers to the Confederacy. Accordingly, he proposed to buy time for building a bigger army by imposing a naval blockade of the Confederacy to starve it economically. The plan was derisively dubbed "Scott's Anaconda," and while it was true that the Union did not have sufficient numbers of ships to make it initially effective, the blockade ultimately proved a useful, albeit never decisive, tactic.

First Battle of Bull Run

In the meantime, on land, the first major battle that followed the fall of Fort Sumter took place near Bull Run Creek, in Virginia, a position controlling the best direct route to Richmond, which was now the Confederate capital. Poorly trained army troops under Major General Irvin McDowell first made contact with the enemy on July 18. The Confederates drove back one Union division, which allowed time for reinforcement of the Confederate line, and the main battle took place on July 21, pitting 35,000 Union troops against almost 30,000 Confederates. McDowell's forces performed well at first, but Confederate troops were rallied by Brigadier General Thomas J. Jackson, who, for his action, earned the nickname "Stonewall." For much of the afternoon, the battle seesawed, until, late in the day, the Confederates delivered a massive counterthrust, which broke the Union lines and triggered a rout.

After the Union defeat at Bull Run, President Lincoln replaced McDowell as commander of the Army of the Potomac with GEORGE BRINTON MCCLELLAN, who had scored two modest victories in western Virginia (at Philippi, June 3, and Rich Mountain, July 11), which secured for the Union the region that would, in 1863, become the new state of West Virginia. McClellan ably trained and drilled the Army of the Potomac, but he was ignominiously defeated at the Battle of Ball's Bluff (October 21), 30 miles up the Potomac from Washington. Worse, McClellan repeatedly delayed taking major offensive action. However, west of the war's principal coastal theater, Brigadier General ULYSSES SIMPSON GRANT, commanding troops at Cairo, Illinois, where the Ohio River joins the Mississippi River, took Paducah, Kentucky. In early 1862, he also took a series of Confederate forts on the Mississippi. With the fall of the river forts, the Confederates were forced to evacuate Nashville, Tennessee, and they also relinquished control over a significant portion of the Mississippi River.

Battle of Shiloh

Unfortunately, the Union forces proved unable to mount a coordinated attack against the Confederates in the area, and Grant exposed his encampment to attack, which came at Shiloh, Tennessee, on April 6, 1862. The battle nearly developed into a Union rout, but one of Grant's subordinate commanders, WILLIAM TECUMSEH SHERMAN, managed to rally the troops. Other army officers also fought heroically and staved off defeat. Nevertheless, costs were staggering: of 62,682 Union army troops engaged, 1,754 were killed, 8,408 wounded, and 2,885 went missing. Confederate losses were 1,723 killed, 8,012 wounded, and 959 missing out of 40,335 men engaged.

Battle of Pea Ridge

Grant's victories and the costly Battle of Shiloh improved the Union's position in Kentucky and Tennessee. Confederate general Sterling Price withdrew his forces into Arkansas, where he was reinforced by units under Ben McCulloch and Earl Van Dorn. In Arkansas, the Confederates now had an army of 17,000 men to oppose the 11,000 troops under Major General Samuel Curtis. Curtis took a defensive position at Pea Ridge, on high ground overlooking Little Sugar Creek. Skirmishing began on March 7 near Elkhorn Tavern, and a full-scale battle soon developed. By March 8, when the battle ended, the Confederates had fled the field, but Curtis had incurred more casualties

than Van Dorn. Of 11,250 Federal troops engaged at Pea Ridge, 1,384 were killed, wounded, or missing. Of some 14,000 Confederates, 800 became casualties.

The Situation in the Far West

At the beginning of the war, Confederate lieutenant colonel John Robert Baylor swept through the southern New Mexico Territory, all the way from the Rio Grande to California, and proclaimed the Confederate Territory of Arizona, which encompassed all of present-day Arizona and New Mexico south of the 34th parallel. His virtually unopposed advance was followed during the winter of 1861–62 by a larger Confederate invasion led by Henry Hopkins Sibley. At La Glorietta Pass through the Sangre de Cristo Mountains, on March 26, 1862, Union troops under Colonel John Slough, reinforced by Colorado volunteers commanded by Major John M. Chivington, met Sibley's Texans in a two-day battle. On March 28, Sibley was forced to retreat back to Texas. The battle turned the tide against the Confederates in the Southwest.

Peninsula Campaign

On March 11, 1862, Lincoln relieved McClellan as general in chief of the armies, returning him to command of the Army of the Potomac only. When the president urged him to lead his army directly against Richmond, McClellan responded with a much more roundabout plan: to ferry his troops down to Fort Monroe, near Newport News and Hampton Roads, in the southeastern corner of Virginia, below the rebel capital. His plan was to land, then proceed north toward Richmond via the peninsula separating the York from the James rivers.

Ninety thousand men of the Army of the Potomac landed in Virginia on April 4 and advanced on Yorktown the next day. Based on erroneous intelligence, McClellan believed himself grossly outnumbered and, instead of simply attacking Yorktown, he laid siege to it. This gave the Confederates ample time to reinforce and to construct defensive works around Richmond.

In May, McClellan finally attacked Yorktown, only to discover that Confederate forces had withdrawn from that town to move closer to Richmond. At the end of May 1862, most of McClellan's army was north of the Chickahominy River, except for a corps commanded by Major General Erasmus Darwin Keyes. Perceiving the vulnerability of Keyes's isolated position, Confederate general Joseph E. Johnston attacked him at Fair Oaks and Seven Pines on May 31, 1862. The result was an inconclusive and bloody battle between almost equally matched forces: Of 41,797 Union troops engaged, 5,031 were casualties; of 41,816 Confederates, 6,134 became casualties. Johnston was so severely wounded that he withdrew from action for a time and was replaced by ROBERT E. LEE, hitherto a fairly undistinguished commander. Lee would emerge as the Confederates' de facto general in chief and one of the great captains in all military history.

From June 25 to July 1, McClellan and Lee dueled in a series of bloody battles known as the Seven Days, which proved a costly strategic failure for the Union army, albeit something of a tactical victory. Commanding the larger army, McClellan had sustained about 16,000 casualties, killed and wounded. Lee's smaller force, although it suffered nearly 20,000 casualties, succeeded in saving Richmond. Lincoln was unimpressed and removed McClellan from command of the Army of the Potomac, replacing him with the unpopular and irascible John Pope.

Second Battle of Bull Run

Positioned near the site of the Battle of Bull Run, Pope confidently launched an attack on August 29, 1862, battering Jackson's Confederates, and prompting him prematurely to declare victory. Pope was unaware that half of Lee's divided army, under General Longstreet, had yet to join the battle. On August 30, five divisions under Longstreet rushed the Union flank along a two-mile front, inflicting a costly tactical defeat on Pope. At the Second Battle of Bull Run, Pope commanded 75,696 Union troops against the Confederates' 48,527. He lost 1,724 killed, 8,372 wounded, and

5,958 missing. Confederate losses numbered 1,481 killed, 7,627 wounded, and 89 missing. The defeat prompted Pope's dismissal as commander of the Army of the Potomac. McClellan was returned to command.

Battle of Antietam

Encouraged by the Second Battle of Bull Run, Lee invaded Maryland on September 5, 1862, with the 55,000-man Army of Northern Virginia. As usual, McClellan failed to respond decisively, and Lee was thereby able to set up a defensive line at the western Maryland town of Sharpsburg, behind Antietam Creek.

McClellan's plan was to strike at both of Lee's flanks, then attack the center with his reserves, but he was unable to achieve the proper level of coordination to execute his plan effectively. The initial assault on April 17 was uncoordinated and piecemeal, but McClellan did substantially outnumber the Confederates and, by dint of numbers, drove Lee's forces back to the outskirts of Sharpsburg. Mistakenly believing the Confederates were more numerous than they were, McClellan failed to pursue them, and the Army of Northern Virginia escaped back across the Potomac and into Virginia. The cost of what historians call the single bloodiest day of the war was 2,108 Union troops killed, 9,549 wounded, and 753 missing out of 75,316 engaged. The Confederates fielded 51,844 men and lost some 2,700 killed, 9,024 wounded, and approximately 2,000 missing.

After Antietam, McClellan did nothing, while Lee's dashing cavalry commander J.E.B. Stuart made a daring raid into Pennsylvania during October 9–12. On November 7, 1862, McClellan was officially relieved of command of the Army of the Potomac and was replaced by the modest but mediocre Ambrose Burnside.

Battle of Fredericksburg

Burnside deployed his forces north of the Rappahannock River at Warrenton, Virginia, 30 miles from Lee's army, which consisted of only two corps, commanded by Stonewall Jackson and

Battle of Fredericksburg, Virginia, December 13, 1862. Lithograph by Currier & Ives   *(Library of Congress)*

James Longstreet. Burnside's best chance would have been to attack between the separated wings of Lee's army, defeating each wing in detail. He chose instead to continue to advance on Richmond and attack south of Warrenton, at Fredericksburg. Further delay allowed the Confederates to entrench defensively in the hills south of Fredericksburg. By December 11, 78,000 Confederates were securely dug in on the south bank of the Rappahannock. On this same day, the Union crossing began. In all, on December 13, 1862, Burnside ordered 14 costly and fruitless assaults against the Confederate positions. The Battle of Fredericksburg stands as the worst defeat in history of the army. Of the 106,000 Union soldiers engaged, 12,700 were killed or wounded. Confederate losses were 5,300 killed or wounded out of some 72,500 engaged. On January 26, 1863, President Lincoln replaced Burnside as commander of the Army of the Potomac with Joseph "Fighting Joe" Hooker.

Battle of Chancellorsville

Hooker's Army of the Potomac had been reinforced to a strength of 130,000 men—versus the 60,000 men of Lee's Army of Northern Virginia. Hooker's plan was to deploy about one-third of his forces under John Sedgwick in a diversionary attack across the Rappahannock above Lee's Fredericksburg entrenchments. Simultaneously, Hooker himself would lead another third of the army in a long swing up the Rappahannock to come around to attack Lee on his vulnerable left flank and rear. Except for about 10,000 cavalry troopers, who would be used to disrupt Lee's lines of communication to Richmond, the remainder of the Army of the Potomac would be held in reserve at Chancellorsville, ready to reinforce either Sedgwick's or Hooker's wings, as needed. The first part of Hooker's plan unfolded flawlessly. By April 30, 1863, Hooker had established about 70,000 men in Chancellorsville and had set up headquarters in Chancellor House, a plantation home outside of the town. Hooker then dispatched his cavalry to cut the Richmond, Fredericksburg, and Potomac Railroad.

As good as Hooker's plan was, Lee grasped it immediately and was able to out-general Hooker. On May 4, Lee drove Hooker out of Chancellorsville in full retreat north of the Rappahannock. Facing at Chancellorsville an army less than half the size of his own, Hooker lost 17,000 casualties—about 17 percent of the numbers directly engaged. Lee's 13,000 casualties accounted for an even greater percentage of his much smaller force: about 25 percent. Perhaps the greatest loss of all to Lee was the death of Thomas "Stonewall" Jackson, a victim of friendly fire.

Pennsylvania Invasion

Lee decided to make a swift and massive raid into the North in the hope that it would demolish the Union's will to continue the fight and thereby force a favorably negotiated peace. The invasion began on June 3, 1863, and would culminate in the Battle of Gettysburg.

Vicksburg Campaign

While the war proceeded disappointingly for the Union in the East, Grant and other Union commanders were making good progress near the Mississippi River. Grant was particularly determined to take Vicksburg, Mississippi, a fortress town that occupied a high bluff above the river and enabled the Confederates to control traffic on the Mississippi. But the town was so well situated and defended that Grant campaigned for a year, which included a long siege, before the city finally fell to him on July 4, 1863. Vicksburg's fall put the Mississippi River wholly in Union hands.

The capture of Vicksburg, Mississippi, July 4, 1863. Lithograph by Currier & Ives   *(Library of Congress)*

Battle of Gettysburg

Just as Grant was in the final triumphant stages of the Vicksburg campaign, Lee's Army of Northern Virginia and the Union's Army of the Potomac, under Major General GEORGE GORDON MEADE, fought a desperate three-day battle at the crossroads town of Gettysburg, Pennsylvania. Lee nearly achieved victory on the first day of fighting, but he failed to break the Union line on the second day. On the third day, July 3, Lee ordered a massive infantry charge of some 15,000 men, which resulted in 10,000 casualties and brought the battle to a tragic end for the Confederates. By defeating Lee on Northern territory, the Army of the Potomac turned the tide of the war. There would not be another major invasion of the North. However, in failing to pursue the beaten Lee, Meade sacrificed an extraordinary opportunity to bring the war itself to a close. For without the Army of Northern Virginia, the Confederate cause would have been lost.

The Union fielded 88,289 men at Gettysburg, of whom 3,155 were killed and another 14,529 were wounded, mortally wounded, or captured; 5,365 went missing. Of 75,000 Confederates engaged, 3,903 were killed, 18,735 were wounded, mortally wounded, or captured, and 5,425 were reported missing in action.

Battle of Chickamauga

After Gettysburg, the principal action of the war shifted for a time from Mississippi and Pennsylvania to central Tennessee and northern Georgia.

Union general William Starke Rosecrans, commanding the Army of the Cumberland, took Chattanooga easily before the end of summer 1863. He should have concentrated his forces in Chattanooga, resupplied them, then resumed the offensive against Confederate general Braxton Bragg. Instead, he continued to push his three exhausted corps, which became separated in the mountain passes. Bragg counterattacked at Chickamauga Creek, Georgia, 12 miles south of Chattanooga on September 19. By the 20th, the Union forces had been defeated, but not destroyed. Of 58,222 Union troops engaged, 1,657 were killed, 9,756 wounded, and 4,757 went missing. Confederate losses were 2,312 killed, 14,674 wounded, and 1,468 missing out of 66,326 engaged. It was a tactical victory for Braxton Bragg, but his losses were greater than Rosecrans's, and he could not exploit his tactical gains to create a strategically decisive victory.

Siege of Chattanooga

The Union's Army of the Cumberland was in Chattanooga, Tennessee, and now Bragg's Confederates laid siege to them there. To relieve the army, two army corps were detached from the Army of the Potomac under Joseph Hooker. They arrived on October 2, while Sherman led part of the Army of the Tennessee east from Memphis, and Ulysses S. Grant was given command of all military operations west of the Alleghenies. Grant efficiently punched through a Confederate outpost on the Tennessee River west of Lookout Mountain and opened up a supply route to beleaguered Chattanooga.

Battle of Lookout Mountain

Sherman arrived at the Union rallying point, Bridgeport, Alabama, on November 15. On November 24, Grant ordered Major General Joseph Hooker to take Lookout Mountain, the 1,100-foot prominence looming over the Tennessee River just outside Chattanooga. Hooker commenced an uphill battle from eight in the morning until after midnight. Early on the morning of November 25, soldiers from the 8th Kentucky Regiment scrambled up to the summit and planted the Stars and Stripes. The sun had broken through the fog, creating a spectacle that war correspondents dubbed the "Battle Above the Clouds."

On the afternoon of November 25, Grant ordered Thomas to lead the Army of the Cumberland forward to take the Confederate rifle pits at the base of Missionary Ridge south of Chattanooga and just to the east of Lookout Mountain. Thomas's men, having been trapped so long in Chattanooga, were eager to advance. They not only took the rifle pits, but, on their own initiative, charged up the steep slope of Missionary Ridge and swept all Confederate forces before them, breaking Bragg's line where it was the strongest. Missionary Ridge capped the defeat of the Confederacy in the West.

Grant Becomes General in Chief

After Vicksburg, Abraham Lincoln realized that, in Ulysses S. Grant, he had finally found a general fit to lead the Union armies. On March 9, 1864, Grant was appointed supreme commander of all the Union armies. He introduced a new strategy, which focused not on taking cities or occupying territory, but on killing the enemy armies. Without them, Grant reasoned, the war would end, regardless of who occupied a given town or territory. The two principal armies were Robert E. Lee's Army of Northern Virginia and the Army of Tennessee, now under the command of Joseph E. Johnston, who had replaced Bragg. Grant took on the task of fighting Lee and assigned Johnston to his trusted colleague, William Tecumseh Sherman, who became commander of the Military Division of the Mississippi. Sherman was to move down the route of the Western and Atlantic Railroad, advancing inexorably against Atlanta, in the process eating up the Army of Tennessee. As Sherman advanced on Atlanta, forcing Johnston to fight him in order to defend the city, Grant would advance on Richmond, less with the object of taking the Confederate capital than with the purpose of fighting the Army of Northern Virginia, which would rush to the capital's defense. In addition to the main body of the Army of the Potomac, Grant aimed two other armies at Richmond: the Army of the James, 33,000 men under Ben Butler, and a force in the Shenandoah Valley, led by Franz Sigel. The grand operation began on May 4, 1864.

Grant's Campaign

On May 4, 1864, Grant led the 120,000-man Army of the Potomac across the Rapidan River toward open country south of the river. His target was Lee's badly outnumbered 66,000-man Army of Northern Virginia. Lee, however, seized the initiative by attacking the Federal columns as they passed through the tangled and densely forested area known as the Wilderness, the same Wilderness that had brought such disastrous confusion to "Fighting Joe" Hooker at Chancellorsville almost a year to the day earlier. Without an open field for deployment, Grant could not bring his overwhelming strength to bear at any particular point, nor could he make effective use of his artillery. The main fighting spanned May 5–6, 1864, and, by May 8, Grant was forced to withdraw. His losses were 17,666 (2,246 killed, 12,073 wounded, and the rest missing) out of 101,895 engaged. Two Union generals were killed, two wounded, and another two captured. Confederate records indicate that, of 61,025 engaged, 7,500 were killed, wounded, or missing. Two Confederate generals were killed, another was mortally wounded, and four more were wounded but recovered, including James Longstreet, hit by friendly fire.

Grant did not shrink from the defeat he had suffered at the Wilderness. He reasoned that he could afford to lose men, whereas Lee could not. Therefore, instead of retreating north, Grant advanced southward, to Spotsylvania Court House. There the two armies fought an 11-day battle from May 8 through May 19, holding one another in a kind of death grip. This was followed by one bloody engagement after another, culminating in the Battle of Cold Harbor.

Battle of Cold Harbor

On the night of June 1, Grant and Lee raced toward a crossroads called Cold Harbor, six miles northeast of Richmond. From June 1 to June 3, the two armies fought. On the 3rd, Grant charged the Confederate positions with 60,000 Federal troops. Seven thousand Union soldiers fell in a single hour at Cold Harbor.

Siege of Petersburg

Grant slipped his army out of Cold Harbor under cover of darkness and crossed the Chickahominy. Lee could only assume that he was heading for Richmond and so dispatched most of his troops to the outskirts of the city. But Grant had decided on a new objective: Petersburg, a rail junction vital to the supply of Richmond. The Union commander reasoned that, by taking Petersburg, Richmond would be cut off from the rest of the Confederacy and would fall. However, Petersburg was defended by an elaborate system of trenches, and the campaign turned into a siege that began on June 15, 1864, and did not end until nine months later.

The Atlanta Campaign

As Grant settled into the siege of Petersburg, Sherman began his advance to the key railroad terminus of Atlanta, Georgia. His army marched out of Chattanooga and into Georgia on May 7, 1864. Sherman commanded 100,000 men against Joseph Johnston's 62,000. Johnston steadily retreated, hoping not only to keep his army intact but also to delay the taking of Atlanta long enough to cost Lincoln reelection, thereby bringing in a Democratic administration willing to negotiate a favorable peace. Unwisely, Confederate president Jefferson Davis insisted on a more aggressive response to the invasion, and, on July 17, replaced Johnston with the impetuous John Bell Hood. The hard-fought Battle of Peachtree Creek took place on July 20, followed, beginning on the 22nd, by the Battle of Atlanta proper. Once the city was taken, Sherman fought other local actions to secure this prize. This accomplished, the Union had deprived the Confederacy of a major rail hub and industrial city, and it ensured the reelection of President Lincoln.

His victory in Atlanta had revealed to Sherman that the Confederacy was indeed coming apart. He secured permission from Grant to force it apart faster by taking 60,000 troops in a "March to the Sea." His objective was to cut the Confederacy in two, north and south, and to put his army in a position to attack Lee's Army of Northern Virginia from the south even as Grant continued to bear down on it from the north. Along the way, he intended to wage total war on the civilian population, not to punish them, but to make them so war weary that the South would lay down its arms. On November 11, Sherman ordered everything of military signifi-

cance in Atlanta destroyed and prepared to move out. However, control of the destructive operations was lost, and, as a result, by November 16, fires consumed virtually all of Atlanta.

The March to the Sea

Sherman marched southeast from Atlanta, toward Savannah, Georgia, cutting a broad and terrible swath of destruction as he went. On December 22, 1864, he reached Savannah, which surrendered without a fight. On February 17, 1865, the South Carolina capital of Columbia surrendered as fires destroyed half the town. On February 18, the Confederates abandoned Fort Sumter as Union troops closed in on Charleston.

Battles in Tennessee

As Sherman marched to the sea, Major General George Thomas fought Hood and Forrest in Tennessee, at Spring Hill (November 29, 1864) and Franklin (November 30). Confederate forces here were effectively neutralized.

On to Richmond

While Sherman was taking Atlanta and marching to the sea, and while the Union forces in Tennessee were neutralizing both Hood and Forrest, Grant was still tied down in the long siege of Petersburg. In a desperate bid to reduce Union forces there, Confederate Jubal Early invaded Maryland in July, defeating Federal forces at Monocacy on July 9, then menacing Baltimore. Early next approached Washington, attacking the outer forts of the capital on July 11 but retreating during the night of July 12–13 all the way to the Shenandoah Valley. To neutralize Early, Grant dispatched PHILIP HENRY SHERIDAN with about 48,000 men to "pacify" the valley. Sheridan pursued Early relentlessly, setting fire to barns and crops and killing cattle all along the way. Early was decisively defeated at the Battle of Cedar Creek on October 19, 1864.

Petersburg Falls

By early 1865, the Confederate defenders of Petersburg, who had held out for months against Grant's siege, were starving. On March 31, Sheridan, returned from the Shenandoah Valley, defeated Confederate forces at Five Forks, Virginia, and, on April 2, Grant finally broke through the lines at Petersburg. Lee fell back on Amelia Court House, and Confederate president Jefferson Davis gave the order for the Confederate government to evacuate Richmond for Danville, Virginia.

By this time all that remained of the Army of Northern Virginia were about 50,000 men. Lee hoped to hold out long enough to put the Confederacy in a position to negotiate the most favorable peace possible, so he kept fighting as he made his way to hoped-for supplies at Appomattox Station, on the rail line. Union attacks, however, prompted Lee to send word to Grant that he was prepared to surrender. The two commanders met on April 9, 1865, at the McLean farmhouse at Appomattox Courthouse and negotiated the terms of the surrender of the Army of Northern Virginia.

Although Lee held authority to surrender nothing more than the Army of Northern Virginia, his capitulation, for all practical purposes, ended the Civil War. Montgomery, Alabama, fell on April 12, and Federal troops entered Mobile the same day. On April 13, Sherman occupied Raleigh, North Carolina, where, during April 17–18, he hammered out a broad armistice. Abraham Lincoln had been assassinated on April 14, 1865, so it was the new president, Andrew Johnson, who, repudiating the Sherman agreement, concluded on April 26 a narrower armistice. On May 10, 1865, President Johnson declared that armed resistance was "virtually at an end," but three days later, at Palmito Ranch, near Brownsville, Texas, Confederate troops under Edmund Kirby Smith skirmished with Federals. This small engagement was the last fight of the war. Smith surrendered to General E. R. S. Canby, Union army, on May 26. However, the very last Confederate commander to surrender was Stand Watie, son of a full-blooded Cherokee father and half-blooded Cherokee mother, a Confederate brigadier general from Indian Territory, who laid down arms on June 23, 1865, at Doakville, Indian Territory.

Clark, Mark Wayne (1896–1984) *U.S. Army general*

Widely regarded as one of the most exemplary commanders of WORLD WAR II, Clark was raised in the army, born at Madison Barracks in Sackets Harbor, New York, into the family of a career army officer. He graduated from the UNITED STATES MILITARY ACADEMY in 1917 and in April 1918, as a second lieutenant, was sent to France with the 5th Infantry Division. In WORLD WAR I, he participated in the Aisne-Marne offensive. Wounded in June, he was assigned to FIRST U.S. ARMY staff during the Saint-Mihiel offensive (September 12–16, 1918), and the Meuse-Argonne campaign (September 26–November 11) that closed the war. Clark served in the THIRD U.S. ARMY during the Allied occupation of Germany, returning to the United States in November 1919.

Promoted to captain, Clark served at a variety of posts in the Midwest until he was transferred to the ARMY GENERAL STAFF in Washington, D.C., where he was stationed from 1921 to 1924. He graduated from the Infantry School at Fort Benning, Georgia, in 1925 and was promoted to major in 1933. In 1935, he graduated from the COMMAND AND GENERAL STAFF COLLEGE at Fort Leavenworth, Kansas, and was assigned to direct the Civilian Conservation Corps (CCC) in Omaha, Nebraska (1935–36).

Clark graduated from the U.S. ARMY WAR COLLEGE in 1937 and served on the staff of the 3RD INFANTRY DIVISION until 1940, when he became an instructor at the college. As a member of the faculty, he worked to plan the expansion of the army and its preparation for the army's entry into World War II. Promoted brigadier general in August 1941 and major general in April 1942, he was named chief of staff of Army Ground Forces in May. In July, he became commander of U.S. ground forces in Britain and immediately set about organizing II Corps. He did not stay behind a desk, however, but both planned and led a hazardous espionage mission to obtain intelligence on Vichy French forces in North Africa in preparation for Operation Torch, the U.S. North African landings.

In November 1942, Clark was promoted to lieutenant general and given command of Allied forces in North Africa under DWIGHT D. EISENHOWER. Clark was one of the principal planners of the invasion of Sicily and Italy, which was launched from North Africa. At the head of Fifth Army, he landed at Salerno on September 9. Clark's leadership of the Italian campaign has been a subject of controversy because it proved slow, costly, and was, in great measure, unproductive. Nevertheless, after the German surrender, Clark was named Allied high commissioner for Austria, serving in this capacity from June 1945 to May 1947, when he was assigned to command Sixth Army (1947–49). Elevated to chief of Army Field Forces during 1949–52, Clark became the third overall U.S. commander during the KOREAN WAR, succeeding MATTHEW BUNKER RIDGWAY, who had replaced General DOUGLAS MACARTHUR. Clark remained in command in Korea until after the cease-fire of July 27, 1953.

Clark retired from the army in 1954 and became commandant of the Citadel, South Carolina's prestigious military academy. He served there until 1960, then retired to his home outside of Washington, D.C.

Coastal and Hydraulics Laboratory (CHL)

Located in Vicksburg, Mississippi, and attached to the U.S. ARMY CORPS OF ENGINEERS, the CHL is a civil engineering research and development facility that serves both the civilian and the military communities with flood and storm damage reduction research, integrated systems analysis, hydroenvironmental studies, and navigation support.

Specific military applications of the work of the CHL assist the army and other services with issues of mobility and water supply. Work undertaken includes remote sensing and quantification of precipitation; creation of spatially varying precipitation hydrology models; visualization of results in dam break models; and water location in arid and semi-arid regions.

Cold Regions Research and Engineering Laboratory (CRREL)

The CRREL is a research and engineering facility located in Hanover, New Hampshire, with project offices at Fort Wainwright, Alaska, and Fort Richardson, Alaska. The laboratory's mission is to perform scientific and engineering research in cold regions for practical application by the U.S. ARMY CORPS OF ENGINEERS, the army generally, the Department of Defense, and the nation. The laboratory is the only Department of Defense facility that addresses the problems and opportunities unique to the world's cold regions.

The laboratory's efforts include work in engineering and technology in cold regions, seismic-acoustic physics, and building tools for military combat and survival in cold weather, among others. Research work is performed in the laboratory's special low-temperature facilities as well as in the field, including areas as diverse as the Arctic and Antarctic, the Midwest, the U.S. West, Korea, Greenland, Bosnia, and the Mojave Desert.

colonel   See RANKS AND GRADES.

combat arms branches   See ORGANIZATION BY BRANCH.

combat service support branches   See ORGANIZATION BY BRANCH.

combat support branches   See ORGANIZATION BY BRANCH.

Combined Arms Center (CAC)

Administered by the U.S. ARMY TRAINING AND DOCTRINE COMMAND (TRADOC) and located at Fort Leavenworth, Kansas, the CAC is a center for combined arms education, doctrine, and leadership development. Its mission is to educate officers in the art of command and staff functions of the combined arms at the tactical level, and to educate selected officers in the operational art of war. CAC writes doctrine for warfighting at the division and corps levels and has a training development function for leader development and battle command, and for experimenting with the concepts, methods, procedures, and means of battle command. CAC is also responsible for providing training exercises for commanders and staffs, from brigade through corps levels, in the exercise of battle command.

Two subordinate units are important to the CAC mission. The Threats Directorate reports directly to the CAC commander but serves the entire army as the TRADOC focal point for all matters concerning potential adversaries and the threats they represent, defined as "the ability of an enemy or potential enemy to limit, neutralize, or destroy the effectiveness of a current or projected mission, organization, or item of equipment." The Foreign Military Studies Office (FMSO) researches, writes, and publishes works on the military establishments, doctrines, and strategic, operational, and tactical practices of selected foreign armed forces.

Combined Arms Support Command (CASCOM)

Located at Fort Lee, Virginia, and administered by the U.S. ARMY TRAINING AND DOCTRINE COMMAND (TRADOC), CASCOM provides the army with combat development, training development, and institutional training. It participates in the force structuring process and determines materiel requirements in order to shape the development, acquisition, and fielding processes for combat service support functions.

Command and General Staff College

Located at Fort Leavenworth, Kansas, the Command and General Staff College is administered by the U.S. ARMY TRAINING AND DOCTRINE COMMAND (TRADOC) and is charged with educating leaders in the values and practice of the profession of arms, acting as the executive agent for the Army's

Leader Development Program, developing doctrine, and promoting and supporting the advancement of military art and science.

Instruction is designed to develop in officers reasoning and decision-making ability, character, self-expression, and teamwork. Education is aimed at developing logical, practical, and original reasoning ability in military problem solving.

command sergeant major   See RANKS AND GRADES.

commissioned officer

Any holder of the rank of second lieutenant or above is a commissioned officer, a soldier whose rank and authority are granted under authority of the president of the United States with the confirmation of the U.S. Congress.

See also NONCOMMISSIONED OFFICER.

Communications-Electronics Command (CECOM)

Located at Fort Monmouth, New Jersey, and subordinate to U.S. ARMY MATERIEL COMMAND (AMC), CECOM develops, acquires, and sustains superior information technologies and integrated systems, enabling battlespace dominance for America's warfighters. A special emphasis is joint interoperability and horizontal technology integration throughout the lifecycle of warfighting systems and platforms.

CECOM has seven major organizational components. They include the Research, Development and Engineering Center (RDEC); Software Engineering Center (SEC); Information Systems Engineering Command (ISEC); Deputy for Systems Acquisition/Systems Management Center (DSA/SMC); Logistics and Readiness Center (LRC); Tobyhanna Army Depot; and CECOM Acquisition Center (AC).

company   See ORGANIZATION BY UNITS.

Continental army

The precursor to the U.S. Army, the Continental army was created on June 15, 1775, by the Continental Congress, which authorized companies of riflemen and named GEORGE WASHINGTON commander in chief. In addition, the Continental Congress took over the so-called Boston army, at the time engaged against British forces in Boston, and began commissioning generals. During the AMERICAN REVOLUTION, the Continental army constituted the "regular army," but it never supplanted the many state and local militias that also fought in the war.

Over the course of the entire American Revolution, the Continental army numbered (by modern estimate) 231,771, although nothing approaching this number served at any one time. The Continental army was almost completely disbanded by 1784, a year after the end of the Revolution.

Although many militia companies served under him during the Revolution, Washington constantly begged Congress to fund more troops for the Continental army. Militiamen were usually poorly disciplined and poorly trained, and, worst of all, enlisted for terms as brief as 90 days. The regular Continental army enlistment was a year, which

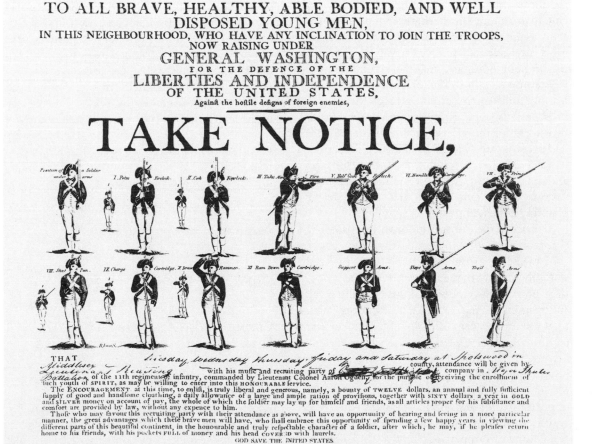

Recruiting poster for the Continental army   *(Dover Publications)*

was much better, though Washington lobbied for three-year enlistments, which Congress finally authorized effective January 1, 1777. The longer enlistments meant that the training of Continental army troops was generally far superior to militia training. Longer service also, of course, answered manpower requirements more effectively than short-term enlistments.

The Continental army was raised by regiments, with each state authorized by Congress to recruit a certain number of regiments to be incorporated under Washington's overall command. Eighty-eight regiments were authorized. Pennsylvania and the New England states were the most zealous in recruiting, so that the so-called Continental army was principally an army of the Northeast. Despite the three-year terms, it became increasingly difficult to maintain the strength of the Continental army as the war dragged on. Desperate state legislatures attempted to induce recruits by increasing recruitment bounties, but, more commonly, the legislatures sought to reinforce the army by transferring militiamen into Continental service for brief periods (typically, the summer only). Indeed, by the end of the 1770s, the three-year enlistment had become largely a matter of theory; most troops had actually been recruited for far briefer terms, and the Continental army became a hodgepodge of various enlistments, a fact that made strategic planning almost impossible.

Service in the Continental army was paid for by a combination of funds authorized by Congress (but raised from the states) and, directly, by the states themselves in the form of recruitment bounties. Sometimes, individual municipalities also contributed to the recruitment bounties, which might be in the form of cash, cattle, land, or some combination of these. As monetary inflation became an increasing problem, more and more bounties were paid in goods, cattle, and land. Many recruits saw the Continental army as a genuine opportunity for economic advancement. Others craved adventure and camaraderie. Doubtless, some joined from patriotic motives and, certainly, many served because of some combination of all of these inducements.

Despite the many problems it faced, the Continental army proved to be a highly effective fighting force. It was intensely loyal to its commander in chief, Washington, and also demonstrated loyalty to regimental commanders, who were typically prominent citizens of the regiment's state. Despite chronic shortages of provisions, shelter, and even basic supplies such as uniforms, the Continental army, under such commanders as ANTHONY WAYNE and Alexander Hamilton, fielded units equal or superior to the best Europe had to offer, whether British or German mercenary ("Hessian").

Continental United States Armies (CONUSAs)

CONUSAs are regional commands with responsibility for the operations, mobilization, and deployment of reserve units from home stations to areas of operation. As of 2005, there were two continental armies, the FIRST U.S. ARMY (headquarters, Fort Gillem, Georgia) and the Fifth U.S. Army (headquarters, Fort Sam Houston, Texas). The territory of the First Army covers the eastern half of the continental United States, as far west as the Mississippi River and the state of Minnesota. The Fifth Army is responsible for all territory west of Minnesota and the Mississippi River.

corporal   See RANKS AND GRADES.

corps   See ORGANIZATION BY UNITS.

Corpus Christi Army Depot (CCAD), Texas   See FORTS AND OTHER INSTALLATIONS.

court-martial

A court-martial is a military court comprised of military personnel and convened on an ad hoc basis to judge military personnel accused of violating military law. Although there are differences between a court-martial and a civilian court, the court-martial is generally governed by U.S. law, the Constitution, and the Bill of Rights.

There are three types of courts-martial:

1. Summary court-martial—Consists of a single officer who unilaterally acts as judge, jury, prosecutor, and defense counsel and presides over minor matters.
2. Special court-martial—Consists of a legally trained judge and three or more panel members who serve as a jury. A special court-martial is convened in cases more serious than those addressed by a summary court-martial. This body can hand down prison sentences of up to six months, reduction in grade, forfeiture of two-thirds pay for six months, or a bad-conduct discharge (see DISCHARGE, BAD CONDUCT).
3. General court-martial—Consists of a military judge, counsel for the prosecution and for the defense (both fully qualified attorneys), and a five-member jury. The general court-martial tries the most serious offenses (murder, rape, desertion, and so on) and may hand down long imprisonments or even the death penalty as well as authorize a dishonorable discharge (see DISCHARGE, DISHONORABLE). The president of the United States must approve all death sentences or sentences pronounced on general officers.

Criminal Investigation Division See U.S. ARMY CRIMINAL INVESTIGATION COMMAND.

Custer, George Armstrong (1839–1876)
U.S. Army general

One of the army's most famous officers, Custer earned spectacular fame as the "Boy General" of the CIVIL WAR and went on to lead the 7th Cavalry in the INDIAN WARS, meeting defeat and death at the Battle of the Little Bighorn.

Born in New Rumley, Ohio, George Armstrong Custer spent part of his childhood with a half-sister in Monroe, Michigan. He attended the UNITED STATES MILITARY ACADEMY at West Point, graduat-

ing, only one demerit shy of dismissal, at the bottom of his class on the eve of the Civil War. Despite his abysmal academic performance, Custer was a dashing officer, a superb field commander, and utterly reckless with his own safety and that of his men. In staff positions with General GEORGE BRINTON MCCLELLAN and, later, General Alfred Pleasonton, Captain Custer so impressively demonstrated his potential that he was jumped in rank to brigadier general of volunteers and given command of a Michigan cavalry brigade. At 23, he was the youngest general officer in the army.

Custer wore his blond hair below shoulder length and sported a gaudy uniform of his own design. From Gettysburg to Appomattox, he earned renown for slashing cavalry charges that often proved decisive in small operations. His personal courage was absolute, and he earned the respect,

A portrait of George and Elizabeth Custer with Custer's brother, captain Thomas W. Custer, also killed at Little Bighorn *(National Archives)*

even the devotion of his men, despite his often harsh treatment of them and his manifest disregard for their safety. By war's end, he was a major general commanding a full division of volunteers.

After the war, Custer reverted to the rank of lieutenant colonel in the REGULAR ARMY. He was assigned to the 7th Cavalry, newly formed to fight the mounted Indian warriors of the western plains. Garbed now in fringed buckskin instead of his former black velvet and gold lace, but still possessed of his mane of yellow hair, Custer was a spectacular embodiment of the dashing Indian fighter. The 7th's commanding colonel was frequently absent, and, for all practical purposes, Custer commanded the regiment.

His first engagement against Indians, in Kansas in 1867, ended in failure. He was unable to defeat the warriors and was even court-martialed on charges of absence without leave and "overmarching" his men. Found guilty, he was sentenced to a year's suspension of rank and pay. Upon his return to duty in 1868, he made a brutal surprise attack on Chief Black Kettle's Cheyenne village on the Washita River in present-day Oklahoma. Although the village was essentially a civilian target, with many women and children, and although Black Kettle himself was an advocate of peace, Custer's operation was greeted by the army and much of the public as a great victory. It became the foundation of his reputation as a consummate Indian fighter.

Custer was a vigorous self-promoter who wrote popular magazine articles and a best-selling memoir, *My Life on the Plains*. A better commander than some, but less successful against the Indians than others, he nevertheless earned a peerless reputation among the public. In 1874, he led the Seventh Cavalry out of its base at Fort Abraham Lincoln to explore the Black Hills of the Dakota Territory. Part of the Great Sioux Reservation, guaranteed to the Sioux by the Treaty of 1868, the Black Hills region had long been coveted by whites who thought it a fertile gold field. When the federal government attempted to buy the Black Hills in order to legalize the gold mining operations there, war broke out with the Sioux under such leaders as Sitting Bull and Crazy Horse. In 1876, Custer led the 7th in an operation against a Sioux village on the Little Bighorn River in Montana Territory. Acting without reconnaissance, he attacked with five companies of his regiment on June 25. Overwhelmed by vastly superior numbers of warriors, he and all the troopers directly under his command were wiped out.

"Custer's Last Stand" stunned and enraged Americans and, ultimately, motivated the conquest of the Sioux and the acquisition of the Black Hills, even as it enshrined Custer in a heroic immortality many believe he did not deserve. Custer's devoted wife Elizabeth, or Libbie, spent the rest of her long life defending as well as glorifying his name in three best-selling biographies.

D

Davis, Benjamin O., Sr. (1877–1970)
U.S. Army general

Benjamin O. Davis, Sr. was the army's first African-American general in the REGULAR ARMY. Born in Washington, D.C., on July 1, 1877, Davis entered military service on July 13, 1898, during the SPANISH-AMERICAN WAR as temporary first lieutenant of the 8th United States Volunteer Infantry. Mustered out on March 6, 1899, he enlisted on June 18, 1899, as a private in Troop I, 9th Cavalry, of the regular army and was promoted to corporal and squadron sergeant major. On February 2, 1901, he was commissioned a second lieutenant of CAVALRY.

He served with the 9th Cavalry on the Island of Samar in the Philippines, then was assigned in August 1901 to the 2nd Squadron, 10th Cavalry and served as adjutant at Fort Washakie, Wyoming. In September 1905, Davis was appointed professor of military science and tactics at Wilberforce University, Ohio, remaining there until 1909, when, after serving briefly at Fort Ethan Allen, Vermont, he was named military attaché to the U.S. legation at Monrovia, Liberia.

In January 1912, Davis was assigned to duty with the 9th Cavalry at Fort D. A. Russell, Wyoming, and at Douglas, Arizona. He was once again assigned in 1915 as professor of military science and tactics at Wilberforce University and, then, in the summer of 1917, he was sent to the Philippines for duty as supply officer of the 9th Cavalry at Camp Stotsenburg. Returning to the

United States in 1920, he was named professor of military science and tactics at Tuskegee Institute, Alabama, where he served until July 1924. In that year, he became instructor of the 372nd Infantry, Ohio National Guard, Cleveland, Ohio. Returning to Wilberforce University as professor of military science and tactics in 1929, he was detailed the

England, 1942: General Benjamin O. Davis, Sr., inspects a soldier's rifle. *(Library of Congress)*

following year to special duty with the Department of State in connection with affairs relating to the Republic of Liberia.

In 1931, Davis returned to Tuskegee as professor of military science and tactics. He taught there until August 1937, when he was transferred to Wilberforce University. In 1938, he was named instructor and commanding officer of the 369th Infantry, New York National Guard, which later became the 369th Coast Artillery (Antiaircraft) Regiment.

Promoted to brigadier general (temporary) on October 25, 1940, he was ordered to Fort Riley, Kansas, in January 1941 as brigade commander with the 2nd Cavalry Division, then assigned to duty in Washington, D.C., as assistant to the Inspector General. Davis was retired on July 31, 1941, then recalled to active duty with the permanent rank of brigadier general the following day, thereby becoming the first African American to hold general officer rank in the regular army. In September 1942, during WORLD WAR II, Davis was sent to the European theater of operations as adviser on Negro problems, assigned to help manage the many difficulties inherent in a segregated army (see AFRICAN AMERICANS IN THE U.S. ARMY).

In November 1944, Davis was made special assistant to the commanding general, communications zone, European theater of operations, and was stationed in Paris. After serving again as assistant to the Inspector General in Washington, D.C., Davis retired on July 14, 1948, having served 50 years.

Davis's son, Lieutenant General Benjamin O. Davis, Jr., USAF, became the fourth African-American graduate of the UNITED STATES MILITARY ACADEMY and the nation's second African-American general officer.

decorations and medals

Members of the army are eligible for decoration with the following medals and commendations, the majority of which may also be awarded to members of the other services as well and, on occasion, members of foreign armed services.

American Campaign Medal

This medal is awarded for service within the American theater between December 7, 1941, and March 2, 1946, under any of the following conditions: permanent assignment outside the continental United States; permanent assignment as an aircrew member of airplanes making frequent flights over ocean waters for a period of 30 consecutive days or 60 days nonconsecutive; duty outside the continental United States in a passenger status or on temporary duty for 30 consecutive days or 60 days nonconsecutive; duty in active combat against the enemy, if awarded a combat decoration or furnished a certificate by the unit commander stating that the individual participated in combat; served within the continental United States for an aggregate period of one year.

American Defense Service Medal

This medal is awarded for any active duty service period completed between September 8, 1939, and December 7, 1941, if the active duty order specified service for a 12-month period or longer. A Foreign Service Clasp is attached to the ribbon and medal if the same requirements are met and the service was performed outside the continental United States.

Antarctica Service Medal

Established by an act of Congress on July 7, 1960, the ribbon was authorized in 1961, and the design of the medal received final approval in 1963. The decoration is awarded to any member of the U.S. armed forces, U.S. citizen, or resident alien of the United States who, after January 1, 1946, to a date to be announced, has served on the Antarctic continent or in support of U.S. operations there.

The first recipients of this award were members of the U.S. Navy operation "High Jump" under Admiral Robert E. Byrd in 1946 and 1947.

Armed Forces Expeditionary Medal

This medal was established on December 4, 1961, to be awarded to members of the U.S. armed forces who, after July 1, 1958, have participated in U.S. military operations and encountered foreign armed opposition, or were in danger of hostile action by foreign armed forces. The medal was awarded for service in South Vietnam, before the Vietnam Service Medal was issued.

Armed Forces Reserve Medal

The medal is awarded to any service member or former service member of the RESERVE COMPONENTS of the U.S. armed forces who completes or has completed a total of 10 years of honorable and satisfactory military service. The service need not be consecutive, as long as the service occurs within a period of 12 consecutive years. An hourglass device on the medal's ribbon denotes each additional 10-year period of service.

Armed Forces Service Medal

Authorized by Executive Order 12985, January 11, 1996, this medal is presented to members of the U.S. armed forces who, after June 1, 1992, participate, or have participated, as members of U.S. military units, in a U.S. military operation deemed by the JOINT CHIEFS OF STAFF to be a significant activity, but encounter no foreign armed opposition or imminent threat of hostile action.

Army of Occupation Medal

This medal was established in 1946 and the order has been amended several times to cover areas not originally authorized. It is awarded for 30 consecutive days at a normal post of duty on assignment to the armies of occupation. Designed with regard to the WORLD WAR II experience, the medal's obverse shows the Remagen bridge abutments, symbolic of Europe, and the reverse shows Mount Fujiyama, symbolic of Asia. Clasps were authorized for wear on the ribbon, with the inscriptions "Germany" or "Japan" to signify that the recipient served in either area of occupation. There were also some unofficial bars, such as "Korea" and the Berlin Airlift Device.

Asiatic-Pacific Campaign Medal

This medal is awarded for service in the Asiatic-Pacific theater of World War II between December 7, 1941, and March 2, 1946, under any of the following conditions: permanent assignment; passenger status or on temporary duty for 30 consecutive days or 60 nonconsecutive days; in active combat against the enemy, if personnel were awarded a combat decoration or furnished a certificate by the unit commander stating that he participated in combat.

Bronze Star

Authorized by Executive Order 9419 on February 4, 1944, this decoration is awarded to personnel in any branch of military service who, while serving on or after December 7, 1941, shall have distinguished himself or herself by heroic or meritorious achievement or service—not involving participation in aerial flight—in connection with military operations against an armed enemy. The award recognizes acts of heroism performed in ground combat if they are of lesser degree than that required for the Silver Star. It also recognizes single acts of merit and meritorious service if the achievement or service is of a lesser degree than that deemed worthy of the Legion of Merit.

Army personnel who, as members of the Armed Forces of the United States between December 7, 1941, and September 2, 1945, were awarded the Combat Infantryman's Badge or Medical Badge for exemplary conduct may, upon application, receive the Bronze Star.

Defense Meritorious Service Medal

This medal was established by President Jimmy Carter (Executive Order 12019) on November 3, 1977, and is awarded to military personnel serving with or assigned to a number of joint activities, including the secretary of defense, organizations of the Joint Chiefs of Staff, and headquarters of joint commands. Also included are other joint activities and specified commands such as military assistance advisory groups and joint missions, and jointly manned staffs within Allied Command Europe, Allied Command Atlantic, the NATO Military Committee, and military agencies associated with functions of the military or other joint activities as may be designated by the secretary of defense. The medal is awarded for noncombat meritorious achievement or for service that is "incontestably exceptional and of magnitude that clearly places the individual above his peers" while serving in one of the assignments for which the medal has been designated.

Defense Superior Service Medal
President Gerald R. Ford established this medal by Executive Order 11904 on February 6, 1976, for award by the secretary of defense to military officers who perform exceptionally with the Office of the Secretary of Defense, the Joint Chiefs of Staff, special or outstanding command in a defense agency, or any other joint activity designated by the secretary.

Euro-African-Middle Eastern Campaign Medal
This medal is awarded for service in the European-African-Middle Eastern theater of World War II between December 7, 1941, and November 8, 1945, under any of the following conditions: permanent assignment; passenger status or on temporary duty for 30 consecutive days or 60 nonconsecutive days; in active combat against the enemy, if individual was awarded a combat decoration or furnished a certificate by the unit commander stating that he participated in combat.

Good Conduct Medal
The Good Conduct Medal—also known in the army as the Army Good Conduct Medal—was authorized by Executive Order 8809, on June 28, 1941, for award to enlisted men who shall have honorably completed three continuous years of active military service subsequent to August 26, 1940, and who are recommended by their commanding officers for exemplary behavior, efficiency, and fidelity. Persons awarded this medal must have had character and efficiency ratings of excellent or higher throughout the qualifying period, including time spent in attendance at service schools, and there must have been no convictions by COURT-MARTIAL. During wartime the Good Conduct Medal may be awarded on completion of one year of continuous service rather than three. This was specified by Executive Order 9323 of March 31, 1943, during World War II, and it was amended by Executive Order 10444 on April 10, 1953, during the KOREAN WAR and applying to any future period in which the United States is at war.

Humanitarian Service Medal
This medal was authorized by Executive Order 11965, January 19, 1977, to honor personnel of the U.S. armed forces who have distinguished themselves by meritorious direct participation in a significant military act or operation of a humanitarian nature, or have rendered a service to mankind.

Many operations are eligible for the award. The first was the Guyana Disaster Relief in Jonestown, Guyana, in 1978. Subsequent operations have included disaster, flood, tornado, snow removal, and earthquake relief work. Also included were Operation Boat People, Evacuation of Laos, Cuban Refugee Resettlement, Beirut Evacuation, Cholera Epidemic in Truk Islands, and operations of humanitarian aid in the United States.

Inter-American Defense Board Medal
The Inter-American Defense Board Medal was established at the 91st session of the Inter-American Defense Board shortly after World War II, on December 11, 1945, and was authorized by Executive Order 11446, January 18, 1969. The medal is presented to USN (and other U.S. military) personnel who have served on the Inter-American Defense Board for at least one year.

Joint Meritorious Unit Award
Authorized by the secretary of defense on June 10, 1981, this award was originally called the Department of Defense Meritorious Unit Award. It is awarded in the name of the secretary of defense to joint activities for meritorious achievement or service, superior to that which is normally expected, for actions in the following situations: combat with an armed enemy of the United States, a declared national emergency, or under extraordinary circumstances that involve national interests.

That this award ribbon is identical to the Department of Defense Superior Service Medal ribbon reflects the fact that the service performed must be similar to warrant the award of this medal to an individual.

Joint Service Achievement Medal

This award was established by the secretary of defense on August 3, 1983, and is presented in the name of the secretary of defense for either outstanding achievement or meritorious service. It takes precedence over the achievement medals of the service branches. Individuals eligible for this award must be members of the armed forces of the United States below the grade of 0-6, and assigned to a qualifying organization such as the defense agencies, headquarters of unified commands, Office of the Joint Chiefs of Staff, and the Office of the Secretary of Defense. The required service or achievement, while of a lesser degree than that required for award of the Joint Service Commendation Medal, must have been accomplished within distinction.

The Joint Service Achievement Medal may not be awarded for any act or period of service for which an achievement medal of a military service branch is awarded. It should not be awarded for retirement.

Joint Service Commendation Medal

Established by the Department of Defense on June 25, 1963, this decoration is awarded by the Office of the Secretary of Defense, the Joint Chiefs of Staff, and other Department of Defense agencies or joint activities reporting through the Joint Chiefs of Staff. Any member of the armed forces who distinguishes himself or herself by meritorious achievement or service while serving in any specified activity after January 1, 1965, is eligible for the award, which, however, is not awarded for any period of service for which any of the commendation medals of the branches of the armed forces are given.

Korean Service Medal

Authorized on November 8, 1950, this medal is awarded to members of the U.S. armed forces for service in Korea for 30 consecutive or 60 nonconsecutive days between June 27, 1950, and July 27,

1954, the Korean War period. The obverse of the medal depicts a Korean gateway, encircled by the inscription "Korean Service."

Kosovo Campaign Medal

On May 3, 2000, President Bill Clinton approved the establishment of the Kosovo Campaign Medal to recognize the accomplishments of military service members participating in or in direct support of Kosovo operations, including the Kosovo Air Campaign (March 24, 1999–June 10, 1999). The area of eligibility encompasses the total land area and air space of Serbia (including Kosovo), Montenegro, Albania, Macedonia, Bosnia, Croatia, Hungary, Romania, Greece, Bulgaria, Italy, and Slovenia, and the waters and air space of the Adriatic and Ionian seas north of the 39th north latitude. The medal may also be awarded to those who participated in or in direct support of the Kosovo Defense Campaign (June 11, 1999–date to be determined) within the total land area and air space of Serbia (including Kosovo), Montenegro, Albania, Macedonia, and the waters and air space of the Adriatic Sea within 12 nautical miles of the Montenegro, Albania, and Croatia coastlines south of 42 degrees and 52 minutes north latitude.

Kuwait Liberation Medal— Government of Kuwait

This award was authorized by the government of Kuwait to members of the U.S. military who participated in Operations Desert Shield and Desert Storm and the liberation of Kuwait. A secretary of defense memorandum of March 16, 1995, authorized the acceptance and wearing of the Kuwait Liberation Medal by members of the U.S. armed forces. To be eligible for this award, U.S. military personnel must have served in support of Operations Desert Shield and Desert Storm between August 2, 1990, and August 31, 1993, in one or more of the following areas: the Persian Gulf, Red Sea, Gulf of Oman, that portion of the Arabian Sea that lies north of 10 degrees north latitude and west of 68 degrees east longitude, Gulf of Aden, or the total land areas of Iraq, Kuwait, Saudi Arabia, Oman, Bahrain, Qatar, and the United Arab Emirates.

Kuwait Liberation Medal— Kingdom of Saudi Arabia

This medal was authorized by the government of Saudi Arabia to members of the coalition forces who participated in Operation Desert Storm and the liberation of Kuwait. A U.S. deputy secretary of defense memorandum dated October 7, 1991, authorized the acceptance and wearing of the Kuwait Liberation Medal by members of the U.S. armed forces.

To be eligible for this award, U.S. military personnel must have served in support of Operation Desert Storm between January 17, 1991, and February 28, 1991, in one or more of the following areas: the Persian Gulf, Red Sea, Gulf of Oman, that portion of the Arabian Sea that lies north of 10 degrees north latitude and west of 68 degrees east longitude, the Gulf of Aden, or the total land areas of Iraq, Kuwait, Saudi Arabia, Oman, Bahrain, Qatar, and the United Arab Emirates.

Legion of Merit

The Legion of Merit is the first U.S. decoration created specifically for award to citizens of other nations. Established by an act of Congress of July 20, 1942, and amended by an executive order of March 15, 1955, it is conferred on officers and enlisted men of the armed forces of the United States and on nationals of other counties "who shall have distinguished themselves by exceptionally meritorious conduct in the performance of outstanding services" since September 8, 1939, the date of President Franklin D. Roosevelt's proclamation of the state of emergency prior to World War II.

The Legion of Merit may be awarded for combat or noncombat services; in the case of American military personnel, if the award is for combat service, it is shown by the wearing of a combat "V."

The Legion of Merit is the first U.S. award distinguished by different degrees. If a holder of the Legion of Merit in one degree is subsequently given another such award, it is never in a degree lower than the original one. The degrees of Chief Commander and Commander are conferred on members of foreign governments only and are awarded for services comparable to those for which the Distinguished Service Medal is given to members of the U.S. armed forces.

Medal of Honor

The highest military honor in the United States, the Medal of Honor has been awarded 3,428 times in the nation's history and is presented by the president in the name of Congress to a person "who distinguishes himself or herself conspicuously by gallantry and intrepidity at the risk of his life or her life above and beyond the call of duty while engaged in an action against an enemy of the United States; while engaged in military operations involving conflict with an opposing foreign force; or while serving with friendly foreign forces engaged in an armed conflict against an opposing armed force in which the United States is not a belligerent party. The deed performed must have been one of personal bravery or self-sacrifice so conspicuous as to clearly distinguish the individual above his comrades and must have involved risk of life. Incontestable proof of the performance of the service will be exacted and each recommendation for the award of this decoration will be considered on the standard of extraordinary merit."

Meritorious Service Medal

Established by Executive Order 11448 on January 16, 1969, the Meritorious Service Medal is awarded to members of the armed forces who distinguish themselves either by outstanding achievement or by meritorious service to the United States. The award is the noncombat counterpart of the Bronze Star Medal.

Military Outstanding Volunteer Service Medal

This award, authorized by Executive Order 12830 on January 9, 1993, may be awarded to members of the U.S. armed forces and their reserve components who, after December 31, 1992, perform outstanding volunteer community service of a sustained, direct, and consequential nature.

Multinational Force and Observers Medal

The Multinational Force and Observers (MFO) Medal was created pursuant to a United Nations resolution to keep the peace between Egypt and Israel in the Sinai Peninsula. In 1984, the Department of Defense authorized the MFO Medal to armed forces personnel who served at least 90 consecutive days with the MFO after August 3, 1981.

National Defense Service Medal

Authorized by Executive Order 10448 on April 22, 1953, and amended by Executive Order 11256 on January 11, 1966, this medal is awarded for honorable active military service as a member of the armed forces of the United States between June 27, 1950, and July 27, 1954 (Korean War period), between January 1, 1961, and August 14, 1974 (VIETNAM WAR period), and between August 2, 1990, and November 30, 1995 (Desert Shield and Desert Storm periods).

NATO Medal— Former Republic of Yugoslavia

This award is authorized by the secretary general of NATO for specific NATO operations relating to the Republic of Yugoslavia. In accordance with Executive Order 11446, the secretary of defense, with concurrence of the secretary of state, has approved acceptance and wear by U.S. service members who meet criteria specified by the secretary general of NATO. Acceptance of the NATO Medal has been approved for U.S. military personnel who serve under NATO command or operational control in direct support of NATO operations in the Former Republic of Yugoslavia, or as designated by Supreme Allied Commander, Europe (SACEUR), from July 1, 1992, to October 12, 1998.

NATO Medal—Kosovo Operations

This award is authorized by the secretary general of NATO for specific NATO operations relating to Kosovo. In accordance with Executive Order 11446, January 16, 1969, the secretary of defense has approved acceptance and wear by U.S. service members who meet criteria specified by the secretary general of NATO effective from October 13, 1998, to a date to be determined. The following Kosovo operations are included: Operations Allied Force (March 24, 1999–June 10, 1999), Joint Guardian (June 11, 1999–date to be determined), Allied Harbour (April 4, 1999–September 1, 1999), Sustain Hope/Shining Hope (April 4, 1999–July 10, 1999), Noble Anvil (March 12, 1999–July 20, 1999). Participation in these Kosovo Task Forces also merit eligibility for the award: Hawk (April 5, 1999–June 24, 1999), Saber (March 31, 1999–July 8, 1999), Falcon (June 11, 1999–date to be determined, coinciding Joint Guardian), and Hunter (April 1, 1999–November 1, 1999).

Philippine Defense Medal

The medal was awarded for combat service in the defense of the Philippines from December 8, 1941, to June 15, 1942, if the person was either a member of the Bataan or Manila Bay forces or of a unit, ship, or airplane under enemy attack, or assigned or stationed in Philippine waters for at least 30 calendar days during this period. A person who meets both conditions is authorized to wear a bronze service star on the ribbon.

Philippine Independence Medal

The medal is awarded to personnel who are recipients of both the Philippine Defense Medal and the Philippine Liberation Medal.

Philippine Liberation Medal

The medal was awarded for participation in the liberation of the Philippines from October 17, 1944, to September 3, 1945, to personnel who participated in the initial landing operations on Leyte or adjoining islands from October 17, 1944, to October 20, 1944; who participated in any engagement against the enemy during the campaign on Leyte and adjoining islands; or who served in the Philippine Islands or on ships in Philippine waters for at least 30 calendar days during October 17, 1944–September 3, 1945. Recipients who meet more than one of these conditions are authorized to wear a bronze service star on the ribbon for each additional condition under which they qualify.

Philippine Presidential Unit Citation

This ribbon was awarded to members of the U.S. armed forces for services culminating in the liberation of the Philippine Islands during World War II. The award was made in the name of the president of the Republic of the Philippines.

Prisoner of War Medal

This medal was authorized by Congress and signed into law by President Ronald Reagan in 1986 and may be awarded to any person who was a prisoner of war after April 5, 1917—the date of U.S. entry into WORLD WAR I. Persons eligible for the award included those taken prisoner or held captive while engaged in an action against an enemy of the United States, while engaged in military operations involving conflict with an opposing armed force, or while serving with friendly forces engaged in armed conflict against an opposing armed force in which the United States was not a belligerent party. The person's conduct while in captivity must have been honorable, and the medal may be awarded posthumously to the next of kin of the recipient.

Purple Heart

This award is a modern form of the original Purple Heart established by General GEORGE WASHINGTON in 1782. It is conferred on any person wounded in action while serving with the armed forces of the United States. It is also awarded posthumously to the next of kin of personnel killed or having died of wounds received in action after April 5, 1917.

The Purple Heart is awarded for wounds or death incurred as a result of an act of any opposing armed force, as a result of an international terrorist attack, or as a result of military operations while serving as part of a peacekeeping force. The decoration was authorized for the army by a War Department order of February 22, 1932.

Second and subsequent awards of the Purple Heart are denoted by a gold star for navy and marine corps personnel and by an oak-leaf cluster for army and air force personnel.

Private First Class Jessica Lynch receives the Purple Heart from Lieutenant General James B. Peake, U.S. Army Surgeon General, during a ceremony at Walter Reed Medical Center, July 21, 2004. Lynch also received the Bronze Star and the Prisoner of War Medal.   *(U.S. Army)*

Republic of Korea Presidential Unit Citation

This unit award was presented to units of the United Nations Command for service in Korea during the Korean War and was awarded in the name of the president of the Republic of Korea. It is a ribbon award with accompanying citation.

Republic of Korea War Service Medal

On August 20, 1999, the secretary of defense approved the acceptance and wearing of the Republic of Korea War Service Medal in recognition of the sacrifices of United States veterans of the Korean War. To receive the medal, military veterans must have served in the country of Korea, its territorial waters, or airspace within the inclusive period of June 25, 1950, to July 27, 1953. Service must have been performed while on permanent assignment in Korea or while on temporary duty in Korea for 30 consecutive days or 60 nonconsecutive days, or while as a crew member of aircraft in flight over Korea participating in actual combat operations or in support of combat operations. Korean War–era veterans who served in Japan, Guam, Okinawa, or the Philippines are not eligible for this award.

Republic of Vietnam Campaign Medal

This medal is awarded to members of the U.S. armed forces who served for six months in South Vietnam during the period March 1, 1961, to March 28, 1973, or served outside the geographical limits of South Vietnam and contributed direct combat support to the RVN Armed Forces for an aggregate of six months, or did not complete six month's length of service, but who were wounded by the enemy (in a military action), captured by the enemy during action or in the line of duty (and were later rescued or released), killed in action or in the line of duty, or who were assigned in Vietnam on January 28, 1973, and who served a minimum of 60 calendar days in Vietnam during the period January 29, 1973, to March 28, 1973.

Republic of Vietnam Gallantry Cross with Palm

This medal was awarded by the Republic of Vietnam to certain units of the U.S. armed forces for valorous combat achievements during the Vietnam War, March 1, 1961, to March 28, 1973.

Silver Star

The Silver Star was authorized by act of Congress (July 9, 1918) for army personnel as a small (3/16-inch diameter) device to indicate "a citation for gallantry in action, published in orders issued from headquarters of a general officer, not warranting the award of a Medal of Honor or Distinguished Service Cross." Known in the army as the "citation star," the award was made retroactive, so that all those cited for gallantry in action in previous campaigns, even as far back as the SPANISH-AMERICAN WAR, were eligible to wear it. In 1920, a similar device was authorized for USN and USMC personnel. On August 8, 1932, Congress authorized the redesign of the Silver Star as a full-sized medal. The

Army Chief of Staff General Peter Schoomaker pins the Silver Star on Staff Sergeant Jeffrey Adamec, September 10, 2004. Adamec was awarded the nation's third-highest medal for valor for destroying four Iraqi armored personnel carriers during Operation Iraqi Freedom. *(U.S. Army)*

medal is currently awarded by all branches of the armed forces to any person who, while serving in any capacity, is cited for gallantry in action against an enemy of the United States while engaged in military operations involving conflict with an opposing foreign force, or while serving with friendly forces against an opposing armed force in which the United States is not a belligerent party.

Southwest Asia Service Medal

Authorized by Executive Order 12754, on March 12, 1991, this medal is awarded to members of the U.S. armed forces who served in support of Operation

Desert Shield or Operation Desert Storm (PERSIAN GULF WAR) between August 2, 1990, and November 30, 1995, in one or more of the following areas: Persian Gulf, Red Sea, Gulf of Oman, Gulf of Aden, that portion of the Arabian Sea that lies north of 10 degrees north latitude and west of 68 degrees east longitude, and the land areas of Iraq, Kuwait, Saudi Arabia, Oman, Bahrain, Qatar, and the United Arab Emirates. Also eligible are individuals who served in Egypt, Israel, Turkey, Syria, and Jordan (including territorial airspace and waters) directly supporting combat operations between January 17, 1991, and November 30, 1995.

Three distinct campaign periods apply to the award: Defense of Saudi Arabia, August 2, 1990–January 16, 1991; Liberation and Defense of Kuwait, January 17, 1991–April 11, 1991; Southwest Asia Cease-Fire Campaign, April 12, 1991–November 30, 1995. A bronze service star is worn for participation in each campaign period.

United Nations Medal

Awarded to service members who are or have been in UN service with one of the following: UN Observation Group in Lebanon; UN Truce Supervision Organization in Palestine; UN Military Observer Group in India and Pakistan; UN Security Forces, Hollandia; UN Transitional Authority in Cambodia; UN Advance Mission in Cambodia; UN Protection Force in Yugoslavia; UN Mission for the Referendum in Western Sahara or UN Operations in Somalia (including U.S. Quick Reaction Force members); UN Iraq/Kuwait Observation Group; and UN Mission in Haiti.

The UN secretary general determines the amount of service required and individual eligibility.

United Nations Service Medal

This medal was authorized by the United Nations General Assembly on December 12, 1950, and the U.S. Department of Defense authorized it for the U.S. armed forces on November 27, 1951. It was awarded to officers and enlisted men of the armed forces of the United States who participated in the action in Korea between June 27, 1950, and July 27,

1954. The medals bear the inscription, "For Service in Defense of the Principles of the Charter of the United Nations."

Vietnam Service Medal

Created by Executive Order 11213, July 8, 1965, this medal was awarded to all service members of the armed forces who, between July 4, 1965, and March 28, 1973, served in the following areas of Southeast Asia: in Vietnam and the contiguous waters and airspace, in Thailand, Laos, or Cambodia, or the airspace over these, or in the direct support of military operations in Vietnam. Personnel previously awarded the Armed Forces Expeditionary Medal for service in Vietnam between July 1958 and July 1965, may, upon request, exchange that medal for the Vietnam Service Medal; no one is authorized to wear both medals solely for services in Vietnam.

Campaign stars worn on the medal's ribbon indicate the number of campaigns participated in during the recipient's service in Vietnam. A total of 17 different campaign periods are recognized.

World War II Victory Medal

This medal is awarded for any service period between December 7, 1941, and December 31, 1946.

Defense Language Institute Foreign Language Center (DLIFLC)

The DLIFLC is located at the Presidio of Monterey and is the primary foreign language training institution within the Department of Defense (DoD). The center conducts full-time foreign language resident training and provides foreign language services to DoD, government agencies, and foreign governments.

Defense Meritorious Service Medal   See
DECORATIONS AND MEDALS.

Defense Superior Service Medal   See
DECORATIONS AND MEDALS.

Delta Force

The Delta Force is officially designated 1st Special Forces Operational Detachment–Delta (1stSFOD-D) and is the army's special operations unit expressly organized for the conduct of missions requiring a rapid response with the surgical application of a variety of skills while maintaining the lowest possible profile of U.S. involvement.

The Delta Force was secretly created in October 1977 by army colonel Charles Beckwith in response to a number of terrorist incidents that had occurred during the decade. Modeled in part on the British army's Special Air Service (SAS), Delta Force was created as an overseas counterterrorist force specializing in hostage rescue, barricade operations, and reconnaissance. Delta soldiers are handpicked and specially trained. The unit conducts worldwide recruitment twice yearly. Candidates are extensively prescreened and then subjected to a three- to four-week Assessment and Selection course. After successful completion of this phase, they are enrolled in a six-month Operator Training course. After graduation from this course, candidates are assigned to an operational position within the unit. Most Delta Force personnel are volunteers drawn from the 82ND AIRBORNE DIVISION, the SPECIAL FORCES (Green Berets), and the RANGERS.

The organizational details of Delta Force are secret, but the unit reportedly consists of three operating squadrons, designated A, B, and C. These, in turn, are subdivided into small groups known as troops. Reportedly, each troop specializes in HALO (High-Altitude, Low-Opening) parachute operations, scuba diving, or other operational skills. Other Delta units specialize in selection and training, logistics, finance, and medical requirements.

Delta units were deployed to Saudi Arabia in 1990 to serve as bodyguards for senior United States officers and, during the PERSIAN GULF WAR, were deployed to locate and destroy mobile SCUD launchers in Iraq's northern deserts. In 1993, Delta Force took part in operations to capture warlord Mohammad Farah Aidid in Mogadishu, Somalia. With the USN's Naval Special Warfare Development Group, Delta is currently responsible for counterterrorist operations outside the United States.

Department of the Army   See HEAD-QUARTERS, DEPARTMENT OF THE ARMY; SECRETARY OF THE ARMY.

depots   See FORTS AND OTHER INSTALLATIONS.

discharge, bad conduct (BCD)

Although similar to a dishonorable discharge (see DISCHARGE, DISHONORABLE), BCD is not perceived by the public to be as severe. The punishment constitutes part of a sentence of a general COURT-MARTIAL. It bars the dischargee from receiving any Veteran's Administration benefits.

See also DISCHARGE, GENERAL; DISCHARGE, HONORABLE.

discharge, dishonorable (DD)

The DD is part of the sentence of a general COURT-MARTIAL and is the worst type of discharge from the army. The person discharged receives no Veteran's Administration benefits and is stigmatized, even in civilian life, as less than honorable.

See also DISCHARGE, BAD CONDUCT; DISCHARGE, GENERAL; DISCHARGE, HONORABLE.

discharge, general (GD)

This administrative discharge from the army is given under honorable conditions for reasons such as unsuitability or ineptitude, but not for criminal or other wrongdoing charges. The recipient of a GD is entitled to Veteran's Administration benefits. The GD is issued to individuals whose performance is consistently substandard, or it is granted for medical or psychiatric reasons. In some cases, individuals who seek treatment for drug dependency avoid COURT-MARTIAL (and a dishonorable discharge) but are separated from the service by GD.

See also DISCHARGE, BAD CONDUCT; DISCHARGE, DISHONORABLE; DISCHARGE, HONORABLE.

discharge, honorable (HD)

This type of discharge is granted to army soldiers who have served satisfactorily or with distinction. It entitles the person discharged to receive all Veteran's Administration benefits, and it is a powerful recommendation to civilian employers. An honorable discharge is given upon expiration of enlistment, dependency, disability, or convenience of the government.

See also DISCHARGE, BAD CONDUCT; DISCHARGE, DISHONORABLE; DISCHARGE, GENERAL.

division   See ORGANIZATION BY UNITS.

dog tag

All members of the U.S. military wear around their necks two oval tags of noncorroding metal stamped with the wearer's name, date of birth, blood type, social security number (which also serves as the wearer's military identification number), and religion (if any). Round dog tags were first issued in 1906.

dream sheet

Dream sheet is the familiar name for the form officers and enlisted personnel fill out to indicate their preference of assignment within their grade or specialty. Preferences are typically with regard to location and type of duty. Since assignments must suit the requirements of the service, preferences are not always honored—hence, the name "dream sheet."

Dugway Proving Ground, Utah   See FORTS AND OTHER INSTALLATIONS.

E

Echelon Above Corps (EAC)

EAC are army organizations above and independent of the level of corps. Examples include ARMY AIR AND MISSILE DEFENSE COMMAND, JOINT TACTICAL GROUND STATION, CHEMICAL SERVICE ORGANIZATION, and Intelligence and Security Command (INSCOM).

Eighth U.S. Army (EUSA)

The current mission of the EUSA, which is deployed to the Republic of Korea (ROK), is to support deterrence of North Korean aggression against the ROK. In the event that this deterrence fails, the EUSA would be tasked to support noncombatant evacuation operations and transition to providing combat support and combat service support to assigned, attached, and other designated forces within the Korean theater of operations. EUSA would also conduct combat operations as ordered.

As presently constituted, EUSA consists of:

19th Theater Support Command; provides logistics support and headquartered at Camp Henry in Daegu

8th Personnel Command, headquartered at Yongsan

516th PSB, headquartered in Yongsan; controls all incoming mail to Korea

1st Replacement Company, Yongsan; controls and processes all incoming soldiers to Korea

EUSA Band, Yongsan

509th PSB at Camp Casey; another postal unit

2nd Infantry Division, headquartered at Camp Red Cloud, Uijongbu; major U.S. ground combat unit in Korea, patrols the border with North Korea

1st Signal Brigade, headquartered at Yongsan; provides strategic and tactical communications, and information management

17th Aviation Brigade, headquartered at Yongsan with subordinate units elsewhere; provides aviation support for all army aviation operations in the region

501st Military Intelligence Brigade; operates throughout ROK to provide combat information and multidiscipline intelligence to joint and combined war fighters

6th Cavalry Brigade; conducts attack helicopter operations 8th Military Police Brigade

8th MP Brigade, headquartered at Yongsan; conducts military police functions throughout the theater

18th Medical Command, headquartered at Yongsan; provides theater medical support

175th Finance Command, Yongsan; provides accounting services and finance support to soldiers, civilian employees, and family members in theater

Combat Support Coordination Team 3; facilitates combat, combat support, and combat service support of army aviation

19th MP Battalion Criminal Investigation Division; conducts criminal investigations of serious, sensitive, or special interest matters, and criminal intelligence, logistics security, counterdrug, antiterrorism, force protection and protective services operations in support of army forces in Korea and Japan

United States Armed Forces Claims Service, Korea, Yongsan; provides technical supervision of U.S. Army claims operations throughout Korea and Japan

Eighth United States Army Band, Seoul

Eighth United States Army Non-Commissioned Officers Academy; provides NCO training and development

UNC Security Battalion-Joint Security Area; provides security to the Demilitarized Zone (border area)

SOCKOR (Special Operations Command Korea); exercises operational control over all assigned or attached special operation forces in the theater

Special Forces Detachment-Korea; serves as liaison between the Korean Special Forces and the U.S. military

Special Operations Theater Support Element; provides forward-deployed logistics planning and coordination

Logistic Support Element Far East (DSAFE); enhances war fighting weapons system readiness

Joint U.S. Military Affairs Group-Korea; assists ROK armed forces in management, logistics, and organization

U.S. Army Corps of Engineers Far East District, headquartered in Seoul; serves as the Department of Defense design and construction agent for Korea

129th Medical Detachment; provides comprehensive veterinary medical treatment for military family pets throughout Korea

The Eighth U.S. Army was officially activated in the United States during WORLD WAR II, on June 10, 1944, and was deployed to the Pacific theater under the command of Lieutenant General Robert L. Eichelberger. It was a major component in executing General DOUGLAS MACARTHUR's "island hopping" strategy, retaking islands from the Japanese in the course of more than 60 amphibious assaults. The Eighth also participated in the liberation of the Philippines, and, on July 1, 1945, conducted mop-up operation throughout the archipelago. The Eighth U.S. Army would have been one of the principal units of the massive Allied forces set to invade the Kanto Plain (Tokyo) of the Japanese main island, had the Japanese not surrendered after the atomic bombing of Hiroshima and Nagasaki. After the Japanese surrender, the Eighth U.S. Army, with the Sixth U.S. Army, served as the ground force for the occupation of Japan under General Douglas MacArthur.

On June 25, 1950, the KOREAN WAR began when North Korean troops invaded the ROK. General MacArthur deployed elements of the 24th Infantry Division of EUSA to Korea on June 30, 1950, and on July 6, the 25TH INFANTRY DIVISION was ordered to Pusan. Eighth Army officially became operational in Korea on July 13, 1950 and fought a retreating campaign to a defensive position that became known as the Pusan Perimeter. The Eighth U.S. Army held the perimeter until MacArthur's landing of X Corps at Inchon initiated a general offensive. EUSA then achieved a breakout and drove northward against badly demoralized resistance. On October 19, the North Korean capital of Pyongyang fell, and ROK troops reached the Yalu River, the border with Manchuria, on October 28, 1950. On November 25, Chinese troops invaded across the Yalu, and pushed the Eighth U.S. Army (and all other United Nations and ROK units) below the 38th Parallel.

On December 23, Lieutenant General MATTHEW BUNKER RIDGWAY assumed command of United Nations ground forces in Korea, including the Eighth U.S. Army. Ridgway was able to reestablish the battle line at the 38th Parallel, which, after two more years of bloody stalemate, became the demilitarized zone (DMZ) that still separates North and South Korea.

After an armistice was signed on July 27, 1953, the Eighth remained in place to help man the cease-fire line and has been carrying out this mission ever since. In 1970, a decision was made to reduce U.S. forces, including EUSA, in Korea. A planned further withdrawal was canceled in 1981 by President Ronald Reagan. At present, the Eighth U.S. Army strength in the ROK at just under 36,000.

80th Division (Institutional Training)

The 80th Division (Institutional Training) consists of 3,000 ARMY NATIONAL GUARD reservists assigned to 40 units in Delaware, Virginia, West Virginia, Pennsylvania, and Maryland. As an institutional training division, the 80th commands and controls 10 Army Reserve Forces Schools. The division is currently organized into seven brigades, four of which give formal classroom and practical training in combat support, combat services support, professional development, and medical services. One brigade trains initial entry soldiers, another trains initial entry military police; and a third furnishes training support to all the other brigades.

The division was activated as the 80th Infantry Division in September 1917, after the United States entered WORLD WAR I, at Camp Lee (now Fort Lee), Virginia. Originally made up of conscripts from Virginia, West Virginia, and Pennsylvania, the new division was nicknamed the "Blue Ridge Division."

At full strength, the 80th Infantry Division totalled 23,000 soldiers, who landed in France on June 8, 1918. By mid-August the division had completed training with the British Third Army and joined forces on the western front, taking part in the Somme and the Meuse-Argonne offensives. The 80th was relieved of frontline duty on November 5, 1918, and the armistice came days later, on November 11. The 80th returned to the United States in May 1919 and was inactivated at Camp Lee on June 26.

Reconstituted into the organized reserve on June 24, 1921, and organized on September 1, 1922, at Richmond, Virginia, the division remained a cadre or skeleton strength unit until July 15, 1942, when it was activated during WORLD WAR II at Camp Forest, Tennessee. Troops were subsequently trained at Camp Phillips, Kansas, and the California-Arizona maneuver area. On July 4, 1944, the division was shipped to Europe, where it was trained in England. The division landed at Utah Beach, Normandy, on August 2, 1944, and fought at LeMans on August 8. Attached to the THIRD U.S. ARMY, the division advanced swiftly across northern France, Belgium, and into Germany. Some units had penetrated into Austria and Czechoslovakia by the time of the German surrender.

The 80th played an important role in the Ardennes Campaign ("Battle of the Bulge"), holding Luxembourg against a German onslaught. With the 4th Armored Division and 26th Infantry Division, elements of the 80th participated in the relief of U.S. forces surrounded at Bastogne, Belgium.

During the first week of February 1945, the division crossed the Our and Sauer rivers into Germany and covered 125 miles in just six days. By early April it crossed the Rhine River and took the city of Kassel. From here, the division advanced to the east, capturing Gotha, Erfurt, and Weimar-Buchenwald, where it liberated the infamous concentration camp. By the German surrender, the 80th Division had seen 277 days of combat and had captured more than 200,000 enemy soldiers.

Returning to the United States in January 1946, the division was inactivated, then redesignated as the Reserve Airborne Division. On May 10, 1952, it was again reorganized as a Reserve Infantry Division, then as a Reserve Training Division on March 1, 1959. On October 1, 1994, the 80th was redesignated as an Institutional Training Division.

In 1990–91, two 80th Division units were called to active duty in support of Operation Desert Shield and Operation Desert Storm during the PERSIAN GULF WAR.

82nd Airborne Division

Based at Fort Bragg, North Carolina, the 82nd is the largest parachute force in the Western alliance. Every 82nd Airborne soldier is a paratrooper, who is fully airborne qualified regardless of specialty.

Also, virtually every piece of the division's combat equipment is air-drop capable.

The 82nd Airborne consists of:

1st Brigade—504 PIR
2nd Brigade—325 AIR
3rd Brigade—505 PIR
Division Artillery
82nd Aviation Brigade
82nd Signal Battalion
Division Support Command
313th Military Intelligence Battalion
Division G1/AG
82nd Soldier Support Battalion
Division Band
82nd Military Police Company
Advanced Airborne School

Formed as the 82nd Infantry Division during WORLD WAR I on August 25, 1917, at Camp Gordon, Georgia, the division was dubbed the "All-Americans" because members were drawn from all 48 states. This is the origin of the division's famous double-A shoulder patch. During WORLD WAR II, on August 15, 1942, the 82nd Infantry became the first airborne division in the army and was redesignated the 82nd Airborne Division.

The 82nd shipped out to North Africa in April 1943 under the command of Major General MATTHEW BUNKER RIDGWAY to participate in the campaign against German and Italian forces there. However, by the time the 82nd arrived, North Africa had been secured, and the division's first two combat operations were parachute and glider assaults into Sicily and Salerno, Italy, on July 9 and September 13, 1943. The 504th Parachute Infantry Regiment, temporarily detached from the Division to fight at Anzio, was dubbed "Devils in Baggy Pants," a sobriquet appropriated from the diary of a captured German officer. The 504th remained in Italy while the rest of the 82nd was moved in November 1943 to the United Kingdom to prepare for Operation Neptune, the airborne phase of

Paratroops of the 82nd Airborne Division prepare to board a C-130 Hercules.   *(U.S. Army)*

An 82nd Airborne trooper jumps from the C-130's cargo ramp. *(U.S. Army)*

Operation Overlord, the amphibious assault on Normandy ("D-day"). The division was reorganized, adding two new parachute infantry regiments, the 507th and the 508th. The paratroopers and glider troops of the 82nd were among the first soldiers to land and fight in Normandy, seeing 33 days of combat and suffering 5,245 casualties.

After the Normandy operation, the 82nd became part of the newly organized XVIII Airborne Corps, consisting of the U.S. 17th, 82nd, and 101ST AIRBORNE DIVISIONS. The division next participated in Operation Market Garden, an assault on German positions in Holland. On September 17, 1944, the 82nd Airborne Division conducted its fourth combat jump, capturing its German-occupied Dutch objectives between Grave and Nijmegen. Although the division succeeded, the operation failed after the defeat of other Allied units at Arnhem, and the 82nd was ordered back to France.

On December 16, 1944, the Germans launched a massive surprise offensive through the Ardennes Forest, which resulted in the Battle of the Bulge,

and, on December 18, the 82nd joined the fighting there.

After V-E Day, troops of the 82nd served in Berlin as part of the occupation force in Germany, returning to the United States on January 3, 1946, and taking up residence at Fort Bragg, where it was designated a regular army division on November 15, 1948.

In April 1965, the 82nd was deployed to the Dominican Republic to intervene in the civil war there. In 1968, during the Tet Offensive of the VIETNAM WAR, the division's 3rd Brigade was sent into action, ultimately spending 22 months in Vietnam, before returning to Fort Bragg on December 12, 1969.

During the 1970s, division units were deployed to the Republic of Korea, Turkey, and Greece for military exercises. On October 25, 1983, elements of the division were deployed in Operation Urgent Fury, the invasion of Grenada—the first time the division had been used as a rapid deployment force. The first division aircraft touched down at Point Salinas, Grenada, a mere 17 hours after notification.

On December 20, 1989, elements of the division conducted their first combat jump since World War II onto Torrijos International Airport, Panama, as part of Operation Just Cause, launched to capture Panamanian dictator Manuel Noriega and bring him to trial in the United States on charges of drug trafficking. Following the night combat jump and seizure of the airport, the 82nd conducted follow-on combat air assault missions in Panama City and the surrounding areas. The paratroopers returned to Fort Bragg on January 12, 1990, only to be called back into action seven months later as the vanguard of deployment to the Middle East as part of Operation Desert Shield. On January 16, 1991, Desert Shield became Operation Desert Storm, the PERSIAN GULF WAR. On February 23, the vehicle-mounted 82nd protected the XVIII Airborne Corps flank as the armor and mechanized units penetrated deep inside Iraq. The ground war was over in 100 hours, and Kuwait, having been invaded by Iraq, was liberated.

In 2003, much of the division was again deployed to Iraq as part of Operation Iraqi

Freedom, the controversial war to overthrow the regime of Saddam Hussein and bring democracy to Iraq.

84th Division (Institutional Training)

The 84th Division (Institutional Training) is a U.S. ARMY RESERVE unit that spans a six-state area, including Wisconsin, Minnesota, Illinois, Michigan, Indiana, and Ohio. Headquarters is in Milwaukee, Wisconsin. The division provides year-round military specialty-skill training to army active duty, army reserve, and ARMY NATIONAL GUARD soldiers throughout the six-state area. The division trains RESERVE OFFICER TRAINING CORPS (ROTC) cadets on university campuses and, at Advanced Camp, provides basic combat training to recruits at various army installations, and furnishes initial soldier inprocess services to various army installations.

The division has eight brigades, three of which conduct initial entry training, while the rest train in a wide variety of subjects, including combat support training, health services training, and professional development training.

The division's nickname, "The Railsplitters," and its distinctive shoulder patch, showing an axe splitting a log for a rail fence, reflects its earliest lineage, which may be traced to the militia company in which Abraham Lincoln briefly served during the Black Hawk War in 1832. However, the division was officially formed on August 5, 1917, during WORLD WAR I, as a combat infantry unit composed of men from Wisconsin, Kentucky, and Illinois. Trained for 13 months before it shipped out to Europe, the division never fought as a unit; rather, it served as a source of replacements for other units. It was also a training unit for replacements heading to the western front.

Inactivated in 1919, the division was not reactivated until October 1942, after the United States entered WORLD WAR II. The division landed in England on September 20, 1944, and then disembarked in France on November 10. From here, it was transported to Belgium, where it became the first unit to break through the northern section of Germany's vaunted Siegfried Line. The 84th also played an important role in the Ardennes offensive, the "Battle of the Bulge," holding fast against Nazi Germany's last onslaught.

In November 1944, the division advanced into Germany, capturing the town of Geilkenkirchen during the offensive against Aachen. From here, the 84th remained in almost continuous action and advance until it reached the Elbe River in April 1945 and made contact with the Soviet Red Army in May.

In January 1946, the division returned to the United States as part of the Army Reserve and became a reserve airborne division in 1947. It was reorganized into a three-brigade training division in 1952, then as a four-brigade training division in 1959. On January 21, 1991, elements of the division were mobilized during the PERSIAN GULF WAR. Deployed to Fort Sill, Oklahoma, division members provided refresher training to several thousand reactivated individual ready reservists. Reorganized in 1993, the 84th Division (TNG) merged with the 85TH DIVISION (TNG) and expanded its area of operation to include Wisconsin, Illinois, Missouri, and Iowa. In April 1995, the division become an institutional training division and further expanded its area of operation to include Wisconsin, Illinois, Missouri, Iowa, and Nebraska. (The 85th Division reorganized as a training support division.)

85th Division (Training Support)

Headquartered in the Chicago suburb of Arlington Heights, Illinois, the 85th provides training services to the RESERVE COMPONENTS through its four brigades.

The division was created in Michigan in 1917 as the 85th Infantry Division after U.S. entry into WORLD WAR I and was named the "Custer Division," after Michigan native GEORGE ARMSTRONG CUSTER. Inactivated after the war, it was reactivated at Camp Shelby, Mississippi, in May 1942 during WORLD WAR II. The division received its combat training at Camp Shelby, in nearby DeSoto

National Forest, in the swamps of Louisiana, and at Camps Coxcomb and Pilot Knob at the Desert Training Area in California. During December 1943–January 1944, the division was sent to North Africa and underwent additional training in the Atlas Mountains of Algeria and then at the Invasion Training Center on the coast of the Mediterranean Sea. In March 1944, forward elements of the division arrived in Italy and went into the line near Minturno. The division entered action as a complete unit on April 14, 1944, and was instrumental in the capture of Rome, the destruction of the German "Gothic Line" in the North Apennines, and the closure of the Brenner Pass in the Italian Alps.

After Germany's surrender, the division performed redeployment duties in Italy until it returned to the United States, where it was inactivated on August 26, 1945. Elements of the division were reactivated in the postwar years, and the division was reconstituted in its present role as a training division.

87th Division (Training Support)

The 87th Division (Training Support) is a U.S. ARMY RESERVE division with headquarters in Birmingham, Alabama, and subordinate units in Florida, Georgia, Mississippi, South Carolina, and Puerto Rico. The division plans, conducts, and evaluates training exercises for Army Reserve and ARMY NATIONAL GUARD units. The division specializes in realistic simulation for combat support and combat service support units and battle command staff training for unit staffs and command elements. Additionally, the division provides training and mobilization support to RESERVE COMPONENTS when mobilized. The 87th also supports Military Assistance to Civilian Authorities (MSCA) missions in times of natural disaster or emergency.

The division was originally activated as the 87th Infantry Division at Camp Pike, Arkansas, on August 15, 1917, during WORLD WAR I. The division was sent to France and entered combat late in the war, therefore, it conducted combat support rather than combat missions, including construc-

tion, guard duty, military police operations, convoy escort, and various logistics and supply duties. The division returned to the United States for deactivation in July 1919 and was reactivated in 1921 as part of the Organized Reserves.

The division was reactivated in the REGULAR ARMY at Camp McCain, Mississippi, on December 15, 1942, during WORLD WAR II. The first elements of the division shipped out for England on October 4, 1944, and final elements arrived on November 13. On November 24, the division left for France. As part of the THIRD U.S. ARMY commanded by GEORGE SMITH PATTON, JR., the division participated in the swift drive across France, Belgium, Luxembourg, and Germany. On May 21, 1945, the division linked up with Red Army forces at the Czechoslovakian border. The division fought in campaigns in the Ardennes, participated in the breakthrough of the Siegfried Line, and engaged in actions at Kyll, on the Moselle River, at Koblenz, on the Rhine River, at Plauen, and on the Mulde River. Because the division was responsible for the capture of the strategically important city of Koblenz, the unit was dubbed the "Liberators of Koblenz."

The division was deactivated after the war, but reactivated in Birmingham as a Reserve Division in November 1946. On February 7, 1957, the division was redesignated the 87th Maneuver Area Command (MAC) until October 1, 1993, when it became the 87th Division (Exercise). In October 1999, the division was yet again reflagged as the 87th Training Support Division.

Eisenhower, Dwight David (1890–1969)
U.S. Army general

The American general who served as supreme Allied commander in the European theater of WORLD WAR II, "Ike" Eisenhower was born in Denison, Texas, and raised in Abilene, Kansas. He graduated from the UNITED STATES MILITARY ACADEMY in 1915, but he was not sent overseas during WORLD WAR I, instead taking on a variety of stateside training missions. Despite his lack of combat experience, his strategic and administrative skills

Dwight D. Eisenhower, Supreme Allied Commander
(Arttoday)

were quickly recognized, and in 1920 he was promoted to major. Two years later, he was posted to Panama, returning to the United States in 1924 to attend COMMAND AND GENERAL STAFF COLLEGE, from which he graduated at the top his class in 1926. In 1928, he graduated from the U.S. ARMY WAR COLLEGE.

From 1933 to 1935, Eisenhower served under General DOUGLAS MACARTHUR in the office of the CHIEF OF STAFF, then accompanied MacArthur to the Philippines, serving there until 1939. After exemplary performance in large-scale maneuvers during the summer of 1941, Eisenhower was promoted to temporary brigadier general, and when the United States entered World War II, he was named assistant chief of the Army War Plans Division (December 1941–June 1942). Jumped to

major general in April 1942, Eisenhower was assigned to command the European theater of operations on June 25. He served as Allied commander for Operation Torch—the invasion of French North Africa—in November, then directed the invasion and conquest of Tunisia from November 17, 1942 to May 13, 1943. The next phase of Allied operations in Europe was the conquest of Sicily, which Eisenhower directed during July 9–August 17, 1944, and the invasion of the Italian mainland, which took place from September 3 to October 8.

After the landings in Italy, Eisenhower traveled to London to take charge of planning the Normandy invasion ("D-day"). He was named supreme commander of the Allied Expeditionary Force in December and directed Operation Overlord, the Allied assault on Normandy (June 6–July 24, 1944). With the beachhead secured, Eisenhower went on to direct the overall advance across northern France (July 25–September 14).

In December 1944, Eisenhower was promoted to general of the army and continued to command and coordinate the Allied campaign in Europe, not only fighting the Germans but also continually juggling the needs and demands of Free French, British, and Russian allies while also endeavoring to serve and satisfy the American commanders. Eisenhower pushed his forces into Germany during a campaign from March 28 to May 8; however, in a controversial political and strategic decision, he essentially relinquished occupation of eastern Germany and Berlin to the Soviet troops of the Red Army.

Following the surrender of Germany on May 7–8, 1945, Eisenhower stayed in Europe through November to command Allied occupation forces. After returning to the United States, he assumed the post of army chief of staff (November 1945–February 1948), then retired to accept the presidency of Columbia University. In December 1950, faced with a critical cold war situation, President Harry S. Truman recalled Eisenhower to active duty as Supreme Allied Commander Europe (SACEUR) and commander of NATO forces. Two years later, Eisenhower again retired, this time to run for president on the Republican Party ticket. He served two terms (1953–61).

Electronic Proving Ground, Utah   See FORTS AND OTHER INSTALLATIONS.

Element Teams   See CHEMICAL SERVICE ORGANIZATION.

engineers

Combat engineers are the first in and the last to leave a battle. Branch members are involved in general engineering, general construction, environmental engineering, civil works, military con-

Combat engineers tighten bolts on a temporary bridge. Rapid bridge building has long been a staple of the U.S. Army engineer's work.   *(U.S. Army)*

struction, and other specialties. In combat, army engineers build bridges, lay minefields, emplace defensive obstacles, conduct demolition operations, and engage in many other tasks as required. Branch headquarters is at Fort Leonard Wood, Missouri.

See also U.S. ARMY CORPS OF ENGINEERS.

Environmental Laboratory (EL)

Operating under the U.S. ARMY CORPS OF ENGINEERS, the EL provides environmental analysis research, development, consultation, technology transfer, direct response, and training support to the Corps of Engineers, the army generally, other Department of Defense elements, and other U.S. government agencies in the fields of environmental quality; resource inventory, analysis, evaluation, and management; water quality; pollution abatement; pollution prevention; hazardous, toxic, and radioactive waste characterization, inventory, treatment, and/or disposal; contaminant mobility; wetlands; fate and effects of environmental risk assessment; aquatic plant control and other nonindigenous species control, such as zebra mussels; dredging and dredged material management; environmental engineering; environmental modeling and simulations; environmental restoration; assessment, treatment, and management of contaminated sediments; environmental chemistry; environmental sensors development; outdoor recreation; and cultural resources.

Euro-African-Middle Eastern Campaign Medal   See DECORATIONS AND MEDALS.

F

field army   See ORGANIZATION BY UNITS.

field artillery

Traditionally dubbed the "king of battle," field artillery is the combat branch of the army that provides the massive firepower necessary for army victory on the modern battlefield. The branch is armed with guns and rockets and also integrates all forms of fire, including field artillery, tactical air fire, naval gunfire, army aviation, and so on. Members of the branch specialize in combined arms operations, controlling the firepower of the big guns while operating in coordination with INFANTRY and ARMOR. Branch headquarters is at Fort Sill, Oklahoma.

Fifth U.S. Army

Headquartered at Fort Sam Houston, Texas, the Fifth U.S. Army oversees the training and monitors the mobilization readiness of ARMY NATIONAL GUARD units within its area of responsibility. Additionally, the organization provides training assistance for RESERVE COMPONENTS when they are preparing for war and other missions. The Fifth U.S. Army includes two training support divisions, the 91st and 75th; six Training Support Brigades (TSBs); two Simulation Brigades (SIMS); and three Field Training Groups (FTGs).

The Fifth U.S. Army was activated during World War II at Oujda, French Morocco, on January 5, 1943. Under the command of Lieutenant General MARK WAYNE CLARK, it fought in the bloody Italian Campaign from the landings at Salerno on September 9, 1943, through the Battle of the Rapido River, the Battles of Monte Cassino, and the assault on Anzio. On June 4, 1944, Fifth U.S. Army units entered Rome, and the Fifth Army thereby became the first American force to liberate a European capital. The army continued to press the Italian campaign northward, reaching the Austrian-Italian border on May 4, 1945. In 602 days of combat, the Fifth U.S. Army suffered 109,642 casualties, including 19,475 killed in action.

The organization was inactivated in October 1945, then reactivated in June 1946, with headquarters at Chicago and, later, at Fort Sheridan, Illinois. On June 30, 1971, the Fifth U.S. Army and the Fourth U.S. Army merged at Fort Sam Houston, and the Fourth U.S. Army was inactivated on the following day.

In 1995, the CONTINENTAL UNITED STATES ARMIES (CONUSA) were realigned, and the Fifth U.S. Army area of responsibility was expanded to 21 states, all of the states west of the Mississippi River, except Minnesota. The FIRST U.S. ARMY is responsible for the states east of the Mississippi River and Minnesota.

Finance Corps

With its home station at Fort Jackson, South Carolina, the Finance Corps is a combat service support branch of the army. Its mission is to sustain the combat soldier and commanders in the field with timely and accurate finance and accounting support, including military and civilian pay, the preparation and payment of travel and commercial vendor vouchers, and accounting for the disbursement of public funds.

fire team   See ORGANIZATION BY UNIT.

1st Armored Division ("Old Ironsides")

The 1st Armored Division, nicknamed "Old Ironsides," combines ARMOR, INFANTRY, and FIELD ARTILLERY elements and was activated at Fort Knox, Kentucky, on July 15, 1940. Its nickname originated with the division's first commander, Major General Bruce R. Magruder, who was inspired by a painting of the USS *Constitution,* popularly known as "Old Ironsides." The name seemed especially appropriate for a unit operating tanks.

The 1st Armored Division participated in Operation Torch, the Allied invasion of French Northwest Africa during WORLD WAR II. Stepping off with the invasion on November 8, 1942, Old Ironsides became the first U.S. armored division to see combat in the war. Suppressing unexpectedly heavy Vichy French opposition, Old Ironsides was instrumental in securing the beachhead within three days.

From the landing, the 1st Armored Division advanced toward Tunisia. The division was put under the control of II Corps in January 1943 and was tasked with defending central Tunisia against a combined German and Italian counterattack. In February, the 1st Armored Division was defeated by a superior German armored force at the Battle of Kasserine Pass. After sustaining heavy losses, the division withdrew and, under II Corps commander GEORGE SMITH PATTON, JR., more than recovered. After three more months of fighting, the division and the Allies achieved victory in North Africa.

The 1st Armored Division advanced from North Africa to Italy, landing, as part of the Fifth Army under General MARK WAYNE CLARK at Salerno on September 9, 1943. The division participated in the capture of Naples on October 1, and, in November, the 1st Armored Division attacked the infamous Winter Line, breaking it, but then becoming bogged down at Cassino. The division participated in an amphibious assault at Anzio on January 23, 1944, and the 1st Armored Division led the Allied breakout from the beachhead on May 23. It then spearheaded the drive to Rome, liberating that city on June 4.

After the liberation of Rome, the 1st Armored Division pressed its pursuit of the Germans all the way to the North Apennines. The division broke through here and into the Po River valley in April 1945. On May 2, 1945, German forces in Italy surrendered.

After the war, the 1st Armored Division was transferred to Germany as part of the Allied occupation forces. The unit returned to the United States in April 1946 and was inactivated at Camp Kilmer, New Jersey. With the escalation of the KOREAN WAR, the division was reactivated at Fort Hood, Texas, on March 7, 1951. However, the division remained in the United States during the war and trained for nuclear warfare, participating in tests of the "Atomic Field Army" at Fort Hood and in Operation Sagebrush, the largest joint maneuver conducted since World War II.

In February 1956, the 1st Armored Division moved to Fort Polk, Louisiana, and was soon reduced in size, moved back to Fort Hood, and assigned as a training cadre for new inductees. In 1962, the division was again returned to full strength and reorganized. The division deployed from Fort Hood to Fort Stewart, Georgia, in response to the Cuban missile crisis in 1962. At Fort Stewart it prepared and trained for a possible amphibious invasion of Cuba. When the crisis passed, the division returned to Fort Hood.

During the VIETNAM WAR, the 1st Armored Division was not committed to combat as a division, but two units, Company A, 501st Aviation, and 1st Squadron, 1st Calvary, served with distinction.

The division played a major role in the PERSIAN GULF WAR during 1990–91, moving 17,400 soldiers and 7,050 pieces of major equipment to Saudi Arabia for Operation Desert Shield and Operation Desert Storm.

On February 24, 1991, the 1st Armored Division crossed into Iraq, leading VII Corps's main flanking attack against divisions of the elite Iraqi Republican Guard.

On December 14, 1995, the 1st Armored Division was ordered to Bosnia-Herzegovina as part of Operation Joint Endeavor, a NATO operation. In April 1999, the division participated in Operation Allied Force in response to the ethnic cleansing and fighting in Kosovo and, in 2000, the division assumed control of the Multinational Brigade-East.

The 1st Armored Division was deployed to Iraq in 2003 as part of U.S. forces in Operation Iraqi Freedom, the second Persian Gulf War.

1st Cavalry Division

The 1st Cavalry Division traces its roots to 1855, when the 2nd Cavalry Regiment was organized. In 1861, this unit was redesignated the 5th Cavalry and fought in such CIVIL WAR battles as First Bull Run, Antietam, Gettysburg, The Wilderness, and Appomattox. After the Civil War, the 5th, 7th, 8th, and 9th Cavalry regiments, which would later be consolidated into the 1st Cavalry Division, fought the INDIAN WARS. In 1916, shortly before the United States's entry into WORLD WAR I, elements of these units participated in the Punitive Expedition against Pancho Villa.

As a result of the National Defense Act, the 1st Cavalry Division was formally activated on September 13, 1921, at Fort Bliss, Texas. The 7th and 8th Cavalry Regiments, then the 5th Cavalry Regiment, were assigned to the division, that also originally included the 82nd Field Artillery Battalion (Horse), the 13th Signal Troops, the 27th Ordnance Company, Division Headquarters, and the 1st Cavalry Division Quartermaster Train (later designated as the 15th Replacement Company). The division's early missions mainly involved patrolling the Mexican border. During the Great Depression, the division provided training for some 62,500 men in the Civilian Conservation Youth Corps.

In 1943, during WORLD WAR II, the 1st Cavalry Division was dismounted and deployed to the Southwest Pacific to function as an infantry unit. After six months of training in Australia, the division sailed on February 29, 1944, for the Admiralty Islands and participated in the taking of this objective. From here, the division participated in combat on Leyte in the Philippines, then moved on to Luzon, the main island of the Philippines. Soldiers of the "First Team" were the first to enter Manila. After the Japanese surrender in World War II, the 1st Cavalry led the Allied occupational army into Tokyo.

Early in the KOREAN WAR, the 1st Cavalry Division landed at Pohangdong, South Korea, on July 18, 1950, executing the first amphibious operation of the war. Crossing the 38th parallel on October 9, 1950, 1st Cavalry troopers overran and captured Pyongyang, the North Korean capital, then fought a desperate defensive battle after the intervention of Communist Chinese forces. The 1st Cavalry played an essential role in the defense of the South Korean capital, Seoul.

In January 1952, after 18 months of continuous fighting, the division was rotated back to Hokkaido, Japan. It returned to Korea in 1957 to patrol the Demilitarized Zone, where it remained until 1965. In that year, the division returned to the United States, but it was soon recast as the army's first "air mobile" division. In this new configuration, the 1st Cavalry served in the VIETNAM WAR.

The Pleiku campaign began on October 29, 1965, and consisted of 35 days of continuous air mobile operations, during which troopers destroyed two of the three regiments of a North Vietnamese division. The division carried out Operation Pershing during 1968, scouring the Bong Son plain, An Lo valley, and the hills of coastal II Corps, seeking out and destroying enemy units. By the end of the operation on January 21, 1969, the enemy had lost 5,401 soldiers and an additional 2,400 prisoners. From this operation, the division moved to I Corps, Vietnam's most northerly tactical zone. The division successfully withstood the infamous Tet Offensive, then went on to liberate Quang Tri and the ancient capital city of Hue. From here, the division marched to the relief of besieged marines at Khe Sann.

The 1st Cavalry invaded Cambodia in May 1970 to interdict the shipment of North Vietnamese supplies. When the division left Vietnam in 1972, it had the distinction of having been the first to arrive in country and the last to leave.

In January 1975, the 1st Cavalry was reorganized a second time as an army armored division. In August 1990, the division began its participation in Operation Desert Shield and, subsequently, Operation Desert Storm, during the first PERSIAN GULF WAR. Deployed to Saudi Arabia, the 1st Cavalry was assigned to draw Iraqi forces away from the main U.S.-coalition invasion. After this mission had been successfully completed, elements of the division attacked 10 miles into Iraq and then penetrated deeper as a reconnaissance-in-force unit. Later in February, the division was tasked with the destruction of the elite Iraqi Republican Guard.

With the end of the Persian Gulf War, the division began its redeployment back to the United States. In April 1998, the division was deployed on a peacekeeping mission to war-torn Bosnia Herzegovina.

Soldiers from the 1st Infantry Division establish a security perimeter in the city of Baqubah, Iraq, on August 4, 2004.   *(Department of Defense)*

1st Infantry Division ("Big Red One")

The 1st Infantry Division (ID) is the oldest continuously serving army division. It began as the First Expeditionary Division, organized in May 1917 during WORLD WAR I from army units in service on the Mexican border and at various posts throughout the United States. Units from the division first sailed from New York and Hoboken, New Jersey, for France on June 14, 1917. Among the first official acts of the division was a July 4th march of 2nd Battalion, 16th Infantry, through the streets of Paris to bolster French morale. It was during this ceremony, when the procession stopped at Lafayette's tomb, that one of General JOHN JOSEPH PERSHING's staff uttered the famous words often misattributed to Pershing himself: "Lafayette, we are here!" The 1st Expeditionary Division was redesignated as the 1st ID two days later.

The newly redesignated unit fired the first American shell of the war on October 23, 1917, and, on October 25, the division suffered the first American casualties of the war. The division won its first victory in April 1918, taking the German-held village of Cantigny. Soissons fell to the 1st ID in July 1918, and the division was also instrumental in clearing the infamous Saint Mihiel salient during continuous combat from September 11 to September 13, 1918. The 1st ID also fought in the Meuse-Argonne campaign, the last major campaign of the war. After this, the division was the first army unit to cross the Rhine River into occupied Germany.

During WORLD WAR II, the 1st ID entered combat early, as part of Operation Torch, the Allied invasion of North Africa and the first U.S. action against Germany. Elements of the division landed near Oran, Algeria, on November 8, 1942, and campaigned in Tunisia. After victory was secured in North Africa, the 1st Infantry participated in Operation Husky, the invasion of Sicily, landing at Gela on July 10, 1943. It was the Big Red One that opened the Allied road to the straits of Messina, the stepping off point for the invasion of the Italian mainland.

Elements of the 1st ID were among the first to make the assault on D-day, June 6, 1944, at Omaha Beach. After an extremely hard-fought breakout from the beachhead, the division advanced through the difficult Norman hedgerow country, then moved northeast to liberate Liège, Belgium. From here, the division pushed on to the German border, crossing through the heavily fortified Siegfried Line to launch the first Allied ground attack against a major German city, Aachen, which surrendered on October 21, 1944.

After taking Aachen, the Big Red One continued the advance into Germany. The division successfully withstood the German counteroffensive known as the Battle of the Bulge in December 1944, and, on January 15, 1945, the division attacked and penetrated the Siegfried Line for a second time, taking, securing, and occupying the Remagen brigehead, over which the Allied advance now rushed. On April 8, 1945, the division crossed the Weser River into Czechoslovakia, and the war was over a month later. The 1st ID remained in Germany on occupation duty until 1955, when it returned to the United States, where it was headquartered at Fort Riley, Kansas.

The next great action in which the 1st Infantry engaged was the VIETNAM WAR. The Big Red One was, in 1965, the first army division to deploy to Vietnam, advance parties landing at Qui Nhon on June 23, 1965. The division's first Vietnam operation began on July 22, 1965, at Bien Hoa, and the main contingent of the division began arriving in country during September 1965. For almost five years, the 1st Infantry Division fought in Vietnam, returning to Fort Riley in April 1970.

The Big Red One was put on alert for deployment on November 8, 1990, during Operation Desert Shield, the prelude to the PERSIAN GULF WAR. The ground phase of Operation Desert Storm (the combat phase of the war) began on February 24, 1991, with the 1st Infantry spearheading the armored attack into Iraq. Through a succession of battles, the division raced toward Kuwait, seizing the highway running north to that country on February 27. This action cut off the possibility of escape for the Iraqi invaders. The war ended on the following day with complete Iraqi capitulation.

In 1995 through much of 2000, the division was deployed to Bosnia to enforce the Dayton Peace Accords, and, in 1999, it was deployed to Kosovo to enforce a cease-fire agreement there. In 2003, much of the division had been deployed to Iraq, fighting the insurgent war that ensued following the principal combat phase of Operation Iraqi Freedom.

first lieutenant　See RANKS AND GRADES.

first sergeant　See RANKS AND GRADES.

First U.S. Army

Currently headquartered at Fort Gillem, Georgia, the First U.S. Army trains, mobilizes, and deploys U.S. ARMY RESERVE and ARMY NATIONAL GUARD units in the eastern United States, Puerto Rico, and the U.S. Virgin Islands. An important First U.S. Army mission is, when directed, to conduct homeland security operations.

The First U.S. Army was formed during WORLD WAR I in France on August 10, 1918, under the command of General JOHN JOSEPH PERSHING. It was the first U.S. army to be identified by number. During the war, the First fought in the reduction of the St. Mihiel salient and in the Meuse-Argonne offensive. The First U.S. Army was deactivated shortly after the war, in 1919, but was reactivated at Fort Jay, New York, in 1933, as a training and readiness organization.

The First U.S. Army was under the command of General OMAR NELSON BRADLEY during WORLD WAR II and was the first major unit landed at

Omaha and Utah beaches during the Normandy invasion (D-day), June 6, 1944. The First was also the first U.S. army to break out of the Normandy beachhead, and it was the first U.S. army to march into Paris when that city was liberated. The First had the distinction of breaking through Germany's vaunted "West Wall" defenses, the so-called Siegfried Line, and it was also the first U.S. army to cross the Rhine. Soldiers of the First were the first Allied troops to link up with Soviet Red Army troops advancing from the east.

The First U.S. Army moved its headquarters after World War II to Governor's Island in New York Harbor, and on January 1, 1966, the First and Second U.S. armies merged, with First Army headquarters moving to Fort Meade, Maryland.

In 1973, First U.S. Army was assigned to improve the readiness of the RESERVE COMPONENTS. In 1983, Second U.S. Army was reactivated at Fort Gillem, Georgia, and assumed responsibility for Reserve Component affairs in seven states and two territories formerly belonging to the First U.S. Army. In 1991, Fourth U.S. Army was deactivated and its seven midwestern states became part of the First U.S. Army. Four years later, the First U.S. Army left Fort Meade, Maryland and was reorganized at Fort Gillem, absorbing the Second U.S. Army.

forts and other installations

The term *fort* is used to describe most major permanent army installations. In addition to forts, the army maintains four army airfields, five active arsenals, three barracks, a variable number of camps (a term typically applied to temporary or semipermanent base installations, often in foreign countries), nine active depots, and four proving grounds.

As of 2005, army forts included:

Fort A. P. Hill, Virginia

Fort A. P. Hill is part of the Military District of Washington (MDW). Established in 1942, the fort consists of 76,000 acres and is located 20 miles southeast of Fredericksburg. It is used for general military training. Approximately 230,000 troops train here annually.

Further reading: Fort A. P. Hill Web site, www.aphill.army.mil.

Fort Belvoir, Virginia

Established in 1912 on 8,656 acres about 16 miles southwest of Washington, D.C., Fort Belvoir is home to a wide array of important army and Department of Defense activities, including the Defense Systems Management College; Defense Mapping School; Headquarters, Criminal Investigation Command; Defense Logistics Agency; Defense Contract Audit Agency; Army Management Staff College; Night Vision and Electronic Sensors Directorate; 701st Military Police Group; Davison Army Airfield; Force Integration Management Support Agency; and DeWitt Army Community Hospital.

Further reading: Fort Belvoir Web site, www.belvoir.army.mil.

Fort Benning, Georgia

This large installation occupies 182,000 acres outside of Columbus, Georgia. Established in 1918, it is now home to the U.S. Army Infantry Center and School; 75th Ranger Regiment headquarters, 36th Engineer Group; Infantry Training Brigade; Basic Combat Training Brigade; Ranger Training Brigade headquarters; Western Hemisphere Institute for Social Change; and Martin Army Community Hospital.

Further reading: Fort Benning Web site, www.benning.army.mil.

Fort Bliss, Texas

Historic Fort Bliss was created in 1848 and today occupies 1,000,000 acres north of El Paso. It is home to the U.S. Army Air Defense Artillery Center and School; the 6th, 11th, 31st, 35th, and 108th Air Defense Artillery Brigades; 32nd Army Air and Missile Defense Command; Joint Task Force 6 headquarters; U.S. Army SERGEANT MAJOR ACADEMY; German Air Force Air Defense School; and William Beaumont Army Medical Center.

Further reading: Fort Bliss Web site, www.bliss.army.mil.

Fort Bragg, North Carolina

Fort Bragg is located 10 miles northwest of Fayetteville on 148,609 acres. Established in 1918, it is now home to XVIII Airborne Corps headquarters; 82ND AIRBORNE DIVISION; U.S. ARMY SPECIAL OPERATIONS COMMAND; U.S. Army SPECIAL FORCES Command; XVIII Airborne Corps Artillery; John F. Kennedy Special Warfare Center and School; 1st Corps Support Command (Airborne); 16th MP Brigade; 18th Aviation Brigade (Airborne); 18th Soldier Support Group; 229th Aviation Regiment (Attack); 20th Engineer Brigade (Combat)(Airborne); 35th Signal Brigade (Airborne); 44th Medical Brigade (Airborne); 1st Special Warfare Training Group (Airborne); 3rd Special Forces Group (Airborne); 7th Special Forces Group (Airborne); 1st Special Forces Operational Detachment-Delta; U.S. ARMY CIVIL AFFAIRS AND PSYCHOLOGICAL OPERATIONS COMMAND; 4th Psychological Operations Group (Airborne); 525th Military Intelligence Brigade (Airborne); 1st ROTC Region headquarters; Readiness Group-Bragg; U.S. Army Airborne and Special Operations Test Board; and Womack Army Medical Center.

Further reading: Fort Bragg Web site, www. bragg.army.mil.

Fort Buchanan, Puerto Rico

Fort Buchanan is the home station of U.S. ARMY, SOUTH (USARSO) and is a subinstallation of Fort McPherson. All fort activities are related to the support of USARSO.

Further reading: Fort Buchanan Web site, www. buchanan.army.mil.

Fort Campbell, Kentucky

Fort Campbell is located astride the Kentucky-Tennessee state line. Established during WORLD WAR II in 1942, it occupies 105,000 acres and is home to the 101ST AIRBORNE DIVISION (Air Assault); 5th Special Forces Group (Airborne); 160th Special Operations Aviation Regiment (Airborne); Air Assault School; and the Florence Blanchfield Army Community Hospital.

Further reading: Fort Campbell Web site, www. campbell.army.mil.

Fort Carson, Colorado

Established in 1945, Fort Carson occupies 137,000 acres just four miles outside of Colorado Springs. In addition to the fort proper, the installation maintains 244,000 acres of maneuver area, Pinon Canyon Maneuver Site, just east of Trinidad.

Fort Carson is home to 7TH INFANTRY DIVISION headquarters; 3rd Armored Cavalry Regiment; 10th Special Forces Group (Airborne); and 43rd Area Support Group.

Further reading: Fort Carson Web site, www. carson.army.mil.

Fort Detrick, Maryland

The installation was established during World War II in 1943 and is located on 1,200 acres outside of Frederick, Maryland. Major activities here include the U.S. Army Medical Research and Materiel Command (MRMC) and the National Cancer Institute, in addition to numerous other tenant commands relating to biomedical research, medical materiel management, and global telecommunications.

Further reading: Fort Detrick Web site, www. detrick.army.mil.

Fort Dix, New Jersey

Fort Dix was established during WORLD WAR I, in 1917, near Wrightstown, New Jersey. The major activities of this 31,000-acre post are now all related to RESERVE COMPONENTS training. Also housed here is 2nd Brigade, First ROTC Region. The fort is collocated with McGuire Air Force Base and is home to Watson Air Force Clinic.

Further reading: Fort Dix Web site, www. dix.army.mil.

Fort Drum, New York

Although established in 1780 near Watertown, the 107,000-acre Fort Drum is a very modern post, which is home to the 10TH MOUNTAIN DIVISION

(Light Infantry). Additionally, it is a major training center, with special facilities for cold weather training.

Further reading: Fort Drum Web site, www. drum.army.mil.

Fort Eustis, Virginia

Fort Eustis was established during World War I in 1918 between Williamsburg and Newport News. The 8,200-acre post is home to the U.S. Army Transportation Center and School; U.S. Army Aviation Logistics School; U.S. Army Training Support Center; Military Traffic Management Command–Deployment Support Command; 7th Transportation Group (Composite); 8th Transportation Brigade; and McDonald Army Community Hospital.

Further reading: Fort Eustis Web site, www. eustis.army.mil.

Fort Gillem, Georgia

Fort Gillem was established in 1941, just before U.S. entry into World War II. Located southeast of Atlanta, it functions as a subsidiary of nearby Fort McPherson and houses the headquarters of FIRST U.S. ARMY, 3rd Military Police Group (CID), and the U.S. Army Second Recruiting Brigade.

Further reading: Fort Gillem Web site, www. mcpherson.army.mil/Fort_Gillem.htm.

Fort Gordon, Georgia

Fort Gordon was established on the eve of American entry into World War II in 1941 and occupies 56,000 acres south of Augusta. It is home to the U.S. Army Signal Center and School; 15th Signal Brigade; 513th Military Intelligence Brigade; 702nd Military Intelligence Group; and the Dwight D. Eisenhower Army Medical Center.

Further reading: Fort Gordon Web site, www. gordon.army.mil.

Fort Greely, Alaska

Established during World War II in 1942, Fort Greely is located 100 miles southeast of Fairbanks

and covers 677,000 acres. Long home to the U.S. Army Warfare Training Center and U.S. Army Cold Regions Test Center, Fort Greely is scheduled to become the site of a portion of a national missile defense system. This proposal is controversial, since it may contravene the 1972 Anti-Ballistic Missile Treaty. As of early 2004, however, the plan to use the fort for this purpose remains in place.

Further reading: Fort Greely information available at U.S. Army–Alaska Web site, www.usarak.army.mil.

Fort Hamilton, New York

This venerable facility, established in 1825, occupies 170 acres in Brooklyn, close to the Verrazano-Narrows Bridge, and it serves as headquarters of the New York Area Command, providing administrative and logistical support for army activities in the New York City metropolitan area.

Further reading: Fort Hamilton Web site, www. hamilton.army.mil.

Fort Hood, Texas

Occupying 217,337 acres 50 miles south of Waco, Fort Hood was established during World War II in 1942 and is home of III Corps headquarters; 1ST CAVALRY DIVISION, 4TH INFANTRY DIVISION (Mechanized); 3rd Personnel Group; 3rd Signal Brigade; 13th Corps Support Command (COSCOM); 13th Finance Group; 89th Military Police Brigade; 504th Military Intelligence Brigade; 21st Cavalry Brigade (Air Combat); and the Durnall Army Community Hospital.

Further reading: Fort Hood Web site, www. hood.army.mil.

Fort Huachuca, Arizona

Located 70 miles southeast of Tucson, this facility was established as a frontier army outpost in 1877 and now covers 73,000 acres. It is home to the U.S. Army Intelligence Career School; U.S. Army Electronic Proving Ground; U.S. Army Information Systems Engineering Command; CONUS Theater Network Operations and Security Center; Joint Interoperability Test Command, U.S. Army Signal

Colonel James Hickey, commander of the 1st Brigade Combat Team, leads part of the brigade in the pass and review portion of a ceremony marking the official return to Fort Hood of the 4th Infantry Division. 1st BCT soldiers played a role in the capture of Iraqi president Saddam Hussein during Operation Iraqi Freedom. *(U.S. Army)*

Command; 11th Signal Brigade; and the 111th and 112th Military Intelligence Brigades.

Further reading: Fort Huachuca Web site, http://huachuca-www.army.mil.

Fort Irwin, California

Established on 642,000 acres northeast of Barstow, Fort Irwin was opened in 1940 and is now home to the U.S. Army National Training Center; 11th Armored Cavalry Regiment; and Weed Army Community Hospital.

Further reading: Fort Irwin Web site, www.irwin.army.mil.

Fort Jackson, South Carolina

Fort Jackson was created in 1917, shortly after the United States entered World War I, and comprises a 52,000-acre post within Columbia, the state capital. It houses the U.S. Army Training Center; U.S. Army Soldier Support Institute (ADJUTANT GENERAL SCHOOL and Finance School); U.S. Army Chaplain Center and School; Recruiting and Retention School; 1st Basic Training Brigade; 4th Training Brigade; TRADO Pre-Command Course; and Moncrief Army Community Hospital.

Further reading: Fort Jackson Web site, www.jackson.army.mil.

Fort Knox, Kentucky

Because it houses the U.S. Bullion Depository, Fort Knox is one of the most famous of American military installations. In addition to the depository, however, the fort is also home to the U.S. Army Armor Center and School; headquarters, Second ROTC Region; and headquarters, U.S. Army Recruiting Command. It is also the home of Ireland Army Hospital.

The fort was established during World War I in 1918 and occupies 110,000 acres 45 miles south of Louisville.

Further reading: Fort Knox Web site, www. knox.army.mil.

Fort Leavenworth, Kansas

An early frontier outpost, established in 1827, Fort Leavenworth now occupies 5,634 acres north of the city of Leavenworth. Best known as the site of the U.S. Disciplinary Barracks, the facility is also home to the U.S. Army Combined Arms Center–Combined Arms Training; U.S. Army COMMAND AND GENERAL STAFF COLLEGE; TRADOC Analysis Center; National Simulation Center; and the Mason Army Community Hospital.

Further reading: Fort Leavenworth Web site, www.leavenworth.army.mil.

Fort Lee, Virginia

Established on the eve of U.S. entry into World War II, in 1941, Fort Lee is located outside of Petersburg on almost 6,000 acres. It is home to the U.S. Army Combined Arms Support Command; U.S. Army Logistics Management College; U.S. Army Quartermaster Center and School; Defense Commissary Agency; 23rd Quartermaster Brigade; 49th Quartermaster Group; Readiness Group Lee; and Kenner Army Community Hospital.

Further reading: Fort Lee Web site, www.lee. army.mil.

Fort Leonard Wood, Missouri

Established in 1940, this 63,000-acre post is located near Waynesville. It is home to the U.S. Army Engineer Center and School; U.S. Army Chemical School; U.S. Army Military Police School; 1st Engineer Brigade; 3rd Training Brigade; 3rd Chemical Brigade; and the General Leonard Wood Army Community Hospital.

Further reading: Fort Leonard Wood Web site, www.wood.army.mil.

Fort Lewis, Washington

Fort Lewis was established during World War I in 1917 and now consists of 86,000 acres along Puget Sound. Its activities include serving as home to the headquarters of I Corps; 1st Brigade, 25TH INFANTRY DIVISION (Light); 3rd Brigade, 2ND INFANTRY DIVISION; 1st Special Forces Group (Airborne); headquarters, Fifth Army (West); headquarters, Fourth ROTC Region; 2nd Battalion (Ranger), 75th Infantry; 6th Military Police Group; 555th Engineer Group; 201st Military Intelligence Brigade; 1st Military Police Brigade (Provisional); 1st Personnel Support Group; 593rd Corps Support Group; 62nd Medical Group; Madigan Army Medical Center; and Yakima Training Center and Vancouver Barracks.

Further reading: Fort Lewis Web site, www. lewis.army.mil.

Fort McCoy, Wisconsin

Established in 1909, Fort McCoy occupies 60,000 acres in west-central Wisconsin and is currently a Total Force Warfighting Training Center. As such, it is the largest mobilization site for RESERVE COMPONENTS.

Further reading: Fort McCoy Web site, www. mccoy.army.mil.

Fort McNair, District of Columbia

Fort McNair was created in 1791 and is now situated on 99 acres along the Potomac River in southwest Washington, D.C. It is the headquarters of the Military District of Washington (MDW) and also houses the National Defense University, which includes the National War College and the

Industrial College of the Armed Forces. The Inter-American Defense Board is also located at the fort.

Further reading: Fort McNair Web site, www.fmmc.army.mil.

Fort McPherson, Georgia

Fort McPherson was established after the CIVIL WAR in 1866 in southwest Atlanta. The fort proper encompasses 487 acres and includes the subposts Fort Gillem and Fort Buchanan. Fort McPherson is headquarters of Forces Command (FORSCOM); U.S. Army Reserve Command (USARC); and Third Army Forces Central Command headquarters.

Further reading: Fort McPherson Web site, www.mcpherson.army.mil.

Fort Meade, Maryland

Established during World War I in 1917, Fort Meade occupies 13,500 acres in the Baltimore–Washington, D.C., area and is home to the National Security Agency (NSA) as well as headquarters, FIRST U.S. ARMY (EAST). The Defense Information School is here, along with headquarters, U.S. ARMY INTELLIGENCE AND SECURITY COMMAND (INSCOM); Defense Courier Service; and U.S. Army Field Band.

Further reading: Fort Meade Web site, www.ftmeade.army.mil.

Fort Monmouth, New Jersey

Established during World War I in 1917, Fort Monmouth is located in Monmouth County. A facility of 1,100 acres, it is home to headquarters, Communications-Electronics Command (CECOM), U.S. Military Academy Preparatory School; and Patterson Army Community Hospital.

Further reading: Fort Monmouth Web site, www.monmouth.army.mil.

Fort Monroe, Virginia

Established in 1823, historic Fort Monroe is located on 1,000 acres adjacent to Hampton on Hampton Roads. It is home to U.S. ARMY TRAINING AND DOCTRINE COMMAND (TRADOC) headquarters; Cadet Command; and the Joint Warfighting Center.

Further reading: Fort Monroe Web site, www.monroe.army.mil/monroe.

Fort Myer, Virginia

Established in 1862, Fort Myer occupies a 250-acre site in Arlington, Virginia, beside Arlington National Cemetery. It is the home of First Battalion, 3rd Infantry (The Old Guard); 1101st Signal Brigade; and U.S. Army Band (Pershing's Own).

Further reading: Fort Myer Web site, www.fmmc.army.mil.

Fort Polk, Louisiana

Fort Polk was opened in 1941 on nearly 200,000 acres in west-central Louisiana. It houses the JOINT READINESS TRAINING CENTER; 2nd Armored Cavalry Regiment (Light); Warrior Brigade; and the Bayne-Jones Army Community Hospital.

Further reading: Fort Polk Web site, www.jrtc.polk.army.mil.

Fort Richardson, Alaska

Headquarters of the U.S. Army, Alaska, Fort Richardson is a 62,500-acre post adjacent to Anchorage. It was established in 1940.

Further reading: Fort Richardson information at U.S. Army, Alaska Web site, www.usarak.army.mil.

Fort Riley, Kansas

Established as a frontier outpost in 1853, Fort Riley today occupies 100,000 acres east of Junction City and is home to the 24th Infantry Division (Mechanized); 1st Brigade, 1ST INFANTRY DIVISION (Mechanized); 3rd Brigade, 1ST ARMORED DIVISION; 937th Engineer Group; and Irwin Army Community Hospital.

Further reading: Fort Riley Web site, www.riley.army.mil.

Fort Rucker, Alabama

Opened during World War II in 1942, Fort Rucker occupies 64,500 acres 20 miles northwest of Dolan. It is home to the U.S. Army Aviation Center and School; 1st Aviation Brigade; Aviation Training Brigade; and U.S. Army Safety Center.

Further reading: Fort Rucker Web site, http://www-rucker.army.mil.

Fort Sam Houston, Texas

The fort was created in 1845 and now includes 2,900 acres within San Antonio in addition to Camp Bullis, 24 miles to the northwest, a site of 27,000 acres. The fort is the headquarters of Fifth Army; headquarters, U.S. ARMY MEDICAL COMMAND; headquarters, U.S. Army Medical Department Center and School; 5th Brigade, Fourth Region (ROTC); and Brooke Army Medical Center.

Further reading: Medical Command (Fort Sam Houston) Web site, www.cs.amedd.army.mil.

Fort Shafter, Hawaii

Established in 1905, Fort Shafter occupies 1,400 acres just outside of Honolulu. It is headquarters of the U.S. ARMY, PACIFIC (USARPAC) and houses the Tripler Army Medical Center.

Further reading: USARPAC (Fort Shafter) Web site, www.usarpac.army.mil.

Fort Sill, Oklahoma

Established as a frontier post in 1869 when Oklahoma was Indian Territory, Fort Sill now occupies 94,220 acres north of Lawton. Its major activities include the U.S. Army Field Artillery Training Center; III Corps Artillery; 17th, 75th, 212th, and 214th Field Artillery Brigades; Henry Post Army Airfield; and Reynolds Army Community Hospital.

Further reading: Fort Sill Web site, http://sill-www.army.mil.

Fort Stewart, Georgia

Fort Stewart was established in 1940 on 279,000 acres 40 miles southwest of Savannah. It is home to the 3RD INFANTRY DIVISION and Winn Army Community Hospital.

Further reading: Fort Stewart Web site, www.stewart.army.mil/homepage.htm.

Fort Story, Virginia

Established in 1914, Fort Story is situated on 1,451 acres adjacent to Virginia Beach. It is a subinstallation of Fort Eustis and is the site of amphibious training as well as a testing site for the army's Logistics-over-the-Shore assets.

Further reading: Fort Eustis (also Fort Story) Web site, www.eustis.army.mil/fort_story.

Fort Wainwright, Alaska

Located on 963,000 acres just east of Fairbanks, this installation was established as an Army Air Field in 1940, was Ladd Air Force Base for a time, then was designated Fort Wainwright in 1961. It is home to the 1st Battalion, 17th Infantry; 4th Battalion, 9th Infantry; 172nd Infantry Brigade (Separate); 11th Field Artillery Battalion; 4th Battalion; 123rd Aviation Brigade; and the Cold Regions Research and Engineering Laboratory, as well as the Alaska Fire Service and Bassett Army Community hospital.

Further reading: U.S. Army, Alaska (Fort Wainwright) Web site, www.usark.army.mil.

As of 2005, army airfields included:

Biggs Army Airfield, Texas

Located adjacent to Fort Bliss, Texas, Biggs Army Airfield provides full airfield services with 24-hour capability for the aviation assets of all four military services, the Department of Justice, and other government flight detachments. The airfield also supports other nonflying federal and local agencies. Secondarily, Biggs provides MEDEVAC support to Fort Bliss, west Texas, and southern New Mexico. Biggs is used for major interservice exercises as well as for USAF readiness tests.

Biggs is situated on about 4,000 acres and has a 13,572-foot runway and about 9.7 miles of taxiways.

Biggs Airfield lies at the historical heart of military aviation, which may be said to have begun at Fort Bliss in 1916 when the First Aero Squadron was attached to General JOHN JOSEPH PERSHING's punitive expedition in pursuit of Pancho Villa. In June 1919, two squadrons of DeHaviland DH-4 bombers replaced the frail Jennys and became the first aircraft of the Border Air Patrol. In 1920, the 8th Airship Company was activated at Camp Owen Bierne, a mile northeast of Bliss Field, but was deactivated in 1922. The facility was officially named for Lieutenant James Berthes "Buster" Biggs on January 25, 1925. A native El Paso aviator, he was killed in 1918 during World War I when his plane crashed at Belrain, France.

The field was greatly expanded during World War II and functioned as a training and transient base throughout the war. In 1947, Biggs was transferred to the newly independent USAF as home base for heavy strategic bombers. It was returned to army control in 1966 and reactivated as an army airfield in 1973 and is now the largest active army airfield in the world.

Further reading: Biggs Army Airfield Web site, www.bliss.army.mil/Other%20Sites%20at%20Ft%20Bliss/airfield/enter.htm.

Hunter Army Airfield, Georgia

Located adjacent to Savannah, this 5,400-acre facility is a subinstallation of Fort Stewart and supports the 3rd Infantry Division (Mechanized) as well as a ranger battalion.

Further reading: Hunter Army Airfield Web site, see Fort Stewart Web site, www.stewart.army.mil.

Lawson Army Airfield, Georgia

Lawson Army Airfield is the airport for Fort Benning.

Simmons Army Airfield, North Carolina

Simmons Army Airfield is the airport for Fort Bragg.

As of 2005, army arsenals included:

Picatinny Arsenal, New Jersey

Established in 1880, the 6,500-acre arsenal is located at Dover, New Jersey, and is the site of headquarters, U.S. Army TACOM Armament Research, Development, and Engineering Center (TACOM-ARDEC).

Further reading: Picatinny Arsenal Web site, www.pica.army.mil/picatinny.

Pine Bluff Arsenal, Arkansas

The arsenal was established in 1941 on 15,000 acres near Pine Bluff and is dedicated to the design and manufacture of smoke, riot-control, and incendiary munitions as well as the demilitarization of surplus munitions. The arsenal also serves as a center for the development of equipment to defend against chemical and biological weapons.

Further reading: Pine Bluff Arsenal Web site, www.pba.army.mil.

Redstone Arsenal, Alabama

Redstone is administered by the U.S. ARMY MATERIEL COMMAND (AMC) and is home to the AVIATION AND MISSILE COMMAND (AMCOM). Redstone is the site of army activities relating to missiles and missile munitions. It was also the site of the army's early involvement in the space race during the late 1950s and early 1960s.

Further reading: Redstone Arsenal, "Redstone Arsenal: A Tradition of Excellence," at www.redstone.army.mil.

Rock Island Arsenal, Illinois

The arsenal was established during the CIVIL WAR in 1862 on a 946-acre island in the Mississippi River between Moline, Illinois, and Davenport, Iowa. It is headquarters of the INDUSTRIAL OPERATIONS COMMAND, which directs activities for three arsenals and 28 depots.

Further reading: Rock Island Arsenal Web site, www.ria.army.mil.

Watervliet Arsenal, New York

The arsenal was established in 1813, during the WAR OF 1812, and occupies 42 acres in the town of Watervliet. Home of the army's BENÉT LABORATORIES, Watervliet is the only cannon manufacturing plant in the United States.

Further reading: GlobalSecurity.Org, "Watervliet Arsenal, Watervliet, New York," www.globalsecurity.org/military/facility/watervliet.htm.

As of 2005, army barracks included:

Carlisle Barracks, Pennsylvania

Established during the French and Indian War in 1757, Carlisle Barracks occupies 400 acres on the edge of the town of Carlisle, Pennsylvania, and is home to the U.S. ARMY WAR COLLEGE; Strategic Studies Institute; Center for Strategic Leadership; U.S. ARMY MILITARY HISTORY INSTITUTE; U.S. Army Peacekeeping Institute; and Dunham Army Health Clinic.

Further reading: Carlisle Barracks Web site, www.carlisle.army.mil.

Schofield Barracks, Hawaii

Established in 1908, Schofield Barracks lies 17 miles northwest of Honolulu on a 14,000-acre site. Wheeler Army Airfield and Helemano Army Reservation are subinstallations of the facility. It serves as headquarters for the 25th Infantry Division (Light) and the 45th Corps Support Group (Forward).

Further reading: Schofield Barracks Web site at 25th Infantry Web site, www.25idl.army.mil.

U.S. Army Disciplinary Barracks, Kansas

Located at Fort Leavenworth, the Disciplinary Barracks are the army's only maximum-security prison. The facility is used to house convicts from all of the services.

As of 2005, the army camps included:

Camp Able Sentry, Macedonia
Camp Bondsteel, Kosovo

Camp Bonifas, Korea
Camp Carroll, Korea
Camp Casey, Korea
Camp Castle, Korea
Camp Comanche, Bosnia
Camp Dobol, Bosnia
Camp Doha, Kuwait
Camp Eagle, Korea
Camp Edwards, Korea
Camp Essayons, Korea
Camp Garry Owen, Korea
Camp George, Korea
Camp Giant, Korea
Camp Greaves, Korea
Camp Henry, Korea
Camp Hialeah, Korea
Camp Hovey, Korea
Camp Howze, Korea
Camp Humphreys, Korea
Camp Kyle, Korea
Camp LaGuardia, Korea
Camp Long, Korea
Camp Market, Korea
Camp McGovern, Bosnia
Camp Mobile, Korea
Camp Monteith, Kosovo
Camp Nimble, Korea
Camp Page, Korea
Camp Red Cloud, Korea
Camp Sears, Korea
Camp Shelby, Mississippi, USA
Camp Stanley, Korea
Camp Stanton, Korea
Camp Walker, Korea
Camp Zama, Japan

As of 2005, army depot facilities included:

Anniston Army Depot (ANAD), Alabama

Anniston Army Depot is the only army depot where maintenance on both heavy and light-tracked combat vehicles and their components is performed. In addition to maintaining and repairing tanks (including the M-1A Abrams), the depot has assumed responsibility for towed and self-propelled artillery as well as the M-113 Family of

Vehicles (FOV). The depot also performs maintenance on individual and crew-served weapons as well as land combat missiles and small arms. Additionally, the depot maintains and stores conventional ammunition and missiles, as well as 7 percent of the nation's chemical munitions stockpile (until this stockpile is demilitarized). The maintenance mission includes a wide range of vehicle conversions and upgrades.

Principal tenant organizations at the depot include the Defense Distribution Depot, Anniston (DDAA), the Anniston Munitions Center (ANMC), the Anniston Chemical Activity (ANCA), the Program Manager for Chemical Demilitarization (PMCD), the Center of Military History Clearing House, the 722nd Ordnance Company (Explosive Ordnance Disposal-EOD), and the Defense Reutilization and Marketing Office (DRMO).

Anniston Army Depot is located in the foothills of the Appalachian Mountains in northeast Alabama and occupies over 25 square miles of land, including more than 18,000 acres of woodland and 10 acres of lakes and streams. The facility was established in 1942 as a storage depot during World War II. The depot has 2,647 employees and includes 2,100 buildings/structures, 266 miles of roadway, and 46 miles of railroad.

Further reading: Anniston Army Depot Web site, www.anad.army.mil.

Corpus Christi Army Depot (CCAD), Texas

The Corpus Christi Army Depot (CCAD) serves as a center for the overhaul, repair, modification, retrofitting, testing, and modernization of helicopters and helicopter engines and components for the army and other services as well as foreign military customers. The facility services the AH-1W Super Cobra, CH-47D Chinook, MH-60 Pavehawk, OH-58D Kiowa, AH-64A Apache, SH-60 Seahawk, UH-1N Huey, and UH-60 Blackhawk helicopters. Additionally, Corpus Christi Army Depot serves as the depot training base for active duty ARMY, ARMY NATIONAL GUARD, Army Reserve, and foreign military personnel. The facility provides onsite maintenance services, aircraft crash analysis, lubricating oil analysis, and chemical, metallurgical, and training support worldwide.

Further reading: Corpus Christi Army Depot Web site, www.ccad.army.mil.

Deseret Chemical Depot, Utah

Deseret Chemical Depot stores a large percentage of the United States' stockpile of chemical munitions. The depot also supports weapons demilitarization, including research and development activities.

Further reading: Deseret Chemical Storage Depot information, www.hazardouswaste.utah.gov/CDS/DCDHP1.HTM.

Letterkenny Army Depot, Pennsylvania

Letterkenny Army Depot, Pennsylvania, is the army's center for tactical missile repair and maintenance as well as repair and maintenance of ground support and radar equipment associated with army tactical missiles. These missiles and missile systems include the Patriot, Avenger, Hawk, MLRS, and TOW.

Located in south-central Pennsylvania near Chambersburg, Letterkenny encompasses more than 17,500 acres, much of which is used to conduct maintenance, modification, storage, and demilitarization operations on tactical missiles and ammunition. The range of the facilities capabilities include machining, sheet metal work, welding, heat treatment, hydraulics, blasting, painting, plating, metal finishing, engine overhaul, generator overhaul, nondestructive testing, precision measurement, upholstery, woodworking, electronic systems integration, wiring harness fabrication, fiber optic cable work, military-standard soldering, multilayer circuit board fabrication, motor rebuild, antenna pattern testing, radar testing, phased array antenna testing, shielded room environment capability, clean room environment capability, and dielectric fluid reprocessing.

Further reading: Letterkenny Army Depot Web site, www.letterkenny.army.mil.

Pueblo Chemical Depot, Colorado

The Pueblo Chemical Depot is located in south-eastern Colorado, about 14 miles east of the city of Pueblo. The 23,000-acre facility is now used for the storage of chemical weapons.

Further reading: Pueblo Chemical Depot information, www.globalsecurity.org/wmd/facility/pueblo.

Red River Army Depot (RRAD), Texas

Located in Bowie County, Texas, near Texarkana, staff at the Red River Army Depot (RRAD) conduct ground combat, air defense, and tactical systems maintenance, certification, and related support services worldwide for the army, components of the Department of Defense, and various foreign nations. Supported equipment includes the M-2 Bradley Fighting Vehicle, the MLRS, various trucks, the M-977 HEMTT (Heavy Expanded Mobility Tactical Truck), the 25-ton crane, and the M-998 HMMWV (High-Mobility Multipurpose Wheeled Vehicle), as well as the Patriot missile system.

Further reading: Red River Army Depot Web site, www.redriver.army.mil.

Sierra Army Depot, California

Located southeast of Susanville, California, near the Nevada state line, the Sierra Army Depot serves as the army's Rapid Delivery Logistics Facility and Department of Defense strategic power projection support platform to provide worldwide maintenance, assembly, and containerization of critical operational project stocks, including deployable medical systems, medical supplies, petroleum and water systems, aviation systems, force provider, and other items. The depot stores and performs caretaker services for demilitarization account ammunition. When so directed, the depot performs resource recovery, recycle, and reuse of demilitarized ammunition.

The Sierra Army Depot was established during World War II on February 2, 1942.

Further reading: Sierra Army Depot Web site, www.sierra.army.mil.

Tobyhanna Army Depot, Pennsylvania

Located near Scranton, Pennsylvania, Tobyhanna Army Depot is the army's "C^{4}ISR [Command, Control, Communications, Computer, Intelligence, Surveillance, and Reconnaissance] Logistics Support Center for Warfighter Readiness and Transformation." It maintains devices ranging from handheld radios to satellite communications and is a full-service repair, overhaul, and fabrication facility.

The origin of the depot goes back to 1912, when the army established Camp Summerall, Camp Tobyhanna, and the Tobyhanna Artillery Target Range here. Tobyhanna was closed down after World War II, but, on January 17, 1951, the army announced its plan to reacquire 1,400 acres of the former Tobyhanna Military Reservation for a SIGNAL CORPS supply depot. The depot was opened on February 1, 1953.

Further reading: Tobyhanna Army Depot Web site, www.tobyhanna.army.mil.

Tooele Army Depot, Utah

Tooele Army Depot is a joint ammunition storage site, which is responsible for shipping, storing, receiving, inspecting, and maintaining training and war reserve conventional ammunition. When so directed, the depot also demilitarizes (destroys or otherwise inactivates) surplus or obsolete ammunition. The Ammunition Equipment Directorate located at Tooele designs and manufacturers equipment used in the maintenance and demilitarization of munitions for all of the Department of Defense (DoD).

Further reading: Tooele Army Depot information, www.globalsecurity.org/military/facility/tooele.htm.

As of 2005, the army operated the following proving grounds:

Aberdeen Proving Ground (APG), Maryland

Aberdeen Proving Ground was created in Aberdeen, Maryland, on October 20, 1917, six months after the United States entered World War

I, as a facility for the design and testing of ordnance. Today, the facility occupies more than 72,500 acres in Harford County, Maryland, and comprises two principal areas, separated by the Bush River: the northern area, called the Aberdeen Area, and the southern area, called the Edgewood Area.

Among the 50 tenants at the facility are the U.S. Army Soldier, Biological and Chemical Command, U.S. Army Ordnance Center and School, U.S Army Developmental Test Command, U.S. Army Aberdeen Test Center, U.S. Army Center for Health Promotion and Preventive Medicine, Northeast Region Civilian Personnel Operations Center, U.S. Army Medical Research Institute of Chemical Defense, Program Manager for Chemical Demilitarization, 203rd Technical Intelligence Unit, and major elements of the ARMY RESEARCH LABORATORY.

More than 7,500 civilians and 3,900 military personnel work at Aberdeen Proving Ground.

Further reading: "Aberdeen Proving Ground," www.apg.army.mil/aberdeen_proving_ground. htm.

Dugway Proving Ground, Utah

Established in 1942, Dugway covers 1,300 square miles of west-central Utah and has as its mission the testing of army equipment and weapons systems, including artillery and chemical and biological defenses.

Further reading: Dugway Proving Ground Web site, www.dugway.army.mil.

Electronic Proving Ground (EPG), Arizona

Located at Fort Huachuca, Arizona, the EPG is responsible for much of the army's electronic instrumentation development, rapid prototyping of electronic devices, development and testing of software systems, experiment design, and electronic modeling and simulation testing.

Further reading: Electronic Proving Ground, www.epg.army.mil.

Yuma Proving Ground, Arizona

The Yuma Test Branch was established here in 1943 during World War II, and the current proving ground occupies some 1,300 square miles. The proving ground serves the U.S. Army Test and Evaluation Command for general-purpose testing of weapons systems.

Further reading: Yuma Proving Ground Web site, www.yuma.army.mil.

4th Infantry Division (Mechanized)

Stationed at Fort Hood, Texas, the 4th Infantry Division (ID) has as its mission deployment to an area of operations anywhere in the world, where it executes sustained, decisive full-spectrum operations.

The 4th ID was nicknamed the "Ivy Division" after the design of its shoulder patch—four green ivy leaves joined at the stem and opening at the four corners. That emblem is a play on the roman numeral four, IV, and thus "Ivy." Moreover, ivy leaves are traditional symbols of tenacity and fidelity and are the basis of the division's motto, "Steadfast and Loyal."

The division was formed in December 1917 during WORLD WAR I and went into action in the Aisne-Marne campaign during July 1918. Units of the division were deployed piecemeal and attached to several French infantry divisions. However, before the campaign ended, the division was reunited and fought as a unit during the culminating weeks of the action on the Aisne-Marne front. The 4th Infantry Division earned the distinction of being the only U.S. unit to serve in both the French and British sectors of the western front.

During WORLD WAR II, the 4th Infantry was deployed to staging areas in England to train for a major role in Operation Overlord, the D-day amphibious invasion of Normandy. On June 6, 1944, the division's 8th Infantry Regiment became the first Allied unit to assault German forces on the Normandy coast. The regiment landed at Utah Beach and, for 26 days, advanced inland, securing positions for the breakout across France. The division was the first U.S. unit to participate in the liberation of Paris.

From Paris, the 4th Infantry moved into the Hurtgen Forest and fought what proved to be its fiercest battle there. During the Battle of the Bulge, the division managed to hold its ground and, the battle won, advanced across the Rhine. Penetrating deep into southern Germany, it crossed the Danube and, finally, halted its advance at the Isar River in southern Germany. At this point, the war in Europe ended.

The 4th Infantry Division was not deployed in the next major conflict, the KOREAN WAR, but was sent to Vietnam early in the VIETNAM WAR, in September 1966. Its brigades were deployed to different locations, the 1st Brigade near the South China Sea, the 2nd Brigade in the central highlands, and the 3rd Brigade in the Mekong Delta. From these positions, the 4th Infantry Division took part in 11 major campaigns during five years in Vietnam.

After returning from Vietnam in December 1970, the 4th Infantry Division was settled at Fort Carson, Colorado, where it was reorganized as a mechanized unit. It remained here for 25 years, during which period the nickname of the division changed from the Ivy Division to the Ironhorse Division, reflecting its new mechanized status and its mission of readiness for contingency deployment worldwide. In December 1995, the division transferred to Fort Hood, Texas, its present home. In 2003, elements of the 4th Infantry were deployed to Iraq to participate in Operation Iraqi Freedom.

40th Infantry Division (Mechanized)

The 40th Infantry Division (ID) is the principal unit of the California ARMY NATIONAL GUARD, headquartered at Camp Roberts, Los Alamitos, California. The unit was organized at Camp Kearney, near San Diego, California, on September 16, 1917, after the U.S. entry into WORLD WAR I. As originally established, the 40th ID was composed of National Guard organizations of the states of Arizona, California, Colorado, Nevada, New Mexico, and Utah. Its emblem, a sunburst symbol, gave the division its nickname: the "Sunburst Division."

During World War I, the division was deployed to France on August 3, 1918, and redesignated the 6th Depot Division, charged with receiving, equipping, training, and forwarding replacements to the front. The division returned to the United States on June 30, 1919, and was inactivated until March 3, 1941, shortly before U.S. entry into WORLD WAR II. At this time, the 40th ID was composed of National Guard organizations from California and Utah.

During World War II, the division was deployed to the Pacific theater on August 23, 1942, and fought in the Bismarck Archipelago, southern Philippines, and Luzon campaigns, receiving three Distinguished Unit Citations. Returning to the United States on April 7, 1946, the division was also inactivated on that date.

Initially, the 40th Infantry Division was assigned to defend the outer islands of Hawaii. During its deployment there, the division underwent intensive amphibious and jungle training. On December 20, 1943, the first units left for Guadalcanal, and by mid-January 1944, movement was completed. On April 24, 1944, the 40th ID left Guadalcanal for New Britain and took positions at Talasea on the northern side of the island, at Arawe on the southern side, and at Cape Gloucester near the western end. Patrols were sufficient to neutralize the enemy here; no major battle was fought.

Relieved on New Britain on November 27, the 40th began training for the Luzon (Philippines) landing. The division sailed from Borgen Bay on December 9, 1944, and made an assault landing at Lingayen, Luzon, then advanced to occupy Lingayen airfield, the Bolinao Peninsula, and San Miguel. From here it was on to Manila, on the way toward which the division encountered heavy fighting.

The division left Luzon on March 15, 1945, and was landed on Panay Island to cut behind the Japanese positions. After knocking out Japanese resistance and seizing airfields at Santa Barbara and Mandurriao, the division saw action on

Negros Island, then returned to Panay in June and July 1945.

With the end of the war, the 40th ID was transferred to Korea for occupation duty.

After World War II, the 40th ID was returned to state control. After the terrorist attacks on the United States in 2001, various 40th ID units were deployed in support of Operation Noble Eagle (homeland defense operations) and deployed overseas to Afghanistan. In 2003, some units were deployed to Iraq to support Operation Iraqi Freedom.

42nd Infantry Division ("Rainbow")

Part of the ARMY NATIONAL GUARD, the 42nd Infantry Division is headquartered at Troy, New York, and was organized in September 1917 after the United States entered WORLD WAR I. In the headlong rush to mobilize, many states competed with each other for the honor to be the first to send their National Guard units to fight in Europe. Federal and army officials, wishing to stem any negative effects of such competition, created a division composed of handpicked National Guard units from 26 states and the District of Columbia. This was the 42nd, which was established at Camp Mills, Long Island, New York. Colonel DOUGLAS MACARTHUR, instrumental in forming the division, remarked: "The 42nd Division stretches like a Rainbow from one end of America to the other," and from that point forward the unit was known as the "Rainbow Division."

The division arrived in France in November 1917 and entered the front line in March 1918, where it remained in contact with the enemy for 174 days, fighting in six major campaigns. The division suffered one out of 16 American Expeditionary Force casualties during the war.

The 42nd Division was sent home after the war in May 1919 and was not reactivated until July 1943, during WORLD WAR II. The division landed in France in December 1944, and, as part of the Seventh Army, advanced through France and entered Germany in March 1945. It was the 42nd

Division, along with elements of the 45th Infantry Division, that liberated the infamous Dachau concentration camp, revealing to the world for the first time the full horror of the Holocaust.

The war record of the 42nd Division was admirable. It was the first division in its corps to enter Germany, the first to penetrate the Siegfried Line, and the first to enter Munich, birthplace of the Nazi movement. Division troops seized more than 6,000 square miles of enemy territory. After the German surrender, the division served as occupation forces in Austria and then was inactivated in June 1946.

In 1993, the 42nd Division consolidated with elements of the 26th and 50th divisions to form one Army National Guard division, which has units in nine states, including New York, Vermont, New Jersey, Massachusetts, Rhode Island, Kentucky, Florida, Illinois, and Michigan.

After the terrorist attacks against the United States on September 11, 2001, elements of the division from New York City armories—the 1st Battalion, 69th Infantry; 1st Battalion, 101st Cavalry; the 642nd Division Aviation Support Battalion; and the 1st Battalion, 258th Field Artillery Regiment—provided immediate emergency response and assisted in sustained security and recovery operations in Manhattan as part of JOINT TASK FORCE 42. Some 42nd Infantry Division troops were federally mobilized and deployed to Afghanistan in support of Operation Enduring Freedom, while others were assigned to Operation Noble Eagle, providing homeland security.

49th Armored Division

The 49th Armored Division (AD) was organized after WORLD WAR II as a unit of the Texas ARMY NATIONAL GUARD and was made up primarily of combat veterans. The division trained together for the first time at Fort Hood, Texas, in 1948. By 1949, the organization of the division was complete, and the first tank gunners fired for final qualification. Once it was deemed combat ready, the 49th AD became one of the six divisions assigned to the

Ready Reserve Strategic Army Force, a ready reserve component.

The 49th AD was mobilized for federal service on October 15, 1961, during the Berlin crisis—the showdown between the United States and the Soviet Union over the division of the German capital following erection of the Berlin Wall. The 49th was sent to Fort Polk, Louisiana, for the next 10 months. In May 1962, while at Fort Polk, the 49th AD staged a massive maneuver code-named Iron Dragoon, which was perhaps the most ambitious National Guard armor exercise ever. At this time, the 49th became the first Army National Guard unit to fire the Honest John ballistic missile.

The 49th AD was deactivated in 1968 and reformed into the 36th, 71st, and 72nd separate brigades. It was reactivated as a division on November 1, 1973, and headquartered at Camp Mabry, Austin, Texas. In the 1990s, the division was deployed to lead Task Force Eagle in Bosnia, and in March 2000 about 1,000 49th AD soldiers become the first National Guard unit since World War II to provide the command and control for an active army maneuver outfit. The division troops, reinforced by 200 guardsmen from Maryland, directed the peacekeeping efforts of up to 3,000 3rd Cavalry soldiers in the American sector of Bosnia-Herzegovina. Deployment in Bosnia took place in February 2000 with a return in October.

forward observer
Artillery liaison officer attached to an infantry unit in the field for the purpose of directing artillery fire against the enemy.

frag
A verb meaning to kill a fellow soldier with an explosive device. Victims of fragging are typically unpopular officers. The most common method of fragging is to toss a grenade into the officer's quarters while he or she sleeps. "Frag" is also used more generally as a synonym for the assassination ("fratricide") of a fellow soldier, regardless of the means employed.

fresh meat
Crude nickname for a replacement soldier in time of war or sustained combat.

G

general See RANKS AND GRADES.

general of the armies See RANKS AND GRADES.

general of the army See RANKS AND GRADES.

Geotechnical and Structures Laboratory (GSL)

Part of the U.S. ARMY CORPS OF ENGINEERS U.S. Army Engineer Research and Development Center, the Geotechnical and Structures Laboratory conducts research in the areas of soil mechanics, engineering geology and rock mechanics, earthquake engineering, geophysics, concrete and materials, and centrifuge modeling.

The laboratory researches, tests, and furnishes advice on airfields and pavements, concrete and cement, and also provides a general Materials Testing Center. The laboratory also works on earthquake engineering and the geosciences. GSL works directly for army components as well as elements of the other services and for the civilian and government communities.

Gibbon, John (1827–1896) *U.S. Army general*
A master artillerist in the CIVIL WAR, Gibbon was one of the army's leading commanders during the INDIAN WARS. He was a Philadelphia-area native,

but was raised in Charleston, South Carolina. After graduating from the UNITED STATES MILITARY ACADEMY in 1847, he was commissioned in the artillery and sent to the front to fight in the UNITED STATES–MEXICAN WAR. By the time he arrived, however, the war was essentially over, and his first taste of combat came in sporadic action against the Seminole Indians in Florida during 1849.

Promoted to first lieutenant in 1850, Gibbon was assigned to the military academy as an artillery instructor, serving in this capacity from 1854 to 1859 and writing during this time the *Artillerist's Manual* (1859), which became a standard reference. He was promoted to captain in November 1859 and sent to Utah, only to be recalled east at the outbreak of the Civil War. Assigned to the division of Major General Irvin McDowell as chief of artillery in October 1861, he was promoted to brigadier general of volunteers in May 1862. He led the 1st Brigade, 1st Division, I Corps at the Second Battle of Bull Run (August 29–30, 1862), South Mountain near Frederick, Maryland (September 14), and at Antietam (September 17), where a journalist dubbed his command the "Iron Brigade."

On December 13, while commanding 2nd Division of I Corps at Fredericksburg, Gibbon was gravely wounded, but he was able to return to duty to command the 2nd Division of Major General WINFIELD SCOTT's II Corps at the Battle of Gettysburg during July 1–3, 1863. It was Gibbon's division that took the full force of Pickett's charge. On the last day of battle, Gibbon was again seriously wounded, returning to duty months later to lead the 2nd Division at the Battle of the Wilderness (May 5–6, 1864), Spotsylvania (May 8–19), and Cold Harbor (June 1–3).

After receiving promotion to major general of volunteers following Cold Harbor, Gibbon fought at Petersburg (June 15–18), then was appointed commander of XXIV Corps in the Army of the James in January 1865. He led this unit until the end of the war.

After the war, Gibbon was mustered out of volunteer service in January 1866 and reverted to the rank of colonel in the REGULAR ARMY. He was put in command of the 36th Infantry in July, then transferred to the 7th Infantry in 1869. Stationed with his command in Montana, he campaigned against the Sioux during 1876. It was Gibbon's regiment that was the first to arrive at the Little Bighorn battlefield on June 27 in the aftermath of GEORGE ARMSTRONG CUSTER's defeat, and it was they who relieved the survivors.

In 1877, Gibbon took part in the long pursuit of the Nez Perce. He suffered the third serious wound of his career in this engagement.

Promoted to brigadier general in 1885, Gibbon was given command of the army's Department of the Pacific the following year. He served until his retirement, in 1891, at headquarters in San Francisco.

Golden Knights

Stationed at Fort Bragg, North Carolina, the Golden Knights is the army exhibition, demonstration, and competition parachute team. Ninety handpicked and specially trained soldiers make up the Golden Knights, who specialize in performing precision aerial maneuvers and landing on target. The team is generally considered the best in the world.

The origin of the Golden Knights can be traced to 1959, when Brigadier General JOSEPH WARREN STILWELL, CHIEF OF STAFF of XVIII Airborne Corps, formed the Strategic Army Corps Parachute Team.

On June 1, 1961, the army redesigned and activated the team as the United States Army Parachute Team, and in 1962 the team officially adopted the nickname "Golden Knights" because of their record of gold medals won in competition.

The team's mission is threefold: To perform live aerial demonstrations for the public and to promote the army's public relations and recruitment efforts; to compete in national and international parachuting competitions; and to test and evaluate new parachuting equipment and techniques for improved operation and safety.

The Golden Knights consists of the Black and Gold Demonstration Teams, the Formation Skydiving Team, the Style and Accuracy Team, an aviation section, and a headquarters section.

The Black and Gold Teams spend more than 230 days each year entertaining more than 12 million people at air shows and special events around the country and the world. As of 2004, the teams have performed more than 8,500 live aerial demonstrations in all 50 states and 47 countries.

In addition to the Black and Gold Teams, the two parachute competition teams—the Formation Skydiving Team and the Style and Accuracy Team—tour the world competing in parachuting competitions. As of 2004, these teams have produced 408 national champions and 65 world champions, and have won 14 national and six world team titles in formation skydiving, making them the most-winning parachute team in the world.

The Golden Knights aviation section consists of six fixed-wing aircraft and a team of highly experienced pilots and crew members who ensure that the parachutists make it into the air safely and quickly. The headquarters section has a highly skilled team of soldiers and civilians working on the administration, budget, media relations, operations, parachute maintenance, and supply concerns of the team.

Good Conduct Medal   See DECORATIONS AND MEDALS.

grade   See RANKS AND GRADES.

Grant, Ulysses Simpson (1822–1885)
*U.S. Army general, president of the
United States*

As general in chief of the Union army, Grant led
the Union forces to victory in the CIVIL WAR. He
was born Hiram Ulysses Grant at Point Pleasant,
Ohio, the son of farmer Jesse B. Grant and received
an appointment to the UNITED STATES MILITARY
ACADEMY in 1839. He was listed on the academy's
rolls as Ulysses (a name he often went by) Simpson
(his mother's maiden name), and he adopted
Ulysses Simpson Grant as his name henceforth.

A mediocre cadet, Grant graduated in 1843,
21st in a class of 39. Commissioned a second lieutenant, he was assigned to the 4th Infantry and, two
years later, during September 1845, was sent as part
of Zachary Taylor's command to Texas as Mexico
and the United States stood at the brink of the
UNITED STATES–MEXICAN WAR. In that conflict,
Grant fought with distinction at most of the major
battles, earning a brevet promotion to first lieu-

General Ulysses S. Grant   *(Arttoday)*

tenant for his performance at the Battle of Molino
del Rey on September 8, 1847. Distinguishing himself again at Chapultepec on September 13, 1847,
he was breveted captain, and, on September 16, he
was formally commissioned first lieutenant.

After the war, Grant returned to the United
States and was variously posted, earning regular
promotion to captain in August 1853. Despite this,
he grew impatient with the slow pace of promotion
and resigned his commission in 1854, only to discover that he had little talent for anything other
than soldiering. By 1860, having failed at several
business ventures, he moved to Galena, Illinois,
where he joined his father and brothers in the family tannery. With the outbreak of the Civil War in
1861, Grant was chosen to train the Galena militia
company, then moved to the Illinois state capital,
Springfield, to work in the state ADJUTANT GEN-
ERAL's office. In June 1861, he was appointed
colonel of the 21st Illinois Volunteer Infantry regiment and, in August, was promoted to brigadier
general of volunteers and given command of the
District of Southeast Missouri, headquartered at
Cairo, the southernmost tip of Illinois.

Acting entirely on his own initiative, Grant
seized Paducah, Kentucky, on September 6, 1861,
but he was forced to retreat from Belmont, Missouri, on November 7. Grant persuaded his cautious commanding officer, Henry Wager Halleck,
to allow him to move against Fort Henry on the
Tennessee River, which he took on February 6,
1862. This action put the Union forces in position
to seize the initiative in the West.

Grant's next objective was Fort Donelson on
the Cumberland River, which he invested on February 14. The next day, the Confederate garrison
mounted a massive breakout attempt, which Grant
was barely able to check. By the 16th, however, the
garrison surrendered. Grant had presented his
terms, stating that nothing less than "unconditional surrender" would be acceptable. From that
point on, Grant acquired a new nickname—U.S.—
for "Unconditional Surrender."

Unimpressed with Grant's triumphs, Henry
Halleck felt that Grant had verged on insubordination and he temporarily relieved him from com-

mand but restored him to his position late in March. Confederate general Albert Sidney Johnston surprised Grant at Shiloh (April 6–7, 1862), but Grant was able to save the day, despite heavy losses. Nevertheless, Halleck took direct command of western forces after Shiloh, and Grant was cast into the background until Halleck was made general in chief of the Union army in July and Grant was assigned command not only of his own army but that of William Starke Rosecrans as well.

From December 1862 through July 1863, Grant tried various tactics to lay effective siege against the strategically vital Mississippi River fortress town of Vicksburg. The town did not fall to him until July 4, 1863. Together with the simultaneous Union victory at Gettysburg, Vicksburg was the definitive turning point of the Civil War.

After Vicksburg, Grant was promoted to major general in the REGULAR ARMY and was assigned command of the Military Division of the Mississippi on October 4, 1863. He and his subordinates George Thomas and WILLIAM TECUMSEH SHERMAN broke the siege during October 25–28, then went on to defeat the army of Braxton Bragg in the "Battle Above the Clouds" at Lookout Mountain and Missionary Ridge during November 24–25.

Vicksburg and Chattanooga catapulted Grant to prominence and prompted President Abraham Lincoln to promote him to lieutenant general and give him overall command of all Union forces. In contrast to previous overall commanders, Grant fought with singular aggressiveness. Even in defeat, as at the Battle of the Wilderness during May 4–7, 1864, he refused to retreat, but waded steadily southward to reengage the enemy. He was grimly willing to trade casualties for strategic objectives, and he understood the central statistical fact of the Civil War: the North had far more men and resources than the South. Therefore, continual offensive operations would win the war, regardless of cost.

Grant campaigned steadily against the Army of Northern Virginia under ROBERT EDWARD LEE, always sidestepping his way toward Richmond, which he invaded in April 1865. Grant then pressed the pursuit of the Army of Northern Virginia, finally accepting Lee's surrender at Appomattox Court House on April 9, 1865. For all practical purposes, this ended the Civil War.

After the war ended, Grant returned to Washington, where he oversaw a massive demobilization and also directed the military role in postwar Reconstruction. In recognition of his services to the nation, he was promoted to the newly created rank of general of the army in July 1866.

Grant served briefly as interim secretary of war under President Andrew Johnson during 1867–68, but his insistence on measures to protect the army of occupation in the South caused a permanent rift with Johnson, who was a Tennessean. Grant then embraced the strong (and often punitive) Reconstruction policies of the radical wing of the Republican Party, and he easily achieved the Republican nomination for president in 1868. Winning election, he served two terms, which were notorious for their corruption and scandal. Through all this, no one impugned Grant's integrity, but it was clear that he had little political sense and was often the victim of his cabinet and his advisers. He retired to private life after the close of his second term, settling in New York in 1881. Once again, he failed in a series of business ventures and went bankrupt by 1884. At the urging of humorist Mark Twain, Grant, racked by poverty and throat cancer, wrote his *Memoirs*. Completed only four days before his death, the work is a literary masterpiece and an extraordinary living history of the Civil War.

Green Berets See SPECIAL FORCES.

group

In the army, a group is a flexible administrative and tactical unit composed of two or more battalions. The term may also be applied to support and service support units. Often, a brigade and a group are terms that describe much the same single-arm, support, or service support unit.

grunt

In the army and marine corps, a grunt is an enlisted infantryman.

H

hard stripe

The insignia chevrons of a NONCOMMISSIONED OFFI-CER. Although the term is used in the USMC, it has even greater significance in the U.S. Army because it is contrasted with "soft stripe," the insignia of the specialist grades, which consist of arcs and eagles instead of chevrons.

Headquarters, Department of the Army

Located in the Pentagon in Arlington, Virginia, Headquarters, Department of the Army is the nerve center of the army and the place of ultimate decision regarding army affairs and missions. The SECRETARY OF THE ARMY has his offices here, as do the command and control elements of the USN and USAF as well as the Department of Defense. This facilitates full coordination of action among the services.

history, U.S. Army

The immediate precursor of the U.S. Army was the CONTINENTAL ARMY, created by the Continental Congress on June 15, 1775, to fight in the AMERI-CAN REVOLUTION. This force was disbanded after the war in 1783, and the U.S. Army proper was created by Congress under the Articles of Confederation on June 3, 1784, as a single regiment of 700 officers and enlisted men. It was conceived primarily as a frontier constabulary, responsible for patrolling the Old Northwest, the federal territory of the Ohio region. When the powers of the federal government were multiplied under the Constitution in 1789, the army was expanded. In 1792, it consisted of the so-called American Legion, a frontier force of 5,000, which prosecuted warfare against the Indians primarily in the Old Northwest.

The first substantial increase in the size of the army came in 1808, when the force was increased to 9,921 officers and men. The WAR OF 1812 brought further increases, and in 1814 Congress authorized 62,674 men—although the force never reached this size during the war. The war made vividly clear the inadequacy of militia forces and the necessity of a viable federal army even as it also exposed the generally poor quality of that army—although a few fine commanders did emerge, most notably WINFIELD SCOTT.

Despite the lessons of the war, Congress reduced the army to 12,383 men after the Treaty of Ghent in 1815 and then to a paltry 6,126 in 1821. However, this force consisted of a cadre of veterans and a high proportion of officers. It was intended to serve as the core around which a larger force could be rapidly built up if the need arose.

After the War of 1812 and until the CIVIL WAR of 1861–65, the forces of the army were mostly broadcast among far-flung western outposts in an effort to control conflict with the Indians. Throughout much of the 19th century, the primary mission of the army involved combat with the

Indians, beginning with the Seminoles in the East and concentrating mostly on various tribes in the West (see INDIAN WARS). In 1846, however, the UNITED STATES–MEXICAN WAR broke out, which brought the REGULAR ARMY to a strength of 17,812 men. This still-modest force was supplemented by the U.S. Volunteers, some 70,000 citizen-soldiers.

From an institutional point of view, the most important aspect of the U.S.-Mexican War was as an impetus to the ongoing professionalization of the army. The UNITED STATES MILITARY ACADEMY had been founded in 1802, and, as a result, the war with Mexico was led by highly professional officers who compiled an impressive record of victory.

Despite triumph in the war with Mexico, morale dwindled in the army, largely because it was underfunded and presented very little opportunity for advancement. Promotions typically proceeded at a glacial pace, and most of the promising young officers who had fought in Mexico left the service before the start of the Civil War—though some of the best, including ULYSSES SIMPSON GRANT and WILLIAM TECUMSEH SHERMAN, returned at the outbreak of war.

The Civil War brought the army to an unprecedented level of strength, at over a million men. A large fraction of the prewar officer corps left the U.S. Army to join the provisional Confederate army, and all too many senior commanders were appointed for political reasons rather than for their professional military merits. A few great officers emerged, Grant, Sherman, and PHILIP HENRY SHERIDAN among them, but, much of the time, the Union army was poorly led. Nevertheless, it was such a mighty force that the cause of the South was doomed.

As had occurred after other major wars, demobilization came quickly after 1865. By 1871, the army consisted of 29,000 officers and men very thinly distributed, for the most part, across the West and assigned to fight the later Indian Wars. The SPANISH-AMERICAN WAR demonstrated the unpreparedness of the army for an engagement outside of the national borders. The army quickly swelled to 200,000 regulars and volunteers, but the war was over before most had been deployed to

Cuba and the Philippines. After the war, the force was reduced to about 80,000, and shortly before U.S. entry into WORLD WAR I in 1917, the nation had only the 15th-largest army in the world, at just over 100,000 men. As a result of a spectacular mobilization, which, for the second time in U.S. history included a military draft (the Civil War occasioned the first U.S. conscription), army strength reached 4 million, of whom about half were ultimately deployed to fight in Europe.

Yet again, demobilization rapidly and drastically reduced the army after World War I. Strength was down to 150,000 by 1921, and morale in the interwar force was low. Moreover, the army fell behind European armies in the development of new weapons technologies, including ARMOR and, especially, AIRCRAFT. However, the small officer corps continually honed strategy and tactics. As WORLD WAR II loomed in Europe, President Franklin Roosevelt agitated for military preparedness. Congress authorized an increase in the size of the force, and, in 1935, a weapons development program and buildup were commenced. After the fall of France in June 1940, Congress enacted the nation's first peacetime draft, and FDR federalized the ARMY NATIONAL GUARD. The later belief that the United States had been unprepared for war when the Japanese attacked Pearl Harbor on December 7, 1941, is a popular misconception. Although there would be much catching up to do, the nation had never been better prepared for battle, its army consisting of 1.5 million men—a number that would grow to more than 8 million before the war ended in September 1945.

World War II made the United States unmistakably the free world's preeminent superpower. Nevertheless, demobilization soon after the war dissolved the 8 million-man army to a force of 590,000 organized into 10 understrength divisions. This meant that the army had again to scramble when a new conflict, the KOREAN WAR, broke out in 1950. By the armistice of 1953, the army had reached 1.5 million men, reduced to 873,000 during the presidency of DWIGHT DAVID EISENHOWER, then increased to a million under President John F. Kennedy in an effort to enable the armed forces to wield a "flexible response" in meeting any number of crises and brushfire wars spawned by the ongoing cold war conflict with the Soviet Union and Communist China.

Among the most dramatic changes in the postwar army was the racial integration of the force (see AFRICAN AMERICANS IN THE U.S. ARMY).

After the Korean War and during the 1950s and early 1960s, army forces were deployed mainly in Europe, as the largest component of NATO, and in South Korea, as a defense against renewed aggression there. The rest of the army was stationed throughout the United States. Escalation of the VIETNAM WAR after 1965 brought many troops into this theater, more than 500,000 by 1968. Throughout the 1960s, the force that fought in Vietnam was probably better trained and better equipped than any army force in history. Initially, morale was high. However, as tactical success repeatedly failed to produce strategic victory and as the antiwar movement gained overwhelming momentum in the American street and ultimately in Congress, morale eroded. After 1968, ground troops were steadily withdrawn from Vietnam, and, in 1973, Melvin Laird, secretary of defense in the administration of President Richard M. Nixon, announced an end to the military draft and the creation of the "all-volunteer force."

For the army, the Vietnam War constituted a tactical victory but a strategic defeat. The war ended in 1975 with reunification of the North and South under a communist regime. The specter of this failure—though not, strictly speaking, a military failure—haunted the army during the remainder of the 1970s and throughout the 1980s. Nevertheless, the all-volunteer force proved highly successful, as demonstrated in Operations Desert Shield and Desert Storm (the PERSIAN GULF WAR) of 1990–91. Success also came in the first phase of Operation Iraqi Freedom, the invasion of Iraq and the overthrow of its dictator Saddam Hussein, in 2003; however, occupation of the nation following the "major combat" phase proved far more problematic and caused many to question the capacity of the army as an occupying force. As of 2005, the occupation of Iraq, bedeviled by chronic violence, was sorely testing army morale, and Pentagon officials expressed increasingly deep concern over maintaining rates of recruitment and retention. Stop-loss orders involuntarily extended the tours of many soldiers in Iraq, and civilian as well as military officials voiced some concern over the future adequacy of the all-volunteer force.

homosexuals in the military

Reflecting the mainstream social values that prevailed generally through most of U.S. history, little is known about the history and extent of homosexuality in the American military. Documents from the CONTINENTAL ARMY record that a Lieutenant Gotthold Frederick Enslin became the first U.S. soldier to be drummed out of the service for sodomy on March 11, 1778. It is also well known that a number of lesbians (and, presumably, some heterosexual women as well) disguised themselves as men and fought on both sides during the CIVIL WAR. However, the military concerned itself very little with homosexuality until WORLD WAR II, when official policy held that homosexuals were not fit for combat service. New regulations authorized screening procedures to exclude homosexuals, not only on the basis of proven "acts of sodomy" but also on the basis of any manifestations of what today would be called a gay identity. During the war, 4,000 to 5,000 men and a few women were rejected for service on the basis of homosexuality. Because these totals comprise only a very small number out of some 18 million individuals examined during the period, it must be assumed that the screening program had little actual success in excluding gays and lesbians. Indeed, by the time the war ended, some 9,000 individuals had been given general discharges (see DISCHARGE, GENERAL) or dishonorable discharges (see DISCHARGE, DISHONORABLE) for homosexual habits, traits, or behavior. Such discharges disqualified these soldiers from receiving veteran's benefits.

In 1950, Congress passed the Uniform Code of Military Justice, which included severe penalties for homosexual acts (oral or anal sex); namely, five years' imprisonment and dishonorable discharge. From time to time, various sections of the military conducted "witch hunts," including campaigns of intimidation, to uncover homosexuals. Overall, between 1941 and 1996, the armed services discharged some 100,000 gay men and lesbian women.

Beginning in 1973, gay and lesbian military personnel resorted to the courts to challenge the constitutionality of antigay regulations in the services, particularly the arbitrary and inconsistent nature of the regulations and their execution. The Department of Defense responded in 1981 with Directive 1332.14, which did not liberalize policy but, on the contrary, sought to remove ambiguity in the treatment of homosexual personnel by simply making discharge mandatory in all cases.

During his campaign for the White House in 1992, Bill Clinton pledged an end to discrimination against gay men and lesbians in the U.S. military. Once in office, however, he encountered significant opposition from the Department of Defense, which claimed that gay and lesbian soldiers frequently suffered from mental illness, that they were especially vulnerable to blackmail and therefore presented a higher than average security risk, and that their presence would substantially damage morale. In response, President Clinton compromised by formulating a "don't ask, don't tell" policy, barring military officials from inquiring into the sexual orientation of personnel, but also requiring that gay men and women refrain from openly expressing their sexuality while in military service. This included a prohibition against all "homosexual conduct."

Policy Concerning Homosexuality in the Armed Forces was passed by the Senate on September 9, 1993, and by the House on September 28, 1993, as Section 654, Chapter 37 of Title 10, United States Code. Holding that military life makes demands distinct from that of civilian life and is therefore properly subject to regulations that differ from the laws that pertain to civilians, Section 654 states, in part:

> The presence in the armed forces of persons who demonstrate a propensity or intent to engage in homosexual acts would create an unacceptable risk to the high standards of morale, good order and discipline, and unit cohesion that are the essence of military capability.

The key word and concept is *demonstrate.* Individuals who refrain from any demonstration of their homosexual orientation may be retained in the service. Their homosexual identity will remain hidden because the law also bars officials from asking recruits about their sexual orientation.

As of 2005, "don't ask, don't tell" remains the policy of the U.S. military, and there are no signs that this will change any time soon. Between the implementation of the policy in 1994 and 2004 nearly 11,000 men and women have been discharged on the grounds of their homosexuality. Far from reducing the number of gays and lesbians separated from the service, the policy has increased it. For example, in 2002, 1,250 gay men and lesbian women were discharged, about twice the number discharged in 1993, the year before the policy went into effect.

howitzer

Howitzer is the general term for any short-barreled artillery weapon firing breech-loaded, medium-velocity, medium-range shells. These weapons have been and continue to be extensively employed today by the army.

See also INDIRECT FIRE SYSTEMS.

Humanitarian Service Medal   See DECORATIONS AND MEDALS.

Hunter Army Airfield, Georgia   See FORTS AND OTHER INSTALLATIONS.

I

Indian Wars (1866–1891)

Warfare between Indians and whites began in 1493 and continued, almost without interruption, through early 1891; however, the period from 1866 to 1891 is typically identified with what the army referred to as the "Indian Wars" and intensely occupied the tiny post–CIVIL WAR army operating from garrisons throughout the American West.

War for the Bozeman Trail (1866–1868)

In 1866, Chief Red Cloud of the Oglala Sioux refused to yield to demands that he sell to the government the land traversed by the Bozeman Trail, from Julesburg, Colorado, to the gold fields of Virginia City, Montana. Red Cloud further warned that he would not permit whites to use the trail. In response, Colonel Henry B. Carrington marched out of Fort Laramie, Wyoming, on June 17, 1866, and began garrisoning three forts along the Bozeman Trail: Fort Reno at the forks of the Powder River, Fort Phil Kearny (his headquarters) at the forks of Piney Creek, and Fort C. F. Smith near the Bighorn River, in Montana. Red Cloud struck the forts before they were completed, prompting one of Carrington's officers, Captain William J. Fetterman, to launch an expedition against the Indians on December 21. Fetterman and his command, 80 men, were killed in what the nation's newspapers called the "Fetterman Massacre." Although the army counterattacked effectively, the Indians refused to make peace, which led to Hancock's War.

Hancock's War (1867)

WILLIAM TECUMSEH SHERMAN sent Winfield Scott Hancock to campaign against the Southern Cheyennes, the Southern Arapahos, Kiowas, and the Oglala and Southern Brulé Sioux. From April through July, Colonel GEORGE ARMSTRONG CUSTER and his 7th Cavalry pursued the Indians, who now terrorized Kansas. Exhausted, Custer withdrew, and what had begun as an offensive campaign degenerated into a succession of futile attempts to defend civilian settlements. It was a doomed effort, since Hancock's 4,000 troops were thinly broadcast over 1,500 miles of major trails, which they could not hope to patrol effectively.

Hancock's War prompted the federal government to negotiate peace terms with the tribes of the southern and central plains, ostensibly giving to Red Cloud most of what he had fought for, including white abandonment of the Bozeman Trail forts. However, this was far less of a concession that it appeared on its face, since the transcontinental railroad was about to render the Bozeman Trail obsolete. Nor did the treaty succeed in ending the wars in the West.

Snake War (1866–1868)

In the Northwest, violence erupted among the Yahuskin and Walpapi bands of the Northern Paiutes, popularly known as the Snakes, who inhabited southeastern Oregon and southwestern Idaho. The Snake War was not a series of formal

This painting depicts a scene from the Battle of Washita, showing the 7th U.S. Cavalry attacking a Cheyenne encampment.   *(Library of Congress)*

battles, but a continuous pursuit punctuated by numerous guerrilla actions. During a two-year period, Brevet Major General George Crook and his 23rd Infantry engaged the Snakes at least 49 times and, more important, kept them on the run in what amounted to a war of attrition. By the middle of 1868, the Snakes had lost 329 killed, 20 wounded, and 225 captured. Most of the Snakes sued for peace, but a minority joined the Bannocks and Cayuses in what became the Bannock War of 1878.

Sheridan's Campaign (1868–1869)

After Cheyenne attacks along the Saline and Solomon rivers in 1868, William Tecumseh Sherman and his immediate subordinate, PHILIP HENRY SHERIDAN, launched a major campaign against the Plains Sioux. In the early autumn of 1868, Sheridan dispatched Major George A. Forsyth with 50 hand-picked plainsmen to patrol settlements and travel routes. On September 17, the small company encountered 600–700 "Dog Soldiers" (young militant warriors) and Oglala Sioux in western Kansas. Forsyth's greatly outnumbered party took refuge on an island in the nearly dry Arikara Fork of the Republican River. Forsyth's sole advantage was possession of modern repeating carbines. Rapid fire twice turned back the Indians' headlong charges, and the battle ended when a major war chief, Roman Nose, was killed.

Sheridan's winter campaign deployed one column from Fort Bascom, New Mexico, another from Fort Lyon, Colorado, and a third, under Custer, from Fort Dodge, Kansas. They would converge on the Indians' winter camps on the Canadian and Washita Rivers, in Indian Territory. Thanks to a combination of relentless military pressure and the rigors of winter, the Indians submitted to confinement on reservations, and the influence of the Dog Soldiers was forever ended in Kansas.

Modoc War (1872–1873)

The Modocs were a small tribe, numbering no more than 400–500 individuals, living in the rugged Lost River Valley of northern California and southern Oregon. They occupied lava beds along the Lost River, near Tule Lake. Eventually, white settlers coveted even this barren land, and when the Modocs refused to accept life on a reservation, a small-scale but intense war broke out late in 1872. Under a leader known to the whites as Captain Jack, the Modocs repeatedly eluded all army forces sent after them. Unable to dislodge the Modocs, President ULYSSES SIMPSON GRANT appointed a peace commission to meet with them. For part of March 1873 and well into April, the commissioners ineffectually negotiated. On Good Friday, April 11, 1873, Captain Jack, pressured by other warriors, assassinated Major General E. R. S. Canby and another negotiator and wounded a third, then fled with his warriors to the lava beds. The assassination of Canby, the highest-ranking army officer killed in the Indian Wars, moved General Sherman to authorize an all-out campaign against the Modocs, who nevertheless continued to inflict a toll against their pursuers. Still, the continual warfare progressively wore them down, and, on May 28, assisted by a captured Modoc, troops ran to ground Captain Jack, his family, and a number of followers. They were captured on June 3. Captain Jack and three others identified as rebellion ringleaders were tried, convicted, and hanged.

Red River, or Kiowa, War (1874–1875)

The Red River (Kiowa) War was an ambitious army offensive against the Indians of the southern plains, which followed a June 27, 1874, Comanche and Cheyenne raid on a white hunter village at Adobe Walls in the Texas Panhandle and a July 12 Kiowa ambush of Texas Rangers at Lost Valley. Generals John C. Pope (in command of forces in Kansas, New Mexico, parts of Colorado, and Indian Territory) and Christopher C. Augur (commanding Texas and parts of Indian Territory) were ordered to converge on the Staked Plains region of the Texas Panhandle. Colonel Nelson A. Miles, one of Pope's best field commanders, led eight troops of the 6th Cavalry and four companies of the 5th Infantry south from the Canadian River into Indian Territory. As this force of 774 troopers approached the Staked Plains escarpment on August 30, it encountered some 600 Cheyenne. The running battle was fought across 12 miles of the Staked Plains during five hours and culminated in a Cheyenne stand at Tule Canyon. The Indians were exhausted as well as demoralized, but Miles, by this point, also realized that he had insufficient supplies to press the attack further. Reluctantly, he withdrew to resupply his force, destroying abandoned Indian villages as he did so.

Both sides were greatly hampered by drought alternating with torrential rain, but the army kept up the pursuit and the destruction of Indian villages and crops. During the late fall and winter of 1874–75, with their villages in ruins and their people cold and hungry, Kiowas and Cheyennes began to straggle into Forts Sill and Darlington, to accept confinement to reservations. In this way, the war ground to a close.

Apache War (1876–1886)

In 1875–76, an uprising developed among Apache Indians at the San Carlos reservation in Arizona. Victorio (a Warm Springs Apache chief) made the first break from San Carlos on September 2, 1877, leading more than 300 Warm Springs Apaches and a few Chiricahuas out of the reservation. Victorio terrorized the Mexican state of Chihuahua, much of western Texas, southern New Mexico, and Arizona. Mexican and United States forces cooperated in pursuit of Victorio, who managed to elude them for over a year. By the fall of 1880, however, Victorio's warriors began to wear out, but Victorio and a group of diehards united with Geronimo, a Chiricahua who had been leading warriors in resistance to the reservation off and on since 1877. By 1882, the army had defeated various Apache bands and faced only the Chiricahuas and the Warm Springs Apaches, led principally by Geronimo. In September 1882, Brigadier General George Crook began operations against Geronimo, even penetrating far into Mexico in pursuit of him. However, the campaign proved to be long and frustrating, and it was August 1886 before Geronimo and his small band were captured. He and other Apache leaders were imprisoned for a time in Florida, but Geronimo was later allowed to return to a reservation in Indian Territory. Geronimo died, aged 80, at Fort Sill, Oklahoma, in 1909.

Sioux War for the Black Hills (1876–1877)

Provoked by continued incursions into their lands, the Sioux of the northern plains routinely raided settlements in Montana, Wyoming, and Nebraska during the 1870s. In 1874, George Armstrong Custer led a military expedition into the Black Hills and discovered gold. Within a year, in violation of the Treaty of Fort Laramie (April 29, 1868), thousands of prospectors swarmed into the Black Hills, which led to the war of 1876–77. The most notorious battle of this war took place on June 25, 1876, at the Little Bighorn River, where Sioux warriors under Gall and Crazy Horse killed more than 200 members of the 7th Cavalry, including Custer.

The "Custer Massacre" shocked the nation, and Congress not only authorized an increase in the army's strength but also gave the military direct control of the Sioux reservations. After a long campaign, Crazy Horse was confined to a reservation and, on September 5, 1877, was stabbed to death in a scuffle involving soldiers and Indians.

Although the Northern Cheyenne reported to the Cheyenne and Arapaho Agency in Indian Territory during August 1877, they rebelled during fall 1878, but were soon suppressed by a combination of army troops and citizen volunteers. The most

venerable of all Sioux chiefs, Sitting Bull, withdrew into Canada with a small band of followers.

Nez Perce War (1877)

The Nez Perce tribe lived in and about the Wallowa Valley of Washington State. When a portion of the tribe led by Chief Joseph the Younger refused to move to a reservation, army forces under Major General Oliver O. Howard campaigned against them beginning on June 17, 1877. A pattern of pursuit and skirmish developed, covering some 1,700 miles and stretching from June to September 30, when, with 350–400 men, Nelson A. Miles attacked some 650 Nez Perces at the Battle of Bear Paw Mountain. The Indians surrendered on October 5 and were consigned to the Colville Reservation, Washington.

Bannock War (1878)

White incursions into Bannock lands southeast of Boise, Idaho, led to an uprising under Chief Buffalo Horn beginning on May 30, 1878, with the shooting of two white settlers. The chief led about 200 warriors, including Northern Paiutes and Umatillas in addition to Bannocks in raiding southern Idaho. On June 8, civilian volunteers killed the chief in a skirmish near Silver City, southwest of Boise, whereupon the surviving warriors rode to Steens Mountain, in Oregon, to unite with Northern Paiute followers of a militant medicine man named Oytes and a chief called Egan. Some 450 warriors now waged war against a slightly larger number of soldiers led by Howard, who pursued the Bannocks (as the mixed group was indiscriminately dubbed) until September 12, 1878, when a final battle was fought in Wyoming, and the surviving Indians withdrew to a reservation.

Sheepeater War (1879)

Even after Oytes and Egan surrendered, some Bannocks took refuge among the Sheepeaters, a collective name for renegade Shoshonis and Bannocks in the Salmon River Mountains of Idaho. After these Indians raided a prospectors' camp on Loon Creek in May 1879, a troop of the 1st Cavalry was dispatched to track them down. The result was the Sheepeater War, conducted against a mere handful of warriors, perhaps no more than 35 men, but also waged against the inhospitable terrain of the Idaho mountains. The conflict petered out early in October with the surrender of a handful of Sheepeaters and Bannocks.

Ute War (1879)

The Utes of western Colorado and eastern Utah resisted proposed removal to Indian Territory (present-day Oklahoma) and menaced their white Indian agent, Nathan C. Meeker, who called for aid from the army. Major Thomas T. "Tip" Thornburgh, commanding a mixed unit of 153 infantry and cavalrymen, supplemented by an additional 25 civilian volunteers, arrived on the scene, but succeeded only in provoking combat on September 25, in which Thornburgh and others were killed. This triggered a war in which many Indians as well as Meeker and nine other agency employees were killed. In the end, Secretary of the Interior Carl Schurz, an Indian agent named Charles Adams, and an old Ute chief named Ouray managed to negotiate the release of white captives (October 21), and, by 1880, Chief Ouray agreed to lead the Utes to reservations in eastern Utah and southwestern Colorado.

Sioux War (1890–1891)

By the mid 1880s, the major fighting of the Indian Wars had come to an end with almost a quarter of a million Indians confined to reservations. Presiding over the Hunkpapa Sioux at the Standing Rock Reservation on the South Dakota–North Dakota border, Chief Sitting Bull refused to cooperate with the agent in charge and did all he could to avoid contact with the white world. At this time, too, a new Native American religious movement swept the reservations. Whites called it the Ghost Dance, and it foretold of a new world coming, one in which only Indians dwelled and in which buffalo were again plentiful. Some followers of the Ghost Dance, notably the Teton Sioux chiefs Short Bull and Kicking Bear, urged an armed uprising to hasten the coming of this new order.

White authorities became alarmed by the Ghost Dance movement and, on November 20, 1890, cavalry and infantry reinforcements arrived at the Pine Ridge and Rosebud reservations. This served only to prompt some 3,000 Indians to gather on a plateau ("the Stronghold") at the northwest corner of the Pine Ridge Reservation, presumably to prepare resistance. Hoping to preempt this, the Pine Ridge superintendent dispatched 43 reservation policemen to arrest Sitting Bull on December 15, 1890. In a scuffle during the arrest, Sitting Bull was fatally shot, and an uprising seemed inevitable.

In addition to Sitting Bull, General Miles had another Ghost Dance leader to contend with. Big Foot was the highest standing chief of the Miniconjou Sioux, who were living on the Cheyenne River. Unknown to Miles, Big Foot had recently renounced the Ghost Dance, and Miles was also unaware that Chief Red Cloud, a Pine Ridge leader friendly to the whites, had asked Big Foot to come to the reservation to use his influence to persuade the Stronghold party to surrender. Miles knew only that Big Foot was headed for the Stronghold, and he assumed that his intention was to join the other hostiles. Accordingly, Miles deployed troopers across the prairies and badlands to intercept all Miniconjous and, in particular, Big Foot. A squadron of the 7th Cavalry located the chief and about 350 followers on December 28, 1890, camped near a stream called Wounded Knee. By the morning of December 29, 500 soldiers, under Colonel James W. Forsyth, surrounded Big Foot's camp. Four Hotchkiss guns—small, rapid-fire HOWITZERS—were trained on the camp from the surrounding hills. Forsyth was to disarm the Indians and take them to the railroad, so that they could be removed from the "zone of military operations." In the process of disarming them, resistance broke out. Although few of the Indians were now armed, both sides opened fire, and the Indians began to flee. To contain them, troops opened up on the camp with the Hotchkiss guns, firing at the rate of almost a shell a second. In less than an hour the "Battle" of Wounded Knee was over. Big Foot and 153 other Miniconjous were known to have been killed. So many others staggered, limped, or crawled away that it is impossible to determine just how many died. Most authorities believe that 300 of the 350 who had been camped at Wounded Knee Creek lost their lives. Casualties among the 7th Cavalry were 25 killed and 39 wounded, mostly victims of "friendly fire."

The Wounded Knee Massacre prompted "hostile" and hitherto "friendly" Sioux factions to unite in a December 30 ambush of the 7th Cavalry near the Pine Ridge Agency. Elements of the 9th Cavalry came to the rescue, and General Miles subsequently marshaled 3,500 troops (out of a total force of 5,000) to surround the Sioux, who had assembled 15 miles north of the Pine Ridge Agency along White Clay Creek. This show of overwhelming force was sufficient to move the Sioux to surrender on January 15, 1891. This marked the end of the Indian Wars.

indirect fire systems

Indirect fire is fire delivered against a target that cannot be physically seen by the aimer. Currently (2005), the U.S. Army inventory includes the following indirect fire systems.

M-101 105-mm Howitzer

The direct predecessor of the M-101 was the M-1, a weapon designed in the 1920s and used in large quantity during WORLD WAR II as the M-2. The M-101 was replaced by the M-119 105-mm HOWITZER in 1989. The general characteristics of the M-101 include:

Weight: 4,980 lb
Barrel length: 8 ft 5 in
Muzzle velocity: 1,801 fps
Rate of fire: 10 rounds/min maximum
Crew: 8

M-102 105-mm Lightweight Howitzer

This towed howitzer was introduced in 1965 and is used by army airmobile and airborne units. It has replaced the M-101 105-mm howitzer because it is lighter and has greater range. The general characteristics of the weapon include:

Weight: 3,400 lb
Length of barrel: 11 ft 1 in

Muzzle velocity: 1,801 fps
Rate of fire: 10 rounds/min maximum
Range: 16,514 yd
Crew: 8

M-109 Paladin

The M-109—currently designated as the M-109A6—Paladin is a howitzer designed to provide the primary artillery support for armored and mechanized infantry divisions. It was introduced in 1963 as the M-109 and, in its A6 configuration and iteration, is the most technologically advanced self-propelled cannon system in the army inventory. The "A6" version incorporates numerous changes to the standard model to provide improvements to weapon survivability, responsiveness, reliability, availability and maintainability, armament, and terminal effects. The weapon features a fully automated fire-control system, which provides accurate position location, azimuth reference, and on-board ballistic solutions of fire missions. The A6 iteration features a servo-driven, computer-controlled gun drive with manual backup.

Paladin incorporates a number of advanced features. They include, most notably, "shoot and scoot" capability, which significantly improves survivability. The vehicle also incorporates improved ballistic, nuclear, biological, and chemical protection. The weapon is capable of responsive fire. It can fire within 45 seconds from complete stop with on-board communications, remote travel lock, and automated cannon slew capability. The Paladin is capable of highly accurate fire controlled by on-board POSNAV and technical fire control. The A6 iteration is capable of extended range: 33,000 yards, using HE RAP and M-203 propellant. This latest version of the weapon also offers increased reliability thanks to an improved engine, track, and diagnostics. Additionally, the weapon has been upgraded with global positioning system-aided self-location, the M-93 Muzzle Velocity System, and a commercial, off-the-shelf-based computerprocessor.

General specifications of the Paladin include:

Maximum unassisted range: 24,000 yd
Maximum assisted range: 33,000 yd

Minimum range: 4,375 yd

Maximum rate of fire: 4 rounds/min for 3 minutes

Sustained rate of fire: 1 round/min, depending on the use of thermal warning devices

Maximum speed: 38 mph (highway)

Weight, empty: 56,400 lb

Weight, combat loaded: approximately 63,615 lb

Crew: 4 (accompanying M-992 FAASV-5)

M-114 155-mm Howitzer

This towed weapon is an update of the M-2 of World War II and was the principal 155-mm howitzer for both the army and USMC until the introduction of the M-198 155-mm howitzer during the 1980s. The venerable design dates to 1919. The gun's general characteristics include:

Weight: 16,755 lb

Barrel length: 12 ft 5 in

Muzzle velocity: 1,850 fps

Rate of fire: 40 rounds/hour

Range: 15,914 yd; in its 39-caliber reconfiguration, 33,246 yd

Crew: 11

M-119 105-mm Howitzer

This is an American-built version of the British L118 Light Gun. While it has not fully replaced the M-102 105-mm lightweight howitzer in army air-mobile units, it has replaced the M-101 105-mm howitzer, and airborne and light infantry units have widely adopted it. General characteristics of the weapon include:

Weight: 4,100 lb

Length of barrel: 9 ft 1 in

Muzzle velocity: 1,801 fps

Rate of fire: 8 rounds/min maximum

Range: 21,325 yd

Crew: 10

M-120/121 120-mm Mortar

The M-120 is a towed weapon, and the M-121 is mounted on the M-106 armored personnel carrier. Both were purchased from Israel (K6 and TT6 mortars) and have the following general characteristics:

Weight: 319 lb

Length: 5 ft 9 in

Rate of fire: 19–20 rounds/min maximum

Range: 7,918 yd maximum

Crew: 4

M-198 Towed Howitzer

Introduced into the army inventory in 1979, the M-198 Towed Howitzer is designed to provide destructive, suppressive, and protective indirect and direct field artillery fire in support of combined arms operations. A 155-mm medium-artillery system, this towed howitzer provides direct support fires on an interim basis to the Stryker Brigade Combat Teams and direct general support fires to light and special-purpose forces, such as airborne and air assault units. The weapon replaces the older M-114 155-mm howitzer, which was first fielded in World War II. The newer weapon provides major improvements in lethality, range, reliability, availability, emplacement, and movement.

The M-198 is intended to be towed by a five-ton truck; however, the versatile weapon system can also be dropped by parachute or transported by a CH-47 Chinook helicopter or C-130 Hercules transport aircraft.

The carriage of the M-198 has a fully retractable suspension system and features a top carriage that can be rotated 180 degrees. This decreases overall length to facilitate shipment or storage. The fire control equipment fitted to the weapon may be used by one or two crewmen for direct or indirect fire. The gunner on the left side of the weapon controls left and right (traversing) settings, and the assistant gunner, stationed on the right side, controls up and down (elevation) settings.

General specifications of the weapon system include:

Length: 40.7 ft, in tow; 36.2 ft, when in firing position

Width: 9.2 ft, in tow

Height: 9.5 ft, in tow

Weight: 16,000 lb

Crew: 10

Range, standard: 24,500 yd

Range, rocket-assisted: 30,000 yd
Maximum rate of fire: 4 rounds/min for first 2 min
Sustained rate of fire: 2 rounds/min
Ammunition: The weapon fires all current 155-mm NATO-standard ammunition, including high explosive (HE), smoke (HC, WP), dual-purpose, improved conventional munitions (DPICM), the family of scatterable mines (FASCAM), cannon-launched guided projectiles (Copperhead), and illumination. The standard HE round weighs 95 pounds.
Manufacturer: Rock Island Arsenal

M-224 60-mm Mortar

This mortar was developed beginning in 1970 and was first deployed in 1981. Initially, the army acquired 1,590 of the weapon. It is lightweight and reliable, firing an M-720 high-explosive round as well as other rounds. General characteristics include:

Weight: 46.5 lb (conventional); 18 lb (handheld)
Rate of fire: 30 rounds/min for 4 min
Range: 3,817 yd (conventional); 984 yd (handheld)

M-252 81-mm Mortar

This was purchased from a British manufacturer for use by the army and the U.S. Marine Corps and fires all M-29 projectiles as well as M-821 high-explosive bombs. The mortar is designed to be vehicle-mounted. The first were delivered in 1987.

General characteristics include:

Weight: 91 lb
Length: 4 ft 6 in
Rate of fire: 33 rounds/min maximum
Range: 6,124 yd with M-29 ammunition
Crew: 5

M-270 MLRS Self-Propelled Loader/Launcher (SPLL)

The MLRS is an all-weather, indirect, area-fire weapon system intended to strike counterfire, air defense, armored formations, and other targets. The primary missions of MLRS are the suppression, neutralization, and destruction of threat fire

The M-270 MLRS Self-Propelled Loader/Launcher *(U.S. Army)*

support and forward area air defense targets. The army uses a modified MLRS to launch the ARMY TACTICAL MISSILE SYSTEM (ATACMS).

MLRS is intended to complement cannon artillery by providing large amounts of firepower in a short time against such targets as enemy artillery, air defense systems, mechanized units, and personnel. A key element of MLRS is "shoot and scoot" capability. Unlike emplaced artillery, the highly mobile MLRS can quickly move to avoid counterattack.

The MLRS M-270 is derived from the M-2 Bradley Fighting Vehicle. The basic M-270 is a full-tracked, self-propelled launcher/loader designed to launch 12 tactical rockets. For general characteristics of the Bradley, see M-2 Bradley Fighting Vehicle.

Industrial Operations Command (IOC)

IOC is the largest subordinate command of the U.S. ARMY MATERIEL COMMAND. It maintains, revamps, and ships the army's weapon systems, vehicles, and ammunition. IOC headquarters is at Rock Island Arsenal, Illinois, with installations and activities spread across 28 states and 11 countries.

Combat Equipment Group-Europe stores prepositioned materiel at sites in Belgium, Italy, Luxembourg, and the Netherlands. In Italy, Combat Equipment Battalion-South and its 24th Combat Equipment Company at Leghorn Army Depot, Livorno, maintain enough prepositioned equipment and ammunition to outfit a heavy brigade of two armor and two mechanized infantry battalions.

The Lake City Army Ammunition Plant, near Kansas City, Missouri, produces all of the army's small-arms ammunition, and the Crane Army Ammunition Activity near Bloomington, Indiana, manufactures other munitions, from flares to 40,000-pound shock charges. The Rock Island Arsenal, a three-and-a-half-mile-long island in the Mississippi River, is the world's largest weapons factory, which produces an estimated $100 million worth of army equipment annually. The Watervliet (New York) Arsenal produces all of the army's M-1A1 Abrams and A-2 tank guns, and the Let-terkenny (Pennsylvania) Army Depot maintains tactical missiles.

infantry

Historically the "Queen of Battle," the infantry is any unit or body of soldiers who fight on foot. In the USMC and the army, infantry constitute the major force. Most infantry troops are riflemen. "Infantry" is also the name of the oldest and most basic combat branch of the army, its mission to gain and retain ground and "to close with the enemy by fire and maneuver to destroy or capture him, and to repel his assault by fire, close combat, and counterattack."

Traditionally, infantrymen moved on foot. Today, however, they move by land, sea, or air, and they may go into a fight on foot, by parachute, helicopter, assault boat, or aboard such conveyances as the M-2 Bradley Fighting Vehicle. Headquarters for the branch is at Fort Benning, Georgia.

Information Technology Laboratory (ITL)

The ITL is the premier Department of Defense laboratory for the development and application of advanced information technology for military engineering and army civil works mission areas. The laboratory supports the research missions of the U.S. ARMY CORPS OF ENGINEERS, U.S. Army Engineer Research and Development Center (ERDC), other corps activities, the army generally, the Department of Defense, and other agencies by conceiving, planning, managing, conducting, and coordinating research and development in high-performance computing, computer-aided, and interdisciplinary engineering, computer science, information technology, and instrumentation systems.

The ITL began as a small Automated Data Processing Center in the U.S. Army Engineer Waterways Experiment Station, and in 1986 it became a full-fledged laboratory. In 1999, it consolidated with seven other U.S. Army Corps of Engineers laboratories.

Integrated Materiel Management Center (IMMC)

The IMMC, located at the Sparkman Center of the Redstone Arsenal, Alabama, provides logistics support worldwide to users of the army's missile systems and aviation. Collaborating with project executive officers and program managers, warfighters, and industry, the IMMC develops, acquires, fields, and sustains worldwide logistics support to ensure the readiness of the army's weapon systems for any operation.

Inter-American Defense Board Medal

See DECORATIONS AND MEDALS.

J

Japanese-American soldiers in World War II

At the time of the attack on Pearl Harbor, December 7, 1941, some 120,000 persons of immediate Japanese descent were residents in the continental United States. Of these, about 80,000 had been born in this country and were citizens. Within four days after Pearl Harbor, the Federal Bureau of Investigation (FBI) arrested and detained 1,370 Japanese Americans as "dangerous enemy aliens," despite their being American citizens. On January 5, 1942, U.S. draft boards summarily classified all Japanese-American selective service registrants as enemy aliens, and many Japanese Americans who were already serving were discharged or restricted to menial labor duties. On January 23, Japanese-American soldiers and sailors on the U.S. mainland were segregated out of their units.

On January 20, 1942, Leland Ford, a congressman from the district encompassing Los Angeles, sent a telegram to Secretary of State Cordell Hull, asking that all Japanese Americans be removed from the West Coast, and, on January 29, U.S. Attorney General Francis Biddle established "prohibited zones," areas forbidden to all enemy aliens. Early the next month, the army designated 12 "restricted areas" in which enemy aliens were to be subject to a curfew from 9 P.M. to 6 A.M. and in which they were permitted to travel only to and from work, never going more than five miles from

their homes. By February 19, 1942, the FBI held 2,192 Japanese Americans, and, on that day, President Franklin D. Roosevelt signed Executive Order 9066, authorizing the secretary of war to define military areas "from which any or all persons may be excluded as deemed necessary or desirable." This prompted Secretary of War Henry Stimson to order Lieutenant General John DeWitt to effect what was termed the "evacuation" of Japanese Americans, citizens and noncitizens alike, Nisei (those born in the United States) and Issei (immigrants), living within 200 miles of the Pacific Coast. In all, some 110,000 persons were moved to internment camps in California, Idaho, Utah, Arizona, Wyoming, Colorado, and Arkansas.

Although conditions in the camps were hardly inhumane, they were spartan; many internees suffered significant to catastrophic financial hardship and loss, and many more regarded the evacuation as profoundly humiliating as well as a betrayal by their country. During their confinement, some 1,200 young Japanese men secured release from the camps by enlisting in the army. The overwhelming majority of these young men were segregated in the 442nd Regimental Combat Team, which, activated on February 1, 1943, also included about 10,000 Japanese-Hawaiian volunteers. (Japanese Hawaiians had not been subject to Executive Order 9066.) The 442nd was sent to Europe and fought valiantly in Italy, France, and Germany, emerging from the war as the most highly decorated unit of its size and length of service in American military history.

In the meantime, on February 25, 1942, the all-Nisei Varsity Victory Volunteers (known as the "Triple V") was formed in Hawaii as part of the 34th Combat Engineers Regiment. However, on the West Coast of the mainland, the War Department discontinued the induction of Japanese Americans as of March 30, 1942.

Shortly before Pearl Harbor, on November 1, 1941, the War Department had opened a secret language school under the control of the Fourth Army in San Francisco. The school was staffed by four Nisei instructors and had 60 students, of whom 58 were Nisei. These individuals would make up the first class of the Military Intelligence Language School. During the war, many of the school's graduates were sent to the Aleutian Islands and the South Pacific as Japanese linguists and as intelligence operatives. The language school was moved from San Francisco to Camp Savage, Minnesota, on May 25 in compliance with the order excluding all Japanese Americans from the West Coast.

On May 26, 1942, General GEORGE CATLETT MARSHALL established the Hawaii Provisional Infantry Battalion, made up of Japanese Americans from the Hawaii National Guard. On June 5, the battalion left Honolulu for San Francisco and, on the 12th, it was activated in the REGULAR ARMY as the 100th Infantry Battalion. Just five days later, the War Department announced that it would not accept for service any Japanese or persons of Japanese extraction, regardless of citizenship status. Before the end of the month, however, on June 26, army policy makers recommended the formation of a Board of Military Utilization of U.S. Citizens of Japanese Ancestry, to determine whether a Japanese American unit should be sent to fight in Europe. In October, Elmer Davis, director of the Office of War Information, recommended to President Roosevelt that Japanese Americans be allowed to enlist.

While army policy shifted back and forth, 26 members of the 100th Infantry Battalion were sent to Ship Island and Cat Island off the Mississippi Gulf Coast to be used to train dogs to recognize and attack Japanese. This assignment was based on what white officers believed was the unique scent of the Japanese.

On February 1, 1943, the army acted on the question of Japanese-American enlistment by activating the 442nd Regimental Combat Team (RCT), an all Japanese-American force. The members of the Triple V unit formed the core of the 442nd, which began training in Mississippi in May.

Although the 442nd was destined to become the most celebrated Japanese-American unit, it was not the first to see action. On September 2, 1943, the 100th Infantry Battalion landed in Oran, North Africa, and was assigned to guard supply trains from Casablanca to Tunisia. Later, the unit was assigned to the 34TH INFANTRY DIVISION and, on September 22, 1943, landed on the beach at Salerno, Italy, as part of the 133rd Infantry Regiment, 34th Infantry Division. In November, the battalion participated in an offensive against the Germans crossing the Volturno River south of Naples, and, in January 1944, it fought in the Battle of Cassino. From this engagement, in March, the battalion landed at Anzio.

Generally, army policy was to use Japanese-American combat troops exclusively in the European theater; however, in late 1943, 14 Nisei were assigned to Merrill's Marauders, the famed commando unit operating in North Burma. In April 1944, the 1399th Engineering Construction Battalion, exclusively a Japanese-American unit, was formed to work on noncombat construction and maintenance projects in Hawaii. Throughout much of the Pacific and Asian war, Japanese-American graduates of the Military Intelligence Language School were deployed, typically in the front lines, as interpreters, translators, and intelligence operators.

The 442nd Regimental Combat Team finally shipped out of Hampton Roads, Virginia, bound for Europe on May 1, 1944, while the 100th continued to fight in Italy. Arriving in Italy on June 26, 1944, the 442nd RCT was assigned to the Fifth Army and attached to the 34th Division. At this point, the 100th Infantry Battalion was attached to the 442nd and, thus configured, the 442nd RCT was committed to battle near Belvedere, Italy. On July 27, 1944, General MARK WAYNE CLARK, commanding the Fifth Army, personally presented the Distinguished Presidential Unit Citation to the 100th Infantry Battalion for action at Belvedere.

The 442nd's Antitank Company was detached from the RCT and assigned to the 1st Airborne Task Force for glider training. On August 15, 1944, the unit participated in the invasion of southern France, then rejoined the 442nd on October 11.

The 442nd left Italy for France on September 26, 1944, and, as part of the Seventh Army, fought in the Vosges Mountains. In March 1945, the 442nd left France to return to Italy, where it joined the all African-American 92nd Infantry Division. The following month, the 442nd made a spectacular surprise attack on Nazi mountainside positions, breaking through the infamous Gothic Line in a single day. The unit then pursued the retreating Germans, driving them up the Italian coast to Genoa and Turin.

Detached from the 442nd, the 522nd Field Artillery Battalion participated in the liberation of Jewish prisoners of the Landsberg-Kaufering and Dachau death camps.

After the German surrender on May 2, 1945, the 442nd participated in occupation duty, then returned to the United States in July 1946. On July 15, in Washington, D.C., President Harry S. Truman presented the 442nd RCT with a Presidential Unit Citation. "You fought not only the enemy," the president remarked, "but you fought prejudice— and you have won."

In addition to the Japanese-American men who rendered distinguished service in WORLD WAR II, beginning in October 1943, Japanese-American women were accepted into the WOMEN'S ARMY CORPS (WAC). Some 300 would serve during the war and immediately afterward.

Joint Chiefs of Staff (JCS)

JCS is a statutory agency within the Department of Defense consisting of O-10-grade members, including a chairman and vice chairman, the chiefs of staff of the air force and army, the chief of naval operations, and the commandant of the marine corps. The JCS advises the secretary of defense on various military matters. Originally established in 1942, during WORLD WAR II, JCS was reestablished in 1949.

Joint Meritorious Unit Award   See DECORATIONS AND MEDALS.

Joint POW/MIA Accounting Command (JPAC)

The JPAC is located at Oahu, Hawaii, and was activated on October 1, 2003, with the mission of achieving the fullest possible accounting of all Americans missing as a result of the nation's previous conflicts. The highest priority of JPAC is the return of any living Americans who remain prisoners of war.

The JPAC was created from the merger of the 30-year-old U.S. Army Central Identification Laboratory, Hawaii, and the 11-year-old Joint Task Force-Full Accounting. The command is jointly manned by personnel from the U.S. Army, USAF, USN, and USMC, in addition to civilian experts. The laboratory portion of the command, the Central Identification Laboratory (CIL), is the world's largest forensic anthropology laboratory.

WORLD WAR II produced some 78,000 American service members reported as missing, of whom about 35,000 are deemed recoverable. The KOREAN WAR produced 8,100 missing, the VIETNAM WAR 1,800, and cold war conflicts 120. One serviceman is missing from the PERSIAN GULF WAR. In an effort to account for these individuals, the JPAC is organized to support five main areas: analysis, negotiations, investigations, recovery, and identification.

Analysis begins with historians and analysts gathering information from multiple sources, primarily in archives. A loss incident case file is created for each unaccounted service member. Analysts provide the operations and laboratory sections of JPAC with all available information regarding the loss, and an investigative or recovery team deploys.

Negotiations are often necessary with representatives of foreign governments, including Russia, Germany, France, Vietnam, Cambodia, Laos, North Korea, China, Papua New Guinea, Burma, and other nations to ensure positive in-country conditions are created for JPAC investigative and recovery operations.

Investigations are carried out by field investigative teams, which deploy to locations around the world to attain three primary goals: to document and survey potential recovery sites, to generate new leads that may result in future recoveries, and to assist in the planning of future recovery selections. JPAC maintains six investigative teams consisting of four to nine members with specialized skills, including a team leader, assistant team leader, analyst, linguist, and a medic. In some cases an anthropologist, explosive ordnance technician, and/or a life support technician augments the team.

Recovery proceeds in all cases recommended for recovery. The recovery process gets under way after adequate information has been collected and analyzed. JPAC has 18 recovery teams, 10 of which are dedicated to those missing from the Vietnam War, five teams dedicated to the Korean War, and three teams to recovering missing Americans from World War II, the cold war, and the Persian Gulf War. A typical recovery team size is 10 to 14 personnel, and it is commanded by the team leader and includes a team sergeant (typically an army sergeant first class trained in mortuary affairs) and a civilian forensic anthropologist. Additional team members may include a linguist, medic, life support technician, forensic photographer, explosive ordnance disposal technician, and several mortuary affairs specialists.

Identification is made when the remains recovered are brought back to the laboratory. Identification techniques include the entire range of forensic methods, including analysis of skeletal and dental remains, mitochondrial DNA (mtDNA), material evidence, personal effects, and life-support equipment.

Joint Readiness Training Center (JRTC)

JRTC began operations in 1987 at Fort Chaffee, Arkansas, and, since 1993, has been headquartered at Fort Polk, Louisiana. As the name implies, the JRTC emphasizes integration of training among the services, especially the army and USAF. The emphasis is on combined arms training involving airlift, close-air support, and aerial resupply. Special operations soldiers, including SPECIAL FORCES and RANGERS, receive joint training here.

Joint Service Achievement Medal   See

DECORATIONS AND MEDALS.

Joint Service Commendation Medal   See

DECORATIONS AND MEDALS.

Joint Service Lightweight Integrated Suit Technology   See NUCLEAR-BIOLOGICAL-CHEMICAL DEFENSE EQUIPMENT.

Joint STARS E-8C

The E-8C Joint Surveillance Target Attack Radar System (Joint STARS) is a joint USAF–Army platform for airborne battle management and command and control. Joint STARS is an E-8C aircraft, a military modification of the Boeing 707-300 commercial airliner, equipped with a special suite of radar, communications, operations, and control subsystems designed to develop an understanding of the enemy situation in support of attack operations and targeting.

The E-8C is equipped with a large radome under the forward fuselage that houses a side-looking phased-array radar antenna, the heart of the surveillance system. The E-8C can fly a mission profile for nine hours without refueling, and it is capable of in-flight refueling. All information gathered is relayed in near-real time to the army's common ground stations via a secure jam-resistant surveillance and control data link.

Joint Tactical Ground Station (JTAGS)

These units are designated as AIR DEFENSE ARTILLERY Detachments and are assigned the mission of providing a strategically and tactically deployable, in-theater capability to receive and process defense support program (DSP) sensor information about theater ballistic missiles (TBM) and other infrared events of interest. JTAGS are assigned to a joint task force or a theater.

A JTAG unit provides two joint tactical ground station sections capable of independent operations at separate locations within a theater. The sections furnish in-theater missile warning data and real-time warning and alerting data for dissemination to in-theater tactical forces and population centers.

Joint Task Force (JTF)

A JTF is composed of assigned or attached elements of the army, USN, USN, or USMC, and the USAF, or two or more of these services to operate in conjunction as ordered by the Secretary of Defense or the appropriate military commander.

Judge Advocate General's Corps

The army entrusts its legal affairs to this special branch, which is staffed by officers who hold law degrees and which provides legal services for the army and its soldiers. Judge advocates serve as prosecutors and defense attorneys for criminal trials, and practice international, operation, labor, contract, environmental, tort, and administrative law. The Judge Advocate General's Corps is responsible for administering the Uniform Code of Military Justice.

Junior Reserve Officers Training Corps (JROTC)

Administered by the ROTC CADET COMMAND, Junior Reserve Officers Training Corps is the high school version of the college-level ROTC program. JROTC prepares high school students for military leadership roles as well as making them aware of their rights, responsibilities, and privileges as American citizens. JROTC is a four-year curriculum.

K

King Air 90   See AIRCRAFT.

Knox, Henry (1750–1806) *U.S. Army general*
Knox was a general in the AMERICAN REVOLUTION who is considered the father of army artillery and was the principal founder of the UNITED STATES MILITARY ACADEMY. Born in Boston, Henry Knox was a bookseller who joined the Massachusetts militia in 1768 and the CONTINENTAL ARMY in 1775. He became colonel of the Continental Regiment of

Henry Knox, father of U.S. Army artillery and of the United States Military Academy   *(Arttoday)*

Artillery on November 17 of that year. Knox managed to transport some 60 captured British artillery pieces (weighing about 120,000 pounds, with shot) by sledge over 300 miles from Fort Ticonderoga, New York, through the snow to Cambridge, Massachusetts (December 5, 1775–January 25, 1776). This action was instrumental in driving the British from Boston (April 19, 1775–May 17, 1776), and the captured guns became the core of American artillery in the Revolution.

Knox's regiment fought at Long Island (August 27, 1776) and covered Washington's long retreat through New York and New Jersey. Knox's artillery played a key role in Patriot victories at Trenton on December 26 and at Princeton on January 3, 1777. Following the Trenton victory, Knox was promoted to brigadier general.

During January–May 1777, with his army in winter quarters, Knox established the Springfield Arsenal in Springfield, Massachusetts, and, at Morristown, New Jersey, the Academy Artillery School, direct precursor of the United States Military Academy.

When active combat recommenced, Knox fought at the Battle of the Brandywine on September 11, but drew criticism for his role in the lost Battle of Germantown on October 4. However, at Monmouth Courthouse (June 28, 1778) and at Yorktown (May–October 17, 1781), it was clear that he had trained his artillerymen well. Triumphs here were crucial to the outcome of the war.

On March 22, 1782, Knox became the youngest major general in the army and, on August 29, was appointed the first commandant of the new military academy at West Point. Indeed, Knox is generally credited with having founded the academy.

When Washington left the Continental army to become president of the United States, Knox replaced him as commander in chief of the army. He was appointed first U.S. secretary of war under Washington and served from September 12, 1789, to December 31, 1794.

Knox retired to his estate at Thomaston, Maine, in 1795, but he accepted an appointment as major general during the crisis with France in 1798.

Korean Service Medal   See DECORATIONS AND MEDALS.

Korean War (1950–1953)

At 4 A.M. (local time), June 25, 1950, the North Korean People's Army (NKPA) of Communist-controlled North Korea (Democratic Republic of Korea, or DRK) crossed the 38th parallel to invade U.S.-allied, pro-Western South Korea (Republic of Korea, or ROK). The main invading force advanced on Seoul, the South Korean capital, about 35 miles below the parallel, while smaller forces moved down the center of the Korean Peninsula and along the east coast. Inferior South Korean forces retreated in great disorder before the advance, and the North Koreans soon took Seoul. In response, President Harry S. Truman ordered General DOUGLAS MACARTHUR, commander of the U.S. Far East Command, to supply the ROK with equipment and ammunition, the ROK army having abandoned much of its supplies in the retreat.

The outbreak of the Korean War put the United States in an extraordinarily difficult position, committed to containing communist aggression without escalating Korea into a major war involving the Soviets and the Communist Chinese. Truman ordered the U.S. Seventh Fleet to protect Taiwan in anticipation of an attempted Chinese attack against the Chinese Nationalists there. The president also directed MacArthur to make air and naval strikes against North Korean positions below the 38th parallel. On June 30, he authorized MacArthur to use all available U.S. forces to aid the ROK. In the post–WORLD WAR II rush to demobilize, all that was available were units of the Eighth U.S. Army as well as the 29th Regimental Combat Team, units that were understrength and not fully combat ready. Much the same was the case with the Far East Air Force and the modest naval forces in the area. Nevertheless, Truman obtained a United Nations sanction for action to contain the northern aggression, and he named MacArthur commander of U.S. and UN forces.

Army troops began arriving in Korea just six days after the June 25 invasion. By this time, the NKPA had crossed the Han River *south* of Seoul and was still on the move. By July 3, Kimpo Airfield and the port of Inchon were in communist hands. Deciding that he had no time to consolidate his forces for a massed attack, MacArthur deployed a unit designated Task Force Smith just above the southern port city of Pusan on July 5. The NKPA pushed the task force into a disorganized retreat, whereupon MacArthur deployed three more units, also to no avail. By July 13, the NKPA had pushed ROK and U.S. forces to Taejon, in south central South Korea. MacArthur rushed to build up forces in Japan. Two divisions were moved to South Korea on July 18, but Taejon was lost to the NKPA on July 20.

Although the defeats were serious, MacArthur understood that, in advancing so far and so fast, the NKPA had dangerously stretched its lines of communication and supply. The USAF began interdicting these supply lines, and a naval blockade also proved effective. Now Lieutenant General Walton H. Walker, commander of the EIGHTH U.S. ARMY, resolved to make a stand along a line north of Pusan, the 140-mile-long "Pusan perimeter," extending in an arc from the Korea Strait to the Sea of Japan. Walker's defense proved very costly to the vulnerable NKPA and bought MacArthur the time he needed to build up forces sufficient for an offensive thrust.

MacArthur designed a high-risk amphibious assault at Inchon, a position *north* of the enemy, which would allow U.S. forces to squeeze the NKPA between the Eighth Army and the Inchon invaders. The problem was that Inchon was subject to extremely hazardous tides and other adverse natural conditions. Many experts advised that a landing here was virtually impossible. Nevertheless, on September 15, 1950, the landing was made with great success and is generally considered the tactical masterpiece of MacArthur's military career. Within two weeks, Seoul was once again in ROK hands, and the NKPA lines were blocked. During September 16–23, General Walker's Eighth Army began to fight its way out of the Pusan perimeter, meeting very heavy resistance at first, but ultimately forcing the NKPA to withdraw. The Eighth Army pursued it, meeting up with the landing force on September 26, and driving the NKPA northward. It was neutralized as a fighting force in South Korea.

After the Inchon triumph, MacArthur secured permission to cross the 38th parallel and invade North Korea. By the 19th, I Corps, Eighth Army, had cleared Pyongyang, the North Korean capital, and, by October 24, I Corps was just 50 miles outside of Manchuria. ROK forces were also now positioned close to the Chinese border.

When China threatened to intervene, President Truman conferred with MacArthur, who declared with great assurance that the Chinese threats were empty. By the end of October, however, it became clear that the Chinese had, in fact, come to the aid of North Korea, and, on November 25, 1950, some 300,000 Chinese troops crossed the Yalu River into North Korea, beginning a drive that pushed U.S. and other United Nations forces back into South Korea. Once again, Seoul fell to the Communists.

General MacArthur clamored for authority to expand the war into China itself. The Truman administration sought to limit the war, even to the point of withdrawing from the Korean Peninsula, should that become necessary. MacArthur publicly opposed this. Truman ordered him and MATTHEW BUNKER RIDGWAY, commander of the Eighth Army, to begin a slow and methodical offensive—dubbed the "meatgrinder" by frontline G.I.s—on January 25, 1951. This brutal but limited approach regained Seoul by the middle of March 1951, and, by the 21st, UN troops were back at the 38th parallel, where they halted. The UN member nations now agreed that securing South Korea below the 38th parallel was an acceptable outcome of the war.

When Truman informed MacArthur that he would announce willingness to commence negotiations with the Chinese and North Koreans on the basis of current positions, the general preempted Truman's announcement by publicly declaring that, if the UN would expand the conflict to North Korea's coastal areas and interior strongholds, the Chinese would realize that they were at serious risk of suffering military defeat. Then, on April 5, 1951, Republican House leader Joseph W. Martin read into the *Congressional Record* a letter from MacArthur stating the necessity of opening up a second front against China itself. This act of insubordination moved Truman to relieve Douglas MacArthur as commander on April 11, 1951, and replace him with Ridgway, who, in turn, gave command of the Eighth Army to Lieutenant General James A. Van Fleet.

On April 22, a new Chinese–North Korean offensive was launched, but was skillfully repulsed by Van Fleet at great cost to Communist forces. After this, the Communists adopted a new strategy of stealthy hit-and-run attacks by small units for the purpose of wearing down U.S. and UN forces. Van Fleet responded by taking the offensive and advancing on May 22, 1951. He was, however, ordered to halt and hold his position because UN allies feared the possibility of Soviet entry into the war. Van Fleet reluctantly consolidated his position just north of the 38th parallel.

At this point, cease-fire talks began, but they were destined to drag on for the next two years, during which time inconclusive combat continued. An armistice was finally signed on July 27, 1953, on the basis of a division of North and South Korea along the 38th parallel.

How many Chinese and North Korean troops were killed in the Korean War is unknown, but estimates range between 1.5 and 2 million, in addition to at least 1 million civilians. The UN command lost 88,000 killed, of whom 23,300 were American. Many more were wounded. As of 2005, Korea remains divided, and friction with North Korea now believed to possess some nuclear weapons is an ever-present danger.

Kosovo Campaign Medal   See DECORATIONS AND MEDALS.

Krueger, Walter (1881–1967) *U.S. Army general*

Krueger holds a place in army history as one of the great tactician-planners of WORLD WAR II. A native of Platow, West Prussia, he immigrated to the United States with his family in 1889. Raised in Cincinnati, Ohio, he dropped out of high school to enlist as a volunteer in the army during the SPANISH-AMERICAN WAR (1898), then joined the REGULAR ARMY in mid-1899. He was dispatched to the Philippines during the insurrection there (1899–1903) and was promoted to second lieutenant in the 30th Infantry in June 1901. Krueger attended Infantry and Cavalry School, graduating in 1906, then went on to the COMMAND AND GENERAL STAFF COLLEGE, from which he graduated in 1907. After a second tour in the Philippines during 1908–09, he served on the faculty of the Army Service School from 1909 to 1912 and, during this period, translated several German works on tactics, becoming an authority on the German army and its military practices.

Krueger was promoted to captain in 1916 and served under General JOHN JOSEPH PERSHING during the punitive expedition against Mexico's Pancho Villa from March 1916 to February 1917. He was sent to France during WORLD WAR I in February 1918 and attended the General Staff College at Langres, becoming assistant chief of operations for the 26th Division after graduation. Krueger transferred to the 84TH DIVISION and became chief of staff of the Tank Corps during the Meuse-Argonne offensive in October.

Krueger remained in France after the armistice as chief of staff for VI Corps, then became chief of staff for IV Corps in Germany. He held the temporary rank of colonel, but reverted to captain when he returned to the United States in July 1919. Krueger graduated from the U.S. ARMY WAR COLLEGE in 1921 and was assigned to the War Plans Division of the General Staff, where he served from 1923 to 1925. In 1926, he graduated from the Naval War College and taught there from 1928 to 1932, when he was promoted to colonel. Four years later came promotion to brigadier general and appointment as assistant chief of staff for war plans. Krueger left this staff post in 1938 to assume command of 16th Brigade at Fort Meade, Maryland. Promoted to major general in February 1939, he was assigned command of the 2nd Division, and then VIII Staff Corps in October 1940. Promoted to temporary lieutenant general, Krueger was appointed commander of the Third Army and Southern Defense Command in May 1941. Once World War II began, the Sixth Army was activated under his command, and he took it to Australia in January 1943, commanding it through a series of combat operations in the Southwest Pacific theater under General DOUGLAS MACARTHUR. Krueger had charge of the landings on Kiriwina and Woodlark Islands on June 30, 1943, then directed the invasion of New Britain from December 15, 1943, to March 1944. This invasion was followed by operations on the Admiralty Islands and along the northern coast of New Guinea during February–August 1944. Krueger was in command during the seizure of Morotai, the last of the islands taken before the landings in the Philippines in October.

Krueger directed the landings on Leyte on October 20, beginning the process that saw the return of U.S. forces to the Philippines. He was in charge of landings on Mindoro (December 15) and on Luzon (January 9, 1945). Fighting in central Luzon stretched from February to August. In March, Krueger was promoted to general, just after the fall of Manila to U.S. troops on March 14. Krueger's men drove the remnants of Japanese resistance into the mountains of northeastern

Luzon and liberated most of the island by late June.

Krueger remained in the Pacific after the surrender of Japan, leading the Sixth Army in occupation duty on Honshu in September 1945, but he retired less than a year later, in July 1946.

Kuwait Liberation Medal—Government of Kuwait   See DECORATIONS AND MEDALS.

Kuwait Liberation Medal—Kingdom of Saudi Arabia   See DECORATIONS AND MEDALS.

L

laboratories

The U.S. Army operates 15 major laboratories that conduct research into many aspects of warfighting. Their purpose is to advance the state of the military art to enable the army to carry out its various missions more effectively and, where appropriate, even to define new missions.

> *Air Maneuver Battle Lab* (AMBL)
> *Army Research Laboratory* (ARL), Adelphi, Maryland
> *Battle Command Battle Laboratory*—Fort Gordon
> *Battle Command Battle Laboratory*—Fort Huachuca
> BATTLE COMMAND BATTLE LABORATORY—FORT LEAVENWORTH
> BENÉT LABS
> *Central Identification Laboratory* (see JOINT POW/MIA ACCOUNTING COMMAND)
> COASTAL AND HYDRAULICS LABORATORY (CHL)
> COLD REGIONS RESEARCH AND ENGINEERING LABORATORY (CRREL)
> *Combat Service Support Battle Lab*
> *Construction Engineering Research Laboratory*
> *Depth and Simultaneous Attack Battle Laboratory* (DSABL)
> ENVIRONMENTAL LABORATORY (EL)
> GEOTECHNICAL AND STRUCTURES LABORATORY
> INFORMATION TECHNOLOGY LABORATORY (ITL)
> TOPOGRAPHIC ENGINEERING CENTER (TEC)

Landstuhl Regional Medical Center, Heidelberg, Germany

Landstuhl Regional Medical Center is located at Landstuhl Post, a permanent U.S. military installation in the German state of Rheinland-Pfalz, 11 kilometers west of Kaiserslautern and five kilometers south of Ramstein Air Base. The hospital is the largest American hospital outside of the United States, and it is the only American tertiary-care hospital in Europe. Landstuhl provides primary and tertiary care, hospitalization, and treatment for more than 52,000 American military personnel and their families. The center also provides specialized care for more than 250,000 additional American military personnel and their families in the European theater.

Specialties unique to the European theater include hematology/oncology, pediatric cardiology, rheumatology, burn stabilization, neurosurgery, nuclear medicine, addiction treatment facility, neonatal intensive care, and magnetic resonance imaging. Half the Landstuhl staff are army personnel, 15 percent air force, and 35 percent civilian. The hospital has 162 beds and neonatal bassinets, with an expansion capability in excess of 310 beds.

As of 2005, Landstuhl was providing medical treatment to casualties injured during Operation Enduring Freedom in Afghanistan and Operation Iraqi Freedom. Typically, casualties from the Middle East are sent to Landstuhl and may be sent from there to rehabilitation facilities in the United States.

Lee, Robert Edward (1807–1870) *Confederate general*

Although Lee resigned his army commission for military service with the Confederacy during the CIVIL WAR, he remains perhaps the most universally respected, admired, and beloved military commander in American history. He was born at Strafford, Virginia, the third son of AMERICAN REVOLUTION hero Henry "Lighthorse Harry" Lee and his second wife, Ann Hill Carter. After graduating from the UNITED STATES MILITARY ACADEMY second in the class of 1829, Lee was commissioned in the Corps of Engineers and posted to service along the southeastern coast.

Had it not been for his extraordinary leadership of the Army of Northern Virginia during the Civil War, Lee would have earned a place in army history as a brilliant military engineer, whose work on the Mississippi at St. Louis and the New York harbor defenses during 1836–46 was masterful. Lee served under John E. Wool during the UNITED STATES–MEXICAN WAR as military engineer from September 26 to December 21, 1846; he then joined Major General WINFIELD SCOTT at the Brazos River during January 1847 as a staff officer at the capture of Veracruz on March 27 and at Cerro Gordo on April 18. Lee proved himself an invaluable reconnaissance officer during the closing engagements of the war.

After the United States–Mexican War, Lee was appointed superintendent of the United States Military Academy, serving there from 1852 to 1855. Promoted to colonel, Lee commanded the 2nd Cavalry, headquartered in St. Louis, from 1855 to 1857, and served in Texas and the Southwest before he was recalled to Virginia after the death of his father-in-law in 1857. Lee was still in Virginia when he was ordered to Harpers Ferry to lead a small contingent of U.S. Marines (the only available troops) in putting down John Brown's raid. This mission, the only instance in which an army officer led marines into combat, was successfully completed on October 18, 1859.

From February 1860 to February 1861, Lee commanded the Department of Texas and was then recalled to Washington on February 4. He resigned his commission when Virginia seceded from the Union, despite Abraham Lincoln's offer of overall command of federal forces.

Lee assumed command of Virginia's military and naval forces and also served as Confederate president Jefferson Davis's personal military adviser. Lee enjoyed little success in his first field command in western Virginia, but, when called on to replace General Joseph E. Johnston (who was wounded at Seven Pines during May 31–June 1), Lee created the Army of Northern Virginia and led it in a successful defense against GEORGE BRINTON MCCLELLAN in the Seven Days (June 26–July 2). Lee also spectacularly outgeneraled John Pope, humiliating him at Second Bull Run during August 29–30. Lee took the offensive by invading Maryland and was attacked by McClellan at Antietam on September 17. The battle was in most respects a bloody draw. Lee repulsed McClellan, but he himself was forced to retreat to Virginia.

In Virginia, Lee confronted Ambrose Burnside, whom he defeated at Fredericksburg on December 13, 1862. At Chancellorsville, during May 2–4, 1863, Lee scored a brilliant victory over Joseph Hooker, then invaded the North again. He was, however, defeated by General GEORGE GORDON MEADE at the make-or-break Battle of Gettysburg (July 1–3, 1863), which was the turning point of the war. Lee was forced to withdraw into Virginia, and the North was secure from invasion.

Lee conducted no more major campaigns until General ULYSSES SIMPSON GRANT was made Union general in chief on March 9, 1864. He then employed a brilliantly successful defense against Grant at the Wilderness during May 5–6, 1864. Lee bested Grant again at Spotsylvania (May 8–12), but he was then forced out of his entrenchments at the North Anna River on May 23 when Grant enveloped him. However, Lee successfully repulsed Grant's assault at Cold Harbor on June 3, but suffered envelopment that forced him back across the James River, which Grant crossed during June 12–16. Lee mounted a desperate defense of Petersburg, but the long siege there badly weakened the Army of Northern Virginia (June 1864–April 1865).

Jefferson Davis named Lee general in chief of the Confederate armies on February 3, 1865, but after the failure of John Brown Gordon's surprise assault on Fort Stedman (near Petersburg) on March 27, 1865, Lee once again found himself outflanked by Grant (at Five Forks, during March 29–31). He withdrew from Richmond and Petersburg during April 2–3, 1865, with Grant in hot pursuit. With his route of escape through the Carolinas blocked, Lee surrendered the Army of Northern Virginia to Grant at Appomattox Court House on April 9, 1865. For all intents and purposes, this ended the Civil War.

Lee was made a prisoner of war for a short period before he was paroled. In September 1865, he accepted the presidency of Washington College (later renamed Washington and Lee University) in Lexington, Virginia. Prematurely aged and suffering from a heart ailment, he died five years later.

Legion of Merit   See DECORATIONS AND MEDALS.

Letterkenny Army Depot, Pennsylvania
See FORTS AND OTHER INSTALLATIONS.

lieutenant colonel   See RANKS AND GRADES.

lieutenant general   See RANKS AND GRADES.

Liggett, Hunter (1857–1935) *U.S. Army general*
As director of the U.S. ARMY WAR COLLEGE, Hunter Liggett was instrumental in making it an effective center for the study of battlefield problems. He was born in Reading, Pennsylvania, and graduated from the UNITED STATES MILITARY ACADEMY in 1879 with a commission in the INFANTRY. He served on the Western frontier and was promoted to first lieutenant in June 1884 and captain in June 1897. With the outbreak of the SPANISH-AMERICAN WAR in April 1898, Liggett accepted a volunteer commission as major and assistant ADJUTANT GENERAL. Throughout the war, he served as a division adjutant in Florida, Alabama, and Georgia from June 1898 through April 1899. During April–October 1899, after the war had ended, he was posted to Cuba, then sent to the Philippines in December 1899, where he commanded a subdistrict on Mindanao from 1900 to 1901.

Returning to the United States, Liggett rejoined the 5th Infantry at his permanent, REGULAR ARMY rank of captain in October 1901, but he was promoted to major the following year and transferred to 21st Infantry in Minnesota. He was appointed adjutant general of the Department of the Lakes, serving in this post from 1903 to September 1907, when he was given command of a battalion in the 13th Infantry, headquartered in Kansas. Promoted to lieutenant colonel in June 1909, he graduated from the U.S. Army War College the following year, then remained at the school as its director from 1910 to 1913 and as its president from 1913 to 1914. During his tenure, he introduced a program of thorough and logical study of battlefield problems, helping to make the Army War College the army's most prestigious training school and the focus of army strategic planning. Liggett also played a major role in creating the army officer education program and was instrumental in preparing plans for intervention in Mexico and the Caribbean, as well as for the defense of the Philippines.

Liggett was promoted to colonel in March 1912 and to brigadier general in February 1913. In 1914, he assumed command of 4th Brigade, 2nd Division in Texas, then was sent to the Philippines in 1915. The following year, he was appointed commander of the Philippines Department. On March 4, 1917, he was promoted to major general and returned to the United States in May as commander of the Western Department.

In September 1917, Liggett was appointed to command the 41st Division, which he took to France in October. In Europe, he was named commander of I Corps on January 20, 1918, and had administrative control of the handful of American units in action during the spring. Liggett led I Corps (which included the 2nd and 26th U.S. and the 167th French divisions) into action near Château-Thierry on July 4, 1918. I Corps played a key role in the Aisne-Marne offensive of July 18–August 5.

Liggett and his corps were transferred to Lorraine, where he prepared for the first major American offensive of WORLD WAR I: reduction of the Saint-Mihiel salient (September 12–16). He also participated in the first phase of the Meuse-Argonne campaign during September 26–October 12, then replaced General JOHN JOSEPH PERSHING as commander of the FIRST U.S. ARMY on October 16. Liggett prepared and reorganized First Army for the second phase of Meuse-Argonne (October 16–31), which proved a great success and, in its final phase (November 1–11), the culminating battle of the war.

Hunter Liggett stayed on in Europe after the armistice as commander of First Army until it was disbanded on April 20, 1919. He then commanded THIRD U.S. ARMY, the occupation force in Germany, from May 2 to July 2, 1919. After returning to the United States, he resumed command of the

Hunter Liggett, U.S. Army   *(Arttoday)*

Western Department until his retirement, with the rank of major general, on March 21, 1921. In June 1930, he was advanced to lieutenant general on the retired list.

M

M-1A1 Abrams Main Battle Tank See TRACKED VEHICLES.

M-2 Bradley Fighting Vehicle See TRACKED VEHICLES.

M-3/M-5 Stuart Tank See TRACKED VEHICLES.

M-4 Carbine See WEAPONS, INDIVIDUAL AND CREW-SERVED.

M-4 Sherman Tank See TRACKED VEHICLES.

M-9 Armored Combat Earthmover See TRACKED VEHICLES.

M-9 Pistol See WEAPONS, INDIVIDUAL AND CREW-SERVED.

M-16 Assault Rifle See WEAPONS, INDIVIDUAL AND CREW-SERVED.

M-26 Pershing Main Battle Tank See TRACKED VEHICLES.

M-40/M-42 Field Protective Mask See NUCLEAR-BIOLOGICAL-CHEMICAL DEFENSE EQUIPMENT.

M-42A1 Skysweeper See AIR DEFENSE ARTILLERY.

M-47 Dragon See ANTIARMOR WEAPONS.

M-48 Chaparral See AIR DEFENSE ARTILLERY.

M-60A1 Main Battle Tank See TRACKED VEHICLES.

M-68 105-mm Tank Gun See TRACKED VEHICLES.

M-88A2 Hercules See TRACKED VEHICLES.

M-93/M-93A1 Nuclear, Biological, and Chemical Reconnaissance System See NUCLEAR-BIOLOGICAL-CHEMICAL DEFENSE EQUIPMENT.

M-101 105-mm Howitzer See INDIRECT FIRE SYSTEMS.

M-102 105-mm Lightweight Howitzer
See INDIRECT FIRE SYSTEMS.

M-107 175-mm Gun   See INDIRECT FIRE SYSTEMS.

M-109 Paladin   See INDIRECT FIRE SYSTEMS.

M-110A2 203-mm Howitzer   See TRACKED VEHICLES.

M-113 Armored Personnel Carrier   See TRACKED VEHICLES.

M-114 155-mm howitzer   See INDIRECT FIRE SYSTEMS.

M-119 105-mm Howitzer   See INDIRECT FIRE SYSTEMS.

M-120/121 120-mm Mortar   See INDIRECT FIRE SYSTEMS.

M-167 20-mm Vulcan Gatling Antiaircraft Mount   See AIR DEFENSE ARTILLERY.

M-203/M-203A1 Grenade Launcher   See WEAPONS, INDIVIDUAL AND CREW-SERVED.

M-224 60-mm Mortar   See INDIRECT FIRE SYSTEMS.

M-240B Machine Gun   See WEAPONS, INDIVIDUAL AND CREW-SERVED.

M-249 Squad Automatic Weapon (SAW)
See WEAPONS, INDIVIDUAL AND CREW-SERVED.

M-256 120-mm Tank Gun   See TRACKED VEHICLES.

M-256A1 Chemical Agent Detector Kit
See NUCLEAR-BIOLOGICAL-CHEMICAL DEFENSE EQUIPMENT.

M-270 MLRS Self-Propelled Loader/ Launcher (SPLL)   See INDIRECT FIRE SYSTEMS.

M-578 Light Armored Recovery Vehicle
See TRACKED VEHICLES.

M-712 Copperhead   See ANTIARMOR WEAPON

M-977 HEMTT (Heavy Expanded Mobility Tactical Truck)   See WHEELED VEHICLES.

M-992 Field Artillery Ammunition Support Vehicle   See WHEELED VEHICLES.

M-998 HMMWV (High-Mobility Multipurpose Wheeled Vehicle)   See WHEELED VEHICLES.

M-1070 Heavy Equipment Transporter (HET)   See WHEELED VEHICLES.

M-1075 Palletized Load System   See WHEELED VEHICLES.

M-11078 Medium Tactical Vehicles   See WHEELED VEHICLES.

MacArthur, Douglas (1880–1964) *U.S. Army general*

MacArthur was Supreme Allied Commander in the Pacific during WORLD WAR II and, for a time, supreme commander of United Nations forces during the KOREAN WAR. He was the son of the nearly legendary General Arthur MacArthur, born at Little Rock Barracks, Arkansas. After graduation, first in his class, from the UNITED STATES MILITARY ACADEMY (USMA) in 1903, MacArthur was commissioned a second lieutenant of engineers and sent to the Philippines. During 1905–06, he served as aide to his father during a military tour of Asia, then, during 1906–07, he served as aide to President Theodore Roosevelt. In 1908, he assumed command of a company of the 3rd Engineers at Fort Leavenworth, moving on as an instructor in the General Service and Cavalry schools in 1909.

In September 1913, MacArthur served on the ARMY GENERAL STAFF, and with the United States's entry into WORLD WAR I, MacArthur was instrumental in creating the 42ND INFANTRY DIVISION ("Rainbow"), serving as the unit's chief of staff when it was sent to France in October 1917. MacArthur served with the 42nd at Aisne-Marne (July 25–August 2), then commanded a brigade during the assault on the Saint-Mihiel salient from September 12 to September 17. He led a brigade at Meuse-Argonne (October 4–November 11, 1918), and commanded the entire division in the "race to Sedan" at the end of the war (November 6–11).

After the armistice, MacArthur served with occupation forces in Germany, returning to the United States in April 1919, when he received appointment as superintendent of the USMA. He left West Point in 1922 to accept a command, as major general, in the Philippines and remained there until January 1925. MacArthur returned to the States, but he left again for the Philippines, as commander of the Department of the Philippines, in 1928.

In 1930, MacArthur returned to the United States again, this time as chief of staff of the army. He served in this high post through 1935, but he brought down upon himself and the army a storm

General Douglas MacArthur in a widely published World War II publicity photo   *(Arttoday)*

of controversy when, in the summer of 1932, he personally led a detachment of troops against the so-called Bonus Army (Depression-ridden World War I veterans demanding early payment of promised government benefits) camped in and around Washington, D.C. Many condemned his actions as brutal.

In October 1935, MacArthur was sent back to the Philippines to organize its defenses in preparation for the islands' scheduled independence from the United States. The new Philippine government appointed MacArthur field marshal in August 1936, and he resigned his commission in the army to accept the appointment. He did not want to be transferred from the Philippines before completing preparations for its defense. However, he accepted recall to American service on the eve of war with Japan (July 26, 1941) and was promoted to lieutenant general, with overall command of army forces in the Far East. He was headquartered in the Philippines.

Like other senior American officers, MacArthur was surprised by the Japanese bombing of

Pearl Harbor on December 7, 1941, and by air attacks on Clark and Iba airfields in the Philippines on the following day. Although hopelessly undermanned and underequipped, MacArthur mounted a skillful defense, withdrawing to fortified positions on Bataan during a long retreat (December 23, 1941–January 1, 1942) that he made very costly to Japanese ground forces. MacArthur personally commanded the defense of Bataan and the Manila Bay forts until President Franklin D. Roosevelt ordered his evacuation to Australia. He left on March 11, reluctantly, promising "I shall return."

Decorated with the Medal of Honor for his defense of the Philippines, he was made supreme commander of Allied forces in the Southwest Pacific area in April 1942. Working closely with the USN, he directed the reconquest of New Guinea as a first step in the liberation of the Pacific. He successfully directed the repulse of a strong Japanese assault on Port Moresby during July–September 1942, then took the offensive in an advance across the Owen Stanley Range during September–November, ultimately assaulting and taking the Buna-Gona fortifications during November 20, 1942–January 22, 1943. Following this hard-won gain, MacArthur directed the "island-hopping" strategy by which the Allied forces retook the captured Pacific islands, advancing inexorably against mainland Japan.

After campaigning along the north coast of New Guinea, MacArthur invaded western New Britain during December 15–30, 1943, cutting off the major Japanese base at Rabaul. Next came victories at Hollandia, Jayapura, and Aitape, which isolated the Japanese Eighteenth Army in April 1944. Moving west along the New Guinea coast, MacArthur coordinated a massive offensive with Admiral Chester Nimitz in the central Pacific. MacArthur's forces took Morotai in the Molucca Islands while Nimitz pounded and then invaded the Palau Islands (Carolines). On October 20, 1944, MacArthur personally commanded ground forces invading Leyte, thereby redeeming his pledge to return to the Philippines.

Intent on liberating the Philippine Islands, MacArthur concentrated on expansion of Philippine operations to Mindoro on December 1 and Luzon on January 9, 1945. (Critics thought that his concentration on the Philippines compromised other aspects of the Pacific war effort.) Following the Luzon campaign (February 3–August 15, 1945), MacArthur went on to liberate the rest of the Philippines. Simultaneously, on Borneo, he took the coastal oilfields that fueled much of the Japanese war effort.

In April 1945, MacArthur was named commander of all U.S. ground forces in the Pacific. He would have had overall charge of the anticipated invasion of Japan; however, the dropping of newly developed atomic bombs on Hiroshima and Nagasaki in August prompted the Japanese to surrender before the invasion was launched. Promoted to general of the army, MacArthur was accorded the honor of accepting the Japanese surrender, which took place aboard the battleship USS *Missouri* riding at anchor in Tokyo Bay on September 2, 1945.

MacArthur next served masterfully as supreme commander of Allied occupation forces in Japan, governing the broken nation with a strong hand tempered by benevolence. MacArthur administered both the rebuilding and the democratization of Japan. In most quarters throughout the conquered nation, MacArthur became a popular figure.

On June 25, 1950, communist North Korean troops invaded South Korea, and MacArthur was named supreme commander of United Nations forces in Korea by a UN Security Council resolution of July 8. He set about directing the defense of the Pusan perimeter during August 5–September 15, then staged perhaps the greatest military operation of his career by landing a force at Inchon on September 15, thereby enveloping the North Koreans and ultimately destroying North Korean forces in South Korea. He next secured the approval of the United Nations and President Truman to invade North Korea in October, and pushed the communist forces deep into the north, all the way to the Yalu River, the border with China. However, during November 25–26, communist Chinese forces entered the war, pushing the United Nations and South Korean armies southward. MacArthur conducted a fighting withdrawal and settled into a defensive front just south of the South Korean capital of Seoul.

Thus embattled, MacArthur publicly advocated bombing targets in China itself (even with nuclear weapons), a move that American politicians, chief among them President Harry S. Truman, feared would trigger a third world war. When MacArthur persisted in insubordination and flatly refused to conduct a limited war, Truman relieved him of command on April 11, 1951—despite the fact that he had just recaptured Seoul on March 14.

Replaced in Korea by Lieutenant General MATTHEW BUNKER RIDGWAY, MacArthur returned to the United States, where he was hailed as a national hero. On April 19, 1951, he delivered a stirring retirement address to Congress in which he declared that "old soldiers never die, they just fade away." Although there was much talk of his entering politics at the presidential level, he retired from public life.

Mahan, Dennis Hart (1802–1871) *military instructor and theorist*

Mahan was a seminal army instructor and military science author at the UNITED STATES MILITARY ACADEMY (USMA). He was born in New York City, the son of Irish immigrants. Growing up poor, his lofty ambition was to be an artist, toward which end he secured an appointment to USMA mainly to take advantage of the extensive drawing courses required as part of the engineering program. He excelled intellectually, and Major Sylvanus Thayer made him acting assistant professor of mathematics during his second year. He graduated first in the class of 1824 and was commissioned in the engineers, but he remained at West Point as an instructor during 1824–26.

From 1826 to 1830, Mahan studied at Metz, France, at the School for Application for Engineers and Artillery. He then returned to USMA as assistant professor of engineering in 1830. After he achieved an appointment as full professor, he resigned his second lieutenant's commission on January 1, 1832, and taught at West Point as a civilian. His most significant contribution to the USMA curriculum was his fourth-year course in military science: "Engineering and the Science of War." He wrote the texts for the course, and, in 1836, he published *Complete Treatise on Field Fortification* and, the following year, *Elementary Course on Civil Engineering*. His *Elementary Treatise on Advance-Guard, Out-Post, and Detachment Service of Troops* was published in editions that appeared in 1847, 1853, and 1863. It was nothing less than a comprehensive treatment of tactics and strategy.

Mahan believed that an offensive campaign of maneuver was generally the most effective means of winning a war, and he stressed the necessity of outposts and reconnaissance. His ideas influenced all of the major commanders of the CIVIL WAR, on both the Union and Confederate sides, and they have remained a durable part of army doctrine.

In addition to the books just mentioned, Mahan was the author of *Industrial Drawing* (1852), *Descriptive Geometry as Applied to the Drawing of Fortification and Stereotomy* (1864), and *An Elementary Course of Military Engineering* (1866–67).

In 1871, when the USMA Board of Visitors recommended Mahan's retirement because of advanced age, the profoundly depressed Mahan leaped off a steamboat to his death in the Hudson River near Stony Point, New York.

major   See RANKS AND GRADES.

major army field commands

The army designates nine commands as major army field commands. At the heart of the army mission, the commands are:

> U.S. ARMY FORCES COMMAND (FORSCOM)
> U.S. ARMY TRAINING AND DOCTRINE COMMAND (TRADOC)

U.S. ARMY MATERIEL COMMAND (AMC)

U.S. ARMY INTELLIGENCE AND SECURITY COMMAND (INSCOM)

U.S. ARMY INFORMATION SYSTEMS ENGINEERING COMMAND (USAISEC)

U.S. ARMY CRIMINAL INVESTIGATION COMMAND (USACIC)

U.S. ARMY MILITARY DISTRICT OF WASHINGTON (MDW)

U.S. ARMY MEDICAL COMMAND (MEDCOM)

U.S. ARMY CORPS OF ENGINEERS (USACE)

major general   See RANKS AND GRADES.

Marshall, George Catlett (1880–1959) *U.S. Army general and World War II Chief of Staff*

Army chief of staff during WORLD WAR II, Marshall served in the Truman cabinet after the war and, as secretary of state, became architect of the Marshall Plan for the postwar relief of Europe. He was born in Uniontown, Pennsylvania, and graduated from Virginia Military Institute in 1901. Commissioned a second lieutenant of INFANTRY on February 3, 1902, Marshall served in the Philippines during the conclusion of the insurrection on Mindoro (1902–03). Returned to the United States, he attended infantry and CAVALRY school at Fort Leavenworth, graduating at the top of the class of 1907 and staying on at the Staff College during 1907–08. Promoted to first lieutenant in 1907, he taught as an instructor at the schools from 1908 to 1910, then, after serving in a variety of miscellaneous assignments during 1910–13, Marshall returned to the Philippines for three years, where he served as aide to General HUNTER LIGGETT.

Promoted to captain in 1916, Marshall returned to the United States as aide to General James F. Bell, in the Western Department, and then in the Eastern Department in 1917. In June 1917, Marshall shipped out to France as a staff officer with the 1st Division. Assigned as division operations officer, he was one of the planners of the first U.S. offensive of the war in May 1918.

Promoted to temporary colonel in July, Marshall was attached in August to JOHN JOSEPH PERSHING's General Headquarters at Chaumont, where he was the key member of the team that planned the massive Saint-Mihiel offensive of September 12–16. He was also in charge of the transfer of half a million men from the neutralized Saint-Mihiel salient to the Meuse-Argonne front. The movement was accomplished so swiftly that Marshall earned praise as a logistician and was named chief of operations for the First Army in October. The next month, he was made chief of staff of VIII Corps.

With the end of the war, Marshall was assigned to service with the army of occupation in Germany. In September 1919, he returned to the United States and reverted to his prewar rank of captain, but he was appointed aide to Pershing, who was now army CHIEF OF STAFF. Marshall served in this capacity through 1924 and collaborated with Pershing on aspects of the National Defense Act. He was also instrumental in writing the general's reports on the American Expeditionary Force in the war.

Marshall was promoted to major in July 1920 and lieutenant colonel three years later. After leaving Pershing's staff, he served in Tientsin, China, as executive officer of the 15th Infantry, then returned to the United States in 1927 and became assistant commandant of the Infantry School at Fort Benning, Georgia, through 1932. He was promoted to colonel and worked with the Civilian Conservation Corps (CCC) in 1933, then became senior instructor to the Illinois National Guard from 1933 to 1936, when he was promoted to brigadier general and given command of 5th Infantry Brigade at Vancouver Barracks, Washington. He left this assignment in 1938 to move to Washington, D.C., as head of the War Plans Division of the ARMY GENERAL STAFF. Promoted to major general in July, Marshall was appointed deputy chief of staff. On September 1, he was made a temporary general and appointed chief of staff. From this position, he launched a rapid expansion of the army preparatory to war. It was under Marshall's leadership that the army grew from its prewar strength of 200,000 to 8 million soldiers during the war.

After Pearl Harbor and U.S. entry into World War II, Marshall reorganized the Army General Staff and, by March 1942, effected the restructuring of the army into three major commands: Army Ground Forces, Army Service Forces, and Army Air Forces. Serving on the JOINT CHIEFS OF STAFF, he was a principal military adviser to President Franklin D. Roosevelt, and he was present at all the great Allied conferences of the war, first with Roosevelt and then with President Truman. Marshall was one of the key architects of American and Allied military strategy, as well as U.S. political strategy bearing on the war.

In December 1944, Marshall was elevated to the rank of general of the army and concluded his military service as Chief of Staff, on November 20, 1945. Just five days after he resigned as chief, however, President Truman sent him to China as his special envoy. Marshall attempted to mediate a peace between Jiang Jieshi (Chiang Kai-shek) (and his KMT) and Mao Zedong (Mao Tse-tung) (and the Chinese Communist Party), but without success. After his return to the United States, he replaced James F. Byrnes as secretary of state in Truman's cabinet on January 1947 and left as his most enduring monument the program of economic aid to rebuild war-ravaged Europe that was popularly called the Marshall Plan.

Marshall resigned from the cabinet in January 1949, but he returned in September of the next year as secretary of defense and served in that post during the opening of the KOREAN WAR. In ill health, Marshall stepped down as secretary of defense and retired from public life in September 1951. Three years later, in December 1953, he was awarded the Nobel Prize for Peace, chiefly in recognition of the Marshall Plan. He was the first soldier ever honored with the prize.

master sergeant   See RANKS AND GRADES.

master warrant officer 5   See RANKS AND GRADES.

McClellan, George Brinton (1826–1885)
Army general

Popular with his troops and a brilliant administrator, McClellan proved to be an overly cautious commander as general in chief of the Union army in the CIVIL WAR. A native of Philadelphia, McClellan graduated, second in his class, from the UNITED STATES MILITARY ACADEMY (USMA) in 1846, just in time to serve under WINFIELD SCOTT in the UNITED STATES–MEXICAN WAR. The young second lieutenant of engineers distinguished himself at Contreras and Churubusco (August 19–20, 1847), for which he was breveted first lieutenant, then fought with conspicuous gallantry once again at Chapultepec (September 13) and was breveted captain.

George B. McClellan whipped the Army of the Potomac into shape but then was fatally overcautious in how he used it.   *(Arttoday)*

McClellan returned to USMA after the war as an instructor in engineering (1848–51), then was assigned as chief engineer for the erection of Fort Delaware (near Delaware City, Delaware) during 1851–54. Promoted to the regular rank of captain, he was assigned to CAVALRY in March 1855 and was dispatched to the Crimea as a U.S. observer of the ongoing Crimean War.

Even as a cavalryman, McClellan thought like an engineer. He designed a new saddle, which was adopted by the army in 1856. The "McClellan saddle" is still widely used.

McClellan resigned his commission in January 1857 to become chief engineer of the expanding Illinois Central Railroad, then left that position to become president of the Ohio & Mississippi Railroad in 1860. However, with the outbreak of the Civil War, he accepted an appointment as major general of Ohio Volunteers in April 1861. The next month he was commissioned a major general of regulars and given command of the Department of the Ohio, winning a minor victory in his first engagement, at Rich Mountain (in present-day West Virginia) on July 11.

McClellan was hailed in the popular press as the "Young Napoleon" and was immediately tapped as commander of the Department (later called Army) of the Potomac. In November, he was named to replace the superannuated Winfield Scott as general in chief of the entire Union army.

McClellan transformed the Army of the Potomac from an inefficient rabble to a well-trained and highly capable military force. However, while he proved an excellent administrator and organizer, he was habitually overcautious as a field commander. He launched the Peninsula Campaign with the object of taking the Confederate capital of Richmond, but he repeatedly hesitated, always asking for reinforcements and grossly overestimating Confederate strength. In March 1862, after McClellan's constant and costly hesitations and half-measures, Abraham Lincoln relieved him of his position as general in chief, although he remained in command of the Army of the Potomac.

During April 5–May 4, 1862, McClellan laid siege to Yorktown, Virginia, which finally fell to him. He successfully repulsed J. E. Johnston at Fair Oaks on May 31, then fought ROBERT E. LEE to a draw at Mechanicsville on June 26, but he declined to press his advantage, choosing instead to withdraw. He then fought the bloody series of battles known as the Seven Days during June 25–July 1, ultimately driving Lee back at Malvern Hill.

McClellan was put in charge of preparing defenses for Washington, D.C., which was continually threatened by the Confederates. He checked Lee's ill-conceived invasion of Maryland, defeating the Confederates at South Mountain on September 14 and earning a terribly costly and very narrow victory at Antietam on September 17. Yet, once again, he did not capitalize on what he had gained and, in November 1862, Lincoln relieved McClellan of command.

In 1864, McClellan ran against Lincoln as Democratic candidate for president and was soundly defeated. Resigning his commission, he took a protracted European tour, then returned to the United States as chief engineer for New York City's Department of Docks. Simultaneously, he served the Atlantic & Great Western Railroad as trustee, then president (1872). He was elected governor of New Jersey in 1877 and served until 1881.

McNair, Lesley James (1883–1944) *U.S. Army general*

One of the principal architects of the WORLD WAR II–era army, McNair was born in Verndale, Minnesota, and graduated from the UNITED STATES MILITARY ACADEMY near the top of his class in 1904. He served in Utah, Massachusetts, New Jersey, and Washington, D.C., through 1909, gaining promotion to first lieutenant in June 1905 and captain in May 1907. After service with the 4th Artillery Regiment in the West from 1909 to 1913, he was sent to France to observe artillery training techniques, then returned to the United States in time to participate in the expedition to Veracruz (April 30–November 23, 1914). He also took part in JOHN JOSEPH PERSHING's punitive expedition into Mexico in pursuit of Pancho Villa from March 1916 to February 1917.

McNair was promoted to major in May 1917 and was assigned detached duty with the ARMY GENERAL STAFF. He shipped out to France with the 1st Division during WORLD WAR I and, in August, was transferred to General Headquarters, American Expeditionary Force, with the rank of lieutenant colonel. In June 1918, he was promoted to colonel, and, in October, became a brigadier general—at the time the youngest general officer in the army.

After the armistice, McNair served as senior artillery officer in the General Staff's Training Section, but then he reverted to his permanent rank of major. Upon his return to the United States, he taught at the General Service School (1919–21), then transferred into a staff post in Hawaii, serving there from 1921 to 1924. He returned to the mainland as a professor of military science at Purdue University from 1924 to 1928, when he was promoted to lieutenant colonel and sent to the U.S. ARMY WAR COLLEGE. After graduation in 1929, he was named assistant commandant of the Field Artillery School and also worked with the depression-era Civilian Conservation Corps (CCC).

Promoted to colonel in May 1935, McNair was given command of the 2nd Field Artillery Brigade in Texas in March 1937, and he was promoted once again, to brigadier general (March 1937). Named commandant of the prestigious COMMAND AND GENERAL STAFF COLLEGE at Fort Leavenworth in April 1939, he served until October 1940, also functioning in the capacity of chief of the newly organized General Headquarters. His responsibilities included training, organization, and mobilization, and McNair became responsible for shaping much of the army as it would enter World War II.

Promoted to major general in September 1940, he was again quickly promoted, to temporary lieutenant general, in June 1941. Later, when General GEORGE CATLETT MARSHALL instituted a sweeping reorganization of the army, McNair was named chief of Army Ground Forces (AGF) in March 1942. Headquartered at the Army War College, McNair directed the expansion of AGF from 780,000 men to its maximum wartime strength of 2.2 million in July 1943. He was an energetic,

hands-on commander, who traveled throughout the country and to the various war theaters to ensure that his troops were combat ready. On one of these trips, in Tunisia, he was severely wounded by a shell fragment in 1943.

McNair was dispatched to England in June 1944, to free up Lieutenant General GEORGE SMITH PATTON, JR., for invasion operations in France. McNair replaced him as commander of the decoy "1st U.S. Army Group," designed to mislead the Germans as to the intended entry point for the D-day invasion. The next month, while McNair was in Normandy, observing the Eighth Air Force bomb German positions, he was killed by bombs that fell short.

The loss to the army was severe. McNair had already streamlined the army's traditional two-brigade, four-regiment "square" division into a three-regiment "triangular" division, which proved much more flexible in highly mobile World War II combat. Doubtless, he would have contributed even more to army doctrine and tactics.

Meade, George Gordon (1815–1872) *Army general and Gettysburg commander*

Regarded as a solid, if cautious and often irascible officer, Meade commanded the Union's Army of the Potomac when it achieved the single most significant victory of the CIVIL WAR, at Gettysburg, Pennsylvania.

He was born in Cadiz, Spain, to the family of an American naval agent, but he was raised in Philadelphia and graduated from the UNITED STATES MILITARY ACADEMY in 1835. His initial commission was in the artillery, and his first posting was to Florida, where he served during the opening of the Second Seminole War. Felled by fever, he was forced to return north and was so severely debilitated by his illness that he resigned his commission on October 26, 1836 to become a civil engineer. He rejoined the army on May 10, 1842, and was once again commissioned a second lieutenant, this time of engineers. Four years later, with the outbreak of the UNITED STATES–MEXICAN WAR, Meade served under General ZACHARY TAYLOR and fought at Palo

Alto (May 8, 1848) and Resaca de la Palma (May 9). He performed with distinction at Monterrey during September 20–24, for which he was breveted first lieutenant.

After the conclusion of the war with Mexico, Meade led survey work for the army in the Great Lakes region, in Philadelphia, and in Florida. He was promoted to captain in May 1856, but with the outbreak of the Civil War, he was jumped to brigadier general of the Pennsylvania volunteers and rushed to an assignment as part of the defense forces around Washington. He then served under GEORGE BRINTON MCCLELLAN in the Peninsula Campaign (April–July 1862), but was badly wounded on June 30 at Frayser's Farm, outside of Richmond, during the Seven Days. Recovering by late summer, Meade participated in Second Bull Run during August 29–30, 1862, then was assigned to divisional command. He fought at South Mountain, Maryland, on September 14, then took command of I Corps at Antietam after General Joseph Hooker was disabled on September 17. In November, Meade was promoted to major general of volunteers and given command of 3rd Division, I Corps at Fredericksburg, where his troops eked out a temporary success on the Union left (December 13).

Following Fredericksburg, Meade was given command of V Corps, then commanded the Center Grand Division (III and VI Corps) of the Army of the Potomac in December. With the recovery of Hooker, Meade reverted to command of V Corps. Meade was present at Chancellorsville during May 1–6, 1863, but he was not heavily engaged. However, after Hooker's miserable performance there, Meade was named to replace him as commander of the Army of the Potomac. In the meantime, Lee invaded Maryland on June 28, and marched on into Pennsylvania. At Gettysburg, Pennsylvania, Meade engaged in a momentous battle with Lee. Like Meade, Lee had not planned on fighting at Gettysburg, but he believed that a victory there would turn the tide of the war by once and for all breaking the Northern will to fight. He therefore committed his forces to it in a major effort. For his part, Meade assumed a defensive strategy, which

was brilliantly executed. With an engineer's eye, he sized up the terrain and used it as an ally during the July 1–3 battle. However, after the disastrous failure of George Pickett's charge—the final Confederate attack—Meade failed to press a counterattack. He did chase Lee's beaten army cautiously, but he failed to inflict a decisive blow against it. Although President Abraham Lincoln expressed profound disappointment at this absence of follow-through, Meade was promoted to regular army brigadier general as of July 3 and remained in command of the Army of the Potomac. When General ULYSSES S. GRANT became general in chief and field commander in March 1864, Meade's authority was reduced to that of Grant's executive officer. Meade served well in the subordinate command role, fighting at the Wilderness (May 5–6,), Spotsylvania (May 8–18), and Cold Harbor (May 31–June 12). At Petersburg, Virginia, he directed the long and arduous trench warfare campaign around that city from July 1864 to April of the next year. He also directed the final operations of the army during the Five Forks–Appomattox campaign of March 30–April 9 and was among those present when Grant accepted Lee's surrender at Appomattox on April 9, 1865.

After the war, Meade remained with the army as commander of the Third Military District (encompassing Alabama, Georgia, and Florida), and was one of very few Northern military governors who was committed to discharging his office with justice and humanity. In 1869, Meade became commander of the Military Division of the East, but he never fully recovered from the wound he had received early in the war. In 1872, he developed pneumonia and succumbed to it.

Medal of Honor   See DECORATIONS AND MEDALS.

Medical Regional Commands
The army is one of the world's biggest providers of medical services. Its regional commands and associated facilities include:

Europe Regional Medical Command

LANDSTUHL REGIONAL MEDICAL CENTER, HEI-DELBERG, GERMANY

Great Plains Command

Bayne-Jones Army Community Hospital, Fort Polk, Louisiana

Brooke Army Medical Center, Fort Sam Houston, Texas

Darnall Army Community Hospital, Fort Hood, Texas

Evans Army Hospital, Fort Carson, Colorado

General Leonard Wood Army Community Hospital, Fort Leonard Wood, Missouri

Irwin Army Community Hospital, Fort Riley, Kansas

Munson Army Health Center, Fort Leavenworth, Kansas

Raymond W. Bliss Army Health Clinic, Fort Huachuca, Arizona

Reynolds Army Community Hospital, Fort Sill, Oklahoma

William Beaumont Army Medical Center, Fort Bliss, Texas

North Atlantic Command

Andrew Rader Health Clinic, Fort Myer, Virginia

DeWitt Army Community Hospital, Fort Belvoir, Virginia

DiLorenzo Tricare Health Clinic, Washington, D.C.

Ireland Army Community Hospital, Fort Knox, Kentucky

Keller Army Community Hospital, West Point, New York

Kenner Army Health Clinic, Fort Lee, Virginia

Kimbrough Ambulatory Care Center, Fort Meade, Maryland

McDonald Army Community Hospital, Fort Eustis, Virginia

Patterson Army Health Clinic, Fort Monmouth, New Jersey

WALTER REED ARMY MEDICAL CENTER, Washington, D.C.

Womack Army Medical Center, Fort Bragg, North Carolina

Pacific Command

18th Medical Command, Seoul, Korea

Tripler Army Medical Center, Honolulu, Hawaii

U.S. Army Medical Department Activity, Tokyo, Japan

Southeast Command

Blanchfield Army Community Hospital, Fort Campbell, Kentucky

Dwight D. Eisenhower Army Medical Center, Fort Gordon, Georgia

Fox Army Health Center, Redstone Arsenal, Alabama

Lawrence Joel Army Health Clinic, Fort McPherson, Georgia

Martin Army Community Hospital, Fort Benning

Moncrief Army Community Hospital, Fort Jackson, South Carolina

Rodriguez Army Health Clinic, Fort Buchanan, Puerto Rico

Southern Command Army Health Clinic

United States Army Aeromedical Center, Fort Rucker, Alabama

Winn Army Community Hospital, Fort Stewart, Georgia

Western Command

Army Medical Department, Alaska

Madigan Army Medical Center, Tacoma, Washington

Weed Army Community Hospital, Fort Irwin, California

Medical Service Corps

A combat service support branch of the army, the Medical Service Corps provides highly skilled and dedicated leaders who perform the clinical, scientific, administrative, command, and support services essential to efficiently and effectively manage a quality, world-class health-care system in support of the army. The branch includes a wide variety of professional specialties, including, for example, health services personnel officer, hospital administrator, clinical psychologist, information systems officer, hospital architect, medical logistician, patient administrator, health services operations officer, health services comptroller, and aeromedical evacuation officer. Units operate at the platoon, company, and corps level. The home station of the Medical Service Corps is at Fort Sam Houston, Texas.

Meritorious Service Medal   See DECORATIONS AND MEDALS.

Merrill, Frank Dow (1903–1955) *U.S. Army general*

Merrill's leadership during the arduous Burma campaign of WORLD WAR II constitutes a landmark in army unconventional warfare. Born in Hopkinton, Massachusetts, Merrill enlisted in the army in 1922, serving in Panama through 1925. Appointed to the UNITED STATES MILITARY ACADEMY, he graduated in 1929 and was commissioned a second lieutenant of CAVALRY. He attended Ordnance School during 1931–32 and Cavalry School from 1934 to 1935, becoming an instructor there and serving until 1938, when he was attached to the U.S. embassy in Tokyo. During this assignment, Merrill studied both the Japanese language and imperial military organization.

Promoted to captain in 1939, Merrill left the embassy assignment in 1940 and joined the intelligence staff of DOUGLAS MACARTHUR's Philippine Command. In 1941, he was promoted to temporary major and was on a mission in Rangoon when the United States entered World War II on December 8, 1941. Remaining in Burma, he joined the command of Lieutenant General JOSEPH WARREN STILWELL when Stilwell broke through to Burma with Chinese forces in March 1942. Merrill served with Stilwell during the first Burma campaign, and he accompanied his retreat to India in May. He was promoted to temporary lieutenant colonel at that time and then to full colonel early the following year. Stilwell chose him to command a provisional U.S. infantry regiment, which he sent into combat in northern Burma as part of the joint American-Chinese offensive to reopen the Burma Road in February 1944. Merrill's troops marched a hundred miles into Burma and spearheaded a broad Chinese-American envelopment action.

During this arduous jungle campaign, Merrill suffered from heart trouble and had to be hospitalized twice. At last, in mid August, he was transferred to lead a liaison group of the Allied Southwest Asia Command in Ceylon and was promoted to major general in September. He was then appointed chief of staff of General Simon B. Buckner's Tenth Army in the Okinawa campaign from April 1 to June 22, 1945, then served under Stilwell again when he took over after Buckner's death.

After the war, Merrill served as chief of staff of the Sixth Army, headquartered in San Francisco. In 1947 he was appointed chief of the American Advisory Military Mission to the Philippines. He retired from the army in July 1948 and served the state of New Hampshire as commissioner of roads and public highways.

MH-60K Blackhawk SOF   See AIRCRAFT.

Miles, Nelson Appleton (1839–1925) *U.S. Army general*

Miles was perhaps the army's single most effective Indian fighter. He was born near Westminster, Massachusetts, and attended school there and in Boston. While in Boston, at the outbreak of the CIVIL WAR, the enterprising Miles borrowed funds to raise a volunteer company. However, he was soon commissioned in the REGULAR ARMY as a first lieutenant in the 22nd Massachusetts Regiment in 1861 and was quickly chosen as an aide to General Oliver O. Howard, whom he accompanied during GEORGE BRINTON MCCLELLAN's Peninsula campaign (April–July 1862).

From the beginning, Miles earned a reputation as a dashing officer of boundless courage, and promotion came swiftly. He was promoted to lieutenant colonel in the field at Fair Oaks on May 31 and was then jumped to colonel when he took command of the 61st New York at Antietam on September 17. Wounded at Fredericksburg on December 13, he was fit for duty again in the spring of 1863 and fought at Chancellorsville during May 2–4. He was again wounded in that battle and was later awarded the Medal of Honor, in 1892.

Promoted to brigadier general of volunteers in May 1864, Miles commanded a brigade in the Battle of the Wilderness during May 5–6; at Spotsylvania, May 8–18; Cold Harbor, May 31–June 12; and at Petersburg, June 15–18. He fought with such distinction at Ream's Station, near Petersburg, on June 22, that he was breveted to major general in August and, during March–April 1865, was given command of a division during the last phase of operations around Petersburg.

In the aftermath of the war, during October 1865, Miles was promoted to major general of volunteers and made commander of II Corps. He also served as commandant of Fort Monroe, Virginia, and was therefore assigned as the jailer of the Confederacy's president, Jefferson Davis. Miles earned a degree of public censure for his treatment of Davis, whom he closely confined and shackled.

Miles earned a commission as colonel in the regular army and was assigned in July 1866 to command the newly formed 40th Infantry, an African-American regiment. This assignment displeased Miles, as did the duties of civil government and police work required by Reconstruction policies. Miles lobbied for a change of command, and, during this period, in 1868, he made an advantageous marriage, to Mary Sherman, niece of both Senator John Sherman of Ohio and his brother, General WILLIAM TECUMSEH SHERMAN. The following year, in March 1869, Miles was given command of the 5th Infantry in the West, an assignment very much to his liking.

The colonel took charge of one of four columns sent against the Comanches, Kiowas, and southern Cheyennes during the Red River War on 1874–75.

When GEORGE ARMSTRONG CUSTER and his command were annihilated at the Little Bighorn on June 25, 1876, Miles was one of few army officers who remained undemoralized and eager to take the offensive. His vigorous campaigning against the Sioux and northern Cheyenne resulted in their withdrawal to assigned reservations or their flight into Canada. On January 8, 1877, he defeated Crazy Horse—one of those closely associated with the Custer battle—at Wolf Mountain (near present-day Miles City, Montana).

Miles's next major victory came when General Oliver O. Howard called him to Eagle Creek in the Bear Paw Mountains (near Chinook, Montana) to coordinate with him in the encirclement of a band of Nez Perces led by Chief Joseph the Younger. The battle, which took place in driving snow during October 1–5, 1877, resulted in the surrender of Joseph and his band, who withdrew to a reservation.

Miles was promoted to regular army brigadier general in 1880 and replaced General George Crook as commander of U.S. forces in Arizona. Miles took up the pursuit of Geronimo and his band of renegade Apaches with great singleness of purpose during 1885–86. However, Geronimo repeatedly evaded capture. He did not succeed in running the Indian leader to ground until August 1887. Promoted to major general in 1890, Miles commanded the final operation of the INDIAN WARS. He directed the suppression of the much-feared Ghost Dance cult uprising in 1890. The massacre of Sioux at Wounded Knee Creek, perpetrated by the 7th Cavalry under Colonel James W. Forsyth, had not been ordered by Miles, who, in fact, condemned it and relieved Forsyth of command following it. Miles ordered a court of inquiry and was outraged when the court exonerated Forsyth. Over Miles's protests, General John M. Schofield, Miles's superior, reinstated Forsyth. Nevertheless, Miles's public reputation was badly tarnished by Wounded Knee, although his military career forged ahead. In 1895, he was appointed commanding General of the Army, in which post he carried on a stormy relationship with Secretary of War Russell A. Alger. In bad odor with the civilian administration, he was denied a major role in the SPANISH-AMERICAN WAR, which commenced in April 1898. He did direct the conquest of Puerto Rico, an operation he planned and executed with great precision during July 25–August 13.

The Spanish-American War occasioned yet another dispute between Miles and the War Department, which he publicly accused of supplying spoiled beef to the troops in Cuba—charges that were subsequently substantiated and led to a major reform movement not only in government but also in federal regulation of food handling and processing generally.

Miles was promoted to lieutenant general in February 1901, but he found himself repeatedly embroiled in controversy. When he insisted on meeting with rebel leaders while touring the Philippines during the insurrection of 1902, Secretary of War Elihu Root became so enraged that, in 1903, he effectively forced Miles into retirement.

Military Intelligence (MI)

With a home station at Fort Huachuca, Arizona, MI is a combat support branch of the army. Its mission is to determine the enemy's plans before the plans are put into action. MI units are deployed worldwide in support of force projection, and they conduct operations of tactical intelligence, counterintelligence, signals intelligence and electronic warfare, security, interrogation, as well as reconnaissance and surveillance. Much of the work is of a highly technical and advanced nature, using radio communications intercept, direction-finding, computer analysis, digital imagery, and satellite communications.

military occupational specialty

A soldier's military occupational specialty (MOS) is a group of related skills that, taken together, define the soldier's job.

Military Outstanding Volunteer Service Medal   See DECORATIONS AND MEDALS.

Sergeant Michelle Whitty, Electronic Warfare Team One, Alpha Company, 101st Military Intelligence, 1st Infantry Division, conducts security during a mission in Kosovo, Yugoslavia. Whitty and her team monitor air traffic in the area.   *(U.S. Army)*

Military Police (MP)

A combat support branch of the army, MP executes a dual mission. The branch prepares for war by leading and training combat-ready MP forces capable of conducting operations against enemy forces in the rear area and expediting battlefield movement of critical resources. The second aspect of the mission—law enforcement, criminal investigation, terrorism, counterterrorism, physical security, corrections, and crime prevention—is carried out in the peacetime garrison environment. Home station of Military Police is Fort Leonard Wood, Missouri.

Military Traffic Management Command (MTMC)

Headquartered at Falls Church, Virginia, MTMC is the army component of the U.S. Transportation

Command, a unified joint command. It is the Department of Defense manager of military traffic, including land transport and common-user ocean terminal service within CONUS (the continental United States). MTMC also manages worldwide movement and storage of household goods for the Department of Defense.

MIM-23 Hawk   See AIR DEFENSE ARTILLERY.

MIM-104 Patriot   See AIR DEFENSE ARTILLERY.

Multinational Force and Observers Medal
See DECORATIONS AND MEDALS.

N

★

Natick Soldier Center (NSC) See U.S. ARMY SOLDIER SYSTEMS CENTER.

National Defense Service Medal See DECORATIONS AND MEDALS.

National Training Center (NTC)
Located at Fort Irwin, California, the NTC is a desert training center for armored and mechanized task forces. The site was selected in 1979 because it offers more than 1,000 square miles for maneuver and ranges, as well as an uncluttered electromagnetic spectrum for communications and instrumentation training, ample airspace restricted to military use, and isolation from densely populated areas. NTC was activated on October 16, 1980. In addition to desert training, NTC offers urban terrain training.

Although isolated, Fort Irwin is open to the public and maintains the NTC and 11th ACR Museum, which presents the history of this military reservation from 1901 to the present.

NATO Medal—Former Republic of Yugoslavia See DECORATIONS AND MEDALS.

NATO Medal—Kosovo Operations See DECORATIONS AND MEDALS.

NBC Elements See CHEMICAL SERVICE ORGANIZATION.

91st Division (Training Support)
Headquartered at Dublin, California, the 91st Division (Training Support) plans, staffs, conducts, and evaluates training exercises, including small unit collective training, for ARMY NATIONAL GUARD and U.S. ARMY RESERVE Combat Support and Combat Service Support Units at the squad, platoon/section, and company/battery levels and above. When these units are mobilized, the 91st Division assists in the validation of units as they prepare for deployment.

The 91st—the "Wild West"—Division was created as an infantry division during WORLD WAR I on August 5, 1917, at Camp Lewis, Washington. The division shipped out to England in the summer of 1918 and was committed to battle in September 1918, at the Saint Mihiel offensive. The division also fought in the Meuse-Argonne offensive and was victorious against the German First Guard Division. In 1919, the division was deactivated at the Presidio, San Francisco, then was reconstituted in 1921 as part of the Organized Reserves. For the next two decades, the division constituted an administrative control center rather than a full INFANTRY division. It was reactivated early in 1942 during WORLD WAR II at Camp White, Oregon, and sent to Europe. The division fought in the Italian campaign, and, in September

1944, elements of the division crossed the Sieve River, outflanked the infamous Gothic Line, and captured the Futa Pass.

After the war, the division was deactivated at Fort Rucker, Alabama, in December 1945 and was reactivated in December 1946 at the Presidio of San Francisco as part of the U.S. Army Reserve. In 1959, the division was reorganized and redesignated as the 91st Division (Training), and in 1993 it was again reorganized and redesignated, this time as the 91st Division (Training Support).

95th Division (Institutional Training)

The 95th Division (Institutional Training) is a command of the U.S. ARMY RESERVE and is headquartered at the Harry L. Twaddle U.S. Armed Forces Reserve Center in Oklahoma City, Oklahoma. More than 3,500 soldiers are assigned to the division at Army Reserve centers throughout Oklahoma, Arkansas, Louisiana, Texas, Kansas, Nebraska, New Mexico, Missouri, and Iowa. The division consists of an Infantry (BCT) Brigade, an Artillery (FAOSUT) Brigade, a Training Support Brigade, four Institutional (TASS) School Brigades, a Senior ROTC Brigade, a Drill Sergeant School, the Division Headquarters and Headquarters Company, and the 95th Division Band.

The peacetime mission of the 95th Division (Institutional Training) is to support the U.S. Army's TRAINING AND DOCTRINE COMMAND (TRADOC) by conducting field artillery initial entry training and basic combat initial entry training at the Field Artillery Training Center, Fort Sill, Oklahoma. The division's Institutional Training Brigades provide soldiers of the Army Reserve, ARMY NATIONAL GUARD, and Active Army with MILITARY OCCUPATIONAL SPECIALTY (MOS) and Professional Development courses. During mobilization, the division provides drill sergeants and instructors to augment TRADOC installations and the ARMY MEDICAL DEPARTMENT (AMEDD) Center and School, as well as continues to provide instruction to members of the Army Reserve not affected by the mobilization.

The 95th Division was created on September 5, 1918, as the 95th Infantry Division during WORLD WAR I. Constituted too late to see action, it was soon demobilized, on December 22, 1918, only to be reconstituted at Oklahoma City, Oklahoma, on June 24, 1921, as part of the organized reserves. During WORLD WAR II, on July 14, 1942, the division was activated at Camp Swift, Texas. It served overseas in northern France, the Rhineland, the Ardennes and Alsace regions, and in central Europe, then was inactivated on October 12, 1945, at Camp Shelby, Mississippi. Two years later, on May 13, 1947, the division was again reconstituted as part of the organized reserves in Oklahoma City, Oklahoma. On April 1, 1959, it was redesignated as a training division and, in 1995, as an institutional training division in 1995.

98th Division (Institutional Training)

The 98th Division (Institutional Training) is a command of the U.S. ARMY RESERVE and is headquartered at Rochester, New York. The division consists of more than 3,300 soldiers stationed at Army Reserve centers throughout New England, New York, and New Jersey. Eight brigades incorporate U.S. Army Reserve Forces Schools, a Reserve Forces Training Site-Maintenance, a Reserve Forces Intelligence School, a Noncommissioned Officer Academy, and an ROTC Training detachment.

The 98th Division, called the Iroquois Division, was partially organized on July 23, 1918, during WORLD WAR I at Fort McClellan, Alabama. The armistice of November 11, 1918, was concluded before the division was fully formed, and it was demobilized. On June 24, 1921, the 98th was reestablished, this time as a component of the Organized Reserve. On September 15, 1942, it was activated for service in WORLD WAR II and was deployed to Oahu, Hawaii, on April 19, 1944. The division relieved the 33rd Division as defenders of the Hawaiian Islands and, while performing this duty, simultaneously trained for Asiatic deployment. The 98th was earmarked for participation in the planned invasion of Japan, a mission that was rendered unnecessary by Japan's surrender after atomic bombs were dropped on Hiroshima and Nagasaki in August 1945.

The 98th returned to reserve status in 1947 and was designated a training division in 1959. In 1994, after reorganization, the 98th became the 98th Division (Institutional Training).

noncommissioned officer

Any soldier holding rank from pay grade E-4 to E-9. The noncom's appointment is not signed by the president of the United States, in contrast to that of a COMMISSIONED OFFICER.

Northern Warfare Training Center

Based at Fort Wainwright, Alaska, the Northern Warfare Training Center trains units and leaders in cold weather and mountain operations to increase war-fighting capabilities in these environments. The center conducts basic cold weather and mountain training, maintains a core of advanced cold weather and mountain instructors, and assists in the development and refinement of army mountain and cold weather doctrine.

The origins of the center may be traced to the eve of WORLD WAR II, when, in November 1941, the 87th Mountain Infantry and the Mountain and Winter Warfare Board were activated at Fort Lewis, Washington. These organizations conducted training and testing at Mount Rainier, Washington, throughout the winter of 1941–42, and the units trained here would become the nucleus for the first cold weather and mountain training center to be established by the army.

In 1942, the Mountain Training Center was established at Camp Hale, Colorado, with members of the 87th Mountain Infantry as a cadre. Training of the 10TH MOUNTAIN DIVISION for its role of fighting in the mountains of Italy was the prime World War II achievement of the Mountain Training Center, which also sent training detachments to such locations as Camp McCoy, Wisconsin; Pine Camp, New York; Elkins, West Virginia;

and Adak Island, Alaska, to assist in the training of units in the unique requirements of mountain and cold weather operations.

At the end of World War II, the Mountain Training Center was moved to Camp Carson, Colorado. Then, in November the Army Arctic School was established at Big Delta, Fort Greely, Alaska. Training provided here included arctic survival, mountaineering, skiing, and solutions to tactical, technical, and logistical problems in cold regions. In July 1949, the Army Arctic School was redesignated the Army Arctic Indoctrination School.

In 1957, the Arctic Indoctrination School was redesignated the U.S. Army Cold Weather and Mountain School and was given the mission not only of training soldiers for cold weather and mountain deployment but also of developing cold weather and mountain warfare doctrine, tactics, and techniques. In April 1963, the school was again redesignated, this time as the Northern Warfare Training Center and was given the mission of training individuals as well as units in the conduct of warfare in cold and mountainous regions. Today, this mission continues, and the center is responsible for maintaining the army's state-of-the-art training in cold weather and mountain warfare.

Nuclear-Biological-Chemical (NBC) See CHEMICAL SERVICE ORGANIZATION.

nuclear-biological-chemical (NBC) defense equipment

NBC weapons are a significant threat on the modern battlefield. Currently (2005), the army inventory includes the following NBC defense equipment.

M-40/M-42 Field Protective Mask

Adopted by the army in 1992, the M-40/M-42 Field Protective Mask provides respiratory, eye, and face protection against chemical and biological agents, as well as radioactive fallout particles and other battlefield contaminants. It replaces the M-17-series protective mask as the standard army field mask. Improvements include enhanced comfort, fit, and protection.

The mask consists of a silicone rubber face piece with an in-turned peripheral face seal, binocular rigid eye lens system, and elastic head harness. Other features include front and side voicemitters, which allow clear communication, particularly when operating FM communications. A drink tube is included for a drinking capability while the mask is worn. Clear and tinted lens inserts are provided, as is a filter canister with special NATO standard threads to insure interoperability among all NATO forces. Because of its comfort features, the mask can be worn continuously for eight to 12 hours.

The face-mounted canister (gas and aerosol filter) can be worn on either the left or the right cheek, and is designed to withstand a maximum of 15 nerve, choking, and blister agent attacks. The canister will also withstand a maximum of two blood agent attacks. Biological agents do not degrade the filter, which can therefore withstand an indeterminate number of such attacks.

The M-40A1 is the mask issued to dismounted soldiers and is available in small, medium, and large sizes. The M-42A2 Combat Vehicle Crewman Mask has the same components as the M-40A1, but includes an additional built-in microphone for wire communication. The filter canister is attached to the end of the hose with an adapter for the CPFU connection.

The M-45 Protective Mask is issued to Blackhawk crew members and provides protection without the aid of forced ventilation air. It is compatible with all aircraft sighting systems and night vision devices. It incorporates close fitting eyepieces, a voicemitter, drink tube, and a low-profile filter canister.

The M-48 and M-49 protective masks are issued to Apache crew members. They are an upgrade of the M-43 Type I mask and include an improved blower that is chest-mounted, lighter, less bulky, and battery powered.

All versions of the mask are manufactured by ILC Dover, Frederica, Delaware.

M-93/M-93A1 Nuclear, Biological, and Chemical Reconnaissance System

The M-93/M-93A1 Nuclear, Biological, and Chemical Reconnaissance System, which entered army service in 1998, is designed to detect, identify, and mark areas of nuclear and chemical contamination, to sample soil, water, and vegetation for nuclear, biological, and chemical contamination, and to report accurate information to supported commanders in real time.

The M-93 is a fully integrated nuclear-biological-chemical (NBC) reconnaissance system, which incorporates a dedicated system of NBC detection, warning, and sampling equipment integrated into a six-wheeled, all-wheel-drive armored vehicle. Informally, the system is called the "Fox NBC Reconnaissance System." It was originally developed in Germany for use by the German military. The U.S. military initiated a detailed requirement for the Fox system, which was generated in the late 1980s in response to a perceived need to quickly field a chemical reconnaissance vehicle to U.S. forces in Europe. The German-designed and -produced vehicles (designated the XM-93) met many of the U.S. requirements and were modified for adoption by the army. A System Improvement Phase provided vehicles (designated the XM-93E1) for testing to ensure they satisfied all U.S. requirements of operational capability, and a Block 1 modification phase upgraded all XM-93 vehicles to the M-93A1 configuration. The first army unit was equipped with the NBCRS-Fox Block 1 system, the M-93A1, in October 1998.

The M-93A1 iteration of the vehicle contains an enhanced NBC sensor suite that consists of the M-21 Remote Sensing Chemical Agent Alarm (RSCAAL), MM-1 Mobile Mass Spectrometer, Chemical Agent Monitor/Improved Chemical Agent Monitor (CAM/ICAM), AN/VDR-2 Beta Radiac, and M-22 Automatic Chemical Agent Detector/Alarm (ACADA). The NBC sensor suite is digitally linked with the communications and navigation subsystems by a dual-purpose central processor system known as the Multipurpose Integrated Chemical Agent Detector (MICAD). The MICAD processor fully automates NBC warning and reporting functions and provides the crew commander with full situational awareness of the Fox's NBC sensors, navigation, and communications systems. Additionally, the M-93A1 Fox is equipped with an advanced position navigation system—including a Global Positioning System (GPS) and an Autonomous Navigation System (ANAV)—that enables the Fox system to locate and report agent contamination with a high degree of accuracy.

The vehicle is equipped with an overpressure filtration system to permit the crew to operate in a shirt-sleeve environment that is nevertheless fully protected from the effects of NBC agents and contamination outside the vehicle. Moreover, the automated features of the M-93A1 reduce the crew requirements to just three soldiers from the four soldiers required to operate the original M-93 Fox.

The M-93A1 is capable of detecting chemical contamination in its immediate environment through point detection. It can detect contamination at a distance through the use of the M-21 RSCAAL. The Fox system then automatically integrates contamination information from sensors with input from on-board navigation and meteorological systems and rapidly transmits (via SINCGARS radios) its digital NBC warning messages to warn follow-on forces.

In normal operation, two Fox reconnaissance systems, working as a team, precede the movement of troops and materiel and are tasked with locating and marking contaminated areas.

The M-93/M-93A1 Nuclear, Biological, and Chemical Reconnaissance System is fully amphibious and is capable of swimming speeds up to six miles per hour. Other general specifications include:

Weight: 17 tons
Length: 22.25 ft
Height: 8.1 ft
Maximum speed: 65 mph on-road
Powerplant: Mercedes-Benz OM 402A V-8 diesel
Horsepower: 320 hp
Crew: 3

Manufacturer: General Dynamics Land Systems (Detroit, Michigan, and Anniston, Alabama) and Henschel Wehrtechnik (Kassel, Germany)

M-256A1 Chemical Agent Detector Kit

The M-256A1 Chemical Agent Detector Kit was acquired by the army in 1978 to provide everything necessary for the detection and identification of blood, blister, and nerve agents present environmentally either as liquid or as vapor. The kit may be used to determine when it is safe to unmask, to locate and identify chemical hazards during reconnaissance missions, and to monitor decontamination effectiveness. The M-256 kit is not an alarm; rather, it is a tool intended for use after soldiers have received other warnings about the possible presence of chemical warfare agents and after they have responded by putting on their chemical protective clothing.

The M-256 kit consists of a carrying case, a booklet of M-8 paper, 12 disposable sampler-detectors individually sealed in plastic laminated foil envelopes, and a set of instruction cards attached by a lanyard to the plastic carrying case. The case is made from molded, high impact plastic and has a nylon carrying strap and a nylon belt attachment. The case measures just seven inches high, five inches wide, and three inches in depth. The entire M-256 kit weighs 1.2 pounds. Operation is compatible with temperatures ranging from minus 25 degrees Fahrenheit (–32 degrees Celsius) to 120 degrees Fahrenheit (49 degrees Celsius).

The M-8 paper included in the kit is used to test liquid substances for the presence of nerve agents and blister agents. M-8 paper is similar in principle to litmus (pH) paper used in any chemistry laboratory. Like the litmus paper, the M-8 paper changes color in the presence of a positive test substance. The M-8 paper is specifically designed—it is impregnated with special dyes—to react to nerve agents and blister agents in liquid form. Indeed, soldiers are separately issued their own supply of M-8 paper as part of their standard chemical detection equipment. To perform the test, the soldier blots the M-8 paper on the suspect liquid and inspects for color change, comparing the resulting hue to a color chart included inside the front cover of the booklet that accompanies each packet of paper.

Each sampler-detector included in the kit contains a square impregnated spot capable of reacting with blister agents, a circular test spot designed to react with blood agents, a star-shaped test spot that responds to nerve agents, and a lewisite detecting tablet and rubbing tab. The test spots are made of standard laboratory filter paper. There are eight glass ampoules, six containing reagents for testing and two in an attached chemical heater. When the ampoules are crushed between the fingers, formed channels in the plastic sheets direct the flow of liquid reagent to wet the test spots. Each test spot or detecting tablet develops a distinctive color to indicate whether a chemical agent is or is not present in the air.

The kit contains reagents that use eel enzyme for the nerve test. This replaces the horse enzyme formerly used and thereby provides for an improvement by detecting lower levels of nerve agent. Any type of mustard agent is also detectable, provided that vapor is present.

Using the directions on the foil packets or in the instruction booklet, any soldier can conduct a complete test with the liquid-sensitive M-8 paper and the vapor-sensitive sampler-detector in no more than 20 minutes. To increase proficiency in conducting tests, a M-256A1 trainer simulator was developed to provide realistic training while avoiding unnecessary exposure to potentially carcinogenic reagents in the working M-256A1 detector kit. The M-256A1 trainer contains 36 pre-engineered detector tickets and an instruction booklet. The pre-engineered detector tickets show color changes comparable to those seen when the M-256A1 detector kit is used in clean or contaminated environments.

Specifications of the working kit include:

Agents Detected: hydrogen cyanide (AC), cyanogen chloride (CK), mustard (H), nitrogen mustard (HN), distilled mustard (HD), phosgene oxime (CX), lewisite (L), and nerve agents (V and G series).

Joint Service Lightweight Integrated Suit Technology (JSLIST)

The JSLIST was developed in 1997 and entered army service that year. Designed to be worn in combination with a Chemical Protective Mask, the JSLIST suit provides protection against chemical and biological agents, as well as radioactive fallout particles and other battlefield contaminants.

The JSLIST suit was developed jointly by all the armed services and includes a lightweight chemical/biological (CB) protective garment and multipurpose overboots and gloves. Each of these components is based on state-of-the-art materiel technologies, which have been subjected to extensive user evaluation and field and laboratory testing. The objective of the new suit technology was to create equipment that reduced heat stress, that was compatible with all interfacing equipment, that allowed for longer wear, and that incorporated a high degree of washability. The JSLIST replaces the earlier Battle Dress Overgarment (BDO).

The JSLIST overgarment is a universal, lightweight, two-piece, front-opening suit, wearable as an overgarment or as a primary uniform over underwear. It features an integral hood, bellows-type sockets, high-waist trousers, adjustable suspenders, adjustable waistband, and a waist-length jacket, which not only enhances system comfort but also improves system acceptance and maximizes compatibility with the individual user equipment. On the waist-length coat, a flap fastened with Velcro covers the zipper. The sleeves also have Velcro wrist-closure adjustment tabs, and the left sleeve has an outside expandable pocket with flap. The JSLIST system includes a liner of a nonwoven front, laminated to activate carbon spheres and bonded to a knitted back, which absorbs chemical agents. The earlier BDO liner consisted of charcoal-impregnated polyurethane foam and nylon tricot laminate. The problem with this system was that the BDO foam deteriorated as the wearer rubbed against it.

The bulky charcoal layer of the older BDO has been replaced in the new system with a selectively permeable membrane that is lighter and that is engineered to block harmful substances, rather than absorb them. The new material and construction also allows more perspiration to escape.

With a weight of just under six pounds, the new suit is about half the weight of the BDO. It is available in a four-color Woodland or a three-color desert camouflage pattern and can be worn in an uncontaminated environment for 45 days with up to six launderings or for over 120 days with no launderings. The JSLIST suit can be worn in a contaminated environment for 24 hours. Each soldier is issued two JSLIST suits.

The Multipurpose Rain/Snow/CB Overboot (MULO), which is part of the JSLIST system, replaces the older black vinyl overboot/ green vinyl overboot (BVO/GVO). The MULO is manufactured by injection molding an elastomer blend, which is compounded to provide maximum chemical and environmental protection required. The boot incorporates two quick-release side buckles and is designed to be worn over the standard issue combat boot, jungle boot, and intermediate cold/wet boot. The MULO provides 60 days of durability and 24 hours of protection against liquid chemical agents. The MULO boot is capable of being decontaminated to an operationally safe level using standard field decontaminates. Environmental protection is provided against water, snow, and mud, in addition to petroleum, oil, and lubricant (POL). The boot offers a high degree of flame resistance.

The Joint Service Lightweight Integrated Suit Technology is manufactured by the National Center for the Employment of the Disabled (El Paso, Texas); Group Home Foundation (Belfast, Maine); Creative Apparel (Belfast, Maine); South Eastern Kentucky Rehabilitation Industries (Corbin, Kentucky); Peckham Vocational Industries (Lansing, Michigan); and Battelle (Stafford, Virginia).

Office of the Chief Army Reserve (OCAR)
See U.S. ARMY RESERVE.

OH-6 Cayuse See AIRCRAFT.

OH-58 Kiowa See AIRCRAFT.

100th Division (Institutional Training)

The 100th Division (Institutional Training) is headquartered in Louisville, Kentucky, and has units in Alabama, Kentucky, Mississippi, and Tennessee. It is organized into eight major subordinate commands with 44 units and 3,000 reservists. The division is a major army training resource.

The division was organized as the 100th Infantry Division in July 1918 at Camp Bowie, Texas, during WORLD WAR I. The armistice of November, 11, 1918, occurred before the division was deployed to Europe, and it was demobilized in 1919, but reconstituted in June 1921 at Wheeling, West Virginia.

The 100th was activated at Fort Jackson, South Carolina, late in 1942 and, late the next year, moved from Fort Jackson to winter maneuvers in the Tennessee mountains. Additional training took place at Fort Bragg, North Carolina, in early 1944. The division was committed to combat in early November 1944 as part of the Seventh U.S. Army's VI Corps,

fighting in the Vosges Mountains on the edge of Alsace. After a hard-fought mountain battle, the division pushed the Germans out onto the Rhine plain and into Germany. A heavy enemy counterattack pushed back all Seventh Army units, except for the 100th, which held its sector and ultimately blunted the German offensive. In March 1945, the 100th resumed the initiative and passed through the Siegfried Line into Germany. Its last major battle was an attack on Heilbronn in April 1945. Urban combat lasted a week, then the division pursued the enemy through Swabia toward Stuttgart.

In 185 days of continuous combat, the 100th Infantry Division liberated more than 400 cities, towns, and villages, defeated major elements of eight German divisions, and took 13,351 prisoners. It sustained casualties of 916 killed, 3,656 wounded, and 180 missing in action.

The division was inactivated in January 1946 at Fort Patrick Henry, Virginia, then reactivated in the fall of 1946 as the 100th Airborne Division under the U.S. ARMY RESERVE. The unit was redesignated as the 100th Infantry Division in 1952, and it became a replacement training division in 1955. It was redesignated the 100th Division for institutional training in 1959, its mission to teach basic, advanced individual, and common training to new soldiers. In 1995, the division was reorganized to include Army Reserve Schools, and it also implemented a distance learning systems approach to military career training.

101st Airborne Division (Air Assault)

One of the most celebrated army units, known as the "Screaming Eagles" after their shoulder emblem, the 101st Airborne was formed during WORLD WAR II on August 19, 1942, and earned its first fame during that struggle, fighting in Europe from D-day through victory.

Based at Fort Campbell, Kentucky, the 101st Airborne Division (Air Assault) is formed of three brigades plus Division Artillery, Division Support Command, the 101st Aviation Brigade, 159th Aviation Brigade, 101st Corps Support Group, and several separate commands. Although originally created as a paratroop unit, the current 101st mission is to provide forcible entry capability through heliborne air assault operations. Typically, the 101st conducts operations 150 to 300 kilometers beyond the line of contact or forward-line-of-own-troops. The division is capable of inserting a 4,000-troop combined-arms task force 150 kilometers into enemy territory in a single lift. The air assault capability of the 101st is unmatched by any force in the world.

During World War II, the 101st Airborne Division parachuted into France on the night before the D-day landings at Normandy to disrupt enemy communications. This action began 30 days of continuous combat, after which the division was returned to England to train for its next mission, Operation Market Garden, a jump into a narrow corridor of Holland to seize several bridges in an effort to expedite the Allied advance into Germany. The 101st jumped on September 17, 1944, and also participated in a massive glider landing. Although the 101st was generally successful in its 72 days in combat in the Netherlands, Operation Market Garden as a whole failed.

The 101st rested in France after its long engagement in Holland, but it was called into action again beginning on December 17, 1944, to hold the Belgian town of Bastogne against a massive surprise German offensive in what became known as the Battle of the Bulge. The 101st traveled 107 miles in open 10-ton trucks to reach the town, then held it against far superior numbers of German troops, who soon enveloped the unit. On December 22, the German commander, Lieutenant General Heinrich von Luttwitz, issued a demand for the surrender of the 101st. To this, division commander General Anthony C. McAuliffe replied with a single word: "Nuts." Severely outnumbered, the 101st held out until December 26, when the 4th U.S. Armored Division broke through.

At the end of March, elements of the 101st advanced into the Ruhr region of Germany, then moved into southern Bavaria, where it occupied Berchtesgaden, Adolf Hitler's mountain retreat. During this operation, the division captured several prominent Nazi political and military leaders. After this, on August 1, 1945, the 101st returned to France to begin training for the invasion of Japan. With Japan's surrender later in the month, however, the invasion became unnecessary, and the division was inactivated on November 30, 1945, at Auxerre, France.

Over the next 11 years, the division was activated and then inactivated three times as a training unit, and, in March 1956, it was finally transferred to Fort Campbell, where it was reorganized as a combat division.

In 1965, elements of the 101st were deployed to Vietnam and fought for almost seven years in the VIETNAM WAR, participating in some 15 campaigns. Gone were the parachutes; the division had now become "airmobile" and used helicopters to transport troops and supplies in an air assault role. The 101st fought in both the Tet Offensive and the Tet Counteroffensive in 1969, and it was the last combat division to leave Vietnam, in 1972. The 101st suffered twice as many casualties in Vietnam as it had in World War II.

On October 4, 1974, the 101st Airborne Division (AirMobile) was officially designated the 101st Airborne Division (Air Assault). Its next major deployment came in March 1982, when elements were sent to the Sinai Desert as part of a multinational peacekeeping force. In August 1990, the 101st was among the very first U.S. units to deploy in Operation Desert Shield, the preparatory phase of the PERSIAN GULF WAR. Indeed, the division fired the first ground-based shots of the war, taking out Iraqi radar sites on January 17, 1991, and the division was sent deep into Iraq to set up a base of operations for further attacks. During the ground war phase of the Persian Gulf War, the 101st made the longest and largest air assault in history, deploying more than 2,000 troops and airlifting 50 transport vehicles, artillery, and tons of fuel and ammunition. A cease-fire was declared within 100 hours of the beginning of the ground war.

Subsequent to the Gulf War, elements of the division have supported humanitarian relief efforts in Rwanda and Somalia and served as peacekeepers in Haiti and Bosnia. In February 2003, elements of the 101st began deploying to Iraq as part of Operation Iraqi Freedom, the controversial invasion of that country for the purpose of disarming and ultimately removing Iraqi dictator Saddam Hussein. As of early 2005, the 101st is still engaged in combat in Iraq.

108th Division (Institutional Training)

The 108th is a U.S. ARMY RESERVE training unit, located in Charlotte, North Carolina, and tasked with instructing military skills and teaching basic training to soldiers. The division's subordinate units are located in North Carolina, South Carolina, Georgia, Florida, and Puerto Rico—3,300 soldiers in 23 cities and towns.

The division was originally activated in 1946, after WORLD WAR II, and was then designated the 108th Airborne Division, headquartered in Atlanta, Georgia. It was the airborne mission that gave the division its nickname, Golden Griffons. However, in 1952, the division was reorganized into an INFANTRY division and its headquarters moved to Charlotte, North Carolina. In 1956, the 108th became the prototype of the army training division.

During the VIETNAM WAR, the 108th Division conducted interim training for soldiers waiting to begin basic training. In January 1991, more than 300 108th Division soldiers were called to active duty to support Operation Desert Storm (PERSIAN GULF WAR)—the first time the division had ever been mobilized. Division soldiers assisted in the retraining of individual soldiers at Fort Jackson who were called back to military duty during the war.

Late in 1993, the 108th Division pioneered a new training concept, the Future Army Schools Twenty-first Century, which entailed the expansion of the 108th Division to Georgia and Florida and added 10 new U.S. Army Reserve Forces Schools to the division's force structure. While the 108th Division continued to conduct initial entry training for new soldiers entering the army, it also began administering specialized skill training for officers and enlisted soldiers in the Southeast. In 1996, the 108th Division was assigned another new mission, which entailed conducting Reserve Officer Training Corps (ROTC) training at three colleges and universities in Florida, Georgia, and South Carolina.

operational command (OPCOM)

OPCOM designates the authority to assign military missions and direct units selected for the missions.

See also OPERATIONAL CONTROL.

operational control (OPCON)

OPCON is the person or headquarters given temporary control over a unit's administration, logistics, and personnel while the unit performs a specific mission.

See also OPERATIONAL COMMAND.

Ordnance Corps

The mission of the Ordnance Corps, an army combat service branch, is to arm and fix the force by providing support for weapons systems and the ammunition required for them. The Ordnance Corps supports the development, production, acquisition, and sustainment of weapons systems and munitions. The corps also provides for explosive ordnance disposal during peace and war. The home station of the Ordnance Corps is Aberdeen Proving Ground, Maryland.

organization, administrative

The chief executive officer of the army is the SECRETARY OF THE ARMY, whose deputy and principal assistant is the UNDER SECRETARY OF THE ARMY. Two deputy under secretaries are assigned to the under secretary. Five ASSISTANT SECRETARIES OF THE ARMY have responsibility for specific areas of administration and report directly to the secretary, as do a host of other assistants, including director of information systems for C4 (Command, Control, Communications, and Computers), inspector general, auditor general, chief of legislative liaison, chief of public affairs, director of office of small and disadvantaged business utilization, and general counsel.

Collectively, the civilian administrators just mentioned constitute the Department of the Army's Secretariat. The next organizational level is the department's ARMY STAFF, which consists of army members, including CHIEF OF STAFF, the ARMY GENERAL STAFF, the SPECIAL STAFF, and the PERSONAL STAFF.

organization by branch

Officers and enlisted personnel are assigned to a basic or special branch of the army as follows:

Combat Arms Branches
AIR DEFENSE ARTILLERY
ARMOR
AVIATION
ENGINEERS
FIELD ARTILLERY
INFANTRY

Combat Support Branches
CHEMICAL CORPS
MILITARY INTELLIGENCE
MILITARY POLICE
SIGNAL CORPS

Combat Service Support Branches
ADJUTANT GENERAL CORPS
FINANCE CORPS
MEDICAL SERVICE CORPS
ARMY NURSE CORPS
ORDNANCE CORPS

QUARTERMASTER CORPS
TRANSPORTATION CORPS

Special Branches
ARMY CHAPLAIN CORPS
JUDGE ADVOCATE GENERAL'S CORPS
ARMY MEDICAL CORPS
ARMY DENTAL CORPS
ARMY VETERINARY CORPS
SPECIAL FORCES

organization by component

The army is organized into three components:

The REGULAR ARMY is the army's permanent, professional force, whose members are full-time soldiers, stationed and assigned duty as directed by military authority.

The army's other two components are RESERVE COMPONENTS. The ARMY NATIONAL GUARD (ARNG) is organized under dual status. In peacetime, it is a state force controlled in each state by the governor. In wartime or national emergency, the ARNG can be mobilized by the president and thereby is federalized and placed under direct army control. The U.S. ARMY RESERVE (USAR) consists of federal, not state-controlled, troops who serve in reserve units and are available for call-up into active service under conditions that vary with their status classification within the USAR.

The term *ACTIVE ARMY* is used to denote that part of the army that is on full-time service at any given time. The regular army is a part of the active army at all times; all or some of the reserve components enter into the active army from time to time, according to need. Collectively, all three army components form the "Total Force," a concept that regards and treats all the components as vital to the national defense and national interests.

organization by major field commands

The army is organized into nine major field commands:

U.S. ARMY FORCES COMMAND (FORSCOM) includes the UNITED STATES ARMY RESERVE

COMMAND (see U.S. ARMY RESERVE), CONTINENTAL UNITED STATES ARMIES (CONUSA), THIRD U.S. ARMY, and two training centers: NATIONAL TRAINING CENTER (NTC) and JOINT READINESS TRAINING CENTER (JRTC).

U.S. ARMY TRAINING AND DOCTRINE COMMAND (TRADOC) provides institutional training for soldiers, sets army training standards, and formulates army doctrine.

U.S. ARMY MATERIEL COMMAND (AMC) equips and sustains the army.

U.S. ARMY INTELLIGENCE AND SECURITY COMMAND (INSCOM) is responsible for intelligence, counterintelligence, and operations security for the army.

U.S. ARMY INFORMATION SYSTEMS ENGINEERING COMMAND (USAISEC) provides information systems and services for the army as well as other Department of Defense organizations.

U.S. ARMY CRIMINAL INVESTIGATION COMMAND (USACIC) controls the investigations of serious crimes for the army and provides investigative services for sensitive and special investigations; it also provides security for selected army and Department of Defense officials.

U.S. ARMY MILITARY DISTRICT OF WASHINGTON (MDW) is responsible for army units and activities in the Washington, D.C., area.

U.S. ARMY MEDICAL COMMAND (MEDCOM) manages army health care delivery and training within the United States. The ARMY MEDICAL DEPARTMENT is the principal operational arm of the command.

U.S. ARMY CORPS OF ENGINEERS (USACE) manages both army real property and engineering projects for the army and air force as well as civil works programs for the army and other federal agencies.

organization by units

Operationally and tactically, the army is organized into units, the constitution of which is specified in the TABLE OF ORGANIZATION AND EQUIPMENT (TOE), established by the DEPARTMENT OF THE ARMY. The most common army units follow, listed in order of ascending size and scope of responsibility:

fire team: The fire team is an informal tactical group, usually consisting of four soldiers and constituting half a squad.

squad: The squad is the army's smallest formal tactical unity, consisting of eight to 12 soldiers. A squad is commanded by a sergeant and is generally subdivided into two fire teams of four men each. Four squads make up a platoon.

platoon: Generally, a group of four squads under a lieutenant. Two platoons generally make up a company, under a captain. In some applications, "platoon" is used to describe any small group assigned a specific function.

company: A company is a command level below a battalion and above a platoon. In the army, it is the basic administrative as well as tactical unit. A company is commanded by a captain; three to four companies plus a special headquarters company constitute a battalion. In the army, an artillery company is called an artillery battery.

battalion: The battalion is a unit, usually commanded by a lieutenant colonel, composed of two or more companies in addition to a headquarters company. When it is part of a regiment, the battalion has only tactical functions. When it exists as a separate unit, the battalion incorporates both administrative and tactical functions. A battalion numbers anywhere from 300 to 1,000 soldiers.

regiment: Regiment is a traditional unit term no longer officially used by the army or marine corps (having been supplanted by brigade), but still used unofficially in deference to tradition.

brigade: In the army, a brigade is smaller than a division and may be comprised of battalions or smaller units. The brigade is usually a single-arm unit, such as a brigade of FIELD

ARTILLERY or SPECIAL FORCES. A brigade is usually commanded by a colonel.

division: An army division is a major administrative and tactical unit that combines in itself the necessary arms and services for sustained combat. It is larger than a regiment or brigade and smaller than a corps (which usually consists of two or more divisions). Light INFANTRY divisions typically number 11,000 troops, whereas armored and mechanized divisions may muster 16,500.

corps: As defined by the Department of Defense, an army corps is a tactical unit larger than a division and smaller than a field army. It usually consists of two or more divisions together with auxiliary arms and services.

field army: An administrative and tactical organization consisting of a headquarters, certain organic army troops, service support troops as may be required, a variable number of corps, and a variable number of divisions.

theater army: A theater army is the army component of a unified joint command in a theater of operations. It is an ECHELON ABOVE CORPS (EAC) and provides combat support and combat service support for army forces in the theater. A theater army is not a permanent organization, but is constituted according to the requirements of the theater in question.

P

Patton, George Smith, Jr. (1885–1945)

U.S. Army general

One of the most famous names among army commanders, George Patton led the THIRD U.S. ARMY in WORLD WAR II across France and Germany and as far east as Czechoslovakia. He was a brilliant tactician, quite probably the finest in the entire war, and a flamboyant as well as controversial leader.

Born at San Gabriel, California, Patton attended Virginia Military Institute in 1904 before securing an appointment to the UNITED STATES MILITARY ACADEMY. He graduated after a difficult five years (he repeated his first year) and was recognized, among other things, as a superb horseman. Commissioned a second lieutenant in the CAVALRY, he served in a number of army posts. Excelling as an athlete, Patton represented the army on the United States pentathlon team at the 1912 Stockholm Olympics. He was also honored with an appointment to study at Saumur, the prestigious French cavalry school. He then graduated from the Mounted Service School at Fort Riley, Kansas, in 1913. From 1914 to 1916, Patton served as an instructor at the school. An expert swordsman, he wrote the army's saber manual and even designed the still-current official army saber.

In 1916, Patton was assigned to General JOHN JOSEPH PERSHING's punitive expedition to Mexico in pursuit of Pancho Villa, at the conclusion of which, in 1917, he was promoted to captain. Patton worshiped Pershing as a model military officer and was thrilled to be appointed to his staff and sent with him to France in May 1917, after the U.S. entry into WORLD WAR I.

In Europe, Patton became the first American officer to receive tank training, and he became an enthusiastic convert to the potential of mechanized warfare. He set up the AEF Tank School at Langres in November 1917. Promoted to temporary lieutenant colonel, then temporary colonel, he organized and led the 1st Tank Brigade in the assault on the Saint-Mihiel salient during September 12–17, 1918. Wounded in this engagement, he quickly recovered and fought at Meuse-Argonne (September 26–November 11).

Like many other officers, Patton reverted to his prewar rank on his return to the United States following the armistice. However, he was soon promoted to major (1919) and given command of the 304th Tank Brigade at Fort Meade, Maryland. In this command, he formulated, honed, and perfected armored tactics during 1919–21.

From 1921 to 1922, Patton was posted with the 3rd Cavalry Regiment to Fort Myer, Virginia, and he graduated at the top of his class from the COMMAND AND GENERAL STAFF College in 1923. He served on the ARMY GENERAL STAFF from 1923 to 1927, then as chief of cavalry from 1928 to 1931, when he left to attend the U.S. ARMY WAR COLLEGE. Patton was made executive officer of the 3rd Cavalry and promoted to lieutenant colonel in 1934. He returned to service on the General Staff

Two top USA commanders in the European theater, World War II: George S. Patton (left) and Omar Bradley *(National Archives and Records Administration)*

in 1935, with a promotion to colonel coming in 1937.

From December 1938 to July 1940, Patton commanded the 3rd Cavalry, and then took command of the 2nd Armored Brigade during July–November 1940. Promoted to temporary brigadier general on October 2, 1940, he became acting commanding general of the 2nd Armored Division in November. The appointment was made permanent on April 4, 1941, and Patton was also promoted to temporary major general. He led his division in the massive war maneuvers conducted in Tennessee during the summer and fall of 1941.

Shortly after U.S. entry into World War II, Patton was named commander of I Armored Corps (January 15, 1942), and he was then assigned to create and command the Desert Training Center at Indio, California, from March 26 to July 30, 1942, in preparation for combat in North Africa. Patton was instrumental in the final planning for Operation Torch (July 30–August 21), the conquest of North Africa, and he commanded the Western Task Force in landings there on November 8, 1942. He was named to replace General Lloyd R. Fredendall as commander of II Corps on March 3, 1943, after Fredendall was disastrously defeated by Panzer general Erwin Rommel at the Kasserine Pass. Patton was promoted to temporary lieutenant general on March 12, only to be relieved of command three days later after a dispute with his British colleagues. Patton's arrogance and outspoken, impulsive nature would plague him throughout the war. Friction with the Allies, the press, and with superiors would prove chronic.

Soon after this incident, Patton was given command of I Armored Corps, which became the Seventh Army on July 10. Patton led it with extraordinary drive during the invasion of Sicily from July 10 through August 17. On the 16th, while visiting wounded soldiers in a field hospital, Patton encountered a soldier suffering from battle fatigue. He accused the man of cowardice and slapped him. Two weeks later, a similar slapping incident occurred. The public and Patton's superiors were scandalized by these outbursts, and Patton was sent to England in disgrace on January 22, 1944.

Patton publicly apologized for the incidents, but he was nevertheless temporarily sidelined in England. The planners of the Normandy invasion used Patton's presence in England to dupe the Germans into thinking that he was going to lead an invading army by way of Calais—not Normandy. Once the D-day invasion was actually put into motion, Patton was given command of the newly formed Third Army and arrived with it in France on July 6.

It was in the operations that followed that Patton became one of the great heroes of World War II. He led the Third Army during the breakout from Normandy and the lightning advance across France through the summer of 1944, collecting retroactive promotions to brigadier general and to major general in the process. He liberated town after town, delivering ruinous blows to the retreating German army.

When the Germans launched their desperate surprise offensive in Belgium in the Ardennes (December 16, 1944–January 1945)—the so-called Battle of the Bulge—Patton performed a tactical miracle by wheeling the entire Third Army, exhausted from months of forced marching and battle, 90 degrees north and launching a bold counterattack into the southern flank of the German penetration. By this action, he relieved Bastogne on December 26, 1944, ended the Battle of the Bulge, and then poised his army for the final push to the Rhine.

After encountering stiff resistance during January–March 1945, the Third Army crossed the Rhine at Oppenheim on March 22 and advanced into central Germany and northern Bavaria by April. Units of the Third reached Linz, Austria, on May 5 and Pilsen, Czechoslovakia, on May 6—even before the Germans surrendered.

With the war in Europe won, indiscreet expression of political opinions once again caused trouble for Patton. He outspokenly criticized the Soviet allies and, even worse, as military governor of Bavaria, he opposed de-Nazification policies because (he said) they left the conquered territories without qualified officials to maintain order. The Allied command yielded to public and diplomatic pressure and relieved Patton of command of the Third Army and removed him from the governorship of Bavaria.

Although Patton desperately wanted to be sent to the Pacific to fight the war against Japan, he was appointed commander of the Fifteenth Army—essentially a "paper army," an administrative unit set up to collect records and compile a history of the war. On December 9, 1945, he broke his neck in an otherwise trivial automobile accident near Mannheim. Paralyzed from the neck down, he was hospitalized. Pulmonary edema and congestive heart failure developed, and he died on December 21.

pay, basic military

Basic military pay is the same for all the armed services. Basic pay level is pegged to grade (sometimes called "pay grade") and to years in grade. While the nomenclature of ranks varies more or less from one service to another (see RANKS AND GRADES), grades are standardized. For example, a navy captain is equivalent in rank to an army colonel, a fact reflected in the grade they share, O-6. (An army captain is grade O-3, equivalent to a navy lieutenant.)

The following charts, which are current as of January 2004, show basic military pay for officers (O), warrant officers (W), and enlisted personnel (E). Personnel receive additional compensation, either in the form of salary or in other compensation (such as special living allowances) based on special duties or special qualifications. In addition

COMMISSIONED OFFICERS					
	Years of Service				
Pay grade	Under 2	Over 2	Over 3	Over 4	Over 6
O–10	—	—	—	—	—
O–9	—	—	—	—	—
O–8	7,751.10	8,004.90	8,173.20	8,220.60	8,430.30
O–7	6,440.70	6,739.80	6,878.40	6,988.50	7,187.40
O–6	4,773.60	5,244.30	5,588.40	5,588.40	5,609.70
O–5	3,979.50	4,482.90	4,793.40	4,851.60	5,044.80
O–4	3,433.50	3,974.70	4,239.90	4,299.00	4,545.30
O–3	3,018.90	3,422.40	3,693.90	4,027.20	4,220.10
O–2	2,608.20	2,970.60	3,421.50	3,537.00	3,609.90
O–1	2,264.40	2,356.50	2,848.50	2,848.50	2,848.50

to basic pay, all personnel receive compensation in the form of housing (or housing subsidies), meals, uniforms (or uniform allowances), medical benefits, and educational benefits.

COMMISSIONED OFFICERS

Pay grade	Over 8	Over 10	Over 12	Over 14	Over 16
O–10	—	—	—	—	—
O–9	—	—	—	—	—
O–8	8,781.90	8,863.50	9,197.10	9,292.80	9,579.90
O–7	7,384.20	7,611.90	7,839.00	8,066.70	8,781.90
O–6	5,850.00	5,882.10	5,882.10	6,216.30	6,807.30
O–5	5,161.20	5,415.90	5,602.80	5,844.00	6,213.60
O–4	4,809.30	5,137.80	5,394.00	5,571.60	5,673.60
O–3	4,431.60	4,568.70	4,794.30	4,911.30	4,911.30
O–2	3,609.90	3,609.90	3,609.90	3,609.90	3,609.90
O–1	2,848.50	2,848.50	2,848.50	2,848.50	2,848.50

Years of Service

COMMISSIONED OFFICERS

Pay grade	Over 18	Over 20	Over 22	Over 24	Over 26
O–10	—	12,524.70	12,586.20	12,847.80	13,303.80
O–9	—	10,954.50	11,112.30	11,340.30	11,738.40
O–8	9,995.70	10,379.10	10,635.30	10,635.30	10,635.30
O–7	9,386.10	9,386.10	9,386.10	9,386.10	9,433.50
O–6	7,154.10	7,500.90	7,698.30	7,897.80	8,285.40
O–5	6,389.70	6,563.40	6,760.80	6,760.80	6,760.80
O–4	5,733.00	5,733.00	5,733.00	5,733.00	5,733.00
O–3	4,911.30	4,911.30	4,911.30	4,911.30	4,911.30
O 2	3,609.90	3,609.90	3,609.90	3,609.90	3,609.90
O–1	2,848.50	2,848.50	2,848.50	2,848.50	2,848.50

Years of Service

COMMISSIONED OFFICERS WITH OVER 4 YEARS OF ACTIVE SERVICE AS AN ENLISTED MEMBER OR WARRANT OFFICER

	Under 2	Over 2	Over 3	Over 4	Over 6
O–3E	—	—	—	4,027.20	4,220.10
O–2E	—	—	—	3,537.00	3,609.90
O–1E	—	—	—	2,848.50	3,042.30

COMMISSIONED OFFICERS WITH OVER 4 YEARS OF ACTIVE SERVICE AS AN ENLISTED MEMBER OR WARRANT OFFICER

	Over 8	Over 10	Over 12	Over 14	Over 16
O–3E	4,431.60	4,568.70	4,794.30	4,984.20	5,092.80
O–2E	3,724.80	3,918.60	4,068.60	4,180.20	4,180.20
O–1E	3,154.50	3,269.40	3,382.20	3,537.00	3,537.00

COMMISSIONED OFFICERS WITH OVER 4 YEARS OF ACTIVE SERVICE AS AN ENLISTED MEMBER OR WARRANT OFFICER

	Over 18	Over 20	Over 22	Over 24	Over 26
O–3E	5,241.30	5,241.30	5,241.30	5,241.30	5,241.30
O–2E	4,180.20	4,180.20	4,180.20	4,180.20	4,180.20
O–1E	3,537.00	3,537.00	3,537.00	3,537.00	3,537.00

WARRANT OFFICERS

	Under 2	Over 2	Over 3	Over 4	Over 6
W–5	—	—	—	—	—
W–4	3,119.40	3,355.80	3,452.40	3,547.20	3,710.40
W–3	2,848.80	2,967.90	3,089.40	3,129.30	3,257.10
W–2	2,505.90	2,649.00	2,774.10	2,865.30	2,943.30
W–1	2,212.80	2,394.00	2,515.20	2,593.50	2,802.30

WARRANT OFFICERS

	Over 8	Over 10	Over 12	Over 14	Over 16
W–5	—	—	—	—	—
W–4	3,871.50	4,035.00	4,194.30	4,359.00	4,617.30
W–3	3,403.20	3,595.80	3,786.30	3,988.80	4,140.60
W–2	3,157.80	3,321.60	3,443.40	3,562.20	3,643.80
W–1	2,928.30	3,039.90	3,164.70	3,247.20	3,321.90

WARRANT OFFICERS

	Over 18	Over 20	Over 22	Over 24	Over 26
W–5	—	5,360.70	5,544.30	5,728.80	5,914.20
W–4	4,782.60	4,944.30	5,112.00	5,277.00	5,445.90
W–3	4,291.80	4,356.90	4,424.10	4,570.20	4,716.30
W–2	3,712.50	3,843.00	3,972.60	4,103.70	4,103.70
W–1	3,443.70	3,535.80	3,535.80	3,535.80	3,535.80

ENLISTED PERSONNEL

Pay grade	Under 2	Over 2	Over 3	Over 4	Over 6
			Years of Service		
E–9	—	—	—	—	—
E–8	—	—	—	—	—
E–7	2,145.00	2,341.20	2,430.60	2,549.70	2,642.10
E–6	1,855.50	2,041.20	2,131.20	2,218.80	2,310.00
E–5	1,700.10	1,813.50	1,901.10	1,991.10	2,130.00
E–4	1,558.20	1,638.30	1,726.80	1,814.10	1,891.50
E–3	1,407.00	1,495.50	1,585.50	1,585.50	1,585.50
E–2	1,337.70	1,337.70	1,337.70	1,337.70	1,337.70
E–1	1,193.40	1,193.40	1,193.40	1,193.40	1,193.40
E–1 <4 months	1,086.00	—	—	—	—

Pay grade	Over 8	Over 10	Over 12	Over 14	Over 16
			Years of Service		
E–9	—	3,769.20	3,854.70	3,962.40	4,089.30
E–8	3,085.50	3,222.00	3,306.30	3,407.70	3,517.50
E–7	2,801.40	2,891.10	2,980.20	3,139.80	3,219.60
E–6	2,516.10	2,596.20	2,685.30	2,763.30	2,790.90
E–5	2,250.90	2,339.70	2,367.90	2,367.90	2,367.90
E–4	1,891.50	1,891.50	1,891.50	1,891.50	1,891.50
E–3	1,585.50	1,585.50	1,585.50	1,585.50	1,585.50
E–2	1,337.70	1,337.70	1,337.70	1,337.70	1,337.70
E–1	1,193.40	1,193.40	1,193.40	1,193.40	1,193.40

	Over 18	Over 20	Over 22	Over 24	Over 26
			Years of Service		
E–9	4,216.50	4,421.10	4,594.20	4,776.60	5,054.70
E–8	3,715.50	3,815.70	3,986.40	4,081.20	4,314.30
E–7	3,295.50	3,341.70	3,498.00	3,599.10	3,855.00
E–6	2,809.80	2,809.80	2,809.80	2,809.80	2,809.80
E–5	2,367.90	2,367.90	2,367.90	2,367.90	2,367.90
E–4	1,891.50	1,891.50	1,891.50	1,891.50	1,891.50
E–3	1,585.50	1,585.50	1,585.50	1,585.50	1,585.50
E–2	1,337.70	1,337.70	1,337.70	1,337.70	1,337.70
E–1	1,193.40	1,193.40	1,193.40	1,193.40	1,193.40

Pershing, John Joseph (1860–1948) *U.S. Army general who led the AEF in World War I*

Pershing was the general who led the American Expeditionary Force (AEF) in WORLD WAR I. He was born in Laclede, Missouri, and was raised on a farm there. He worked as a schoolteacher from 1878 to 1882, when he obtained an appointment to the UNITED STATES MILITARY ACADEMY (USMA), from which he graduated in 1886. His first posting was as a second lieutenant in the 6th Cavalry Regiment, serving in the West during the late phase of the INDIAN WARS. From 1891 to 1895, Pershing taught at the University of Nebraska as commandant of cadets. Promoted to first lieutenant in 1892, he took time out to earn a law degree (awarded June 1898), then saw service with the 10th Cavalry—a black regiment of "BUFFALO SOLDIERS" commanded by white officers. It was from this assignment that Pershing earned the nick-

General John J. Pershing, commander of the American Expeditionary Force, World War I   *(U.S. Army)*

name destined to stick throughout his career, Black Jack.

Pershing served with the 10th from October 1895 to October 1896, when he was appointed aide to general NELSON APPLETON MILES. From June 1897 to April 1898, Pershing returned to USMA as an instructor in tactics, then returned to the 10th Cavalry as its QUARTERMASTER. During the SPANISH-AMERICAN WAR, he fought at El Caney–San Juan Hill (July 1–3, 1898), but he was felled by malaria. He was briefly assigned quiet duty at the War Department toward the end of his convalescence in August 1898, then was appointed chief of the Bureau of Insular Affairs, serving from September 1898 to August 1899.

In 1899, Pershing requested a posting to the Philippines, where he served on northern Mindanao. From December 1899 to May 1903, he was engaged in the pacification of the Moros, an indigenous, mostly Islamic people who militantly resisted American authority. Pershing returned to Washington and staff duty shortly before his marriage to Helen Francis Warren on January 25, 1905.

From March 5, 1905, to September of 1906, Pershing was stationed in Japan as a military attaché and observer in the Russo-Japanese War. The assignment turned out to be Pershing's great opportunity, because it brought him into contact with President Theodore Roosevelt, who, greatly impressed with Captain Pershing, supported his promotion—in one leap—to brigadier general on September 20, 1906.

From December 1906 to June 1908, Pershing commanded a brigade at Fort McKinley, near Manila, then accepted an appointment as military commander of Moro Province in the Philippines in November 1909. He served in this post until early 1914, continually conducting small-scale operations against recalcitrant Moro rebels.

In April 1914, Pershing was assigned command of 8th Brigade in San Francisco, but he was almost immediately dispatched to the Mexican border during the civil war in Mexico. On August 27, 1915, while Pershing was in Texas, on the Mexican border, a fire swept through his family's quarters in the Presidio at San Francisco. Pershing was devastated to learn that his wife and three of their daughters had perished. Francisco "Pancho" Villa, whom Pershing would soon be assigned to capture, was among the many who wrote or wired their condolences.

On March 9, 1916, Villa raided Columbus, New Mexico, leaving 17 U.S. citizens dead. President Woodrow Wilson ordered Pershing to invade Mexico and capture Villa. Commanding a force of 4,800, he chased Villa and his men for 10 months until he was ordered home on January 27, 1917. Although his "punitive expedition" did not succeed in capturing Villa, it did track down and kill most of Villa's key commanders, effectively neutralizing Villa's band as a military threat to the United States.

On May 12, 1917, Pershing was named commander of the American Expeditionary Force (AEF), which was to be sent to Europe to fight in World War I. Pershing arrived in France well in advance of the force, on June 23, and directed the massive American buildup from August 1917 through October 1918. Apart from fighting Germans, his greatest challenge was preserving the independence of the AEF. It was unacceptable to him—and to the American people—for an American army to be commanded by French generals. With great difficulty, Pershing prevailed. He then went on to conduct three major offensives: Aisne-Marne (July 25–August 2, 1918), Saint-Mihiel (September 12–17), and the Meuse-Argonne (September 26–November 11). All were costly, but effective. The Americans had arrived at a time of Allied exhaustion. Their presence turned the tide of the war. On his triumphal return to the United States, Pershing was promoted to general of the armies—a *six*-star general—and judiciously avoided offers to enter politics. He remained in the military as CHIEF OF STAFF (appointed on July 21, 1921) and held that post until his retirement on September 13, 1924. He published his memoirs in 1931. Pershing nearly succumbed to a debilitating illness in 1938, but he recovered—though never completely. By 1941, his health had deteriorated so severely that he took up permanent residence in Walter Reed Hospital.

Persian Gulf War

On August 2, 1990, the fourth-largest ground force in the world, the army of Iraq, a nation long under the brutal dictatorship of Saddam Hussein, invaded its oil-rich neighbor, Kuwait, pursuant to Hussein's proclamation of annexation. Militarily overwhelmed, Kuwait fell to the invasion within a week. The invasion sent shockwaves throughout the Middle East and the Western nations, including the United States and its allies, who feared that Iraq would continue its aggression southward into Saudi Arabia. Among other issues, vast oil fields were in jeopardy.

The United States responded to the invasion by freezing Iraqi assets in American banks and by cutting off trade with the country. The administration of President George H. W. Bush acted to obtain U.N. resolutions condemning the invasion and supporting military action against it. Bush and Secretary of State James Baker forged an unprecedented military and diplomatic coalition among 48 nations. Of these, 30 provided military forces, with the United States making the largest contribution; 18 other nations provided economic, humanitarian, and other noncombat assistance. Saudi Arabia and other Arab states near Iraq provided port facilities, airfields, and staging areas for the buildup of ground forces. Because it was felt that the participation of Israel would unduly provoke the Arab members of the coalition, that nation agreed to refrain from military action, except in direct self-defense.

The U.S. buildup in the Middle East began on August 7, 1990, in response to a Saudi request for military aid to defend against possible Iraqi invasion. Dubbed Operation Desert Shield, the buildup was intended to deploy sufficient forces to deter further Iraqi aggression and to defend Saudi Arabia. The first step was a naval blockade of Iraq. On August 8, U.S. Air Force fighters began to arrive at Saudi air bases, and lead elements of the army, primarily the 82ND AIRBORNE DIVISION (part of the VIII Airborne Corps), arrived on August 9. By September, these forces were augmented by those of other coalition members and were now at sufficient strength to deter an invasion of Saudi Arabia.

By the end of October, 210,000 army and U.S. Marine Corps troops had been deployed, in addition to 65,000 troops from other coalition nations. Beginning in mid-November, the army brought in heavy armor units from European bases, and all coalition forces were put under the overall command of army general H. NORMAN SCHWARZKOPF.

With forces in place, the United States and the coalition countries attempted to effect diplomatic negotiation of an Iraqi withdrawal from Kuwait. When Saddam Hussein proved unresponsive, Bush and the State Department successfully lobbied for a United Nations resolution authorizing military force to expel Iraq from Kuwait. Secured on November 29, the resolution set a withdrawal deadline of January 15, 1991. By this time, army commanders and those of the other services and other members of the coalition planned to have 450,000 coalition troops on the ground. These would oppose a larger Iraqi force of some 530,000 men, who, however, were far less well equipped than the troops of the coalition. Ground operations would be preceded by massive air assault and naval bombardment, and the coalition enjoyed the overwhelming advantage of more than 170 warships deployed, including six aircraft carriers and two battleships. Air power consisted of 2,200 combat craft.

When the deadline passed, Operation Desert Shield, the buildup phase of the coalition's operations, became Operation Desert Storm, the PERSIAN GULF WAR. On the morning of January 16, a massive five-week, 88,000-sortie air campaign was unleashed against Iraq and Iraqi positions in Kuwait. During this phase of the war, Iraqi air defenses were quickly neutralized, and the Iraqi air force proved entirely ineffective. The Iraqis did launch attacks with obsolescent Soviet-made Scud surface-to-surface missiles, directed against Israel and Saudi Arabia. The army deployed mobile Patriot missile launchers to intercept the Scud attacks (see AIR DEFENSE ARTILLERY). The performance of the Patriots would became a subject of controversy in after-war analysis. During the action, Defense Department analysts claimed an 80 percent success rate in intercepting Scuds in Saudi Arabia and a 50 percent rate in Israel. After the war, these claims were officially scaled back to 70 percent and 40 percent, but subsequent congressional investigations put these figures much lower, approaching 0 percent. It was probably the crudeness of the Scud system itself, not the success of attempts to intercept the missiles, that accounted for the fact that relatively few hit their intended targets.

The overwhelming air supremacy achieved by the coalition prevented Iraqi reconnaissance aircraft from operating, which meant that Iraqi commanders had no intelligence concerning the deployment of army and other coalition ground troops. The coalition ground offensive stepped off at 4 A.M., February 24, 1991. The plan was for the army's XVIII Airborne Corps to be positioned on the coalition's left flank. This unit would move into Iraq on the far west and, striking deep within the country, cut off the Iraqi army in Kuwait, isolating it from any support or reinforcement from the north. The French 6th Light Armored Division covered the left flank of the XVIII Airborne Corps. The center of the ground force consisted of the U.S. VII Corps, the U.S. 2nd Armored Cavalry, and the British 1st Armored Division. The center units were to move north into Iraq after the left and right flanks had been secured, then make a sharp right turn to advance into Kuwait from the west to attack Iraqi units there, including the elite Republican Guard. The right flank was also charged with breaching Iraqi lines in Kuwait. The units composing this flank were mainly U.S. Marines.

The attacks on the first day, mainly by marines, were intended, in part, to screen the main attack and to deceive the Iraqis into thinking that the principal assault would come on the coast of Kuwait. Although Iraqi defenses were well developed, relatively light resistance was offered, and many Iraqi prisoners were quickly taken. By the second day of the ground war, French troops had secured the left flank of the coalition advance, and the U.S. forces had neatly cut off all avenues of Iraqi retreat and reinforcement. The U.S. 24th Division ended its advance in Basra, Iraq, which sealed the remaining avenue of escape from Kuwait.

With the Iraqis in Kuwait occupied on the right, the XVIII Airborne Corps made a surprise attack on the left, in the west. By nightfall of February 25, well ahead of schedule, the XVIII Airborne Corps was already turning east into Kuwait. When the corps encountered units of the vaunted Republican Guard, this elite Iraqi unit simply fled. By February 27, however, after the 24th Infantry had taken Basra, the Republican Guard was bottled up. Its Hammurabi Division, the most celebrated of the Republican Guard, did attempt to engage the XVIII Airborne Corps in a delaying action intended to allow the remainder of the Republican Guard to escape, but the Hammurabi Division was almost completely destroyed.

The ground war was over within 100 hours. On February 28, 1991, at 8 A.M., a cease-fire was declared. Shortly afterward, Iraq capitulated on U.S. terms. Kuwait had been liberated with minimal coalition casualties: 95 killed, 368 wounded, 20 missing in action. Iraqi casualties were perhaps as many as 50,000 killed and another 50,000 wounded; 60,000 Iraqi troops were taken prisoner. Massive quantities of Iraqi military hardware were destroyed, as were communication equipment and military bases, barracks, and other facilities. Saddam Hussein, however, remained in power, and his nation would become in 2003 the target of a second invasion—this one conducted mainly by the United States and the United Kingdom—that would result in an army occupation of Iraq, the dictator's removal from office, and protracted combat against so-called insurgents—foreign terrorists, Saddam loyalists, and others.

Personal Staff

Officers of the Personal Staff assist the CHIEF OF STAFF directly and consists of aides to the Chief of Staff as well as other officers whom the chief desires to work with directly or who have charge of activities the chief desires to administer or coordinate directly.

Philippine Defense Medal   See DECORATIONS AND MEDALS.

Philippine Independence Medal   See DECORATIONS AND MEDALS.

Philippine Liberation Medal   See DECORATIONS AND MEDALS.

Philippine Presidential Unit Citation   See DECORATIONS AND MEDALS.

Picatinny Arsenal   See FORTS AND OTHER INSTALLATIONS.

Pine Bluff Arsenal   See FORTS AND OTHER INSTALLATIONS.

platoon   See ORGANIZATION BY UNITS.

Powell, Colin Luther (1937–   ) *U.S. Army general, secretary of state*
Powell attained high public visibility as chairman of the JOINT CHIEFS OF STAFF during the PERSIAN GULF WAR. He was born in New York City, the son of Jamaican immigrants, and he graduated from the City University of New York in 1958. He had enrolled in an ROTC program at the university and was commissioned a second lieutenant in the army on graduation. His first assignment was as a platoon leader and company commander in Germany during 1959–62. He was sent to South Vietnam during 1962–63 as part of a contingent of U.S. military advisers to the Army of the Republic of Vietnam (ARVN). He returned to South Vietnam during the height of the VIETNAM WAR, (1968–70), as an INFANTRY battalion executive officer and assistant chief of staff (G-3) with the 23rd (American) Infantry Division.

In 1971, Powell earned an M.B.A. degree from George Washington University and was also honored by selection as a White House Fellow. He was made special assistant to the deputy director of the Office of the President, serving in that capacity during 1972–73. Promoted to lieutenant colonel, Powell returned to field command during 1973–75, as commander of the 1st Battalion, 32nd Infantry in South Korea. He returned to the United States to attend the U.S. ARMY WAR COLLEGE, from which he graduated in June 1976. Promoted to colonel, he was assigned command of the 2nd Brigade, 101ST AIRBORNE DIVISION (Air Assault) at Fort Campbell, Kentucky, during 1976–77, then returned to Washington, D.C., where he was assigned to the Office of the Secretary of Defense. Powell served for a brief time as executive assistant to the secretary of energy in 1979, then was appointed senior military assistant to the deputy secretary of defense, a post in which he served from 1979 to 1981.

Powell returned to field command again in 1981 as assistant division commander, 4TH INFANTRY DIVISION (Mechanized), at Fort Carson, Colorado, returning to Washington in 1983 as senior military adviser to Secretary of Defense Caspar Weinberger until 1985. The following year, he was put in command of U.S. V Corps in West Germany, returning to the United States in 1987 as deputy assistant for national security affairs to President Ronald Reagan and, subsequently, assistant for national security affairs to Presidents Reagan and George H. W. Bush from December 1987 to January 1989.

On October 1, 1989, President George H. W. Bush selected Powell to serve as chairman of the Joint Chiefs of Staff as well as commander in chief, U.S. ARMY FORCES COMMAND. He was the first African American to hold these positions.

The first major action he directed in this latter post was the December 1989 Operation Just Cause, an expedition into Panama to apprehend the nation's dictator, Manuel Noriega, and bring him back to the United States to stand trial on drug trafficking charges. From August 1990 to March 1991, Powell directed U.S. participation in United Nations operations against Iraqi dictator Saddam Hussein, including during the PERSIAN GULF WAR of 1990–91. This massive operation gained Powell a great deal of public exposure and approval. The highest-ranking African American in the U.S. armed forces, Powell was seen as an intelligent and politically attractive figure. Many Americans hoped that he would declare himself a candidate for president when he retired from the military in 1993. He chose not to do so at the time; rather, in 2001, he became secretary of state under President George W. Bush and served throughout Bush's first term.

Presidential Unit Citation   See DECORATIONS AND MEDALS.

Presidio of Monterey, California   See FORTS AND OTHER INSTALLATIONS.

Prisoner of War Medal   See DECORATIONS AND MEDALS.

private   See RANKS AND GRADES.

private first class   See RANKS AND GRADES.

proving grounds   See FORTS AND OTHER INSTALLATIONS.

Purple Heart   See DECORATIONS AND MEDALS.

Q

quartermaster

The quartermaster is the officer responsible for procuring food, clothing, and equipment for troops—that is, for looking after troop quarters. Abbreviation is QM

Quartermaster Corps

With its home station at Fort Lee, Virginia, the Quartermaster Corps, an army combat service support branch, plans and directs the processes and activities that provide soldiers with food, water, petroleum, repair parts, weapon systems, and a variety of field services. The Quartermaster Corps is the main driver of U.S. Army logistics, charged with efficiently providing soldiers with the right items, at the right place, at the right time.

R

Rangers

Army Rangers are airborne troops under the command of U.S. ARMY SPECIAL OPERATIONS COMMAND (USASOC), trained to be members of an elite, light, and highly proficient INFANTRY battalion. The 75th Ranger Regiment is headquartered at Fort Benning, Georgia, which is also the home of the Ranger School.

Rangers specialize in direct action missions, especially seizing enemy airfields and staging raids on enemy forces and facilities. Ranger units are elite light infantry troops who focus on mission-essential tasks that include movement to contact, ambush, reconnaissance, airborne and air assaults, and hasty defense. Because Rangers rely heavily on external fire support, Ranger fire-support personnel are extensively trained in the employment of close air support (CAS), attack helicopters, naval gunfire, the use of AC-130 gunships, and the use of artillery in concert with Ranger ground operations.

Rangers undergo the most rigorous training of any USA soldiers. *(U.S. Army)*

ranks and grades

"Rank" refers to a person's official position within the military hierarchy. "Grade" is an alphanumeric symbol associated with rank, which is keyed to pay level (and is therefore often called "pay grade"). Officer grades range from O-1 to O-10, warrant officer grades from W-1 to W-5, and enlisted grades from E-1 to E-9. For basic pay associated with these grades, see PAY, BASIC MILITARY.

U.S. Army ranks and grades fall into three groups: COMMISSIONED OFFICERS, warrant officers, and enlisted personnel.

Commissioned Officers (in descending order)

General of the armies (O-10)

This rank has been achieved by only one 20th-century commander, JOHN JOSEPH PERSHING; however, Generals ULYSSES SIMPSON GRANT, WILLIAM TECUMSEH SHERMAN, and PHILIP HENRY SHERIDAN were variously designated general of the armies or general of the army. A 1976 act of Congress posthumously recognized GEORGE WASHINGTON as general of the armies. The insignia is six stars. There is no equivalent in the other services.

General of the army (O-10)
Rarely held, this general officer wears an insignia of five stars. The U.S. Navy (USN) equivalent is fleet admiral, and the U.S. Air Force (USAF) equivalent is general of the air force. There is no U.S. Marine Corps (USMC) equivalent. The following officers achieved this rank: GEORGE CATLETT MARSHALL, DOUGLAS MACARTHUR, DWIGHT DAVID EISENHOWER, Henry H. Arnold (redesignated general of the air force in 1949), and OMAR NELSON BRADLEY.

General (O-10)
Except for general of the army (a rank rarely held) and general of the armies (awarded only twice in army history), general is the senior officer rank in the army. The USN equivalent is admiral, and the USAF and USMC equivalent is general. Insignia is four stars.

Lieutenant general (O-9)
The army lieutenant general is the equivalent of a USN vice admiral and a USAF and USMC lieutenant general. Insignia is three stars.

Major general (O-8)
The army major general is the equivalent of a USN rear admiral (upper) and a USAF and USMC major general. Insignia is two stars.

Brigadier general (O-7)
The army brigadier general is the equivalent of a USN rear admiral (lower) and a USAF and USMC brigadier general. Insignia is a single star.

Colonel (O-6)
The army colonel is the equivalent of a USN captain and a USAF and USMC colonel. Insignia is an eagle.

Lieutenant colonel (O-5)
The army lieutenant colonel is the equivalent of a USN commander and a USAF and USMC lieutenant colonel. Insignia is a silver oak leaf.

Major (O-4)
The army major is the equivalent of a USN lieutenant commander and a USAF and USMC major. Insignia is a gold oak leaf.

Captain (O-3)
The army captain is equivalent to a USN lieutenant and a USAF and USMC captain. Insignia is a pair of parallel silver bars.

First lieutenant (O-2)
The army first lieutenant is the equivalent of a USN lieutenant junior grade and a USAF and USMC first lieutenant. Insignia is a silver bar.

Second lieutenant (O-1)
The second lieutenant is the lowest-ranking commissioned officer in the army and is equivalent to a USN ensign and a second lieutenant in the USAF and USMC. Insignia is a gold bar.

Warrant Officers (in descending order)
In the army, warrant officers are technicians of such highly specialized skills as to merit officer rank without the command responsibilities assigned to commissioned officers. There are five grades of warrant officer:

> master warrant officer 5 (W-5)
> chief warrant officer 4 (W-4)
> chief warrant officer 3 (W-3)
> chief warrant officer 2 (W-2)
> warrant officer 1 (W-1)

Insignia for all five ranks is a silver bar. The W-1 bar has a black square in the middle; the W-2 bar has two black squares separated by a broad silver divider; the W-3 bar is three black squares on a silver background; the W-4 bar consists of four black rectangles on a silver background; and the W-5 bar shows four silver rectangles outlined in black against a silver bar.

Enlisted Personnel (in descending order)

Sergeant major of the army (E-9)
The sergeant major of the army is the senior NONCOMMISSIONED OFFICER in the army. The rank shares the E-9 pay grade with sergeant major and com-

mand sergeant major and is the equivalent of the USN master chief petty officer of the navy, the USAF chief master sergeant of the air force, and the USMC sergeant major of the marine corps. Insignia is three chevrons above three rockers with an eagle and star device between the chevrons and the rockers.

Command sergeant major (E-9)
The army command sergeant major is senior to the sergeant major but holds the same E-9 pay grade. The USN equivalent is the master chief petty officer; the USAF equivalent is the command chief master sergeant; and the USMC equivalent is the sergeant major. Insignia is three chevrons above three rockers with a star and leaf device between the chevrons and the rockers.

Sergeant major (E-9)
The army sergeant major holds a pay grade of E-9 and is equivalent in rank to a USAF chief master sergeant and a USMC master gunnery sergeant. Insignia is three chevrons above three rockers with a star device between the chevrons and the rockers.

Master sergeant (E-8)
Like the army first sergeant, the master sergeant is an E-8, equivalent to a USN senior chief petty officer, a USAF senior master sergeant, and a USMC master sergeant. Insignia is three chevrons above three rockers.

First sergeant (E-8)
Like the army master sergeant, the first sergeant is at pay grade E-8 and is the equivalent of a USN senior chief petty officer, a USAF senior master sergeant, and a USMC first sergeant. Insignia is three chevrons above three rockers with a diamond device between the chevrons and rockers.

Sergeant first class (E-7)
The army sergeant first class is equivalent in rank to a USN chief petty officer, a USAF master sergeant, and a USMC gunnery sergeant. Insignia is three chevrons above two rockers.

Specialist Seven (E-7)
A noncommissioned officer with specialized training, the Specialist Seven wears an insignia with three arcs above an eagle device.

Specialist Six (E-6)
The insignia is two arcs above an eagle device.

Staff sergeant (E-6)
An army staff sergeant is equivalent in rank to a USN petty officer first class, a USAF technical sergeant, and a USMC staff sergeant. Insignia is three chevrons over a single rocker.

Sergeant (E-5)
The army sergeant is the equivalent of a USN petty officer second class, a USAF staff sergeant, and a USMC sergeant. Insignia is three chevrons.

Specialist Five (E-5)
The insignia is one arc above an eagle device.

Corporal (E-4)
An army corporal is equivalent to a USN petty officer third class, a USAF senior airman, and a USMC, corporal. Insignia is two chevrons.

Specialist Four (E-4)
The insignia is an eagle device.

Private first class (E-3)
The army private first class is equivalent to a USN seaman, USAF airman first class, and USMC lance corporal. The insignia is a single chevron above a single rocker.

Private (E-1 or E-2)
A newly enlisted private is assigned the pay grade of E-1 and wears no insignia. Following basic training, the private is assigned grade E-2 and wears a single chevron. An E-1 private is the army equivalent of a USN seaman recruit, a USAF airman basic, and a USMC private. An army E-2 private is equivalent to a USN seaman apprentice, a USAF airman, and a USMC private first class.

RC-12/RU-21 Guardrail   See AIRCRAFT.

Red River Army Depot (RRAD)   See FORTS AND OTHER INSTALLATIONS.

Redstone Arsenal   See FORTS AND OTHER INSTALLATIONS.

regiment   See ORGANIZATION BY UNITS.

regular army

The "regular army" is the permanent, professional army force. Regular army members, all volunteers, are on active, full-time military duty.

See also RESERVE COMPONENTS, ACTIVE ARMY, ARMY NATIONAL GUARD, and U.S. ARMY RESERVE.

Republic of Korea Presidential Unit Citation   See DECORATIONS AND MEDALS.

Republic of Korea War Service Medal

See DECORATIONS AND MEDALS.

Republic of Vietnam Campaign Medal

See DECORATIONS AND MEDALS.

Republic of Vietnam Gallantry Cross with Palm   See DECORATIONS AND MEDALS.

reserve components

The reserve components of the army are the ARMY NATIONAL GUARD (ARNG) and U.S. ARMY RESERVE (USAR). Members of the reserve components may perform part-time military service while residing in their homes and working civilian jobs. When the president determines the need, however, they may be called into full-time service under full military control.

Ridgway, Matthew Bunker (1895–1993)
U.S. Army general

Ridgway was the army general who planned and executed the world's first airborne assault—on Sicily, during WORLD WAR II—and who assumed the difficult role of taking over supreme command of KOREAN WAR operations from DOUGLAS MACARTHUR.

Born at Fort Monroe, Virginia, Ridgway graduated from the UNITED STATES MILITARY ACADEMY (USMA) in 1917 and was dispatched to a United States–Mexican border post with the 3RD INFANTRY DIVISION. By August 1918, he had been promoted to acting captain and given command of the regimental headquarters company. Toward the end of WORLD WAR I, in September 1918, he returned to USMA as an instructor in French and Spanish. Promoted to the permanent rank of captain, he was sent to Infantry School, from which he graduated in 1925.

From 1925 to 1930, Ridgway served variously in China, Texas, Nicaragua, the Canal Zone, and the Philippines. He returned to the United States and took the Infantry School advanced course in 1930. Promoted to major in 1932, he graduated from the COMMAND AND GENERAL STAFF COLLEGE in 1935, then served on the staffs of VI Corps and Second Army in Chicago. Ridgway graduated from the U.S. ARMY WAR COLLEGE in 1937 and served briefly with the Fourth Army based in San Francisco, then joined the War Plans Division of the War Department in September 1939. After promotion to lieutenant colonel in July 1940, temporary colonel in December 1941, and temporary brigadier general in January 1942, Ridgway was appointed assistant division commander of the 82nd Infantry Division based in Louisiana in March 1942. He directed the unit's conversion to the 82ND AIRBORNE DIVISION by August, and, promoted to temporary major general, he accompanied the division to the Mediterranean early in 1943.

Ridgway planned and executed the first-ever army airborne assault. A portion of the division parachuted into Sicily during July 9–10, 1943. Ridgway led elements of the division into combat around Salerno on September 13, then, just before dawn on June 6, 1944, he parachuted into France with his troops in support of the Normandy (D-day) invasion.

Ridgway's command was expanded to the XVIII Airborne Corps (the combined 82ND and 101ST AIRBORNE DIVISIONS) in August. He led the airborne contingent of the failed Operation Market Garden masterminded by British field marshal Bernard Law Montgomery in September. Ridgway's corps was far more successful at the Battle of the Bulge, where it was instrumental in checking the last great German offensive of World War II from December 16, 1944 to January 15, 1945.

From January to April 1945, Ridgway served in the Rhineland and Ruhr campaigns. At the end of the war, he was promoted to lieutenant general (June 1945) and was given command of the Mediterranean region from November 1945 to January 1946. Following the war, he was appointed to the United Nations Military Staff Committee in January 1946 and subsequently directed the Caribbean Defense Command from July 1948 to August 1949, when he was appointed deputy chief of staff of the army.

Ridgway took over command of the EIGHTH U.S. ARMY in Korea shortly after the death of General Walton H. Walker and the great Chinese counteroffensive at the end of 1950, which pushed the U.S.-UN forces relentlessly southward. Taking over a badly beaten and demoralized force, Ridgway managed to bring the Chinese counteroffensive to a standstill 75 miles south of Seoul. With the arrival of reinforcements, he was able to commence his own counteroffensive, taking advantage of the fact that Chinese lines of communication and supply were stretched to the breaking point. The Ridgway counteroffensive began on January 25, 1951, and he had liberated Seoul by March 14–15. On March 30, U.S. and UN troops advanced north of the 35th parallel, halting the drive on April 22. At this point, President Harry S. Truman concluded his dispute with General Douglas MacArthur over goals and strategy by firing MacArthur and naming Ridgway to replace him as UN commander and commander in chief Far East on April 11.

In June, Ridgway commenced negotiations with the North Koreans, which continued after he left in May 1952 to succeed General DWIGHT DAVID EISENHOWER as NATO supreme Allied commander Europe. With this appointment came a promotion to general. The following year, Ridgway returned to the United States as army CHIEF OF STAFF and was immediately embroiled in the red-baiting accusations of Senator Joseph McCarthy, who charged that the army was riddled with Communists and

"fellow travelers." Ridgway parried McCarthy's thrusts masterfully and survived—along with the army—to see McCarthy suffer censure from his Senate colleagues for his reckless behavior.

In the cold war climate that followed World War II and Korea, in which armed conflict was often on a local scale, Ridgway became concerned that the United States relied too heavily on strategic nuclear weapons programs at the expense of developing and maintaining tactical conventional warfare capability. In advocating this position, at the end of his career, he came into increasingly sharp conflict with U.S. Secretary of Defense Charles Wilson, a proponent of reducing conventional forces and allocating increased funding to nuclear weapons development.

Ridgway stepped down in June 1955 and retired from the army. In 1956, he published his memoirs, *Soldier,* and entered into private business in an executive capacity.

rocket-assisted projectile (RAP)

This type of artillery shell is equipped with a small rocket motor to increase both velocity and range. RAPs are used by the army and marine corps.

Rock Island Arsenal   See FORTS AND OTHER INSTALLATIONS.

rock 'n' roll

Used chiefly in the army and marine corps as slang for cocking and chambering ammunition in preparation for firing. The phrase is also used as an instruction to set weapons to full automatic position for continuous firing.

Rocky Mountain Arsenal   See FORTS AND OTHER INSTALLATIONS.

ROTC

Administered by the ROTC CADET COMMAND, ROTC (Reserve Officers Training Corps) is a college-based program that produces 75 percent of all army officers. ROTC was founded in 1916, and, as of 2003, the program had produced more than 500,000 second lieutenants for the army.

The full ROTC course carries an obligation for military service after graduation; however, the program can be taken as a college elective for up to two years without obligation.

See also JUNIOR RESERVE OFFICERS TRAINING CORPS.

ROTC Cadet Command

Headquartered at Fort Monroe, Virginia, and administered by the U.S. ARMY TRAINING AND DOCTRINE COMMAND (TRADOC), the ROTC Cadet Command is responsible for administering the Army ROTC and JROTC programs to commission the future officer leadership of the army and to motivate young people to become better citizens.

S

Schofield Barracks   See FORTS AND OTHER INSTALLATIONS.

Schwarzkopf, H(erbert) Norman (1934–   )
U.S. Army general

As an army general and CINC U.S. Central Command, Schwarzkopf successfully led Operation Desert Shield and Operation Desert Storm during the PERSIAN GULF WAR against Iraq in 1990–91.

Born in Trenton, New Jersey, on August 22, 1934, Schwarzkopf was the son of a WORLD WAR I army officer who went on to head the New Jersey State Police from 1921 to 1936 before returning to active duty in the army during WORLD WAR II. H. Norman Schwarzkopf was commissioned second lieutenant after graduating from the UNITED STATES MILITARY ACADEMY in 1956.

In addition to numerous staff strategic and personnel management assignments, Schwarzkopf saw two combat tours in the VIETNAM WAR, 1965–66 and 1969–70, then commanded a brigade in Alaska (1974–76). Schwarzkopf also served as deputy commander of U.S. forces in the 1983 invasion of Grenada. He became widely known to the American public as overall commander of Persian Gulf operations Desert Shield and Desert Storm (August 2, 1990–April 10, 1991), after which he retired—triumphantly—from the military.

Scott, Winfield (1786–1866) *U.S. Army general*

The military career of Winfield Scott spanned the WAR OF 1812 to the early months of the CIVIL WAR. Scott was one of the great forces that shaped the army in the 19th century.

Scott was born near Petersburg, Virginia, and he was educated briefly at the College of William and Mary in 1805, then apprenticed himself to a lawyer. In 1807, he enlisted in a local CAVALRY troop during the patriotic fervor that followed the *Chesapeake-Leopard* affair, which raised the issue of British impressment of American sailors and would ultimately contribute to the commencement of the War of 1812.

Scott was commissioned a captain of light artillery and dispatched to New Orleans in May 1808, but he fell afoul of his commander, the extravagantly corrupt General James Wilkinson, the following year and was suspended from 1809 to 1810. He returned to service in New Orleans during 1811–12, then returned to Washington, D.C., where he obtained promotion to lieutenant colonel in July 1812. Joining the army of General Stephen Van Rensselaer at Niagara in October 1812, he commanded a small detachment of volunteers at Queenston on October 13, where he was captured. Soon freed in a prisoner exchange, he was promoted to colonel and made adjutant to Henry Dearborn in March 1813. He planned and led a successful attack on Fort George, Ontario, on May

Winfield Scott, "Old Fuss and Feathers," was one of the great officers of the 19th-century U.S. Army.   *(Arttoday)*

27, suffering a wound in the battle. He was given command of the captured fort, then joined Wilkinson's advance on Montreal in October and fought at Chrysler's Farm (near Cornwall, Ontario) on November 11, 1813.

Scott was promoted to brigadier general in March 1814 and devoted himself to training a brigade in Buffalo. Under General Jacob Brown, he led his brigade into Canada on July 3, achieving a victory at Chippewa on July 5, 1814. At the major battle of Lundy's Lane on July 25, 1814, he was twice wounded and became a national hero. Breveted to major general, Scott was appointed to head the board of inquiry on General William H. Winder's conduct in the ignominious defeat at Bladensburg, Maryland, which had led to the burning of Washington, D.C. Scott at this time was also one of the authors of the army's first standard drill book.

Appointed to command of the army's Northern Department in 1815, following the war, Scott twice visited Europe to observe military developments

there. He was disappointed when he failed to be promoted to commanding general following the death of Jacob Brown in February 1828, and he tendered his resignation, which was refused. Instead, he was made commander of the Eastern Division in 1829.

Scott was called on to lead a force during the Black Hawk War of 1832, but many of his troops were stricken in camp by a cholera epidemic. Delayed, Scott did not arrive in Wisconsin until Chief Black Hawk and his followers had been neutralized. However, he was instrumental in negotiating the Treaty of Fort Armstrong with the Sac and Fox tribes on September 21, 1832. Late that year, President Andrew Jackson prudently sent Scott to South Carolina to observe the military situation there during the Nullification Crisis (a prelude to the Civil War, in which South Carolina defied a federal tariff, on constitutional grounds). Scott saw to the reinforcement of the federal garrisons around Charleston, yet he did so in a subtle manner that avoided stirring local passions.

In 1836, Scott was dispatched to Florida to fight the Seminoles, who were resisting removal to Indian Territory (modern Oklahoma) as prescribed by treaties most of the tribe had repudiated but which the federal government held as binding. Scott was plagued by ill-trained and downright insubordinate troops, as well as a lack of supplies. Soon relieved of command and replaced by General Thomas S. Jesup, he was brought up on charges before a board of inquiry, which, however, cleared him in 1837. Following this, during January–May 1838, Scott was sent to Maine during the border dispute with Britain known as the Aroostook War. He exercised admirable diplomacy and thereby avoided a shooting war.

During the late summer and early fall of 1838, Scott was assigned to oversee the forcible removal of the Cherokees from Georgia, South Carolina, and Tennessee to Indian Territory. Through no fault of his own, the operation was marked by corruption and brutality and has been recorded in Native American memory as the "Trail of Tears."

Scott was sent back to Maine as the border dispute flared up there again in January 1839. He parleyed with the lieutenant governor of New Brunswick and, once again, avoided outright war.

On July 5, 1841, Scott was at last appointed commanding general of the army. With the outbreak of the UNITED STATES–MEXICAN WAR, Scott at first supported General ZACHARY TAYLOR's position in Texas and northern Mexico, but he soon became convinced that something more aggressive was called for and proposed an invasion of Mexico City itself. President James Polk approved Scott's plan and replaced Taylor with Scott, who carefully laid plans for a landing at Veracruz. Accomplished on March 9, 1847, the Veracruz assault was the first amphibious operation ever undertaken by the army. The city of Veracruz fell on March 27 after a brief siege. Scott marched inland, trouncing General Santa Anna's much larger army at Cerro Gordo on April 18 and occupying Puebla on May 15. He resupplied and reinforced his army there, then set off for Mexico City on August 7. In a bold maneuver that no less an international figure than the Duke of Wellington pronounced hopelessly foolhardy, Scott severed his line of supply so that he could rapidly circle south. Thus positioned, he defeated Santa Anna at Contreras and Churubusco during August 19–20. Scott pushed Santa Anna back into Mexico City.

Scott suspended operations during peace negotiations, which commenced on August 25. The discussions broke down on September 6, whereupon Scott dealt the Mexican forces a blow at Molino del Rey on September 8 and Chapultepec on September 13. The following day, he took Mexico City itself. Scott held authority in the Mexican capital as military governor until he returned to the United States on April 22, 1848. Accused of exceeding his authority in the course of the invasion, he was quickly cleared of misconduct. He was, in fact, a national hero, who narrowly lost the Whig presidential nomination to Zachary Taylor in 1848. Scott ran for the presidency under the banner of a breakaway Whig faction in 1852, but he lost by a wide margin to Democrat Franklin Pierce.

Breveted to lieutenant general in February 1855, Scott was sent to negotiate during an Anglo-American boundary crisis over possession of San Juan Island in Puget Sound during September 1859. As the clouds of civil war gathered on the horizon, Scott returned to the East and advised on preparing for the conflict. His counsel fell on deaf ears, as the administration of President James Buchanan did little more than mark time. In January 1861, Scott transferred his headquarters to Washington, D.C., and, when war began, he supervised the opening engagements. His boldest stroke was the so-called Anaconda Plan, a proposed naval blockade of Confederate ports. However, Scott was aged, obese, and infirm—called, half derisively, half affectionately, "Old Fuss and Feathers." He retired from the army on November 1, 1861, and was replaced as general in chief by GEORGE BRINTON MCCLELLAN.

2nd Infantry Division

The 2nd Infantry Division is posted in the Republic of Korea (South Korea) as a strategic instrument of national policy to deter and assist in the defense of South Korea against any invasion from North Korea. The soldiers of the 2nd Infantry Division are prepared to become operational immediately and, in the event of an attack, expand the battle space until other U.S. warfighting divisions arrive (as scheduled) 120 hours later.

The 2nd Infantry Division is one of very few active U.S. units that was organized on foreign soil. The division came into being on October 26, 1917, at Beaumont, France, during WORLD WAR I. Dubbed the Indianhead Division (after its distinctive shoulder patch emblem), the division was originally composed of one brigade of U.S. Infantry, one brigade of U.S. Marines, an artillery brigade, and an array of supporting units. Unique in the history of the army, the division was twice commanded by USMC generals, Major General C. A. Doyen and Major General John A. Lejune, respectively.

The division trained during the winter of 1917–18, then was committed to combat in the spring of 1918 at the Battle of Belleau Wood and the Château-Thierry campaign. The division was victorious at Soissons and Mont Blanc, then participated in the Meuse-Argonne offensive, which brought the war to a close. After the armistice, the 2nd Infantry Division entered Germany and performed occupation duties until April 1919.

After returning to the United States, the division was stationed at Fort Sam Houston, Texas, and spent the interwar years as an experimental unit, testing new concepts and innovations for the army. In 1940 the 2nd Infantry Division became the first command to be reorganized under the "triangular concept," which provided for three separate regiments in each division and became the organizing principle behind the army of WORLD WAR II.

In November 1941 the division moved to Camp McCoy, Wisconsin, training for winter warfare. With World War II under way, in September 1943, the division moved to a staging area at Camp Shanks, New York, then sailed on October 7 for Europe as part of the buildup for Operation Overlord, the Normandy "D-day" invasion. The division landed at Omaha Beach on June 7, 1944, D-day + 1, and fought through to a breakout in the Normandy hedgerow country. The division liberated its first objective, the strategically key port of Brest, on September 18, 1944, then lingered to mop up Normandy. These operations completed, the division advanced through France and then to St. Vith, Belgium, from which, on December 11, 1944, the division pierced the Siegfried Line but was forced to withdraw when counterattacked by the Germans in the offensive that gave rise to the Battle of the Bulge. The division held, preventing the enemy from seizing the roads to Liège and Antwerp.

After successfully defending its positions during the Battle of the Bulge, the division resumed the offensive on February 6, 1945, advancing rapidly across Germany and, by the end of the war, into Czechoslovakia as far as Pilsen, where it met the Red Army advancing from the east.

Had it not been for the atomic bombs dropped on Hiroshima and Nagasaki, which ended the war in the Pacific in August 1945, the 2nd Infantry Division would have been shipped to that theater.

Instead, it returned to Fort Lewis, Washington, conducting Arctic, air transportability, amphibious, and maneuver training. The division deployed to Korea at the outbreak of the KOREAN WAR, arriving at Pusan on July 23, 1950, the first unit to reach Korea directly from the United States. The division successfully repelled a desperate North Korean human wave attack on the night of August 31, which resulted in a 16-day battle. The division was also the first U.S. unit to break out of the Pusan defensive perimeter. The Indianheads led the spectacular EIGHTH U.S. ARMY drive to the Manchurian border. When the Chinese counterattacked across the border, the 2nd Infantry Division was assigned to protect the rear and right flank of the retreating Eighth Army. The Chinese winter offensive was finally blunted by the 2nd Infantry Division on January 31, 1951, at Wonju. This achieved, the division seized the initiative and launched a two-prong attack in February 1951. The division was instrumental in neutralizing the communist spring offensive. The division was rotated back to the United States beginning on August 20, 1954, after four years in Korea.

After the war, the division was stationed briefly in Alaska, then, on November 8, 1957, effectively deactivated, only to be reactivated in the spring at Fort Benning, Georgia. The division was returned to the Republic of Korea in July 1965 as the major land component for the defense of the border between the North and the South.

second lieutenant   See RANKS AND GRADES.

secretary of the army

By federal statute, the secretary of the army is responsible for and has the authority to conduct all the affairs of the DEPARTMENT OF THE ARMY, including recruiting, organizing, supplying, equipping, training, mobilizing, and demobilizing. The secretary has overall responsibility for formulating and implementing policies and programs consistent with the national security policies and objectives established by the president and the secretary of defense. By law a civilian, the secretary of the army is appointed by the president with the advice and consent of the Senate.

Security Assistance Command (USASAC)

Headquartered at Alexandria, Virginia, and subordinate to the U.S. ARMY MATERIEL COMMAND (AMC), the Security Assistance Command provides total program management, including planning, delivery, and life-cycle support of equipment, services, and training to, and coproduction, with U.S. allies and other international partners. The command negotiates and implements coproduction agreements and serves as a proponent for army security assistance information management and financial policy. The command also provides logistics procedural guidance to the army security assistance community. Additionally, the command supports federal emergency assistance and humanitarian relief operations.

sergeant   See RANKS AND GRADES.

sergeant first class   See RANKS AND GRADES.

sergeant major   See RANKS AND GRADES.

Sergeant Major Academy

Headquartered at Fort Bliss, Texas, the Sergeant Major Academy was established in 1972 to administer the top level of the Noncommissioned Officer Education System (NCOES) and, as of 1981, all of the advanced NONCOMMISSIONED OFFICER courses. Five major subject areas are addressed: leadership, communications, training management, professional skills, and military studies.

The academy also maintains operational control over the Army First Sergeant Course (FSC), a five-week program that trains master sergeants,

first sergeants, and sergeants first class promotable in the finer points of performing present or future duties as a first sergeant. Additionally, the academy developed the common leader training for all Basic NCO Courses (BNCOC). In 1989, the academy began conducting the Command Sergeant Major Course (CSMC), a one-week course for newly assigned command sergeants major and CSM designees. Other academy courses include the CSM Spouse Course and the Battle Staff Noncommissioned Officer Course (BSNCOC).

The Sergeant Major Academy administers the United States Army Museum of the Noncommissioned Officer, which traces the history of the noncommissioned officer ranks through 200 years of army history.

sergeant major of the army   See RANKS AND GRADES.

7th Infantry Division

Since June, 4, 1999, when it was reactivated, the 7th Infantry Division (ID) has been based at Fort Carson, Colorado. The unit, dubbed "the Bayonet," was organized in 1918, during WORLD WAR I, but, because it was formed relatively late in the war, did not see action in France until October 11, a month before the armistice. The division was about to assault the Hindenburg Line, Germany's last-ditch defensive position, when hostilities ceased. After just 33 days in the line, the 7th Division had suffered 1,988 casualties.

The division returned to the United States during June 1919 and was demobilized and, in 1921, inactivated. It was not until July 1940 when a skeleton force of officers and enlisted men arrived at Ford Ord, California, to reactivate the 7th ID initially under the command of Major General JOSEPH WARREN STILWELL. The division was made up mostly of new inductees. The 7th ID trained in amphibious assault under a new commander, Major General C. H. White, and, after U.S. entry into WORLD WAR II, the 7th ID was redesignated as the 7th Motorized Division and trained for desert warfare. However, the unit was once again trained in amphibious warfare. Deployed to Alaska, elements of the 7th ID landed at "Red Beach" on Attu in the Aleutians and commenced a hard-fought campaign against Japanese invaders of U.S. territory. After Attu had been secured, the division turned to another Aleutian Island, Kiska, only to find that the Japanese had evacuated.

From Alaska, the division was redeployed for training in Hawaii, and on January 22, 1944, the division embarked for Kwajalein Atoll, to attack and take this Japanese-held island in what military historians have described as the most nearly perfect amphibious operation in history. Kwajalein was secured within three days, and, by February 7, most of the division returned to Hawaii for rest and further training.

The 7th ID landed on Leyte, Philippines, on October 20, 1944. After a very hard-fought campaign, Leyte was declared secure on February 6, 1945. The next month, the division trained in the Philippines for the assault on the Ryukyu Islands, and, on April 1, 1945, the division landed on Okinawa. This enormously daunting objective was secured by June 21. Army staff calculated that the 7th ID had killed between 25,000 and 28,000 Japanese soldiers in the Okinawa campaign and had taken 4,584 prisoners. Division casualties were 1,116 killed and nearly 6,000 wounded.

After the Japanese surrender, the 7th ID was deployed to Korea to participate in the occupation of the peninsula south of the 38th parallel.

Occupation duty ended in 1948 for the 7th ID, and the division was stationed in Japan. Although understrength, it was redeployed to Korea after the outbreak of the KOREAN WAR in 1950 as part of the Inchon landing on September 17. It was during this war that the 7th Division received its nickname, Bayonet. The division advanced from Inchon to Seoul, which was secured on September 30, after which the division was moved to Pusan for training. From here, it made an amphibious landing at Iwon and advanced to the Yalu River, the border with China.

On November 27, Chinese Communist Forces (CCF) intervened in the war, and the 7th ID fought a desperate rearguard action.

During the rest of the war, the 7th ID fought in all of the major actions and, after the armistice of July 27, 1953, was tasked with defense duty along the 38th parallel.

The division was deactivated at Fort Lewis, Washington, on April 2, 1971, and was reactivated on October 21, 1974, at Fort Ord. On October 1, 1985, it was redesignated the 7th Infantry Division (Light), and, in March 1988, conducted Operation Golden Pheasant to counter Nicaraguan incursions into Honduras. On December 29, 1989, it participated in Operation Just Cause, an invasion of Panama for the purpose of apprehending Panama's strongman president Manuel Noriega, who was under indictment in the United States on charges of drug trafficking.

The division was inactivated on June 15, 1994, then reactivated at Fort Carson on June 4, 1999, and it remains active.

75th Division (Training Support)

The 75th Division (Training Support) consists of 799 active component soldiers, 2,265 RESERVE COMPONENT soldiers, 35 ARMY NATIONAL GUARD soldiers, and 80 civilians. Operational command and control headquarters is the FIFTH U.S. ARMY at Fort Sam Houston, Texas. The mission of the division is to provide battle command staff training for 39 brigade and battalion-level headquarters and to provide training support and mobilization assistance for a large number of units throughout the U.S. ARMY RESERVE and Army National Guard. On January 27, 2003, the 75th DIV(TS) was mobilized for the first time since WORLD WAR II in support of Operation Enduring Freedom and the war against terrorism. At this time, the division mobilized and trained thousands of soldiers, providing high-fidelity, realistic training, assessment, and mobilization.

The 75th Division (Training Support) was activated in April 1943 during World War II as the 75th

Infantry Division, based at Fort Leonard Wood, Missouri, and with an authorized strength of 15,514. In November 1944, the division deployed by sea to England, then moved next month to France and was immediately committed to combat in the Ardennes campaign, or the "Battle of the Bulge," the desperate effort to crush the last great German offensive of the war. In January 1945, 75th Division units attached to 3rd Armor Division made contact with the enemy near Ocquier, Belgium, and had its bloodiest day of combat on January 15. In February, the division was assigned to the Seventh U.S. Army and was deployed to Alsace, France, to attack the so-called Colmar Pocket, the last major concentration of German soldiers in France.

After the Colmar Pocket was cleaned out, later in February 1945, the division deployed to Holland as part of the VIII Corps of the Second British Army and participated in the battle of the Ruhr from March 31 to April 15. After the German surrender, the 75th Infantry Division assumed security and military government duties in Westphalia, Germany. Division casualties during the war included 817 killed in action, 3,314 wounded in action, and 111 who died from their wounds.

The division was deactivated in November 1945 at Camp Patrick Henry, Virginia, and was reactivated in November 1950 as an Army Reserve Division at Houston, Texas. In 1955, the division became the 75th Infantry Division (Maneuver Area Command), its mission to train commanders and staffs of battalion- and corps-level units. In 1966, MAC took on the responsibility of performing army training tests and command post exercises at platoon level, and, by the 1970s, the 75th specialized in simulation exercises, pioneering computer-based simulations. In 1993, the 75th Division (MAC) was redesignated as the 75th Division (Exercise) and provided simulation exercises, and command and staff training for all reserve component battalion and higher headquarters in its area of operation. In October 1999 the division was again redesignated, this time as the 75th Division (Training Support). It continued to provide simulation and other training, but also integrated active component and reserve component soldiers into a single unit.

77th Infantry Division (Reinforcement Training Unit [RTU])

As a Reinforcement Training Unit, the 77th Infantry Division (ID) is composed of personnel in the RESERVE COMPONENT who, because of business or personal reasons, cannot devote the time required to belong to an active reserve unit. Membership in the 77th ID is also home to personnel who are close to retirement but do not have a position in another unit. The mission of the 77th Infantry Division (RTU) is to administer the assigned and attached reinforcement training units and supervise training, maintaining the professional expertise of the Individual Ready Reserve personnel attached to it. Members of the 77th are assigned to various senior Army and Joint commands, including (for example), Office of the Chief of Staff; Office of the Chief, Army Reserve; Deputy Chief of Staff for Logistics; Office of the Assistant Secretary of the Army for Finance and Management; Office of the Assistant Secretary of the Army for Research, Development, and Acquisition; the Army Concepts and Analysis Agency; Headquarters Military Traffic Management Command; Special Operations Command–Korea, and so on.

The mission of the 77th is to train and maintain the expertise of the individual members so that they may accomplish their assignments as individual mobilization assets (IMA). The unit conducts training on current army and Department of Defense policy and doctrine and carries out briefings that utilize the special knowledge of attached personnel to instruct unit members regarding the intricacies of each individual's area of specialization.

The parent Command is the 77th Regional Support Command, Fort Totten, New York.

78th Division (Training Support)

The 78th Division (Training Support) is headquartered at the Sergeant Joyce Kilmer U.S. Army

Reserve Center in Edison, New Jersey, with four subordinate brigades located in Edison, New Jersey; Fort Drum, New York; Fort Meade, Maryland; and Fort Bragg, North Carolina. The division reports to the FIRST U.S. ARMY. Its mission is to provide training assistance and support to RESERVE COMPONENTS through command and staff training exercises and simulations and to coordinate and synchronize mobilization assistance and support to reserve component units.

Called the "Lightning Division," the 78th has as its insignia a red semicircle with a white lightning bolt streaking through it. The origin of the name is uncertain. Some believe that, in WORLD WAR I, the French compared the action of the 78th to a bolt of lightning that seared the field through which it raced. Others hold that the name is a tribute to Burlington County, New Jersey, the county in which the division was organized and which was famous for the highly alcoholic Jersey Applejack—"white lightning"—produced there.

The division was activated on August 23, 1917, at Camp Dix, New Jersey, with an initial strength of 20,000 in four infantry regiments—the 309th, 310th, 311th, and 312th—and three artillery regiments—the 307th, 308th, and 309th. Deployed to France in the summer and fall of 1918, it served as the "point of the wedge" in the final offensive against Germany. The division fought in three major campaigns: Meuse-Argonne, Saint-Mihiel, and Lorraine. After the armistice, the 78th was demobilized during June 1919 and was not reactivated until WORLD WAR II, at Camp Butner, North Carolina, on August 15, 1942. The division functioned for two years as a training division, then was deployed to Europe, where it saw combat in Belgium, France, and Germany. After the German surrender, the division was assigned to six months of occupation duty and was deactivated in May 1946.

In November 1946, the 78th ID was reactivated at Newark, New Jersey, and in May 1959 was reorganized as a Training Division. It was not deployed again until 1990–91 during the PERSIAN GULF WAR, when its 920th Transportation Company (Medium, Petroleum) was sent to Southwest Asia. The 1018th reception battalion, the 2nd Brigade

OSUT Headquarters, and the 1st and 3rd Battalion of the 310th Regiment as well as the 1st Brigade's 3rd Battalion, 309th Regiment, with a composite detachment from the 78th Training Support Brigade, provided assistance in necessary training base expansion at Fort Dix, and the 348th MP Detachment conducted protective service missions for key national leaders throughout the world during the mobilization period.

In 1992 the 78th became an Exercise Division, conducting small unit collective training and computerized battle simulation exercises for the First U.S. Army. On October 17, 1999 the 78th was transformed into a Training Support Division, one of five in the army, tasked with providing training support, assistance, and evaluation as directed by First U.S. Army for designated Reserve and National Guard units.

After the terrorist attacks on the United States on September 11, 2001, the 78th Division provided military assistance to civil authorities. Later, the unit was mobilized to fight the "war on terrorism," providing the final training soldiers receive before deployment and also ensuring that deploying units have all the equipment and protective gear necessary.

Sheridan, Philip Henry (1831–1888) *U.S. Army general*

Sheridan forged the army CAVALRY into a highly effective force during the CIVIL WAR and served extensively in the INDIAN WARS. He was born in Albany, New York, and graduated from the UNITED STATES MILITARY ACADEMY in 1853. His first service was with the 1st Infantry Regiment in Texas and the 4th Infantry in Oregon, fighting Indians. Promoted to first lieutenant in March 1861, he rose to captain in May and fought in the Corinth (Mississippi) campaign of 1862 during the Civil War. After winning appointment as colonel of the 2nd Michigan Cavalry in May 1862, he led a daring raid on Booneville, Mississippi, on July 1, for which he was promoted to brigadier general of volunteers. As commander of the 11th Division of the Army of the Ohio, he fought extremely well at Perryville

(October 8) and at Stones River (December 31, 1862–January 3, 1863). Promoted to major general of volunteers in 1863, he served with the Army of the Cumberland in the Tullahoma campaign of 1863, then led the XX Corps to support General George Henry Thomas at Chickamauga during September 19–20. He fought the rearguard for Thomas's retreat as well.

During November 24–25, Sheridan charged up Missionary Ridge at the battle of Chattanooga and, by April 1864, had gained an appointment as commander of Cavalry Corps, Army of the Potomac. In this assignment, he fought under ULYSSES SIMPSON GRANT in the Battle of the Wilderness (May 5–6) and at Spotsylvania Court House (May 8–18). His raid against rebel lines of supply and communications during Spotsylvania resulted in the defeat of J. E. B. Stuart at Todd's Tavern on May 7 and, again, at Yellow Tavern on May 11. Assigned to destroy rail lines near Charlottesville, Virginia, he engaged Confederate units at Haw's Shop on May 28 and at Trevilian Station on June 11–12.

Sheridan was assigned command of Union forces in the Shenandoah Valley in August and conducted his finest campaign of the war through this valley, defeating the Confederate army at Winchester on September 19 and at Fisher's Hill on September 22, then cutting a swath through the Shenandoah that made this "breadbasket of the Confederacy" useless to the enemy.

Sheridan was promoted to brigadier general of regulars in September. That month, while he was absent from his army, they were surprised at Cedar Creek on October 19. Hearing of the attack, Sheridan galloped 20 miles to the battle—an action immortalized as Sheridan's Ride—and managed personally to regroup and rally his troops, who succeeded in repulsing the enemy. In November, he was promoted to major general of regulars.

Sheridan received the thanks of Congress in February 1865, then went on to raid Petersburg during February 27–March 24. Joining up with Grant, he turned ROBERT EDWARD LEE's flank at Five Forks on April 1, then engaged Lee's rearguard at Sayler's Creek on April 6. By this action, he blocked Lee's avenue of retreat at Appomattox Courthouse, and there, on April 9, Lee surrendered the Army of Northern Virginia—effectively ending the Civil War.

Named commander of the Military Division of the Gulf in May 1865, Sheridan was later appointed commander of the Fifth Military District in March 1867, to which was added the vast Department of the Missouri in September. He initiated a campaign against the Indian tribes of the Washita Valley in Oklahoma during 1868–69. In March 1869, Sheridan was promoted to lieutenant general with command of the Division of the Missouri. He was detached from this post during the Franco-Prussian War of 1870–71, when he was sent to Europe as an observer and as a liaison officer with the Prussians.

During 1876–77, Sheridan directed the campaign against the Southern Plains Indians, then became commander of the Military Divisions of the West and Southwest in 1878. In November 1883, he replaced his old friend and mentor WILLIAM TECUMSEH SHERMAN as commanding general of the army. He was promoted to general two months before his death.

Sherman, William Tecumseh (1820–1891)
U.S. Army general

ULYSSES SIMPSON GRANT's right hand during the CIVIL WAR, Sherman brought an uncompromising "total war" approach to the conflict. Afterward, he applied this same approach to prosecution of the INDIAN WARS in the American West.

Sherman was a native of Lancaster, Ohio, the son of an Ohio Supreme Court judge. Appointed to the UNITED STATES MILITARY ACADEMY, he graduated in 1840 with a commission in the artillery and was posted to Florida to serve against the Seminoles. He was promoted to first lieutenant in November 1841, and, with the outbreak of the UNITED STATES–MEXICAN WAR in 1846, he was assigned to the staff of Stephen Watts Kearny, only to be disappointed when he saw no battle action during 1846–47. He served most of the war as an administrative officer in California until that territory joined the Union in 1848.

Sherman became a commissary captain in September 1850 and, feeling profound dissatisfaction with his career, resigned his commission to start a building firm in 1853. His business failed, and he moved to Leavenworth, Kansas, where he set up as a lawyer in 1857. His practice likewise failed, but he finally found a satisfying position as superintendent of the newly established Alexandria Military Academy, which later became the Louisiana Military Academy, and, finally, Louisiana State University in Baton Rouge. He served here from October 1859 until January 1861, when it became clear that the country was about to fight a civil war.

Sherman returned to duty as colonel of the 13th Infantry in May 1861, then was appointed to a brigade command at First Bull Run (July 21). In August, he became a brigadier general of volunteers and was then given command of Union forces in Kentucky in October. He faltered badly in this assignment and seemed on the verge of a nervous collapse. However, he was transferred to the Western Department in November and pulled himself together. In February 1862, he was assigned as a division commander in the Army of the Tennessee, commanded by Ulysses S. Grant, and fought with great distinction at Shiloh during April 6–7. Indeed, Shiloh wholly redeemed Sherman after his problems in Kentucky, and, in May, he was promoted to major general of volunteers. He fought under Grant in the Corinth (Mississippi) campaign during May–June and began operations against the fortified Mississippi River town of Vicksburg. However, he suffered a defeat at Chickasaw Bluffs on December 29, which stopped his advance. Transferred to command of XV Corps, Army of the Mississippi, he took Arkansas Post on January 11, 1863, then transferred with XV Corps to the Army of the Tennessee. In this capacity, he returned to Vicksburg to support Grant's siege of the town during January 1863–July 1864. He took Jackson, Mississippi, on May 14.

Promoted to brigadier general of regulars in July, Sherman rushed to the relief of William Rose-

crans at Chattanooga, then succeeded Grant as commander of the Army of the Tennessee in October. He played a strong supporting role in coordinating with George Henry Thomas's Army of the Cumberland, and he was in command of the Union left at Chattanooga during November 24–25. In December, he marched to the relief of Ambrose Burnside, who, with characteristic ineptitude, had managed to get himself besieged in Knoxville.

Named commander of the Military Division of the Mississippi in March 1864, he now controlled the Armies of the Cumberland, the Tennessee, and the Ohio. He consolidated these forces—some 100,000 men—in a spectacular drive toward Atlanta, which he coordinated with Grant's advance on Richmond. Sherman advanced 100 miles in 74 days, pushing the army of Confederate general J. E. Johnston before him, fighting battles at Dalton, Georgia, on May 8–12, at Resaca, on May 15–16, at New Hope Church on May 24–28, and at

Grant's right hand in the Civil War, William Tecumseh Sherman took an uncompromising view of warfare as necessarily aggressive.   *(Arttoday)*

Dallas, on May 25–28, closing inexorably on Atlanta. Although he suffered a reverse at Kennesaw Mountain on June 27, he beat John Bell Hood at the Battle of Peachtree Creek, at the time just outside of Atlanta, on July 20. Northwest of the city, he triumphed at Ezra Church on July 28, and, on September 2, occupied the city.

Atlanta was razed by a fire, which Sherman's troops may or may not have started. Whoever actually set the blaze, the fire was a fitting prelude to the devastation that followed. An advocate of what today would be called "total war"—the policy of carrying combat to the civilian population rather than confining it to a contest of armies—Sherman commenced his infamous "March to the Sea" on November 16. His soldiers looted and destroyed all that lay before them, clear through to the coast. Sherman's army occupied Savannah on December 21. This accomplished, Sherman turned to the Carolinas, beginning a drive on February 1, 1865, which culminated in the capture and burning of Columbia, South Carolina, on February 17. The burning was blamed on Sherman's troops, though it is more likely that retreating rebel troops set the blazes.

Sherman successfully repulsed a surprise attack by Johnston at Bentonville, North Carolina, during March 19–20. This threat neutralized, he captured Raleigh on April 13, then, two weeks later, on April 26, he received Johnston's surrender near Durham Station, North Carolina. With Grant's acceptance of ROBERT EDWARD LEE's surrender at Appomattox (on April 9), this victory marked the end of the Civil War.

After the war, Sherman was appointed commander of the Division of the Missouri in June and was promoted to lieutenant general of regulars in July 1866. From his headquarters in Chicago, he directed much of the strategy and policy of the Indian Wars—though he participated in no battles personally. In November 1869, he became commanding general of the army and received a promotion to general. He held this often largely ceremonial post until his retirement in 1884. Sherman published a fine memoir in 1875 and created an army officer training center at Fort Leavenworth, Kansas, during the year of his retirement.

Sierra Army Depot   See FORTS AND OTHER INSTALLATIONS.

Signal Corps

A combat support branch of the army, the Signal Corps has as its mission the provision of seamless, secure, consistent, and dynamic worldwide information systems and communication networks for real-time command and control of army, joint, and combined forces in tactical, garrison, and strategic operations. Signal Corps officers plan, employ, and operate state-of-the-art voice, imagery, and data distribution systems and networks. Home station for the Signal Corps is Fort Gordon, Georgia.

Silver Star   See DECORATIONS AND MEDALS.

Simulation, Training, and Instrumentation Command (STRICOM)

Headquartered at Orlando, Florida, and subordinate to the U.S. ARMY MATERIEL COMMAND (AMC), STRICOM develops and manages training devices, training simulations and simulators, instrumentation, targets, and threat simulators for the army.

Southwest Asia Service Medal   See DECORATIONS AND MEDALS.

Spanish-American War (1898)

Early in the 19th century, Spain's Central and South American colonies won their independence. Late in the century, Cuba, a Spanish colony, became increasingly rebellious, prompting the Spanish government to send, in 1896, General Valeriano Weyler to govern the island and restore order. The general took an iron fist approach, rounding up rebels and sympathizers and incarcerating them in "reconcentration camps." The U.S. government looked on warily, but newspapers, especially those controlled by Joseph Pulitzer and William Randolph Hearst, stirred American popular opinion against Spain and in favor of the "liberation" of Cuba. This position was also supported by a variety of American business interests in Cuban sugar and fruit plantations. At length, President William McKinley ordered the battleship *Maine* into Havana Harbor to protect American citizens and property there.

On February 9, 1898, Hearst published a purloined private letter in which the Spanish minister to the United States insulted President McKinley. The nation was already stirred to outrage when, on February 15, the battleship *Maine* suddenly exploded, with the loss of 266 crewmen. A naval court of inquiry concluded that the ship had struck a Spanish mine (modern analysts believe that the ship's powder magazine spontaneously exploded through no hostile action), and the Hearst and Pulitzer papers vied with one another to demonize Spain. The war cry "Remember the *Maine* . . . to hell with Spain!" was soon rampant, and, on April 24, 1898, the United States went to war with Spain.

The army favored the USN's proposal to prosecute the war chiefly through a naval blockade of Cuba, but Congress and the public clamored for an invasion. At the time, the army consisted of no more than 26,000 officers and men and a National Guard that enrolled about 100,000 more, most poorly trained and ill equipped. Moreover, army strategists had no standing plan for a foreign invasion, since the army was considered an exclusively defensive force. In belated preparation for war, Congress passed a Mobilization Act on April 22, 1898, which enabled the mobilization of National Guard units outside of U.S. borders. The act also provided for the recruitment of 125,000 volunteers, to which an additional 75,000 were soon added. A special 10,000-man force, christened the "Immunes" and consisting of persons "possessing immunity from diseases incident to tropical climates," was also authorized. The act also more than doubled the authorized strength of the REGULAR

ARMY, to about 65,000. By the end of the 10-week war, in August 1898, the regular army numbered 59,000, and the volunteer forces 216,000.

In the short term, logistics were strained to the breaking point, but, fortunately, the navy was more fully manned and equipped, and was thereby able to strike the first blows. On May 1, 1898, the navy attacked and destroyed the Spanish fleet in Manila Harbor, Philippines.

By May 1898, General NELSON APPLETON MILES was prepared to lead army units from Tampa, Florida, against Cuba. The marine corps coordinated with the navy to neutralize Spanish batteries guarding Havana harbor, and, on June 14, V Corps, consisting of three divisions, 17,000 men, mostly regular army, under Major General William R. Shafter, left Tampa. It was June 20 before the transport convoy arrived near Santiago, the troops having suffered under brutal tropical heat and in overcrowded, unsanitary conditions. Admiral William T. Sampson wanted General Shafter to land at Santiago Bay and immediately storm the fort on the east side of the entrance to the bay to drive the Spanish from their guns, but Shafter had not transported heavy artillery and therefore doubted that his troops could take the fort. He decided instead on a less direct approach. He landed at Daiquirí, east of Santiago Bay. Disembarkation began on June 22 and was not concluded until June 25 amid great confusion. Cavalry mounts were tossed overboard, left to swim ashore on their own. Many horses swam out to sea and were lost. Had the Spanish commanders responded appropriately, they might have taken advantage of the prevailing chaos to wipe out the landing force. Spain had at least 200,000 troops in Cuba, of which 36,000 were stationed in Santiago. Combined with about 5,000 local insurgents (under General Calixto Garcia), army forces numbered only 22,000. Fortunately, for the Americans, the Spanish did nothing to resist the inept landings, and elements of V Corps advanced west toward the high ground of San Juan, a series of ridges east of Santiago. On June 23, Brigadier General Henry W. Lawton led the army vanguard along the coast from Daiquirí to take and hold Siboney, which became the principal base of operations. On June 24, Brigadier General Joseph Wheeler took his dismounted CAVALRY units inland along the road to Santiago and captured Las Guasimas, engaging briefly the rear guard of a retreating Spanish force. V Corps units, now just five miles outside of San Juan Heights, paused to await the arrival of the rest of Shafter's divisions, but Shafter became concerned about the debilitating effect the tropical conditions had on his troops. He decided on an immediate frontal attack against San Juan Heights, which stepped off at dawn on July 1. At first, the attack went badly as troops fell victim to the heat and to Spanish artillery. Nevertheless, by midday U.S. forces made a vigorous assault on the heights. Among the army units participating were the 9th and 10th Cavalry—both African-American regiments—and the volunteer regiment known as the Rough Riders and commanded by the dashing lieutenant colonel Theodore Roosevelt. These three cavalry regiments, all unmounted, seized and occupied Kettle Hill, as infantry charged up San Juan Hill and overwhelmed the defenders. Short of food, water, and ammunition, the Spaniards abandoned San Juan. Simultaneously, USN ships engaged and destroyed the Spanish fleet, and, on July 16, Spanish commanders in Cuba surrendered.

Next, on July 21–25, General Nelson A. Miles led more than 3,000 troops out of Guantánamo to a landing at Guánica on the southeastern coast of Puerto Rico. Meeting virtually no resistance, they advanced to the port town of Ponce. Miles secured this as a base of operations and led four columns toward San Juan, brushing aside the inconsequential resistance he encountered. The campaign was suspended on August 13, when news reached Miles that Spain had signed a peace protocol.

Shortly after the army and USN triumphed in Cuba and Puerto Rico, VIII Corps, about 13,000 volunteers and 2,000 regulars under Major General Wesley Merritt, began landing near Manila, the Philippines. By the beginning of August, 11,000 U.S. troops were arrayed to the rear of the Filipino insurgents just outside the city. Within Manila, as many as 15,000 Spanish troops were ready to make a defensive stand. Both Admiral Dewey and General Merritt appealed to Madrid for a bloodless surrender, but the cause of Spanish honor seemed to demand at least a show of resistance. Therefore, on August 13, VIII Corps attacked, supported by Dewey's naval bombardment, forcing the Spanish garrison to surrender. On August 14, the Manila surrender was formalized, although, in fact, Madrid had signed a general peace protocol on August 12. This was followed by the Treaty of Paris, signed on December 10, 1898, which secured Spain's grant of independence for Cuba. President McKinley pressed his negotiators to obtain cession of Puerto Rico, Guam, and the Philippine Islands, which were secured for the United States.

Special Branches   See ORGANIZATION BY BRANCH.

Special Forces

Popularly known as the Green Berets, after their distinctive headgear, Special Forces is a special branch of the army, with a home station at Fort Bragg, North Carolina. The Special Forces Command is subordinate to U.S. ARMY SPECIAL OPERATIONS COMMAND (USASOC) and controls five active component groups and two ARMY NATIONAL GUARD groups. Special Forces has five primary missions: foreign internal defense, unconventional warfare, special reconnaissance, direct action, and counterterrorism.

In peacetime, foreign internal defense is the principal mission. This is carried out by assisting friendly developing nations to improve their technical skills and ensure protection of human rights issues. Special Operations also assists with humanitarian and civic action projects.

The unconventional warfare mission includes military and paramilitary operations carried out in enemy-held and enemy-controlled areas. Operations include guerrilla warfare, evasion and escape, sabotage, subversion, and other operations of a clandestine nature.

Special reconnaissance is carried out behind hostile borders to provide theater commanders with intelligence concerning enemy capabilities and actions, local populace, and terrain.

Direct action includes short-duration strikes and small-scale offensive actions, whether of an overt or covert nature.

The counterterrorism mission includes offensive measures taken to prevent, deter, or respond to terrorism.

The Special Operational Detachment A (SFOD A, or "A Team") is the basic Special Forces unit, consisting of a 12-man team fully prepared to equip, train, advise, organize, and support indigenous military or paramilitary forces in unconventional warfare and internal defense. The "B Detachment" (SFOD B) is the company headquarters, which incorporates multipurpose command and control that can deploy SF teams by itself without the need for augmentation. The "C Detachment" (SFOD C), the battalion command and control authority, provides staff planning, supervision, and administration to the A Team and B Detachment. SFOD C also advises and assists in the employment of Special Forces units in the Joint Special Operations Task Force.

Army Special Forces was organized in 1952 and was a development of RANGER and commando units first fielded during WORLD WAR II. Special Forces truly came into its own in the early 1960s, during the presidency of President John F. Kennedy, whose administration saw the Green Berets as an answer to the guerrilla-style combat of the many cold war–era "brushfire wars" that burst into flame in Latin America, the Middle East, Africa, and Southeast Asia. These small, elite units were used in operations to counter communist insurgencies throughout the developing world. The 5th Special Forces Group was especially active early in the VIETNAM WAR and established the Green Beret presence there. Green Beret units would continue to conduct many operations throughout the entire war.

During the 1960s, Special Forces received little support from the army hierarchy, which was reluctant to sanction an essentially autonomous elite

force. It was largely due to the personal sponsorship and intervention of President Kennedy that the Green Berets developed into a significant force, which, to this day, remains popular with chief executives as a means of conducting military operations well short of outright war. After Vietnam, army commanders substantially reduced the size of Special Forces, only to restore the units to full strength during the 1980s, when they were used chiefly for liaison, rescue, and reconnaissance. These were the roles that were also most important for Special Forces during the PERSIAN GULF WAR of 1990–91.

See also DELTA FORCE.

specialist   See RANKS AND GRADES.

Special Staff

Made up of senior officers, the Special Staff reports to the CHIEF OF STAFF and has responsibility for the army's special activities. The Special Staff includes the Chief of Engineers, Chief, National Guard Bureau, Chief, Army Reserve, and the Army Surgeon General.

squad   See ORGANIZATION BY UNITS.

staff sergeant   See RANKS AND GRADES.

Steuben, Baron Friedrich Wilhelm von
(1730–1794) *Continental army officer*
This Prussian officer was instrumental in training the CONTINENTAL ARMY during the AMERICAN REVOLUTION and thereby laid the foundation for a professional army. He was born in Magdeburg, Prussia, the son of a distinguished military family. In 1747, Steuben entered the Prussian army and served with it during the Seven Years' War, both as a field officer in the infantry and as a staff officer. He was assigned confidential diplomatic missions and was then attached to the staff of Emperor

Frederick the Great from 1757 to 1763, when he resigned (with the rank of captain) to become chamberlain at the petty court of Hohenzollern-Hechingen. He served in this capacity until 1771, then journeyed to France with the Hohenzollern prince to raise money for the court during 1771–75. When this came to nothing, Steuben tried to enter, in succession, the French, Austrian, and Baden armies, but he was admitted to none. At last, he returned to France in 1777 to enter the American service, and, bearing a recommendation from Benjamin Franklin to GEORGE WASHINGTON, he sailed from Marseilles on September 26 and arrived in Portsmouth, New Hampshire, on December 1.

On February 5, the Continental Congress accepted Steuben's offer to serve as a volunteer, and he hastened to join Washington at Valley Forge,

Baron von Steuben, a Prussian military officer, was indispensable during the American Revolution in training the soldiers of the Continental army, the direct precursor of U.S. Army.   *(Arttoday)*

Pennsylvania, on February 23. Steuben set about training Washington's regulars, beginning with a model company of 100. His methods spread throughout the Continental army quickly, despite the fact that Steuben knew no English and had to use interpreters to make himself understood. His charisma transcended the language barrier, and he was highly successful at training and motivating troops.

Appointed major general and inspector general by Congress in May, he participated in the Battle of Monmouth on June 28, then, from 1778 to 1779, he wrote *Regulations for the Order and Discipline of the Troops of the United States,* a manual that served the American army for three decades.

Steuben went to Virginia in the spring of 1780 to raise troops and supplies and to organize local defenses against the depredations of turncoat Benedict Arnold along the coast during the fall of 1780 and into the spring of the following year. Steuben fell ill and turned over his command to the Marquis de Lafayette on June 19, but he recovered in time to join the army in September just prior to Yorktown. He took command of a division at Yorktown from September 28 to October 19.

At the conclusion of the American Revolution, Steuben tried with little success to secure the surrender of British posts on the frontier during the spring and summer of 1783. He left the Continental army on March 24 of the following year and lived a lavish retirement in upstate New York. Soon weighed down by debt, he secured a well-deserved pension from the government in June 1790 and was thereby narrowly saved from destitution. From his retirement, he remained active in U.S. military affairs and was instrumental in urging the creation of a national military academy. He also advocated a standing militia to supplement a small professional army.

Stilwell, Joseph Warren (1883–1946) *U.S. Army general*

Nicknamed "Vinegar Joe" because of his acidic and irascible temperament, Stilwell had the thankless task of leading troops on the chronically undersupplied China-Burma-India (C-B-I) front in WORLD WAR II. In this, he became an inspiration to all army officers for the success with which he accomplished much using very little.

A native of Palatka, Florida, Stilwell was raised in Yonkers, New York, and graduated from the UNITED STATES MILITARY ACADEMY (USMA) in June 1904 as a second lieutenant in the infantry. He requested duty in the Philippines and was posted to the 12th Infantry Regiment, which saw action on Samar against the rebel leader Puljanes during February–April 1905.

In 1906, Stilwell returned to the USMA as a foreign language instructor, an assignment that ultimately spanned four years and grew to include the teaching of history and tactics in addition to coaching athletics and teaching languages. In 1911, Stilwell finally transferred back to the Philippines and was promoted to first lieutenant soon afterward. During November and December, he visited China for the first time.

Returning again to West Point as a language instructor, he served there from 1913 to 1916 and was promoted to captain in September 1916. Named brigade adjutant in the 80th Division after promotion to temporary major in July 1917, he shipped out to France in January 1918 during WORLD WAR I. He was appointed to a post as staff intelligence officer. During March 20–April 28, he was attached to the French XVII Corps near Verdun, then received an assignment as deputy chief of staff for intelligence under General Joseph T. Dickman in IV Corps during the Meuse-Argonne campaign (September 26–November 11). Stilwell was promoted to temporary lieutenant colonel on September 11, 1918, then temporary colonel in October. After the armistice, he served in occupation duties until May 1919. Not wishing to return immediately to the United States, Stilwell next requested an assignment to China as a language officer. He served there from August 6, 1919, to July 1923. During this chaotic period in Chinese history, Stilwell made an important ally in the warlord Feng Yuxiang (Feng Yu-hsiang).

"Vinegar Joe" Stilwell accomplished prodigies with few men and fewer supplies in the always hard-pressed China-Burma-India theater of World War II. *(Arttoday)*

After returning to the United States in 1923, Stilwell attended Infantry School at Fort Benning. He graduated in 1924 and enrolled in the COMMAND AND GENERAL STAFF COLLEGE at Fort Leavenworth from 1925 to 1926. He was then returned to China in command of a battalion of the 15th Infantry at Tientsin in August 1926. There he met GEORGE CATLETT MARSHALL.

Promoted to regular lieutenant colonel in March 1928, Stilwell became head of the tactical section of the Infantry School in July 1929, largely through the influence of Marshall.

Stilwell left the Infantry School in 1933 to become training officer for the IX Corps reserves from 1933 to 1935. After this, he was appointed military attaché to China and was promoted to colonel on August 1, 1935. During his assignment in China, Stilwell became intimately familiar with vast regions of the country, and he was a keen observer of the developing Sino-Japanese War. He returned to the United States in 1939 and, en route, received a promotion to brigadier general.

Assigned command of the 3rd Brigade, 2nd Division in September 1939, Stilwell played a major role in the Third Army's maneuvers of January 1940, then commanded the "red" forces in the massive Louisiana-Texas maneuvers of May 1940. His superiors recognized his genius for moving troops quickly and in unexpected ways, and, following the maneuvers, Stilwell was assigned, on July 1, 1940, to command the newly created 7th Division stationed at Fort Ord, California. In September, he was promoted to temporary major general and was moved up to command of III Corps in July 1941.

After Pearl Harbor propelled the United States into World War II, Stilwell was promoted to lieutenant general and appointed commanding general of U.S. Army forces in the China-Burma-India theater in January 1942. He set up a headquarters at Chungking (Chongqing), China, where he made an ally of the Nationalist Chinese leader Jiang Jieshi (Chiang Kai-shek), who, on March 6, 1942, agreed to Stilwell's taking command of Chinese forces in Burma. Arriving in Burma on March 11 with a single Chinese division, Stilwell soon raised eight more.

Like his British counterpart in the C-B-I theater, General William Slim, Stilwell suffered from chronic shortages of supply and reinforcements. He also had to contend with conflicting orders from Jiang. Ultimately, he was forced to withdraw from Burma to India during May 11–30. After the disappointment in Burma, Stilwell turned his attention to training and equipping the three Chinese divisions in India and to creating "the Hump,"

an airlift chain to supply Kunming during January and February 1943.

In July 1943, Stilwell was appointed deputy supreme Allied commander in the C-B-I under British supreme commander Lord Louis Mountbatten. Stilwell advocated the Salween-Myitkyina Mogaung offensive of March–August 1944, which was a hard-won success that ended in the capture of Myitkyina on August 3 and the subsequent liberation of all of northern Burma. Following this, Stilwell was promoted to temporary general, but he found it impossible to maintain a working relationship with Jiang Jieshi, and, at Jiang's request, President Franklin D. Roosevelt recalled him on October 19, 1944.

Back in the United States, Stilwell was named commander of army ground forces on January 23, 1945, and was decorated with the Legion of Merit and the Oak Leaf cluster of the DSM on February 10, 1945. Dispatched to Okinawa, he took command of the Tenth Army there on June 23 and was among those present at the Japanese surrender ceremony in Tokyo Bay on September 2, 1945.

After the war, Stilwell became president of the War Equipment Board and then commander of the Sixth Army and the Western Defense Command in January 1946, succumbing later in the year to stomach cancer.

Stinger   See WEAPONS, INDIVIDUAL AND CREW-SERVED.

Stryker Eight-wheel-drive Armored Combat Vehicles   See WHEELED VEHICLES.

T

Table of Organization and Equipment (TOE)

The TOE is an army document that prescribes the wartime mission, capabilities, organizational structure, and mission-essential personnel and equipment requirements for specific military units.

Each TOE is identified by a unique number composed of a nine-position, alphanumeric code consisting of the following:

Series: A 2-position numeric code indicating the branch or major nonbranch subdivision to which the TOE applies. These are:

01 Aviation/Aviation Logistics
03 Chemical
05 Engineer
06 Field Artillery
07 Infantry
08 Medical
09 Ordnance (Missile/Munitions)
10 Quartermaster
11 Signal
12 Adjutant General/Band
14 Finance
16 Chaplain
17 Armor
19 Military Police
20 General
27 Judge Advocate
29 Composite Units and Activities (CSS)
30 Military Intelligence
31 Special Forces
32 Security
33 Psychological Operations
34 Combat Electronics Warfare and Intelligence
37 Mechanized Units
41 Civil Affairs
42 Supply
43 Maintenance (except Missile)
44 Air Defense Artillery
45 Public Affairs
51 Army
52 Corps
54 Logistics Organizations & Operations
55 Transportation
57 Airborne Division
63 Combat Service Support
67 Air Assault Division
77 Light Infantry Division
87 Heavy Division/Brigade

Organizational elements: A 3-position numeric code indicating the organizational elements of the branch or major subdivision follows the series number. The three digits in positions 3, 4, and 5 of the TOE number include:

Position 3 (ECHELON): Identifies the type unit within the branch or major subdivision.

- 0, 1, 2, and 3—Divisional/brigade and equivalent
- 4—Corps units
- 5—Teams (generic)

- 6—ECHELONS ABOVE CORPS (EAC)/theater army
- 7, 8, and 9—Unique (e.g., 9 is used with series 01 to identify aviation maintenance TOEs)

Position 4 (UNIQUE): Specifies the TOE within the categories outlined above.

Position 5 (TYPE ORG): Identifies the type of organization:

- 0: Corps, division, brigade, or modular company (recapitulation).
- 1: Corps headquarters and headquarters company (HHC) or similar or associated unit (headquarters and headquarters battery [HHB] corps artillery, headquarters and headquarters engineer command, rear area operations center [RAOC], etc.).
- 2: Brigade, group, regiment, division artillery, or similar organization HHC/HHB/ headquarters and headquarters detachment (HHD)/ headquarters and headquarters troop (HHT).
- 3: Separate companies within brigade, division, or corps subgroups.
- 4: Division HHC and, if required, some separate companies.
- 5: Battalion or similar organization (recapitulation).
- 6: Battalion or similar organization HHC, HHD, HHB, and HHT.
- 7, 8, and 9: Company or similar organization within a battalion.

Position 6: Indicates the TOE edition, as follows:

L-edition identifies all TOEs that incorporate Army of Excellence [AOE] concepts and doctrine.

A-edition TOEs incorporate Force Projection Army concepts and doctrine.

F-edition identifies Force XXI TOEs.

B-edition indicates audit.

C-edition TOEs are those undergoing cyclic review, but not yet DA approved.

E-edition TOEs identify unique TOEs where there is a long-standing HQDA approved requirement, based on unique mission, geog-

raphy, climate, or equipment, but no equivalent A-, F-, or L-edition TOE exists.

S-edition indicates an automated unit reference sheet (AURS).

H- and J-editions are obsolete.

Position 7 (VARIATION): Identifies variations or teams.

Positions 8 and 9: Reserved for future use.

Tank-Automotive and Armaments Command (TACOM)

Administered by the U.S. ARMY MATERIEL COMMAND (AMC) and located in Warren, Michigan, TACOM carries out weapon systems research, development, and sustainment in the areas of ground combat, automotive, marine, and armaments technologies. TACOM researches, develops, engineers, leverages, and provides advanced ground systems and serves as a conduit among the army, industry, academia, and other federal agencies to develop advanced technologies.

Taylor, Zachary (1784–1850) *U.S. Army general, president of the United States*

One of the army's early heroes, Zachary Taylor led combined REGULAR ARMY and militia forces in the WAR OF 1812 and in the opening moves of the UNITED STATES–MEXICAN WAR. He was born in Orange County, Virginia, but was raised near Louisville, Kentucky. After a catch-as-catch-can education, he enlisted in the Kentucky militia as a short-term volunteer in 1806, then joined the army as a first lieutenant in the 7th Infantry in March 1808. Two years later, he was promoted to captain, and, in 1811, he served under General William Henry Harrison against Tecumseh's band of Shawnee and other Indians of the Old Northwest.

With the outbreak of the War of 1812, Taylor made a valiant defense of Fort Harrison on the Wabash River on September 4, 1812, which earned him a brevet to major. He continued to serve on the frontier, and he commanded an expedition down the Mississippi River to assert federal authority on the fringes of the wilderness. However, in the rush to demobilize that followed the end of the War of 1812, Taylor was reduced in rank to captain in June 1815. Indignant, he resigned his commission, but he was coaxed back to the army when his friend President James Madison engineered the restoration of the rank of major.

From 1817 to 1819, Taylor served garrison duty with the 3rd Infantry at Green Bay, Wisconsin Territory, then assumed command of Fort Winnebago. Promoted to lieutenant colonel in April 1819, he transferred to Louisiana in 1822. There he built Fort Jesup, near Natchitoches. From 1829 to 1832, Taylor was at Fort Snelling (present-day St. Paul, Minnesota), where he served as Indian superintendent, then moved into the Wisconsin-Illinois area to fight Chief Black Hawk. He fought with distinction at the decisive battle of Bad Axe River on August 2, 1832, which ended the so-called Black Hawk War.

In July 1837, Taylor was dispatched in command of a force to fight the Seminoles, who were resisting federally mandated "removal" to Indian Territory (modern Oklahoma). After he managed to lure the Seminoles into open battle at Lake Okeechobee, he scored a signal victory on December 25. In a war characterized by guerrilla encounters, a full-out field battle such as this was a rarity.

Breveted to brigadier general in 1838, Taylor could not lure the Indians into open conflict again and, therefore, was unable to end the war decisively. In April 1840, at his own request, he was relieved. In May 1841, he was named commander of the Second Department, Western Division, headquartered at Fort Smith, Arkansas. In May 1844, as war clouds gathered over Texas, Taylor put together a combat force at Fort Jesup and was ordered to march to Texas when the republic was annexed to the United States in June 1845. With a force of 4,000, he established his headquarters at Corpus Christi in October.

Taylor and his army were dispatched to the Rio Grande River during February 1846 and occupied territory claimed by Mexico. The United States-Mexican War commenced with hostilities near Fort Brown on April 25. On May 8, at Palo Alto, Taylor defeated a vastly superior Mexican force, then he defeated the Mexicans again on the next day at Resaca de la Palma. Taylor occupied Matamoros on May 18.

Breveted major general and elevated to command of the Army of the Rio Grande in July, Taylor crossed the Rio Grande and invaded Mexico with 6,200 men. He attacked Monterrey, but agreed to an armistice on September 24. President James Polk repudiated the armistice and ordered Taylor to press his advance more deeply into Mexico. Following orders, Taylor captured Saltillo in November, but he then sent most of his regular troops —4,000 strong—and many volunteers to General WINFIELD SCOTT, whose army was invading central Mexico during the winter of 1846–47.

Taylor used his remaining troops—4,600 green volunteers—to continue his own advance. He confronted a 15,000-man army under Mexican general Santa Anna at Buena Vista on February 21. The Mexican commander demanded his surrender. Refusing, Taylor instead launched into combat, repulsing the Mexicans in a bloody two-day battle during February 21–22.

Buena Vista made Taylor a national hero. He capitalized on this renown to become the Whig candidate for president in June 1848. Winning handily, he took office in March 1829, only to die of heatstroke the following year.

10th Mountain Division (Light Infantry)

Headquartered at Fort Drum, New York, the 10th Mountain Division (Light Infantry) grew out of the 87th Mountain Infantry Battalion, which was created on December 8, 1941, at Fort Lewis, Washington, as the army's first mountain unit, specializing both in cold weather combat and in mountain combat. Indeed, it was 10th Mountain Division veterans of WORLD WAR II who were largely responsible for the development of skiing as a popular American sport beginning during the 1950s.

Inactivated on June 14, 1958, the division was reactivated on February 13, 1985, at Fort Drum,

New York. Its purpose is to meet a wide range of worldwide INFANTRY-intensive contingency missions using equipment oriented toward reduced size and weight in order to achieve greater strategic and tactical mobility.

Test and Evaluation Command (TECOM)

Headquartered at Aberdeen Proving Ground, TECOM is the army's principal materiel testing organization for weapons and equipment. Command facilities test a wide variety of military hardware, including vehicles; munitions; weapons and their components; rockets and guided missile systems and components; communications and electronics; command control and intelligence equipment; army aircraft; aircraft system components and related ground-support equipment; as well as training devices and soldiers' clothing and individual equipment.

TH-67 New Training Helicopter   See

AIRCRAFT.

Theater army   See ORGANIZATION BY UNITS.

3rd Infantry Division (Mechanized)

Stationed at Fort Stewart, Georgia, the 3rd Infantry Division (ID) has as its mission the capability to deploy rapidly to a contingency area by air, land, and sea to conduct mobile, combined arms offensive and defensive operations worldwide.

The division was initially activated in November 1917 during WORLD WAR I at Camp Greene, North Carolina, and was sent into combat in France eight months later. On July 14, 1918, the division was heavily engaged in the Aisne-Marne offensive and was assigned to protect Paris with a position on the banks of the Marne River. As surrounding Allied units retreated under the German onslaught, the 3rd ID remained solid and earned the enduring sobriquet "Rock of the Marne."

During WORLD WAR II, the division fought in North Africa, Sicily, Italy, France, Germany, and Austria, compiling a total of 531 consecutive days of combat, its soldiers earning 36 Medals of Honor during the war. At Anzio, the 3rd ID fought off attacks by no fewer than three German divisions, suffering in a single day of the onslaught 900 casualties, more in one day than any division fighting in any theater of the war. The most highly decorated soldier of World War II, Audie Murphy, served with the division's 15th Infantry Regiment.

During the KOREAN WAR, the 3rd Infantry earned a new nickname, "the Fire Brigade," because of its rapid response to the multiple crises in that conflict. The division fought throughout the war, and 11 of its soldiers received Medals of Honor.

The 3rd ID was stationed in Germany from April 1958 to April 1996, and it served as an important deterrent element during the cold war.

In November 1990, the division sent more than 6,000 men and women to serve with the 1ST ARMORED DIVISION in the PERSIAN GULF WAR (Operation Desert Storm). After the war in Iraq ended, some 1,000 3rd ID troops were deployed to southeastern Turkey and northern Iraq to provide humanitarian relief to Kurdish refugees. An additional contingent of 1,000 was deployed as part of Task Force Victory to assist in the rebuilding of Kuwait, which had been ravaged by the Iraqi invaders.

In 1996, the division was restationed at Fort Stewart, Fort Benning, and Hunter Army Airfield, Georgia, but it retained a battalion and, later, a brigade task force in Kuwait. Following the September 11, 2001, terrorist attacks on the United States, 3rd ID units have been deployed to Afghanistan, Pakistan, and other Middle Eastern countries in support of the war on terrorism. In 2003, the 3rd ID constituted a major force in the invasion of Iraq during Operation Iraqi Freedom, fighting its way to Baghdad in early April. As of 2005, elements of the division remain in Iraq, fighting the guerrilla war that ensued after the close of major combat in that country.

Third U.S. Army

Part of the U.S. ARMY FORCES COMMAND (FORSCOM), the Third U.S. Army is located at Fort McPherson, Georgia and is the army component headquarters of the U.S. CENTRAL COMMAND (USCENTCOM). The Third U.S. Army mission is to plan, exercise, and deploy army forces in response to contingencies threatening U.S. interests in Southwest Asia.

Third U.S. Army functions as a Joint Forces Land Component Command (JFLCC) or Coalition Joint Task Force (C/JTF) when designated by Commander in Chief, U.S. Central Command. It also executes operational and tactical control of forces operating within the CENTCOM area of responsibility.

The Third Army was activated during WORLD WAR I in 1918 and deactivated after the armistice, but it was reactivated as a reserve organization in 1921. Withdrawn from the reserves in 1932, it was returned to the REGULAR ARMY as an inactive unit, then was reactivated in 1933. During WORLD WAR II, under the command of Lieutenant General GEORGE SMITH PATTON, JR., the Third Army compiled an extraordinary record in its breakout from the Normandy beachheads through France and into Germany and Czechoslovakia. Inactivated in 1973, it was reactivated in its present role in 1982.

34th Infantry Division

The 34th Infantry "Red Bull" Division is currently an ARMY NATIONAL GUARD division with about 11,000 troops located across five states, Minnesota, Iowa, North Dakota, Colorado, and Michigan. Headquarters are located at Rosemount, Minnesota (just south of Minneapolis–St. Paul).

The 34th Infantry Division (ID) was created by drawing on National Guard troops from Minnesota, Iowa, the Dakotas, and Nebraska late in the summer of 1917 during WORLD WAR I. It was deployed to France in October 1918, a month before the armistice and too late to be committed to battle.

The division was reactivated on February 10, 1941, as the United States prepared for possible entry into WORLD WAR II. The division participated in the extensive Louisiana maneuvers on the eve of war, and it was the first American division actually shipped overseas after the nation entered the war.

The 34th ID participated in six major army campaigns in North Africa, Sicily, and Italy and is credited with amassing 517 days of continuous frontline combat, more than any other division in the European theater (portions of the division are credited with more than 600 days of frontline combat). During the war, the division suffered 21,362 casualties, including 3,737 killed. Members of the division received 11 Medals of Honor and 98 Distinguished Service Crosses.

It was within the 34th ID that the RANGERS were first formed. The 1st Ranger Battalion was created under the command of one of the division's officers, Captain William Darby, and 80 percent of the battalion's volunteers were drawn from the 34th. These men soon earned substantial fame as "Darby's Rangers."

The 34th Infantry Division was reorganized as an active National Guard division on February 10, 1991, replacing the 47th Infantry (Viking) Division.

35th Infantry Division (Mechanized)

The 35th Infantry Division (ID) is an ARMY NATIONAL GUARD organization headquartered at Fort Leavenworth, Kansas, with units in Alabama, Arkansas, Colorado, Florida, Georgia, Illinois, Kansas, Kentucky, Missouri, Nebraska, Oklahoma, and Washington.

The division was created on August 25, 1917, at Camp Doniphan, Oklahoma, made up of National Guard units from Kansas and Missouri. Early on, the division was nicknamed the Santa Fe Division and a "wagon wheel" patch was adopted. Both the name and the symbol were derived from the Santa Fe Trail, which began in Missouri and ran through Kansas, the eastern end located near Camp Doniphan.

The division was deployed to France in May 1918 during WORLD WAR I and fought in the Meuse-Argonne offensive and in Alsace and Lorraine. Among the most famous soldiers in the division was Captain Harry S. Truman, who commanded a battery of Missouri's 129th Field Artillery. The division returned to the United States and was inactivated in May 1919, then, on July 1, 1926, was reorganized with units from Missouri, Kansas, and Nebraska. Another famous division soldier, Captain Charles Lindbergh, a pilot in the 110th Observation Squadron, received a Medal of Honor for his solo flight across the Atlantic Ocean in 1927.

With WORLD WAR II raging in Europe, President Franklin D. Roosevelt mobilized the 35th ID on December 23, 1940. However, the division underwent training for the next four years and was not committed to combat until it landed on Omaha Beach on July 5, 1944, during the invasion of Normandy. Over the following eight months of continuous combat, the 35th ID fought in Normandy, through northern France, and into Alsace, the Ardennes, the Rhineland, and central Europe. The division returned to the United States in July 1945 and was inactivated in December 1945. In 264 days of combat, the division lost 2,947 men killed in action and 12,935 wounded in action.

The 35th ID was reorganized in October 1946 with units from Kansas and Missouri, then was inactivated in 1963 and not reorganized until 1984, this time with units from Missouri, Kansas, Nebraska, Kentucky, and Colorado, at which time its headquarters was established at Fort Leavenworth. In October 2002, the division was reorganized again, with National Guard units from Kansas, Illinois, Kentucky, Missouri, Nebraska, Arkansas, Oklahoma, Georgia, Alabama, Florida, Colorado, Washington, and Hawaii.

In January 2003, many 35th Infantry Division soldiers were deployed to Bosnia-Herzegovina to perform peacekeeping duty as Stabilization Force 13.

38th Infantry Division (Mechanized)

The 38th Infantry Division (ID) is composed of the Indiana ARMY NATIONAL GUARD and is headquartered in Indianapolis, Indiana. The division was created on August 25, 1917, at Camp Shelby, Mississippi, formed from National Guard units mobilized from three states. Indiana furnished most of the troops, followed by Kentucky and West Virginia. From April through June 1918, more than 6,200 soldiers from the division were sent to Europe as individual combat replacements for other divisions already there. Replacements were drawn not only from Indiana, Kentucky, and West Virginia but also from Alabama, Arkansas, Florida, Illinois, Louisiana, Mississippi, Tennessee, Wisconsin, and the District of Columbia.

The 38th ID was deployed to Europe starting in early September 1918. By October 25, the full division was ashore in France. Due to the demand for replacements at the front, the division was deployed piecemeal rather than as a unit, and, indeed, many 38th ID soldiers never saw action before the armistice of November 11, 1918. The division's scattered units were returned to the United States and not reconstituted. On March 8, 1919, the division was formally deactivated.

As early as 1920, the 38th Infantry Division began reorganizing in the National Guard. As WORLD WAR II raged in Europe, the U.S. Department of War began a program of increased training and readiness. From August 11 to August 31, 1940, the 38th Division participated in Second Army maneuvers and was then mobilized. During August–October 1941, the 38th Division prepared for and participated in major field maneuvers, then, with the outbreak of war, entered a long period of training. Late in 1943, the division was ordered to San Francisco for transport to the Pacific theater. Orders were changed, however, and the division was sent to New Orleans over the 1943–44 holidays, and, during the first week of January 1944, was conveyed via the Panama Canal to Hawaii. The 38th relieved the 6th Infantry Division of its ground defense mission on the island. Simultaneously, the division underwent intensive jungle combat training. The division was landed on Leyte, in the Philippines, on December 6, 1944, under heavy fire. The island was declared secure on

Christmas Day, and by the first week of January 1945 the 38th was well into the process of reassembling itself.

From Leyte, the 38th proceeded to Luzon, landing on January 9, 1945, its mission to participate in the capture of Manila. From late January through early September 1945 the 38th Infantry Division was engaged in combat operations on Luzon.

After the war, the 38th ID was reorganized within the National Guard, and Indiana was allotted the entire division. In 1961, the division was nearly federalized again during the Berlin crisis, the showdown between the United States and the Soviet Union over the divided German City. The following year, the division was almost mobilized again, during the Cuban missile crisis. However, the division has not actually been mobilized since the end of World War II.

three-striper

Army and marine corps slang for a sergeant (grade E-5), whose rank is indicated by three chevrons.

Tobyhanna Army Depot   See FORTS AND OTHER INSTALLATIONS.

top

Also called top kick or top sergeant, the army and marine corps nickname for a first sergeant (grade E-8).

Topographic Engineering Center (TEC)

The mission of the Topographic Engineering Center (TEC) is to provide the army warfighter with a superior knowledge of the battlefield and to support the nation's civil and environmental initiatives through research, development, and the application of expertise in the topographic and related sciences.

This laboratory is part of the U.S. ARMY CORPS OF ENGINEERS. Its Topography, Imagery and Geospatial (TIG) Research Division includes a Data Representation Branch, a Geospatial Applications Branch, a Data and Signature Analysis Branch, and an Information Generation and Management Branch. The Topography, Imagery and Geospatial Systems Division encompasses a Force Projection Branch, an Imagery Systems Branch, and a Topographic Systems Branch. The Topography, Imagery and Geospatial Operations Division includes an Analytical Services Branch, Hydrologic and Environmental Analysis Branch, Terrain Analysis Branch, Information Services Branch, and a Geospatial Information and Imagery (GII) Requirements Branch.

TOW   See ANTIARMOR WEAPONS.

tracked vehicles

Tracked vehicles, including tanks, have been the mainstay of U.S. Army armored weapons since WORLD WAR II. Following are the tracked vehicles currently (2005) in the army inventory and significant earlier vehicles. Also included are the most significant tank guns in use today.

M-1A1 Abrams Main Battle Tank

The M-1A1 Abrams entered army service in 1980 and is designed to provide heavy ARMOR superiority on the battlefield by integrating mobility, firepower, and shock effect. The M-1A1 mounts a 120-mm main gun and is powered by a 1,500-hp turbine. It is also clad in specially designed armor. Additionally, the M-1A1 has been upgraded and modernized with increased armor protection, improvements to the suspension system, and an NBC (nuclear, biological, chemical) protection system. The M-1A1D version adds an advanced computer as well as far-target-designation capability. The M-1A2 version now includes a commander's independent thermal viewer, an improved commander's weapon station, position navigation equipment, distributed data and power architecture, an embedded diagnostic system, and improved fire control systems. Additionally, the M-1A2 System Enhancement Program (SEP) features upgraded thermal sensors and other sensors and electronics, allowing for rapid data communication.

The Abrams main battle rank in action   *(U.S. Army)*

General characteristics of the Abram tank include (for M-1/IPM-1, M-1A1, M-1A2, and M-1A2 SEP versions):

Weight: 61.4/62.8 tons, 67.6 tons, 68.4 tons, 69.5 tons
Length: all 32.04 ft
Width: all 12 ft
Height: 7.79 ft, 8.0 ft, 8.0 ft, 8.0 ft
Top speed: 45 mph, 41.5 mph, 41.5 mph, 42 mph
Main armament: 105 mm, 120 mm, 120 mm, 120 mm
Crew: all 4

M-2 Bradley Fighting Vehicle

The Bradley underwent a long and controversial development, beginning in 1964 and finally achieving operational capability in 1983. The Bradley has supplemented and in large measure replaced the M-113 armored personnel carrier and represents a compromise between an armored troop carrier and a genuine fighting vehicle with especially capable self-defense facilities. The Bradley is armed with a

The M-2 Bradley Fighting Vehicle   *(U.S. Army)*

25-mm M-242 chain gun and carries up to 600 rounds of ammunition. This leaves room for only six troops in addition to a three-man operating crew. Other general characteristics of the Bradley include:

Weight: 66,000 lb
Hull length: 21 ft 6 in
Width: 11 ft
Height: 9 ft 9 in
Power plant: Cummins VTA-903T 600-hp V-8
  diesel
Maximum speed: 42 mph

M-3/M-5 Stuart Tank

The M-3 was designed early in 1940, on the eve of U.S. entry into World War II and went into production in March 1941. The major innovation was augmented armor. The M-3 version was designed to take a Continental gasoline engine, but supply problems led to modifications for diesel engines. The M-5 model, introduced late in 1942, was powered by two gasoline-fueled Cadillac engines.

Crewed by four, the Stuart weighed 12 tons and had a maximum speed of 37 miles per hour. Armament consisted of a 37-mm main gun and two .30-caliber machine guns. The army found that the tank performed poorly against advanced German armor in the Mediterranean and European theaters, but, in the Pacific, where the USMC used the Stuart, it was more than a match for Japanese tanks. However, tank duels were rare in the Pacific, and the USMC used the Stuart mainly to support infantry assaults against fixed Japanese defenses.

M-4 Sherman Tank

The Sherman tank was introduced early in World War II, and between 1942 and 1946, 49,324 were produced. It was the principal army and marine corps battle tank during the war. Weighing 35 tons, armed with a 75-mm cannon and three machine guns, and crewed by five, the Sherman marked a substantial improvement over its predecessor, the M-3 Grant, but it was substantially inferior to all of the German tanks fielded against it. However, the Shermans were produced and deployed in overwhelming numbers, and tank commanders soon developed effective formation strategies for coordinated attacks, which made up for many of the Sherman's technical deficiencies. Moreover,

while inferior in armor and firepower to the German tanks, the Sherman was simpler and more reliable than the typically overengineered German weapons.

In the Pacific, where both the army and marine corps used the tanks, the Shermans proved superior to the Japanese tanks; however, tank battles were rare in the Pacific theater. Far more often, the Sherman was used as a mobile artillery platform to support infantry actions.

M-9 Armored Combat Earthmover

Although planned as early as 1958, production of the M-9 did not begin until 1985. The vehicle is a fast armored earthmover used for constructing weapons positions, for building, and for recovering vehicles. The M-9 is a combination bulldozer and front-end loader, capable of holding 237 square feet of fill. The vehicle is also amphibious.

General characteristics of the M-9 include:

Weight: 54,000 lb
Hull length: 20 ft 6 in
Width: 10 ft 6 in
Height to top of cupola: 9 ft 10 in
Power plant: Cummins V903C 295-hp V8
  diesel
Maximum speed: 30 mph
Crew: 1

M-26 Pershing Main Battle Tank

The Pershing was developed at the end of World War II and was used by the army and marines; however, postwar cutbacks meant that many USMC units retained the earlier M-4 Sherman Tank, which proved no match for the Russian-built tanks used by the North Koreans and Chinese during the KOREAN WAR. Pershings fared much better against the enemy in that war.

The M-26 Pershing was armed with a 90-mm main gun; supplemental weapons were two .50-caliber machine guns. Crewed by five, weighing 42 tons, and achieving 30 miles per hour, the Pershing was very heavily armored and an extremely effective weapon.

M-60A1 Main Battle Tank

Although the M-60 is now in army service only in ARMY NATIONAL GUARD and U.S. ARMY RESERVE units, it has proven itself to be one of the world's great main battle tanks. Between 1960 and 1987, the Chrysler Corporation produced more than 15,000 for the U.S. Army as well as the armies of 21 other nations. The weapon has been repeatedly upgraded with cutting-edge weapon control, new ammunition, improved armor, and more powerful engines.

The M-60A1, introduced in 1962, incorporated a new turret, thicker armor, and a redesigned ammunition stowage system. The M-60A2 introduced another new turret fitted with a 152-mm gun and missile launcher, but development was stopped in order to create the M-60A3, which added improvements to fire control. The M-60A3 entered service in 1978.

The general characteristics of the M-60A3 include:

Weight: 116,000 lb
Hull length: 22 ft 9 in
Width: 11 ft 11 in
Height: 10 ft 9 in
Main gun: 105-mm/51-caliber M-68 rifled gun, 63 rounds
Secondary weapons: 7.62-mm M-240 coaxial machine gun, 5,950 rounds; 12.7-mm M-85 antiaircraft gun, 900 rounds
Power plant: Continental AVDS-1790-2C 750-hp V-12 multifuel engine
Maximum speed: 30 mph
Crew: 4 (commander, gunner, loader, driver)

M-68 105-mm Tank Gun

This weapon is the U.S. Army version of the British L7 gun and is now used as the main armament of the M-60 Battle Tank and the first version of the M-1 Abrams. The gun entered army service in 1962. It can fire a wide array of projectiles, including the M-392 Armor-Piercing Discarding Sabot with Tracer, as well as depleted-uranium rounds, high-explosive projectiles, and a variety of antipersonnel projectiles. The gun's general characteristics include:

Weight: 2,489 lb
Overall length: 18 ft 3 in
Muzzle velocity: 4,955 fps
Range: 2,187 yd
Rate of fire: 9 rounds/min

M-88A2 Hercules

HERCULES stands for Heavy Equipment Recovery Combat Utility Lift and Evacuation System. It was adopted by the army in 1997 to provide towing, winching, and hoisting operations to support battlefield recovery operations and evacuation of heavy tanks and other tracked combat vehicles.

The M-88A2 Hercules is a full-tracked armored vehicle, which uses the existing M-88A1 chassis but improves its towing, winching, lifting, and braking characteristics. Hercules is the primary recovery support for the M-1 Abrams tank fleet and other heavy vehicles, including heavy self-propelled artillery.

General specifications of the M-88A2 Hercules include:

Length: 338 in
Height: 123 in
Width: 144 in
Weight: 70 tons
Speed: 25 mph without load; 17 mph with load
Cruising range: 200 miles
Boom capacity: 35 tons
Winch capacity: 70 tons/670 feet
Draw bar pull: 70 tons
Armament: 1 .50-caliber machine gun
Power Train: 12 cylinder, 1050-hp air-cooled diesel engine with 3-speed automatic transmission
Crew: 3
Manufacturer: United Defense, L.P., York, Pennsylvania

M-107 175-mm Gun

The M-107 was the largest self-propelled gun ever fielded by the U.S. Army. It began service in 1965 and was discontinued in 1981. General characteristics include:

Weight: 62,100 lb
Barrel length: 34 ft 6 in
Maximum muzzle velocity of gun: 3,028 fps
Rate of fire: 2 rounds/min (intense mode)
Range: 35,761 yd (maximum charge)
Powerplant of vehicle: Detroit Diesel 8V-71T 405-hp V8
Speed: 35 mph
Range: 450 miles
Crew: 5 minimum, 13 maximum

M-110A2 203-mm Howitzer

Currently, the M-110A2 is the heaviest piece of field artillery in the army and marine corps. Production of the weapon began in 1962 and some 2,000 have been built. The future of the weapon is in doubt because current doctrine favors lighter and more versatile weapons, such as the 155-mm HOWITZERS. General characteristics of the weapon include:

Weight: 62,500 lb
Barrel length: 27 ft 1/2 in
Muzzle velocity: 2,333 fps
Rate of fire: 2+ rounds/min maximum
Range: 32,808 yd
Vehicle power plant: Detroit Diesel 8V-71T 405-hp V8 diesel
Maximum speed: 34 mph
Crew: 5 minimum, 13 maximum

M-113 Armored Personnel Carrier

This is a widely used armored personnel carrier, developed between 1959 and 1965, with more than 78,000 produced for some 50 countries. Although the M-2 Bradley Fighting Vehicle has largely replaced the M-113 in its basic configuration, several variants continue to be important. The M-548 is a cargo carrier, and the M-577 and M-1068 are mobile command posts. The M-901 is an Improved TOW Vehicle, which fires two TOW Antitank Missiles. The M-981 Fire Support Vehicle incorporates a laser target designator, and the M-1015 Electronic Warfare Systems Carrier is used in electronic warfare applications. Additionally, there is an M-1059 Smoke Generator Carrier.

General characteristics of the basic M-113 include:

Weight: 24,986 lb
Hull length: 15 ft 11 in
Width: 8 ft 10 in
Height: 8 ft 3 in
Power plant: Detroit Diesel 6V53 215-hp diesel
Maximum speed: 38 mph
Crew: 2
Passengers: 11 troops

M-242 Bushmaster 25-mm Cannon

This weapon is the army's principal armament for light armored vehicles. The gun began development at Hughes Helicopters in 1976 and became operational in 1983. Its general characteristics include:

Weight: 244 lb
Overall length: 9 ft 1 in
Muzzle velocity: 4,412 fps
Range: 2,187+ yd
Rate of fire: 500 rounds/min maximum

M-256 120-mm Tank Gun

Designed by the German firm of Rheinmetall, this smooth-bore tank gun is the main armament of the M-1A1 Abrams Main Battle Tank. The choice of smooth bore rather than rifled design was made in the interest of achieving greater muzzle velocity without compromising barrel life. The gun can fire a wide variety of projectiles, including M-829 Armor-Piercing Fin-Stabilized Discarding Sabot with a depleted-uranium penetrator. Development of the gun began in 1964 and the weapon was approved by the USA in 1984. General characteristics include:

Weight (total system): 6,649 lb
Barrel length: 17 ft 5 in
Muzzle velocity: 5,616 fps
Range: 3,281 yd

M-548 Cargo Carrier

Based on the M-113 Armored Personnel Carrier, the M-548 is used primarily for ammunition resupply, although it can also carry other cargo. Modified M-548s carry missile systems and radar stations. The vehicle became operational in 1966. Its general characteristics include:

Weight: 28,400 lb
Payload: 12,000 lb
Hull length: 18 ft 10 1/2 in
Width: 8 ft 10 in
Height: 8 ft 11 in
Armament: ring mount accommodates 7.62-mm machine gun or 12.7-mm machine gun
Maximum speed: 40 mph
Crew: 4

M-578 Light Armored Recovery Vehicle

The M-578 is based on the M-107/M-110 chassis and is designed to recover disabled vehicles in the field. It is also used in the field to make major repairs, such as changing engines, transmissions, and so on. The M-578 is intended to service light armored vehicles and includes a hydraulic crane mounted on a turret as well as a heavy-duty towing winch. The vehicle became operational in 1963, and its general characteristics include:

Weight: 53,572 lb
Hull length: 18 ft 4 in
Width: 10 ft 4 in
Height to top of cupola: 9 ft 7 in
Armament: 12.7-mm M-2 HB antiaircraft machine gun
Power plant: Detroit Diesel 8V7IT 425-hp V-8 diesel
Maximum speed: 34 mph
Crew: 3

TRADOC Analysis Command (TRAC)

Located at Fort Leavenworth, Kansas, and administered by the U.S. ARMY TRAINING AND DOCTRINE COMMAND (TRADOC), TRAC is an analysis agency that conducts research on potential military operations worldwide to inform decisions about the most challenging issues facing the army and the Department of Defense. The TRAC staff consists of military and civilian personnel who conduct operations research on both contemporary and future (five to 15 years out) topics. The research is used to help determine how army units should be organized, what new systems should be procured, how soldiers and commanders should be trained, and so on. Emphasis is put on the development of scenarios for education, training, and force development. TRAC also builds and applies models and simulations that include table-top map games, human-in-the-loop (HITL) simulations and simulators, closed-form models and simulations, and controlled field experiments.

Transportation Corps

The Transportation Corps, "Spearhead of Logistics," is a combat service support branch of the army and has its home station at Fort Eustis, Virginia. Its mission is to project combat power to the right place at the right time with terminal, rail, truck, and marine operations.

25th Infantry Division (Light)

Stationed primarily at Schofield Barracks, Hawaii (with a subordinate command at Fort Lewis, Washington), the 25th Infantry Division (ID) prepares for deployment to a theater of operations to perform combat operations as part of a corps counterattack. When ordered, the division conducts theaterwide deployment within 54 hours of notification.

The origin of the 25th ID may be traced to 1872, when Major General John M. Schofield first identified Hawaii as strategically vital to U.S. interests. On August 12, 1898, during the SPANISH-AMERICAN WAR, Hawaii was annexed as a U.S. territory, and, four days later, 1,300 troops of the 1st New York Volunteer Infantry Regiment and 3rd Battalion, 2nd U.S. Volunteer Engineers, landed near Diamond Head to set up the first military base. This led to the creation of the Hawaiian Division, which was inactivated on October 1, 1941, and was replaced by the 24th Infantry Division, which integrated the 19th and 21st Infantry Regiments, as well as the 229th Infantry Regiment of the Hawaiian Army National Guard, and by the newly created 25th Infantry Division, which incorporated the 27th and the 35th Infantry Regiments, the 298th Infantry Regiment of the Hawaiian National Guard, plus a field artillery brigade.

Following the attack on Pearl Harbor on December 7, 1941, the 24th and the 25th Divisions were dispatched to their defensive positions, the 24th deploying to the north shore of Oahu and the 25th to the beaches on the south side of the island. These units spent all of 1942, the first full year of U.S. involvement in WORLD WAR II, in these defensive positions while also training for jungle warfare.

The 25th Infantry Division embarked for the South Pacific on November 25, 1942, and made an assault on Guadalcanal during December 17, 1942–January 4, 1943, joining a fight that had been ongoing for five months. Within a month of the arrival of the 25th ID, victory was won, and the division was dubbed "Tropic Lightning" in recognition of the speed with which it had transformed the battle.

After Guadalcanal, the division fought actions in the North Solomon Islands, defeating Japanese Forces on Arundel (Kohinggo) and Kolombangera Islands and participating in the capture of Vella LaVella before retiring to New Zealand and then New Caledonia for rest and training. After this interval, on January 11, 1945, the division landed on Luzon, largest of the Philippine Islands. The fighting was extremely costly, and, by the time the 25th captured the Balete Pass, it had suffered more combat deaths than any other U.S. division in the Philippines.

After the conclusion of the Battle of Luzon, the division was moved to Camp Patrick to prepare for the invasion of Japan, an invasion made unnecessary by the atomic bombing of Hiroshima and Nagasaki, which brought an end to the war in August 1945. The 25th ID now took part in the occupation of Japan.

Between July 5 and July 18, 1950, the 25th ID moved from its base in Japan to Korea, successfully blocking the approaches to the port city of Pusan. Afterward, the division participated in the breakout from the Pusan defensive perimeter and drove deep into North Korea in October 1950, participating in the push to the Yalu River, the border of Korea and China. With all other U.S. and United Nations units, however, the 25th ID withdrew in the face of a massive Chinese incursion into Korea. The division assumed defensive positions on the south bank of the Chongchon River on November 30, 1950, then withdrew south of Osan, holding here until a new offensive was launched on January 15, 1951.

The division participated next in Operation Ripper, driving the enemy across the Han River. Other offensives, Operations Dauntless, Detonate, and Piledriver, in spring 1951, secured part of the infamous Iron Triangle, which gave the United Nations a strong position from which to negotiate an armistice.

The division remained in Korea until 1954 and returned to Hawaii from September through October of that year.

In Hawaii, the division conducted intensive training programs in jungle warfare and became the only trained counterguerrilla unit in the army. A small number of helicopter door-gunners were sent to the Republic of South Vietnam in early 1963, and thus the division's involvement in the VIETNAM WAR began. In August 1965, the 65th Engineer Battalion was sent to South Vietnam to assist in the construction of port facilities at Cam Ranh Bay. In December, division personnel participated in Operation Blue Light, a massive airlift into Vietnam, and from April 1966 until 1969 the 25th Infantry Division became increasingly engaged throughout the entire area of operations in Southeast Asia. Soldiers of the division were instrumental in defending the besieged city of Saigon during the 1968–69 Tet Offensive, after which the division devoted an increasing amount of time to training Army of the Republic of Vietnam (ARVN) in the Vietnamization program that accompanied the phased withdrawal of U.S. ground forces.

During April through June 1970, 25th ID soldiers participated in thrusts deep into enemy sanctuaries located in Cambodia, then resumed its work on Vietnamization before beginning redeployment to Schofield Barracks in December 1970. The last units of the division left Vietnam in May 1971.

After returning from Vietnam, the division was radically downsized to a single brigade of 4,000 men, but it was fully reactivated in March 1972. In 1985, the division began reorganization from a conventional infantry division to a light infantry division, a unit primed for mission flexibility, rapid deployment, and combat readiness at 100 percent strength with a Pacific Basin orientation.

Elements of the division were deployed to Saudi Arabia in 1990 as part of Operation Desert Shield and were in the forefront of the ground assault during Operation Desert Storm (PERSIAN GULF WAR) in 1990–91.

More than 3,700 soldiers from the 25th Infantry Division (Light) were deployed to Haiti in January 1995 to participate in the peacekeeping mission Operation Uphold Democracy.

28th Infantry Division (Mechanized)

The 28th Infantry Division (ID) is an ARMY NATIONAL GUARD division that maintains armories in 84 cities throughout Pennsylvania with a strength of more than 15,000 soldiers. Primary division elements include three Combat Brigades, Division Artillery, Division Support Command, Combat Aviation Brigade, Combat Engineer Brigade, and several separate battalions and company-sized elements.

The 28th ID is the oldest division in the army, having been established on March 12, 1879. However, the origins of the division may be traced to colonial America, to 1747, when Benjamin Franklin organized a battalion of "Associators" in Philadelphia. The lineage of the 28th ID extends through the AMERICAN REVOLUTION, the WAR OF 1812, the UNITED STATES–MEXICAN WAR, and the

CIVIL WAR. The division was mustered into federal service in 1898 during the SPANISH-AMERICAN WAR, and elements of the division fought in Puerto Rico and the Philippines.

Units of the 28th ID, known then as the 7th Division, fought in the punitive expedition against Pancho Villa in 1916–17, and, during WORLD WAR I, on October 11, 1917, the division was reorganized as the 28th Division while it trained in Georgia for deployment to France. The division arrived in France on May 18, 1918, and was first committed to battle on July 14. Elements of the 28th ID fought in six major World War I campaigns, Champagne, Champagne-Marne, Aisne-Marne, Oise-Marne, Lorraine, and Meuse-Argonne, suffering more than 14,000 battle casualties and earning the epithet "Iron Division" from no less a figure than General JOHN JOSEPH PERSHING.

The division did not participate in WORLD WAR II, and early in 1946 it was reorganized as part of the Pennsylvania National Guard. Four years later, in 1950, it was called into federal service to become part of U.S. NATO forces in Germany after the outbreak of the KOREAN WAR. The division returned to the United States and to state control on June 15, 1954.

During the early months of the VIETNAM WAR, in October 1965, the 28th Infantry Division was one of three Army National Guard divisions selected as part of the Army Selected Reserve force. Maintained at a high state of readiness, the division was not committed to battle. Nor was the division deployed to the Middle East during the PERSIAN GULF WAR, although division volunteers were deployed to that theater, including the 121st Transportation Company, which served in Saudi Arabia during the war.

The division's artillery sent forward observers to support NATO peacekeeping forces in Bosnia in 1996, and the Target Acquisition Battery of the 109th Field Artillery was mobilized for the peacekeeping mission two years later. In 1999, the division's Company H, 104th Aviation (Air Traffic Control) was activated, with its tour of duty extending into 2000.

29th Infantry Division (Light)

The "Blue and Gray" Division is the only light infantry division in the entire RESERVE COMPONENT. Headquartered at Fort Belvoir, Virginia, the 29th has units in Virginia, Maryland, Massachusetts, North Carolina, and Connecticut.

The division was created on July 26, 1917, when Virginia ARMY NATIONAL GUARD troops were joined with guardsmen from New Jersey, Maryland, and the District of Columbia as the 29th Infantry Division (ID), which was activated on August 25. After training, the division began shipping out to France in 1918, its advance detachment arriving in Brest on June 8. The main body sailed in separate convoys during June and July. Less its artillery, the division assembled near Prauthoy, France, then was deployed to a "quiet" sector of the western front for final training under combat conditions.

On July 25, the division relieved the 32nd Division near Belfort in Alsace, just north of the Swiss border, and, in late September, the division participated in the Meuse-Argonne offensive. The division experienced 21 days of combat before the November 11 armistice, having advanced seven kilometers, captured 2,148 prisoners, and knocked out over 250 machine guns or artillery pieces. One-third of its members were casualties, 170 officers and 5,691 men.

On the eve of WORLD WAR II, the 29th ID was moved to Fort Meade, Maryland. Various units of the division were deployed piecemeal as required, but the bulk of the division trained from April through September 1942, then moved secretly by train to a staging area at Camp Kilmer, New Jersey, for deployment overseas. Most of the division left aboard the ocean liner *Queen Mary* on September 26, the rest following on the *Queen Elizabeth* on October 5. After landing in Scotland, the troops were transported to Tidworth Barracks, in southern England, where they underwent intensive training.

The division took part in Operation Overlord, the D-day invasion of Normandy, landing with the 1ST INFANTRY DIVISION at Omaha Beach on June 6, 1944. Elements of the division took heavy casualties from fierce German resistance. After securing the beachhead, the division advanced on its next objective, the crossroads village of St. Lô. The advance consumed five bloody weeks, after which the division participated in an assault on the port city of Brest.

After a short rest, the 29th ID moved by train across France and Belgium to a part of Holland near the German border. From here, the division made a slow advance into western Germany. München-Gladbach (present-day Münchengladbach) fell to the division on March 1, 1945, and the division advanced to the Elbe River, where it met Soviet troops advancing from the east.

After the German surrender, the 29th ID performed occupation duties, then was inactivated in January 1946 and returned to state control. The 29th ID did not participate in the KOREAN WAR as a unit, although many Army National Guardsmen attached to the division did serve there. On February 1, 1968, members of the 29th ID joined Maryland and Pennsylvania in manning the 28TH INFANTRY DIVISION. The division was not reactivated until June 6, 1984.

twink

A second lieutenant. His or her brand-new gold bar twinkles.

U

UH-1 Huey/Iroquois   See AIRCRAFT.

UH-1N Huey/Iroquois   See AIRCRAFT.

under secretary of the army

The under secretary serves as deputy to the SECRETARY OF THE ARMY and is also the chief acquisition executive for the army. He or she reports directly to the under secretary of defense for acquisition.

unified commands

Unified commands, or unified joint service commands, form the bulk of organization in today's army. These commands are components of joint service commands, which typically include army and USAF components and, often, USN and USMC components as well.

U.S. Army components of major unified commands include:

MILITARY TRAFFIC MANAGEMENT COMMAND (MTMC): army component of U.S. Transportation Command

THIRD U.S. ARMY: army component of U.S. Central Command

U.S. ARMY, EUROPE (USAREUR): army component of U.S. European Command

U.S. ARMY, PACIFIC (USARPAC): army component of U.S. Pacific Command

U.S. ARMY, SOUTH (USARSO): army component of U.S. Southern Command

U.S. ARMY FORCES COMMAND (FORSCOM): army component of U.S. Joint Forces Command

U.S. ARMY SPACE AND MISSILE DEFENSE COMMAND (SMDC): army component of the U.S. Strategic Command

U.S. ARMY SPECIAL OPERATIONS COMMAND (USASOC): army component of U.S. Special Operations Command

See also JOINT TASK FORCE.

uniforms

Today's soldier may wear a variety of BDU (battle dress uniforms), especially designed for specific fighting environments: cold climates, forest, urban, desert, and so on. In addition, army front-line soldiers are typically equipped with advanced body armor and lightweight but strong Kevlar helmets. The Soldier Systems Center in Massachusetts continually develops and tests new clothing and personal equipment for the army. It was not until the late 19th century, however, that the army began to provide clothing intended expressly for battle as opposed to parade and general duty. The army soldier of the AMERICAN REVOLUTION and WAR OF 1812 wore a single uniform. In the Revolution, blue was chosen for the CONTINENTAL ARMY soldier, to distinguish him from the British (who wore predominantly scarlet) and the French (mainly white). The blue coat featured turned-back lapels and cuffs faced, usually, in buff. Infantrymen had uniforms with white metal buttons, artillerists had yellow buttons. Crossed white shoulder belts (which were kept white through laborious application of pipe clay) held up a BAYONET and cartridge box.

By the early 19th century, army uniforms were greatly influenced by European styles of the Napoleonic era. The long coat was reduced to a coat with a cut-in skirt. The three-cornered or cocked hat of the Revolutionary-era soldier was replaced by a shako cap, which, beginning in 1832, was adorned with a metal branch insignia. Whereas Revolutionary troops wore white trousers to contrast with their blue coats, 19th-century troops were issued trousers of sky-blue color.

Beginning in the mid-19th century, the army followed French styles closely, adopting the French frock coat with full skirt and black accoutrements by 1851. Branch colors appeared in details such as lace and piping. During the Civil War, the French kepi, or visored cap, became standard issue, and Union troops wore blue sack-coat fatigue blouses.

As the 19th century drew to a close, the French forage cap replaced the kepi, and, in the field, broadbrimmed campaign hats were frequently worn. The uniform blouse became more form-fitting and buttoned up to a high "choke collar," on which branch insignia and the letters "U.S." were featured. In the field, depending on climate and other conditions, soldiers might shed their uniform blouses and wear cambric shirts. Also depending on unit and duty, the traditional blue uniform might be exchanged for a uniform of khaki, with blouse and trousers of the same khaki-colored wool. Campaign hats might be worn, but British-style pith helmets were also common.

It was at the turn of the 20th century that battle dress became increasingly distinct from parade dress. Army dress uniforms adopted Prussian-style spiked leather helmets, sometimes complete with plume. Field-grade officers might wear cocked hats, again with plume. On the more practical side,

the SPANISH-AMERICAN WAR made clear the desirability of seasonal uniforms. It was in 1902 that cotton khaki became universal in summer, and olive drab wool was worn in the winter. Both of these uniforms were chosen to provide a degree of battlefield concealment in an emerging era of smokeless gunpowder. The traditional army blue was not rejected, but it was confined to dress uniforms only. At this time, too, the forage cap was universally adopted as the service cap. Breeches were pegged and tucked into leggings.

The army soldier entered WORLD WAR I in olive drab. The uniform blouse was loosely fitted and featured many pockets. Leather belting had been replaced for the most part by lighter and more practical web belts, and leggings gave way to cloth puttees for enlisted men and riding boots for officers. The doughboys shipped to France without steel helmets, but, at the insistence of the Allies, soon adopted the British-style "wash-basin" helmet. Officers generally shunned the helmet, but did adopt the leather Sam Browne belt of the British, along with British-style "pinks and green," a uniform in which the blouse contrasted with the trousers.

WORLD WAR II and the era leading up to it saw a revolution in the army uniform, with far more thought given to efficient and protective battle dress. The worldwide nature of the war required wide variation in fabric weight and style. Blouses and trousers (cargo pants) were loose-fitting, and special attention was paid to boots—the combat boot was adapted from the paratrooper boot and designed for comfort as well as support and protection—and to headgear. Early in the war, a new helmet was adopted, the M-1, which came in two parts: a separate liner and an outer steel shell. In the middle of the war, the M-1943 field jacket was introduced, which featured a layered arrangement that could be worn comfortably in a wide range of temperatures and weather conditions.

The olive drab of World War II gave way to Army Green-44 in 1956, although khaki continued to be worn in the summer until 1985. Perhaps the most dramatic change in uniform policy came in 1946, when the so-called Doolittle Board directed an end to distinctive uniforms for officers and soldiers. Although rank insignia would remain distinctive, enlisted men and officers were to wear the same field uniforms. Dress uniforms were also nearly identical, with officers distinguished only by a black trouser stripe and a gold chin strap and visor cap embroidery.

Garrison uniforms were introduced in 1949. In the early 1950s, the green-107 starched olive-drab fatigue uniform was adopted for garrison duty, and in 1954 name tags and "U.S. Army" were added to the fatigue blouse. The VIETNAM WAR called for development of tropical combat clothing, new camouflage styles, and generally muted treatment of all insignia. In 1961, SPECIAL FORCES troops were distinguished by a green beret. RANGERS adopted black berets in 1975, and airborne troops maroon berets in 1980. In 2001, black berets were authorized for all soldiers—a move that created considerable controversy in some quarters.

United Nations Medal　See DECORATIONS AND MEDALS.

United Nations Service Medal　See DECORATIONS AND MEDALS.

United States Army Reserve Command (USARC)

USARC, a major subordinate command of U.S. ARMY FORCES COMMAND (FORSCOM), commands, controls, and supports all U.S. ARMY RESERVE troop units in the continental United States, except for Psychological Operations and Civil Affairs units. USARC prepares and ensures the readiness of nearly 1,700 units under its command through a command and control structure that focuses on training, readiness, supporting mobilization, and the ability to provide military support to other federal agencies.

USARC is divided into 11 Regional Readiness Commands (RRCs) located throughout the United States, which provide resources, logistics, and personnel management services to all Army Reserve units within their region. In addition, three Regional Support Groups (RSGs) assist the RRCs in providing administrative, logistics, and general support services. Army Garrison Units manage Active Component garrisons during mobilization.

USARC also commands a network of seven institutional training and five exercise divisions, which train new soldiers during mobilization and provide valuable peacetime training for active and reserve soldiers. The USARC also supervises specific troop units such as military police and signal commands through a system of 25 General Officer Commands (GOCOM).

USARC in-residence training facilities, correspondence schools, and distance-learning hubs are located at Fort McCoy, Wisconsin; Fort Hunter-Liggett, California; Camp Parks, California; and Fort Dix, New Jersey. Additionally, USARC manages 500 Army Reserve units that are part of the Army's Force Support Package (FSP). The FSP is designed for immediate activation in case of mobilization. The Tiered Resourcing Program, implemented and managed by the USARC, improves unit readiness and ensures FSP units receive the highest priority for all resources. USARC also manages the overseas deployment for training (ODT) program, which allows Army Reserve units to perform mission-related training while providing mission-essential medical, transportation, maintenance, and engineering capabilities to the army.

United States–Mexican War

After the U.S. Congress resolved on March 1, 1845, to admit the Republic of Texas as a state to the Union, Mexico, which had repudiated the treaty by which it had granted Texas independence in 1836, severed diplomatic relations with the United States. Although President Polk continued efforts to negotiate U.S. claims to Texas as well as to Upper California (in 1845 still a Mexican province), he ordered Brigadier General ZACHARY TAYLOR, U.S. Army, to take up a position on or near the Rio

Grande to repel an anticipated invasion. Beginning on July 23, 1845, Taylor transported most of his 1,500-man force by steamboat from New Orleans to the plain at the mouth of the Nueces River near Corpus Christi. Throughout the rest of the summer and into the fall, more troops arrived, creating a force of about 4,000. When negotiations between the United States and Mexico broke down in February 1846, Taylor was ordered to advance 100 miles down the coast to the Rio Grande. He deployed most of his troops 18 miles southwest of Point Isabel, on the Rio Grande, just opposite the Mexican border town of Matamoros. On April 25, 1846, General Mariano Arista led a substantial Mexican force across the river and into Texas, where he attacked an advance detachment of 60 army dragoons under Captain Seth B. Thornton. Eleven soldiers were killed, and the other troops, including Thornton, were captured; many were wounded.

Taylor called on Texas and Louisiana for 5,000 militia volunteers to supplement his army forces. On May 8, with only 2,300 troops (even fewer available for combat), Taylor engaged an advancing Mexican army of 4,000. Nevertheless, Taylor enjoyed the advantages of superior artillery and excellent young officers, including ULYSSES SIMPSON GRANT. Taylor used his artillery to good advantage and drove the Mexicans from the field. A more aggressive commander would have pursued the defeated enemy; Taylor, however, first strengthened defenses around his supply train, then, at a more leisurely pace, set off after Arista's army.

On May 9, at a dry riverbed called Resaca de la Palma, five miles from Palo Alto, Taylor engaged the Mexicans in a battle that began as an artillery brawl and soon developed into hand-to-hand combat and another army victory. Yet again, however, Taylor did not give chase to finish off Arista's entire force.

With war already under way, Congress voted a declaration of war and President Polk signed it on May 12, 1846. The strength of the regular army was increased from about 8,500 men to 15,540. In addi-

tion a call-up of 50,000 one-year volunteers was also authorized. Polk's major objective was to obtain all Mexican territory north of the Rio Grande and Gila rivers, west to the Pacific Ocean. The army's most senior commander, Major General WINFIELD SCOTT, a hero of the WAR OF 1812, drew up a three-pronged plan. Taylor would march west from Matamoros to Monterrey, Mexico; once Monterrey was taken, all of northern Mexico was vulnerable. At the same time, Brigadier General John E. Wool would march from San Antonio to Chihuahua, Mexico; from here, he could advance farther south, to Saltillo, near Taylor's force at Monterrey. Finally, Colonel Stephen Watts Kearney would advance out of Fort Leavenworth, Kansas, to take Santa Fe and, from here, continue all the way to San Diego, California. This third prong would later be modified, as part of Kearny's force, under Colonel Alexander W. Doniphan, would make a remarkable advance deep into Mexico, via Chihuahua to Parras. Initially, there was no plan to capture the Mexican capital, Mexico City, because Polk and Scott hoped that achieving the objectives of the three-pronged strategy would force Mexico to capitulate quickly without the necessity for a deeper invasion.

Taylor had to deal with the illness of many troops in sweltering temperatures. When he began his overland advance from camp at Camargo to Monterrey, he did so with fewer than half the troops originally available to him: 3,080 army regulars and 3,150 militiamen. This force reached Monterrey on September 19 and took the town by September 23. Unwisely, Taylor then granted the Mexican commander's request for an eight-week armistice. The Mexicans took advantage of this to rebuild their forces, and President Polk, on October 11, condemned Taylor for having allowed the Mexican army to escape. On November 13, Taylor dispatched 1,000 men to Saltillo to seize control of the only road to Mexico City from the north and the road to Chihuahua. Next, on November 15, naval forces took the town of Tampico, and, in December, Brigadier General Wool arrived from San Antonio with 2,500 army troops. Headed for

Chihuahua, he learned that the Mexicans had abandoned the town, so he united with Taylor's main force at Monterrey.

Taylor wanted to deploy a defensive line connecting Parras, Saltillo, Monterrey, and Victoria, but he was informed that President Polk had authorized Scott to make an amphibious assault on Veracruz. Eight thousand of Taylor's troops were to be detached to join Scott's force. Left with 7,000 men, mostly volunteers, Taylor was ordered to evacuate Saltillo and go on the defensive at Monterrey. Taylor deemed these orders mere "advice" and, instead of following them, left small garrisons at Monterrey and Saltillo, then sent 4,650 men 18 miles south of Saltillo to Agua Nueva. Unknown to him, Santa Anna was only 35 miles from Agua Nueva. This led to the Battle of Buena Vista, on February 22–23, 1847. The forces of Mexican commander Santa Anna outnumbered Taylor's command three to one, but Taylor refused Santa Anna's demand for surrender. Santa Anna fired his artillery, then the two armies jockeyed for position. Despite the disparity in their numbers, superior American artillery and bold leadership won the day for the Americans.

While Taylor fought in Mexico, Colonel Stephen Watts Kearny led a spectacular march from Fort Leavenworth, Kansas, to Santa Fe, New Mexico, which fell to Kearny without a shot. From Santa Fe, Kearny marched on to California, reaching San Diego in December 1846 only to find that a U.S. naval squadron had already secured the California ports.

By March 2, 1847, when Scott commenced operations leading to the landing at Veracruz—the first amphibious landing in army history—the Americans were in control of northern Mexico. Scott landed 10,000 men at Veracruz during the night of March 9. He took Veracruz, then advanced on Jalapa, moving toward Mexico City. On April 17, Scott defeated a superior force at Cerro Gordo, moved on to Jalapa, and then to Puebla, the second largest city in Mexico. Its citizens, who hated Santa Anna, surrendered to Scott without resistance on May 15, 1847.

While Scott prepared to march out of Puebla and on to Mexico City, State Department official Nicholas P. Trist opened treaty negotiations with Santa Anna. Wishing to apply maximum pressure to Santa Anna, Scott decided to commit all of his troops to the advance, which meant leaving his line of communication, from Veracruz to Puebla, entirely undefended. He moved out on August 7 and won the Battle of Contreras on August 20 and the Battle of Churubusco several days later.

On September 8, Scott stormed and seized El Molino del Rey, a cannon foundry just west of Chapultepec Castle outside of Mexico City. On September 13, he began an assault on Chapultepec with an artillery barrage, then sent three columns over the approaches to the hilltop fortress, which was soon taken. Mexico City itself fell on September 14, 1847. This hastened peace negotiations and, on February 2, 1848, the Treaty of Guadalupe Hidalgo was concluded.

By terms of the treaty, in return for the cession to the United States of "New Mexico"—the present state of New Mexico and portions of the present states of Utah, Nevada, Arizona, and Colorado—and California, as well as the renunciation of claims to Texas above the Rio Grande, Mexico was to be paid $15 million, and the United States agreed to assume all claims of U.S. citizens against Mexico.

United States Military Academy (USMA)

The United States Military Academy, popularly known as West Point, was founded on March 16, 1802, and charged with producing commissioned leaders of character for the army. Its official mission is "to educate, train, and inspire the Corps of Cadets so that each graduate is a commissioned leader of character committed to the values of Duty, Honor, Country; professional growth throughout a career as an officer in the United States Army; and a lifetime of selfless service to the nation." This is achieved through a four-year academic program consisting of a core of 31 courses designed to provide a balanced education in the arts and sciences. Beyond the core curriculum, cadets choose electives

Graduation day at West Point, United States Military Academy   *(U.S. Army)*

that allow for the exploration of a given field or major in greater depth. Graduates receive a Bachelor of Science degree, as well as a commission as second lieutenant in the army.

In addition to academic courses, cadets follow a rigorous physical program, which includes physical education classes and competitive athletics. Every cadet participates in an intercollegiate, club, or intramural sport each semester. Additionally, cadets are taught basic military skills, including leadership, through the military program. Most of the military training takes place during the summer, with new cadets undergoing cadet basic training (known as "Beast Barracks") the first year, followed by cadet field training at Camp Buckner

the second year. During their third and fourth summers at West Point, cadets serve in ACTIVE ARMY units around the world. They attend advanced training courses such as airborne, air assault, or northern warfare. Some serve in a leadership cadre, training first- and second-year cadets. Military training is combined with military science instruction, providing a thorough foundation for officership.

Moral and ethical components are highly important in the West Point program. These include formal instruction in the important values of the military profession, voluntary religious programs, interaction with staff and faculty role models, and a vigorous guest speaker program.

Although admission is open to all young men and women, it is extremely competitive. All applicants must be nominated by a member of Congress or by the DEPARTMENT OF THE ARMY. Nominees are then evaluated on academic, physical, and leadership potential. More than 900 second lieutenants are graduated annually, a figure that accounts for about 25 percent of the new officers required by the army annually. The entire Corps of Cadets numbers 4,000, of which approximately 15 percent are women.

U.S. Army, Europe (USAREUR)

USAREUR commands army forces of the European Command. At present these number some 30,000 ground troops. Headquarters of USAREUR is in Heidelberg, Germany. The command is the army component of the unified U.S. European Command, a joint service command, and includes the Seventh U.S. Army, a RESERVE COMPONENT command.

U.S. Army, Pacific (USARPAC)

USARPAC is headquartered at Fort Shafter, Hawaii, and is the army component of the U.S. Pacific Command, a unified joint service command.

USARPAC provides trained-and-ready combat and enabling forces and has sent peacekeeping forces to the Sinai Peninsula, Haiti, East Timor, and Bosnia. The 196th Infantry Brigade provides training support to ARMY NATIONAL GUARD and U.S. ARMY RESERVE forces in Alaska, Hawaii, Guam, and American Samoa, as well as humanitarian assistance, disaster relief, and military support to civil authorities. The 9th Regional Support Command commands Army Reserve forces throughout the region.

U.S. Army, South (USARSO)

Headquartered at Fort Buchanan, Puerto Rico, USARSO is the army component of the U.S. Southern Command (USSOUTHCOM), a unified joint service command. USARSO is in charge of all army operations within the 12-million-square-mile USSOUTHCOM area of responsibility, which encompasses all of Latin America, totalling some 32 countries.

U.S. Army Accessions Command (USAAC)

The USAAC is responsible for the accession of soldiers "from first handshake through the completion of individual training." The mission of the command is to transform volunteers into quality soldiers, leaders, and team members imbued with a warrior and winning spirit. The command is tasked with meeting the army's manpower and readiness requirements and standards by providing soldiers and leaders who graduate from training immediately able to contribute to the success of their unit. Moreover, the command seeks to train soldiers of character as well as competence. In short, the USAAC sees to it that the army gets the right soldier at the right time, in the right place, with all the right competencies.

The command includes six major directorates, centers, and activities: an Operations and Training Directorate, a Strategic Outreach Directorate (to direct recruitment advertising and outreach), the Army Center for Accessions Research (an organization devoted to marketing the army to prospective recruits), a Personnel Directorate, an Information Support Activity, and a Resource and Logistics Management Directorate.

U.S. Army Air Defense Artillery Center and School   See FORTS AND OTHER INSTALLATIONS.

U.S. Army bands

The premier band of the army is the United States Army Band (Pershing's Own). Some army divisions also have their own bands. In addition, other army organizations, such as the U.S. Army Reserve —Europe, often have bands.

The U.S. Army bands trace their lineage to pre-Revolutionary times, specifically to a drum corps in colonial Virginia, in existence about 1633. The first known "complete" military band in the colonies was organized in New Hampshire in 1653 and consisted of 15 hautbois (oboes) and two drums. By the 18th century, officers funded bands for the militia units they commanded.

Military music was important from the very beginning of the AMERICAN REVOLUTION. Musicians formed part of the famed "Minuteman" militia companies, and it is recorded that, on April 19, 1775, one William Diamond (or Dinman) beat To Arms for the Lexington, Massachusetts, militia company. Also present at the Battle of Lexington was a fifer, Jonathan Harrington. When the Second Continental Congress met in Philadelphia at the start of the Revolution, the arriving delegates were welcomed by a military band, and, throughout the war, although CONTINENTAL ARMY troops often lacked the most basic supplies and provisions, bands were attached to at least seven regiments. They marched with the regiments, and they also gave frequent civilian concerts.

GEORGE WASHINGTON, commanding general of the Continental army, was genuinely concerned about the poor quality of music in the force. Marching drill depended on music and poor music made drill difficult. Washington instituted rigorous training for his musicians, and he demanded that only after a musician was approved by a drum or fife major would he be allowed to perform with the regiment. Moreover, well-trained musicians were perceived as evidence of a well-trained fighting force. In the 1777 Battle of Bennington, for example, American commander colonel John Stark had his fifes and drummers play even as his forces closed with the enemy. Bennington was a great Patriot victory.

BARON FRIEDRICH WILHELM VON STEUBEN, the German officer who provided invaluable training to the Continental army and wrote that force's first set of regulations, *Regulations for the Order and Discipline of the Troops of the United States* (1779), specified one fife and one drummer to be assigned to each company. The *Regulations* standardized the drum calls that regulated the soldier's day and largely substituted for verbal commands. To administer Continental army music, Washington appointed Lieutenant John Hiwell inspector and superintendent of music in the army, his duties to organize rehearsals, set performance standards, requisition musical supplies, inspect instruments for proper maintenance, and supervise all drum and fife majors.

After the Revolution, bands continued to figure importantly in army and militia forces and on the parade grounds of the newly established UNITED STATES MILITARY ACADEMY at West Point, New York. In 1821, when Congress created legislation to reorganize the REGULAR ARMY, legislators provided for bandsmen to be attached to regiments and paid as privates. Officers were still obliged to provide instruments—if they wanted a band. However, the bands were, for the first time, officially recognized as a separate squad in each regiment. In 1825, a regimental fund was created to finance all aspects of the bands, including their instruments. The bands were combined with the drums of the regimental field music to form a single complete unit consisting of from 15 to 24 musicians.

In 1832, the army promulgated new regulations, which included authorization for regimental bands limited to 10 musicians with the rank of private and a chief musician. All bandsmen were liable for regular military training and, in an emergency, were to serve in the ranks as regular soldiers. In 1841, the size of the regimental band was increased to 12 musicians and, during the UNITED STATES–MEXICAN WAR (1846–48), the size of bands was increased to 16 musicians. Bandsmen were no longer required to muster with other troops, although they were often called on to perform such nonmusical roles as stretcher bearers, field messengers, and water carriers. Many bandsmen never played their instruments during the war.

The run-up to the CIVIL WAR saw an influx of well-trained musicians, mostly from Germany, and great improvements in brass instruments, which soon came to dominate military marching bands. The transition from keyless bugles to keyed trumpets and cornets greatly simplified playing and therefore opened the ranks of the regimental bands to more musicians.

By the time of the Civil War, a School of Practice for U.S.A. Field Musicians was established at Governor's Island, in New York harbor. The school consisted of a barracks and the school facilities, and the work done here helped to standardize the army bands. On July 22, 1861, Congress passed legislation authorizing each regular army regiment of infantry two principal musicians per company and 24 musicians for a band. Each cavalry and artillery regiment was authorized two musicians per company or battery. Each artillery band was permitted 24 musicians and each cavalry band was permitted 16 musicians. In 1862, the secretary of war calculated that the War Department spent $4 million on 618 bands, a ratio of one musician to every 41 soldiers. On July 17, 1862, Congress passed Public Law 165, which replaced regimental bands with brigade bands (one band for every four regiments), thereby reducing the number of bands to approximately 60 and the number of musicians to about 2,500.

Civil War bandsmen performed at concerts, parades, reviews, and guard mount ceremonies. They drummed soldiers out of the army and performed for funerals and executions. They played for troops marching into battle and were often positioned at the front. Under some commanders, bands were required to play under fire, with combat soldiers on the line, in order to encourage the troops.

After the Civil War, Congress drastically reduced funding for the maintenance of military bands and, for the most part, uniformed civilian bands replaced soldier-staffed bands throughout the army. Soldier-staffed bands did not return to the army until early in the 20th century, when Congress authorized a school for army bandleaders at Governor's Island. The school began operations in 1911, and, from this point forward, army bands assumed increasing importance, especially during WORLD WAR I, when General JOHN JOSEPH PERSHING personally advocated a major increase in the number of bands and even established a band school in France. Band strength varied from 28 to 48 pieces during this period.

After the war, in February 1920, the Army Music School at Fort Jay, Governor's Island, was reorganized, and in 1921 it was moved to the U.S. ARMY WAR COLLEGE, Washington D.C. It offered a two-year bandleader course, a one-year preparatory bandleader course, a one-year advanced instrumentalist course, and a one-year bandsmen course. However, budget constraints closed the school in 1928. With U.S. entry into WORLD WAR II, however, the number of army bands exploded to more than 500, with the United States Army Band (Pershing's Own), the U.S. Military Academy Band, and the U.S. Army Air Corps Band designated special. The kinds of music played by the bands was extremely varied. In addition to traditional marching music, bands played jazz and swing (popular bandleader Glenn Miller served in the army as a captain, then major), as well as social dance music and classical music.

Since World War II, bands have continued to figure importantly in the army, and many divisions have their own bands. Musicians are highly trained professionals, and the level of performance throughout the service is very high.

U.S. Army Civil Affairs and Psychological Operations Command

The U.S. Army Civil Affairs and Psychological Operations Command (Airborne) is the headquarters for Army Civil Affairs and Psychological Operations units. The command is composed of about 9,000 soldiers and provides support to all theater commanders in meeting their global commitments.

The command consists of one active-duty Psychological Operations unit: the 4th Psychological Operations Group (Airborne), with six battalions; and one active-duty Civil Affairs unit: the 96th Civil Affairs Battalion (Airborne), with six companies. Both units are located at Fort Bragg, North Carolina.

U.S. Army Corps of Engineers (USACE)

Headquartered in Washington, D.C. as a major army command, USACE is staffed overwhelmingly by civilians: about 34,600 of them; only about 650 USACE personnel are military. USACE specialists include biologists, engineers, geologists, hydrologists, natural resource managers, and others essential to providing engineering services that include planning, designing, building, and operating water resources and other civil works projects relating to navigation, flood control, environmental protection, disaster response, and so on; designing and managing the construction of military facilities for the army and USAF; and providing design and construction management support for other federal agencies, including the Department of Defense.

Over the years, important USACE projects have included road construction, beginning with the National (Cumberland) Road in 1811; surveying American road and canal routes pursuant to the great General Survey Act of 1824; cleaning and dredging selected waterways and engineering various harbor improvements, beginning in 1826 and extending into the present day; flood control, especially along the Mississippi River, beginning in the mid-1850s and continuing through the present; construction of such public projects as customs houses, marine hospitals (for the treatment of merchant marine sailors), lighthouses, bridges, water supply improvements for Washington, D.C., and significant participation in the construction of such Washington, D.C., structures as the Washington Monument, the Executive Office Building, the Lincoln Memorial, the Library of Congress, and the Government Printing Office. Beginning in the early 20th century, USACE engineers, pursuant to the General Dam Act of 1906, began to oversee many aspects of dam construction and operation. The corps pioneered the construction of hydroelectric generating facilities associated with several dams. The USACE has assumed major responsibility nationwide for flood and erosion control and has provided major response capability and management in natural disasters. Between 1989 and 1992, for example, USACE responded to the *Exxon Valdez* disaster, the largest and most destructive oil spill in U.S. history in Prince William Sound,

Alaska; USACE responded in the aftermath of major hurricanes, including Andrew and Iniki in 1992 and 1995, respectively; and California's Northridge earthquake in 1994. In addition, USACE is responsible for many projects in wartime, including domestic construction and construction in combat theaters.

U.S. Army Criminal Investigation Command (USACIC)

Headquartered at Falls Church, Virginia, USACIC commands army investigations of serious crimes and also provides personal security for selected army and Department of Defense officials.

U.S. Army Disciplinary Barracks

The U.S. Army Disciplinary Barracks, located at Fort Leavenworth, Kansas, is run by the army but is more properly called the United States Disciplinary Barracks, because it confines not only army offenders but also offenders from the USAF, USN, USMC, and USCG. The disciplinary barracks not only incarcerates inmates but also provides an extensive vocational training industry program to furnish inmates the opportunity to acquire marketable job skills and return to civilian life as useful, productive citizens.

The U.S. Army Disciplinary Barracks was originally designated the United States Military Prison when it was established by Congress in 1874. It has been in operation at Fort Leavenworth since May 15, 1875. This facility was the first in the nation to establish a vocational training program, and it is currently the only long-term prison in the Department of Defense. A new Disciplinary Barracks was completed at Fort Leavenworth in 2002.

U.S. Army Forces Command (FORSCOM)

FORSCOM is the largest of the army's nine MAJOR ARMY FIELD COMMANDS. It is charged with supervising the training of some 800,000 active, reserve, and NATIONAL GUARD troops to prepare for combat. FORSCOM provides army support to Joint Forces Command. Its mission is fourfold:

1. To supply combat-ready units
2. To execute contingency missions as ordered
3. To defend the United States landmass
4. To respond to federal, state, and local officials during emergencies, including disasters and antidrug operations

FORSCOM administers the UNITED STATES ARMY RESERVE COMMAND (USARC), the CONTINENTAL UNITED STATES ARMIES (CONUSAs), the THIRD U.S. ARMY, and two major training centers, the NATIONAL TRAINING CENTER (NTC), and the JOINT READINESS TRAINING CENTER (JRTC).

U.S. Army Infantry Center and School

See FORTS AND OTHER INSTALLATIONS.

U.S. Army Information Systems Engineering Command (USAISEC)

Headquartered at Fort Huachuca, Arizona, USAISEC provides information systems and services to the army and other Department of Defense organizations. The command's primary mission is system engineering and integration of information systems for the army, including the design, engineering, integration, development, sustainment, installation, testing, and acceptance of information systems.

U.S. Army Intelligence and Security Command (INSCOM)

INSCOM is a major army command charged with conducting dominant intelligence, security, and information operations for military commanders and national decision makers. Headquartered at Fort Belvoir, Virginia, INSCOM is a global command incorporating 14 major subordinate commands and a variety of smaller units with personnel dispersed at over 180 locations worldwide. INSCOM was organized on January 1, 1977.

INSCOM provides warfighters with the seamless intelligence needed to understand the battlefield and to focus and leverage combat power. The command collects intelligence information in all intelligence disciplines and also has major responsibilities in the areas of counterintelligence and force protection, electronic warfare and information warfare, and support to force modernization and training.

U.S. Army Materiel Command (AMC)

Headquartered in Alexandria, Virginia, AMC is an army major command tasked with providing superior technology, acquisition support, and logistics to ensure dominant land force capability of the army and allied forces. AMC equips and sustains a ready army.

Subordinate AMC organizations include the INDUSTRIAL OPERATIONS COMMAND at Rock Island, Illinois; the AVIATION AND MISSILE COMMAND at St. Louis; the COMMUNICATIONS-ELECTRONICS COMMAND at Aberdeen Proving Ground, Maryland; the ARMY RESEARCH LABORATORY at Adelphi, Maryland; the AVIATION AND MISSILE COMMAND at Redstone Arsenal, Alabama; the TANK-AUTOMOTIVE AND ARMAMENTS COMMAND at Warren, Michigan; the TEST AND EVALUATION COMMAND at Aberdeen Proving Ground; the SECURITY ASSISTANCE COMMAND at Alexandria, Virginia; the SIMULATION, TRAINING, AND INSTRUMENTATION COMMAND at Orlando, Florida; U.S. ARMY SOLDIER SYSTEMS CENTER at Natick, Massachusetts; and AMC-Europe (Seckenheim, Germany) and AMC–Far East (Seoul, South Korea).

U.S. Army Medical Command (MEDCOM)

MEDCOM, headquartered at Fort Sam Houston, Texas, administers the army's fixed hospitals and dental facilities; preventive health, medical research, development and training institutions; and a veterinary command that provides food inspection and animal care services for the entire Department of Defense. MEDCOM also supervises all army medical training.

U.S. Army Military District of Washington (MDW)

MDW commands army units, activities, and installations in and around the nation's capital. Although its geographic area is small for a major army command, its mission is critical and highly visible. MDW responds to crisis, disaster, or security requirements in the national capital region; MDW conducts official ceremonies and public events, not only locally but also worldwide; MDW provides base operations support for army and Department of Defense organizations throughout the capital area and in New York City. Specialized support services include personal property shipping and storage services for the region, rotary-wing airlift, and operation of the Arlington National Cemetery.

The command's five major installations are the Fort Myer Military Community, which includes Fort Lesley J. McNair in Washington, D.C., and Fort Myer, Virginia; Fort Belvoir, Virginia; Fort A. P. Hill, Virginia; Fort Hamilton, New York; and Fort Meade, Maryland. MDW administers Arlington National Cemetery; 3rd U.S. Infantry (The Old Guard); The U.S. ARMY BAND ("Pershing's Own"); the 12th Aviation Battalion; the Joint Personal Property Shipping Office, Washington Area; the White House Transportation Agency; and the Army Signal Activity–MDW (ASA-MDW).

U.S. Army Military History Institute (USAMHI)

Located at Carlisle Barracks, Pennsylvania, and administered by the U.S. ARMY WAR COLLEGE, USAMHI is tasked with preserving army history and ensuring access to historical research materials. Toward this end, USAMHI collects, organizes, preserves, and makes available source materials on American military history to the defense community, academic researchers, and the public.

USAMHI holds over nine million items documenting army and military history in collections that include books, rare books, periodicals, photographs, manuscripts (diaries, letters, memoirs), military publications and manuals, maps, and oral histories. Although USAMHI is not a museum, it does maintain some historical displays, which are free and open to the public, including the General of the Army OMAR NELSON BRADLEY Museum, commemorating the service of General Bradley.

U.S. Army Reserve (USAR)

Unlike the ARMY NATIONAL GUARD (ARNG), USAR members are federal troops, although both the ARNG and USAR are part of the RESERVE COMPONENTS, joining the ACTIVE ARMY only when activated by the president of the United States.

The modern USAR was created in 1952, replacing the Officers Reserve Corps and Enlisted Reserve Corps. Most USAR units specialize in combat support and combat service support missions. USAR is the army's main source for transportation, medical, civil affairs, and logistics personnel.

USAR consists of the Selected Reserve, the Individual Ready Reserve (IRR), and the Retired Reserve, a total of more than 1,000,000 soldiers, subject to call by the president when needed. USAR units total more than 2,000 in the United States, Guam, Virgin Islands, Puerto Rico, and Germany. Within the United States, USAR units are commanded by the Army Reserve Command and Army Civil Affairs and Psychological Operations Command.

Unless activated, USAR members live and work in their civilian community, drilling at regular intervals in some 1,500 Army Reserve centers located throughout the country.

The Office of the Chief Army Reserve (OCAR), located in the Pentagon, develops and executes USAR plans, policies, and programs, and also administers USAR personnel, operations, and construction funds. OCAR commands the Army Reserve Personnel Command (AR-PERSCOM).

United States Army Reserve Command (USARC), headquartered in Atlanta, Georgia, commands all continental United States USAR units except for civil affairs and psychological operations units, which are administered by the U.S. Army Civil Affairs and Psychological Operations Command (USACAPOC). USAR units are divided into a dozen Regional Readiness Commands.

The Selected Reserve consists of Troop Program Units (TPUs), Active Guard and Reserve (AGR) soldiers, and Individual Mobilization Augmentees (IMAs). These are the reservists most readily available for activation. There are about 2,000 Troop Program Units in the Selected Reserve, in which members train on selected weekends and perform two or more weeks of annual training.

Active Guard/Reserve soldiers serve on active duty in units and organizations that directly support the Army Reserve.

Individual Mobilization Augmentees are assigned to high-level headquarters and train annually for two weeks.

Individual Ready Reserve are trained soldiers who may be called on to replace soldiers in active and reserve units. Many IRR members are soldiers who have left active duty recently and who still have a reserve commitment.

The Retired Reserve consists of approximately 737,000 retirees from the army, who are available for callup if necessary.

U.S. Army Soldier Systems Center (SSC)

Established in 1953 in Natick, Massachusetts, and administered by the U.S. ARMY MATERIEL COMMAND, SSC is a soldier-support organization responsible for researching, developing, fielding, and managing food, clothing, shelters, airdrop systems, and other soldier-support items with the objective of providing America's soldiers with the best equipment in the world.

The principal component of SSC is the Natick Soldier Center (NSC), popularly called Natick Labs, and commanded by the army's Research, Development and Engineering Command (RDECOM). The mission of the Natick Soldier Center is to maximize the soldier's survivability, sustainability, mobility, combat effectiveness, and quality of life by treating the soldier as a system.

Natick Soldier Center performs basic and applied research, technology development and demonstration, and engineering of combat clothing and individual equipment, rations and food service equipment, airdrop systems, shelters, and organizational equipment. The center also integrates and transitions the technologies for combat-essential elements of command and control, survivability, lethality, sustainability, and mobility into the soldier system and warrior systems for other services and agencies.

U.S. Army Space and Missile Defense Command (SMDC)

Headquartered in Arlington, Virginia, SMDC is the army component of the U.S. Strategic Command and has the following primary missions: commanding and controlling army space forces, providing integrated missile defense and computer network operations, conducting strategic information operations, and enabling with C^4ISR (Command, Control, Communications, Computers, Intelligence, Surveillance, and Reconnaissance) global strike, space operations, and integrated missile defense.

As the army proponent for space and national missile defense, and as the army integrator for theater missile defense, SMDC ensures that army warfighters have access to space assets and products to win decisively with minimum casualties. Additionally, SMDC works to ensure an effective missile defense to protect the United States, deployed forces, and the forces of allies.

Subordinate commands include:

U.S. Army Space Command (ARSPACE), Colorado Springs, Colorado: the principal army component of the U.S. Space Command

1st Space Battalion's Theater Missile Warning Company: provides theater CINCs with in-theater tactical ballistic missile warning capability on the battlefield

Space and Missile Defense Technical Center (SMDTC), Huntsville, Alabama: research and development element of the command

Space and Missile Defense Battle Lab (SMDBL), Huntsville, Alabama, and Colorado Springs, Colorado: designs and conducts advanced simulations

TRADOC System Manager (TSM) for Ground-based Midcourse Defense (GMD), Arlington, Virginia: integrates and manages GMD user activities within the army

Office of Technical Integration and Interoperability (OTII): sets interoperability requirements for effective theater and missile defense

Force Development and Integration Center (FDIC), Arlington, Virginia: develops the army's space and missile defense concepts, validates requirements, and ensures solution integration throughout the army

Reagan Test Site, central Pacific Ocean: radars, instrumentation, and test support facilities for ballistic missile testing and space-object tracking

High Energy Laser Systems Test Facility (HEL-STF), White Sands Missile Range, New Mexico: national center for high-energy laser research, development, testing, and evaluation

U.S. Army Special Operations Command (USASOC)

USASOC, established on December 1, 1989, and headquartered at Fort Bragg, North Carolina, is the army component of U.S. Special Operations Command, a unified joint services command. USASOC trains, equips, deploys, and sustains army special-operations forces for worldwide special operations supporting regional combatant commanders and country ambassadors. These forces consist of SPECIAL FORCES, RANGERS, Psychological Operations, Civil Affairs, Special Operations Aviation units (160th Special Operations Aviation Regiment), and Special Mission units.

U.S. Army Training and Doctrine Command (TRADOC)

TRADOC is headquartered at Fort Monroe, Virginia, and is tasked with acquiring and providing institutional training for army soldiers, setting training standards and requirements, and preparing the army for the future. TRADOC administers training for officers, from basic officer courses through the COMMAND AND GENERAL STAFF COLLEGE. It administers enlisted training from BASIC TRAINING through the most senior school, the SERGEANT MAJOR ACADEMY.

TRADOC operates through four major subordinate organizations: COMBINED ARMS CENTER (CAC), COMBINED ARMS SUPPORT COMMAND (CASCOM), TRADOC ANALYSIS COMMAND (TRAC), and the ROTC CADET COMMAND.

U.S. Army Transportation School

Located at Fort Eustis, Virginia, the U.S. Army Transportation School trains TRANSPORTATION CORPS soldiers and civilians for the army transportation mission.

During WORLD WAR II, four schools were established to train Transportation Corps soldiers. The first school was established in 1943 at Mississippi State College under the supervision of the ADJUTANT GENERAL. The school moved to Hanahan, Louisiana, and then to New Orleans Army Base on February 1, 1944. The original curriculum included transportation modes, terminal operations, and cargo/personnel movement.

After the war, in 1946, Fort Eustis was established as the centralized training installation for the Transportation Corps and became the home of the Transportation School. The first Transportation Officer Advanced Course (TOAC) opened in the fall of 1947.

The primary mission of the school is to train transportation competencies. Today, the curriculum includes company grade officer qualification courses, company and field grade officer professional development courses, enlisted military occupational specialty-qualification courses, enlisted professional development courses, and a wide range of power projection courses for all branches of service and Department of Defense civilians. All Transportation Corps military occupational specialties are taught at the Transportation School. Additionally, the Transportation School develops and fields army driver unit training programs, and provides advice to Motor Transport Operator Course trainers at Fort Leonard Wood and Fort Bliss.

U.S. Army War College (USAWC)

Located at Carlisle Barracks, Pennsylvania, the U.S. Army War College has prepared senior military officers and civilians for strategic leadership responsibilities since its establishment in 1901. At this institution, senior military, civilian, and international leaders from all military services and government agencies come to study and confer on the strategic application of land power. Per Army Regulation 10-44, the Army War College prepares "selected military, civilian, and international leaders for the responsibilities of strategic leadership; educate[s] current and future leaders on the development and employment of landpower in a joint, multinational and interagency environment; conduct[s] research[es] and publish[es] on national security and military strategy; and engage[s] in activities in support of the army's strategic communication efforts."

Components of the Army War College include:

Directorate of Academic Affairs
Department of Distance Education
Department of Command, Leadership and Management
Department of Military Strategy, Planning and Operations
Department of National Security and Strategy
International Fellows Program
Advanced Strategic Arts Program
USAWC Library
Center for Strategic Leadership
Strategic Studies Institute
Army Heritage and Education Center
U.S. ARMY MILITARY HISTORY INSTITUTE

U.S. Central Command (USCENTCOM)

USCENTCOM is headquartered at MacDill Air Force Base, Tampa, Florida, and is the unified command responsible for U.S. security interests in 25 nations, from the Horn of Africa through the Arabian Gulf region and into Central Asia. It is a unified command of the Department of Defense and is comprised of components from the army, USMC, USN, and USAF. The army headquarters component of USCENTCOM is the THIRD U.S. ARMY headquartered at Fort McPherson, Georgia.

V

V150 Commando   See WHEELED VEHICLES.

Vietnam Service Medal   See DECORATIONS AND MEDALS.

Vietnam War (1954–1975)

Origins and Early U.S. Involvement

The United States became involved in Vietnam for the same reason it fought the KOREAN WAR: to contain the expansion of communism. By the time the French reasserted colonial control of Vietnam after WORLD WAR II, the colony-nation was in the throes of a revolution. By the early 1950s, the charismatic popular leader Ho Chi Minh achieved a high degree of control over the North, while the South remained in French hands. President Harry S. Truman and, afterward, President DWIGHT DAVID EISENHOWER provided military advisers and materiel aid to the French in an effort to defeat the communist forces of Ho Chi Minh. However, in 1954, the French found themselves besieged at Dien Bien Phu. President Eisenhower stepped up military aid, explaining on April 7, 1954, that Vietnam was like a domino: allow it to fall, and many other countries would follow, one after the other, like so many more dominoes. This so-called domino theory would surface in the 1960s as a rationale for ever-deepening U.S. involvement in the Vietnam War.

Despite U.S. aid, Dien Bien Phu fell to the forces of Ho Chi Minh on May 7, 1954, and was quickly followed by additional Viet Minh (communist) victories. In July, France and the Viet Minh agreed to divide Vietnam along the 17th parallel and concluded an armistice, which called for a reunification plebiscite to be held in July 1956. Believing such a plebiscite would result in unification under communist rule, South Vietnam refused to proceed. U.S. officials braced for an anticipated invasion from the north—it did not come—and President Eisenhower committed the United States to a long-term advisory role. In the meantime, North Vietnamese insurgency into South Vietnam developed into a guerrilla war conducted by the Vietcong (VC, communist guerrillas incorporating elements of the Viet Minh). In 1960, the United States expanded its Military Advisory and Assistance Group (MAAG) to 685 men, including Army SPECIAL FORCES teams assigned to train Vietnamese rangers. Despite this, the insurgency increased. On April 29, 1961, President John F. Kennedy authorized an additional 100 advisers, the establishment of a combat development and test center in Vietnam, increased economic aid, and other measures. On May 11, he committed 400 U.S. Special Forces troops. U.S. Air Force (USAF) personnel also began to arrive in increasing numbers. In the earliest stages of American involvement in the war, it was the USAF that had the greatest in-country presence.

Beginning in January 1962, USAF and army personnel conducted Operation Mule Train, transporting large quantities of cargo and personnel into Vietnam, and, soon, army and U.S. Marine Corps (USMC) helicopters and personnel were being used to transport small ARVN (Army of the Republic of Vietnam) units into offensive operations against the communist insurgents. By the end of 1962, there were more than 11,000 American military personnel in Vietnam. Vietcong attacks increased during 1963.

Gulf of Tonkin Resolution

President Kennedy was assassinated on November 22, 1963. The new president, Lyndon B. Johnson, escalated the war in Vietnam, beginning with the Gulf of Tonkin Resolution of August 7, 1964. The resolution was passed following reported attacks on U.S. destroyers conducting surveillance in international waters in the Gulf of Tonkin. The Senate resolution gave the president great latitude in expanding the war as he might see fit. (The validity and even the veracity of the Gulf of Tonkin attacks were later challenged.)

After his election to the presidency in his own right in November 1964, Johnson authorized restricted air strikes on targets in Laos. Insurgency operations continued to increase, and the United States found itself propping up a series of unpopular—albeit anticommunist—South Vietnamese regimes.

On February 7, 1965, Vietcong mortar squads and demolition teams attacked U.S. advisory forces and Camp Holloway, headquarters of the Army 52nd Aviation Battalion, near Pleiku, killing nine Americans and wounding 108. This set the Johnson administration on a course of rapid escalation, beginning mainly with USAF air strikes. The hope was to wage primarily an air war with the object not of reunifying Vietnam but of keeping South Vietnam independent. Although the initial phases of major U.S. combat involvement were primarily air oriented, army general William Westmoreland was put in overall command of U.S. forces in Vietnam. He argued that bombing alone would have little effect on the North Vietnamese and that a

blocking force was necessary on the ground. Although Washington opposed this, it approved of the development and use of army "air cavalry." Accordingly, the 1st Cavalry Division (Airmobile) was equipped with more than 400 helicopters, which were used in the campaign for the Central Highlands during late 1965 and early 1966.

On June 28, 1965, the first major army ground operation was launched. The 173rd Airborne Brigade airlifted two ARVN battalions and two battalions of the 503rd Infantry Brigade into battle in Bien Hoa Province, just 20 miles northeast of Saigon. During October 23–November 20, 1965, the 1st Cavalry Division (Airmobile) defeated VC (Vietcong) and NVA (North Vietnamese army) forces in western Pleiku Province. Both sides suffered heavy casualties, but the U.S. forces blocked a North Vietnamese attempt to seize this region and thereby cut South Vietnam in half.

Further Escalation, 1966–1967

The year 1966 began with Operation Marauder, in which the 173rd Airborne Brigade engaged the VC in the Mekong Delta. This was followed during January 19–February 21 by Operation Van Buren, in which the 1st Brigade of the 101ST AIRBORNE DIVISION and ARVN units secured Phu Yen Province in the central coastal region. The operation set the pattern for the "search-and-destroy" actions that General Westmoreland favored as the leading tactic of the war. Indeed, many of these missions were highly successful; however, American military planners had yet to appreciate the North Vietnamese willingness to absorb catastrophic casualties and thus to persist in fighting.

During the spring and summer of 1966, the 25th Infantry Division, 1st Cavalry Division (Airmobile), and ARVN units moved into Pleiku Province to interdict infiltration from North Vietnam as well as through Cambodia. Simultaneously, the 101st Airborne fought in Kontum Province, and, in June and July, the 1st Division, in concert with the 5th ARVN Division, was heavily engaged in Binh Long Province, 70 miles north of Saigon. The object of such operations was to use "main force" to overwhelm the insurgents wherever and whenever they surfaced. There was no specific strategic goal other than to meet force with overwhelming force. Such operations continued throughout 1966–67, always resulting in far more North Vietnamese than U.S. casualties, but failing to bring about any resolution.

While the army, USMC, and USAF prosecuted the "main force" war, ARVN pursued a "pacification program," intended to win the "hearts and minds" of the South Vietnamese peasantry and turn them against the communist insurgents. Pacification included not only military components but also education, land reform, communications, agriculture, and other civil measures. The program produced measurable results, but it failed to be decisive, and, by 1967, a widespread antiwar movement was growing among the increasingly frustrated people of the United States. From this point forward, popular support for the Vietnam War eroded, and the United States suffered deep political, social, and cultural divisions.

The Tet Offensive and Its Consequences

Beginning on January 30, 1968—Tet, a Vietnamese lunar holiday—North Vietnamese forces struck major cities and military bases from Quang Tri and Khe Sanh, near the Demilitarized Zone (DMZ) in the northern region of South Vietnam, to Quang Long near the country's southern tip. The offensive was massive and widespread, but it proved far costlier to the NVA and VC than to U.S. and ARVN forces. Of an estimated 84,000 attackers, as many as 45,000 were killed. Yet, in the United States, the three-week offensive scored a devastating psychological victory for the communists and persuaded many Americans, including key politicians and policy makers, that the Vietnam War was unwinnable. With American casualties at 2,000 a month in February 1968, and the publication of a somewhat distorted news story in March, announcing that General Westmoreland was asking for 200,000 more men, a wave of outrage swept the American public. Antiwar demonstrations became increasingly frequent, bigger, and more boisterous. By the end of 1968, the number of U.S. troops in Vietnam, mostly army soldiers, would reach a high of 536,000. However, before this, Lyndon Johnson pulled himself out of the 1968 presidential race and, in an olive branch offered to the North, announced that he would restrict bombing above the 20th parallel. Cease-fire negotiations began in May, stalled, then resumed.

President Nixon Widens the War

Richard M. Nixon triumphed over Democratic challenger Hubert H. Humphrey in the 1968 election and, after he took office, sought to implement a foreign policy designed to cut off North Vietnam from both Soviet and Chinese support. This approach, Nixon believed, would free America's hand to negotiate "peace with honor" in Vietnam. Simultaneously, Nixon sought to widen the war even as he pursued a program of "Vietnamization," an effort to train and equip ARVN forces to take over combat duties from U.S. forces, which would be progressively withdrawn and reduced.

Army (and USAF) personnel engaged increasingly in missions intended to train and develop ARVN forces. However, it soon became heartbreakingly apparent that ARVN personnel were largely ineffective against the far more committed North Vietnamese. Despite this, in May 1969, the withdrawal of army ground units from Vietnam began in earnest. The Paris Peace Talks, initiated in fall 1968 under President Johnson, droned on, and the Nixon strategy aimed at cutting North Vietnam loose from the Soviets collapsed as the USSR announced recognition of the Provisional Revolutionary Government (PRG) formed by North Vietnam's National Liberation Front (NLF) in June 1969. In a climate of increasing hopelessness, the morale of army forces in Vietnam sharply deteriorated, as no soldier was eager to die for a lost cause. Drug and alcohol abuse became epidemic, as did a pervasive attitude of defeatism.

Withdrawal and Defeat

By the end of 1971, withdrawals had reduced U.S. troop strength to 175,000 in Vietnam, calming protests at home even as it eroded frontline morale. Early in 1972, President Nixon decided to compensate for the reduced army ground presence by stepping up the air war, mining Haiphong harbor, and establishing a naval blockade of the North. It was hoped that the bombing would force North Vietnamese negotiators to come to a settlement in the Paris Peace Talks. In fact, the Paris Peace Accords were signed on January 27, 1973, but they did not bring an end to the fighting. Both sides repeatedly violated the terms of the accords. Nevertheless, on January 27, Secretary of Defense Melvin Laird announced an end to the military draft, and, on March 29, the last army troops departed Vietnam.

The Nixon administration continued to send massive amounts of aid to the Thieu government, and both North and South Vietnam continued to violate the Paris accords. Bombing was resumed, but a war-weary Congress turned against the president, whose administration was disintegrating under the emerging evidence of its involvement in the Watergate scandal. In 1974, U.S. aid to South Vietnam was reduced from $2.56 billion to $907 million, and to $700 million in 1975. President Nixon resigned in August 1974, and, although President Gerald Ford sought $300 million in "supplemental aid" to South Vietnam, Congress rejected the request and, from early 1975 on, the South suffered one military defeat after another. Lieutenant General Duong Van Minh surrendered South Vietnam to the forces of North Vietnam on April 30, 1975.

W

Walter Reed Army Medical Center

Located in Washington, D.C., the center, the premier army medical facility, was established in 1909. It is the headquarters of the North Atlantic Regional Medical Command; Walter Reed Army Medical Center; Walter Reed Institute of Research; Armed Forces Institute of Pathology; Army Medical Biochemical Research Laboratory; and Army Physical Disability Agency.

War of 1812 (1812–1815)

Despite the terms of the Treaty of Paris (1783), ending the AMERICAN REVOLUTION, and the subsequent Jay's Treaty (1794), intended to resolve lingering territorial disputes, British fur trappers and traders repeatedly "invaded" United States territory on the western frontier during the early 19th century. Moreover, British interests deliberately incited Indian hostility against American settlers in the West, and the Royal Navy routinely "impressed" (abducted for naval service) American merchant sailors on the high seas. These provocations, coupled with the young republic's insatiable hunger for new territory, provoked the War of 1812.

In 1812, the region known as Spanish Florida extended as far west as the Mississippi River. Because Spain was an ally of Great Britain against Napoleon Bonaparte, American "War Hawks" (congressmen and others who favored war) reasoned that victory in a war against Britain would result in the acquisition of its ally's territory, which would be joined to the vast western territories already acquired under terms of the Louisiana Purchase (1803). A triumphant war would greatly expand the size of the United States, and, on June 18, 1812, the United States declared war on Great Britain.

The War Hawks gave little thought to the fact that the strength of the army was only 12,000 regular troops, who were broadcast across a vast territory and who were led by generals of very uneven ability, most having attained their rank through political connections rather than demonstrated military ability. Relying on militia companies to swell the ranks of the land army, American strategists devised grandiose plans for a three-pronged invasion of Canada: a penetration from Lake Champlain to Montreal; another across the Niagara frontier; and a third into Upper Canada from Detroit. Undermanned, poorly led, and thoroughly uncoordinated, all three prongs failed.

The first failure was that of William Hull, aging governor of Michigan Territory and a minor hero of the American Revolution. He commanded American forces north of the Ohio River—300 army regulars and 1,200 Kentucky and Ohio militiamen (who soon deserted and had to be replaced by Michigan volunteers). He led his forces across the Detroit River into Canada on July 12, 1812, with the objective of taking Fort Malden, which guarded the entrance to Lake Erie. Believing himself outnumbered, Hull repeatedly delayed his attack, thereby giving the British time to attack preemptively the American garrison at Fort Michilimackinac, guarding the Mackinac Straits between Lake Huron and Lake Michigan, on July 17, 1812. On August 2, the brilliant Shawnee political and war leader Tecumseh began harassing and ambushing Hull's columns. Terrified, the American commander, still believing himself vastly outnumbered (at this time, Tecumseh actually led only about 700 warriors), withdrew from Canada and headed back to Fort Detroit, which he surrendered without a shot, on August 16. The day troops and settlers evacuated the fort, Potawatomi Indians attacked, killing 35 men, women, and children, mainly by torture.

In the Northeast, New York militia general Stephen Van Rensselaer led 2,270 militiamen and 900 army regulars in an assault on Queenston Heights, Canada, just across the Niagara River. The army regulars succeeded in crossing the river before they were pinned down on October 13 by the British. At this juncture, the rest of the militia refused to cross the international boundary and stood by as 600 British regulars and 400 Canadian militiamen overwhelmed their comrades. The result was a humiliating American defeat.

The rapid collapse of Detroit and Fort Dearborn, coupled with the total failure of the Canadian campaign, laid the Midwest open to Indian assault and British invasion. ZACHARY TAYLOR led army forces in driving off a Potawatomie Indian assault on Fort Wayne, Indiana Territory, on September 5, 1812, but most of the so-called Old Northwest (corresponding to much of the present-day Midwest) nevertheless fell under Indian control. Army general William Henry Harrison mounted effective counterattacks, and, as 1812 closed, Harrison destroyed villages of the Miami Indians near Fort Wayne and raided Indian refugee camps near present-day Peru, Indiana.

In January 1813, Harrison moved against Fort Malden, advancing across frozen Lake Erie, only to suffer a major defeat on January 21. By the fall of 1813, 4,000 Americans, mostly militiamen, had been killed or captured, compared to combined British and Indian losses of no more than 500.

In 1813, renewed American attempts to invade Canada failed, and the Niagara frontier was stalemated. In the Old Northwest, the American situation became somewhat brighter. After the January disaster at Fort Malden, William Henry Harrison set about rebuilding and even enlarging his army, which grew into a force of 8,000 by the late summer of 1813. While Harrison resurrected U.S. land forces, a dashing young naval officer named Oliver Hazard Perry hastily cobbled together an inland navy. By coordinating operations with Perry, Harrison scored a major victory at the Battle of the Thames on October 5, 1813, in which the great Indian leader Tecumseh fell.

The victories of Perry and Harrison suggested that the tide of war might be turning. But then, in Europe, Paris fell (March 30, 1814), Napoleon's marshals mutinied (April 1), and the emperor abdicated (April 4, 1814). Napoleon was exiled to the island of Elba, and, it seemed, the long series of Napoleonic Wars were at an end. The British could now turn their full attention to the war in North America. They made plans to attack in three principal areas: in New York, along Lake Champlain and the Hudson River, which would sever New England from the rest of the Union; at New Orleans, which would block the vital Mississippi artery; and in Chesapeake Bay, to threaten Washington and to create a diversion that would draw off and pin down U.S. manpower. By the summer of 1814, the American situation looked bleak. Strangled by blockade, threatened on three fronts, the United States was hurtling toward economic ruin. Late in the summer, American resistance to the attack in Chesapeake Bay folded, and the British, under Major General Robert Ross, triumphed in Maryland at the Battle of Bladensburg (August 24). Green Maryland militiamen commanded by the inept William H. Winder broke and ran under fire. Ross then easily invaded Washington, D.C., where he burned most of the public buildings, including the Capitol and the White House. President Madison and most of the government fled into the countryside. From Washington, Ross advanced north on Baltimore. His amphibious forces bombarded Fort McHenry, in Baltimore harbor, during September 13–14, 1814, which, however, held out.

The salvation of Baltimore was a hopeful sign. Nevertheless, while Washington burned and Baltimore fell under attack, 10,000 British veterans of the Napoleonic Wars advanced into the United States from Montreal. Opposing them on land was an inferior American force, but, on September 11, 1814, American naval captain Thomas MacDonough engaged the British squadron on Lake Champlain. The result of this critical battle was the destruction of the squadron. Thus deprived of a vital link in communication and supply, the British army retreated, and the offensive along Lake Champlain collapsed.

President Madison responded favorably to British peace feelers in January 1814 and, in July, treaty negotiations were convened at Ghent, Belgium. The Treaty of Ghent, signed on December 24, 1814, officially restored the status quo antebellum, and the document was unanimously ratified by the U.S. Senate on February 17, 1815. Beyond ending the war, little was definitively resolved by the Treaty of Ghent, although it did establish a joint U.S.-British commission to set a definitive boundary between the United States and Canada.

Word of the Treaty of Ghent did not reach General Andrew Jackson, who was marching on New Orleans, to engage the 5,300 British regulars under General Edward Pakenham. Jackson did not command army personnel, but rather 3,100 Tennessee and Kentucky volunteers, in addition to New Orleans militiamen and a collection of locals (including "free colored" volunteers), bringing his total force to about 4,700 men. He managed to win a spectacular victory on January 8, 1815, which was so glorious that, to most Americans, it mattered little that the Battle of New Orleans had been fought *after* the Treaty of Ghent had officially concluded the war.

warrant officers   See RANKS AND GRADES.

Washington, George (1732–1799) *commander in chief of the Continental army, first president of the United States*

The general who created and commanded the CONTINENTAL ARMY during the AMERICAN REVOLUTION, Washington went on to become the first president of the United States and was hailed, even in his own time, as the "Father of His Country." He was born in Westmoreland County, Virginia, and, after the death of his father on April 12, 1743, was raised by his eldest brother, Lawrence, at Mount Vernon, a handsome Virginia estate. Given a catch-as-catch-can education, Washington diligently learned the surveyor's trade and was from 1749 to 1751 surveyor for Culpeper County. After Lawrence Washington

George Washington. Painting by Charles Willson Peale *(West Point Collections, United States Military Academy)*

died in July 1752 (and with the death of Lawrence's only daughter two months later), Washington inherited Mount Vernon and, as a major Virginia property holder, was appointed adjutant for southern Virginia and given the militia rank of major in November 1752. He was also appointed adjutant of Northern Neck—between the Rappahannock and the Potomac rivers—and the Eastern Shore in 1753.

On the eve of the French and Indian War, Virginia governor Robert Dinwiddie sent Washington to assess French military activity in the Ohio Valley and to evict the French from the region. The expedition, which spanned October 31, 1753, to January 16, 1754, progressed from coastal Williamsburg, Virginia, through the wilderness to Fort Duquesne (on the site of modern Pittsburgh, Pennsylvania). Washington won an initial skirmish with a small French party, but French troops out of Fort Duquesne drove him back to a hastily constructed stockade Washington had dubbed Fort Necessity. Outnumbered, Washington surrendered to the French on July 3, 1754, and returned to Virginia. These two small battles marked the commencement of the French and Indian War.

Washington was assigned as aide-de-camp to British general Edward Braddock and was promoted to the local rank of colonel in March 1755. Leading Virginia volunteers, Washington marched with Braddock to retake Fort Duquesne during May–July. On July 9, 1755, Braddock and his troops, including Washington, were attacked by a mixed French and Indian force. Although the British regulars panicked, Washington's Virginians fought well and most survived the catastrophic battle.

For his leadership in the battle, Washington was hailed as a hero and given command of all Virginia forces. He and his troops accompanied another British general, John Forbes, in a successful expedition against Fort Duquesne during July–November 1758.

In 1758, Washington was elected to the Virginia House of Burgesses. The next year he married Martha Dandridge Custis, a wealthy, childless widow, served as justice of the peace for Fairfax County (1760–74), and prospered as a plantation owner. Washington also became a key member of the first Virginia provincial congress in August 1774 and was chosen as one of seven Virginia delegates to the First Continental Congress in September 1774. He served as a member of the Second Congress in May 1775. With the outbreak of the Revolutionary War, Congress asked Washington to accept a commission as general in chief of the Continental army.

On June 15, 1775, he directed the blockade of Boston, then formally took command of the army at Cambridge, Massachusetts, on July 3, 1775. Washington scored an important victory at Boston when he successfully fought to gain Dorchester Heights on March 4, 1776, which ultimately forced the British commander, Richard Howe, to withdraw from the Massachusetts capital.

Far less successful was Washington's defense of Long Island and New York City during August–November 1776, and it soon became apparent that Washington's grasp of tactics was less than masterful. Nevertheless, it also became clear that he was a great leader of men. He understood that the fledgling Continental army and militias could not defeat the armed forces of the most powerful nation on earth, but, Washington believed, if he could hold the army together, he could exhaust the British and win a favorable negotiated peace. In retreat, Washington drew the British far from supply as he moved across the Hudson River and into New Jersey and, in November, Pennsylvania. Then, suddenly, on December 25–26, 1776, he recrossed the Delaware and caught unawares the mercenary Hessian troops at Trenton, New Jersey. This remarkable victory was a blow to the British and a great boost both to the Continental army and to the American Revolution generally. Washington triumphed next at the Battle of Princeton, routing three British regiments on January 3, 1777, before retiring into winter quarters at Morristown, New Jersey, on January 6.

Washington next dispatched many of his best troops and ablest officers into upstate New York to check a British advance there while he remained in New Jersey to engage Howe and prevent his capture of Philadelphia. However, Washington lost the Battle of Brandywine Creek on September 11, 1777, relinquishing Philadelphia to the British, but he mounted a surprise counterattack at Germantown on October 4. This action also failed, but French observers were impressed by Washington's gallantry, and the move did much to motivate a Franco-American alliance.

Washington managed to hold the Continental army together at Valley Forge, Pennsylvania, during the harsh winter of November 1777–April 1778, and he survived the so-called Conway Cabal, a scheme to replace him as commander with General Horatio Gates. With the coming of spring, Washington engaged General Sir Henry Clinton in a battle at Monmouth, New Jersey, that resulted in a costly draw on June 28, 1778. He made judicious leadership choices in the South and began to turn the tide of war there. In concert with French general Jean Baptiste Rochambeau, Washington planned the Yorktown (Virginia) campaign against the army of Charles Cornwallis. Executed during August 21–September 26, 1781, the Yorktown campaign succeeded brilliantly, forcing the surrender of Cornwallis on October 19, 1781. Although the American Revolution continued, Yorktown virtually ensured a favorable outcome in the Peace of Paris of September 3, 1783.

In an eloquent ceremony, Washington took leave of his troops at Fraunces Tavern, Manhattan, on December 4, 1783, and retired to Mount Vernon. He was elected president of the Constitutional Convention in Philadelphia in 1787 and, in February 1789, was unanimously elected as the first president of the United States. Washington was inaugurated on April 30 and was reelected to a second term in December 1792.

As president, Washington shaped the office of the nation's chief executive, setting a high and highly democratic standard. Refusing a third term, Washington returned to Mount Vernon in March 1797, then briefly served as commander in chief during the so-called Quasi-War with France in 1798. At the end of that year, Washington took ill with severe laryngitis and died.

Watervliet Arsenal   See FORTS AND OTHER INSTALLATIONS.

Wayne, Anthony (1745–1796) *Continental army general*

One of the army's great early generals and a hero of the AMERICAN REVOLUTION, "Mad Anthony" Wayne brought a degree of peace to the Old Northwest frontier in the turbulent years following independence.

Born in Waynesboro, Chester County, Pennsylvania, Wayne made his early living as a surveyor and land agent in Nova Scotia, beginning in 1765. He returned to Pennsylvania in 1767 to take over his father's prosperous tannery, which he ran until 1774, when he was elected to the Pennsylvania legislature. An ardent patriot, Wayne served on Pennsylvania's Committee of Public Safety during the run-up to the Revolution. He resigned his legislative seat in 1775 to raise a regiment of volunteers and, on January 3, 1776, was formally commissioned colonel of the 4th Pennsylvania Battalion.

Wayne participated in the unsuccessful invasion of Canada early in the Revolution and was wounded at Trois Rivières on June 8, 1776. Assigned to command Fort Ticonderoga, he was promoted to brigadier general on February 21, 1777, and he commanded the Pennsylvania Line at Brandywine on September 11. He suffered a bloody defeat during a surprise night attack on his encampment at Paoli, Pennsylvania (the "Paoli Massacre"), on September 21. This misfortune cast doubts on his fitness for command, and he demanded a COURT-MARTIAL on the matter to clear his name. Duly acquitted of any wrongdoing, Wayne resumed his command and fought bravely at the Battle of Germantown (Pennsylvania) on October 4, sustaining a minor wound in this action. He wintered with the army at Valley Forge during 1777–78, then participated in the victory at Monmouth Courthouse (New Jersey) on June 28, 1778, leading the initial attack and successfully defending the center against the British counterattack. But it was the daring and spectacular night attack on Stony Point, New York, on July 16, 1779, that earned Wayne his early reputation. He secured this important strongpoint from the British garrison without firing a single shot. Wayne's famous sobriquet—"Mad Anthony"—was born at about this time as well, but it had nothing to do with the action at Stony Point. A neighbor of Wayne's deserted from the CONTINENTAL ARMY. Arrested, he told the authorities to contact Wayne, who would vouch for him. Not only did General Wayne refuse to help the deserter, he denied knowing him at all. "He must be mad," the deserter responded incredulously. The epithet stuck.

Wayne was commanding operations along the lower Hudson River in 1780 when he suffered defeat at Bull's Ferry during July 20–21. Early the following year, he responded immediately to news of Benedict Arnold's treachery—Arnold had turned coat to join the British—by rushing to defend imperiled West Point. Through force of personality, Wayne succeeded in suppressing a mutiny in the Pennsylvania Line during January 1–10, 1781, but he was less successful later that year in Virginia, when he was defeated at Green Spring on July 6. Even in defeat, however, he managed to save his army from annihilation by the greatly superior British force.

Wayne participated in the victory at Yorktown (Virginia) during May–October 17, 1781, then, fighting under General Nathanael Greene, he led an effective expedition into Georgia against British-allied Creek and Cherokee Indians during January–July 1782.

Wayne was breveted to the rank of major general on September 30, 1783, but he retired from the army at the end of the Revolution to take up a quiet life as a farmer. He was active in politics as Chester County's representative to the Pennsylvania General Assembly during 1784–85, and he was then elected by Georgians—who were familiar with his exploits against the Creeks and Cherokees—as one of their representatives to Congress on March 4, 1791. He did not serve, however, because his seat was declared vacant on March 21 on the grounds of election fraud as well as failure to meet residency requirements.

Nevertheless, Wayne's life as a farmer did not long endure. On March 5, 1792, he was appointed major general and commander in chief of the army in the Old Northwest (the area encompassing present-day Ohio and the upper Midwest). His mission was to contain the Indians of that region, the Shawnee chiefs Little Turtle and Blue Jacket having recently dealt severe defeats to two previous commanders, Joshua Harmar and Arthur St. Clair, inexperienced leaders who led poorly trained units. Determined not to let this happen again, Wayne patiently and thoroughly prepared his troops before he maneuvered them into an advantageous position. On August 20, 1794, he met Little Turtle at the Battle of Fallen Timbers and soundly defeated him. The battle led to the conclusion of the Treaty of Greenville, by which the Shawnee ceded vast tracts of land to the government, thereby opening most of the Ohio country to settlement and bringing to the Old Northwest some 14 years of relative calm.

As a result of Wayne's victory over the Indians, British traders in the Ohio region lost their allies and were compelled to surrender to Wayne the British forts on the Great Lakes during 1796. Unfortunately, the general did not have long to bask in his triumphs. He succumbed to sudden illness at the end of 1796.

weapons, individual and crew-served

Currently (as of 2005), the major U.S. Army individual and crew-served weapons include:

M-4 Carbine

The M-4 Carbine entered army service in 1997. A compact version of the M-16A2 rifle, the M-4 is intended to be used by individuals and small units to engage targets with accurate, lethal, direct fire. The weapon features a collapsible stock, a flat-top upper receiver accessory rail, and a detachable handle/rear aperture site assembly. The M-4 Carbine is intended to be used in close quarters to engage targets at extended range with accurate, lethal fire. Moreover, as a compact version of the M-16, the

M-4 achieves greater than 85 percent commonality with the rifle.

The M-4 is a 5.56-mm caliber weapon weighing 7.5 pounds, loaded, with sling and one magazine. Maximum effective range is 600 meters against an area target and 500 meters against a point target. The weapon is manufactured by Colt Manufacturing of Hartford, Connecticut.

M-9 Pistol

The M-9 Pistol was adopted by the army in 1990 and is used by individuals and small units to engage targets with accurate, lethal, direct fire. The pistol is a semiautomatic, single-action/double-action weapon and is now the primary sidearm of the entire U.S. military, replacing the venerable .45 caliber model M-1911A1.

The M-9 has a 15-round staggered magazine with a reversible magazine release button, which can be positioned for either right- or left-handed shooters. Other general specifications of the weapons include:

Caliber: 9 mm
Overall length: 8 1/2 in
Barrel length: 5 in
Weight, unloaded: 2.1 lb
Weight, fully loaded: 2.6 lb
Range: 164 ft
Manufacturer: Beretta USA

M-16 Assault Rifle

The M-16 Assault Rifle is the standard-issue shoulder weapon in the army and throughout the U.S. military. It is a comparatively simple weapon—one pull, three shot—and is both light and durable. The M-16 was developed from the AR-15 designed by Eugene Stoner of the ArmaLite Company about 1956. The design was licensed to the Colt Arms Company and was adopted in 1962 by the secretary of defense as the 5.56-mm M-16 rifle. In 1965, the M-16 became the military's basic service rifle and was in very widespread use by the following year.

The M-16A1 Semiautomatic Rifle version was adopted by the U.S. Army in 1967. Improvements

U.S. Army troops marching with their M-16A3 assault rifles *(U.S. Army)*

over the original included a positive forward assist to help close the bolt when dirty, chromium-plated chamber and bore to resist corrosion, and an improved gas system with a new bolt buffer designed to reduce the rate of fire on full auto. These improvements made the weapon far more reliable. Some 3.69 million M-16A1s have been manufactured.

The M-16A2 Semiautomatic Rifle version replaced the M-16A1 in 1983 in U.S. Army service. It fires a three-round burst in semiautomatic operation and incorporates an adjustable rear sight, which corrects for both wind and elevation. The weapon has a heavier barrel and a muzzle compensator to prevent muzzle climb during semiautomatic operation.

General characteristics of the M-16A2 include:

Manufacturer: Colt Manufacturing and Fabrique Nationale Manufacturing Inc.
Length: 39.63 in
Weight, with 30-round magazine: 8.79 lb
Bore diameter: 5.56 mm
Maximum range: 11,800 ft
Muzzle velocity: 2,798 ft per second
Rate of fire, cyclic: 800 rounds/min
Rate of fire, sustained: 12–15 rounds/min
Rate of fire, semiautomatic: 45 rounds/min
Rate of fire, burst: 90 rounds/min
Magazine capacity: 30 rounds

Another M-16 variant is the M-16A2 Squad Advanced Marksman Rifle (SAMR), which incorporates the Trijicon Advanced Combat Optical Gunsight.

The M-16A3 replaced the M-16A2 in 1994 and is essentially an M-16A2 with full-automatic capability. The M-16A4 is identical to the M-16A3, but it can fire single shots or three-round bursts; there is no full auto option.

A special variant is the M-4/M-4A1 5.56-mm Carbine, a shortened variant of the M-16A2 rifle for use in close quarters.

M-19-3 40-mm Grenade Machine Gun
The M-19-3 Grenade Machine Gun entered U.S. Army service in 1983 as a weapon to enable individuals and small units to engage targets with accurate, lethal, automatic indirect fire. The gun is a self-powered, air-cooled, belt-fed, blowback-operated weapon designed to deliver decisive firepower not only against enemy personnel but also against lightly armored vehicles. For selected units, it is a replacement for the M-2 heavy machine gun and is intended to serve as the primary suppressive weapon for combat support and combat service support units.

The MK-19-3 may be mounted on the M-998 HMMWV (High-Mobility Multipurpose Wheeled Vehicle) family of vehicles, the M-113 Armored Personnel Carrier, various five-ton trucks, and some other vehicles. The 40-mm weapon weighs 72.5 pounds and has a maximum effective range of 2,200 meters against area targets. It is manufactured by General Dynamics of Saco, Maine.

M-203/M-203A1 Grenade Launcher
This weapon entered service with the army in the early 1970s. It is designed to be used by individuals and small units to engage targets with accurate, lethal grenade fire. The M-203 is a single-shot weapon that is intended for use with the M-16 Series Rifle. It fires a 40-mm grenade. The M-203A1 is a single-shot weapon designed for use with the M-4 Series Carbine. Like the M-203, it fires a 40-mm grenade. Both versions of the weapon have a leaf sight and a quadrant sight.

In addition to launching standard 40-mm grenades, the M-203 may be used as the delivery system for a growing array of less-than-lethal munitions.

General specifications of both weapons include:

Weight: 3 lb, empty; 3.6 lb, loaded
Overall length: 15 in
Barrel length: 12 in
Ammunition type: CN/CS/OC tear gas rounds, smoke, nonlethal projectiles, signal and practice rounds as well as standard 40-mm rounds.
Effective range: approximately 350 yd
Manufacturer: Colt Manufacturing, Inc., Hartford, Connecticut

M-240B Machine Gun

The M-240 Machine Gun entered service with the army in 1997 as a weapon designed to enable individuals and small units to engage targets with accurate, lethal, direct automatic fire. The weapon is ground-mounted, gas-operated, and crew-served. It is an extremely reliable 7.62-mm machine gun, which is capable of delivering more energy to the target than the smaller caliber M-249 Squad Automatic Weapon (SAW) and is being issued to infantry, armor, combat engineer, SPECIAL FORCES, RANGERS, and selected field artillery units that require medium support fire. It is intended to replace the army's ground-mounted M-60 series machine guns.

General specifications of the M-240B Machine Gun include:

Caliber: 7.62 mm
Weight: 27.6 lb
Maximum effective range: 6,000 ft against an area target; 2,625 ft against a point target
Rate of fire: 200–600 rounds/min
Manufacturer: FN Manufacturing, Columbia, South Carolina

M-249 Squad Automatic Weapon (SAW)

The M-249 Squad Automatic Weapon (SAW) was adopted by the army in 1987 as a weapon to enable individuals and small units to engage targets with accurate, lethal, direct automatic fire. The SAW is a lightweight, gas-operated, one-man-portable automatic weapon that is capable of delivering a large volume of effective fire at ranges up to 800 meters. Each infantry squad is issued two M-249 SAWs. The weapon is intended to replace the M-60 7.62 medium machine gun in certain units.

General specifications of the M-249 Squad Automatic Weapon include:

Caliber: 5.56 mm
Weight: 16.5 lb
Maximum effective range: 3,280 ft against area targets; 2,000 ft against point targets
Rate of fire: 750 rounds/min
Manufacturer: FN Manufacturing, Columbia, South Carolina

Stinger

The FIM-92 Stinger is the army's system for short-range air defense, providing protection against low-altitude airborne targets, including fixed-wing aircraft, helicopters, unmanned aerial vehicles, and cruise missiles. The Stinger missile may be launched from modified versions of the M-2 Bradley Fighting Vehicle (Bradley Stinger Fighting Vehicle or Bradley Linebacker), from the Avenger, and from helicopters. In its man-portable configuration, it may be shoulder launched (Man Portable Air Defense—MANPADS).

Reaching operational capability in 1981, the Stinger is a "fire-and-forget" weapon, which uses a passive infrared seeker and proportional navigation system to find its designated target. Latest-generation Stingers also incorporate all-aspect engagement capability and IFF (Identification-Friend-or-Foe).

The Stinger system consists of a missile packaged within a disposable launch tube. The only reusable component is a detachable gripstock.

General characteristics of the Stinger include:

Primary contractors: Hughes Missile System Company and General Dynamics/Raytheon Corporation
Propulsion: dual-thrust solid fuel rocket motor
Length: 5 ft
Width: 5.5 in
Weight, fully armed: 34.5 lb
Range: 0.5–5 mi
Ceiling: 10,000 ft
Crew: 2 enlisted

Westmoreland, William Childs (1914–   )
U.S. Army general

Westmoreland was the principal U.S. commander in the VIETNAM WAR. A native of Spartanburg, South Carolina, Westmoreland spent a year at the South Carolina military academy known as The Citadel, then entered the UNITED STATES MILITARY ACADEMY, from which he graduated in 1936. Commissioned a second lieutenant in the artillery, he saw service in Oklahoma, Hawaii, and North Carolina before the United States entered WORLD WAR II. Promoted to major in April 1942, he commanded an artillery battalion in Tunisia from November 8, 1942, to May 13, 1943. Westmoreland distinguished himself in the disastrous battle of Kasserine Pass during February 14–22, 1943, and subsequently commanded his battalion in the Sicily campaign from July 9 to August 17.

Westmoreland participated in the invasion of Normandy as part of the 9th Infantry Division, hitting the beach on June 10, 1944. The following month, he was promoted to colonel and made divisional chief of staff, serving with the 9th in its advance across northern France and into Germany to the Elbe River during July 1944 to May 1945.

After Germany's surrender, Westmoreland commanded the 60th Infantry Regiment in occupation duty into early 1946, then transferred to the 71st Division through March 1946. Next, after undergoing parachute training, Westmoreland assumed command of the 504th Parachute Infantry Regiment. This was followed by appointment as chief of staff of the 82ND AIRBORNE DIVISION, a post he held from 1947 to 1950, when he was assigned as an instructor at the COMMAND AND GENERAL STAFF COLLEGE and at the U.S. ARMY WAR COLLEGE.

Westmoreland left the service schools in August 1952 to command the 187th Airborne Regimental Combat Team in Korea. He was promoted to brigadier general in November and served on the ARMY GENERAL STAFF from 1953 to 1958, becoming secretary of the general staff in December 1956, after promotion to major general.

In 1958, Westmoreland was made commander of the 101ST AIRBORNE DIVISION at Fort Campbell, Kentucky. He served in this post through July 1960, when he returned to West Point as the academy's superintendent. During these cold war years, he oversaw the expansion of the cadet program, approximately doubling the number of students by the time he left in 1963—as a lieutenant general—to resume airborne command, now as commander of the XVIII Airborne Corps.

In June 1964, Westmoreland began what was undoubtedly his most fateful assignment, taking over from General Paul D. Harkin as commander of the U.S. Military Assistance Command in Vietnam (MACV). Promoted to general in August, he served in Vietnam through mid-1968 and oversaw the massive escalation of U.S. involvement in the war, from a relatively small cadre of military "advisers" to more than half a million U.S. troops. Westmoreland pursued a strategy of attrition against an enemy that was willing to suffer and die in great number. As the war ground on, U.S. popular and political support for the effort waned. During January–April 1968, the Vietcong launched the infamous Tet offensive, a massive attack on many fronts. Although American forces sustained substantial losses, they dealt the communists a much harder blow. By any military standard, Westmoreland had presided over a tactical victory; however, the communists refused to quit, and the Tet offensive was almost universally regarded as a moral victory for the North. This greatly escalated the tempo and scope of antiwar protest in the United States, and President Lyndon Johnson took the first steps to reduce American participation in the war. He began by, in effect, promoting Westmoreland out of command, bringing him home as army chief of staff and replacing him in Vietnam with General CREIGHTON WILLIAMS ABRAMS, JR. Westmoreland served as CHIEF OF STAFF until his retirement in July 1972.

wheeled vehicles

This article discusses the major wheeled vehicles currently (2005) used by the army; however, one historical vehicle requires at least cursory mention, although it is no longer used. In 1939 the army issued a request for proposal to 135 companies for a new military vehicle to replace the service's aging and heterogenous fleet of motorcycles and Ford Model T trucks. Only three companies actually submitted proposals: Ford Motor Company, Willys-Overland, and American Bantam Car Company. The army awarded a contract to Bantam, but their delivered prototypes failed under rigorous field testing. In the end, Willys won the contract in July 1941, and the Jeep, certainly the most famous American wheeled military vehicle in history, was born. (Ford also built Jeeps, under Willys license, and Bantam designed and built trailers to be towed by the Willys vehicle.)

The origin of the vehicle's name has long been a subject of controversy. Some authorities believe that, although Willys beat out Ford, it was Ford's designation for the vehicle, "GP," for general purpose, that stuck. Slurred, "GP" came out as "jeep." Others reject this etymology, claiming that the vehicle name was borrowed from that of a wily little character in the very popular "Thimble Theater" newspaper comic strip by E. C. Segar. Segar's Jeep could appear and disappear, walk through walls, and generally go anywhere.

The original Willys Jeep was powered by a four-cylinder engine that could run at 4,000 rpm for 100 hours straight. The transmission comprised a three-speed manual, with a four-wheel-drive transfer case with high and low gears. The open-topped vehicle had a fold-up cloth roof. Top speed was 60 miles per hour, and the vehicle could climb a 40-degree slope, turn around in a 30-foot circle, and tilt up to 50 degrees to either side without tipping over. When equipped with snorkels for air intake and exhaust, the Jeep could run under water. More than 350,000 Jeeps were built in WORLD WAR II, and the vehicle was continually modified and produced for army use until 1981, when it was replaced by the High Mobility Multipurpose Wheeled Vehicle (HUMVEE).

M-977 HEMTT
(Heavy Expanded Mobility Tactical Truck)

The M-977 is a 10-ton 8 by 8 truck that can accommodate a payload of 22,000 pounds and that incorporates an integral crane for loading and unloading in field conditions. Variants of the cargo version include the M-978, a 2,500-gallon tanker, and the M-984A1 Wrecker. The M-977 became operational in 1983 and has proved very successful, with the army acquiring almost 13,000 vehicles

from the manufacturer, Oshkosh Truck Corporation of Oshkosh, Wisconsin. General characteristics of the vehicle include:

Weight: 62,000 lb
Length: 33 ft 4 1/2 in
Width: 8 ft
Cab height: 8 ft 5 in
Power plant: Detroit Diesel 8V-92TA 445-hp V-8 diesel
Maximum speed: 55 mph
Crew: 2

M-992 FAASV (Field Artillery Ammunition Support Vehicle)

The FAASV—"Fas-Vee"—is based on the M-109 155-mm self-propelled howitzer chassis and is used for in-field ammunition resupply. The vehicle carries 93 projectiles, 99 charges, and 104 fuses in specially designed honeycomb storage racks and incorporates a conveyor belt for offloading. The vehicle became operational in 1985. Its general characteristics include:

Weight (loaded): 58,500 lb
Length: 22 ft 3 i
Width: 10 ft 4 in
Height: 10 ft 6 in
Power plant: Detroit Diesel 8V-71T 405-hp diesel V-8
Maximum speed: 35 mph
Crew: 2
Passengers: 6 troops

M-998 HMMWV (High-Mobility Multipurpose Wheeled Vehicle)

Beginning in 1985, the "Humvee" began rapidly displacing the Jeep as the ubiquitous general-purpose military vehicle. Manufactured by AM General, the Humvee is a 4 by 4 trucklike vehicle that can be readily modified for many purposes, ranging from missile carrier, to troop carrier, to ambulance. Before the middle of the 1990s, some 90,000 Humvees had been delivered to the army.

General characteristics of the M-998 include:

Weight: 5,200 lb basic configuration
Payload: 2,500 lb
Hull length: 15 ft
Width: 7 ft 1 in
Height: 5 ft 9 in
Power plant: Detroit Diesel 150-hp V-8 diesel
Maximum speed: 65 mph
Crew: 1 driver
Passengers or other crew: 3–7

M-1070 HET
(Heavy Equipment Transporter)

The M-1070 Heavy Equipment Transporter, or HET, entered army service in 1993 to transport, deploy, recover, and evacuate combat-loaded main battle tanks and other heavy tracked and wheeled vehicles.

The complete Heavy Equipment Transport System (HETS) consists of the M-1070 Truck Tractor plus the M-1000 Heavy Equipment Transporter Semitrailer. The system is capable of transporting payloads up to 70 tons and is intended to transport the M-1A1 Abrams Main Battle Tank. The truck and trailer can operate on major highways worldwide as well as on secondary roads and, off road, cross-country. Special features of the HETS include front- and rear-axle steering on the tractor, a central tire-inflation system, and cab space for six personnel to accommodate the two HETS operators and four tank crewmen. The M-1000 semitrailer component has automatically steerable axles and an advanced load-leveling hydraulic suspension.

General specifications of the entire system include:

Tractor length: 358 in
Tractor width: 102 in
Trailer length: 622 in
Trailer width, at rear bumper: 144.8 in
Tractor curb weight: 41,000 lb
Trailer curb weight: 50,000 lb
Payload: 140,000 lb
Engine: 500 horsepower Detroit Diesel engine
Transmission: 5-speed automatic
Speed, on highway: 40–45 mph, unloaded; 25–30 mph, with 70-ton payload

Range: 300 mi
Fording: 28 in of water
Air transportability: C-5A and C-17 cargo transports
Manufacturer, tractor: Oshkosh Truck, Oshkosh, Wisconsin
Manufacturer, semitrailer: Systems and Electronics, Inc, St. Louis, Missouri

M-1075 Palletized Load System (PLS)

PLS was developed to expedite bulk resupply of battlefield forces. The PLS vehicle modifies the M-977 HEMTT (Heavy Expanded Mobility Tactical Truck) to carry a "flatrack," a demountable cargo bed while towing a trailer also loaded with a flatrack. The vehicle has an integral multilift hoist, which pulls the entire flatrack onto the truck. Thus, in a single operation, 24 pallets of ammunition or other material can be loaded onto the truck.

PLS became operational in 1993. Its general characteristics include:

Gross weight: 86,595 lb
Length: 24 ft
Width: 8 ft
Height to cab: 9 ft 6 in
Power plant: Detroit Diesel 8V-92TA 500-hp V-8 diesel
Maximum speed: 55 mph
Range: 336 miles

M-1078 Medium Tactical Vehicles

The FMVT series consists of the 4-by-4 Light Medium Tactical Vehicle (LMTV) and the 6-by-6 Medium Tactical Vehicle (MTV), which have been produced in several variants to replace the army's venerable deuce-and-a-half (2 1/2 ton) trucks and five-ton trucks. LMTV variants include the M-1078 cargo truck, the M-1079 van, the M-1081 LAPES-capable cargo truck, and the M-1080 chassis, which can be mated to a variety of bodies. MTV variants include the M-1083 cargo truck, M-1084 cargo with crane, M-1085 long-bed cargo, M-1086 long-bed cargo with crane, M-1087 van, M-1088 tractor, M-1089 wrecker, M-1090 dump truck, M-1091 tanker, and other specialized variants.

General characteristics of the LMTV include:

Payload: 5,000 lb
Length: 21 ft 2 in
Width: 8 ft
Height to cab: 9 ft 1 in
Power plant: Caterpillar 3116 ATAAC 225-hp
  6 cylinder diesel
Maximum speed: 55 mph

General characteristics of the MTV include:

Payload: 10,000 lb
Length: 22 ft 10 in
Width: 8 ft
Height to cab: 9 ft 1 in
Power plant: Caterpillar 3116 ATAAC 290-hp
  6 cylinder diesel
Maximum speed: 55 mph

V-150 Commando

The Commando has been produced in a number of variants for use as lightly armored reconnaissance vehicles. The basic vehicle is a 4-by-4 without vertical surfaces and a very low superstructure. It can be fitted with a range of weapons, from 7.62-mm machine guns to a 90-mm cannon. The original version became operational in 1964.

General characteristics of the V-150 include:

Weight: 21,800 lb
Hull length: 18 ft 8 in
Width: 7 ft 5 in
Height: 6 ft 6 in
Power plant: Chrysler 191-hp gasoline engine
  or Cummins V-504 202-hp diesel
Maximum speed: 55 mph
Crew: 3
Passengers: 2 troops

White Sands Missile Range   See FORTS AND OTHER INSTALLATIONS.

Women's Army Auxiliary Corps (WAAC)

See WOMEN'S ARMY CORPS.

women in the U.S. Army

Until WORLD WAR I the role of women in the U.S. Army was informal, and women were not considered members or even auxiliary members of the service. In World War I, an Army Nurse Corps was created, although the nurses did not hold military rank. It was not until WORLD WAR II and the creation of the Women's Auxiliary Army Corps and the WOMEN'S ARMY CORPS (WAC) that women were given clear official status in the army. The WAC was made a permanent separate corps of the army in 1948 by authority of the Women's Armed Services Integration Act. This law defined women's roles in the military. It limited the number of women who could serve to no more than 2 percent of active duty personnel. It stipulated that while women would hold full rank and privileges, they could not be promoted above the level of lieutenant colonel in the army, marines, or air force (or commander in the navy). Most significantly, women were excluded from combat roles. While the recruitment ceiling and the cap on promotions were repealed in 1967, the prohibition against combat service remained in effect until the late 1990s—except for female pilots (including army aviators), who began serving in combat in the early 1990s. In 1978, the WAC was disbanded, and women were fully integrated into the REGULAR ARMY.

During the VIETNAM WAR, women began serving in increasing numbers, forming 1.6 percent of active duty personnel by 1971 and 5 percent by the end of the war. Beginning in 1973, with the elimination of the military draft and the creation of the all-volunteer army, women were more actively recruited. Progress in advancing women's rights in the army paralleled progress achieved by women in the civilian sector, notably in the workplace, during this period. Before the 1970s were out, women officers were permitted to command units that included both men and women, pregnant women were no longer automatically discharged from the army, segregated training of men and women was ended, and spouse entitlements were equalized for married servicemen and servicewomen. The first female army pilots earned their wings in 1974, and the first female cadets were admitted to the UNITED STATES MILITARY ACADEMY and the other service academies in 1978.

In 1970, Colonel Anna Mae Hays, chief of the Army Nurse Corps, was promoted to brigadier general, becoming the first woman in army history to attain general officer rank. On May 21, 1997, Claudia J. Kennedy, deputy chief of staff for intelligence, became the first female army lieutenant general.

Some 500 WACs served in Vietnam during the Vietnam War, and most of the 6,000 military nurses in Vietnam were female army officers. In 1989, 800 women soldiers were among the 18,400 U.S. troops deployed to Panama for Operation Just Cause, and from August 1990 to February 1991, 41,000 military women, about three-quarters of them army soldiers, served in Operations Desert Shield and Desert Storm (the PERSIAN GULF WAR). Thirteen women were among the 375 U.S. military personnel killed in that conflict.

In Operation Iraqi Freedom, the controversial invasion of Iraq for the purpose of removing Saddam Hussein from power, approximately 37,000 women, most of them army soldiers, were deployed. They constituted about 15 percent of the United States forces there. By February 2004, of 558 U.S. soldiers killed in Iraq, 15 were women.

As of 2003, women accounted for nearly 16 percent of the ACTIVE ARMY and were serving in almost all (90 percent+) army positions, including limited frontline combat roles.

Women's Army Corps (WAC)

The WAC was established as the Women's Army Auxiliary Corps (WAAC) by Congress on May 14, 1941, primarily to furnish the army with clerks, typists, switchboard operators, and the like, thereby freeing up men for combat and other service. Oveta Culp Hobby was appointed as the first director of the WAAC, which soon recruited its authorized limit of 150,000 women, of whom 35,000 were trained as officers. Initially, most "auxiliaries" (as the WAACs were called) worked as file clerks, typists, stenographers, or motor pool drivers. Later, positions became more diverse, especially in the U.S. Army Air Forces, where WAACs worked as weather observers and forecasters, cryptographers, radio operators and repairers, sheet metal workers, parachute riggers, Link Trainer instructors, bombsight maintenance specialists, aerial photograph analysts, and control tower operators. More than a thousand women ran the tabulating machines used to keep track of personnel records.

On July 3, 1943, the Women's Army Auxiliary Corps became the Women's Army Corps, and the personnel were no longer considered auxiliaries, but members of the REGULAR ARMY. During this same month, the first battalion of WACs to reach the European theater of operations arrived in London, 557 enlisted women and 19 officers assigned to duty with the Eighth Air Force. A second battalion arrived during September and October. Most of the women worked as telephone switchboard operators, clerks, typists, secretaries, and motor pool drivers, while WAC officers served as executive secretaries, cryptographers, and photo interpreters. A detachment of 300 WACs served with Supreme Headquarters, Allied Expeditionary Force (SHAEF), often handling highly classified materials. In February 1945, a battalion of 800 African-American WACs, the 6888th Central Postal Battalion, was sent to Europe, responsible for the redirection of mail to all U.S. personnel in the European theater of operations (army, navy, marine corps, civilians, and Red Cross workers). WACs were also assigned extensively to the Pacific theater.

Most of the WACs were demobilized after V-J Day in August 1945. However, early in 1946, the army asked Congress for authority to establish the Women's Army Corps as a permanent part of the regular army. Authorization came by act of Congress on June 12, 1948. The WAC became a separate corps of the regular army and remained part of the army organization until 1978, when women were fully assimilated into all but the combat branches of the service.

Wood, Leonard (1860–1927) *U.S. Army general*

An extraordinary army officer, Wood began his career as a medical officer and became CHIEF OF STAFF of the army. He was born in Winchester, New Hampshire, and graduated from Harvard Medical School in 1884. After practicing briefly in Boston, he joined the army in June 1885 as acting assistant surgeon with the rank of second lieutenant. Promoted to assistant surgeon at the rank of first lieutenant in January 1886, he participated in the expedition against the Apache leader Geronimo during May through September of that year. In 1891, he was promoted to captain and was posted to Washington, D.C., becoming White House physician to President Grover Cleveland in 1895. He also served in this capacity for a time during the administration of William McKinley.

While Wood was on the White House staff, he became a close personal friend of Theodore Roosevelt, who was at the time assistant secretary of the navy. With Roosevelt, he organized the 1st Volunteer Cavalry—the famed Rough Riders—for service in the SPANISH-AMERICAN WAR in May 1898. Appointed colonel of volunteers, Wood led the Rough Riders to Cuba in June. He was soon promoted to command of the 2nd Brigade—which included the 1st Volunteers and the 1st and 50th Cavalry regiments—and personally led the 2nd Brigade at the make-or-break Battle of San Juan Hill on July 1. He was also in command during subsequent actions, culminating in the capture of Santiago de Cuba on July 17. At this time, he was promoted to brigadier general and was named military governor of Santiago on July 18. In this post, the physician in Wood came to the fore, as he worked tirelessly to improve sanitation as well as to restore civil order. In October, his appointment as governor was extended to the entire province.

Wood was promoted to major general in December 1898, but he reverted to brigadier general after the war, in April 1899; however, when he became governor of all of Cuba, he was reinstated as a major general. Wood worked vigorously to improve the Cuban infrastructure by building

Leonard Wood was a medical officer who went on to become the U.S. Army's senior commander. *(Arttoday)*

roads, schools, and communications. He collaborated closely with Major William C. Gorgas in combating yellow fever, which was endemic to the region. Wood also drew up a constitution and legal code for Cuba, then stepped down as governor when the newly elected president, Tomás Estrada Palma, took office on May 20, 1902.

Wood was next appointed governor of the rebellious Moro Province of the Philippines in March 1903 and then was made commander of the Department of the Philippines at Manila in April 1906. Returning to the United States in November 1908, he became commander of the Department of the East and, in April 1910, was appointed chief of staff for the army. His tenure was a stormy one, as he worked tirelessly to reform and shake up the sleepy peacetime army. A proponent of preparedness when WORLD WAR I broke out in Europe in

1914, Wood created civilian training camps in Plattsburgh, New York, albeit without the cooperation or consent of the War Department. While this alienated the department, it did help to ensure that the army was at least on the road to preparedness when the nation entered the war in 1917. Wood himself was passed over for major command during the war, however, and served during part of 1918 as commander of the 89th Infantry Division at Camp Funston (now part of Fort Riley), Kansas. After the war, in January 1919, he was appointed commander of the Central Department, headquartered in Chicago.

Wood sought the nomination as Republican candidate for president in 1920, but he lost to Warren G. Harding, who subsequently sent him to the Philippines as governor general. He served there until his death in 1927.

World War I (U.S. participation, 1917–1918)

World War I began in July 1914 and ended in November 1918. The United States did not enter the war until April 6, 1917, and, at that, had not massed sufficient numbers of troops to take a major role in combat until 1918. Entry into the war was spurred by growing pro-Allied sentiment, among both the public and the highest levels of government, but it was specifically precipitated by repeated German violations of U.S. neutrality rights. These included attacks on U.S. merchant vessels, attacks on the commercial vessels of other nations with consequent loss of American lives and property, and, finally, attacks on U.S. warships. Also, in February 1917, British intelligence authorities turned over to President Woodrow Wilson a telegram that had been intercepted between Germany's foreign minister, Alfred Zimmermann, and the German ambassador to Mexico. Transmitted on January 16, 1917, the "Zimmermann Telegram" authorized the ambassador to propose a German-Mexican alliance against the United States. Although Mexican president Venustiano Carranza did not take Germany up on its offer, the Zimmer-

mann Telegram, together with the maritime attacks, were sufficient to prompt Wilson to ask Congress for a declaration of war against Germany on April 2, 1917.

The United States entered the war at a low point for the Allies. Every major Allied offensive had failed, and the Central Powers possessed vast tracts of Allied territory. The Allies pressed the United States for an immediate influx of men. To meet this need, the Selective Service Act of 1917 was signed into law on May 18, and, over the next two years, 23.9 million men were registered for the draft and 2.8 million were drafted, most of them into the army, which expanded from 133,000 men in 1916 to 4.5 million by Armistice Day, November 11, 1918. Nevertheless, tensions between the U.S. general in chief, JOHN JOSEPH PERSHING, and the French and British allies were often high because Pershing insisted on maintaining direct control of the American Expeditionary Force (AEF) rather than committing units and men to battle in a piecemeal fashion.

General Pershing arrived in Paris with a small staff on June 14, 1917. Despite a massive transport effort, only 175,000 army troops were in Europe by the end of 1917. Recognizing that it would take some time for Americans to arrive in significant numbers, Germany's generalissimo Erich Ludendorff launched an all-out series of offensives on the western front in an effort to make a timely breakthrough. The pressure on the Allies was terrific and demoralizing.

The first of the Ludendorff offensives, on the Somme, began on March 21, 1918, and inflicted at least 240,000 Allied casualties, although it was equally costly to the Germans. Undeterred by his own heavy casualties, Ludendorff mounted a second offensive, against the British at the Lys River, forming part of the Belgian-French border. By April 29, when Ludendorff broke off this offensive, British losses were 239,000, and the Germans had nearly broken through to a decisive victory, but they suffered a staggering 348,300 killed and wounded. The third offensive, on the Aisne River, began on May 27 against lightly held French positions on the Chemin des Dames ridge. This was begun as nothing more than a diversionary attack, but it was so successful that it became the major effort of the offensive. In 24 hours, the Germans advanced 20 miles, and, by May 30, they had reached the Marne, less than 50 miles outside of Paris. Again, the war hung in the balance, and, this time, the army played a minor role in assisting the British on the Lys.

The first truly significant army action occurred on April 20, when two companies of the 26th Division came under heavy attack near Seicheprey along the Saint-Mihiel salient. About 2,800 regular German troops spearheaded by 600 elite shock troops overran the American positions. A large number of Americans were taken prisoner, and 669 others were either killed or wounded. Unshaken, General Pershing rushed the 2nd and 3rd divisions to reinforce the French along the Marne. In the meantime, Major General Robert Lee Bullard launched the first army offensive of the war, at the village of Cantigny, some 50 miles northwest of the action at Chemin des Dames and about 60 miles north of Paris. Cantigny was the site of a German advance observation point and was very strongly fortified. On May 28, the U.S. 1st Division attacked the village and drove the Germans out. Later in the day and on the next day, the Americans successfully repulsed German counterattacks.

The vanguard of the German offensive was at Château-Thierry, on the Marne. The U.S. 2nd and 3rd divisions were rushed in to block the Germans from crossing the Marne at this point. The 3rd Division defended the Marne bridges, successfully holding them against the Germans, then counterattacking. The French 10th Colonial Division, inspirited by the performance of the Americans, joined the action, pushing the German onslaught back across the Marne at Jaulgonne.

Deserters from the increasingly demoralized German army revealed to French captors the strategy behind Ludendorff's next two projected offensives. The next assault would come at Noyon and Montdidier, just southeast of Cantigny and northwest of Château-Thierry. The French command prepared thoroughly for the assault, which came on June 9. A Franco-American counterattack checked the advance of the German Eighteenth Army by June 11, and, on June 12, the Allies repulsed an attack by the German Seventh.

By spring 1918, more than 250,000 U.S. troops, almost all army soldiers, were arriving in France each month. In desperation, Ludendorff launched his fifth offensive in five months, aiming to destroy the British army in Flanders. He preceded this intended main thrust with a preliminary offensive against the French and Americans in the Champagne region, focusing the attack on the fortified city of Reims. The French arrested the advance of German shock troops during the night of July 14–15 east of Reims, but, west of the city, the Germans punched through to the Marne and crossed it with 14 divisions. Here the U.S. 3rd Division earned the nickname "Rock of the Marne" for its defense of the region west of Reims.

On July 17, 1918, French overall commander Ferdinand Foch concluded that Ludendorff was beginning to pull troops out of the Marne sector to send them north, against the British. In this movement Foch saw an opportunity for an Allied counteroffensive. The counteroffensive stepped off at 4:35 on the morning of July 18, 1918. The French Tenth, Sixth, and Fifth armies, from left to right along the front, made the assault, while the French Ninth Army waited in reserve. U.S. forces were also active in the Second Battle of the Marne. The American 1st and 2nd divisions spearheaded General Mangin's main assault, and six other divisions also fought valiantly. Ludendorff began to withdraw east across the Marne on the night of July 18.

British commander Sir Douglas Haig proposed an Anglo-French attack east of Amiens in northwestern France, along the Somme River to free up the rail network in the area. The French and English took more than 15,000 prisoners and captured 400 guns on August 8, 1918, a day Ludendorff later called the "Black Day" of the German army. Yet the German army remained intact, and, on August 21, the British Third Army, on the left, and the French armies, on the right, again attacked. Ludendorff now withdrew from the Lys salient in Flanders and from Amiens. ANZAC (Australia–New Zealand Army Corps) and Canadian troops forced a German withdrawal all the way back to the last-ditch Hindenburg Line. With German casualties from the Amiens offensive topping 100,000 killed, wounded, or taken prisoner, Ludendorff personally recommended to Kaiser Wilhelm II an end to the war.

The U.S. First Army, with the French II Colonial Corps attached to it, was assigned to the Saint-Mihiel sector on August 30. Its mission was to push back this bulge or incursion of German strength, which had held since 1915. On September 8, Ludendorff ordered withdrawal from the salient, to begin on September 11. If his troops were allowed to retreat to the Hindenburg Line, the salient would be vacated, but the German army would also be saved. General Pershing was determined to prevent Ludendorff from withdrawing without a fight, and, early on the morning of September 12, 16 army divisions attacked, supported by French artillery and French tanks, as well as a mixed force of American, French, Italian, and Portuguese pilots flying some 600 planes (out of 1,400 deployed) under the command of Colonel William "Billy" Mitchell of the U.S. Army Air Service.

The Allies fought an epic 36-hour battle, ultimately forcing the Germans to surrender en masse, thereby clearing the Saint-Mihiel Salient and dealing the German army an irrecoverable blow. The reduction of the Saint-Mihiel Salient by half a million army soldiers was the largest U.S. military operation since the CIVIL WAR. It was followed immediately by the Meuse-Argonne Offensive. To participate, Pershing moved the entire First U.S. Army, unrested, 60 miles to the Verdun area. Foch's plan was for the Franco-American forces to drive forward from Verdun toward Mézières, a key German rail junction and supply depot. Simultaneously, British units would attack between Péronne and Lens, with the objective of controlling the rail junction at Aulnoye. These operations would gain control of German lines of supply along the western front. Pershing brilliantly executed the transfer

of a 500,000-man army, by night, into position for the attack that would initiate the offensive. It began at 5:25 on the morning of September 26 against extremely well prepared and heavily fortified defenses in rugged, heavily wooded terrain. The initial advance rapidly penetrated the first two German lines, but then slowed along the line between Apremont and Brieulles by October 3. By October 4, it was apparent that the dense Argonne Forest offered no room for maneuver so that Pershing's only option was to make repeated and costly frontal assaults. The Argonne operation therefore stretched through nearly the end of October before the third German line was broken.

During the first 11 days of November 1918, the army, having broken out of the Argonne Forest, raced through the final German positions in the Meuse River valley. Pershing—and the other Allied commanders—wanted to exert maximum pressure even as peace seemed at hand. The U.S. 1st Division was about to take Sedan on November 6 when higher command ordered a halt. The honor of conquering that city, it was decreed, must be French. On November 10, the U.S. Second Army, under Major General Robert Lee Bullard, launched an attack in its drive toward the village of Montmédy, only to break it off the next day, November 11, at 11 A.M. sharp, the hour of armistice. World War I had ended.

World War II (U.S. participation, 1941–1945)

This article primarily discusses army land, amphibious, and airborne operations in World War II. It does not include U.S. Army Air Forces operations.

World War II began in Europe on September 1, 1939, when forces of Adolf Hitler's Germany invaded Poland. Following this, France and Britain declared war on Germany, and Germany next invaded the Netherlands, Belgium, and Luxembourg (May 10, 1940). France fell to German occupation on June 22, 1940, and, on June 22, 1941, Hitler's armies invaded the Soviet Union. Italy, under the dictatorship of Benito Mussolini, emerged as Germany's most important European ally, and Japan was tied to Italy and Germany by a military alliance. The United States remained neutral, although U.S. president Franklin D. Roosevelt conducted a policy that clearly and increasingly favored the allies, including Britain and the Soviet Union, which the United States supplied with arms and other materiel.

Attack on Pearl Harbor

War finally came to the United States not via Europe, but from the Pacific. At 7:55 A.M., December 7, 1941, amid deteriorating relations between Japan and the United States, some 200 Japanese carrier-launched dive bombers and torpedo planes attacked the USN and army facilities at Pearl Harbor, Hawaiian Territory, devastating the USN battleship fleet and destroying many U.S. Army Air Corps aircraft on the ground. Casualties totaled more than 3,400 men, including 2,403 killed. A U.S. declaration of war followed on December 8, 1941. Since Japan was a member of the so-called Berlin-Rome-Tokyo Axis, the declaration constituted a de facto declaration against Germany and Italy as well. (Germany declared war against the United States on December 11, and Italy followed suit.

Japanese Victories

Immediately after Pearl Harbor, Japanese forces attacked U.S. and British holdings in the Pacific. In December, Wake Island and Guam, both defended by small garrisons of marines and sailors, fell. In Asia, British-held Hong Kong fell, as did Malaya and Singapore.

The U.S. territory of the Philippines was occupied by about 130,000 troops under the command of General DOUGLAS MACARTHUR, including 22,400 army regulars (among them 12,000 Philippine Scouts), 3,000 members of the Philippine Constabulary, and the Philippine army, consisting of 107,000 men, many of whom were virtually untrained, unorganized, and unarmed. MacArthur also commanded the U.S. Far East Air Force, including 35 B-17 bombers and about 90 other combat aircraft. MacArthur deployed most of his forces north of Manila under Major General Jonathan M. Wainwright to resist an invasion via Lingayen Gulf. His plan was to use the B-17s to hit Formosa by way of counterattack in the hope of resisting the invasion long enough to receive reinforcements. Japan's aim was to overwhelm the defenders before any reinforcement was possible.

The Japanese attack came on December 8 and was devastating. More than half of the B-17s were destroyed on the ground, along with 56 fighters and other aircraft. This prevented MacArthur's planned air assault on Formosa. Next, beginning on December 10, Japanese bombers destroyed the naval base at Cavite while Japanese troops began to land at Luzon, in the northern Philippines. The Japanese invaders also secured beachheads in the south, at Mindanao and Jolo. As the main invasion of Luzon commenced on December 22, most of the Philippine army collapsed, but army and Philippine army Scout units retreated in an orderly fashion, inflicting heavy casualties on the Japanese. However, on December 24, another Japanese landing was made, at Limon Bay, and MacArthur decided to save his troops by abandoning Manila and withdrawing to Bataan. The Philippine capital was occupied by the Japanese on December 26 without resistance.

By January 7, 1942, American and Filipino forces were dug into well-prepared positions across the upper Bataan Peninsula and offered valiant resistance, which significantly delayed the Japanese conquest of the islands. In mid-March, MacArthur evacuated the Philippines on orders from President Roosevelt, leaving Wainwright in command and pledging, "I shall return." On May 5, Wainwright surrendered and was forced to lead 78,000 American and Filipino POWs, many already starving, on a "death march" from Bataan to a prison camp 65 miles away. Some 10,000 POWs died en route.

January 1942 brought the final British defeat on the Malay Peninsula, followed during February 8–15 by the Japanese conquest of Singapore. Thailand and Burma were invaded during January–March. Working in concert with Chinese forces under the command of army general JOSEPH STIL-WELL, the Allies reorganized but retreated from Mandalay and from Burma. Cut off from overland supply, China was kept supplied by a hazardous airlift ("the Hump") organized by General Stilwell.

Battles of Coral Sea and Midway

Early in 1942, the Japanese formulated a plan to seize Tulagi, in the Solomon Islands, and Port Moresby in New Guinea while the Imperial Combined Fleet engaged and destroyed the American fleet, then captured Midway Island. The object was to establish a defensive chain from the Aleutian Islands, through Midway, Wake, and the Marshalls and Gilberts. Once this chain was forged, the Japanese could invade New Caledonia, the Fijis, and Samoa. The first step was to destroy the American fleet, especially the aircraft carriers. The plan was put into operation in May 1942; however, the USN arrested the Japanese advance at the Battle of the Coral Sea (albeit at great cost) in May and, at the Battle of Midway, forced the withdrawal of Japanese forces on June 5. Midway was the turning point of the Pacific war. Although the USN lost 307 men, 150 planes, a destroyer, and the carrier *Yorktown,* the Japanese lost 275 planes, four carriers, a cruiser, and about 4,800 men. For U.S. forces, the battle transformed the Pacific war from a defensive to an offensive operation.

Battle of Guadalcanal

The Japanese defeat at Midway prompted imperial military planners to abandon the plan to take New Caledonia, the Fijis, and Samoa, and, instead, to invade Port Moresby overland, using troops landed at Buna-Gona, New Guinea. When the Japanese began building an airfield on Guadalcanal, more than 600 miles southeast of their large base at Rabaul in the Solomon chain, the USN and USMC made an assault on Guadalcanal and Tulagi. Army troops soon joined the marines on Guadalcanal, which, after a bloody six-month struggle, was secured. As Midway had turned the tide in the sea war, the victory at Guadalcanal was the turning point in the war on land in the Pacific theater.

Operation Torch

American popular opinion favored concentrating the U.S. war effort against Japan to avenge Pearl Harbor; however, American military planners understood the importance of aiding Britain and the Soviet Union in defeating Hitler's Germany. While U.S. strategists wanted to use England as a staging area from which to launch a massive cross-channel invasion of Europe, the British favored invading via what Prime Minister Winston Churchill called the "soft underbelly of Europe," defeating German forces in North Africa, then using North Africa as a staging area from which to invade Sicily, the Italian mainland, and, finally, all of Europe. Once southern Europe had been secured, another invasion force could be launched from the west. This would surround the Axis powers on the west, south, and east. More immediately, the brilliant German tank commander, General Erwin Rommel, had scored victories against the British in North Africa and was menacing the Suez Canal, without which Allied supplies would quickly dry up.

Field Marshal Bernard Law Montgomery led the British Eighth Army to a hard-fought victory against Germany's vaunted Afrika Korps at the second Battle of El Alamein during October–November 1942. On November 13, Tobruk fell to Montgomery, followed by Tripoli on January 23, 1943. Montgomery pursued Rommel's Afrika Korps across the Tunisian frontier during February. In the meantime, army forces under General DWIGHT DAVID EISENHOWER began Operation Torch on November 8, 1942, landing in North Africa. Using Morocco and Algeria as bases, army units were to launch operations eastward against Tunisia, into which Montgomery was already forcing Rommel's Afrika Korps. However, the first engagement between army troops and the Afrika Korps, at Kasserine Pass, Tunisia, during February 14–22, 1943, brought a humiliating defeat for the poorly led and poorly trained Americans. Fortunately, Rommel withdrew, leaving the U.S. forces intact, and Eisenhower called in Major General GEORGE SMITH PATTON, JR., to take over command of the U.S. II Corps after Kasserine. Patton revitalized the corps and, working in concert with Montgomery, pushed the Afrika Korps into full retreat from its positions in Tunisia.

As Patton was readied to command the invasion of Sicily, Major General OMAR BRADLEY was given command of the army in North Africa. The U.S. and Free French armies attacked a combined German-Italian army from the north while Montgomery's British Eighth Army came up from the south. On May 13, the Italian First Army surrendered to Montgomery, signaling the collapse of the entire Axis position in North Africa. The stage was now set for the Allied invasion of Europe via Sicily.

Operation Husky

Operation Husky, the invasion of Sicily from North Africa, began on the night of July 9–10, 1943. Three thousand ships and landing craft carried 14,000 vehicles, 600 tanks, 1,800 guns, and 160,000 men of the Fifteenth Army Group to a landing in Sicily. German and Italian land forces numbered about 350,000, but beachheads were quickly secured, and the British Eighth Army captured Siracusa on July 12, followed by Augusta on July 14. At Catania the advance was halted by Axis defenders occupying the slopes of Mt. Etna. While the British forces were stalled, Lieutenant General GEORGE S. PATTON captured the port of Licata, then beat back a counterattack at Gela. The U.S. II Corps, under Omar Bradley, drove up the center of Sicily, taking San Stefano. Now the U.S. thrust turned east in two columns, one along the coast, the other inland. This drew off pressure from the British Eighth Army, which was thereby able to take Catania. The capture of Messina by Patton ended the 38-day battle for Sicily. Axis casualties numbered 167,000, mostly Italian; the Allies lost 31,158 men, including 11,923 Americans. Not only did the Sicily invasion bring Allied forces to the backdoor of Europe, it forced the overthrow of Italy's fascist dictator and Hitler ally Benito Mussolini. The new Italian government, under Marshal Pietro Badoglio, began secretly to seek a separate peace with the Allies.

Nevertheless, Hitler rushed large German forces into the Italian mainland, which ended Allied hopes that a rapid conquest of Italy would quickly bring them into the rest of Europe.

The South Pacific, 1943

The invasion of Sicily, followed by landings on the Italian mainland, penetrated Hitler's defensive perimeter, just as Allied victories on Guadalcanal and New Guinea pierced Japan's first line of defenses. The Japanese responded by reinforcing Rabaul and other positions held in the South and Southwest Pacific. To leverage their resources, the Allies adopted an "island hopping" strategy, selectively targeting some Japanese-held islands for conquest while "hopping over" others, which were cut off and rendered militarily useless by virtue of the other conquests.

To neutralize Rabaul, the main Japanese base in the South Pacific, General Douglas MacArthur was given overall command of forces in the region. He directed a two-pronged offensive, in which Admiral William "Bull" Halsey's fleet drove northwestward through the Solomon Islands, while General WALTER KRUEGER led the Sixth U.S. Army through New Guinea and New Britain toward Rabaul. By the end of June 1943, American forces had landed at Nassau Bay, New Guinea. This was followed by operations at Lae and Salamaua, New Guinea, by combined Australian and American troops, who drove the Japanese out of Salamaua by the middle of September. After Finschafen was surrounded on September 22 and fell on October 2, southeastern New Guinea became a staging area for an assault on New Britain during October through December. By the end of the year a firm beachhead had been established on that island.

Simultaneously with the operations in New Guinea and New Britain, U.S. land and naval forces set off from Guadalcanal to take the central and northern Solomon Islands. Russell Island was the first in the chain to fall, on February 11, 1943, followed by Rendova Island on June 30. From Rendova, army, USMC, and USN forces assaulted New Georgia during July 2–August 25. Resistance ended only after the Japanese troops on the island had been virtually wiped out.

Overlapping the assault on New Georgia was an attack on Vella Lavella, which developed into another hard-fought campaign spanning August 15 to October 7. In the end, however, the central Solomons fell to the Americans—at a cost of 1,136 U.S. troops killed and 4,140 wounded. Of the 8,000 Japanese troops forming the Vella Lavella garrison, at least 2,500 died. The victory here provided a jumping-off point for an attack on Bougainville, which, with Rabaul and Choiseul, was the last Japanese bastion in the Solomons. By December, Bougainville had not only been taken but became a major Allied naval and air base.

Central Pacific, 1943

While the army worked with the navy and marines in the South Pacific, most of the Central Pacific campaign during 1943 was conducted by the navy and marines with much support from U.S. Army Air Forces bombers. The marines' conquest of Tarawa, at great cost, put U.S. forces in position to take the major Japanese forces installed at Truk.

North Pacific, 1943

In the North Pacific, Japanese forces held Attu and Kiska, the westernmost of the Aleutian Islands, and the only part of the North American continent the Japanese succeeded in invading. Combined navy, army, and Canadian army forces battled to evict the Japanese here.

Italian Campaign, 1943

Marshal Pietro Badoglio concluded an armistice with the Allies on September 8, and, on September 9, the Fifth U.S. Army under Lieutenant General MARK WAYNE CLARK landed at Salerno against fierce German resistance. It was not until September 18 that British and American operations achieved sufficient coordination to enable the Fifth U.S. Army to secure the Salerno beachhead. German general Albert von Kesselring had inflicted more than 15,000 casualties on the Allies.

During September and early October, the Fifth U.S. and Eighth British armies advanced north-

ward, always against hard resistance. The Allied advance was stalled in the rugged, snowbound terrain southeast of the Rapido River.

C-B-I Theater, 1944

Throughout the Pacific and Asian campaigns, the China-Burma-India (C-B-I) theater was given short shrift, and Allied commanders had to make do and improvise with often woefully meager resources. At the start of 1944, the British advanced into Arakan, western Burma, and were very nearly pushed back by a Japanese counterattack during February 4–12. A British counterattack against the Japanese encircling force resulted in the envelopment of the Japanese attackers, but the entire front ground to a halt for the balance of 1944 with the onset of the monsoon in May.

In north Burma, the major effort was directed against the Japanese stronghold of Myitkyina, which combined U.S. and Chinese forces under General Joseph Stilwell attacked during May 17–18, only to be repulsed. Myitkyina did not surrender to Stilwell until August 3.

In the meantime, in central Burma, British forces repelled a Japanese invasion of India, virtually destroying the Japanese Fifteenth Army by September. The British then advanced into central Burma.

China Theater, 1944

By early 1944, General Claire Chennault's Flying Tigers—now officially the Fourteenth U.S. Air Force—were proving extremely effective against the Japanese in China. To check Chennault, the Japanese commenced a counteroffensive in east China. Seven of the 12 Fourteenth Air Force airfields were captured, and the cities of Kunming and Chungking were in danger of falling. At the request of China's premier Jiang Jieshi (Chiang Kai-shek), General Stilwell was recalled and replaced by Gen. Albert C. Wedemeyer. By December, combined army and Chinese forces, with air support from Chennault, brought the Japanese advances to a halt.

South and Southwest Pacific, 1944

By the end of March, the Solomons and the St. Mathias group of islands were solidly in Allied hands, and Rabaul was completely cut off. To the east, Saidor, the Admiralties, and New Britain all fell under Allied control early in the year. However, the Japanese resolved to hold on to western New Guinea at all costs. During March and April, combined U.S. and Australian forces encircled the Japanese position at Hollandia, New Guinea, inflicting extremely heavy casualties. From here, the islands of Wakde (May 17), Biak (May 27–June 29), Wewak and Aitape (June 28–August 5), Noemfoor (July 2–7), and Sansapor (July 30) were either neutralized or captured.

Central Pacific, 1944

Navy, marine, and army forces secured Kwajalein Island, in the Marshalls group, by February 7. Marines and army troops landed in the Eniwetok atoll on the island of Engebi. From here, they jumped off to Eniwetok Island and Parry Island, where, as usual, they had to overcome suicidal resistance. Eniwetok was secured as the rallying point for the large V Amphibious Force, a collection of warships and landing craft capable of delivering 127,000 men. From Eniwetok, a massive joint marine-army landing at Saipan was commenced on June 15. Although little air support was available, the ground forces slowly took Saipan, successfully fending off a suicidal counterattack on July 9. The conquest of this island was one of the bloodiest campaigns of the Central Pacific war. More than 3,000 Americans were killed and 13,160 wounded, while Japanese losses amounted to 27,000, including many hundreds of civilians who had committed suicide by jumping off the island's cliffs, having been told by the Japanese troops that the American soldiers would torture and even cannibalize them.

Amphibious and Ground Operations in the Philippines

"I shall return," General MacArthur promised when he left the Philippines at the outset of the war. The Saipan landings and the Battle of the Philippine Sea put American forces in a position to redeem that pledge. On September 15, 1944, MacArthur made a surprise landing on the island of Morotai, south of the Philippines. In coordination with this landing, Admiral Nimitz attacked Peleliu. There marines met much more formidable resistance from some 10,000 Japanese dug into coral caves and caverns, which afforded ideal defensive positions. It took a month of bitter fighting to reduce Peleliu, and then only with reinforcements from an army regiment.

Originally, the plan had been to advance from Morotai and Peleliu to Mindanao and Yap, but Admiral Halsey now recommended skipping these intermediate steps and immediately launching an invasion of Leyte, at the very center of the Philippine archipelago. This would split the 250,000-man Japanese army there. Thus divided, the enemy could be defeated first on Leyte, then on Luzon, and finally on Mindanao. The Leyte landings commenced on October 20 and extended through October 22. MacArthur arrived a few hours after a beachhead was established. After wading ashore, he mounted a radio truck and broadcast—"People of the Philippines: I have returned! By the grace of Almighty God our forces stand again on Philippine soil—soil consecrated in the blood of our two people. Rally to me!"

Retaking the Philippines was a slow and costly struggle, calling on the full resources of the navy, marines, and army. Naval operations prevented the Japanese from reinforcing the Philippines, and, on December 7, 1944, General Walter Krueger's army troops had joined advance U.S. forces already landed on Leyte. The island fell to the Americans before the end of the month. From here, MacArthur launched his assault against Luzon, and thence to Bataan. Manila fell in January, and the last Japanese garrison on the islands, at Corregidor, surrendered in February 1945. Mop-up operations, especially on Mindanao, continued almost to the very end of the war. It was not until July 5, 1945, that MacArthur formally declared that the Philippines had been retaken.

Italy, 1944

During January, the Fifth U.S. Army and British Eighth Army remained pinned down at the Rapido River. On January 22, an Anglo-American force of

50,000 landed at Anzio, virtually unopposed. Instead of immediately driving inland, however, Major General John P. Lucas delayed in consolidating his forces, a decision that allowed the German commander, Kesselring, to reinforce his positions in Anzio. During February 16–29, the Germans counterattacked, forcing Lucas into retreat. He was relieved by Major General Lucius K. Truscott, Jr. Although Truscott was a much more aggressive commander than Lucas, valuable momentum had been lost, and Anzio hardened into a costly stalemate.

Along the Rapido, the Fifth U.S. Army made three costly and futile assaults against the German line, which produced 23,860 U.S. and 9,203 British casualties before a massive frontal assault during May 11–25 finally broke through toward Rome, which Mark Clark entered on June 4. However, the Tenth German Army remained intact and continued to take a heavy toll on the Allies.

After the fall of Rome, the Allies advanced quickly to the Arno River during the summer of 1944. The Fifth U.S. Army crossed the river on August 26; however, although the Eighth British Army took Rimini on September 21, Clark was unable to capture Bologna during an October assault.

Operation Overlord

On June 6, 1944, the greatest invasion in history was launched against five beaches in Normandy. The two westernmost, designated Utah Beach and Omaha, were the targets of Omar Bradley's First U.S. Army. East of Omaha Beach were beaches designated Gold, Juno, and Sword, on which the Second British Army (with a Canadian corps attached) landed. Overall command of the invasion, the landing phase of which was designated Operation Overlord, was under General Dwight D. Eisenhower, and command of ground forces was given to British field marshal Sir Bernard Law Montgomery. The initial landing force consisted of about a million men, supported by another million troops in logistical formations. Two-thirds of the invasion force was American. In the initial landings, 176,000 troops were conveyed by 4,000 ships and landing craft escorted by 600 warships. Air support was provided by 2,500 heavy bombers and 7,000 fighters. Five divisions were ashore by nightfall, and beachheads were firmly established everywhere except on Omaha Beach, where German resistance was heaviest.

During June 7–18, the Allied invasion expanded, but the breakout from Normandy was impeded by the topography of the region, which was dense with *bocage,* hedgerows. By the end of the initial phases of the invasion—the conclusion of Operation Overlord—the Allies had suffered 122,000 casualties, whereas the German defenders lost perhaps 114,000 men.

Beginning on July 25, Operation Overlord gave way to Operation Cobra, the full breakout from the Normandy beachheads, as General Omar Bradley led the First U.S. Army against the German defenses west of St.-Lô. On August 1, the newly organized Third U.S. Army, under George S. Patton, took the Allied right and led the main breakout through Brittany by way of Avranches. This was the beginning of an extraordinary drive through France and, ultimately, Germany itself. Patton's armor swept through Brittany, then wheeled south into the Loire River valley while his infantry moved to the left toward Le Mans. Behind the Third Army, the First Army pivoted left.

On August 25, U.S. Army and Free French troops liberated Paris, marking a critical milestone in the invasion, and, by the early autumn, German forces were now isolated in western France. In the meantime, on August 15, Operation Anvil-Dragon got under way with landings on the Côte d'Azur by the Seventh U.S. Army (including elements of Free French forces) under Lieutenant General Alexander Patch. The campaign in southern France and the Rhône Valley cleared the Germans from southern France by the end of August. From here, the Seventh U.S. Army advanced north to the Vosges, linking up with Patton's Third Army and other elements as part of the general drive eastward. While American (and Free French) forces were advancing through central and southern France, the British concentrated on the north, pursuing the retreating Germans into the Low Countries. Unfortunately, this required diversion of fuel and other supplies from Bradley's army group (including Patton's Third Army), so that, on August 30, Third Army crossed the Meuse River, only, quite literally, to run out of gas.

Despite the slowdowns caused by logistical problems, the Allies closed in on the German frontier. British field marshal Montgomery's Operation Market Garden, a plan to seize intact the Rhine crossing at Arnhem and to secure the other bridges into Germany, failed, but Montgomery did enjoy other successes in the Low Countries.

In the meantime, Bradley's army group attacked the great German defenses of the Siegfried Line along Germany's western frontier. The Third U.S. Army reached Metz on October 3, and the First U.S. Army captured Aachen on October 21. Throughout November, the Allies conducted an all-out offensive against German forces west of the Rhine. During November 16–December 15, the Roer River–Hürtgen Forest region was heavily contested. South of this, Patton's Third Army swept through Lorraine while Allied forces, including the Free French, conducted operations in Alsace that resulted in the liberation of Mulhouse and Strasbourg.

Battle of the Bulge
By December 1944, it seemed as if Germany would soon collapse. However, Hitler mounted one final—and entirely unanticipated—counteroffensive aimed at delivering a violent blow that would split the Allies, then defeat them in detail north of the line formed by Antwerp, Brussels, and Bastogne. This Ardennes offensive, popularly called the Battle of the Bulge, commenced on December 16—a massive assault by 20 German divisions. Outnumbered and overwhelmed, the Allied forces scrambled to recover. Bradley ordered the U.S. 101ST AIRBORNE to join the 10th Armored Division to hold Bastogne. It was a desperate stand, but it bought time for Patton and the Third Army to turn 90 degrees to the north and advance against the German southern flank in the Ardennes. This turned the tide of the Battle of the Bulge, which, by January 1945, was over and won. The cost to the Allies was 7,000 killed, 33,400 wounded, and

21,000 captured or missing. German losses were about 120,000 killed, wounded, or captured. Except for a relatively minor action in Alsace and Lorraine during January 1945, the Ardennes action was the last German offensive of the war. As the British, Americans, and French closed in from the west, the Russians advanced from the east. Germany was squeezed between the jaws of a great Allied pincer.

Japan Fights On, 1945
By early 1945, it was clear that Germany was in irreversible collapse. In any meaningful military sense, Japan had also lost the war by this time. Yet surrender was an alien concept to the Japanese warrior class, and the war not only continued but, even as the Allied victories mounted, the toll of Allied casualties actually increased. Amid a naval blockade and continuous bombing, the army prepared to mount a full-scale—and, doubtless, monumentally costly—invasion of the Japanese homeland.

Iwo Jima, Okinawa
Possession of Iwo Jima, a rocky island in the Bonin group, only eight square miles in area, was vital to the ongoing U.S. advance against the Japanese mainland. The Japanese used it as a base for fighter aircraft to intercept incoming American bombers. The Americans wanted to clear the Japanese out and then, in turn, use Iwo Jima as a forward air base. The invasion of Iwo Jima began on February 19 and was carried out by the USMC, which completed the conquest on March 24, 1945.

Beginning in March, Operation Iceberg went into action: the conquest of the Ryukyu island group, midway between Formosa and Kyushu, the southernmost island of Japan itself. Admiral Raymond Spruance was designated to lead the Fifth Fleet in a massive amphibious movement to land the Tenth U.S. Army, XXIV Corps, and III Marine Amphibious Corps on Okinawa. Japanese defenses were extremely formidable, the Japanese Thirty-second Army numbering 130,000 and deployed within a carefully prepared system of defenses. After long initial preparation by naval and aerial bombardment, the landings took place during April 1–4. By the end of April, a stalemate stalled the advance on land, but once Japanese artillery has been neutralized, the invaders resumed the full offensive during May 11–31, which culminated in June when the Japanese headquarters was overrun. The commanders on both side perished in the great battle. General Simon Bolivar Buckner, Jr., was killed by an artillery round and Japan's Mitsuru Ushijima committed hara-kiri just before his headquarters was captured. Japanese casualties totaled 107,500 dead (it is believed an additional 20,000 were sealed—and therefore entombed—in their defensive caves during the fighting) and American casualties were in excess of 12,000 killed and 37,000 wounded. The fall of Okinawa brought with it the loss of what remained of Japan's navy and air force.

Victory in Italy

If the final Pacific battles were heartbreakingly slow and abundantly bloody, much the same can be said for Allied progress in Italy. It was April 1945 before the British Eighth Army managed to strike the German Tenth southeast of Bologna and, shortly after this, the Fifth U.S. Army broke into the Po Valley, sending the remaining German defenders into full retreat. The Fifth U.S. Army and the British Eighth pursued the retreating Germans far into northern Italy.

Advance to the Rhine

By early February 1945, the "Colmar Pocket," a position in the Vosges Mountains held by the German Nineteenth Army, was cleared, and British and American forces went on to clear the Rhineland through March.

On March 7, a task force of the U.S. 9th Armored Division in the vanguard of the First Army's advance found that the railroad bridge across the Rhine at Remagen had not been demolished by the enemy. They took and held the bridge, which greatly accelerated the Allied advance across the Rhine. On March 22, General Patton led the 5th Division across the Rhine at Oppenheim in a surprise crossing that met with virtually no resistance.

Within two days, army engineers had thrown multiple bridges across the river, and the Third Army began rolling into Germany en masse. Just behind Patton was British commander Montgomery, who crossed his forces above the Ruhr, north of the point where Patton crossed. On March 24, the Ninth U.S. Army breached the river at Dinslaken. The First U.S. Army broke out of Remagen on March 25 and moved over the Rhine there. Additional crossings followed before the end of the month.

As both the Western allies and the Russians raced through Germany, the army and the government collapsed. Adolf Hitler committed suicide on April 30, having appointed Admiral Karl Doenitz as his successor. Under Doenitz, an unconditional surrender was concluded during May 7–8 and an armistice put in place on May 8–9. World War II was ended in Europe.

Japan Surrenders

The capture of Iwo Jima enabled fighter aircraft to escort U.S. bombers round-trip into and out of Japan, greatly increasing the effectiveness of the air raids. All of Japan's major cities and industrial installations were hit and hit again. While fire rained from the sky, USN forces tightened the blockade around Japan, even as General MacArthur and Admiral Nimitz assembled an amphibious invasion force that would dwarf the forces that had landed at Normandy. However, the use of two newly developed atomic bombs, on Hiroshima (August 6) and Nagasaki (August 9), made the invasion (Operation Olympic and Operation Coronet) unnecessary. On August 14, Japanese emperor Hirohito accepted the Allied terms, a cease-fire was declared on August 15, and, on September 2, 1945, General MacArthur presided over the Japanese signing of the formal surrender document on the deck of the U.S. battleship *Missouri*, anchored in Tokyo Bay. World War II was over.

World War II Victory Medal   See DECORATIONS AND MEDALS.

X-Y

XM-8 Armored Gun System   See TRACKED
VEHICLES.

Yakima Training Center   See FORTS AND
OTHER INSTALLATIONS.

Yuma Proving Ground   See FORTS AND OTHER
INSTALLATIONS.

U.S. Army
Abbreviations and Acronyms

★ ───

AAC Army Acquisition Corps
ACDUTRA Active Duty for Training
ADA Air Defense Artillery
AERS Army Education Requirements System
AG Adjutant General (also abbreviation for "army green")
AGC Adjutant General Corps
AMC U.S. Army Materiel Command
AMCOM Aviation and Missile Command
AMD Air and Missile Defense
AMEDD Army Medical Department
AOR Area of Responsibility
AOS Area of Concentration
APC Armored Personnel Carrier
APFT Army Physical Fitness Test
APO Army Post office
AR Army Regulation
ARNG Army National Guard
AUSA Association of the United States Army
AWC U.S. Army War College
AWOL absent without leave
BCD discharge, bad conduct
BDU Battle Dress Uniform
BOQ Bachelor Officer Quarters
CAC Combined Arms Center
CASCOM Combined Arms Support Command
CECOM Communications-Electronics Command
CGSC Command and General Staff College

CIB Combat Infantryman Badge
CID Criminal Investigation Division
COLA cost-of-living allowance
CONUS Continental United States
CONUSA Continental United States Army
CONUSAs Continental United States Armies
CS Chief of Staff
CSA Chief of Staff, Army
CVC Combat Vehicle Crewman
DA Department of the Army
DBDU Desert Battle Dress Uniform
DCSI Deputy Chief of Staff for Intelligence
DCSLOG Deputy Chief of Staff for Logistics
DCSOPS Deputy Chief of Staff for Operations and Plans
DCSPER Deputy Chief of Staff for Personnel
DD discharge, dishonorable
DoD Department of Defense
DUI Distinctive Unit Insignia
DVQ Distinguished Visitor Quarters
EAC Echelon Above Corps
ECWCS Extended Cold-Weather Clothing System
EOD Explosive Ordnance Disposal
FM Field Manual
FORSCOM U.S. Army Forces Command
FTX Field Training Exercise
GCM general court-martial
GD discharge, general

HD   discharge, honorable
HEAP   High-Explosive-Armor-Piercing
HHC   Headquarters and Headquarters Company
HQ   Headquarters
HQDA   Headquarters, Department of the Army
ICAF   Industrial College of the Armed Forces
IG   Inspector General
INSCOM   U.S. Army Intelligence and Security Command
IOC   Industrial Operations Command
ITOW   Improved TOW
JAG   Judge Advocate General
JCS   Joint Chiefs of Staff
JDA   Joint Duty Assignment
JRTC   Joint Readiness Training Center
JSO   Joint Specialty Officer
JTAGS   Joint Tactical Ground Station
JTF   Joint Task Force
KP   Kitchen Police
MACOM   Major Army Command
MDW   U.S. Army Military District of Washington
MECH   Mechanized
MEDCOM   U.S. Army Medical Command
MEL   Military Education Level
MI   Military Intelligence
MOOTW   Military Operations Other Than War
MOS   Military Occupational Specialty
MP   Military Police
MSA   Morale Support Activity
MSC   Medical Service Corps
MTMC   Military Traffic Management Command
MWR   Morale, Welfare, and Recreation
NBC   Nuclear, Biological, Chemical
NCO   noncommissioned officer
NTC   National Training Center
OCO   Office, Chief of Ordnance
OCONUS   Outside the Continental United States
OCS   Officer Candidate School
OER   Officer Evaluation Report
OIC   Officer in Charge
OJT   on-the-job training
OMPF   Official Military Personnel File
OPMS   Officer Personnel Management System

OTRA   Other Than Regular Army
PAC   Personnel and Administration Center
PAO   Public Affairs Officer
PERSCOM   U.S. Total Army Personnel Command
PIO   Public Information Office
PM   Preventive Maintenance
PX   Post Exchange
QM   Quartermaster
QMC   Quartermaster Corps
R&R   rest and recuperation
RA   regular army
RDI   Regimental Distinctive Insignia
REMBASS   Remotely Monitored Battlefield Sensor System
RSO   Reconnaissance Staff Officer
SAM   Surface-to-Air Missile
SOP   Standing Operating Procedure
SSC   U.S. Army Soldier Systems Center
SSI   Shoulder Sleeve Insignia
STRICOM   Simulation, Training, and Instrumentation Command
TACOM   Tank-Automotive and Armaments Command
TAD   Temporary Additional Duty
TDY   Temporary Duty
TECOM   Test and Evaluation Command
TIG   Time in Grade
TIS   Time in Service
TM   Technical Manual
TOE   Table of Organization and Equipment
TOW   Tube-launched, Optically tracked, Wire-guided
TRAC   TRADOC Analysis Command
TRADOC   U.S. Army Training and Doctrine Command
TRANSCOM   Transportation Command
TWI   Training with Industry
TWOS   Total Warrant Officer System
UCMJ   Uniform Code of Military Justice
USA   United States Army
USACE   U.S. Army Corps of Engineers
USACIC   U.S. Army Criminal Investigation Command
USAISEC   U.S. Army Information Systems Engineering Command

USAMHI   U.S. Army Military History Institute
USAR   U.S. Army Reserve
USARC   United States Army Reserve Command
USAREUR   U.S. Army, Europe
USARJ   U.S. Army, Japan
USARPAC   U.S. Army, Pacific
USARSO   U.S. Army, South (USARSO)
USASAC   Security Assistance Command
USASOC   U.S. Army Special Operations Command

USAWC   U.S. Army War College
USMA   United States Military Academy (West Point)
USSOCOM   U.S. Special Operations Command
VOQ   Visiting Officer Quarters
VSI   Voluntary Separation Incentive
WAC   Women's Army Corps
WO   Warrant Officer
WOS   Warrant Officer Service

United States
Air Force

ENTRIES A–Z

Aerial Achievement Medal   See DECORA-
TIONS AND MEDALS.

Aeronautical Division, U.S. Army Signal Corps

Established on August 1, 1907, the Aeronautical Division of the U.S. Army Signal Corps was the earliest antecedent organization of the USAF. The commanding officer was Captain CHARLES DeFOR-EST CHANDLER, who was assigned two enlisted men—one of whom deserted.

The Aeronautical Division was primarily concerned with balloon operations (see BALLOONS AND DIRIGIBLES) until 1911. In July 1914, it was replaced by the AVIATION SECTION, U.S. ARMY SIGNAL CORPS.

Aerospace Defense Command (ADC)

Originally designated the Air Defense Command when it was established in 1946, the ADC was replaced during 1948–51 by CONTINENTAL AIR COMMAND (CONAC), then reestablished in 1951 as a MAJCOM. Its redesignation as the Aerospace Defense Command (ADC) came in 1965. ADC was responsible for the air defense of the continental United States, and, when NORAD was activated in 1957, integrating U.S. defense with that of Canada, ADC became a part of this command.

Over the years, the role of ADC was increasingly transferred to the AIR NATIONAL GUARD and the AIR FORCE RESERVE, and ADC was inactivated in 1980.

African Americans in the U.S. Air Force

African Americans have served in every war fought by the United States since the American Revolution. Typically, however, much of that service was performed in segregated units, and African Americans were afforded little opportunity to attain officer status or, indeed, to progress very far in a military career. Some 900,000 African Americans served during WORLD WAR II, mainly in the army. The exigencies of the war, however, together with a desire to demonstrate opposition to Nazi racist ideology, motivated the U.S. Coast Guard and, to a lesser extent, the U.S. Navy to integrate shipboard service. The marines and the army, including the U.S. ARMY AIR FORCES, remained segregated.

In 1940, President Franklin D. Roosevelt promoted Colonel BENJAMIN O. DAVIS, Sr., to brigadier general—the first African American of this rank—and opened the U.S. ARMY AIR CORPS to black pilots. One of these men, Davis's son, Benjamin O. Davis, Jr., was among the first of the TUSKEGEE AIR-MEN, a segregated unit of African-American fighter pilots trained at an airfield established at the Tuskegee Institute in Alabama. The Tuskegee Airmen served with distinction in the North African and Italian theaters, but they remained segregated throughout the war.

In 1948, President Harry S. Truman issued Executive Order 9981, which mandated an end to segregation in the military and a universal policy of equal treatment and opportunity regardless of race. Among the services, the USAF (an independent service as of 1947) stood at the forefront of implementing the integration policy. The army and the marines continued to maintain all-black units until 1951, during the KOREAN WAR—although the officer corps remained overwhelmingly white. As of 2005, African Americans make up about 15 percent of the total USAF population. Six percent of USAF officer are African American.

In 1975 Daniel "Chappie" James, Jr., one of the Tuskegee Airmen of World War II, became the first African-American four-star general in the USAF. In 1973, Thomas N. Barnes became the USAF's first African American CHIEF MASTER SERGEANT OF THE AIR FORCE, the highest noncommissioned rank in the service.

Air Combat Command (ACC)

ACC is a MAJCOM responsible for fighters, bombers, and reconnaissance aircraft based in the continental United States (CONUS) and for CONUS command, control, communications, and intelligence platforms. ACC also controls some theater AIRLIFT and tanker/refueling operations. ACC provides forces to unified commands and augments theater forces already deployed.

ACC was created in 1992 from elements of STRATEGIC AIR COMMAND (SAC), TACTICAL AIR COMMAND (TAC), and MILITARY AIRLIFT COMMAND

Gunners of the U.S. Fifth Air Force in Korea, September 1952   *(National Archives and Records Administration)*

A KC-135R Stratotanker has just refueled an F-16 Fighting Falcon. Three more F-16s wait their turn, as does an F-15C Eagle (the plane with the twin vertical stabilizers). *(U.S. Air Force)*

(MAC). It is headquartered at Langley AFB, Virginia.

Air Corps Act of 1926

On the recommendation of the President's Advisory Board, the Air Corps Act of 1926 raised the U.S. ARMY AIR SERVICE to a corps and renamed it the U.S. ARMY AIR CORPS. The act created the post of assistant secretary of war (for air), provided for air sections on the general staff, and authorized the addition of two general officers as assistant chiefs of the air corps. Rank, promotion, and pay status were raised for USAAC officers and enlisted men, and a five-year program was introduced to expand the USAAC from 919 to 1,650 officers, from 8,725 to 15,000 enlisted men, and from 1,254 aircraft to 1,800.

The approach and onset of the Great Depression reduced the funding authorized by the Air Corps Act by 55 percent, which meant that the goals of the five-year program were not realized by 1931; however, the quality, if not the quantity, of USAAC aircraft was substantially improved under the act.

Air Corps Training Center, San Antonio

Pursuant to the AIR CORPS ACT OF 1926, Brigadier General FRANK P. LAHM was put in command of U.S. ARMY AIR CORPS training. He wanted to concentrate training at a single airfield, and, in 1929, construction began on Randolph Field outside of San Antonio, Texas. The base became headquarters of the Air Corps Training Center in 1931 and, dubbed the "West Point of the Air," handled all primary flight training. Advanced flight training remained at Kelly Field, Texas. With the expansion of the USAAC in 1938 and later, training was extended to other facilities, and the mission of Randolph Field became mainly the training of instructor pilots. Further expansion of the USAAC in 1940 brought extensive reorganization of training under a new Training and Operations Division of the Office, Chief of Air Corps, and three Air Corps Training Centers were established, at Maxwell Field, Alabama, at Moffett Field, California, and at Randolph.

aircraft, cold war and after

The cold war spanned roughly 1948 through the collapse of the Soviet Union in 1991. This period encompasses the KOREAN WAR and the VIETNAM WAR (see AIRCRAFT, KOREAN WAR and AIRCRAFT, VIETNAM WAR), and some of the aircraft described in this article were used in those conflicts; however, most of the aircraft included here were intended primarily for strategic roles or other roles directly related to cold war conflicts.

Attack (designated "A") Aircraft

A-10 Thunderbolt II: Korea, Vietnam, and various "brushfire" conflicts of the cold war period pointed up the need for the strategically oriented USAF to add specially designed tactical aircraft to its inventory. The A/OA-10 Thunderbolt II was the first USAF aircraft specially designed for CLOSE AIR SUPPORT of ground forces. The aircraft has excellent maneuverability at low air speeds and altitude and serves as a highly accurate weapons-delivery platform. Advanced electronics give A-10s night-vision capability, and redundant primary structural sections endow it with the kind of survivability necessary in close air support. Armament includes a 30-mm GAU-8/A Gatling gun, which can fire 3,900 rounds a minute, and AGM-65 Maverick and AIM-9 Sidewinder missiles (see MISSILES, TACTICAL).

Fairchild Republic delivered the first production A-10A in October 1975. The aircraft saw extensive service in the PERSIAN GULF WAR, launching 90 percent of the AGM-65 Maverick missiles used in the conflict. Top speed is 420 mph, ceiling is 45,000 feet, and range is 800 miles. The aircraft can carry up to 16,000 pounds of mixed ordnance on eight underwing and three under-fuselage pylon stations,

The XB-70 Valkyrie lands on the main, 15,000-foot runway of Edwards AFB, California, during the 1960s. *(U.S. Air Force)*

including 500 pounds of Mk-82 and 2,000 pounds of Mk-84 series low/high drag bombs, incendiary cluster bombs, combined effects munitions, mine dispensing munitions, AGM-65 Maverick missiles, and laser-guided/electro-optically guided bombs, infrared countermeasure flares, electronic counter-measure chaff, jammer pods, 2.75-inch (6.99-centimeter) rockets, illumination flares, and AIM-9 Sidewinder missiles.

Bomber (designated "B") Aircraft

B-52 Stratofortress (see AIRCRAFT, VIETNAM WAR)

B-57 Canberra: The Martin Company derived, under licenses, the B-57 from a British design, English Electric's Canberra B.Mk.2, and it was thus the only non-U.S. design used in the USAF after WORLD WAR II. The B-57A first flew in 1953 and entered service the following year. Sixteen B-57Bs were later converted for night intruder operations and 11 aircraft saw Vietnam service. Most extensively used in operations directly relating to the cold war was the reconnaissance version, the RB-57D, which was the principal USAF "spy" plane before the U-2. Other Canberras were converted into EB-57Es, for aerospace electronic warfare. The last Canberras left service (with the AIR NATIONAL GUARD) in 1982. Top speed was 598 mph, service ceiling was 40,100 feet, and range was 2,300 miles. The Canberra could carry 9,200 pounds of bombs, including nuclear weapons.

B-70 Valkyrie: Conceived in the 1950s, the B-70 was intended for use by the STRATEGIC AIR COMMAND (SAC) as its principal high-altitude bomber, which could fly at Mach 3, and would replace the subsonic B-52 as a nuclear weapons delivery platform. Funding cutbacks aborted production, however, and only two were built, with XB-70 designations, indicating their status as research aircraft for the advanced study of aerodynamics, propulsion, and other issues related to large supersonic aircraft. The Valkyrie was built largely of stainless-steel honeycomb sandwich panels and titanium. The Number 1 XB-70 made its initial flight on September 21, 1964, and achieved Mach 3 flight on October 14, 1965. The Number 2 airplane first flew on July 17, 1965, but crashed on June 8,

1966, following a mid-air collision. Number 1 was retired on February 4, 1969.

This beautiful aircraft has a delta-wing span of 105 feet and a fuselage length of almost 186 feet. Its six jet engines propel it to a top speed of 2,056 mph (Mach 3.1). Range is 4,288 miles and service ceiling is 77,350 feet.

B-1 Lancer: The B-1, now the backbone of the USAF's long-range bomber force, had a difficult birth. The original B-1A model never went into production, although the USAF acquired four prototype flight test models in the 1970s and continued tests through 1981. In that year, President Ronald Reagan approved production of the improved variant B-1B, and the first production model flew in October 1984, with the first delivery made in June 1985. The final B-1B was delivered on May 2, 1988.

The B-1B is of an advanced blended wing/body configuration, and it features variable-geometry design to maximize performance at sub- and supersonic speeds. The aircraft was first used in combat against Iraq during Operation Desert Fox in December 1998. The aircraft have been used in Operation Allied Force and in the campaign in Afghanistan in response to the September 11, 2001, terrorist attacks on the United States. Built by Boeing, the B-1B has a top speed in excess of 900 mph and an intercontinental range. Its service ceiling is in excess of 30,000 feet. Three internal weapons bays can accommodate up to 84 Mk-82 general purpose bombs or Mk-62 naval mines, 30 CBU-87/89 cluster munitions or CBU-97 sensor-fused weapons and up to 24 GBU-31 JDAM GPS guided bombs or Mk-84 general purpose bombs. The USAF has acquired more than 70 of the aircraft.

B-2 Spirit: One of two radar-foiling "stealth" aircraft in the USAF inventory (see F-117 Nighthawk), the B-2 Spirit is a multirole bomber capable of delivering both conventional and nuclear munitions. The bomber's stealth characteristics (reduced infrared, acoustic, electromagnetic, visual, and radar signatures) make it ideal for penetrating deep into enemy airspace.

The aircraft was developed in deep secrecy, and the first B-2 was publicly displayed on November

22, 1988. Its first flight came on July 17, 1989, and the first operational aircraft was delivered on December 17, 1993. The principal contractor is Northrop Grumman Integrated Systems Sector, with Boeing Military Airplanes Company, Hughes Radar Systems Group, General Electric Aircraft Engine Group, and Vought Aircraft Industries, Inc. Capable of reaching high subsonic speeds, with a service ceiling of 50,000 feet, the B-2 carries a 40,000-pound payload of conventional or nuclear weapons. The USAF inventory includes 21 operational aircraft, in addition to one test aircraft.

Cargo and Transport (designated "C") Aircraft

C-10A Extender: This modification of the McDonnell Douglas DC-10 commercial transport for military tanker and cargo use first flew in 1980, with active service beginning the next year; 59 were built. The three-engine jet aircraft can carry a 169,000-pound payload over 4,370 miles at about 600 mph and to a service ceiling of 42,000 feet.

C-17A Globemaster: The Boeing C-17 is capable of rapid strategic delivery of troops and all types of cargo to main operating bases or directly to forward bases in the deployment area. In addition, the aircraft can perform tactical airlift and airdrop missions. Measuring 174 feet long with a wingspan of 169 feet, 10 inches, the aircraft is powered by four jet engines. Cargo is loaded through a large aft door that accommodates military vehicles and palletized cargo, to a maximum payload of 170,900 pounds. Unrefueled range is 2,400 nautical miles; cruise speed is approximately 450 knots (.74 Mach). Despite its size, the aircraft can operate through short, poorly improved airfields.

First flight was on September 15, 1991, and the first production model was delivered on June 14, 1993.

C-18: This designation was applied to eight Boeing 707-323Cs acquired by the USAF from American Airlines for training and support missions. They were subsequently modified as EC-18B Advanced Range Instrumentation Aircraft, for use in the U.S. space program as telemetry platforms. Two were further modified to EC-18C Joint STAR aircraft (see E-8A Joint STARS, below).

C-25: These two aircraft are military variants of the Boeing 747-200 "jumbo jet" commercial transports. Further modified as VC-25A in 1990, they are used for presidential airlift as AIR FORCE ONE. The aircraft are capable of in-air refueling.

C-47 Skytrain (see AIRCRAFT, WORLD WAR II)

C-54 Skymaster (see AIRCRAFT, WORLD WAR II)

C-121 Constellation (see AIRCRAFT, KOREAN WAR)

C-135 Stratolifter: The Boeing C-135 Stratolifter was the first USAF strategic jet transport. It went into service in 1961. Although originally designed as a cargo transport, 732 of 820 actually built were tankers. Others were converted for use in a variety of roles: In 1961, the Strategic Air Command (SAC) used an EC-135 conversion as the "Looking Glass" electronic warfare aircraft, an airborne command and control post to be used in the event that the SAC underground command center and other alternates were lost. Although the last plane was delivered in 1965, special reconnaissance missions still use RC-135s, and another modification, the NKC-135A, is flown in test programs for AIR FORCE SYSTEMS COMMAND (AFSC). AIR COMBAT COMMAND (ACC) operates the OC-135s as an observation platform in compliance with the Open Skies Treaty. Top speed is 600 mph, service ceiling, 45,000 feet, and range, 4,625. The aircraft can carry 126 troops or 44 litter patients and 48 ambulatory, with six attendants.

C-137 and VC-137: Based on the Boeing 707-153, the C-137 is a military passenger transport. In 1959, a VC-137 became the first jet aircraft to be used for presidential airlift as Air Force One. Modified as EC-137Ds, the aircraft became the backbone of the AWACS system. See E-3 Sentry (AWACS), next.

Electronic Warfare (designated "E") Aircraft

E-3 Sentry (AWACS): The E-3 Sentry is an airborne warning and control system (AWACS) aircraft that provides all-weather surveillance, command, control, and communications needed by commanders of U.S., NATO, and other allied air defense forces. The E-3 Sentry is a modified Boeing 707/320 commercial airframe equipped most conspicuously with a large rotating radar dome housing a radar subsystem that permits surveillance from the earth's surface up into the stratosphere, over land or water. The E-3 fleet is continuously upgraded with cutting-edge electronics to gather and present broad and detailed battlefield information in real time.

Engineering, test, and evaluation began on the first E-3 Sentry in October 1975; first deliveries came in March 1977. The USAF has 33 E-3s in its inventory. The aircraft's optimum cruising speed is 360 mph with a ceiling above 29,000 feet. Unrefueled endurance is in excess of eight hours.

E-4: This modification of the Boeing 747-200 commercial transport was selected for service as the Advanced Airborne National Command Post (AANCP), the communications link between the U.S. National Command Authority and the armed forces. The latest iteration is the E-4B. Like the C-25 and VC-25, these aircraft can be refueled in flight for unlimited endurance.

E-8A Joint STARS: A modification of ED-18D aircraft (also see *C-137 and VC-137*), two aircraft serve in the Joint Surveillance and Target Attack Radar System (Joint STARS) mission. The E-8A first flew in 1988. A joint undertaking of the USAF and U.S. Army, JSTARS directs attacks by ground forces with extreme precision. The aircraft performed extraordinary service in the Persian Gulf War, and, as of 2002, a program was under way to build at least 22 E-8As.

Fighter (designated "F") Aircraft

F-106 Delta Dart: This all-weather interceptor was developed by Convair from its F-102 "Delta Dagger" and was originally designated the F-102B. The first flight was December 26, 1956, and deliveries to the USAF began in July 1959. Production ended in late 1960, after 277 F-106As and 63 F-106Bs had been built. Top speed was 1,525 mph, range, 1,500 miles, and service ceiling, 53,000 feet.

F-15 Eagle: This all-weather air-superiority fighter was built by McDonnell during the early

1970s and first flew in July 1972. Deliveries began in November 1974. The single-seat F-15C and two-seat F-15D models entered the USAF inventory beginning in 1979. The aircraft have been continuously upgraded with an improved central computer; a programmable armament control set, allowing for advanced versions of the AIM-7, AIM-9, and AIM-120A missiles; and an expanded tactical electronic warfare system, which provides improvements to the ALR-56C radar warning receiver and ALQ-135 countermeasure set; and a highly advanced radar system. F-15C, D, and E models were deployed during the Persian Gulf War and achieved a confirmed 26:0 kill ratio, accounting for 36 of the 39 USAF air-to-air victories. Top speed of the F-15 is 1,875 mph, ceiling is 65,000 feet, and range is 3,450 with conformal fuel tanks and three external fuel tanks. The aircraft is typically armed with one internally mounted M-61A1 20-mm six-barrel cannon with 940 rounds of ammunition; four AIM-9L/M Sidewinder and four AIM-7F/M Sparrow air-to-air missiles, or eight AIM-120 AMRAAMs, carried externally.

F-16 Fighting Falcon: The sleek, compact, highly agile F-16 is a multirole fighter used in air-to-air combat and air-to-surface attack. The F-16A first flew in December 1976, and the first operational F-16A was delivered in January 1979. The F-16B is a two-seat model with tandem cockpits. Many iterations have kept the F-16 at the cutting edge of avionics and weapons delivery. In the Persian Gulf War, F-16s flew more sorties than any other aircraft and were used to attack airfields, military production facilities, Scud missiles sites, and a variety of other targets. Produced by Lockheed Martin, the F-16 reaches 1,500 mph and has a ceiling above 50,000 feet. Its ferry range exceeds 2,000 miles. Typically, the aircraft is armed with one M-61A1 20-mm multibarrel cannon with 500 rounds; external stations can carry up to six air-to-air missiles, conventional air-to-air and air-to-surface munitions, and electronic countermeasure pods.

F-111 Aardvark: Development of the F-111 took place amid much controversy over effectiveness and cost. Its principal feature is its variable-

An F-16C Fighting Falcon banks right, revealing the dome of its ordnance load.   *(U.S. Air Force)*

sweep wings, which allow the pilot to fly from slow approach speeds to supersonic velocity at sea level and more than twice the speed of sound at higher altitudes. Using internal fuel only, the plane has a range of more than 2,500 nautical miles and can carry conventional as well as nuclear weapons. The aircraft first flew in December 1964 and delivery began in October 1967. Some aircraft were used in Vietnam. F-111F models were deployed during the Persian Gulf War. The last F model was delivered to the USAF in November 1976.

The F-111F reaches Mach 2.5 at its ceiling of 60,000 feet and has a range of 3,565 miles with external fuel tanks. It can carry up to four nuclear bombs on four pivoting wing pylons, and two in an internal weapons bay. Wing pylons carry a total external load of 25,000 pounds of bombs, rockets, missiles, or fuel tanks. After 30 years of service, the F-111 was retired in 1997.

F-117A Nighthawk: The F-117A Nighthawk was the world's first "stealth" aircraft, designed to be virtually invisible to radar, infrared, and other detection technologies. A single-seat, twin-engine fighter, the F-117A was first delivered in 1982 by Lockheed. The last delivery was in the summer of 1990. Its exact speed is classified, but known to be in the high subsonic range. It was used with great success in the Persian Gulf War and in subsequent conflicts.

YF-22 Raptor: In conjunction with Lockheed Martin (now Lockheed-Boeing-General Dynamics) and Pratt and Whitney, Boeing developed the F-22 Raptor as a replacement for the F-15C. As of the end of 2001, USAF plans were to procure 339 F-22s, and production was scheduled to run through 2013. Budget constraints for F-Y2006 may limit acquisition to 180 aircraft at a staggering cost of $330 million each.

The stealthy air superiority fighter began delivery in November 2001. It first flew in May 1998. Maximum speed is in excess of Mach 1.8, and ceiling is above 50,000 feet.

Reconnaissance and Surveillance (designated "U" and "SR") Aircraft

U-2: The most famous "spy" plane in history, the peculiar designation of this Lockheed craft, "U," for "utility," was used to *disguise,* not to express, its

U-2 "Dragon Lady"   *(National Archives)*

purpose: high-altitude surveillance deep in enemy (primarily Soviet) airspace. The aircraft was a fixture of the cold war (made most famous when one, piloted by Francis Gary Powers, was shot down over the USSR in 1960), played a central role in the Cuban missile crisis of 1962, and served in Vietnam and the Persian Gulf War as well as other conflicts. The "Skunk Works" team of famed Lockheed designer Kelly Johnson began work on the U-2 in 1954, first flight was 1955, and delivery began soon afterward. The U-2R, a major redesign, was executed in 1966.

The U-2 has a single jet and is relatively slow—top speed 528 mph—but capable of reaching very high altitude—70,000 feet. Its range is also great at 4,600 miles.

SR-71 "Blackbird": This "strategic reconnaissance" aircraft is one of aviation's truly spectacular achievements. With a maximum speed in excess of 2,000 mph, it is the fastest jet aircraft ever built. Its

The SR-71 Blackbird aircraft   *(National Archives)*

range is 2,900 miles, and its service ceiling is 85,000 feet, higher than any other conventional jet and at the very edge of what an air-breathing engine is capable of operating in. The first flight took place on December 22, 1964, and the first SR-71 entered service in January 1966. The fleet was retired on January 26, 1990, but some aircraft were returned to service in 1995 and began flying operational missions in January 1997. Recently, the SR-71 was permanently retired by the USAF, although NASA still uses one for experimental purposes.

From 80,000 feet, the SR-71 could survey 100,000 square miles of the earth's surface each hour. The jet is unarmed.

Helicopter (designated "H")

HH-60G Pave Hawk: The Sikorsky HH-60G Pave Hawk is designed to conduct day or night operations into hostile environments to recover downed aircrew or other isolated personnel during war. The helicopter also performs civil search and rescue, emergency aeromedical evacuation (MEDEVAC), disaster relief, international aid, counterdrug activities, and NASA space shuttle support. It is a highly modified version of the U.S. Army Black Hawk helicopter, with upgraded communications and navigation equipment, automatic flight control system, night vision goggles, and a forward looking infrared (FLIR) system. It can be refueled in flight and is armed with two crew-served 7.62-mm machine guns. The twin-engine helicopter achieves a 184 mph top speed and has a range of 445 miles (with in-air refueling, unlimited). It was first deployed in 1982. USAF inventory currently includes 64, with 18 in the Air National Guard, and 23 in the Air Force Reserve.

aircraft, interwar period (1919–1940)

Even after WORLD WAR I demonstrated the importance of the airplane in combat, the United States was slow to develop military aviation. The aircraft included in this entry are planes developed and *used* after World War I but before World War II. A number of famous planes were developed before World War II but were manufactured and used pri-

marily during that war; these are treated in AIRCRAFT, WORLD WAR II.

Attack (designated "A") Aircraft

A-12 Shrike: Attack aircraft are primarily intended for the CLOSE AIR SUPPORT role. The A-12 entered service in 1932 as an all-metal monoplane built by Curtiss. It served into the early months of World War II—until 1942—and was capable of a 177 mph top speed with a 15,150-foot service ceiling. Its bomb load was 400 pounds.

A-17: The Northrup A-17 became the principal attack plane of the U.S. ARMY AIR CORPS during the interwar years. It entered service in 1935 and could hit 220 mph with a service ceiling of 19,400 feet. It carried 400 pounds in bombs.

Bomber (designated "B") Aircraft

Martin bombers: The series of bombers designed by Glenn Martin of the Glenn L. Martin Company immediately following World War I came in response to a U.S. ARMY AIR SERVICE order for a bomber superior to Britain's famed Handley Page. The MB-1 first flew in 1918, but it was never used as a bomber; a few were used as observation planes and at least one as a transport. The MB-2, derived from the MB-1, went into production in 1920. It was MB-2s that WILLIAM MITCHELL used in 1921 to demonstrate the effectiveness of aerial bombardment against large naval vessels. The aircraft carried a 2,000-pound bomb load at 99 mph to a ceiling of 8,500 feet.

Keystone Bomber: Used by the USAAS and then the U.S. ARMY AIR CORPS from 1923 to 1933, the Keystone Bomber (manufactured by the Keystone Aircraft Corporation) replaced the MB-2 and was produced in several versions. The LB-6 ("Light Bomber") achieved 114 mph and had a service ceiling of 11,650 feet. It carried a bomb load of 2,000 pounds and was especially significant as the vehicle the USAAC used to develop its early doctrine of strategic bombing (see BOMBING, STRATEGIC).

B-9: This Boeing design was the first all-metal monoplane bomber used by the USAAC. It was based on the design of the company's Model 200 Monomail commercial transport and first flew in

1931. The twin-engine craft had a top speed of 188 mph and a service ceiling of 20,750 feet. Bomb load was 2,260 pounds.

B-10: Built by the Glenn L. Martin Company, the twin-engine B-10 (followed by the B-12 and B-14) was the first *mass-produced* all-metal bomber used by the USAAC. The aircraft entered production in 1934 and was capable of 213 mph and could reach a service ceiling of 24,200 feet with a bomb load of 2,260 pounds.

B-15: Boeing built the four-engine B-15 in response to a USAAC order for a bomber that could hit targets as far away as Alaska and Hawaii. It first flew in 1937 and had a range of 5,130 miles, a top speed of 200 mph, and a service ceiling of 18,900 feet. Underpowered, it was not used as a bomber in World War II but did serve as a transport. Lessons learned in designing the aircraft were incorporated into the famed B-17 Flying Fortress, which is discussed in AIRCRAFT, WORLD WAR II.

B-18 Bolo: This Douglas Aircraft Company twin-engine design was intended to replace the B-10 by doubling its bomb load and range. Capable of flying at 215 mph, with a service ceiling of 10,000 feet, the B-18 could carry a 6,500-pound bomb load over a range of 1,150 miles. The USAAC ordered 217, making the B-18 the most common bomber in the service during the mid-1930s. Production stopped just before World War II, in 1940, but some were converted to transport use (as the C-58) during the war.

B-19: The Douglas B-19 never entered production, but, designed in 1935 and first flown in 1941, it was an important experiment in long-range bomber design and prefigured the B-29 of World War II and the B-36 of the KOREAN WAR and Cold War eras. The four-engine B-19 had a spectacular 212-foot wingspan, could hit 224 mph, reach 39,000 feet, and carry a 37,100-pound bomb load over 7,710 miles.

Fighter (designated "FM" for fighter, multiplace) and Pursuit (designated "P") Aircraft

FM-1 Airacuda: Bell Aircraft Corporation built only a dozen twin-engine Airacudas during the 1930s as long-range interceptors. The design was unique, with the props mounted as pushers rather than tractors and a gunner armed with a 37-mm and .30-caliber gun forward of each engine. In the fuselage, there were .50-caliber and .30-caliber guns as well. The Airacuda carried a small bomb load. Although faster (270 mph) than the bombers of the day, the Airacuda was not as fast as most single-engine pursuit and fighter craft.

P-1, P-3, P-5, P-6, P-23: These aircraft, all built by Curtiss, were the principal USAAC fighters (then designated "pursuit" planes) of the 1920s. The P-6 was the most advanced of this series (the P-23 was simply a modification of the P-6) and emerged in 1927. With a top speed of 193 mph, the P-6 had a service ceiling of 23,900 feet and a range of 244 miles. The Curtiss company called the series the "Hawks," but this never became an official USAAC designation.

P-12: This Boeing design first flew in 1929 and would be the last of the biplane fighters. The U.S. Navy also adopted the aircraft, as the F4B. The P-12 had a top speed of 189 mph and a service ceiling of 29,300 feet.

P-26: As the P-12 was the last biplane fighter in the USAAC inventory, so the P-26 was the first monoplane fighter produced for the service. Built by Boeing, it first flew in 1932 and was produced in a total quantity of 184. Top speed was 234 mph, with a service ceiling of 27,400 feet, and a range of 360 miles.

P-35: Designed by Seversky Aircraft Corporation (subsequently renamed Republic Aircraft Corporation), the P-35 was accepted by the USAAC in 1937; 77 were ordered before production ended in 1940. Forty-eight of these aircraft were lost when the Japanese attacked the Philippines in 1941. Capable of a 290 mph top speed and a 31,400-foot service ceiling, the P-35 had a range of 950 miles.

P-36: Curtiss-Wright received a USAAC contract for 210 P-36s, to that time, the largest order the service had ever placed. The all-aluminum aircraft was the USAAC's frontline fighter through the first months of World War II. It could reach 323 mph and attain a service ceiling of 32,700 feet. Range was 650 miles.

Observation (designated "O") Aircraft

O-1 Falcon: A Curtiss Aeroplane and Motor Company update of the kind of observation planes common in World War I, the O-1 Falcon was accepted by the USAAC in 1925 and was produced in relatively small numbers, but in several variations. Top speed was 140 mph; service ceiling, 15,300 feet.

O-47: A single-engine, canopied monoplane, this observation aircraft accommodated three crewmembers: pilot, observer, and gunner. General Aviation Company, renamed North American Aviation, began production in 1937, the first model flew the following year, and the plane became the standard observation craft for the USAAC. By the time World War II began, the O-47 was already obsolete. The plane could reach 221 mph and had a service ceiling of 23,200 feet.

Trainer (designated "PT," primary trainer) Aircraft

PT-1: Consolidated Aircraft Corporation built 171 PT-1s for USAAS and USAAC during the 1920s and into the 1930s. The aircraft design went through many iterations, finally becoming the BT-7, a basic trainer. The most typical version, PT-3A, flew at 102 mph to a ceiling of 14,000 feet.

PT-13 Kaydet: Built by Stearman Aircraft Company, the PT-13 Kaydet was one of the most successful trainers ever built. It was first ordered by the USAAC in 1936 and was used throughout World War II. Some 5,000 were built for the USAAC and USAAF; the U.S. Navy also ordered many, as did foreign air forces. After the war, the Kaydets, more familiarly called Stearmans, were frequently used as crop dusters and for aerobatics in air shows. Top speed was 135 mph, and the service ceiling was 13,200 feet.

aircraft, Korean War

While many of the aircraft flown during this war had also been used in WORLD WAR II (see AIRCRAFT, WORLD WAR II), the KOREAN WAR saw the transition from piston power to jet propulsion, especially in the realm of the fighter.

Bomber (designated "B") Aircraft

B-26 Invader (see AIRCRAFT, WORLD WAR II)

B-35: Developed on the eve of the Korean War era, this "flying wing," designed by Jack Northrup of Northrop Aviation, was intended as the new wave of bomber design. Stability problems caused cancellation of production; however, the concept of a plane without a traditional fuselage and tail section, or with the fuselage incorporated into the wing as a "lifting body," concepts pioneered in this aircraft and in the B-49, would emerge again in the B-2 and F-117 stealth aircraft of the late cold war era (see AIRCRAFT, COLD WAR AND AFTER).

B-49: The B-49, converted from the B-35, addressed stability problems with the "flying wing" design—but not satisfactorily enough to warrant full production. The USAF opted for the far more conservative and conventional B-36 Peacemaker.

The B-49 was powered by six turbojets and could achieve a top speed of 520 mph.

B-36 Peacemaker: The B-36 was a hybrid transition between the age of piston power and the age of the jet. Built by Consolidated-Vultee, it was intended to replace the B-29 as the platform from which nuclear weapons could be deployed. Design work began as early as 1941, and the plane first flew in 1946. Operational during the Korean War, it was never used in combat. Its main purpose was as a bomber for the STRATEGIC AIR COMMAND (SAC), capable of carrying nuclear weapons to the Soviet Union.

The B-36 was enormous, heavy, and ungainly in appearance. It had a 230-foot wingspan and a fuselage 162 feet long. Gross weight was 410,000 pounds. While its six pusher piston engines and four turbojets allowed it to carry five tons of bombs over 6,800 miles, it was slow at 411 mph and had a limited service ceiling of 36,400 feet, making it very vulnerable to Soviet fighters, which could fly faster and higher. A total of 385 of the aircraft were built.

B-45 Tornado: Built by North American, the Tornado was the first U.S. production jet bomber. It was also the first aircraft to combine a tactical role with the ability to carry nuclear weapons. Design work had begun in 1945, before World War

II ended, and the plane made its first flight in 1947. It served for 10 years, between 1948 and 1958, and 143 were delivered. In addition to the bomber configuration, a reconnaissance version, RB-45, was also built. The B-45 was used in Korea, but not in areas controlled by MiGs. The B-45 was the first aircraft to demonstrate the feasibility of in-air refueling, in 1950.

Capable of making 589 mph and with a service ceiling of 43,200 feet, the B-45 could carry 22,000 pounds of bombs over 1,910 miles.

B-47 Stratojet: This medium-range jet bomber prefigured the great strategic warhorse, the B-52 Stratofortress (see AIRCRAFT, VIETNAM WAR). With a three-man crew, and powered by six turbojets, it could carry 20,000 pounds of bombs (including nuclear weapons) at 606 mph over a 4,000-mile range. Service ceiling was 40,500 feet.

The B-47 first flew in 1947 and was produced by Douglas and, under license, by Lockheed in large numbers: 2,040 planes. An RB-47 variant was used for photo reconnaissance. By 1965, the Stratojet was withdrawn from Strategic Air Command service as nuclear deterrence became increasingly invested in missiles (see MISSILES, STRATEGIC).

B-50 Superfortress: The B-50, a piston-driven bomber (some variants added two turbojets), resembled the B-29, but with greater power. It was intended as an interim bomber until the B-47 could be made fully operational. Between 1945 and 1953, 370 were produced. Although fully operational during the Korean War, the B-50 was not used in combat. It did appear briefly during the VIETNAM WAR, in 1964–65, just as it was being retired.

The B-50's top speed was 380 mph, its service ceiling 36,700 feet, range 4,900 miles, and bomb capacity 20,000 pounds.

Cargo and Transport (designated "C") Aircraft

C-46 Commando (see AIRCRAFT, WORLD WAR II)

C-47 Skytrain (see AIRCRAFT, WORLD WAR II)

C-82 Packet: The Fairchild Packet was designed in 1941 and first flew in 1944. The 100 ordered arrived too late for service in World War II, but they were used in Korea for tactical airlift. Between 1945 and 1948, 220 were built. The principal feature of this two-engine freighter was its large cargo hold, which gave direct access for ground-level loading. Top speed was 248 mph, service ceiling was 21,200 feet, and range 1,920 miles.

C-119 Flying Boxcar: This Fairchild design was developed from the C-82 Packet and produced by Fairchild and, under license, by the Kaiser Manufacturing Corporation. It made its first flight it 1947 and, by the time production ceased in 1955, more than 1,100 had been built. The C-119 was used extensively in Korea in paratroop drops as well as in aerial resupply. In the Vietnam War, the C-119 was used as a gunship, the AC-119, in two variants, the AC-119G (with four 7.62-mm Gatling guns) and the AC-119K (with two M-61s and two turbojets for added thrust).

The standard C-119 had a top speed of 281 mph, a service ceiling of 21,580, a range of 1,630 miles, and a payload of 62 troops, with equipment.

C-121 Constellation: The Constellation was a highly successful passenger transport, which the USAAF commandeered from Lockheed production lines for military service. In World War II, the aircraft began service in 1943 as the C-69. An improved design appeared after the war and, in addition to the extensive civilian production, it was used as a military passenger transport, designated C-121A and VC-121A. The latter configuration was used to transport VIPs, including Dwight Eisenhower, first as NATO commander and then as U.S. president, and Douglas MacArthur. In 1953, a larger version, the C-121C, was modified as the RC-121C, the TC-121C, and the EC-121C, all reconnaissance aircraft. The EC-121C was equipped with advanced electronics and served during the Vietnam War as the "College Eye" surveillance aircraft.

The C-121G (corresponding to the civilian Super-G Constellation) had four engines, a distinctive tailplane with three vertical stabilizers, and a 123-foot wingspan. Its top speed was 368 mph with a service ceiling of 22,300 feet and a range of 2,100 miles.

C-124 Globemaster II: Designed in 1949 as a larger improvement on the C-74 Globemaster, the Globemaster II was the first of the USAF's "heavy lifters." It first flew in 1949 and deliveries began in 1950. Built by Douglas, it had a double-decker cargo hold, equipped with ramps and elevators to accommodate vehicles and cargo on both decks. Two hundred troops, with equipment, could be accommodated—a total payload of 26,375 pounds. Top speed was 271 mph, service ceiling 18,400 feet, and range 4,030 miles.

Fighter (designated "F") Aircraft

F-80 Shooting Star: The USAF's first operational jet fighter, the F-80 was also modified as the T-33 trainer and the F-94 Starfire interceptor. The first Shooting Star flew in January 1944, but it saw no combat in World War II. It came into its own during the Korean War and engaged in the first dogfight between jets, on November 15, 1950,

when an F-80 shot down a MiG-15. The F-94 Starfire, the last of the F-80 line, was retired in 1959.

With a top speed of 543 mph, the F-80 had a service ceiling of 47,500 feet.

F-84 Thunderjet, Thunderstreak, and Thunderflash: The Republic Aviation Corporation began design work on the F-84 in 1944, essentially modifying a piston-driven design to accommodate a jet engine. The first flight of the F-84 took place in 1946 and service began two years later. F-84s served in the Korean War as B-29 escorts, but they soon proved too vulnerable to the superior MiG-15. F-84 use was restricted to an attack role. Republic built 4,457 Thunderjets, but also worked on a redesign with swept wings. This resulted in the F-84F Thunderstreak, which began service in 1954; 2,711 were built. Another variant was the F-84F Thunderflash, built by General Motors. Yet another variant, the RF-84F Thunderflash, was modified

A formation of four Shooting Stars in their training configuration, as T-33As   *(U.S. Air Force)*

with a retractable hook, so that it could be launched and retrieved from a trapeze device on the B-36. These "parasite fighters" were intended to defend the slow and vulnerable B-36 from fighter attack.

The F-84G Thunderflash, the last version of the aircraft, could make 622 mph and reach 40,500 feet. Its range was 2,000 miles, and it carried an ordnance load of 2,000 pounds.

F-86 Sabre: The poor performance of the F-80 and F-84 against the Russian MiG-15 in the Korean War quickly persuaded USAF planners of the need for a high-performance swept wing aircraft. They turned to North American's F-86 Sabre, which had first flown in 1947 and was based on advanced Luftwaffe wing designs, captured at the end of World War II. In 1948, a Sabre exceeded Mach I, becoming the USAF's first supersonic fighter. It entered active service the following year, and, in 1950, the F-86E was rushed into Korean War service. At low altitudes, the F-86E had the edge over the MiG-15, but, at higher altitudes, the MiG-15 was superior. Armament also proved a problem, as the range of the F-86E's six Browning machine guns was inadequate to jet-age speeds. Nevertheless, in the hands of more highly skilled U.S. pilots, the Sabre performed very well against the MiG: 792 MiG-15s were shot down, with the loss of 78 F-86s. North American produced 5,893 F-86s before production ended in 1956. Top speed was 690 mph with a service ceiling of 50,000 feet and a range of 1,270 miles carrying 2,000 pounds of ordnance.

F-89 Scorpion: Northrup designed this, the USAF's first multiseat jet interceptor. The first flight took place in 1948, and it entered active service in 1951. The plane was relegated to the AIR NATIONAL GUARD in 1960. The plane was never entirely satisfactory and was replaced by the F-102 Delta Dagger (see AIRCRAFT, VIETNAM WAR). Top speed was 636 mph, service ceiling 49,200 feet, and range was 1,370 miles.

F-94 Starfire (see *F-80 Shooting Star*)

F-100 Super Sabre: North American commenced design of a successor to the F-86 Sabre in 1951, and, before the year was out, the USAF ordered production. In 1953, a Super Sabre set a

The F-86 Sabre was the USAF's first swept-wing jet fighter. *(U.S. Air Force)*

world speed record of 755 mph and was the first USAF fighter to break the sound barrier in *level* flight (an F-86 had gone supersonic in a dive). The F-100 became well-known around the nation and the world as the show plane of the THUNDERBIRDS exhibition team. Flown late in the Korean War, it was also used in Vietnam, beginning in 1965. It was withdrawn from USAF service in 1972 and flew with Air National Guard units until 1978. The Super Sabre had a top speed of 864 mph and a service ceiling of 39,600 feet. Its range was limited to 530 miles, but it bristled with ordnance—7,040 pounds of it.

Helicopters (designated "H")

H-19 Chickasaw: Sikorsky designed the Chickasaw in 1948, it first flew in 1949, and it entered active service in 1951, mainly as a rescue aircraft, extensively used in the Korean War. It was retired in 1967. With a top speed of 112 mph, the H-19 had a 360-mile range and could haul 10 troops.

H-21 Workhorse: The tandem-rotor H-21 was built by Piasecki Helicopter Corporation. In naval service, it was used mostly for rescue work, whereas the USAF used it for tactical airlift—as did the U.S. Army. Nicknamed the Flying Banana, because of its distinctive shape, the last H-21 was retired from the USAF in 1970. It served in Korea and in the Vietnam War.

Trainer (designated "T") Aircraft

T-28 Trojan: A piston-powered trainer, the Trojan first flew in 1949 and entered USAF service in 1950. It quickly proved a disappointment and was replaced by the T-37A jet-powered trainer. A version designated AT-28D was modified for close air support, but it was seriously vulnerable to ground fire. Top speed was 283 mph, service ceiling was 24,000 feet, and range, 1,000 miles.

T-29: The Consolidated-Vultee T-29 was used as a navigator trainer. It entered service in 1950 and also appeared in staff transport (VT-29) and electronic warfare variants (ET-29). Two major variants were designated the C-131A, a transport, and the MC-131A Samaritan, an aeromedical evacuation aircraft. The Air National Guard flew some C-131s as late as the 1990s. With a top speed of 296 mph and a service ceiling of 23,500 feet, the twin-engine T-29/C-131 had a range of 1,500 miles.

T-33 (see F-80 Shooting Star)

aircraft, Vietnam War

After the end of WORLD WAR II, which ushered in the nuclear and thermonuclear age, the thrust of USAF planning was mainly toward strategic weaponry. Vietnam, however, was an intensively tactical war, and the USAF found itself scrambling to adopt strategic aircraft (especially the B-52) to tactical roles.

Attack (designated "A") Aircraft and Gunships (designated "AC")

A-1 Skyraider: This was primarily designed as a carrier-based naval aircraft in 1944 and was in production through 1957. However, in 1963, a number of A-1 Skyraiders were assigned to the USAF Special Warfare Center at Eglin AFB and were used as attack (CLOSE AIR SUPPORT) aircraft in Vietnam. A huge single-engine piston plane (wingspan 51 feet, length 39 feet, weight 24,872 pounds), the A-1 made 365 mph and had a service ceiling of 25,000 feet over an impressive 2,700-mile range.

A-7 Corsair II: Vought built the A-7 Corsair II as a naval carrier attack plane in 1963, and the exi-

gencies of the Vietnam War, which called for more tactical aircraft than the USAF had in its inventory, prompted the air force to order A-7s. Although the aircraft entered USAF service in 1970, it did not see action in Vietnam until 1972. It proved highly effective in the close air support role. With a top speed of 698 mph, it had a long range (2,871 miles) and could carry a full 15,000 pounds of ordnance.

A-26/B-26 Invader (see AIRCRAFT, WORLD WAR II)

AC-47 (see C-47 in AIRCRAFT, WORLD WAR II)

AC-119 (see C-119 in AIRCRAFT, KOREAN WAR)

Bomber (designated "B") Aircraft

B-52 Stratofortress: This remarkable aircraft first flew in 1954, and the B-52B model entered service in 1955. A total of 744 B-52s were built; the last, a B-52H, was delivered in October 1962. Only the H model is still in the USAF inventory; however, continually updated with modern technology, the B-52 is projected to continue service *beyond* 2045—a service life approaching a century.

The B-52 Stratofortress was built as the USAF's principal manned strategic bomber; however, in Vietnam, it was pressed into service in a tactical role and is indeed capable of dropping or launching the widest array of weapons in the U.S. inventory. In addition to its intended strategic role, the B-52 performs air interdiction and offensive counter-air and maritime operations. It delivered huge quantities of ordnance in tactical operations in Vietnam and was used again during the PERSIAN GULF WAR and in operations in Afghanistan following the September 11, 2001, terrorist attacks against the United States.

Aerial refueling has given the B-52 a range limited only by crew endurance. Unrefueled, its combat range exceeds 8,800 miles. The B-52 is 159 feet long with a wingspan of 185 feet. Its top speed is 650 mph with a service ceiling of 50,000 feet. A crew of five—aircraft commander, pilot, radar navigator, navigator, and electronic warfare officer— flies the plane.

B-57 Canberra (see AIRCRAFT, COLD WAR AND AFTER)

A B-52H Stratofortress in flight   *(U.S. Air Force)*

B-66 Destroyer: The USAF commissioned Douglas to develop the B-66 from the navy A3D Skywarrior as a tactical light bomber and photo reconnaissance aircraft. It was a reconnaissance version (designated RB-66A) that first flew in 1954. The B-66s became operational in 1956, and production ended in 1958 after 294 had been built. It was the last tactical bomber built for the USAF. For service in Vietnam, some B-66s were modified as electronic countermeasures aircraft to confuse enemy radar defenses.

The plane's top speed was 585 mph, service ceiling was 43,000 feet, and range was 1,800 miles.

Cargo and Transport (designated "C") Aircraft

C-5 Galaxy: Lockheed's C-5 is one of the largest aircraft in the world, developed in the 1960s to carry outsize and oversize cargo over intercontinental distances. Despite its size—wingspan: 222.9 feet; length: 247.1 feet; height: 65.1 feet; cargo capacity: 270,000 pounds; maximum takeoff weight: 769,000 pounds—the C-5 can take off and land in relatively short distances. Moreover, ground crews can load and off-load the C-5 simultaneously at the front and rear cargo openings. The C-5 Galaxy carries nearly all of the U.S. Army's combat equipment, even such items as its 74-ton

mobile scissors bridge, and it can do so from the United States to any point in the world.

Lockheed-Georgia delivered the first operational Galaxy to the 437th Airlift Wing, Charleston AFB, in June 1970. With maintenance and modernization programs, the C-5 is expected to remain operational far into the 21st century. Top speed is 518 mph, and range is 6,320 nautical miles.

C-7 Caribou: Built by DeHavilland Aircraft of Canada, the C-7 is a twin-engine, short takeoff and landing (STOL) utility transport used primarily for tactical airlift missions in forward battle areas with short, unimproved airstrips. It can carry 26 fully equipped paratroops or 20 wounded personnel on litters. In a cargo configuration, the C-7 carries more than three tons. The aircraft first flew in

A C-5A Galaxy prepares to unload   *(U.S. Air Force)*

1958, and, in 1961, 22 were delivered to the U.S. Army. In January 1967, responsibility for all fixed-wing tactical transports was transferred to the USAF—along with the Caribous. The aircraft's STOL capability gave it great utility in Vietnam. Capable of reaching 216 mph and with a range of 1,175 miles, the Caribou has a service ceiling of 24,800 feet.

C-9 Nightingale: A modified version of the Douglas (now Boeing) DC-9 commercial transport, the C-9A is the only USAF aircraft specifically designed to move litter and ambulatory patients. Another configuration, the C-9C, is used to transport high-ranking government and Department of Defense officials for special air missions. A C-9C is often used to transport the vice president or the first lady. The C-9A carries 40 litter patients or 40 ambulatory and four litter patients, or other combinations. It flies at 525 mph over a range of 2,500 miles.

C-46 Commando (see AIRCRAFT, WORLD WAR II)

C-47 Skytrain (see AIRCRAFT, WORLD WAR II)

C-123 Provider: The C-123 is a short-range assault transport used to airlift troops and cargo onto short runways and unprepared airstrips. The Chase Aircraft Company designed the C-123 on the basis of earlier designs for large assault gliders. The first prototype flew on October 14, 1949. Chase began manufacture in 1953, but production was subsequently transferred to Fairchild, which built more than 300 C-123Bs. These began entering service in 1955. Between 1966 and 1969, 184 C-123Bs were converted to C-123Ks with the addition of two J85 jet engines for improved performance. In Vietnam, Providers not only flew troops and cargo but also were used to spray defoliant and insecticide. The C-123B has a top speed of 240 mph, a range of 1,825 miles, and a service ceiling of 28,000 feet.

C-130 Hercules: One of the greatest workhorse cargo aircraft ever built, the C-130 Hercules primarily performs tactical airlift functions. Capable of operating from unimproved airstrips, it is the prime transport for air dropping troops and equipment into hostile areas. The basic C-130 has been modified for various specialized roles, including airlift support, Antarctic ice resupply, aeromedical missions, weather reconnaissance, aerial spray missions, fire-fighting duties for the U.S. Forest Service, and natural disaster relief missions. An attack version, the AC-130, was used extensively in Vietnam as a close air support gunship.

The first C-130 was delivered by Lockheed in 1956 and has gone through several versions. It is still in production. The latest C-130, the C-130J, was introduced in February 1999. It has an advanced six-bladed composite propeller coupled to a Rolls-Royce turboprop engine and, in a stretch version (C-130J-30), it will replace retiring C-130Es.

The C-130E could hit 345 mph, whereas the C-130J achieves 417 mph with a ceiling of 33,000 feet carrying a 45,000-pound payload. Range of the C-130E is 1,838 miles versus 2,897 miles for the stretch C-130J-30. The USAF has 186 C-130s in active service, the AIR NATIONAL GUARD, 217, and the AIR FORCE RESERVE, 107.

C-133 Cargomaster: The Douglas C-133 Cargomaster was a four-engine, turboprop transport, which first flew in 1956. It could fly the equivalent of 22 loaded railroad boxcars nonstop between Los Angeles and New York and was used to carry fully assembled tanks as well as the Thor IRBM (INTERMEDIATE RANGE BALLISTIC MISSILE). The plane went out of production in 1961, after 50 had been delivered to the USAF. Top speed was 359 mph, service ceiling, 19,000 feet, range, 3,975 miles. The C-133 could carry 10 crew and 200 passengers or 80,000 pounds of cargo.

C-135 Stratolifter (see AIRCRAFT, COLD WAR AND AFTER)

KC-135 Stratotanker: A specially modified version of the Boeing 707 commercial transport, the KC-135 Stratotanker is the USAF's principal air-refueling aircraft. It also provides aerial refueling support to navy and Marine Corps aircraft, as well as aircraft of allied nations. In Vietnam, midair refueling was extensively used, bringing even the most distant targets within reach of virtually all attack aircraft.

The first 29 KC-135s were purchased in 1954. The first aircraft flew in 1956, and first deliveries were made in 1957. The last was delivered in 1965. Various updates will keep the KC-135 flying for many more years. The aircraft has also been modified for other applications, ranging from flying command post missions to reconnaissance. The EC-135C is U.S. Strategic Command's flying command post, RC-135s are used for special reconnaissance missions, and NKC-135As are flown in test programs. An OC-135 is used as an observation platform in compliance with the Open Skies Treaty.

Top speed is 530 mph, service ceiling is 50,000 feet, and range, 1,500 miles with 150,000 pounds of transfer fuel. About 732 KC-135s are in the USAF inventory.

C-141 Starlifter: The C-141B, a stretched version of the original C-141A, airlifts combat forces over long distances, resupplies forces, and transports casualties. Lockheed delivered the first C-141A in 1964, and the first C-141B in 1979. It was the first jet transport from which U.S. Army paratroopers jumped, and the first to land in the Antarctic. Top speed is 500 mph, service ceiling, 41,000 feet; with in-flight refueling, range is unlimited. Maximum payload is 200 troops, 155 paratroops, 103 litters, and 14 seats, or 68,725 pounds

of cargo. The USAF has 74 C-141Bs on active duty, the Air National Guard, 28, and the Air Force Reserve, 68.

EC-121C (see C-121 Constellation in AIRCRAFT, KOREAN WAR)

Fighter (designated "F") Aircraft

F-4 Phantom II: First flown in 1958, the Phantom II was developed for the U.S. Navy and entered service in 1961. The following year, the USAF approved a version for close air support, interdiction, and counter-air operations. The USAF version was designated F-4C and made its first flight on May 27, 1963, with first deliveries arriving in November 1963. The F-4 can carry twice the normal bomb load of a World War II B-17 and can also fly in a reconnaissance role and on "Wild Weasel" antiaircraft missile suppression missions. Production ended in 1979, after more than 5,000 had been built, including some 2,600 for the USAF. The first USAF Phantom IIs were sent to Vietnam in 1965.

The Phantom II can carry up to 16,000 pounds of externally carried nuclear or conventional bombs, rockets, missiles, or 20-mm cannon pods in various combinations. Its two General Electric

F-4 Phantom *(U.S. Air Force)*

J-79-GE-15s engine push it to an afterburner top speed of 1,400 mph. Service ceiling is 59,600 feet, range is 1,750 miles without aerial refueling.

F-5 Freedom Fighter: Northrop began development of the F-5 in 1954 in response to the company's evaluation of the defense needs of NATO and SEATO countries. The conclusion was that a lightweight supersonic fighter was called for, one that was relatively inexpensive and easy to maintain, and capable of operating out of short runways. Initially, the USAF saw no need for a lightweight fighter, but it ordered the trainer version of the F-5, the T-38 Talon. The F-5 was used extensively by the U.S. Military Assistance Program to supply NATO and SEATO allies. In October 1965, the USAF decided to test a dozen combat-ready F-5As in Vietnam combat operational service trials. The program was code named Skoshi Tiger (Little Tiger), and, as a result, the F-5 was often called "Tiger." Top speed is 925 mph, range, 1,100 miles, and service ceiling, 50,700 feet.

F-100 Super Sabre (see AIRCRAFT, KOREAN WAR)

F-101 Voodoo: The F-101 was designed as a long-range bomber escort for the STRATEGIC AIR COMMAND, but when high-speed, high-altitude jet bombers such as the B-52 were introduced, escort fighters were no longer needed. Before production began, therefore, the F-101 was redesigned as a tactical and air defense fighter. The prototype first flew on September 29, 1954, and the first production F-101A became operational in May 1957, followed by the F-101C in 1957 and the F-101B in 1959. When production ended in March 1961, McDonnell had built 785 Voodoos, including the two-seat interceptor version and the reconnaissance versions—the world's first supersonic photo reconnaissance aircraft. Capable of a maximum speed of 1,095 mph and a range of 1,754 miles, the Voodoo can reach a service ceiling of 52,100 feet.

F-102 Delta Dagger: The F-102 was the world's first supersonic all-weather jet interceptor—and the first operational delta-wing aircraft in the USAF inventory. The first F-102 flew on October 24, 1953, and became operational in 1956. Convair built 1,101 F-102s, including 975 F-102As and 111

TF-102s as combat trainers with side-by-side seating. The interceptor could carry 24 unguided 2.75 inch rockets and six guided missiles. Maximum speed was 810 mph, range 1,000 miles, and service ceiling 55,000 feet.

F-104 Starfighter: The F-104, a supersonic air superiority fighter, was produced in two major versions. Armed with a six-barrel M-61 20-mm Vulcan cannon, it served as a tactical fighter; equipped additionally with heat-seeking Sidewinder missiles, it was a day-night interceptor. Development at Lockheed began in 1952 and the prototype first flew in 1954. On May 18, 1958, an F-104A set a world speed record of 1,404.19 mph, and, on December 14, 1959, an F-104C set a world altitude record of 103,395 feet. The Starfighter became the first aircraft to hold simultaneous official world records for speed, altitude, and time-to-climb.

About 300 Starfighters in one- and two-seat versions were delivered to the USAF, and more than 1,700 F-104s were built for various allies. Top speed was 1,320 mph, range, 1,250 miles, and service ceiling, 58,000 feet.

F-105 Thunderchief: The F-105 (nicknamed "Thud") began development in 1951 at Republic Aviation. The prototype flew on October 22, 1955, but the first production aircraft, an F-105B, was not delivered to the USAF until 1958. The F-105D version was an all-weather strike fighter, and the two-place F-105F was a dual-purpose trainer-fighter. All F-105 production—833 aircraft—ended in 1964. The F-105 was extensively used in Vietnam, flying more sorties and suffering more losses than any other USAF aircraft there. Although the F-105 scored 137 MiG victories, it was a heavy and hard-to-maneuver plane (carrying as much ordnance as a World War II B-17) and was vulnerable to air superiority fighters and to flak. It was, however, less vulnerable to surface-to-air missiles. Top speed was 831 mph, range, 1,500 miles, and service ceiling, 50,000 feet.

Observation (designated "O") Aircraft

O-1 Bird Dog: The O-1, a two-place observation and liaison aircraft, was developed from the commercial Cessna Model 170 as early as 1949. The USAF, army, and marines used Bird Dogs for artillery spotting, frontline communications, medical evacuation, and pilot training. In Vietnam, USAF Bird Dogs were used by forward air controllers (FACS) for reconnaissance—an extremely hazardous mission in these light planes, which were vulnerable to ground fire of all kinds, including that from small arms. More that 3,200 Bird Dogs were ordered by the USAF, most of which were built between 1950 and 1959. Maximum speed was 150 mph, range was 530 miles, and service ceiling, 20,300 feet.

O-2 Super Skymaster: This military version of the Cessna Model 337 Super Skymaster has twin tail booms and tandem-mounted engines, one forward, one aft, in a tractor-pusher propeller arrangement. The Model 337 went into civilian production in 1965 and was selected by the USAF the following year as a supplement to the O-1 Bird Dog forward air controller (FAC) aircraft then operating in Vietnam. The twin engines made the O-2 more survivable. Deliveries began in March 1967 and ended in June 1970, after 532 had been built for the USAF. Top speed was 199 mph, range, 1,060 miles, service ceiling, 19,300 feet.

OV-10 Bronco: This twin-turboprop short takeoff and landing (STOL) aircraft was designed by North American Aviation in response to a Marine Corps order, but it was developed under a USAF, navy, and Marine Corps tri-service program. The first production OV-10A was ordered in 1966 and the first flight took place in August 1967. The OV-10 was designed to perform observation, forward air control, helicopter escort, armed reconnaissance, gunfire spotting, and utility and limited ground attack. The USAF used it primarily for forward air control, especially in Vietnam. The OV-10 also has limited (3,200-pound) cargo capacity and can accommodate five combat-equipped troops or two litter patients and a medical attendant. OV-10s began Vietnam service in July 1968; 157 were delivered to the USAF before production ended in April 1969. Top speed is 281 mph. Cruising speed: 223 mph, range, 1,240 miles, and service ceiling is 26,000 feet.

Utility (designated "U") Aircraft

U-16 Albatross: This venerable (first flew in 1947) Grumman design was used widely in the Vietnam era and earlier for air-sea rescue. It was also designated SA-16 (and nicknamed "Slobbering Albert"). The USAF bought 302 U-16s, and the aircraft saw service for more than a quarter century. An amphibious design, the U-16 had twin engines that propelled it to 236 mph over a range of 3,220 miles.

Training (designated "T") Aircraft

T-37 Tweet: The T-37 Tweet is a twin-engine jet used for training in the fundamentals of aircraft handling and instrument, formation, and night flying. It was developed by Cessna, first flown in 1954, and entered service in 1957. An attack variant, the A-37, was used in the Vietnam War and is now designated as the OA-37B Dragonfly. This configuration is used for forward air control and for rescue work. But it is as a trainer that the T-37 is still most extensively employed. It is designed to give student pilots a feel for handling the larger, faster T-38 Talon or T-1A Jayhawk, which are used in a later training phase. The instructor and student sit side by side. More than 1,000 T-37s were built, and 419 remain in the USAF inventory. Top speed is 360 mph, ceiling 35,000, and range 460 miles.

T-38 Talon: This twin-engine, high-altitude, supersonic jet trainer was built by Northrop as a vehicle to prepare pilots for a variety of advanced fighters. The T-38 is ideal for aerobatics, formation, night, instrument, and cross-country navigation training. The T-38 is also frequently used as a test bed for such experimental equipment as electronics and weapon systems, and NASA uses the aircraft to train astronauts and to serve as chase planes on programs such as the space shuttle.

The Talon first flew in 1959, and more than 1,100 were delivered to the USAF between 1961 and 1972 when production ended. However, through maintenance and upgrade programs, it is

This T-37 Tweet from the 85th Fighter Training Squadron, Laughlin AFB, Texas, flies over Lake Amistad, Texas, during a training mission. After mastering the Tweet, student pilots move up to the faster, more sophisticated T-38 Talon.   *(U.S. Air Force)*

expected that the Talon will continue to serve at least until 2020. Top speed is 812 mph, service ceiling exceeds 55,000 feet, and range is 1,093 miles. Currently, 509 are in the USAF inventory.

T-39 Sabreliner: This twin-jet, multipurpose aircraft was built by North American for the USAF and U.S. Navy, both of which designate it T-39. Capable of cruising at 500 mph at 40,000 feet, it resembles the F-86 Sabre Jet and the F-100 Super Sabre, but it is capable of carrying a crew of two, with four passengers. Highly modifiable, the T-39 was used as a radar and navigational trainer and as a test bed for various instruments, as well as a small cargo (2,300-pound capacity) and passenger carrier. Active service began in 1960, and the aircraft was retired in 1984.

Helicopters (designated "H")

H-3 Jolly Green Giant: The USAF version of the H-3, the Sikorsky S-61 amphibious transport helicopter originally developed for the U.S. Navy, is the CH-3E. After operating six Navy HSS-2 (SH-3A) versions in 1962, the USAF ordered 75 H-3s, which were modified with a new rear fuselage design incorporating a ramp for vehicles and other cargo. The first USAF CH-3C was flown on June 17, 1963; 41 were updated with more powerful engines in 1966 and were redesignated CH-3Es. Later, 50 CH-3Es were modified for combat rescue missions with armor, defensive armament, self-sealing fuel tanks, a rescue hoist, and in-flight refueling capability. Redesignated HH-3Es, they were used extensively in Vietnam; it was this configuration that was nicknamed the "Jolly Green Giant." Maximum speed was 177 mph, range 779 miles (with external fuel tanks), and service ceiling 21,000 feet.

H-21 Workhorse (see AIRCRAFT, KOREAN WAR)

H-53 Super Jolly: As the Vietnam War continued, the USAF determined a need for a better combat rescue helicopter than the H-3. The Marine Corps already had the Sikorsky H-53 Sea

Stallion, which the USAF ordered modified as the H-53 Super Jolly. It entered service in 1967, a twin-engine helicopter capable of lifting seven tons and equipped with modern avionics and ejection seats. In addition to rescue, H-53s were used for heavy-lift operations, military transport, vertical replenishment, vertical onboard delivery, airborne mine countermeasures, advanced early warning, minesweeping, humanitarian aid, and disaster relief. The helicopters were extensively used for astronaut rescue and space capsule and satellite recovery. Updated in 1987 with Pave Low III Enhanced equipment, including forward-looking infrared (FLIR) and terrain-following and terrain-avoidance radar, the H-53s (designated MH-53J) continue to be used extensively and are the largest and most powerful helicopters in the USAF inventory and the most technologically advanced helicopters in the world. Top speed is 186 mph, service ceiling is 18,550 feet, range is 540 miles. The HH-53C configuration can lift 20,000 pounds.

aircraft, World War I

Although powered flight by heavier-than-air aircraft was born in the United States with the Wright brothers' *Flyer I* of 1903, the nation's military had little interest in aviation as a weapon, and, as a result, the U.S. aircraft industry lagged far behind that of Europe when the nation entered WORLD WAR I in 1917.

U.S. manufacturers began turning out De Haviland DH-4 aircraft under license from the British manufacturer in August 1918, but, before this, the U.S. ARMY AIR SERVICE chiefly flew two French-made aircraft for observation and bombing.

Breguet 14: The aircraft came in two configurations, the 14A for observation and the 14B for bombing. The planes were capable of a top speed of 129 miles per hour. The USAAS used 229 14As, 47 14Bs, and 100 "14E" trainers.

Salmson 2A-2: 705 of these French-built observation planes were used by the USAAS. It was in all respects similar to the Breuget 14.

De Haviland DH-4: Built in the United States under British license by Standard Aircraft Company, Dayton-Wright Company, and General Motors, with a U.S.-designed and built "Liberty Engine," the DH-4, a 1916 design, was, in fact, obsolescent by the time it began rolling off U.S. assembly lines in 1918. A staggering 4,846 were built, but they proved defective in design and so prone to catch fire that the aircraft were nicknamed "Flaming Coffins." A DH-4B version corrected these faults, but the version arrived too late to be flown in combat. The USAAS and U.S. ARMY AIR CORPS flew DH-4Bs until 1931. The aircraft had a top speed of 118 mph and a service ceiling of 12,800 feet. It carried 1,200 pounds of bombs.

Nieuport 28: This French-built fighter was obsolete by the time the United States purchased it for use in combat. Nevertheless, it flew with the 94th and 95th Aero Squadrons and Lieutenant Alan Winslow scored the first U.S. aerial victory of the war in one. In this aircraft, Lieutenant Douglas Campbell became the first U.S.-trained ace of the war.

Spad XIII: This aircraft replaced the obsolete Nieuport 28 and was the favorite fighter of USAAS pilots. The Spad XIII was made especially famous in the United States by the exploits of Captain EDWARD V. RICKENBACKER, the nation's dashing top ace. Capable of making 138 mph (200 mph in a dive), the Spad XIII had an impressive service ceiling of 22,300 feet. The United States purchased 893 of the aircraft.

JN Jenny: Manufactured by the Curtiss Aeroplane and Motor Company, the Jenny was ordered by the AVIATION SECTION, U.S. ARMY SIGNAL CORPS in 1916 and was used (without much success) in the PUNITIVE EXPEDITION against Pancho Villa that year. Although it was not used overseas in World War I—and was hopelessly obsolete as a combat aircraft—it served as the primary trainer for 90 percent of U.S. World War I pilots. More than 8,000 were manufactured. A slow plane, with a top speed of 75 mph as driven by its standard 90-horsepower Curtiss OX-5 engine, it had a service ceiling of 8,000 feet.

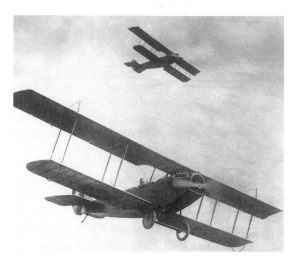

Two Army Service Curtiss JN-4 Jennys *(San Diego Aerospace Museum)*

aircraft, World War II

Listed here are the principal U.S. ARMY AIR CORPS and U.S. ARMY AIR FORCES aircraft used in WORLD WAR II. Some were developed during the interwar period, some during the war itself. Some aircraft developed before the war saw very limited service during the war; these are covered in AIRCRAFT, INTERWAR PERIOD (1919–1940).

Attack (designated "A") Aircraft

A-20 Havoc: This was the principal USAAC and USAAF attack (close ground support) aircraft of World War II. The air arm received 7,230 of them from the Douglas Aircraft Company. The plane went into production at the close of the 1930s and was the first USAAF aircraft type to see action in Europe, arriving there in 1942. The twin-engine craft was nicknamed the "Flying Pike" and had a top speed of 329 mph, a service ceiling of 28,250, and a range of 1,060 miles. Production ended in 1944.

Bomber (designated "B") Aircraft

B-17 Flying Fortress: One of the most celebrated airplanes of World War II, the B-17 was the first U.S. bomber built for strategic operations and was the first U.S. four-engine monoplane bomber. Designed by Boeing, a total of 12,731 of these planes were produced by Boeing and, under license, by Douglas and by Vega, a Lockheed subsidiary. The most successful version, the B-17G, was powered by four 1,200-horsepower Wright R-1820-97 engines that drove the 65,500-pound Fortress at 287 mph and to a service ceiling of 35,600 feet. The aircraft could deliver up to 8,000 pounds of bombs and had a range of 2,000 miles. It bristled with defensive guns and was renowned for its ability to withstand massive damage from enemy fighters and antiaircraft fire.

B-24 Liberator: Less celebrated that the B-17 Flying Fortress, Consolidated Aircraft's B-24 Liberator was nevertheless built in significantly greater numbers—18,482 produced by five manufacturers; no combat aircraft, save the German Bf 109 (a single-engine fighter of World War II), has ever been built in greater quantity.

The B-24 was a notoriously difficult plane to fly, especially in the close formations required for strategic bombing (see BOMBING, STRATEGIC) missions; however, it had two performance edges on the much better loved B-17: top speed was 300 mph (vs. 287 mph for the B-17) and range was 2,100 miles (vs. 2,000). However, the B-17 was capable of greater altitude: 35,600 feet versus 28,000 feet.

B-17 Flying Fortress *(U.S. Air Force)*

B-25 Mitchell: Design work at North American Aviation began in 1938 on this twin-engine medium bomber named in honor of controversial military aviation advocate WILLIAM MITCHELL. It first flew in 1939, and, by the time the war was over, more than 11,000 had been built, 9,815 for the USAAC and USAAF. Considered one of the great bombers of the war, the Mitchell was made spectacularly famous by JAMES HAROLD DOOLITTLE's breathtaking, morale-boosting carrier-launched 1942 raid on Tokyo.

The Mitchell flew at 272 mph with a service ceiling of 24,200 feet and a range of 1,350 miles with a 3,000-pound bomb load. In addition to bombing work, modified B-25s were used as transports and as reconnaissance aircraft, and from 1943 to 1959, they also served as pilot trainers.

B-26 Invader: The Douglas B-26 entered service in World War II in 1944 and proved so successful that it was used in the KOREAN WAR and even in the early phases (1961–64) of the VIETNAM WAR. It was a very fast twin-engine bomber, with a top speed of 372 mph and a service ceiling of 20,450 feet. Carrying a 4,000-pound bomb load, it had a range of 892 miles. Total production of this aircraft was 2,446.

B-26 Marauder: In contrast to the Invader, which bore the same B-26 designation, the Martin Marauder was a difficult plane to master and was soon branded "The Widow Maker," because of the high rate of loss in the hands of inexperienced pilots. Once the aircraft entered full-time service in the war, however, it amply proved itself, and, by the time production stopped in 1945, the USAAF had

B-25C Mitchell *(San Diego Aerospace Museum)*

accepted 5,157 Marauders. The twin-engine medium bomber flew at 283 mph and had a service ceiling of 19,800 feet. Range was 1,100 miles with 4,000 pounds of bombs.

B-29 Superfortress: The most advanced bomber of its time, the B-29 outclassed everything else in the sky and was the only USAAF aircraft capable of delivering atomic weapons, the bomb dropped on Hiroshima on August 6, 1945, and the bomb dropped on Nagasaki on August 9. In effect, then, the B-29 ended World War II.

Design work began at Boeing in 1940, the first flight took place in 1942, and the aircraft was put into service exclusively in the Pacific theater beginning in the last two months of 1944. The TWENTIETH AIR FORCE and the TWENTY-FIRST AIR FORCE were established exclusively to fly the new bomber, whose four engines drove it at 364 mph to a service ceiling of 32,000 feet. Carrying a 20,000-pound bomb load, its range was 4,200 miles, and with a 141-foot wingspan and 99-foot fuselage, it was by far the biggest bomber of the era.

B-32 Dominator: Consolidated Aircraft Company was commissioned to build this four-engine bomber as a kind of hedge against the possible failure of the B-29. However, the B-29 proved a spectacular success, while the B-32 was criticized for basic design and production flaws. Of the 115 built, only 15 saw action, in the Pacific. Most of the scheduled production of 1,588 was canceled before the war ended.

Capable of 357 mph, the B-32 had a service ceiling of 30,700 feet and could carry 10 tons of bombs over 2,400 miles.

Cargo and Military Transport (designated "C") Aircraft

C-46 Commando: Curtiss-Wright designed this aircraft in 1937 as a two-engine commercial passenger plane. On the eve of World War II, the USAAC ordered a model converted for military transport. The aircraft, of which 3,144 were built, was a workhorse that served famously "flying the Hump"—the treacherous Burma-China airlift—and was used after World War II in the Korean War. Although officially retired in 1960, the C-46 was used in the

Vietnam War and in Southeast Asia generally through 1969. With a top speed of 269 mph and a service ceiling of 27,600 feet, the C-46 could carry a payload of 10,000 pounds over 1,200 miles.

C-47 Skytrain: Dwight D. Eisenhower observed that, without the bazooka, the Jeep, the atom bomb, and the C-47, the Allies could not have won World War II. The military variant of the Douglas DC-3, a spectacularly successful and long-lived commercial passenger transport first flown in 1935, the C-47 (in many configurations) was built for the USAAC and USAAF in a quantity of more than 10,000.

The C-47 was used throughout World War II to carry personnel and cargo, to tow gliders, and to drop paratroopers. During the Normandy ("D-day") invasion of June 6, 1944, C-47s dropped 60,000 paratroopers and towed thousands of CG-4 gliders. After the war, the aircraft saw spectacular service in the BERLIN AIRLIFT, in the Korean War, and in the Vietnam War, where it was used not only as a transport but also as an attack gunship (AC-47), nicknamed "Puff the Magic Dragon." The last C-47 was not retired from the USAF until 1975. Commercially, a fair number are still in service.

The twin-engine C-47 flew at 230 mph with a service ceiling of 24,000 feet, a range of 1,600 miles, and a payload of 10,000 pounds.

C-54 Skymaster: Like the C-47, the C-54 was originally developed in the 1930s as a commercial airliner, the four-engine DC-4. The first run of DC-4s was commandeered off the Douglas assembly line by the USAAF in 1942 and redesignated C-54. Before the end of the war, the service bought 1,163 C-54s. This long-range transport was the primary airlifter across the Atlantic and Pacific. By the end of the war, C-54s had made 79,642 crossings of the North Atlantic with the loss of only three aircraft. It was a specially modified C-54 (designated VC-54C), nicknamed *The Sacred Cow*, which became the first aircraft assigned to presidential airlift. It took President Franklin D. Roosevelt to the Yalta Conference. After the war, C-54s were extensively used in the Berlin Airlift and in the Korean War. The aircraft remained in USAF service until 1972.

The C-54 had a top speed of 265 mph, a service ceiling of 22,000 feet, a range of 3,900 miles, and could carry 50 troops with equipment.

C-69: See C-121 Constellation in AIRCRAFT, KOREAN WAR.

Fighter (designated "F" or "P," for pursuit) Aircraft

P-38 Lightning: Lockheed designed this twin-engine fighter with distinctive twin booms (German Luftwaffe pilots called it *Der Gabelschwanz Teufel,* the "Fork-Tailed Devil") and produced a prototype in 1939. By the end of World War II, 9,923 had been delivered to the USAAC and USAAF. The P-38 was more successful flying against Japanese fighters in the Pacific than against German fighters in the European theater. In the Pacific, the top-scoring USAF ace of all time, RICHARD I. BONG, flew a P-38. Its twin engines drove the aircraft at 414 mph, and it could attain a service ceiling of 44,000 feet. Range was 450 miles.

P-39 Airacobra: Bell Aircraft Corporation flew the first prototype Airacobra in 1939, and it was used by the British and the Soviets as well as by the USAAF. In Europe, the P-39 was used mainly in an attack (close air support) role. Early in the war, P-39s also saw action in the Pacific. The fighter was replaced by the F-47 Thunderbolt early in 1944. Capable of a top speed of 399 mph, the P-39 had a service ceiling of 38,500 feet and a range of 750 miles.

P-40 Warhawk: This Curtiss-Wright fighter gained its greatest fame in service with the AMERICAN VOLUNTEER GROUP, the famed "Flying Tigers" serving with the Nationalist Chinese air force against Japan. The distinctive shark-like profile formed by the plane's air scoop was emphasized by the Flying Tigers with a row of tiger teeth. The P-40 was hardly a cutting-edge fighter by the time the war began, but it was ready for production and, in the hands of a capable pilot, held its own against German and Japanese rivals. Some 13,700 were built for the USAAF before production ended in 1944. With a top speed of 378 mph and a service ceiling of 38,000 feet, the P-40 had a limited range of 240 miles.

P-38 Lightning   *(U.S. Air Force)*

P-43 Lancer: Republic Aviation (originally Seversky) produced a small number of this aircraft, which did not perform well against Axis rivals. Speed was 349 mph, service ceiling 38,000 feet, and range 800 miles.

P-59 Airacomet: Bell Aircraft Corporation developed this, the first U.S. jet aircraft, during 1941–42. Thirty were built before production was stopped when the F-80 Shooting Star was introduced just before the end of the war. No U.S. jets saw combat in World War II. P-59 performance was disappointing—inferior to the best piston-powered fighters—and the aircraft was inherently unstable. Top speed was 413 mph, service ceiling 46,200 feet, and range 525 miles.

P-61 Black Widow: The Northrup company built the Black Widow as the USAAF's first night interceptor and the first aircraft specially designed to be equipped with radar. The plane was painted all black for night operations. It first flew in 1942, 732 were built, and it remained in service—as a reconnaissance aircraft—until 1952. The twin-engine P-61 was capable of 366 mph and had a service ceiling of 31,000 feet. Maximum range was 3,000 miles.

P-63 Kingcobra: This Bell Aircraft design was an update of the P-39 Airacobra and first flew in 1942. Although 3,303 were built, the USAAF

Affectionately nicknamed "Jug," the P-47 was one of the most famous AAF fighter planes of World War II. Although originally conceived as a lightweight interceptor, the P-47 developed as a heavyweight fighter.   *(U.S. Air Force)*

North American P-51 Mustang fighter plane over France. Mustangs served in nearly every combat zone. P-51s destroyed 4,950 enemy aircraft in the air, more than any other fighter in Europe. *(U.S. Air Force)*

received relatively few; most were given to the Soviet Union and to France. Top speed was 408 mph with a service ceiling of 43,000 feet and a range of 390 miles.

F-47 Thunderbolt (P-47): More F-47s were built than any other USAAF fighter—15,579 before the end of the war. This Republic design entered service in 1942 and began combat the following year, operating with the EIGHTH AIR FORCE out of England, then with units in the Pacific, and also with the FIFTEENTH AIR FORCE in Italy. Britain and the USSR used many as well. The F-47 was an air-superiority fighter, dominating the skies with a victory rate of 4.6 to 1 (F-47s shot down 3,752 enemy aircraft). The airplane was also well suited to ground attack. After World War II, the AIR NATIONAL GUARD acquired some F-47s, which were returned to the USAF for service in the Korean War, until they were replaced by jets.

A massive single-engine plane, the powerful F-47 could reach 467 mph and had a service ceiling of 43,000 feet. Its range was 800 miles carrying 2,000 pounds in bombs and other ordnance.

F-51 Mustang (P-51): Arguably the finest fighter of World War II, the F-51 was produced by North American and made its first flight in May

1943. Not only was its performance outstanding—437 mph and a service ceiling of 41,900 feet—it had sufficient range (950 miles) to escort bombers deep into enemy territory. A total of 14,490 were produced.

F-82 Twin Mustang. North American developed the Twin Mustang as a very long range (2,240 miles) fighter escort, intended for the great distances of the Pacific theater. The plane was essentially a mating of two P-51s joined by a center wing section and tailplane. Each otherwise independent fuselage had its own engine and pilot. The aircraft did not see action before the end of the war, but did fly after it and, with an order of 250, it was the last piston fighter the USAAF acquired.

Glider (designated "G") Aircraft

G-4: The Waco Aircraft Company built almost 14,000 G-4s, which were made mostly of wood and carried 15 fully equipped troops (or four soldiers and a jeep, or a 75-mm howitzer and crew). It was replaced late in the war by the G-15 Hadrian.

G-15 Hadrian: The G-15 was an improved, more airworthy and sturdier, version of the G-4. Capable of carrying 7,500 pounds, it glided at about 120 mph.

Trainer (designated "PT," primary trainer; "BT," basic trainer; and "T," trainer) Aircraft

PT-16: This version of the Ryan Model S-T was the first monoplane the USAAC used for training. It was ordered in 1940 and was produced in several variants, PT-20, PT-21, and PT-22. Production ended in 1942. The single-engine PT-16 flew at 128 mph to a service ceiling of 15,000 feet over 350 miles.

PT-19: Fairchild (and other manufacturers under license) produced the PT-19 for the USAAC in 1940. There were a number of variants; however, the PT-19 was generally replaced by the more capable PT-13 Kaydet (see AIRCRAFT, INTERWAR PERIOD [1919–1940]). Top speed was 132 mph, service ceiling 15,300 feet, range 400 miles.

BT-13: Basic training was the next step up from primary training. The BT-13, manufactured by Vultee Aircraft, Inc., was the most popular basic trainer. It made 180 mph and had a service ceiling of 21,650 feet over a range of 725 miles.

BT-15 Valiant: This later version of the BT-13 was quite similar to the earlier plane in performance.

T-6 Texan: This North American Aviation design first flew in 1938 and became the USAAF's advanced trainer during World War II. More than 8,000 were acquired. In addition to training, the T-6 was used for forward air control during the Korean War. The plane was and is much loved, with many still flying in the civilian community. Its top speed was 210 mph, its service ceiling 24,200 feet, and its range 629 miles.

Aircraft Identification Codes (AIC)

USAF uses alphabetical prefixes to designate different types of aircraft. The most common prefixes are B, for bomber (e.g., B-52); C, for cargo (e.g., C-5), F, for fighter (e.g., F-16), and T, for trainer (e.g., T-38). Occasionally, two letters are combined for special designations, as in the SR-71 (for "strategic reconnaissance") and the TR-1 (for "tactical reconnaissance").

Air Defense Command   See AEROSPACE DEFENSE COMMAND.

Air Education and Training Command (AETC)

AETC is a MAJCOM responsible for recruiting, accessing, commissioning, and training USAF

A 25th Flying Training Squadron instructor pilot and student walk toward a T-38 Talon at Vance AFB, Oklahoma. *(Department of Defense)*

enlisted and officer personnel. AETC responsibility encompasses basic military training, initial and advanced technical training, and flight training.

AETC integrates a large array of educational operations, including the AIR FORCE RESERVE OFFICER TRAINING CORPS (AFROTC), COMMUNITY COLLEGE OF THE AIR FORCE, and the many operations and responsibilities of the AIR UNIVERSITY. It is headquartered at Randolph AFB, Texas.

Air Force 2000

Air Force 2000 was an important study released in 1982, which envisioned the expansion of the USAF air superiority doctrine into space. With regard to air combat against surface forces, the study advocated development of an advanced tactical fighter (ATF), a conclusion that stood in direct opposition to an army study, *AirLand Battle,* released earlier in the year. The army document foresaw at least partial replacement of manned aircraft by smart weapons and remotely piloted vehicles.

Air Force Achievement Medal See DECORATIONS AND MEDALS.

Air Force Aero-Propulsion Laboratory

See AIR FORCE RESEARCH LABORATORY.

Air Force Agency for Modeling and Simulation (AFAMS)

AFAMS is a FIELD OPERATING AGENCY created in June 1996 to coordinate the USAF's growing requirement for modeling and simulation. The agency's mission is to support implementation and use of the Joint Synthetic Battlespace, a Department of Defense modeling and simulation initiative that is used as a planning and training tool by all of the services. The agency also implements USAF, joint, and Department of Defense policy and standards, it supports corporate USAF modeling and simulation operations, and it coordinates and manages selected modeling and simulation initiatives. AFAMS reports to the director of command and control in the Pentagon, but it is located in Orlando's Central Florida Research Park.

Modeling and simulation have long been used by the USAF to support training, analysis, and operations, but, more recently, the USAF has expanded modeling and simulation activities as a practical solution to improve readiness and lower costs. Modeling and simulation also aid the USAF in improving its warfighting capabilities by allowing real people to conduct operations in a synthetic world.

Air Force Association (AFA)

The AFA was founded on February 4, 1946, and operates today as an international nonprofit organization dedicated to the application of aerospace technology for the betterment of humankind. With 200,000 members and patrons in all 50 states, in Europe, and in the Far East, it publishes *Air Force Magazine,* conducts educational programs, works with industry, sponsors nationwide symposia featuring USAF and Department of Defense leaders, and sponsors the annual Outstanding Airman of the Air Force Program. Its leading mission is to promote public understanding and support of aerospace power in the United States.

The AFA was founded by General of the Air Force HENRY HARLEY ARNOLD and was organized by Major General Edward P. "Ted" Curtis, with Lieutenant General JAMES HAROLD DOOLITTLE as the organization's first president.

Air Force Audit Agency (AFAA)

The AFAA evaluates operations, support, and financial responsibilities for the USAF and is headquartered at Norton AFB, California. Administered by the auditor general of the air force reporting directly to the SECRETARY OF THE AIR FORCE, AFAA consists of three directorates: Acquisitions and Logistics Audit, Financial and Support Audit, and Field Activities.

Air Force bands

Air Force bands provide military and patriotic music for official military and government activities such as ceremonies, formations, and parades, and they provide an essential element for maintaining troop morale, for cultivating positive relations with many communities interacting with USAF units, and for enhancing general public relations.

Air Force bands are classified as either premier bands or regional bands. There are two premier bands: the United States Air Force Band in Washington, D.C., and the United States Air Force Band of the Rockies in Colorado Springs, Colorado. Ten regional bands are found at eight locations in the continental United States and operate from four locations overseas (Germany, Japan, Alaska, and Hawaii). In addition, there are 11 AIR NATIONAL GUARD bands throughout the United States.

Air Force bands are typically organized so that they may be subdivided into several smaller musical units capable of performing autonomously. For example, band members may function as a concert band, a marching or ceremonial band, a jazz or show band, a popular music ensemble, a chamber ensemble, or a "protocol combo" (providing background, dinner, and dance music for official military social functions). Individual musicians, such as buglers, solo vocalists, pianists, and other instrumentalists, may also perform for official functions or ceremonies.

The first known "air force" band, 14 strong, landed in France in September 1917 during WORLD WAR I, their instruments having been purchased from their lieutenant's personal funds. In WORLD WAR II, bands of the U.S. ARMY AIR CORPS and U.S. ARMY AIR FORCES were very active, and, since then, bands have been important adjuncts to USAF morale and presence.

Premier USAF bands:

United States Air Force Band (Bolling AFB)
United States Air Force Band of the Rockies (Peterson AFB)

Regional USAF bands:

For Connecticut, Massachusetts, Maine, New Hampshire, New York, Rhode Island, Vermont: United States Air Force Band of Liberty (Hanscom AFB)

For Louisiana, New Mexico, Oklahoma, Texas: United States Air Force Band of the West (Lackland AFB)

For Delaware, eastern Maryland, eastern Pennsylvania, North Carolina, New Jersey, South Carolina, Virginia: United States Air Force Heritage of America Band (Langley AFB)

For Iowa, Kansas, Minnesota, Montana, North Dakota, Nebraska, South Dakota, Wyoming: United States Air Force Heartland of America Band (Offutt AFB)

For Alabama, Florida, Georgia, Mississippi, Tennessee: Band of the United States Air Force Reserve (Robins AFB)

For Arkansas, Illinois, Missouri, Wisconsin: United States Air Force Band of Mid-America (Scott AFB)

For California, Oregon, Washington: United States Air Force Band of the Golden West (Travis AFB)

For Indiana, Kentucky, Michigan, Ohio, western Maryland, western Pennsylvania, West Virginia: United States Air Force Band of Flight (Wright-Patterson AFB)

For Europe, North Africa, and the Middle East: United States Air Forces in Europe Band (Unit 3315, APO AE 09136-5000)

For Alaska, PACIFIC AIR FORCES, as appropriate: United States Air Force Band of the Pacific (Elmendorf AFB)

For Japan, Pacific Air Forces, as appropriate: United States Air Force Band of the Pacific-Asia, Det 1 (Unit 5075, APO AP 96328-5000)

For Hawaii, Pacific Air Forces, as appropriate: United States Air Force Band of the Pacific-Hawaii (OL-A) (Hickam AFB)

Air Force Base Conversion Agency (AFBCA)

AFBCA is a FIELD OPERATING AGENCY headquartered in Washington, D.C., and serves as the federal real property disposal agent and managing agency for USAF bases as they are closed under the Base Closure and Realignment Act of 1988 and the Defense Base Closure and Realignment Act of 1990. AFBCA works with state and local authorities and communities to help develop reuse opportunities to minimize adverse economic impacts on communities affected by base closings.

Air Force bases

All major USAF installations in the United States and its territories are called Air Force bases, abbreviated AFB. Bases located in foreign countries are called air bases (AB). Two USAF units based in the United Kingdom are known by the name of the host country's base: RAF [Royal Air Force] Lakenheath and RAF Mildenhall.

Altus AFB, Oklahoma

Altus was established as Altus Army Air Field in 1942, was inactivated after WORLD WAR II, then reactivated on August 1, 1953. Currently an AIR EDUCATION AND TRAINING COMMAND (AETC) base and home of the 97th Air Mobility Wing, it operates strategic airlift and aerial flying training schools and maintains and supports C-5, KC-135, C-141, and C-17 aircraft. Approximately 3,500 military personnel are stationed here.

Further reading: Altus AFB Web site, www. altus.af.mil.

Andersen AFB, Guam

Andersen was established as North Field in 1944, during WORLD WAR II and was instrumental in bomber operations against Japan. Today it is a PACIFIC AIR FORCES base and headquarters of the THIRTEENTH AIR FORCE. It is the Pacific center for power projection, regional cooperation, and multinational training, and it serves as a logistics support and staging base for aircraft operating in the Pacific and Indian Oceans. The base is home to 2,163 military personnel and has a USAF clinic and a navy hospital. It was named for General James Roy Andersen, lost at sea on February 26, 1946.

Further reading: Andersen AFB Web site, www. andersen.af.mil.

Andrews AFB, Maryland

Andrews is most famous as the home of AIR FORCE ONE and is the home of the 89th Airlift Wing, which provides mission support to the nation's leaders, including the president. Naval and marine installations are also hosted by the base.

Andrews was established in 1942 as Camp Springs Army Air Field. Located just 12 miles east of Washington, D.C., it served principally as a base for air defense of the capital. It was named for Lieutenant General FRANK MAXWELL ANDREWS, military air power advocate, killed in an aircraft crash on May 3, 1943, in Iceland. The large base is home to 7,400 military personnel and more than 3,000 civilian employees. The base also includes a large hospital.

Further reading: Andrews AFB Web site, www. dcmilitary.com/baseguides/airforce/andrews.

Arnold AFB, Tennessee

This AIR FORCE MATERIEL COMMAND (AFMC) base houses the ARNOLD ENGINEERING DEVELOPMENT CENTER (AEDC), the world's largest test facility for advanced aerodynamics and propulsion systems. The center conducts research, development, and evaluation testing for the USAF and the Department of Defense. Only 123 military personnel work at the base, which is staffed mainly by some 3,000 civilian contract employees.

Dedicated June 25, 1951, the base is named for HENRY HARLEY ARNOLD, WORLD WAR II chief of the U.S. ARMY AIR FORCES.

Further reading: Arnold AFB Web site, www. arnold.af.mil.

This A-10 Thunderbolt from the 81st Fighter Squadron, Spangdahlem AB, Germany, takes off from Aviano AB, Italy.   *(U.S. Air Force)*

Aviano AB, Italy

Located 50 miles north of Venice, Aviano AB is a UNITED STATES AIR FORCES IN EUROPE (USAFE) base, headquarters of the SIXTEENTH AIR FORCE, and host to the 31st Fighter Wing—the only permanent NATO fighter WING in southern Europe.

Aviano has served as an Italian air base since 1911; USAF operations began here in 1954. It is home to 3,163 military personnel.

Further reading: Aviano AB Web site, www. aviano.af.mil.

Barksdale AFB, Louisiana

Located in Bossier City, Louisiana, Barksdale was activated in 1933, principally to provide air defense of the Gulf Coast. It was named for Lieutenant Eugene H. Barksdale, an aviator who died in a crash near Wright Field, Ohio, in 1926. In 1949, Barksdale became a STRATEGIC AIR COMMAND (SAC) base and headquarters for the SECOND AIR FORCE. In 1990, it became the headquarters base for the EIGHTH AIR FORCE and the 2nd Bomb Wing and has continued to serve in these capacities after SAC was disbanded in 1992. The base is also the site of the fine Eighth Air Force Museum.

A very large facility handling mainly B-52 and A-10 operations and the 1307th Civil Engineering (Red Horse) Squadron, Barksdale is home to 5,799 military personnel and 649 civilian employees. Facilities include a 40-bed base hospital.

Further reading: Barksdale AFB Web site, www.barksdale.af.mil.

Beale AFB, California

Home of the 9th Reconnaissance Wing and the 7th Space Warning Squadron, Beale operates U-2 reconnaissance aircraft and T-38 Talon trainers.

Formerly the U.S. Army's Camp Beale (named for Army Brigadier General Edward F. Beale), the facility was acquired by the USAF in 1951 and was first used as a STRATEGIC AIR COMMAND (SAC) base, operating heavy bombers and tankers. More than 3,000 military personnel are assigned to the base.

Further reading: Beale AFB Web site, www. beale.af.mil.

Bolling AFB, Washington, D.C.

Named for Colonel Raynal C. Bolling, first high-ranking U.S. aviator killed in WORLD WAR I, the airfield was established in October 1917. In 1940, part of the base was transferred to the navy as the Anacostia Naval Air Station.

Bolling is now home to the 11th Wing, the USAF Honor Guard, the U.S. Air Force Band, the AIR FORCE OFFICE OF SCIENTIFIC RESEARCH (AFOSR), the Air Force Chief of Chaplains, and the Air Force Surgeon General. It is headquarters of the AIR FORCE HISTORY SUPPORT OFFICE (AFHSO) and headquarters of the AIR FORCE OFFICE OF SPECIAL INVESTIGATIONS (AFOSI), and also houses the AIR FORCE REAL ESTATE AGENCY (AFREA), AIR FORCE MEDICAL OPERATIONS AGENCY (AFMOA), Defense Intelligence Agency, and the AIR FORCE LEGAL SERVICES AGENCY (AFLSA).

Further reading: Bolling AFB Web site, www. bolling.af.mil.

Brooks AFB, Texas

Located in San Antonio, Brooks is an AIR FORCE MATERIEL COMMAND (AFMC) base, which houses the Human Systems Center, the UNITED STATES AIR FORCE SCHOOL OF AEROSPACE MEDICINE, and the Armstrong Laboratory of the Human Systems Program Office. Other units on base are the Systems Acquisition School, AIR FORCE MEDICAL SUPPORT AGENCY (AFMSA), 68th Intelligence Squadron, AIR FORCE CENTER FOR ENVIRONMENTAL EXCELLENCE (AFCEE), and the Medical Systems Implementation and Training Element.

Activated in 1917, the base was named for Cadet Sidney J. Brooks, Jr., who was killed on November 13, 1917, during his commissioning flight. From 1919 to 1923, the field served as a balloon and airship school, and from 1922 to 1931 it was a primary flight training school. The School of Aviation Medicine was established here in 1926. Flight operations ceased at Brooks in 1960.

Further reading: Brooks AFB Web site, www. brooks.af.mil.

Cannon AFB, New Mexico

An AIR COMBAT COMMAND (ACC) base, Cannon is home to the 27th Fighter Wing, with F-16 operations. Activated in August 1942, the base was named for General John K. Cannon, WORLD WAR II Mediterranean theater commander. Cannon was the last USAF base to operate the F-111 "Aardvark," which was retired after 30 years of service in 1996.

Located near Clovis, New Mexico, Cannon is home to almost 5,000 military personnel.

Further reading: Cannon AFB Web site, www. cannon.af.mil.

Carswell AFB

Carswell was activated in 1942 near Fort Worth, Texas, as Tarant Field. Later named Griffiss AFB, it was, in 1948, renamed in honor of Major Horace S. Carswell, Jr., a Fort Worth winner of the Medal of Honor, killed in a B-24 crash landing in China in 1944.

As a STRATEGIC AIR COMMAND (SAC) base, Carswell, home of the 7th Bomb Group, operated B-36 bombers and then B-52s and B-58s. The base was closed in 1991.

Further reading: Carswell AFB information, Global Security.Org, "Carswell AFB," www.globalsecurity. org/wmd/facility/carswell.htm.

Castle AFB

Activated in 1941 at Merced, California, the Castle predecessor installation operated throughout WORLD WAR II as a basic flight training field. In 1946, it was named after Brigadier General Frederick W. Castle, Medal of Honor winner killed in action in 1944, and was inactivated shortly afterward. Reactivated in 1955, as a STRATEGIC AIR COMMAND (SAC) base, it was one of the first installations to operate B-52s. Castle AFB was closed in 1991.

Further reading: Castle AFB information, Global Security.Org, "Castle AFB," at www.globalsecurity. org/wmd/facility/castle.htm.

Chanute AFB, Illinois

Established in 1917 as Rantoul Aviation Field in Rantoul, Illinois, the facility was renamed for aviation pioneer Octave Chanute before the close of the year. During WORLD WAR I, it served as a flight training facility, and, after the war, three military aviation-related training schools were established here, collectively forming the Air Service Technical School. With the advent of WORLD WAR II, Chanute became a major training center for technicians as well as pilots; some 200,000 students passed through schools here.

Renamed Chanute Technical Training Center in 1990, the entire installation was closed in 1993.

Further reading: Chanute AFB information, Octave Chanute Aerospace Museum, "From Swords to Plowshares: The Closure of Chanute," at www. aeromuseum.org/History/plough.html.

Charleston AFB, South Carolina

An AIR FORCE MATERIEL COMMAND (AFMC) base, Charleston is home to the 437th Airlift Wing and other organizations. Activated in October 1942, the base was inactivated in March 1946, then reactivated in August 1953. Charleston AFB is located just outside of Charleston, S.C., and is staffed by 7,352 military personnel and 1,295 civilian employees.

Further reading: Charleston AFB Web site, www. charleston.af.mil.

Clark AB

Located 50 miles north of Manila in the Philippines, Clark was established as Fort Stotsenberg, an army installation, in 1903. In March 1912, Lieutenant FRANK P. LAHM was named to command the Philippine Air School here, with a single aircraft, and in 1919 the installation officially became Clark Field, named in honor of Captain Harold M. Clark, a U.S. Army pilot killed in a crash in Panama. It was in the summer of 1941, on the eve of America's entry into WORLD WAR II, that the 19th Bombardment Group, with B-17s and B-18s, arrived. When the Japanese attacked Clark Field on December 8, 1941, most of the aircraft were destroyed on the ground. Most of the personnel stationed at Clark who survived the initial attack participated in the defense of Bataan, surrendered with the U.S. and Philippine troops under command of Lieutenant General Jonathan Wainwright, and endured the infamous "Bataan Death March" to distant POW camps. U.S. forces began to retake Clark Field late in 1944, forcing the Japanese out by January 1945.

The THIRTEENTH AIR FORCE became resident at Clark AB in 1947, and the base was a central logistics hub during both the KOREAN WAR and the VIETNAM WAR. It was also the first stop for returning U.S. POWs from Vietnam in 1973. During the 1986 revolution against the Philippine's dictatorial president Ferdinand Marcos, Marcos was evacuated through Clark AB, and, in 1989, USAF F-4s, flying from the base, supported Philippine president Corazon Aquino's successful defense in the sixth coup attempt against her.

In 1991, the Philippine Senate rejected an extension of the U.S.-Philippines Military Bases Agreement, which expired on September 16, effectively terminating the American military's lease for Clark AB. The USAF formally transferred Clark AB to the Philippines on November 26, 1991.

Further reading: Clark AB information, Clark Air Base (CAB) home pages, at www.clarkab.org.

Columbus AFB, Mississippi

Activated in 1941 for pilot training, the base is home to the 14th Flying Training Wing and is a location for undergraduate pilot training and an Introduction to Fighter Fundamentals course.

Further reading: Columbus AFB Web site, www. columbus.af.mil.

Davis-Monthan AFB, Arizona

Located within the city limits of Tucson, Davis-Monthan is an AIR COMBAT COMMAND (ACC) base, which houses the 355th Wing and is headquarters of the TWELFTH AIR FORCE. The base is a center for electronic combat training and operations and also hosts a Montana ANG F-16 fighter wing. The base is also the site of the AIR FORCE MATERIEL COMMAND (AFMC) Aerospace Maintenance and Regeneration Center, a storage facility for excess USAF and Department of Defense aerospace vehicles. Almost 6,000 military personnel are stationed here, and the base includes a large military hospital.

Activated in 1927, the base is named for two Tucson-area aviators killed in accidents, Lieutenant Samuel H. Davis (killed December 28, 1921) and Second Lieutenant Oscar Monthan (killed March 27, 1924).

Further reading: Davis-Monthan AFB Web site, www.dm.af.mil.

Dover AFB, Delaware

The largest AIRLIFT aerial post on the East Coast, Dover AFB, an AIR MOBILITY COMMAND (AMC) base, is home to the 436th Airlift Wing. Activated in December 1941, just 10 days after the Japanese attack on Pearl Harbor, the base was inactivated in 1946, then reactivated early in 1951. It was the first airbase to receive the giant C-5 Galaxy transport. More than 7,000 military personnel are stationed here.

Further reading: Dover AFB Web site, www. dover.af.mil.

Dyess AFB, Texas

An AIR COMBAT COMMAND (ACC) base, Dyess is home to the 7th Wing and operates two B-1B bomber squadrons and two C-130 squadrons. All B-1B training is conducted here.

It is named for Lieutenant Colonel William E. Dyess, who escaped from a Japanese POW camp in WORLD WAR II and was subsequently killed in a P-38 crash in December 1943. Almost 5,000 military personnel are stationed here, just outside of Abilene.

Further reading: Dyess AFB Web site, www. dyess.af.mil.

Edwards AFB, California

This AIR FORCE MATERIEL COMMAND (AFMC) base is best known to the public as an advanced aircraft and aerospace vehicle test site and as the secondary landing site for the Space Shuttle. It is home to the AIR FORCE FLIGHT TEST CENTER (AFFTC) and the UNITED STATES AIR FORCE TEST PILOT SCHOOL. Also housed here are the Astronautics Directorate of the Phillips Laboratory and NASA's Ames Dryden Flight Research Facility.

Base activities began here in September 1933 when the site was known as Muroc Army Air Field. It was renamed for Captain Glen W. Edwards, killed on June 5, 1948, while testing the revolutionary YB-49 "Flying Wing." More than 4,200 military personnel are stationed on the base, and government and contract civilian personnel number about 7,400.

Further reading: Edwards AFB Web site, www. edwards.af.mil.

Eglin AFB, Florida

Covering 463,452 acres—two-thirds the size of Rhode Island—Eglin is the nation's largest USAF base. Its host unit is the AIR FORCE DEVELOPMENT TEST CENTER (AFDTC) with an associate unit, the Aeronautical Systems Center. Also located here is the Armament Directorate of the Wright Laboratory. Operational units include 33rd Fighter Wing, 53rd Wing (ACC), 96th Air Base Wing, 46th Test Wing, 9191th Special Operations Wing, 20th Space Surveillance Squadron, 9th Special Operations Squadron, 728th Tactical Control Squadron, a U.S. Army Ranger Training Battalion, a U.S. Navy Explosive Ordnance Disposal School, and the Air Force Armament Museum. Almost 8,500 military personnel are stationed here, and the base also employs 4,303 civilians.

Activated in 1935, the base was subsequently named for Lieutenant Colonel Frederick I. Eglin, a WORLD WAR I pilot killed in an accident on January 1, 1937.

Further reading: Eglin AFB Web site, www. eglin.af.mil.

Eielson AFB, Alaska

A PACIFIC AIR FORCES (PACAF) base, Eielson hosts the 354th Fighter Wing with F-16, A-10, and OA-10 operations. Also operating from Eielson are the Arctic Survival School and the 168th Air Refueling Wing (ANG) as well as a detachment of the AIR FORCE TECHNICAL APPLICATIONS CENTER (AFTAC).

Activated in 1944, the base was named for Carl Ben Eielson, an Arctic aviation pioneer who died on an Arctic rescue mission in November 1929. More than 2,700 military personnel are stationed here.

Further reading: Eielson AFB Web site, www. eielson.af.mil.

Ellsworth AFB, South Dakota

The base is home to the 28th Bomb Wing, with one B1-B squadron, and the South Dakota Air and Space Museum.

Activated in July 1942 as the Rapid City AAB, it was renamed in 1953 for Brigadier General

Richard E. Ellsworth, killed March 18, 1953, in the crash of an RB-36 in Newfoundland. There are 3,724 military personnel stationed here.

Further reading: Ellsworth AFB Web site, www. ellsworth.af.mil.

Elmendorf AFB, Alaska

Located just outside Anchorage, Elmendorf is a PACIFIC AIR FORCES (PACAF) base and a hub for all traffic to and from the Far East. It houses headquarters for the following: ALASKAN AIR COMMAND; ELEVENTH AIR FORCE; and Alaska NORAD Region. The base host unit is the 3rd Wing, with F-15 fighter and C-130 and C-12 airlift operations, as well as E-3 airborne air control operations, and 3rd Medical Group. Associated units also operate from the base, which also hosts various U.S. Army, U.S. Navy, and U.S. Marine activities. More than 6,500 military personnel are stationed at Elmendorf. Facilities include a 60-bed hospital.

Activated in July 1940, the installation was named for Captain Hugh Elmendorf, killed January 13, 1933, at Wright Field, Ohio, while testing a new pursuit aircraft.

Further reading: Elmendorf AFB Web site, www. elmendorf.af.mil.

England AFB, Louisiana

This base was activated near Alexandria, Louisiana, in 1941 and was known as Alexandria AAB until 1955, when it was named for Lieutenant Colonel John B. England, a WORLD WAR II fighter ace killed in a 1954 F-86 accident. He had formerly commanded a bomber unit stationed at Alexandria AAB.

The base was used during World War II for B-17 and B-29 training, was inactivated from 1946 to 1950, then was used by the AIR NATIONAL GUARD until 1953, when the USAF took it over. At the time of its closure in 1992, England AFB was home to the 23rd Tactical Fighter Wing, flying A-10s.

Fairchild AFB, Washington

An AIR FORCE MATERIEL COMMAND (AFMC) base, Fairchild is the air refueling hub to the western

United States. Its host unit is the 92nd Air Refueling Wing, with KC-135 aircraft, and the base also houses tenant units, most notably the 366th Crew Training Group, which operates the AIR EDUCATION AND TRAINING COMMAND (AETC) Survival School. The base is home to 4,316 military personnel.

Activated in 1942 as Galena Field, then renamed Spokane AFB, it was finally named in 1950 after General Muir S. Fairchild, USAF vice chief of staff.

Further reading: Fairchild AFB Web site, www. fairchild.af.mil.

Falcon AFB

Listed under Schriever AFB.

Francis E. Warren AFB, Wyoming

Located just outside of Cheyenne, the base is home to the 90th Missile Wing, with 50 Peacekeeper and 150 Minuteman III missiles. The 37th Air Rescue Flight also operates out of the base. The Air Force ICBM Museum is located on the base.

Activated on July 4, 1867, by the U.S. Army as Fort D. A. Russell, the base was assigned to the USAF in 1947. It had been renamed after the first state governor of Wyoming, Francis Emory Warren, in 1930. The base has no runway; 3,655 military personnel serve here.

Further reading: Francis E. Warren AFB Web site, www.warren.af.mil.

Goodfellow AFB, Texas

This AIR EDUCATION AND TRAINING COMMAND (AETC) base is home to the 17th Training Wing, which provides technical training in intelligence areas, serving not only USAF personnel but members of other services as well as civilian intelligence agencies and members of foreign military services. The wing also trains USAF, U.S. Army, and U.S. Marine Corps personnel in fire protection and fire rescue and conducts USAF special instruments training.

Activated in January 1941, the base was named for Lieutenant John J. Goodfellow, Jr., a WORLD

WAR I pilot killed in action on September 14, 1918. More than 3,000 military personnel are stationed here. The base has no runway.

Further reading: Goodfellow AFB Web site, www.goodfellow.af.mil.

Grand Forks AFB, North Dakota

An AIR FORCE MATERIEL COMMAND (AFMC) base, Grand Forks is home to the 319th Air Refueling Wing and the 321st Missile Group (150 Minuteman III ICBMs). Until the STRATEGIC AIR COMMAND (SAC) was disbanded in 1992, Grand Forks was a SAC base. The base was also home to 319 Bomb Group, which flew B-1 bombers until it was inactivated in May 1994.

Activated in 1956 on land donated to the USAF by the citizens of Grand Forks, the base itself covers 5,418 acres and the missile complex an additional 7,500 square miles. More than 5,000 military personnel are stationed here.

Further reading: Grand Forks AFB Web site, www.grandforks.af.mil.

Griffiss AFB, New York

This longtime STRATEGIC AIR COMMAND (SAC) base was located near Rome, New York, until its phaseout and closure during 1995–98. Activated in 1942 as Rome AAF, it was named in honor of Lieutenant Colonel Townsend E. Griffiss, whose aircraft was shot down by friendly fire during WORLD WAR II in 1942. Its principal unit at the time of its phaseout and closure was the 416th Wing with B-52 bombers and KC-135 tankers.

Further reading: Griffiss AFB information, GlobalSecurity.Org, "Griffiss AFB," at www.globalsecurity.org/military/facility/griffiss.htm.

Grissom AFB, Indiana

Originally a U.S. Navy base near Kokomo, Indiana, then a USAF storage branch from 1951 to 1954, when it became Bunker Hill AFB, it was renamed in honor of Virgil I. "Gus" Grissom, one of America's original seven astronauts, who was killed dur-

ing an Apollo spacecraft test in 1967. The base served both as a STRATEGIC AIR COMMAND (SAC) facility and as a TACTICAL AIR COMMAND (TAC) base, with B-47s and B-58s. At the time of its closure in 1994, it was primarily used by the 305th Air Refueling Wing, flying EC-135s and KC-135s.

Gunter AFB (Gunter Annex)

Listed under Maxwell AFB, Gunter Annex.

Hanscom AFB, Massachusetts

This AIR FORCE MATERIEL COMMAND (AFMC) base is headquarters of the Electronic Systems Center and is responsible for acquisition of C^{4}I (command, control, communications, and intelligence) systems for the USAF and for other services and government agencies. The base is the site for much advanced electronic warfare research and development.

In 1943, the base was named Hanscom Field in honor of Laurence G. Hanscom, an aviation advocate and pioneer killed in a civilian aircraft accident in 1941. More than 2,000 military personnel serve on the base, together with almost 2,000 civilian employees.

Further reading: Hanscom AFB Web site, www.hanscom.af.mil.

Hickam AFB, Hawaii

Located just west of Honolulu, the base was named Hickam Field in 1935 to honor Lieutenant Colonel Horace M. Hickam, killed in an aircraft accident in Texas the year before. Hickam Field was heavily damaged in the December 7, 1941, Japanese attack on Pearl Harbor (157 of 231 planes destroyed or damaged on the ground), but quickly recovered to become a major staging area for WORLD WAR II operations in the Pacific.

In 1957, PACIFIC AIR FORCES (PACAF) headquarters was established at Hickam AFB, which also hosts the 15th Air Base Wing and major tenant units, including 154th Wing (ANG), 201st Combat Communications Group, and 615th Air Mobility Support Group. There are 3,657 military personnel at Hickam AFB and 1,280 civilian employees.

Further reading: Hickam AFB Web site, www2. hickam.af.mil.

Hill AFB, Utah

An AIR FORCE MATERIEL COMMAND (AFMC) base, Hill is headquarters of the Ogden Air Logistics Center, which provides support for silo-based ICBM (INTERCONTINENTAL BALLISTIC MISSILE) weapons—Minutemen and Peacekeepers—and for F-16 and C-130 aircraft, conventional munitions, and other aerospace components, including software and photonics. Other units on base include the 412th Test Wing, which manages the Utah Test and Training Range, the 388th Fighter Wing, the 419th Fighter Wing, and the Defense Megacenter Ogden. The Hill Aerospace Museum is also on base. More than 4,600 military personnel are stationed at Hill, which also employs a large number (9,532) of civilians.

Activated in November 1940, the base was named for Major Ployer P. Hill, killed on October 30, 1935, while testing the first B-17 bomber.

Further reading: Hill AFB Web site, www.hill. af.mil.

Holloman AFB, New Mexico

This AIR COMBAT COMMAND (ACC) base is home to the 49th Fighter Wing, with F-117 Stealth fighter operations. Also on base are F-4E aircrew training (20th Fighter Squadron and 1st German Air Force Training Squadron), AT-38B training, and the 48th Rescue Squadron. Twelve German Tornado aircraft, with 350 German personnel, are permanently assigned to the WING. The base is also home to a number of associated units.

Activated in 1942 as the Alamogordo Bombing and Gunnery Range, the base was named in 1948 in honor of Colonel George Holloman, an instrument flying and missile pioneer who died in a B-17 accident in Formosa in 1946. More than 4,000 military personnel are stationed here.

Further reading: Holloman AFB Web site, www.holloman.af.mil.

Howard AFB, Panama

The 24th Wing, an AIR COMBAT COMMAND (ACC) unit, is headquartered here as the USAF presence throughout Latin America. Also on base are the 640th Air Mobility Support Squadron and the 33rd Intelligence Squadron. Sixteen hundred military personnel are stationed at Howard, which was established in 1928 as Bruja Point Military Reservation, then named for Major Charles H. Howard.

Further reading: Howard AFB information, GlobalSecurity.Org, "Howard AFB," www.globalsecurity.org/military/facility/howard.htm.

Hurlburt Field, Florida

This base is headquarters of the AIR FORCE SPECIAL OPERATIONS COMMAND (AFSOC) and is home to the 16th Special Operations Wing. Also on base are the 505th Command and Control Evaluation Group, which includes the USAF Air Ground Operations School, the USAF Battle Staff Training School (Blue Flag), the 720th Special Tactics Group, the 23rd Special Tactics Squadron, the Joint Warfare Center, the USAF Special Operations School, the 18th Flight Test Squadron, the 823rd Civil Engineering Squadron (Red Horse), a detachment of the 11335th Technical Training Squadron, and a detachment of the AIR WEATHER SERVICE (AWS). More than 7,000 military personnel are stationed at Hurlburt.

Hurlburt was activated in 1941 as an auxiliary field of Eglin AAF (see Eglin AFB) and in 1944 was named in honor of Lieutenant Donald W. Hurlburt, killed while flying from Eglin in 1943.

Further reading: Hurlburt Field Web site, www. hurlburt.af.mil.

Incirlik AB, Turkey

A UNITED STATES AIR FORCES IN EUROPE (USAFE) base, Incirlik, near Ankara, is home to the 39th Wing and operates Combined Task Force assets, including Turkish, British, French, and U.S. combat and tanker aircraft. The base is also home to the 628th Air Mobility Support Squadron, which provides a full aerial port operation.

Activated in May 1954 in what was once a fig orchard (*incirlik* is the Turkish word for fig orchard), the base now has almost 2,500 U.S. military personnel and almost 3,000 civilian employees. It incorporates a medium-sized regional military hospital.

Further reading: Incirlik AB information, GlobalSecurity.Org, "Sixteenth Air Force," at www.globalsecurity.org/military/agency/usaf/16af.htm.

Kadena AB, Japan

A PACIFIC AIR FORCES (PACAF) base, Kadena, is home to the 18th Wing (F-15 operations) and the 909th Air Refueling Squadron (KC-135 operations), the 961st Airborne Air Control Squadron (E-3 operations), and the 33rd Rescue Squadron (HH-60 operations), in addition to associated units.

Kadena was a Japanese airfield during WORLD WAR II when it was taken by U.S. forces invading Okinawa. The USAAF used it as a base from which bombing raids against the Japanese homeland were launched. Kadena was headquarters of the TWENTIETH AIR FORCE during the KOREAN WAR. The base is named for the nearest city. There are some 7,300 military personnel at Kadena and more than 4,000 civilian employees, U.S. nationals, and locals.

Further reading: Kadena AB Web site, www.kadena.af.mil.

Keesler AFB, Mississippi

Located in Biloxi on the Gulf of Mexico, Keesler is an AIR EDUCATION AND TRAINING COMMAND (AETC) base and headquarters of the SECOND AIR FORCE. Housed here is the 81st Training Wing, which specializes in avionics, communications, electronics, and related technical areas, and the Keesler Medical Center (with a 250-bed hospital). The base is also home to the AETC NCO Academy. About 8,300 military personnel are stationed at Keesler, together with more than 4,000 civilian employees.

The base, activated on June 12, 1941, is named for Second Lieutenant Samuel R. Keesler, Jr., a Mis-

sissippi native killed in action as an aerial observer during WORLD WAR I, on October 9, 1918.

Further reading: Keesler AFB Web site, www.keesler.af.mil.

Kelly AFB, Texas

Located outside of San Antonio, Kelly AFB, inactivated in 2001, was an AIR FORCE MATERIEL COMMAND (AFMC) base and the headquarters of the San Antonio Air Logistics Center, which provided logistics management, procurement, and systems support for an array of aircraft, including the C-5 Galaxy. The center managed more than 75 percent of the USAF engine inventory, the fuel and lubricants used by USAF and NASA, and nuclear weapons. The base also housed the headquarters of the AIR INTELLIGENCE AGENCY (AIA) and was home to the AIR FORCE INFORMATION WARFARE CENTER (AFIWC), the Joint Command and Control Warfare Center, the Air Force News Agency, the Defense Commissary Agency, and other agencies and offices. In all, 4,581 military and 14,397 civilian personnel work at Kelly AFB.

Established on November 21, 1916, as Aviation Camp, Fort Houston, Kelly was the oldest continuously active air force base in the United States. It was named for Lieutenant George E. M. Kelly, the first U.S. Army pilot to lose his life flying a military aircraft, killed May 10, 1911.

Further reading: Kelly AFB information, Global Security.Org, "Kelly AFB," at www.globalsecurity.org/military/facility/kelly.htm.

Kirtland AFB, New Mexico

Located in Albuquerque, Kirtland is an AIR FORCE MATERIEL COMMAND (AFMC) base and headquarters of the 377th Air Base Wing. An array of agencies and units are housed here, including 58th Special Operations Wing; AIR FORCE OPERATIONAL TEST AND EVALUATION CENTER (AFOTEC); Philips Laboratory; 150th Fighter Wing (ANG); Field Command's Defense Nuclear Agency; Sandia National Laboratories; Department of Energy's Albuquerque Operations Office; Kirtland NCO

Academy; 898th Munitions Squadron; Air Force Security Police Agency (AFSPA); Defense Nuclear Weapons School; Air Force Inspection Agency; and Air Force Safety Center.

The base is staffed by almost 6,000 military personnel and almost 14,000 civilian employees. It was established in January 1941 as the Albuquerque Army Air Base and was renamed in honor of Colonel Roy C. Kirtland, an air pioneer who died on May 2, 1941.

Further reading: Kirtland AFB Web site, www. kirtland.af.mil.

Kunsan AB, Republic of Korea

A PACIFIC AIR FORCES (PACAF) base, Kunsan is home to the 8th Fighter Wing F-16 operations and also hosts several U.S. Army units. About 2,300 military personnel are stationed at Kunsan, which was built by the Japanese in 1938 and taken over and expanded by the USAF in 1951.

Further reading: Kunsan AB Web site, www. kunsan.af.mil.

Lackland AFB, Texas

This AIR EDUCATION AND TRAINING COMMAND (AETC) base is home to the 37th Training Wing, largest training wing in the USAF, graduating 65,000 students each year. The 737th Training Group provides basic military training. The 37th Training Group conducts more than 250 technical training courses. The Defense Language Institute English Language Center conducts English language training for international and U.S. military students. The INTER-AMERICAN AIR FORCES ACADEMY (IAAFA) offers professional, technical, and management training in Spanish to military forces and government agencies from Latin American and Caribbean nations. Some 6,300 military personnel serve at Lackland, in addition to 6,200 civilian employees, and approximately 8,700 students.

Lackland is also the home of the USAF's largest medical organization, the 59th Medical Wing (Wilford Hall USAF Medical Center), which runs a 592-bed hospital on base.

Activated in 1941 as part of Kelly Field (see Kelly AFB), it was detached in 1942 and, in 1948, was named for Brigadier General Frank D. Lackland, early commandant of Kelly Field, who died in 1943.

Further reading: Lackland AFB Web site, www. lackland.af.mil.

Langley AFB, Virginia

Langley is headquarters of AIR COMBAT COMMAND (ACC) and houses the 1st Fighter Wing F-15 operations. Associate units include Air Operations Squadron, Training Support Squadron, Computer Systems Squadron, the ACC Heritage of America Band, a U.S. Army TRADOC Flight Detachment, the Army/USAF Center for Low-Intensity Conflict, and the AIR FORCE DOCTRINE CENTER (AFDC). NASA's Langley Research Center is adjacent to the base. Almost 8,000 military personnel are stationed at Langley, together with about 1,100 civilian employees.

Activated on December 30, 1916, as an "Aviation Experimental Station and Proving Grounds," the facility was named to honor Samuel P. Langley, aviation pioneer and scientist, who died in 1906.

Further reading: Langley AFB Web site, www. langley.af.mil.

Laughlin AFB, Texas

This AIR EDUCATION AND TRAINING COMMAND (AETC) base is home to the 47th Flying Training Wing, which provides specialized undergraduate pilot training. About 1,200 military personnel are stationed here, along with approximately 1,000 civilian employees. The base was activated in July 1942 and named for First Lieutenant Jack Thomas Laughlin, a native of Del Rio (location of the base), a B-17 pilot killed over Java, January 29, 1942.

Further reading: Laughlin AFB Web site, www. laughlin.af.mil.

Little Rock AFB, Arkansas

An AIR COMBAT COMMAND (ACC) base, Little Rock, is home to the 314th Airlift Wing, the only C-130 training base in the Department of Defense. The base trains USAF crews as well as crews from all service branches and some foreign countries. Tenant organizations include 189th Airlift Wing (ANG); 96th Mobile Aerial Port Squadron; 348th USAF Recruiting Squadron; a detachment of the AIR FORCE OFFICE OF SPECIAL INVESTIGATIONS (AFPSI); a detachment of the 373rd Field Training Squadron; a detachment of the AIR FORCE AUDIT AGENCY (AFAA); and the Combat Aerial Delivery School (ACC). The base is also headquarters for the Arkansas AIR NATIONAL GUARD.

Activated in 1955, the base has 4,450 military personnel and includes a 25-bed hospital.

Further reading: Little Rock AFB Web site, www. littlerock.af.mil.

Los Angeles AFB, California

Located in El Segundo, just outside of Los Angeles, this AIR FORCE MATERIEL COMMAND (AFMC) base is headquarters for AFMC's Space and Missile Systems Center, which is responsible for research, development, acquisition, in-orbit testing, and sustainment of military space and missile systems. The on-base support unit is the 61st Air Base Group. The base has no runway. About 1,500 military personnel are stationed here, together with more than 1,000 civilian employees.

Further reading: Los Angeles AFB Web site, www.losangeles.af.mil.

Malmstrom AFB, Montana

An AIR FORCE SPACE COMMAND (AFSPC) base, Malmstrom's host unit is the 341st Missile Wing, operating Minuteman III missiles. The base tenant unit is the 43rd Air Refueling Group, operating KC-135 tankers. There are 4,350 military personnel stationed at Malmstrom, which was activated on December 15, 1942, as Great Falls AAF and, in 1955, was named for Colonel Einar A. Malmstrom, a WORLD WAR II fighter commander killed in an air accident on August 21, 1954. Malmstrom was the first Minuteman wing of the STRATEGIC AIR COMMAND (SAC).

Further reading: Malmstrom AFB Web site, www.malmstrom.af.mil.

Maxwell AFB, Alabama

An AIR EDUCATION AND TRAINING COMMAND (AETC) base, Maxwell is home to the 42nd Air Base Wing and is the headquarters of AIR UNIVERSITY (AU) as well as home to AIR WAR COLLEGE (AWC), Air Command and Staff College (ACSC), AIR FORCE QUALITY INSTITUTE (AFQI), Air University Library; COLLEGE OF AEROSPACE DOCTRINE, RESEARCH AND EDUCATION; AIR FORCE RESERVE OFFICERS TRAINING CORPS (AFROTC), Officer Training School, and the Ira C. Eaker College for Professional Development. The base is headquarters for the COMMUNITY COLLEGE OF THE AIR FORCE (CCAF) and the CIVIL AIR PATROL (CAP). Also resident here are the Squadron Officer School and the AIR FORCE INSTITUTE OF TECHNOLOGY (AFIT). Associate units base here include 908th Airlift Wing (AIR FORCE RESERVE) and the AIR FORCE HISTORICAL RESEARCH AGENCY (AFHRA). There are 3,729 military personnel stationed at Maxwell, together with 2,986 civilian employees. The base has a 30-bed hospital.

The site of Maxwell AFB, near Montgomery, was a civilian flying school opened by the Wright brothers in 1910. It was activated as a military base in 1918 and was subsequently named for Second Lieutenant William C. Maxwell, killed in air accident on August 12, 1920, in the Philippines. Also see Maxwell AFB, Gunter Annex.

Further reading: Maxwell AFB Web site, www. au.af.mil.

Maxwell AFB, Gunter Annex, Alabama

This AIR EDUCATION AND TRAINING COMMAND (AETC) base is operated under the headquarters of AIR UNIVERSITY (AU). Gunter Annex includes the College for Enlisted Professional Military Education (includes USAF Senior NCO Academy); Extension Course Institute; Standard Systems Group; and AIR FORCE LOGISTICS MANAGEMENT AGENCY (AFLMA). See Maxwell AFB for numbers of personnel on base.

Gunter Annex was activated on August 27, 1940, and was named for William A. Gunter, long-time mayor of Montgomery, Alabama, and a champion of air power, who died in 1940.

Further reading: Maxwell AFB Web site, www.au.af.mil.

McChord AFB, Washington

An AIR MOBILITY COMMAND (AMC) base, McChord's host unit is the 62nd Airlift Wing, and its major tenants include 446th Airlift Wing (AIR FORCE RESERVE) and Western Air Defense Sector (AIR NATIONAL GUARD). The base is responsible for strategic AIRLIFT of personnel and cargo worldwide, on short notice, in support of national objectives. Its primary customer is the U.S. Army's Fort Lewis. There are more than 4,100 military personnel stationed here, together with about 1,300 civilian employees.

Activated on May 5, 1938, the base is named for Colonel William C. McChord, killed August 18, 1937, while attempting a forced landing at Maidens, Virginia.

Further reading: McChord AFB Web site, http://public.mcchord.amc.af.mil.

McClellan AFB, California

Before it was closed in July 2001, this AIR FORCE MATERIEL COMMAND (AFMC) base, located near Sacramento, California, was the headquarters of the Sacramento Air Logistics Center, which provided logistics management, procurement, maintenance, and distribution support for F/EF-111 and A-10 aircraft and, as a second source, for the F-15 and KC-135 weapon systems. The center was program manager for the F-117A stealth fighter and the support center for the F-22. The center supported more than 200 electronic systems and programs as well as eight space systems. It also specialized in very-high-speed integrated circuits, fiber optics, and advanced composites. The center had facilities for robotic nondestructive inspection using X-ray and neutron radiography of F-111-size aircraft. With closure of the base, the USAF contracted many of the center's functions to private industry.

Other major units on base included Defense Depot-McClellan; Defense Information Systems Organization-McClellan; 938th Engineering Installation Squadron; Technical Operations Division, AIR FORCE TECHNICAL APPLICATIONS CENTER (AFTAC); FOURTH AIR FORCE (AIR FORCE RESERVE); and U.S. Coast Guard Air Station, Sacramento.

The base was named for Major Hezekiah McClellan, a pioneer in Arctic aeronautical experiments, who was killed in a crash on May 25, 1936.

Further reading: McClellan AFB information, GlobalSecurity.Org, "McClellan AFB," at www.globalsecurity.org/military/facility/mcclellan.htm.

McConnell AFB, Kansas

An AIR MOBILITY COMMAND (AMC) base, McConnell is home to the 22nd Air Refueling Wing; 931st Air Refueling Group (AIR FORCE RESERVE), and the 184th Bomb Wing (AIR NATIONAL GUARD). Almost 3,000 military personnel are assigned here.

Activated on June 5, 1951, the base is named for Captain Fred J. McConnell, a WORLD WAR II B-24 pilot who died in a crash of a private plane on October 25, 1945, and for his brother, Second Lieutenant Thomas L. McConnell, also a World War II B-24 pilot, who was killed on July 10, 1943, in the Pacific, during an attack on Bougainville.

Further reading: McConnell AFB Web site, www.mcconnell.af.mil.

McGuire AFB, New Jersey

This AIR MOBILITY COMMAND (AMC) base, located near Trenton, is home to the 305th Air Mobility Wing and is headquarters of the TWENTY-FIRST AIR FORCE. Also in residence are the 621st Air Mobility Operations Group, the Air Mobility Warfare Center (at Fort Dix, N.J.), the New Jersey AIR NATIONAL GUARD, the New Jersey CIVIL AIR PATROL, 108th Air Refueling Wing (ANG), 514th Air Mobility Wing (AIR FORCE RESERVE), and the McGuire NCO Academy. Including AFR and ANG units, 10,512 military personnel are assigned to McGuire, along with 1,604 civilian employees.

Activated in 1937 as Fort Dix AFB and adjoining Fort Dix, the installation was renamed in 1948 for Major Thomas B. McGuire, Jr., P-38 pilot, second leading U.S. ace of WORLD WAR II, and recipient of the Medal of Honor, who was killed in action on January 7, 1945, in the Philippines.

Further reading: McGuire AFB Web site, www.mcguire.af.mil.

Minot AFB, North Dakota

An AIR COMBAT COMMAND (ACC) base, Minot is home to the 5th Bomb Wing, operating B-52s, as well as the 91st Missile Wing, with Minuteman III ICBM operations. Other units include the 23rd Bomb Squadron and the 54th Rescue Flight. On base are 3,768 military personnel.

The base was activated in January 1957 and is named after the city of Minot, whose citizens donated $50,000 toward purchase of the land for the USAF. There is a 45-bed hospital on base.

Further reading: Minot AFB Web site, www.minot.af.mil.

Misawa AB, Japan

A PACIFIC AIR FORCES (PACAF) and joint-service base located within the city of Misawa, the base is home to the 35th Fighter Wing, F-16 operations, and includes the 3rd Space Surveillance Squadron, 301st Intelligence Squadron, a Naval Air Facility, a Naval Security Group, a U.S. Army field station, and Company E, U.S. Marine Support Battalion.

The Japanese army built an airfield at Misawa in 1938, and the base was occupied by U.S. forces in September 1945. Currently, more than 4,600 military personnel (USAF, navy, army, marines) are stationed here.

Further reading: Misawa AB Web site, www.misawa.af.mil.

Moody AFB, Georgia

Located in southern Georgia, near Valdosta, this AIR COMBAT COMMAND (ACC) base is home to the 347th Wing, operating F-16 LANTIRN-equipped night fighters, as well as C-130E and A/OA-10 aircraft, and the 71st Air Control Squadron. Tenant units include 336th USAF Recruiting Squadron, a detachment of AIR FORCE OFFICE OF SPECIAL INVESTIGATIONS (AFOSI), and the 332nd Training Detachment. Military personnel on base number 3,752.

The base was activated in June 1941 and named for Major George P. Moody, who had been killed on May 5, 1941, while test-flying a Beech AT-10.

Further reading: Moody AFB Web site, www.moody.af.mil.

Mountain Home AFB, Idaho

This AIR COMBAT COMMAND (ACC) base is home to the 366th Wing, the first and only air-intervention composite WING in the USAF, with F-16C attack, F-15E interdiction, F-15C air superiority, and KC-135R air refueling aircraft prepared to deploy rapidly worldwide for composite air-intervention operations. There are 3,635 military personnel assigned to the base, which was activated in August 1943. A 50-bed hospital is on base.

Further reading: Mountain Home AFB Web site, www.mountainhome.af.mil.

Nellis AFB, Nevada

Located outside of Las Vegas, this AIR COMBAT COMMAND (ACC) base is home to the AIR WARFARE CENTER (AWC) and also has three operational elements: 57th Wing; 99th Air Base Wing; and 53rd Wing (Eglin AFB, Florida). Within 57th Wing are the USAF Weapons School, USAF Air Demonstration Squadron (THUNDERBIRDS), 57th Operations Group, 57th Test Group (including 422nd Test and Evaluation Squadron), and 57th Logistics Group. A-10, F-15E, F-16, and HH-60G aircraft operate out of the base.

A large facility, Nellis is also home to the 414th Combat Training Squadron (Red Flag), 549th Combat Training Squadron (Air Warrior), 547th Intelligence Squadron, 99th Range Group, 820th Civil Engineering Squadron (Red Horse), 896th Munitions Squadron, 11th Reconnaissance Squadron, and 66th Rescue Squadron. More than 7,000 military personnel and almost 1,000 civilians are assigned to the base.

Activated in July 1941 as the AAF Flexible Gunnery School, the base was closed in 1947, then reopened in 1949 and named for First Lieutenant William H. Nellis, a WORLD WAR II P-47 fighter pilot, killed December 27, 1944, in Europe. The main base sprawls over 11,000 acres with a range restricted area of 3.5 million acres, plus 12,000 square miles of airspace over the range and the military operating area. The 119-bed Nellis Federal Hospital is on base, a joint Air Force-Veterans Administration venture assigned to the 99th Medical Group.

Further reading: Nellis AFB Web site, www. nellis.af.mil.

Newark AFB, Ohio

Located at Newark, Ohio, and operated by the AIR FORCE MATERIEL COMMAND (AFMC), the base was closed on September 30, 1996. It was home to the Aerospace Guidance and Metrology Center, which repaired inertial guidance and navigation systems for most USAF missiles and aircraft as well as a variety of inertial systems for other branches of the armed forces. The center also managed the USAF's worldwide measurement and calibration program, providing a link between the National Institutes of Science and Technology and the USAF's 180 precision measurement equipment laboratories at bases around the world.

Activated as a USAF station on November 7, 1962, the facility had no runway.

Further reading: Newark AFB information, Global Security.Org, "Newark AFB," at www.globalsecurity. org/military/facility/newark.htm.

Offutt AFB, Nebraska

Located outside of Omaha, Offut was a major STRATEGIC AIR COMMAND (SAC) base and is now an AIR COMBAT COMMAND (ACC) base and headquarters of the U.S. Strategic Command. It is home to the 55th Wing; Strategic Joint Intelligence Center;

the headquarters of Strategic Communications–Computer Center; Air Force Global Weather Central; 6th Space Operations Squadron; National Airborne Operations Center (NAOC); and the Air Combat Command Heartland of America Band. A very large installation, Offut is staffed by 9,340 military and 1,592 civilian personnel. A 60-bed hospital is on base.

The base was originally activated by the U.S. Army in 1896 as Fort Crook and was first used for balloons in 1918 and for aircraft in 1924. In that year, it was named for First Lieutenant Jarvis J. Offutt, a WORLD WAR I pilot who died on August 13, 1918, in France.

Further reading: Offutt AFB Web site, www. offutt.af.mil.

Osan AB, Republic of Korea

This PACIFIC AIR FORCES base is the headquarters of SEVENTH AIR FORCE. Its host unit is the 51st Fighter Wing, F-16, C-12, A-10, and OA-10 operations, with tenant units including the 303rd Intelligence Squadron, 631st Air Mobility Support Squadron, 5th Reconnaissance Squadron, 31st Special Operations Squadron, and a detachment of the 4th Space Surveillance Squadron. There are 5,538 military personnel stationed at Osan.

The facility was originally designated simply K-55 when its runway was opened in December 1952 during the KOREAN WAR. It was renamed Osan AB in 1956 for the nearby town that was the scene of the first fighting between U.S. and North Korean forces in July 1950.

Further reading: Osan AB Web site, www.osan. af.mil.

Patrick AFB, Florida

Located near Cocoa Beach and the Kennedy Space Center at Cape Canaveral, this AIR FORCE SPACE COMMAND (AFSPC) base is operated by the 45th Space Wing in support of Department of Defense, NASA, and other agency and commercial missile and space programs. Its major tenants include the Defense Equal Opportunity Management Institute; AIR FORCE TECHNICAL APPLICATIONS CENTER (AFTAC); 1st Rescue Group, 41st Rescue Squadron; 71st Rescue Squadron; and the 301st Rescue Squadron (AIR FORCE RESERVE); 741st Consolidated Aircraft Maintenance Squadron; and the Joint Task Force for Joint STARS at Melbourne Regional Airport, Florida. Besides host responsibilities for Patrick AFB and Cape Canaveral AS, the 45th Space Wing also oversees operations at tracking stations on Antigua and Ascension islands. There are 2,700 military and 1,900 civilian personnel at Patrick.

Patrick AFB has supported more than 3,000 space launches from Cape Canaveral since 1950. It was activated in 1940 and named for Major General Mason M. Patrick, chief of the U.S. ARMY AIR SERVICE in WORLD WAR I and chief of the USAAC and U.S. ARMY AIR CORPS from 1921 to 1927.

Further reading: Patrick AFB Web site, www. patrick.af.mil.

Peterson AFB, Colorado

Located near Colorado Springs, Peterson is headquarters of the AIR FORCE SPACE COMMAND (AFSPC). Its host unit is the 21st Space Wing, which supports the headquarters of North American Aerospace Defense Command, U.S. Space Command, and Army Space Command. Also on base is the 302nd Airlift Wing (AIR FORCE RESERVE) and the Edward J. Peterson Air and Space Museum. Active-duty military personnel number 4,299; reserves, 1,260; and civilians 3,065.

The base was activated in 1942 and was soon after named for First Lieutenant Edward J. Peterson, who was killed on August 8, 1942, in an aircraft crash at the base.

Further reading: Peterson AFB Web site, www. peterson.af.mil.

Pope AFB, North Carolina

This AIR COMBAT COMMAND (ACC) base is home to the 23rd Wing; 624th Air Mobility Support Group; 23rd Aeromedical Evacuation Squadron; 23rd Combat Control Squadron; 3rd Aerial Port Squadron; a detachment of MACOS (Combat Control School); 18th Air Support Operations Group; and 24th Special Tactics Squadron. The base adjoins the U.S. Army's Fort Bragg and provides intratheater AIRLIFT and CLOSE AIR SUPPORT for airborne forces and other personnel, equipment, and supplies. More than 4,000 military personnel are stationed at Pope.

Pope was activated in 1919 and named after First Lieutenant Harley H. Pope, a WORLD WAR I pilot killed on January 7, 1917, near Fayetteville, North Carolina.

Further reading: Pope AFB Web site, http:// public.pope.amc.af.mil.

RAF Lakenheath, United Kingdom

This Royal Air Force (RAF) base hosts the 48th Fighter Wing (UNITED STATES AIR FORCES IN EUROPE [USAFE]), which flies the F-15E and the F-15C and trains for and conducts air operations in support of NATO. On base are 5,200 U.S. personnel.

RAF Lakenheath was activated in 1941 and is named after a nearby village.

Further reading: RAF Lakenheath Web site, www.lakenheath.af.mil.

RAF Mildenhall, United Kingdom

This Royal Air Force (RAF) base hosts the headquarters of the THIRD AIR FORCE (UNITED STATES AIR FORCES IN EUROPE [USAFE]). It is home to 100th Air Refueling Wing, KC-135R and European Tanker Task Force operations, with regional logistics support. Associate units on base include 352nd Special Operations Group; 627th Air Mobility Support Squadron; 95th Reconnaissance Squadron; 488th Intelligence Squadron; and a naval air facility. U.S. military personnel here number 4,765.

The base was activated by the RAF in 1934, with a U.S. presence beginning in July 1950. It is named after the nearby town.

Further reading: RAF Mildenhall Web site, www.mildenhall.af.mil.

Ramstein AB, Germany

Ramstein is headquarters of UNITED STATES AIR FORCES IN EUROPE (USAFE) and headquarters of Allied Air Forces Central Europe (NATO). Its host unit is the 86th Airlift Wing, whose 37th Airlift Squadron flies the C-130E Hercules, the 75th Airlift Squadron, the C-9 Nightingale, and the 76th Airlift squadron, the C-20 Gulfstream, C-21 Learjet, and CT-43. Ramstein provides inter- and intratheater operational AIRLIFT, intratheater aeromedical evacuation, and continental U.S. staging and aeromedical evacuation. The wing commander also serves as commander of the Kaiserslautern Military Community, the largest concentration of U.S. citizens (49,300) outside of the United States. KMC encompasses more than 1,000 square miles and 12 USAF and army military installations.

Ramstein was activated with the beginning of the U.S. presence in 1953.

Further reading: Ramstein AB Web site, "AFPC—Ramstein AB," www.afpc.randolph.af.mil/medical/Dental/Maps/ramstein.htm.

Randolph AFB, Texas

Located outside of San Antonio, Randolph is headquarters of the AIR EDUCATION AND TRAINING COMMAND (AEDTC) as well as of the NINETEENTH AIR FORCE. On base is the 12th Flying Training Wing, with T-37, T-38, and T-1A pilot instructor training, and, at Hondo, Texas, T-43 undergraduate navigator training and C-21A AIRLIFT, and T-3 flight screening. Other headquarters located here include AIR FORCE PERSONNEL CENTER (AFPC), AIR FORCE MANAGEMENT ENGINEERING AGENCY (AFMEA), AIR FORCE SERVICES AGENCY (AFSA), and AIR FORCE RECRUITING SERVICE (AFRS). The USAF Occupational Measurement Squadron is also based at Randolph. More than 5,600 military personnel staff the base, along with almost 4,000 civilian employees.

The base was activated in June 1930 and named for Captain William M. Randolph, killed February 17, 1928, when his AF-4 crashed on takeoff.

Further reading: Randolph AFB Web site, www.randolph.af.mil.

Reese AFB, Texas

Located adjacent to Lubbock, this AIR EDUCATION AND TRAINING COMMAND (AETC) base was, until its deactivation in 1997, home to the 64th Flying Training Wing, which provided specialized undergraduate pilot training. More than 1,300 military personnel were active here, along with 1,166 civilian employees and contractors.

Activated in 1942, the base was subsequently named for First Lieutenant Augustus F. Reese, Jr., a P-38 fighter pilot killed during a train-strafing mission at Cagliari, Sardinia, on May 14, 1943.

Further reading: Reese AFB information, Bruce Richardson, "Reese Air Force Base," www.w9fz.com/reeseafb.

Rhein-Main AB, Germany

Located near Frankfurt-am-Rhein, Germany, Rhein-Main AB has been one of the most historically important of U.S. air bases in the postwar world and during the cold war.

The site of Rhein-Mein AB was used for aerial operations as early as 1909, when Count von Zeppelin employed it as a landing area for his great dirigible Z-II. It became a commercial airport in 1936 and the home port of the famed dirigibles *Graf Zeppelin* and *Hindenburg*. On May 6, 1940, the base was converted for military use by the Luftwaffe and was used during WORLD WAR II as a fighter base and as an experimental station for early jet aircraft. Allied bombers heavily damaged the base during late 1944 and early 1945.

In April 1945, the U.S. 826th Engineering Aviation Battalion began clearing rubble and reconstructing major buildings on the base. Army engineers built new runways and extended and widened the existing runways. A passenger terminal was completed in 1946. It was planned to make Rhein-Main a base for NINTH AIR FORCE bombers, but, instead, Rhein-Main became a principal European air transport terminal from 1947 to 1959. Most famously, Rhein-Main served as the main western base for the BERLIN AIRLIFT from June 1948 to September 1949. In April 1959, UNITED STATES AIR FORCES IN EUROPE (USAFE) turned over the northern part of the base to the German government for use as a civilian airport, the *Flughafen*. The rest of the base, under USAFE control, became the principal aerial port for U.S. forces in Germany.

On July 1, 1975, Rhein-Main AB was assigned to MILITARY AIRLIFT COMMAND (MAC), and, by agreement with the German government, only transport aircraft have been stationed at Rhein-Main since May 1975. On April 1, 1992, the base was reassigned to USAFE and functioned as a major hub for U.S. forces deploying and redeploying during the PERSIAN GULF WAR and subsequent international operations. On December 20, 1993, plans were announced to draw down Rhein-Mein AB to half the size and reduce the active duty force by more than two-thirds. This drawdown was completed on April 1, 1995, and Rhein-Mein AB now consists of 2,600 personnel and 30 tenant units. No aircraft are permanently assigned to the base.

Further reading: Rhein-Main AB Web site, www. rheinmain.af.mil.

Robins AFB, Georgia

Located outside of Macon at Warner Robins, this AIR FORCE MATERIEL COMMAND (AFMC) base is the headquarters of Warner Robins Air Logistics Center, which provides worldwide logistics management for the F-15 air-superiority fighter, and for C-130 and C-l41 cargo aircraft, helicopters, missiles, and remotely piloted vehicles. Other management responsibilities include many avionics and most USAF airborne ELECTRONIC WARFARE equipment, airborne communications equipment, airborne bomb- and gun-directing systems, firefighting equipment, general-purpose vehicles, and the Worldwide Military Command and Control System. The base is also home to the 93rd Air Control Wing. Other major units, including AIR FORCE RESERVE headquarters, operate out of Robins AFB.

The base was activated in March 1942 and was named for Brigadier General Augustine Warner Robins, an early chief of the Materiel Division of the U.S. ARMY AIR CORPS, who died on June 16, 1940. Some 4,000 military personnel are stationed at the base, which employs 12,409 civilians.

Further reading: Robins AFB Web site, www. robins.af.mil/fsc.

Schriever AFB, Colorado

Activated in 1985 as Falcon AFB and later renamed, Schriever AFB is located about 10 miles east of Peterson AFB and 12 miles east of Colorado Springs, Colorado. The base is the home of the 50th Space Wing and has tenant units that include the 76th Space Operations Squadron, National Test Facility, and the Space Warfare Center (SWC). Work on the STRATEGIC DEFENSE INITIATIVE (SDI, "Star Wars") project is conducted here. The base has no runway, and it is staffed by more than 4,600 military and civilian personnel.

The 50th Space Wing provides command and control for Department of Defense warning, navigational, and communications satellites. Also housed at Schriever AFB is the Space Warfare Center and the Ballistic Missile Defense Organization, which supports strategic space systems and missile defense programs.

Further reading: Schriever AFB Web site, www. schriever.af.mil.

Scott AFB, Illinois

An AIR MOBILITY COMMAND (AMC) base, Scott is home to the 375th Airlift Wing and is the headquarters of Air Mobility Command as well as of the Air Force C[4] Agency, the U.S. Transportation Command, and the AIR WEATHER SERVICE (AWS), which maintains the Combat Climatology Center here. Also on base is the 932nd Airlift Wing (AIR FORCE RESERVE). Military personnel number about 6,100, civilian employees, 3,550.

Activated on June 14, 1917, the facility was named for Corporal Frank S. Scott, the first enlisted man to die in an aircraft accident, killed September 28, 1912, in a Wright B Flyer at College Park, Maryland.

Further reading: Scott AFB Web site, http:// public.scott.af.mil.

Sembach AB, Germany

Located nine miles from Kaiserslautern, Germany, Sembach is a UNITED STATES AIR FORCES IN EUROPE (USAFE) base. Its origins date back to 1919, when French occupation troops after WORLD WAR I used the area as a landing ground and erected some provisional buildings. The French withdrew in 1930, and Sembach reverted to farmland. In 1951, the French began to build Sembach as an air base, and, on September 1, 1951, U.S. authorities took over construction and named it Sembach Air Auxiliary Field. In 1953, the installation was renamed Sembach AB and became home to reconnaissance and air rescue units. In 1956, the first Matador missile squadron arrived. On September 1, 1959, Sembach became USAFE's primary missile base.

In 1973, Sembach AB became headquarters for the SEVENTEENTH AIR FORCE and served as a base for ELECTRONIC WARFARE operations. On September 30, 1996, the 17AF was inactivated, and most of the base was returned to German control, except for a portion designated the Sembach Annex, which remains under USAFE control.

Further reading: Sembach AB information, "A Brief History of Sembach AB," www.jomo.net/sembach/sabhistory.htm.

Seymour Johnson AFB, North Carolina

Located in Goldsboro, this AIR COMBAT COMMAND (ACC) base is home to the 4th Fighter Wing, F-15E operations and 916th Air Refueling Wing (AIR FORCE RESERVE), KC-135 operations. About 4,600 military personnel are stationed at Seymour Johnson.

The base was activated on June 12, 1942, and named for Lieutenant Seymour A. Johnson, USN, a Goldsboro native killed March 5, 1941, in an aircraft accident in Maryland.

Further reading: Seymour Johnson AFB Web site, www.seymourjohnson.af.mil.

Shaw AFB, South Carolina

Located south of Sumter, this AIR COMBAT COMMAND (ACC) base is home to the 20th Fighter Wing, F-16 fighter operations and A/OA-10 close air support/forward air control operations. It is also the headquarters base of the NINTH AIR FORCE. There are 5,462 military personnel assigned to the base.

Shaw was activated on August 30, 1941, and named for Second Lieutenant Ervin D. Shaw, one of the first Americans to see air action in WORLD WAR I; he was killed in France on July 9, 1918.

Further reading: Shaw AFB Web site, www.shaw.af.mil.

Shemya AFB, Alaska

Today designated Eareckson Air Station, Shemya AFB is located on the island of Shemya, Alaska, and it constitutes the most westerly of the ELEVENTH AIR FORCE bases, approximately 1,500 miles from Anchorage, near the tip of the Aleutian chain. Uninhabited before occupation by U.S. military forces on May 28, 1943, during the Aleutian campaign of WORLD WAR II, the Shemya Island facility was planned as a B-29 base for the bombing of Japan. However, the Joint Chiefs of Staff decided to deploy B-29s from China and the Mariana Islands in the central Pacific, and Shemya was assigned to the 28th Bomber Group, who flew B-24 missions against the northern Kurile Islands and B-25 attacks on Japanese shipping in the North Pacific.

USAF activities at Shemya AB were reduced after World War II, but the base served as a refueling stop on the Great Circle Route, particularly during the KOREAN WAR. The 5021st Air Base Squadron (AAC) provided base support. After the Korean War, Shemya AFB was deactivated on July 1, 1954. In 1958, the USAF resumed operations on Shemya to support strategic intelligence collection activities and to resume support for the Great Circle Route. During the 1970s, the Cobra Dane AN/FPS-108 Phased Array Radar facility was constructed and operated under the AEROSPACE DEFENSE COMMAND (ADC), then the STRATEGIC AIR COMMAND (SAC), and finally the AIR FORCE SPACE COMMAND (AFSPC). Shemya AFB was renamed Eareckson Air Station on April 6, 1993.

Further reading: Shaw AFB information, U.S. Air Force, "Eareckson Air Station History," www.elmendorf.af.mil/units/eareckson/history.htm.

Sheppard AFB, Texas

Located outside of Wichita Falls, Sheppard is an AIR EDUCATION AND TRAINING COMMAND (AEDTC) base and home to the 82nd Training Wing and the 82nd and 782nd Training Groups. These conduct courses in financial management, communications, electronics, aircraft maintenance, munitions, aerospace ground equipment, transportation, civil engineering skills, and education/training career fields. The 882nd Training Group provides training in biomedical sciences, dentistry, health service administration, medical readiness, medicine, nursing, and the Physician Assistant Training program. The 982nd Training Group provides weapon system training at training detachments and operating locations worldwide. Also on base are the 82nd Support Group; 82nd Medical Group, and 82nd Logistics Group.

The 80th Flying Training Wing (AETC), also on base, conducts T-37 and T-38 undergraduate pilot training and instructor pilot training in the Euro-NATO Joint Jet Pilot Training program. The wing also conducts the Introduction to Fighter Fundamentals course with AT-38 aircraft. This large installation has almost 9,000 military personnel on base, together with almost 4,000 civilian employees. A 90-bed hospital is located on base.

The base was activated on June 14, 1941, and named for U.S. senator Morris E. Sheppard of Texas, who died on April 9, 1941.

Further reading: Sheppard AFB Web site, www.sheppard.af.mil.

Soesterberg AB, Netherlands

This Royal Netherlands AB is located 26 miles outside of Amsterdam and has hosted USAF operations since 1954 in a section of the installation called Camp New Amsterdam.

Spangdahlem AB, Germany

A UNITED STATES AIR FORCES IN EUROPE (USAFE) base, Spangdahlem is home to the 52nd Fighter Wing, flying A/OA-lOs, F-15s, and F-16s. The base is manned by almost 6,000 military personnel.

Activated in 1953, the U.S. presence began then as well. It is named after the local town.

Further reading: Spangdahlem AB information, GlobalSecurity.Org, "Spangdahlem AB," www.globalsecurity.org/military/facility/spangdahlem.htm.

Tinker AFB, Oklahoma

Located outside of Oklahoma City, this AIR FORCE MATERIEL COMMAND (AFMC) base is the headquarters of the Oklahoma City Air Logistics Center, which manages and provides logistics support and depot maintenance for more than 850 aircraft, including the B-1B, B-2, B-52, and KC-135. Tinker is home to the 552nd Air Control Wing; 507th Air Refueling Wing (AIR FORCE RESERVE); and Navy Strategic Communications Wing One. Also located here are the Defense Logistics Agency's Defense Distribution Depot Oklahoma City; the 3rd Combat Communications Group; Air Force Electronic Systems Center's 38th Engineering Installation Wing; and the Oklahoma City Megacenter, which manages Tinker's computer systems and services 110 other bases in 46 states. Stationed here are 8,425 military personnel and 12,858 civilian employees. There is a 22-bed hospital on base.

Activated in March 1942, the base was named for Major General Clarence L. Tinker, whose LB-30 (an early model B-24) went down at sea southwest of Midway Island on June 7, 1942.

Further reading: Tinker AFB Web site, http://www-ext.tinker.af.mil.

Travis AFB, California

An AIR MOBILITY COMMAND (AMC) base, Travis is the headquarters of the FIFTEENTH AIR FORCE and home to 60th Air Mobility Wing; 615th Air Mobility Operations Group; 349th Air Mobility Wing (AIR FORCE RESERVE); David Grant Medical Center (with 298-bed hospital); America's Band of the Golden West; and the Air Museum. Well over 12,000 military personnel are stationed at this major base, along with about 2,000 civilian employees.

The base was activated on May 17, 1943, as Fairfield-Suison Army Air Base and was renamed for Brigadier General Robert F. Travis, killed on August 5, 1950, in a B-29 accident.

Further reading: Travis AFB Web site, http://public.travis.amc.af.mil.

Tyndall AFB, Florida

An AIR EDUCATION AND TRAINING COMMAND (AETC) base, Tyndall is home to the 325th Fighter Wing, F-15 operations. The wing provides training for all USAF F-15 air-to-air pilots and maintains readiness for 77 aircraft and assigned operations and support personnel for combat units worldwide. Associate units at Tyndall include the headquarters of the FIRST AIR FORCE; Southeast Air Defense Sector (AIR NATIONAL GUARD); 475th Weapons Evaluation Group; Air Force Civil Engineer Support Agency; and 325th Training Squadron. Military personnel on the base number 5,237, civilians 1,109. There is a 35-bed hospital.

Activated on December 7, 1941, the base was named for First Lieutenant Frank B. Tyndall, a WORLD WAR I fighter pilot killed on July 15, 1930, in a P-1 crash.

Further reading: Tyndall AFB Web site, www.tyndall.af.mil.

Vance AFB, Oklahoma

An AIR EDUCATION AND TRAINING COMMAND (AETC) base located near Enid, Vance is home to the 71st Flying Training Wing, which provides undergraduate pilot training. There are 854 military personnel at Vance, in addition to 1,410 civilian employees.

The base was activated in November 1941 as Enid Army Air Field and was renamed for Lieutenant Colonel Leon R. Vance, Jr., an Enid native and Medal of Honor recipient, who was killed on July 26, 1944, when an air evacuation plane returning to the United States went down in the Atlantic near Iceland.

Further reading: Vance AFB Web site, www.vance.af.mil.

Vandenberg AFB, California

This AIR FORCE SPACE COMMAND (AFSPC) base is the headquarters of the FOURTEENTH AIR FORCE and its host unit, the 30th Space Wing, which conducts polar-orbiting space launches and supports research and development tests for Department of Defense, USAF, and NASA space, ballistic missile, and aeronautical systems. There are 3,255 military personnel on base, together with 1,387 civilians. There is a 45-bed hospital on base.

Originally the U.S. Army's Camp Cooke, activated in October 1941, the base was taken over by the USAF on June 7, 1957, and renamed for General Hoyt S. Vandenberg, second CHIEF OF STAFF, USAF.

Further reading: Vandenberg AFB Web site, www.vandenberg.af.mil.

Whiteman AFB, Missouri

This AIR COMBAT COMMAND (ACC) base, located outside Sedalia, is home to the 509th Bomb Wing, operating B-2 bombers, and the 442nd Fighter Wing (AIR FORCE RESERVE). More than 3,000 military personnel are stationed here. There is a 30-bed hospital on base.

The base was activated in 1942 and named for Sedalia resident Second Lieutenant George A. Whiteman, the first pilot to die in aerial combat during the attack on Pearl Harbor, December 7, 1941.

Further reading: Whiteman AFB Web site, www.whiteman.af.mil.

Wright-Patterson AFB, Ohio

Located outside of Dayton, this is the headquarters of AIR FORCE MATERIEL COMMAND (AFMC) as well as of the Aeronautical Systems Center. Also at

Wright-Patterson are the Wright Laboratory; AIR FORCE INSTITUTE OF TECHNOLOGY (AFIT); Wright-Patterson Medical Center (a 301-bed hospital); 88th Air Base Wing; 445th Airlift Wing (AIR FORCE RESERVE); and some 70 other Department of Defense activities and government agencies. Military personnel here number 8,505; civilians, 14,628.

Originally, Wright Field and Patterson Field were separate facilities. They were merged on January 13, 1948, and named for aviation pioneers Orville and Wilbur Wright and for First Lieutenant Frank S. Patterson, killed on June 19, 1918, in the crash of a DeHaviland DH-4. The base encompasses the site (Huffman Prairie) of much of the Wright brothers' early flying. Now designated Area C of the present base, Huffman Prairie is part of the Dayton Aviation Heritage National Historical Park and is open to the public.

Further reading: Wright-Patterson AFB Web site, www.wpafb.af.mil.

Yokota AB, Japan

This PACIFIC AIR FORCES (PACAF) base is headquarters of U.S. Forces, Japan, as well as of the FIFTH AIR FORCE, 630th Air Mobility Support Squadron. The host unit is the 374th Airlift Wing, with C-130, UH-1N, C-9, and C-21 operations. Yokota is the primary aerial port in Japan. More than 4,000 U.S. military personnel are stationed here, together with 2,563 U.S. civilian employees, and 1,359 local nationals. There is a 30-bed hospital on the base.

The base was opened as Tama Field by the Japanese in 1939.

Further reading: Yokota AB Web site, www.yokota.af.mil.

Air Force Basic Military Training Instructor Ribbon   See DECORATIONS AND MEDALS.

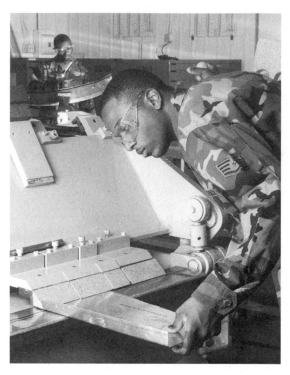

USAF structural maintenance technicians work on parts for a C-130 Hercules at the 374th Maintenance Squadron, Yokota AB, Japan. *(U.S. Air Force)*

Air Force Center for Environmental Excellence (AFCEE)

AFCEE, headquartered at Brooks AFB, is a FIELD OPERATING AGENCY of the Office of the Air Force Civil Engineer. The center provides USAF leaders with the expertise they need to protect, preserve, restore, develop, and sustain our nation's environmental and installation resources. The center provides commanders a full range of technical and professional services in the areas of environmental restoration, pollution prevention, natural and cultural resources conservation, design and construction management, and comprehensive planning. Of the agency's 448 personnel, only 58 are military members; the rest are civilians with degrees in engineering and the sciences, including such fields as architecture, hydrogeology, wildlife biology, and chemistry. AFCEE also relies on contractor employees for technical assistance in computer operations and other areas.

A civilian director heads the center, and an executive director, a USAF colonel (who also serves as the commander of the center's military personnel), assists the director.

In addition to the headquarters-based organizations, the center also has three Regional Environmental Offices located in Dallas (Central Region), Atlanta (Eastern Region), and San Francisco (Western Region). These offices are responsible for keeping USAF commanders advised of all applicable environmental laws and advocate USAF needs to state and federal regulators. They also serve as regional environmental coordinators with the responsibility of coordinating environmental matters among all Department of Defense components within their regions.

The center was created in 1991 as a centralized office to which commanders could go for assistance with their installation's environmental programs.

Air Force Center for Quality and Management Innovation (AFCQMI)

AFCQMI was activated at Randolph AFB, Texas, on December 19, 1996, as a FIELD OPERATING AGENCY merging the Air Force Quality Institute (formerly headquartered at Maxwell AFB, Alabama), with the AIR FORCE MANAGEMENT ENGINEERING AGENCY (at Randolph). AFCQMI focuses on strategic planning, process improvement, applying modern business practices, and analyzing opportunities to outsource and privatize various USAF activities.

Air Force Civil Engineer Support Agency (AFCESA)

Headquartered at Tyndall AFB, AFCESA is a FIELD OPERATING AGENCY that reports to the Office of the Civil Engineer of the Air Force at Headquarters U.S. Air Force, Washington, D.C. The agency provides tools, practices, and professional support to maximize USAF civil engineer capabilities in base and contingency operations. The staff includes specialists in engineering, readiness, training, management analysis, fire protection, systems engineering, computer automation, and equipment and supply management—approximately 215 civilian and military members in all. There are five directorates: Contingency Support, Technical Support, Field Support, Operations Support, and Executive Support. AFCESA also has geographically separated units at Dover AFB, Delaware, and Travis AFB, California.

Contingency Support Directorate (CEX) is responsible for ensuring USAF active-duty and AIR FORCE RESERVE engineer personnel are trained and equipped to deploy anywhere in the world during wartime or peacetime emergencies. The directorate also manages the Air Force Contract Augmentation Program, which allows the USAF to contract a wide-range of noncombatant civil engineer services during disaster response and humanitarian efforts.

The Technical Support Directorate (CES) is responsible for establishing standards and criteria for life-cycle planning, programming, design, construction, operation, maintenance, repair, and revitalization of base infrastructure. It assists MAJCOMs and installations in assessing the condition of infrastructure systems and developing strategies and plans for their upgrade. CES is also home to the Airfield Pavements Evaluation Team and the Utility Rates Management Team.

The Field Support Directorate (CEM) supports base civil engineering units throughout the air force. It provides intermediate- and depot-level repair support on power generation, electrical distribution, heating, ventilating, air conditioning systems, and aircraft arresting systems.

The Operations Support Directorate (CEO) helps increase the capabilities of the base-level civil engineer by enhancing management and logistics practices, systems automation, and training systems. It also provides contracting consultation and manages the Department of Defense–mandated Utilities Privatization Program, which requires the

USAF to turn over most of its water, wastewater, gas, and electric utility systems to private industry by 2003.

The Executive Support Staff (ES) provides internal support to the AFCESA commander and agency staff. The ES staff is made up of diverse career fields including historian, public affairs, graphic support, communications, information management, logistics support, computer support, individual mobilization augmentee support, and financial management. ES also publishes the civil engineer flagship publication *The CE Magazine*.

Air Force Combat Climatology Center (AFCCC)

AFCCC collects, maintains, and applies worldwide weather data, creating climatological analyses to strengthen the combat capability of America's warfighters in all service branches. Operating under the control of the AIR FORCE WEATHER AGENCY (AFWA), AFCCC is located in Asheville, North Carolina.

Air Force Combat Command (AFCC)

AFCC was established under the U.S. ARMY AIR FORCES on June 20, 1941, to take over combat readiness duties from GENERAL HEADQUARTERS (GHQ) AIR FORCE. It was abolished on March 2, 1942, and the groups assigned to it were distributed to other commands.

Air Force Command, Control, Communications, and Computer Agency (AFCCCA)

AFCCCA is headquartered at Scott AFB, Illinois, and develops and validates C⁴ architectures, technical standards, requirements, policies, procedures, and solutions. AFCCCA also ensures full integration of all USAF C⁴ systems. AFCCCA headquarters consists of four major functional areas: Plans and Analysis, Systems and Procedures, Interoperability and Technology, and Resources.

Air Force Commendation Medal   See DE-
CORATIONS AND MEDALS.

Air Force Commissary Service (AFCOMS)

AFCOMS supplies food to the USAF and was established in 1976 as a SEPARATE OPERATING AGENCY. It is headquartered at Kelly AFB, Texas. AFCOMS supplies food to USAF dining facilities and to commissary resale stores.

Air Force Communications Command (AFCC)

AFCC has its origin in the 1938 establishment of the Army Airways Communication System (AACS), which, starting with three officers, 300 enlisted men, and 33 stations, was tasked with providing communication between ground stations and fliers along the airways, disseminating weather information and providing air traffic control. By 1945, AACS had grown to a worldwide organization and had become a MAJCOM—a status soon lost to peacetime budget cutbacks. The organization was restored to MAJCOM status in 1961 as the Air Force Communications Service (AFCS) and in 1979 was renamed the Air Force Communications Command.

Headquartered at Scott AFB, Illinois, its tasks include all aspects of communications and computer support. The command has 700 units at 430 locations throughout the United States and in 26 foreign countries.

Air Force Communications Service   See
AIR FORCE COMMUNICATIONS COMMAND.

Air Force Computer Emergency Response Team (AFCERT)

AFCERT was established by the AIR FORCE INFORMATION WARFARE CENTER (AFIWC), AIR INTELLIGENCE AGENCY (AIA), as the single point of contact in the USAF for reporting and handling computer security incidents and vulnerabilities. AFCERT coordinates the technical resources of AFIWC to assess, analyze, and provide countermeasures for computer security incidents and vulnerabilities reported by USAF computer users, security managers, and system managers.

Air Force Cost Analysis Agency (AFCAA)

AFCAA is based in Arlington, Virginia, and is responsible for developing cost-analysis tools, methods, databases, models, and automated systems. AFCAA products serve the entire USAF.

Air Force Cost Center (AFCSTC)

AFCSTC is a Direct Reporting Unit established in 1985 to apply standard and state-of-the-art cost and economic analysis to estimate costs of acquisitions, operation, and support of weapons systems.

Air Force Council (AFC)

Established in 1951, the Air Force Council serves the CHIEF OF STAFF, USAF, by recommending actions and policies. The AFC also furnishes policy guidance to the AIR STAFF and monitors on an ongoing basis the ability of the USAF to fulfill its mission. The vice chief of staff serves as chair of the AFC.

Air Force: creation as separate service

Well before WORLD WAR II, such U.S. military aviation pioneers as WILLIAM MITCHELL and HENRY

President Truman signs, on September 19, 1951, HR1726, an act "to provide for the organization of the Air Force and the Department of the Air Force," a technicality in the unification plans to make the Air Force Department official. Left to right: Chief of Staff of the Air Force general Hoyt S. Vandenberg, Representative Overton Brooks (D-La.), and Secretary of the Air Force Thomas K. Finletter   *(U.S. Air Force)*

HARLEY ARNOLD advocated the creation of an air force independent from the U.S. Army. These men and those of like mind reasoned that air power required a doctrine distinctly different and separate from the doctrines that governed warfare on land and on the sea; the most thorough and efficient way of creating that doctrine would be in the context of an independent air arm. But it was only after the U.S. ARMY AIR FORCES actually functioned as virtually an independent service in World War II that plans went forward for the creation of an independent USAF.

The process of independence was tied to President Harry S. Truman's 1946 order that the army and navy draft a legislative proposal for the unification of the armed forces. This led, ultimately, to enactment of the NATIONAL SECURITY ACT OF 1947, which created the Department of Defense and much of the structure of the modern defense establishment. The act also called for the creation of an independent air force, which, like the army and navy, would have a civilian-controlled executive department, the DEPARTMENT OF THE AIR FORCE, led by a SECRETARY OF THE AIR FORCE.

The National Security Act was signed into law (PL 253) on July 26, 1947, by President Truman. At the time of signing, he also signed EXECUTIVE ORDER 9877, which completed the administrative actions necessary to implement PL 253, unify the armed forces, and create the USAF. The USAF officially came into existence on September 18, 1947.

Air Force Cross   See DECORATIONS AND MEDALS.

Air Force Development Test Center (AFDTC)

AFDTC is located at Eglin AFB, Florida, and provides a water and land range for weapons testing and firing. On land, the center covers 724 square miles; it also includes the Gulf Test Range, covering an area of 86,500 square miles, encompassing most of the Gulf of Mexico. At AFDTC, testing is carried out for the army, navy, USAF, and Marine Corps as well as for other government, commercial, and international customers. The center is capable of climatic testing, dynamic ground testing, electromagnetic testing, guided projectile testing, gun system testing, inertial guidance testing, radio frequency environment testing, and security system testing.

Air Force Doctrine Center (AFDC)

Headquartered at Maxwell AFB, AFDC is a Direct Reporting Unit to the CHIEF OF STAFF, USAF. It was established on February 24, 1997, as is the "single voice" for all doctrinal matters within the USAF and to the joint community. Its mission is to research, develop, and produce USAF basic and operational doctrine, as well as joint and multinational doctrine, coordinating with the MAJCOMs on their development of tactical doctrine, and assisting the doctrinal development efforts of other services.

AFDC is responsible for reviewing the application of doctrine education for all USAF personnel and is an advocate for the doctrinally correct representation of aerospace power in key USAF, other service, and joint campaign models and exercise scenarios. The center participates in war games and key exercises, and it examines, explores, and advocates methods to better use modeling and simulation to support realistic training, exercises, and studies. AFDC provides research assistance to doctrine development and education and collects and maintains inputs for USAF "Lessons Learned," which arise from exercises and operations.

A major general reporting directly to the Chief of Staff of the Air Force commands the AFDC, which is staffed by 97 active-duty members and civilians. There are three directorates at headquarters, as well as a directorate at Langley AFB, responsible for joint doctrine; an air staff liaison at the Pentagon; five operating locations at major U.S. Army training centers; and an operating location at Nellis AFB. At headquarters, the Doctrine Development Directorate researches, develops, and produces USAF basic and operational doctrine as well as joint and multinational doctrine. The Doctrine Applications Directorate is responsible for effecting the accurate representation of aerospace power in service, joint, and multinational events of doctrinal significance. The Doctrine Deployment Directorate advocates and deploys timely and focused aerospace doctrine, developing and implementing doctrine-specific instruction for USAF senior officers and senior mentors, and providing doctrinal instruction to selected USAF warfighters in preparation for their participation in war games and exercises.

The Joint Integration Directorate at Langley AFB represents the center and provides USAF doctrinal advocacy in the joint arena. The operating locations at Nellis and at army training centers provide USAF representation on matters of aerospace power doctrine, organization, mission, equipment capabilities, tactics, and procedures. Operating Locations include U.S. Army Air Defense Artillery School, Fort Bliss, Texas; U.S. Army Armor Center and School, Fort Knox, Kentucky; U.S. Combined Arms Center, Fort Leavenworth, Kansas; U.S. Army Aviation Center, Fort Rucker, Alabama; U.S. Army Field Artillery School, Fort Sill, Oklahoma; and Nellis AFB, Nevada.

The Joint and Air Staff Liaison Directorate is the liaison between the center, the Joint Staff, Air Staff and the Office of the Secretary of Defense on doctrinal and related issues. It advocates the doctrinally correct representation of aerospace power in publications, models, and exercises, and it oversees the Air and Joint Staff doctrine review processes. It is the conduit with congressional staff offices for the correct representation of aerospace power in national security matters.

Air Force Engineering and Services Center (AFESC)

AFESC was established in 1977 (and was originally called the Air Force Engineering and Services Agency) as a SEPARATE OPERATING AGENCY tasked with assisting MAJCOMs and other USAF installations to operate and maintain their facilities. The center is based at Tyndall AFB, Florida.

Air Force Flight Standards Agency (AFFSA)

AFFSA manages the interoperability of civil and military airspace and air traffic control systems. The agency is based in Washington, D.C.

Air Force Flight Test Center (AFFTC)

AFFTC is located at Edwards AFB, California, on the western edge of the Mojave Desert. Also under the control of AFFTC is the Utah Test and Training Range (UTTR), located in northwestern Utah and northeastern Nevada, about 70 miles west of Salt Lake City, with mission control facilities located off-range at Hill AFB, Utah. In all, AFFTC controls 8,800 square miles of airspace and shares control of 23,800 square miles of airspace with other agencies. Edwards AFB occupies more than 470 square miles, while UTTR covers 2,700 square miles, including the 1,315-square-mile Dugway Proving Ground (DPG).

AFFTC is responsible for flight testing aircraft and aircraft avionics systems for the USAF and other services as well as private and international customers.

Air Force Frequency Management Agency (AFFMA)

AFFMA represents the USAF in all national and international forums concerning the use of the radio frequency electromagnetic spectrum. The agency is based in the Pentagon.

Air Force Global Weather Center   See AIR FORCE WEATHER AGENCY.

Air Force Good Conduct Medal   See DECORATIONS AND MEDALS.

Air Force Historical Foundation

AFHF was founded in 1953 at Maxwell AFB as a nonprofit corporation, which, since its founding, has enjoyed the endorsement of the CHIEF OF STAFF, USAF. The organization is devoted to recording, writing, and publishing the history of American air power and has done so through the journal *Airpower Historian,* begun in 1954, renamed *Aerospace Historian* in 1965, and renamed again *Air Power History* in 1989. In the 1980s, AFHF also began sponsorship of a series of book-length historical studies of the USAF and its antecedents.

Air Force Historical Research Agency (AFHRA)

Based at Maxwell AFB, Alabama, AFHRA provides facilities for research into USAF history. The agency maintains USAF archives and is the principal repository for all USAF historical materials— at present about 3 million documents. Other AFHRA functions include determining USAF lineage and honors and the creation of books and other historical works on the USAF and on military aviation history. AFHRA also serves as adviser regarding declassification of USAF records held at the National Archives and Records Administration.

Air Force History Support Office (AFHSO)

Headquartered in Washington, D.C., AFHSO researches, writes, and publishes books and other materials on the history of the USAF. AFHSO provides historical support through the Air Force historian to USAF headquarters. The agency also publishes books intended to help the USAF in creating strategy, doctrine, and other plans, and to assist in the education of USAF students at professional military schools. AFHSO also provides civilian scholars with research and teaching materials and serves a public-outreach function, to educate and inform the general public about the role of the USAF in national security.

Air Force Information Warfare Center (AFIWC)

The AFIWC is collocated with the AIR INTELLIGENCE AGENCY (AIA) to conduct offensive and defensive counterinformation and information operations. AFIWC was originally activated as the 6901st Special Communication Center in July 1953, then redesignated in August of that year as the Air Force Special Communications Center. It became the Air Force Electronic Warfare Center (AFEWC) in 1975 and the AFIWC on September 10, 1993, combining assets from the former AFEWC, the Air Force Cryptologic Support Center's Securities Directorate, and the former AIR FORCE INTELLIGENCE AGENCY. AFIWC consists of about 1,000 military and civilian specialists in the areas of operations, engineering, operations research, intelligence, radar technology, communications, and computer applications.

AFIWC is divided into eight directorates:

Advanced Programs
Communications-Computer Systems
C^2W Information
Engineering Analysis
Mission Support
Systems Analysis
Operations Support
Information Warfare Battlelab (which identifies innovative and superior ways to plan and employ information warfare capabilities)

Air Force Inspection Agency (AFIA)

The AFIA is headquartered at Kirtland AFB and is a FIELD OPERATING AGENCY that reports to the Secretary of the Air Force Inspector General. Its mission is to provide USAF senior leaders independent assessments of mission capability, health care, and resource management. AFIA recommends improvements to existing USAF processes, policies, and programs for fulfilling peacetime, contingency, and wartime missions. AFIA is staffed by 115 military and 19 civilian personnel and is organized into three inspection directorates, a mission support directorate, and an operations support division.

The Acquisition and Logistics Directorate conducts "Eagle Looks" management reviews of USAF acquisition and logistics processes and programs. The Field Operations Directorate conducts Eagle Looks of a broad range of USAF programs and policies encompassing operations, services, personnel, communications, security, financial management, and civil engineering. The Medical Operations Directorate performs health services inspections of all active duty, AIR FORCE RESERVE, and AIR NATIONAL GUARD medical units. The Mission Support Directorate administers the infrastructure for AFIA and manages the personnel, financial, information systems, logistics, and internal resources to ensure inspectors have the knowledge and equipment to conduct assessments. The Operations Support Division is the single Eagle Look support function for AFIA inspectors, who provide administrative support to inspection teams throughout the Eagle Look process.

AFIA's antecedents include the Inspection Division, established in 1927 under the chief of the U.S. ARMY AIR CORPS. By the end of WORLD WAR II, division functions were aligned under the Office of the Air Inspector, and, in 1948, after USAF independence, the CHIEF OF STAFF, USAF, designated the Office of the Inspector General to oversee all inspection and safety functions. On December 31, 1971, the Air Force Inspection and Safety Center was activated, divided into the Air Force Inspection Agency and the Air Force Safety Agency in August 1991. Both agencies moved to Kirtland AFB in July 1993 after the closure of Norton AFB.

Air Force Inspection and Safety Center (AFISC)

AFISC is a SEPARATE OPERATING AGENCY charged with evaluating the fighting and management effectiveness of the USAF. The center was created in 1971 from the former Office of the Inspector General, which had been established in 1948. Headquartered at Norton AFB, the center has four directorates: one evaluates operational readiness and management; one manages USAF non-nuclear safety programs; one exclusively manages nuclear-related USAF safety programs; and a fourth directorate inspects USAF medical facilities.

Air Force Institute of Technology (AFIT)

AFIT meets USAF needs in graduate education. Located at Wright-Patterson AFB, Ohio, AFIT grants masters and doctoral degrees at its two resident graduate schools and supervises students enrolled in its civilian institutions program. AFIT's Graduate School of Engineering is among the nation's top engineering schools and provides advanced education and research focused on aerospace technology. AFIT's Graduate School of Logistics and Acquisition Management provides officers the advanced expertise they need to manage the life cycles of complex weapons systems. AFIT's Civilian Institutions Program places students in more than 400 civilian universities, research centers, hospitals, and industrial organizations throughout the United States and in several other countries.

AFIT graduates about 800 degree students annually and also operates two resident schools dedicated to short, specialized courses in professional continuing education. These schools also provide expert consultation services to USAF commanders and their staffs. The Civil Engineer and Services School provides engineering, environmental, services, and management courses throughout the Department of Defense and other federal agencies, and the School of Systems and Logistics is responsible for the Air Technology Network, which offers distance learning courses via satellite. More than 30,000 students graduate from the two short-course schools and Air Technology Network programs each year.

Air Force Intelligence Agency (AFIA)

AFIA, headquartered in Washington, D.C., was established in 1972 as the Air Force Intelligence Service (AFIS). It provides AIR STAFF and USAF units with assistance in the use of intelligence and generally collects, processes, analyzes, and disseminates information.

Air Force Legal Services Agency (AFLSA)

This SEPARATE OPERATING AGENCY was established in 1978 to provide specialized legal service to the USAF, both in military and civil contexts. The AFLSA is commanded by the judge advocate general and is headquartered in Washington, D.C. The range of its civil law specialties is suggested by its staff units: Claims and Tort Litigation Staff, General Litigation Division, Contract Law Division, Environmental Law Division, Patents Division, and Preventive Law and Legal Assistance Office. Its military justice divisions include: Court of Military Review, Military Justice Division, Defense Services Division, Trial Judiciary Division, Government Trial and Appellate Counsel Division, and the Clemency, Corrections, and Officer Review Division. Prior to May 1, 1991, AFLSA was called Air Force Legal Services Center (AFLSC).

Air Force Logistics Command (AFLC)

Created in 1921 as the USAAS Property, Maintenance and Cost Compilation Office, AFLC was the Air Service Command (ASC) during WORLD WAR II, was renamed the Air Materiel Command after the war, became the AFLC in 1982, and merged with AIR FORCE SYSTEMS COMMAND in 1992 as the AIR FORCE MATERIEL COMMAND. The mission of the AFLC, now subsumed by the AFMC, was the logistical support of the USAF through buying, supplying, transporting, and maintaining equipment.

Air Force Logistics Management Agency (AFLMA)

AFLMA is located at Gunter Annex to Maxwell AFB, Alabama. Its mission is to enhance USAF readiness and combat capability by conducting studies and developing, testing, analyzing, and recommending

concepts, methods, systems, and procedures to improve logistics efficiency and effectiveness.

Air Force Longevity Service Ribbon   See DECORATIONS AND MEDALS.

Air Force Management Engineering Agency (AFMEA)

Now merged with the Air Force Quality Institute as the AIR FORCE CENTER FOR QUALITY AND MANAGEMENT INNOVATION (AFCQMI), AFMEA develops and maintains USAF manpower standards with the object of improving manpower utilization. The entire AFCQMI is headquartered at Randolph AFB, Texas. Within this organization, AFMEA is responsible for sending and supervising Management Engineering Teams (METs), which use process-analysis and work-measurement techniques to generate recommendations for improving USAF productivity.

Air Force Manpower and Innovation Agency (AFMIA)

Headquartered at Randolph AFB, Texas, AFMIA is tasked with improving USAF mission performance, effectiveness, and resource efficiency by making determinations of current and future peacetime and wartime resource requirements. The principal activity of the agency is to create "objective and innovative" manpower studies and to assists MAJCOMs with competitive sourcing.

Air Force Materiel Command (AFMC)

AFMC is a MAJCOM that researches, develops, tests, acquires, delivers, and logistically supports all USAF weapons systems. The command was created in 1992 as a result of the integration of AIR FORCE LOGISTICS COMMAND and AIR FORCE SYSTEMS COMMAND. AFMC operates logistics centers, test centers, and laboratories and is headquartered at Wright-Patterson AFB, Ohio.

Air Force Medical Operations Agency (AFMOA)

AFMOA is headquartered at Bolling AFB, Washington, D.C., and functions to support the Air Force Surgeon General in creating plans, policies, and programs for all aspects of USAF medicine, including research and clinical areas. In addition to supporting such functions as clinical investigations, aerospace medicine, health promotion, bioenvironmental engineering, family advocacy, and military public health, AFMOA advises on the safe management of radioactive materials.

Air Force Medical Support Agency (AFMSA)

AFMSA assists the Air Force Surgeon General in developing programs, policies, and practices relating to USAF health care. AFMSA divisions include Patient Administration, Health Facilities, Medical Information Systems, and Medical Logistics. The agency is headquartered at Brooks AFB, Texas.

Air Force National Security Emergency Preparedness (AFNSEP)

With facilities in the Pentagon, at Fort McPherson, Atlanta, and at Hickam AFB, Hawaii, AFNSEP oversees—and assists commanders in implementing—the USAF's National Security Emergency Preparedness program, including Domestic Support Operations (DSO) and Continuity of Government (COG) programs. The purpose of these programs is to provide sufficient capabilities at all levels of the USAF to meet essential defense and civilian needs during any national security emergency, in peacetime as well as wartime.

AFNSEP serves as USAF office of primary responsibility for all military support to civil authorities and national security emergency preparedness issues. This includes military support to civilian authorities and military support to civilian law enforcement agencies. In addition to serving as the principal and regional planning agent for military support to civil authorities, AFNSEP approves and coordinates USAF auxiliary activities of the Civil Air Patrol.

Air Force News Agency (AFNEWS)

AFNEWS is headquartered in San Antonio and is a field operating agency of the Office of Public Affairs (SAF/PA) of the secretary of the Air Force. Its mission is to gather, package, and disseminate printed and electronic news and information. The agency manages the Air Force Broadcasting Service and its outlets, Army and Air Force Hometown News Service, and Air Force News Service. AFNEWS has approximately 489 air force, army, navy, and marine military and civilian personnel assigned at more than 26 locations worldwide.

The mission of the Air Force Broadcasting Service is to inform and entertain Department of Defense personnel and their families in Central and Southern Europe, Southwest Asia, Turkey, the United Kingdom, the Azores, and the Pacific Rim. The Army and Air Force Hometown News Service reports on the individual accomplishments of active-duty, guard, reserve members, and Department of Defense civilians. The news service sends news releases to media outlets serving their hometowns. More than 14,000 newspapers, radio, and television stations subscribe to the hometown news service. The Air Force News Service provides USAF and Department of Defense news and information to the USAF community and the public through print, electronic, and Internet-based media.

Air Force News Service creates and distributes the following:

Air Force Link: The USAF official home page on the World Wide Web.

Air Force Link Plus: A multimedia version of the USAF story to a growing Internet audience.

AFNEWS Home Page: Information and links to news service products through the Internet at http://www.afnews.af.mil.

Airman (AFRP 35-1): A nationally recognized monthly feature and information magazine,

Airman reports on events and issues affecting Air Force people.

Air Force Art: A collection of USAF-related artwork created especially for use in base newspapers, briefings, etc.

Air Force Biographies: Accurate, approved biographical information on USAF active-duty general officers, senior civilians, and the chief master sergeant of the air force.

Air Force Fact Sheets: Timely information on USAF aircraft, missiles, major commands, and selected high-interest subjects.

Air Force Policy Letter Digest: A six-page monthly newsletter that is the primary medium for communicating unclassified USAF, DOD, and national policy.

Air Force Print News: USAF and DOD news every weekday. Once each weekday a compilation of the day's news is sent electronically to thousands of subscribers using the e-mail subscription service and is available by FTP.

Air Force Public Affairs Staff Directory: Information about the rank or grade, location, and duties of key public affairs people at USAF.

Air Force Radio News: A five-minute weekday program offering instant access to news and information for and about the USAF community.

Air Force Satellite News: Video news releases produced biweekly on current USAF and DOD issues.

Air Force Speech Series: Original speeches about national days of recognition and special topics.

Air Force Television News: Thirty-minute biweekly television program covering USAF and DOD news and policy issues.

Commander's Call Topics: A monthly publication for use in commander's calls that provides current information on items of interest or importance to USAF military and civilian members and their families.

Internal Talk: Provides USAF base newspaper staffs with tips on journalism and communications technology techniques and ways to improve the communication effectiveness of base newspapers.

Air Force Lithographs: Color reproductions of photographs of USAF subjects. Used for display in buildings, hallways, and common-use areas to promote esprit de corps.

Air Force Nuclear Weapons and Counterproliferation Agency (AFNWCA)

Located at Kirtland Air Force Base, New Mexico, the Air Force Nuclear Weapons and Counterproliferation Agency (AFNWCA) designs and builds systems to enable the air force to operate across the full spectrum of chemical, biological, radiological, nuclear, and explosive (CBRNE) environments. Staffed by scientists, engineers, and program managers, the agency provides air force warfighters with advanced weapons and technical assessments to counter CBRNE threats. In addition, AFNWCA assures the military effectiveness of the air force portion of the nation's nuclear weapon stockpile and oversees stewardship of this stockpile.

AFNWCA is the air force liaison with the National Nuclear Security Administration, and it manages all air force nuclear weapons activities as well as coordinates mission requirements, analyses, and assessments in the areas of counterforce weaponry, passive and active defense, passive and remote detection, target characterization intelligence, and technical issues associated with treaty compliance. AFNWCA also provides technical assessments to support air force warfighting operations and advanced weapons concepts, and it supports requirements for countering chemical, biological, radiological, nuclear, and explosive (CBRNE) weapons of mass destruction.

Air Force Office of Medical Support (AFOMS)

Headquartered at Brooks AFB, Texas, AFOMS is a SEPARATE OPERATING AGENCY that assists the Air Force Surgeon General by preparing plans, programs, studies, policies, and practices for health care in the USAF.

Air Force Office of Scientific Research (AFOSR)

The mission of AFOSR, a technology directorate of the AIR FORCE RESEARCH LABORATORY (AFRL), is to manage all basic research conducted by the USAF. AFOSR solicits proposals for research in numerous broad areas, including:

- Physics
- Solid Mechanics and Structures
- Chemistry
- Mathematics and Computer Sciences
- Electronics
- Structural Materials
- Fluid Mechanics
- Propulsion
- Atmospheric Sciences
- Space Sciences
- Biological Sciences
- Human Performance
- Science and Engineering Education Programs

The directorate manages a number of researcher assistance programs, including the United States Air Force/National Research Council–Resident Research Associateship Program, the University Resident Research Program, and the National Defense Science and Engineering Graduate Fellowship Program, and others. AFOSR is headquartered at Arlington Virginia.

The predecessor organization of AFOSR was created in October 1951 in the headquarters of the Air Research and Development Command. Before this time, USAF had sponsored some basic research under the auspices of the Office of Air Research at the old Air Material Command headquartered at Wright-Patterson AFB and, later, under the Directorate of Research at the newly created Air Research and Development Command (ARDC). The new office was designated AFOSR in August 1955, charged with planning, formulating, initiating, and managing a basic research program. It was the Russians' successful orbit of *Sputnik I* in 1957 that prompted a major budget for AFOSR, and, in the 1950s, the directorate contributed to such notable scientific advancements as providing support to Nobel laureates Richard Hofstadter (for his work on the structure of nuclei and nucleons) and C. H. Townes (for his role in developing microwave amplification by stimulated emission of radiation [MASER]).

Reorganization within the Department of Defense led to the creation of the short-lived Air Force Research Division (AFRD), which, in 1961, became AIR FORCE SYSTEMS COMMAND (AFSC), concentrating on applied research, while AFOSR became part of the Office of Aerospace Research (OAR) and continued to manage research in basic science. However, AFOSR-sponsored basic research typically paid off in applications, such as laser weapons. AFOSR played a central role in managing research for the STRATEGIC DEFENSE INITIATIVE (SDI) program in the 1980s.

Air Force Office of Security Police (AFOSP)

AFOSP is a Separate Operating Agency that sets USAF policy for security, police law enforcement, air base ground defense, information security, and training in small arms. Established in 1979, AFOSP in headquartered at Kirtland AFB, New Mexico.

Air Force Office of Special Investigations (AFOSI)

The USAF's major investigative service since August 1, 1948, AFOSI is a Field Operating Agency with headquarters at Andrews AFB. Reporting to the Inspector General, Office of the SECRETARY OF THE AIR FORCE, AFOSI provides professional investigative service to commanders of all USAF activities. Primary responsibilities include criminal investigative and counterintelligence services: to identify, investigate, and neutralize espionage, terrorism, fraud, and other major criminal activities that may threaten USAF and Department of Defense resources.

AFOSI has 2,274 active-duty officer and enlisted, civilian, and AIR FORCE RESERVE personnel. Of this number, 1,672 are federally credentialed special agents.

In addition to the command's headquarters and U.S. Air Force Special Investigations Academy at Andrews AFB, AFOSI has eight field investigations regions (two of which are overseas), seven field investigations squadrons (six of which are overseas), and more than 160 detachments and operating locations worldwide.

Air Force Officer Training School (OTS)

OTS, located at Maxwell AFB, Alabama, provides a 12-week basic officer training course, designed (as of 2002) to commission 1,700 officers annually, and a four-week commissioned officer training program, which each year provides training for 1,500 new judge advocates, chaplains, and medical officers.

Basic officer training (BOT) is designed for college graduates who seek a USAF commission. Commissioned officer training (COT) is designed for professionals who have received a direct-commissioned appointment as a lawyer, chaplain, or medical practitioner. In addition to the regular COT, OTS offers the Reserve COT course, a two-week intensive program designed for AIR FORCE RESERVE and AIR NATIONAL GUARD medical service officers.

Air Force One

Any aircraft that carries the president of the United States is designated by the radio call sign "Air Force One" when the president is onboard. At present, two VC-25A aircraft, military modifications of the Boeing 747-200B civilian plane, are regularly used for presidential airlift and, when carrying the president, are designated Air Force One. The aircraft is a flying office, living quarters, and command post, which accommodates an aircrew of 23 and 75 passengers. It is equipped with advanced communication equipment (including 85 telephones) and 19 television receivers. The aircraft operate out of Andrews AFB, home of the 89th Airlift Wing.

The routine aerial transport of the president began in 1943, from Miami, Florida, to Morocco for the Casablanca Conference, on board a Navy-operated Boeing 314 flying boat called the *Dixie*

A USAF VC-25A, a modified Boeing 747-200B, serves as the primary aircraft for presidential airlift. It is designated *Air Force One* only when the president is on board.   *(U.S. Air Force)*

Clipper. This led to Project 51, the building of a U.S. ARMY AIR FORCES C-54 Skymaster transport especially for use as a presidential transport. Officially named *The Flying White House,* the aircraft was better known by its nickname, *The Sacred Cow,* and it incorporated special modifications to accommodate President Franklin D. Roosevelt's paraplegic condition.

The Sacred Cow was retired in 1947 and replaced by a Douglas DC-6, designated by the USAF as a C-118, and named the *Independence,* after the Missouri hometown of President Harry S. Truman. In 1948, a Lockheed Constellation (USAF designation C-121) was prepared for Thomas Dewey, who was expected to win election over Truman, and was christened the *Dewdrop.* When, in an upset, Truman won, he continued to use the *Independence,* and it wasn't until President Dwight D. Eisenhower assumed office in 1953 that a C-121, which Eisenhower named the *Columbine II,* was used for presidential airlift. In 1954, the Constellation was replaced by a Super-Constellation, which was designated *Columbine III* and served until President John F. Kennedy chose a Douglas DC-6A (USAF designation VC-118A) as his presidential transport. Kennedy did not name the aircraft. He also used several Boeing 707-153 jet aircraft (USAF designation VC-137A). The jets had been used on occasion for presidential airlift as early as 1959.

The VC-137A aircraft would continue to serve as "Air Force One" through 1990, when they were replaced by the Boeing 747-200B (VC-25A) aircraft.

Air Force Operational Test and Evaluation Center (AFOTEC)

AFOTEC manages USAF operational test and evaluation and may be involved with a weapon system from inception and design through deployment on the flight line.

AFOTEC was established in 1974 at the Air Force Test and Evaluation Center; the word "Operational" was added in 1983. The center's mission is to test and evaluate weapons and other systems independently and under the most realistic conditions possible. AFOTEC's antecedent organization was the Air Proving Ground Command, which existed in various forms from 1941 to 1957, and which emphasized the validation of production and the meeting of specifications rather than rigorous field testing with an eye toward improvement and modification. The disappointing performance and outright failure of certain systems during the VIETNAM WAR motivated creation of AFOTEC, with a far broader mission.

Air Force Operations Group (AFOG)

AFOG monitors on a 24/7 basis all current USAF operations and handles emergencies through the Air Force Operations Center. Headquartered in Washington, D.C., AFOG coordinates action among USAF MAJCOMs, other Field Operating Agencies, and Direct Reporting Units in response to taskings from the Joint Chiefs of Staff National Military Command Center. In addition, AFOG manages the USAF portion of the Worldwide Military Command and Control System Intercomputer Network, the USAF resources and training system database, and the Joint Uniform Lessons Learned database.

Air Force Organization Act of 1951

The NATIONAL SECURITY ACT OF 1947, which authorized the creation of the USAF as an independent air arm, failed to provide a statutory basis for the composition and organization of the USAF. The 1951 act redressed this omission, specifying not only the internal organization of the USAF but also the responsibilities and authority of the SECRETARY OF THE AIR FORCE.

Air Force Organizational Excellence Award   See DECORATIONS AND MEDALS.

Air Force Outstanding Unit Award   See DECORATIONS AND MEDALS.

Air Force Overseas Ribbon–Long Tour

See DECORATIONS AND MEDALS.

Air Force Pentagon Communications Agency (AFPCA)

AFPCA provides C⁴ (Command, Control, Communications, and Computer) systems and services for the Office of the Secretary of Defense, the Joint Chiefs of Staff, the National Military Command Center, the SECRETARY OF THE AIR FORCE, HQ USAF, and other Washington, D.C.-based command centers. Among its other functions, AFPCA maintains secure and nonsecure telecommunications switches, 8,000 telephones, and a network of pagers and cellular telephones. The agency is headquartered in Washington, D.C.

Air Force Personnel Center (AFPC)

Headquartered at Randolph AFB, Texas, AFPC implements personnel programs affecting the nearly 400,000 USAF active-duty members and 185,000 civilian employees through major commands (see MAJCOM) and a worldwide network of military and civilian personnel flights. AFPC also manages some personnel matters affecting more than 109,000 Air National Guardsmen and 78,000 Air Force Reservists.

AFPC began operations on July 25, 1963, and, in 1971, became a Separate Operating Agency. It was renamed the Air Force Manpower and Personnel Center in 1978, then, in October 1985, when the manpower function was separated from personnel, the center was renamed the Air Force Military Personnel Center, effective January 1, 1986. The center became a Field Operating Agency on February 5, 1991.

Air Force Personnel Operations Agency (AFPOA)

AFPOA develops and operates officer, enlisted, and civilian models and databases for management information. The agency manages the Air Force Employee Development Program and the Air Force Relocation, Employee, and Labor Relations Program.

Air Force Program Executive Office (AFPEO)

The Pentagon-based AFPEO consists of six senior USAF officials who manage major and selected USAF acquisition programs in the following areas: Bombers, Missiles, and Trainers; Conventional Strike Systems; Tactical and Airlift Systems; Information Systems; Space Systems; and Command, Control, and Communications Systems.

Air Force Quality Institute   See AIR FORCE CENTER FOR QUALITY AND MANAGEMENT INNOVATION.

Air Force Real Estate Agency (AFREA)

AFREA works with the Office of the Deputy Assistant Secretary for Installations to acquire, manage, and dispose of real property for the USAF. The agency is located at Bolling AFB, Washington, D.C.

Air Force Recognition Ribbon   See DECORATIONS AND MEDALS.

Air Force Recruiter Ribbon   See DECORATIONS AND MEDALS.

Air Force Recruiting Service (AFRS)

Headquartered at Randolph AFB, AFRS is a major component of AIR EDUCATION AND TRAINING COMMAND (AETC), tasked with the mission of recruiting a high-quality volunteer force from a cross-section of America responsive to the personnel needs of the USAF. AFRS is also responsible for recruiting chaplains, physicians, dentists, nurses, health care administrators, and Biomedical Science Corps officers in various specialties, and for obtaining officer candidates for the AIR FORCE RESERVE OFFICER TRAINING CORPS (AFROTC) and AIR FORCE OFFICER TRAINING SCHOOL (OTS).

Headquarters directs four groups and 28 squadrons with approximately 3,350 active-duty and 360 civilian personnel. Every USAF recruiter is a volunteer or is nominated and selected from among the best in his or her career field. Recruiters are trained at the Recruiting School at Lackland AFB, and they staff more than 1,100 recruiting offices around the country and overseas.

When the USAF became an independent service in 1947, it conducted a joint recruiting program with the U.S. Army through the army's recruiting organization. The USAF assumed responsibility for its own recruiting in 1954, assigning the mission to the 3500th USAF Recruiting Wing at Wright-Patterson AFB. This became the U.S. Air Force Recruiting Service in 1959.

Air Force Research Laboratory (AFRL)

The mission of AFRL is to lead the discovery, development, and integration of affordable warfighting technologies for U.S. aerospace forces. AFRL consists of nine technology directorates located throughout the United States, in addition to the AIR FORCE OFFICE OF SCIENTIFIC RESEARCH, and a central staff. However, AFRL also works collaboratively with universities and industry, who receive nearly 80 percent of the AFRL budget.

AFRL staff numbers 5,700 to 5,900 people, responsible for planning and executing the USAF's entire science and technology budget, including basic research, applied research, and advanced technology development. AFRL research sites follow:

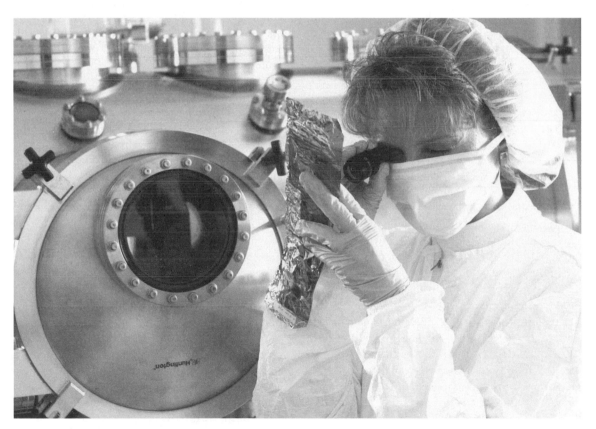

A researcher analyzes an experiment in the Air Force Research Laboratory at Wright-Patterson AFB, Ohio. *(U.S. Air Force)*

- Air Force Office of Scientific Research, head-quartered in Arlington, Virginia
- Wright-Patterson AFB facilities, including research in air vehicles, materials and manufacturing, propulsion, sensors, and human effectiveness
- Tyndall AFB facility for research in materials and manufacturing
- Eglin AFB facility for research in munitions
- Brooks AFB facility for research in human effectiveness
- Williams AFB facility for research in human effectiveness
- Kirtland AFB facilities for research in space vehicles and in directed energy
- Edwards AFB facility for propulsion research
- Rome AFB (New York) facilities for information and sensors research
- Hanscom AFB facilities for research in space vehicles and sensors

Air Force Reserve (AFR)

For a discussion of the basic organization and mission of the AFR, see AIR FORCE RESERVE COMMAND.

Air Force reservists are categorized as Ready Reserve, Standby Reserve, or Retired Reserve.

The *Ready Reserve* is made up of 193,042 trained reservists who may be recalled to active duty to augment active forces in time of war or national emergency. Of this number, 72,195 are members of the Selected Reserve, who train regularly and are paid for their participation in unit or individual programs. These reservists are combat ready and can deploy to anywhere in the world in 72 hours. Additionally, 48,981 are part of the Individual Ready Reserve. IRR members continue to have a service obligation, but they do not train and are not paid. They are subject to recall if needed. The president may recall Ready Reserve personnel from all Department of Defense components for up to 270 days if necessary. Some 24,000 USAF reservists from 220 units were called to active duty during the PERSIAN GULF WAR to work side-by-side with their active-duty counterparts.

Standby Reserve includes reservists whose civilian jobs are considered vital to national defense, or who have temporary disability or personal hardship. Most standby reservists do not train and are not assigned to units. There are 16,858 reservists in this category. *Retired Reserve* includes officers and enlisted personnel—52,057 men and women—who receive pay after retiring from active duty or from the reserve, or are reservists awaiting retirement pay at age 60.

Selected reservists train to active-duty standards, and mission readiness is verified periodically, using active-force inspection criteria. More than 60,000 reservists are assigned to specific AFR units. These are the people who are obligated to report for duty one weekend each month and two weeks of annual training a year. Most work many additional days. Reserve aircrews, for example, average more than 100 duty days a year, often flying in support of national objectives at home and around the world.

Air reserve technicians (ART) are a special group of reservists who work as civil service employees during the week in the same jobs they hold as reservists on drill weekends. ARTs are the full-time backbone of the unit training program, providing day-to-day leadership, administrative, and logistical support, as well as operational continuity for their units. More than 9,500 reservists (in excess of 15 percent of the force) are ARTs. The IMA training program is made up of approximately 13,144 "individual mobilization augmentees." IMAs are assigned to active-duty units in specific wartime positions and train on an individual basis. Their mission is to augment active-duty manning by filling wartime surge requirements.

The AFRC Associate Program provides trained crews and maintenance personnel for active-duty aircraft and space operations. The program pairs an AFR unit with an active-duty unit to share a single set of aircraft. The result is a more cost-effective way to meet increasing mission requirements. Associate aircrews fly C-5 Galaxies, C-141 Starlifters, C-17 Globemaster IIIs, C-9 Nightingales,

KC-10 Extenders, KC-135 Stratotankers, T-1 Jay-hawks, T-37 Tweets, T-38 Talons, F-16 Fighting Falcons, MC-130P Combat Shadows and MC-130 Talon I (Reserve Associate Unit), and E-3 Sentry Airborne Warning and Control System (AWACS) aircraft. Space operations associate units operate Defense Meteorological, Defense Support Program, and Global Positioning System satellites.

USAF reservists are on duty around the world, carrying out the USAF vision of "global engagement." In addition to combat roles, AFR is often engaged in humanitarian relief missions. At the request of local, state, or federal agencies, AFR conducts aerial spray missions using specially equipped C-130s. These missions range from spraying pesticides to control insects to spraying compounds used in the control of oil spills. Other specially equipped C-130s check the spread of forest fires by dropping fire-retardant chemicals. Additional real-world missions include weather reconnaissance, rescue, international missions in support of U.S. Southern Command, and aeromedical evacuation. Recently, AFR has taken an active role in the national counternarcotics effort.

Air Force Reserve Command (AFRC)

AFRC, headquartered at Robins AFB, became a MAJCOM on February 17, 1997, pursuant to the National Defense Authorization Act of Fiscal Year 1997. It supports the USAF mission to defend the United States through control and exploitation of air and space by supporting global engagement. AFRC serves day to day in this mission and is not a force merely held in reserve for possible war or contingency operations.

AFRC consists of 35 flying wings equipped with their own aircraft and nine associate units that share aircraft with an active-duty unit. Four space operations squadrons share satellite control mission with the active force. There also are more than 620 mission support units in the AFRC, equipped and trained to provide a wide range of services, including medical and aeromedical evacuation, aerial port, civil engineer, security force, intelli-

gence, communications, mobility support, logistics and transportation operations, among others. The 447 aircraft assigned to AFRC include the F-16, O/A-10, C-5, C-130, MC-130, HC-130, WC-130, KC-135, B-52, and HH-60. On any given day, 99 percent of these aircraft are mission-ready and able to deploy within 72 hours.

The Office of Air Force Reserve, in the Pentagon, is headed by the Chief of Air Force Reserve, an AIR FORCE RESERVE lieutenant general, who is the principal adviser to the CHIEF OF STAFF of the Air Force for all AFR matters. The Chief of Air Force Reserve establishes AFR policy and initiates plans and programs. In addition to being a senior member of the AIR STAFF, he is also commander of the AFRC. Headquarters AFRC supervises the unit training program, provides logistics support, reviews unit training, and ensures combat readiness. FOURTH AIR FORCE at March Air Reserve Base, California, TENTH AIR FORCE at Carswell Air Reserve Station, Texas, and TWENTY-SECOND AIR FORCE at Dobbins Air Reserve Base, Georgia, report to Headquarters AFRC. They act as operational headquarters for their subordinate units, providing training, operational, logistical and safety support, and regional support for geographically separated units.

The Air Reserve Personnel Center, a Direct Reporting Unit located in Denver, Colorado, provides personnel services to all members of the AFRC and AIR NATIONAL GUARD.

Air Force Reserve Officer Training Corps (AFROTC)

AFROTC, headquartered at Maxwell AFB and administered by the AIR UNIVERSITY, is the largest and oldest source of commissioned officers for the USAF. AFROTC's mission is to produce leaders for the USAF while building better citizens for America. AFROTC is active on more than 144 college and university campuses, and an additional 750 schools offer the AFROTC program under crosstown agreements that allow their students to attend AFROTC classes at an area host school. The program commissions about 1,900 second lieutenants each year and also administers the Air Force Junior ROTC program, which provides citizenship training and an aerospace science program for high school youth. Air Force Junior ROTC programs are offered in 609 high school campuses throughout the nation, as well as in Guam, Puerto Rico, and selected U.S. dependent schools overseas. About 91,000 students are enrolled.

Air Force Review Boards Agency (AFRBA)

AFRBA is based in the Pentagon and manages military and civilian appellate processes for the SECRETARY OF THE AIR FORCE. AFRBA consists of the Air Force Board for Correction of Military Records; the Air Force Civilian Appellate Review Agency; and the Air Force Personnel Council. The council has special authority in examining discharges, decorations, and cases of physical disability.

air forces (organizational units)

Until the USAF underwent a major organizational restructuring in 1993, air forces were organizational units that equated to an army in the U.S. Army. They were subordinate to operational and support commands but superior to a division. There have been numbered air forces and named air forces—as many as 23 numbered air forces and 13 named air forces. After 1993, only the numbered air forces (NAFs) were retained, and these were restructured for strictly warfighting and operational roles; all support functions were allocated elsewhere. Today, a NAF is typically commanded by a major general or lieutenant general, and its staff (about half the pre-1993 strength) is dedicated to operational planning and employment of forces for several wings within the NAF.

In the U.S. ARMY AIR FORCES, before the USAF became an independent service arm (1947), the NAFS were the equivalent of today's Major Commands (MAJCOMs).

Air Force Safety Center (AFSC)

AFSC is a Field Operating Agency with headquarters at Kirtland AFB. The center develops and manages USAF mishap prevention programs and the Nuclear Surety Program. It develops regulatory guidance, provides technical assistance in the flight, ground, and weapons and space safety disciplines, and maintains the USAF database for all safety mishaps. The center oversees all major command mishap investigations and evaluates corrective actions for applicability and implementation USAF-wide. It also develops and directs safety education programs for all safety disciplines.

About 130 people are assigned to AFSC, equally divided between military and civilians. The center is composed of nine divisions, including an AIR STAFF liaison division at the Pentagon.

The Aviation Safety Division manages USAF flight mishap prevention programs for all manned aircraft. The Ground Safety Division develops ground safety programs and procedures to provide a safe work environment for all personnel. The Weapons, Space and Nuclear Safety Division establishes and executes mishap prevention programs for all weapons, reactor, space, and nuclear systems. The division provides nuclear systems design certification, explosive safety standards development, space and weapon safety consultation, as well as system inspection, oversight, education and staff assistance in its areas of responsibility. The Policy, Plans and Programs Division ensures proactive and effective mishap guidance for all safety disciplines. The Computer Operations and Programming Division provides AFSC with the communications and computer infrastructure and expertise. It also maintains the USAF database of all safety mishaps. The Education and Media Division publishes three USAF special publications: *Flying Safety, Road and Rec,* and *Nuclear Surety and Weapons Safety Journal.* The Media Branch is responsible for producing videotape presentations on relevant safety issues to support mishap prevention programs. The Safety Education Branch manages, administers, and sponsors educational courses that encompass the safety disciplines: aviation, ground, weapons, space, and missiles. The branch also manages the USAF Crash Laboratory used as a hands-on training facility with aviation safety courses. The Resource Management, Manpower, and Career Programs Division establishes policy and manages USAF civilian and enlisted safety personnel. The Issues Division, a detachment in the Pentagon, provides a direct interface with members of the Air Staff to facilitate responses to questions on safety-related issues raised by the CHIEF OF STAFF and members of the staff. The Office of the Staff Judge Advocate provides legal advice and general counsel on all aspects of mishap prevention programs and safety investigations.

After the USAF became an independent service, the Office of the Inspector General oversaw all inspection and safety functions. On December 31, 1971, the Air Force Inspection and Safety Center was activated, divided into the AIR FORCE INSPECTION AGENCY and the Air Force Safety Agency in August 1991. Both agencies moved to Kirtland AFB in July 1993 after the closure of Norton AFB. On January 1, 1996, the Air Force Safety Center was activated when the air force chief of safety and staff moved from Washington, D.C., to consolidate all safety functions at Kirtland.

Air Force Scientific Advisory Board (SAB)

Located near the Pentagon in Arlington, Virginia, the SAB is charged with providing independent wisdom and insight to USAF senior leadership on science and technology for continued air and space dominance. The SAB functions as a link between the USAF and the civilian scientific and engineering communities. The board continually reviews and evaluates USAF research and development plans, recommending applications that can be derived from promising scientific and technological developments and discoveries. The board also conducts a variety of studies at the request of senior USAF leadership to assess scientific and engineering aspects of particular operational or acquisition problems or issues. SAB members are

selected on the basis of eminence in scientific fields of interest to the USAF.

Air Force Security Forces Center (AFSFC)

Headquartered at Lackland Air Force Base, Texas, AFSFC was known as the Air Force Security Police Agency before 1991. The AFSFC consists of four major divisions:

> Air Force Corrections Division
> Operations Division
> Force Protection Division
> Training and Combat Arms Division

The Corrections Division is responsible for the transfer and management of Air Force court-martialed members from worldwide confinement facilities for continued confinement in Regional Correctional Facilities (RCFs) operated by the air force, army, navy, and marines. The division maintains court-martial, personnel, and financial data of inmates confined in the Air Force Corrections System as well as for members released on parole or appellate leave.

The Operations Division consists of a Police Services Branch, DoD Canine, an Operations Center, Requirements Branch, Nuclear Security Branch, and an Installation Security Branch.

Police Services administers basic police functions on air force bases and other installations. DoD Canine is responsible for the care, training, management, and deployment of working police dogs. The Operations Center is tasked with maintaining functional management over all USAF Security Forces personnel and equipment to support wartime and peacetime contingencies. The branch is the executive agent responsible for tasking Security Forces through each Major Command (MAJCOM) Security Forces functional manager. Branch personnel also collect, process, analyze and communicate force protection information to assist air force leaders in making informed decisions. During contingencies, crises, and wartime operations, the branch provides force protection recommendations to the Air Force Directory of Security Forces.

Air Force Security Police Agency personnel train in airbase defense and antiterrorism. This security forces airman fires an M-249 during a training exercise at Indian Springs Air Force Auxiliary Field, Nevada. *(U.S. Air Force)*

The Requirements Branch manages current and future requirements, based on operational deficiencies and provides requirement oversight in the development, review and validation, of emerging technology to fulfill operational capabilities. The Nuclear Security Branch develops guidance and policy for the physical security of air force weapons systems worldwide. The Installation Security Branch has primary responsibility for creating systems and policies to ensure the security of air force bases and other facilities.

The Force Protection Division of the Air Force Security Forces Center provides policy, resource advocacy, and guidance in the areas of doctrine, antiterrorism, and training, and also conducts vulnerability assessments.

The Training and Combat Arms Division consist of a Training Branch and a Combat Arms Branch. The Training Branch provides high-quality, cost-effective training to security personnel. The branch also develops policy and guidance for security forces, combat arms, and security awareness and education training programs. The branch also provides professional career development programs for Security Force officers, airmen, and civilians.

The Combat Arms Branch implements policies and procedures for the Air Force Combat Arms Training Program, including ground weapons and munitions. The branch develops ground-weapons training and qualifications programs and establishes qualification standards. It implements field and organizational-level maintenance and repair policies for ground weapons, and implements maintenance policies and procedures and range safety criteria for new types of group weapons.

Air Force Services Agency (AFSVA)

AFSVA, headquartered in San Antonio, Texas, was formed during the reorganization of Morale, Welfare and Recreation and Services functions in 1993 and is tasked with supporting the bases, MAJCOMs, and AIR STAFF by providing technical assistance, fielding new initiatives, developing procedures, and managing selected central support functions to ensure successful services programs. The agency manages USAF central nonappropriated funds and operates central systems for field support such as banking, investments, purchasing, data flow, insurance and benefits programs, and the personnel system. HQ AFSVA supports the Air Force Morale, Welfare, and Recreation Advisory Board. About 400 USAF military and civilian personnel are assigned to AFSVA.

Air Forces Iceland

The smallest of the named air forces, Air Forces Iceland was established in 1952 as the Iceland Air Defense Force under MILITARY AIR TRANSPORT SERVICE (MATS) command and became Air Forces Iceland in 1960 under the AIR DEFENSE COMMAND (ADC). In 1979, it was assigned to TACTICAL AIR COMMAND (TAC) and was reassigned to the FIRST AIR FORCE in 1990.

Air Forces Iceland is important to the defense of the hemisphere because of the strategically critical position Iceland occupies in relation to North Atlantic air and sea routes.

Air Force Space Command (AFSPACECOM)

AFSPACECOM is a USAF MAJCOM as well as a component of the United States Space Command, a unified command of the U.S. armed forces. AFSPACECOM plans, manages, and operates such space assets as ballistic missile warning and offensive attack and spacelift/launch and ground control for Department of Defense satellite operations. AFSPACECOM also serves to coordinate research and development among operational users of USAF space programs. The command is headquartered at Peterson AFB, Colorado.

Air Force Special Operations Command (AFSOC)

AFSOC organizes, trains, and equips USAF special operations forces for worldwide deployment as well as for assignment to regional unified commands. Special operations conducts unconventional warfare, direct action, special reconnaissance, counterterrorism, foreign international defense, humanitarian assistance, psychological operations, personnel recovery, and counternarcotics missions. This MAJCOM is headquartered at Hurlburt Field, Florida.

Air Force Specialty Codes (AFSC)

The USAF developed the AFSC system to identify the duties for all enlisted positions essential to accomplishing the mission of the USAF. Every USAF job—and every USAF member's job qualifications—can be identified by a five-digit code.

* The first character of the AFSC identifies the career grouping.
* The second character identifies the career field.
* The third character identifies a career field subdivision.
* The fourth character identifies the airman's level of qualification (1: helper; 3: apprentice; 5: journeyman; 7: craftsman; 9: superintendent; 0: chief enlisted manager).
* The fifth character denotes the airman's specialty.

Air Force Studies and Analyses Agency (AFSAA)

The Pentagon-based AFSAA assists the SECRETARY OF THE AIR FORCE, the CHIEF OF STAFF, USAF, and other senior staff concerning such issues as force structure, resource allocation, weapons system acquisition and employment, and arms reduction proposals, all in relation to national security policy.

Air Force Systems Command (AFSC)

Since 1992 combined with AIR FORCE LOGISTICS COMMAND as the AIR FORCE MATERIEL COMMAND, AFSC was established in 1950 as the Research and Development Command (RDC). The mission of AFSC, now subsumed by AFMC, is to advise USAF leadership on scientific and technical options available for aerospace equipment needs.

AFSC's antecedent, RDC, was born of the revolutionary technological developments that had burgeoned during WORLD WAR II. U.S. commanders were concerned because a great many of the truly innovative weapons and weapons systems—such as radar, jets, ballistic missiles, and (in its theoretical aspects) even nuclear weaponry—had originated abroad. The mission of the RDC and its successor organizations was, in effect, to get the jump on technology and bring weapons innovations home.

AFSC was especially active during the VIETNAM WAR, when it was called on to develop "instant" solutions for some of the needs of large-scale unconventional warfare. During the Vietnam period, AFSC advanced the development of electronic warfare systems, of gunships, of "smart" (precision-guided) munitions, and of FLIR (forward-looking infrared) sensor technology. AFSC also developed a defense meteorological satellite program during this period.

Air Force Technical Applications Center (AFTAC)

AFTAC is a Direct Reporting Unit originally established in 1959 as the USAF Field Activities Group and redesignated AFTAC in 1980. AFTAC is tasked with the detection of nuclear events, principally the detection of nuclear test detonations in violation of any of several international treaty agreements. One of AFTAC's most vital missions was the detection and tracking of radioactive matter that resulted from the 1986 accident at the Chernobyl nuclear power plant in the former Soviet Union.

AFTAC is headquartered at Patrick AFB, Florida.

Air Force Training Ribbon   See DECORATIONS AND MEDALS.

Air Force Weather Agency (AFWA)

This Field Operating Agency was formed October 15, 1997, and is located at Offutt AFB. Its mission is to enhance our nation's combat capability by arming our forces with quality weather and space products, training, equipment, and communications—anytime, anywhere. AFWA fields well-equipped, well-trained USAF weather units and ensures that USAF weather procedures, practices, and equipment are standardized while leaving units with sufficient flexibility to support their missions. AFWA staff provides specialized training, primarily relating to meteorology, and provides technical assistance as required.

AFWA personnel gather over 140,000 weather reports each day from conventional meteorological sources throughout the world and relay them to AFWA via the Automated Weather Network (AWN). By combining these data with information available from military and civilian meteorological satellites, AFWA constructs a real-time, integrated environmental database. A series of scientific computer programs model the existing atmosphere and project changes. These meteorological tools are made available to technicians for application to specific aerospace environmental problems encountered by operational personnel. AFWA supports the warfighter, the base or post weather station, national programs, command and control agencies and systems, and other operational and planning functions. AFWA exchanges data with the National Weather Service and the Naval Oceanography Command and is the backup agency for two National Weather Service centers.

AFWA is organized into a headquarters element with two subordinate centers. Nearly 574 of the agency's 729 members are located at Offutt AFB.

Air Intelligence Agency (AIA)

Headquartered at Kelly AFB, AIA was activated on October 1, 1993, to gain, exploit, defend, and attack information to ensure superiority in the air, space, and information domains. Approximately 16,000 AIA personnel are stationed worldwide. The agency is organized as follows:

National Air Intelligence Center: Headquartered at Wright-Patterson AFB, the NAIC is the primary Department of Defense producer of foreign aerospace intelligence. The center analyzes all available data on foreign aerospace forces and weapons systems to determine performance characteristics, capabilities, vulnerabilities, and intentions. Its antecedent was the Air Force Systems Command's Foreign Technology Division, organized in 1961.

Air Force Information Warfare Center: Headquartered at Kelly AFB, the AFIWC develops, maintains, and deploys information warfare and command and control warfare capabilities in support of operations, campaign planning, acquisition, and testing. The center is a focal point for intelligence data and provides technical expertise for computer and communications security and for tactical deception and operations security training. Activated on September 10, 1993, the AFIWC combined the Air Force Electronic Warfare Center and elements of the Air Force Cryptologic Support Center's securities directorate.

497th Intelligence Group: Headquartered at Bolling AFB, the group provides worldwide intelligence infrastructure support, physical and personal security, threat support to weapon systems acquisition, and employment and automation support. The group also serves as the Washington, D.C.-area focal point for USAF intelligence planning, logistics, and readiness issues, communications/computer system support, and all military and civilian personnel actions and programs. Formerly the Air Force Intelligence Support Agency, the group was renamed the 497th IG on October 1, 1993.

543rd Intelligence Group: Headquartered at Kelly AFB, the group is a major component of the 67th Intelligence Wing and is headquarters for two Intelligence Squadrons, the 31st IS at Fort Gordon, Georgia, and the 93rd IS, at Lackland AFB.

544th Intelligence Group: Headquartered at Peterson AFB, the group directs, manages, and supports units worldwide in the collection, refinement, and delivery of intelligence.

67th Intelligence Wing: Headquartered at Kelly AFB, the wing manages the agency's global mission and is the only intelligence wing in the USAF. It assists USAF components in the development of concepts, exercises, and employment of AIA forces to support contingency, low-intensity conflict, counterdrug, and special operations. Subordinate to the wing are five intelligence groups located in the continental United States, Hawaii, and Germany. With more than 9,600 personnel assigned, the 67th IW is one of the largest wings in USAF.

Joint Information Operations Center: This is a Joint Chiefs of Staff organization for coordination of joint-service intelligence operations, activities, and needs.

airlift

One of the most important USAF missions, airlift uses large transport aircraft or helicopters to move people, equipment, and supplies. Large-scale strategic airlift supports strategic operations, and smaller-scale tactical airlift supports tactical operations. Formerly, the MILITARY AIRLIFT COMMAND (MAC) managed airlift for the USAF and the Department of Defense. In June 1992, MAC was subsumed by the newly formed AIR MOBILITY COMMAND (AMC), which now manages all Department of Defense airlift.

See also BERLIN AIRLIFT.

Air Materiel Force, European Area

Established as Air Materiel Force, Europe, in 1954 under the UNITED STATES AIR FORCES IN EUROPE (USAFE), this named air force was headquartered at Wiesbaden, Germany, then redesignated Air Materiel Force, European Area, under the AIR MATERIEL COMMAND (AMC) in 1956 and, two years later, moved to Châteauroux Air Station, France. In

The airborne combat team from 1st Battalion, 508th Infantry, jumps from a USAF C-130 Hercules in an exercise over Maniago, Italy.   *(U.S. Air Force)*

1962, it was inactivated because improved distribution systems made this organization's huge supply depots unnecessary.

Air Materiel Force, Pacific Area

The Air Materiel Force, Pacific Area was established in 1944 as the Far East Air Service Command, with headquarters at Brisbane, Australia, and functioning as a named air force under the FAR EAST AIR FORCES (FEAF). In 1946, it was renamed Pacific Air Service Command, U.S. Army, then Far East Air Materiel Command the following year. In 1952, it was redesignated the Far East Air Logistics Forces,

and, in 1955, the Air Materiel Force, Pacific Area, under the AIR MATERIEL COMMAND (AMC). Its headquarters changed location several times, and, at the time of its inactivation in 1962, it was headquartered at Tachikawa AB, with another principal location at Clark AB, Philippines. As with the AIR MATERIEL FORCE, EUROPEAN AREA, also inactivated in 1962, improved distribution systems rendered large remote depots unnecessary.

Air Medal   See DECORATIONS AND MEDALS.

airman   See RANKS AND GRADES.

airman basic   See RANKS AND GRADES.

airman first class   See RANKS AND GRADES.

Airman's Medal   See DECORATIONS AND MEDALS.

Airmen Memorial Museum

Located outside of Washington, D.C., in Suitland, Maryland, the Airmen Memorial Museum was founded in 1988 by the Air Force Sergeants Association and is meant to record and commemorate the service and sacrifices of enlisted airmen from the Signal Corps (1907–18), the U.S. ARMY AIR SERVICE (1918–26), the U.S. ARMY AIR CORPS (1926–41), the U.S. ARMY AIR FORCES (1941–47), and the USAF (1947–present). The museum collects and exhibits artifacts, photographs, diaries, personnel records, letters, books, and other items pertaining to the service of enlisted airmen. Exhibit galleries present text and artifacts that illustrate the history of enlisted airmen from 1907 to the present day.

Airmen Memorial Museum is located at 5211 Auth Road, Suitland, MD 20746; phone: 1-800-638-0594. Web site: www.afsahq.org.

Air Mobility Command (AMC)

Formed in June 1992 from elements of STRATEGIC AIR COMMAND (SAC) and MILITARY AIRLIFT COMMAND (MAC), AMC is a MAJCOM responsible for intertheater AIRLIFT and for most tanker and airlift forces. The rationale behind integrating airlift and tanker operations is to provide truly global mobility and reach, to enhance rapid response, and to enable other services and foreign nations to operate more efficiently with USAF assets. AMC is headquartered at Scott AFB, Illinois.

This C-17 Globemaster III is from the 437th Air Wing, Charleston AFB. The photo was taken from a KC-10 Extender, just after it refueled the Globemaster. *(U.S. Air Force)*

Air National Guard (ANG)

The Air National Guard was established as a separate reserve component of the USAF on September 18, 1947, although National Guard aviators were active in all of America's wars and most of its major contingencies since the era of WORLD WAR I.

Currently, the ANG is administered by the National Guard Bureau, a joint bureau of the departments of the Army and Air Force, located in the Pentagon, Washington, D.C. The ANG is one of the seven reserve components of the U.S. armed forces and has a federal as well as a state mission. In accordance with the U.S. Constitution and federal law, each guardsman holds membership in the National Guard of his or her state as well as the National Guard of the United States.

The ANG's federal mission is to maintain well-trained, well-equipped units available for prompt mobilization during war and to provide assistance during national emergencies, such as natural disasters or civil disturbances. During peacetime, the combat-ready units and support units are assigned to most USAF major commands to carry out missions compatible with training, mobilization readiness, and contingency operations. The ANG provides almost half of the USAF's tactical airlift support, combat communications functions, aeromedical evacuations, and aerial refueling. The ANG has total responsibility for air defense of the entire United States.

When ANG units are not mobilized or under federal control, they report to the governor of their respective state or territory, or, in the case of the District of Columbia, to the commanding general of the District of Columbia National Guard. Each of the 54 ANG organizations is supervised by the adjutant general of the state or territory. Operating under state law, the ANG provides protection of life and property and preserves peace, order, and public safety. State-level missions include emergency relief support during natural disasters such as floods, earthquakes, and forest fires; search and rescue operations; support to civil defense authorities; maintenance of vital public services and antinarcotics operations.

Besides providing 100 percent of the United States air defense interceptor force, the ANG provides:

- air traffic control
- tactical airlift
- air refueling KC-135 tankers
- general purpose fighter force
- rescue and recovery capability
- tactical air support
- weather flights
- bomber force
- strategic airlift forces
- special operations capability

As of 2005, the ANG has more than 107,000 officers and enlisted people who serve in 88 flying units and 280 independent support units.

Air Reserve Personnel Center (ARPC)

ARPC is a Special Operating Agency that was established in 1956 as the Air Reserve Records Center and was redesignated ARPC in 1965. Headquartered in Denver, ARPC handles personnel support

functions for the mobilization and demobilization of the AIR NATIONAL GUARD, AIR FORCE RESERVE, and retired members of the ANG and AFR.

Air Reserves Forces Meritorious Service Medal   See DECORATIONS AND MEDALS.

Air Staff

Air Staff is a headquarters group that advises and assists the top USAF leadership, in addition to the SECRETARY OF THE AIR FORCE, undersecretary and assistant secretaries, and the CHIEF OF STAFF, USAF. The Air Staff is made up of the chief of staff, vice chief of staff, assistant vice chief of staff, and as many as four deputy chiefs of staff, in addition to other members who might be assigned from time to time. The Air Staff antedates the establishment of the independent USAF and was created with the U.S. ARMY AIR FORCES in 1941, becoming active the following year.

Air Superiority Doctrine

The USAF created an air superiority doctrine in 1984, making air superiority the number one priority of the USAF in any conflict, regardless of its nature. The objective of air superiority is to deny the enemy the use of its own air space while allowing U.S. aircraft to accomplish their tasks and missions. The PERSIAN GULF WAR was an extraordinarily dramatic demonstration of the doctrine in action.

Air Transport Command (ATC)   See AIR
MOBILITY COMMAND; MILITARY AIRLIFT COMMAND.

Air University (AU)

Headquartered at Maxwell AFB, Alabama, Air University is a component of the AIR EDUCATION AND TRAINING COMMAND (AETC), which also includes the Air Training Command (ATC), and functions as the USAF's center for professional military education. AU conducts professional military education, graduate education, and professional continuing education for officers, enlisted personnel, and civilians to prepare them for command, staff, leadership, and management responsibilities. AU offers specialized as well as degree-granting programs to serve USAF needs in scientific, technological, managerial, and other areas. AU is also responsible for research in aerospace education, leadership, and management, and it provides precommissioning training and offers courses for enlisted personnel leading to the awarding of select USAF specialty credentials. Finally, AU is also instrumental in the development and testing of USAF doctrine, concepts, and strategy.

The reach of AU extends beyond the active and reserve USAF through such Air University programs as Air Force Junior Reserve Officer Training Corps, AIR FORCE RESERVE OFFICER TRAINING CORPS (AFROTC), and the CIVIL AIR PATROL (CAP).

The AIR FORCE OFFICER TRAINING SCHOOL (OTS), located at Maxwell AFB, provides two officer training programs: Basic Officer Training and Commissioned Officer Training. Basic Officer Training is an intensive thirteen-and-a-half-week program that prepares officer candidates for the technical, physical, and professional requirements of commissioned service. In wartime, OTS may produce as many as 7,000 new second lieutenants in one year. Commissioned officer training, located at Gunter Annex, provides initial officer training for nearly 2,700 USAF judge advocates, chaplains, medical service officers (doctors, nurses, pharmacists, bioenvironmental engineers, and hospital administrators), and medical scholarship recipients each year.

Professional military education for USAF officers begins with Squadron Officer School, where captains study officership, air and space power, leadership tools, and applications. The Air Command and Staff College, the next level of officer professional military education, offers a 40-week curriculum devoted to educating students in the profession of arms, the requisites of command, the nature of war, and the application of air and space power at the theater warfare level. The emphasis is on warfare at the operational and strategic levels. The AIR WAR COLLEGE, senior school in the USAF professional military education system, is treated in a separate entry.

The College for Enlisted Professional Military Education, headquartered at Maxwell's Gunter Annex, is responsible for designing the curriculum taught at Airman Leadership Schools, noncommissioned officer academies, and the Air Force Senior Noncommissioned Officer Academy. The college directly operates the two advanced phases of enlisted professional military education, the stateside NCO academies and the Senior NCO Academy. Major commands operate their own Airman Leadership Schools using curriculum designed by the college. Airman Leadership Schools prepare senior airmen to be noncommissioned officers, and NCO academies prepare technical sergeants to be senior NCOs.

The USAF Senior Noncommissioned Officer Academy is the capstone of enlisted professional military education. Located at Maxwell's Gunter Annex, the school prepares senior enlisted leaders to be chiefs with a curriculum focused on leadership and management, communication skills, and military studies.

In addition to military education, AU administers programs of academic education, including the COMMUNITY COLLEGE OF THE AIR FORCE and the AIR FORCE INSTITUTE OF TECHNOLOGY, both treated in separate entries. Continuing professional education is offered at the Ira C. Eaker College for Professional Development, Air University's largest resident college. The college provides courses for chaplains, commanders, personnel and manpower managers, comptrollers, family support center mangers, judge advocates, first sergeants, and historians. The COLLEGE OF AEROSPACE DOCTRINE, RESEARCH AND EDUCATION (CADRE), another continuing education facility, offers a Contingency Wartime Planning Course and a Joint Doctrine Air Campaign Course, as well as a Joint Flag Officer

Warfighting Course and a Joint Forces Air Component Commanders Course. These two courses prepare general officers from all military services for leadership positions in the joint warfighting environment. CADRE is also a research organization. CADRE doctrine analysts examine both existing and proposed concepts and strategies and deliver the results directly to the AIR FORCE DOCTRINE CENTER. CADRE's Air Force Wargaming Institute conducts numerous games each year to enhance the warfighting skills of both U.S. and international military officers.

Other AU entities are administered through its Office of Academic Support, which directs the Air University Library, the Academic Instructor School, and the International Officer School, tasked with preparing international officers to enter schools and courses. Other organizations under the OAS include: Air University Television, which supports resident and distance learning instruction; the Extension Course Institute, which publishes approximately 330 correspondence courses in specialized, career development, and professional military education; Air University Press, which acquires, edits, and publishes books, monographs, and journals on airpower topics; and Educational Technology.

Air War College (AWC)

The senior school in the USAF professional military education system, the Air War College is part of the AIR UNIVERSITY (AU) system and prepares selected senior officers for key staff and command assignments, in which they will manage and employ aerospace power as a major component of national security.

Air War College curriculum focuses on warfighting and national security issues, with emphasis on the effective employment of aerospace forces in joint and combined combat operations. Each class lasts 44 weeks and enrolls officers from all branches of the armed forces, international officers, and civilians of equivalent rank from U.S. government agencies.

The Air War College operates the National Security Forum, which brings students into contact with business, civic, and professional leaders from throughout the United States to discuss issues affecting national security. The forum is the culmination of the 10-month Air War College course of study.

Air Warfare Center (AWFC)

Located at Nellis AFB, Nevada, the Air Warfare Center manages USAF advanced pilot training and integrates many USAF test and evaluation requirements. The center's first predecessor organization, the USAF Tactical Fighter Weapons Center, was established in 1966. In 1991, the center became the USAF Fighter Weapons Center, and then the USAF Weapons and Tactics Center in 1992. AWFC was created in October 1995.

AWFC uses the Nellis Air Force Range Complex, some 3 million acres, together with another 5-million-acre military operating area, which is shared with civilian aircraft. AWFC also operates at the Eglin AFB range in Florida, which provides over-water and additional electronic expertise.

AWFC oversees operations of four WINGS, the 57th Wing, the 98th Range Wing, and 99th Air Base Wing at Nellis, and the 53rd Wing at Eglin.

The 57th Wing is responsible for such activities as Red Flag, which provides training in a combined air, ground, and electronic threat environment; the USAF Weapons School, which provides USAF graduate-level training for A-10, B-1, B-52, EC-130, F-15, F-15E, F-16, HH-60, RC-135, command and control operations, and intelligence and space weapons. The wing also plans and executes CLOSE AIR SUPPORT missions in support of U.S. Army exercises. In addition, the wing oversees the USAF air demonstration team, the THUNDERBIRDS, and manages the operation and deployment of the Predator, an unmanned reconnaissance aircraft.

The 53rd Wing (Eglin AFB) is the focal point for the combat air forces in electronic combat, armament and avionics, chemical defense, reconnaissance, command and control, and aircrew training devices.

The 99th Air Base Wing is the host wing at Nellis, and the 98th Range Wing manages the operations of the Nellis Air Force Range Complex, including two emergency airfields.

Air Weather Service (AWS)

AWS furnishes technical advice, procedures, and systems for weather support systems. Through various subordinate units, AWS provides weather, climatological, and space support to the USAF. The service is headquartered at Scott AFB, Illinois.

Alaskan Air Command (AAC)

The earliest AAC antecedent was the Alaskan Air Force, activated at Elmendorf Field, Alaska, in January 1942 and redesignated the ELEVENTH AIR FORCE the following month. The organization served in the offensive that liberated the Aleutian Islands from the Japanese, then served in the defense of Alaska. In December 1945, 11AF became the AAC. Somewhat confusingly, a new Eleventh Air Force was formed as part of the Air Defense Command (ADC) and assigned to AAC during 1946–48. In 1990, the AAC became 11AF.

During the cold war period, AAC provided (according to its motto) "Top Cover for America" under NORAD. The command controlled three bases in Alaska, Elmendorf AFB, Eielson AFB, and Shemya AFB, with fighters stationed in forward positions at King Salmon and Galena airports— Galena being the closest U.S. airfield to what was then the Soviet Union. AAC aircraft routinely intercepted Soviet bombers probing U.S. airspace.

Altus AFB, Altus, Oklahoma   See AIR FORCE BASES.

American Volunteer Group (AVG)

In 1940–41, President Franklin D. Roosevelt authorized the creation of a covert U.S. air force to fight for China in the Sino-Japanese War, the conflict that began in 1937 and that ultimately merged with WORLD WAR II. This American Volunteer Group (AVG) was planned to consist of two fighter groups and one medium bomber group. To equip the first of the fighter groups, 100 Tomahawk II-B fighters—equivalent to the Curtiss P-40C pursuit craft—were diverted from British order, and 100 U.S. military pilots and 200 technicians officially resigned from the military to accept private employment as civilian mercenaries with the AVG. The unit, now designated the First American Volunteer Group, was put under the command of a retired U.S. ARMY AIR CORPS captain, CLAIRE L. CHENNAULT, and trained in Burma, then a British colony.

The 1st AVG was not committed to combat until after Pearl Harbor and the U.S. entry into the war in December 1941. America's entry into the war brought the cancellation of the planned second

One of the redoubtable "Flying Tigers" ready to take off in a Curtiss P-40 (Warhawk) fighter plane
(National Archives)

fighter group and the bomber group, but the 1st AVG continued to fly, under Chennault, as what the public came to call the "Flying Tigers." AVG pilots painted a vivid tigerlike mouth and row of jagged teeth on either side of the P-40's distinctive air scoop, and journalists came up with the moniker, which conveyed the aggressive spirit that was in short supply among the Allies during the early days of the Pacific war.

The Flying Tigers played a major role in defending Burma until the Japanese routed the Allies in May 1942. Later in the year, the 1st AVG was instrumental in holding western China until reinforcements reached the Nationalist government. Formally disbanded on July 4, 1942, the AVG was instantly merged into the 23rd Pursuit Group of the U.S. ARMY AIR FORCES. Only five AVG pilots accepted induction in China, but many subsequently rejoined the U.S. military. AVG fliers are credited with having shot down 297 Japanese aircraft; 23 pilots were killed or captured.

Recent historians have concluded that the record of Flying Tiger victories was inflated, but it is beyond dispute that the AVG was highly effective against Japanese air and ground forces during the winter of 1941–42, a period in which all other Allied news in Asia and the Pacific was bleak indeed.

Andersen AFB, Guam   See AIR FORCE BASES.

Andrews, Frank Maxwell (1884–1943) *Air Force general*

A founding father of the USAF, Andrews was born in Nashville, Tennessee, and graduated from the U.S. Military Academy at West Point in 1906, with a commission as a cavalry officer. He entered the U.S. ARMY AIR SERVICE in 1917, received pilot training, and remained in the United States during WORLD WAR I, serving as a training officer. While serving in a series of routine postings during the 1920s, he attended and graduated from both the Air Corps Tactical School (ACTS) and the Com-

mand and General Staff College. During the 1930s, he served a staff tour in Washington, D.C., then attended the Army War College, graduating in 1933. He was assigned to command the 1st Pursuit Group at Selfridge Field, Michigan, but he was recalled to Washington in 1934 to participate in planning the new GENERAL HEADQUARTERS AIR FORCE (GHQ Air Force). In 1935, Andrews was temporarily promoted to brigadier general and took command of the newly created GHQ Air Force, which was the only independent combat unit of the U.S. ARMY AIR CORPS.

As GHQ Air Force commander, Andrews was in a key position to mount a campaign for the establishment of the air force as an independent service arm. He believed that the USAAC had to prove itself by deeds, not theory, in order to achieve independence. Under his command, USAAC personnel staged a number of spectacular exercises to demonstrate the potential of air power. Andrews also focused on developing the B-17 Flying Fortress heavy bomber as the weapon that would transform the air force into an indispensable and highly potent strategic operations force. He laid his career on the line to promote the four-engine bomber over the cheaper B-18, and was passed over for promotion to chief of the USAAC. By 1939, he was returned to his permanent grade of colonel and posted in San Antonio, Texas. However, General George C. Marshall, newly appointed army chief of staff, ended Andrews's exile and brought him to Washington, D.C., as assistant chief of staff for operations and training. In this post, Andrews directed the vital prewar expansion and training of both ground and air forces.

He left this post at the outbreak of WORLD WAR II and served successively as commander of the Panama Canal Air Force, the Caribbean Defense Command, and in Europe. In 1943, his career was cut short when he was killed in a plane crash. Andrews AFB is named in his honor.

Andrews AFB, Maryland   See AIR FORCE BASES.

Appropriations Act of July 24, 1917

This legislative milestone funded U.S. air power in WORLD WAR I to the sum of $640 million, the largest amount of money ever appropriated by Congress for a single purpose up to that time. Funding authorized by the act was used to develop flying fields in the United States and for the manufacture of aircraft intended to equip as many as 345 combat squadrons. Production fell very far short of this goal. By the time of the armistice in November 1918, only 45 U.S. combat squadrons had been committed to action, and these were equipped exclusively with foreign-built planes.

Army Air Forces Antisubmarine Command (AAFAC)

The AAFAC was established at New York City in October 1942 and tasked with countering the German U-boat threat in United States continental waters and elsewhere. AAFAC headquarters was in New York and training facilities were at Langley Field (see Langley AFB), Virginia, but the command operated from three continents in addition to North America and was responsible for the following areas of operation: the north and middle Atlantic, from Newfoundland to Trinidad; the Bay of Biscay; and the approaches to North Africa. AAFAC pilots flew A-20, A-29, B-17, B-18, B-25, and B-34 aircraft, but they relied most heavily on the B-24. Newly developed radar technologies were extensively pioneered by the command.

The AAFAC was active only until August 1943, when its mission was taken over by the U.S. Navy. During its 10 months of operation, U-boats sunk by air action rose from a paltry 10 percent to an impressive 50 percent. Officially, AAFAC pilots were credited with 10 U-boat sinkings.

As of 1986, antisubmarine work once again became a USAF mission, although the navy continues to take primary responsibility for antisubmarine operations. The USAF now uses B-52G bombers equipped with AGM-84 air-to-surface Harpoon missiles for antisubmarine operations.

Army and Air Force Authorization Act of 1950

Passed on July 10, 1950, this act provided the legislative definition of the organization of the USAF, specifying a maximum strength of 502,000 officers and men and an inventory of 24,000 aircraft. On August 3, 1950, with the KOREAN WAR under way, Congress suspended the limitations on strength in anticipation of necessary expansion during the war.

Army Regulation 95-5 (AR 95-5)

Issued on June 20, 1941, AR 95-5 created the U.S. ARMY AIR FORCES. AR 95-5 significantly enhanced the autonomy of the air arm over its former status as the U.S. ARMY AIR CORPS. The USAAF commander reported directly to the army chief of staff, and the AIR FORCE COMBAT COMMAND (AFCC) replaced the cumbersome GENERAL HEADQUARTERS AIR FORCE (GHQ Air Force). The effect of AR 95-5 and subsequent directives was to make the USAAF the functional (if not statutory) equivalent of the army and navy.

Arnold, Henry Harley ("Hap") (1886–1950)
Air Force general

Hap Arnold guided the transformation of the prewar U.S. ARMY AIR CORPS into the mighty U.S. ARMY AIR FORCES of WORLD WAR II and is justly regarded as the father of the independent USAF. He was born in Gladwyne, Pennsylvania, and received an appointment to West Point, from which he graduated in 1907, after which he was assigned to the infantry as a second lieutenant. Arnold served in the Philippines during 1907–09, but, in 1911, he transferred to the AVIATION SECTION, U.S. ARMY SIGNAL CORPS, and volunteered for flight training with the Wright brothers in Dayton, Ohio. In October of the very next year, he became the first to demonstrate how the airplane could be used for reconnaissance, and, for his pioneering efforts, was awarded the first MacKay flying trophy. He also earned the army's first military aviator's badge and expert aviator's certificate, and he established an early world altitude record of 6,540 feet.

Yet Arnold's remarkable achievements did little to spark the army's interest in the airplane as a weapon, and, in April 1913, Arnold was transferred back to the infantry. Returned to the air service in 1916, he was promoted to captain and put in command of the army's aviation training schools in 1917, when the United States entered WORLD WAR I. Arnold directed aviation training from May 1917 through 1919 and earned a reputation as a great teacher. The armistice of November 1918 brought sharp reductions in military funding, which greatly retarded the development of American military aviation. Never one to be discouraged, however, Arnold continued to work toward the goal of creating a credible U.S. Army Air Corps. He attended Command and General Staff College, from which he graduated in 1929 with the rank of

General Henry H. "Hap" Arnold   *(U.S. Air Force)*

lieutenant colonel and in 1931 was given command of the 1st Bomb Wing and the 1st Pursuit Wing at March Field, California, a post he held through February 1935. During July and August 1934, he led a flight of 10 B-10 bombers on a round trip from Washington, D.C., to Fairbanks, Alaska, winning a second MacKay Trophy for having demonstrated the endurance capabilities of the modern bomber.

Promoted to brigadier general, Arnold took command of 1st Wing, GENERAL HEADQUARTERS AIR FORCE (GHQ Air Force) in February 1935 and became assistant chief of staff of the USAAC in December of that year. After the death of General Oscar Westover in September 1938, Arnold was promoted to temporary major general and named chief of staff. From this position, he was able to institute a program to improve the combat readiness of the USAAC, despite inadequate funding and the resistance of tradition-bound military planners. Named acting deputy chief of staff of the army for air matters in October 1940, Arnold became chief of the Air Corps, after it was renamed the U.S. Army Air Forces in June 1941.

Shortly after Pearl Harbor (December 7, 1941), Arnold was promoted to the temporary rank of lieutenant general and was soon afterward named commanding general of the USAAF. He was promoted to the temporary rank of general in 1943. His position as commanding general of the USAAF put Arnold at the very highest level of policy and strategic planning in the United States military. A member of the U.S. Joint Chiefs of Staff, he participated in shaping Allied strategy in Europe and the Pacific.

Among the many organizational innovations Arnold introduced was the creation of the TWENTIETH AIR FORCE in April 1944. His purpose in creating this unit was, first and foremost, to conduct an effective bombing campaign against Japan, but he organized the 20AF so that it reported directly to his command as a representative of the Joint Chiefs. This bold stroke took the USAAF closer to becoming a fully independent service.

In December 1944, along with generals Dwight D. Eisenhower, Douglas MacArthur, and George C. Marshall, Arnold was elevated to the special rank of general of the army. He continued to command the USAAF through the end of the war, retiring in March 1946. A year after his retirement, on September 18, 1947, thanks in large part to all he had done, the USAAF became the USAF, an independent service. To honor its "father," the USAF named Arnold the first general of the air force in May 1949—despite his retired status. Arnold died the following year on his ranch in Sonoma, California.

Arnold AFB, Tennessee   See Air Force bases.

Arnold Engineering Development Center (AEDC)

Located at Arnold AFB, Tennessee, AEDC is the most advanced and largest complex of flight simulation test facilities in the world. Housed here are 58 aerodynamic and propulsion wind tunnels, rocket and turbine engine test cells, space environmental chambers, arc heaters, ballistic ranges, and other specialized units. The mission of the AEDC is to test, evaluate, and troubleshoot aircraft, missile, and space systems and subsystems. AEDC also conducts research to develop advanced testing techniques and instrumentation and to support the design of new test facilities.

The center is named for General of the Air Force Henry Harley Arnold, who set into motion the research program that would become the work of this center. The facility was officially dedicated by President Harry S. Truman on June 25, 1951. AEDC is part of the Air Force Materiel Command (AFMC).

Aviano AB, Italy   See Air Force bases.

aviation medicine

The USAF is active in research into the physical and psychological problems associated with avia-

tion and spaceflight. USAF aviation medicine began in 1917 with the work of Colonel Theodore C. Lyster of the Aviation Section, U.S. Army Signal Corps, but, during World War I, the army relied on civilian physicians contracted to serve as "flight surgeons." In 1918, a Medical Research Laboratory was established at Hazelhurst Field, New York, to research aviation medicine and to train military physicians in the field. By July 1921, the U.S. Army Air Service graduated 46 flight surgeons from Hazelhurst. The following year, the Medical Research Laboratory was transferred to Mitchel Field, New York, as the School of Aviation Medicine. The school moved to Brooks Field, Texas (see Brooks AFB), in 1926, then to Randolph Field (see Randolph AFB).

The principal early work of USAAS aviation medicine was to prevent accidents and illness related to flight, to improve training, to investigate altitude-induced deafness, to test the effects of cold and low air pressure at high altitudes, and even to improve aviator goggles. In 1944, during World War II, the school at Randolph Field expanded to include course work in aeromedical evacuation and to train USAAF nurses.

After World War II, research in aviation medicine expanded and was conducted at the Aero Medical Laboratory at Wright-Patterson AFB; at the Air Force Flight Test Center, Edwards AFB; at the Air Development Center, Holoman AFB. The era of high-speed, high-altitude jet flight brought to prominence more medical issues than ever before. Today, the school, renamed the United States Air Force School of Aerospace Medicine, is located at Brooks AFB, Texas.

Aviation Section, U.S. Army Signal Corps

The first separate U.S. Army unit exclusively devoted to aviation, the Aviation Section was created by act of Congress on July 18, 1914. Its first battle experience came in the Punitive Expedition of 1916 against the Mexican social bandit Pancho Villa, but the performance of its aircraft proved unsatisfactory. It was the Aviation Section that

This E-3 Sentry AWACS from the 966th AWACS, Tinker AFB, Oklahoma, is seen in a training flight over New Mexico.   *(U.S. Air Force)*

struggled to bring U.S. military aviation into WORLD WAR I, and on August 27, 1918, the unit was reorganized as the U.S. ARMY AIR SERVICE.

AWACS (Airborne Warning and Control System)

The predecessor of AWACS, airborne radar, was first used in the VIETNAM WAR on EC-121 "College Eye" aircraft (see AIRCRAFT, VIETNAM WAR). The original EC-121 evolved into the EC-121D, used by the AIR DEFENSE COMMAND (ADC) as part of its early warning system for continental defense. Ultimately, an EC-121T was developed as ASACS (airborne surveillance and control system), which gave way in March 1977 to AWACS, deployed on the E-3 Sentry aircraft. (See also AIRCRAFT, COLD WAR AND AFTER.)

A Boeing 707 modified with large radar dome, the E-3 AWACS provided radar coverage extending from the surface of the earth up to the stratosphere at a range of more than 200 miles—and without the ground clutter that plagues ground-based radar. AWACS has proved invaluable in giving tactical commanders the information required to gain control of air battles as well as CLOSE AIR SUPPORT of ground forces as well as management of interdiction reconnaissance and AIRLIFT operations. AWACS was very extensively used in the PERSIAN GULF WAR.

B

balloons and dirigibles

On November 4, 1782, Joseph-Michel Montgolfier, a French paper manufacturer, filled a taffeta container with hot air and watched it ascend. This was the first recorded practical experiment in ballooning—although as early as 1766, the English scientist Henry Cavendish isolated hydrogen, which led a Scottish chemist named Joseph Black to speculate that if a bladder could be filled with the ultralight gas and both the bladder and the gas weighed less than the air they displaced, the bladder would rise. Neither Cavendish nor Black ever got around to trying the experiment. It was Montgolfier and his brother, Jacques-Étienne, who developed the first practical hot-air balloons, and the French Academy that experimented with the first hydrogen balloons, both in 1783. In that same year, a young physician named Pilâtre de Rozier made the first manned tethered flights in a *Montgolfière,* as the early balloons were called, and a French infantry major, the Marquis d'Arlandes, undertook the first free flight in a balloon on November 21, 1783. Very soon after this, ballooning became the rage in Europe, and Jean-Pierre Blanchard, the first aeronaut-showman, became the most celebrated of the early balloonists. He brought his balloon to America and made an ascension from the yard of the old Walnut Street Prison on January 9, 1793, a flight witnessed by President George Washington, Alexander Hamilton, John Adams, Thomas Jefferson, and James Monroe. After reaching a maximum altitude of 5,812, Blanchard landed, 46 minutes after liftoff, across the Delaware River near Woodbury, New Jersey. He had introduced aviation to the United States.

Although, after witnessing the flight of the Montgolfiers in France, Benjamin Franklin predicted that the balloon would quickly find military applications, it was not until 1840, during the Second Seminole War, that U.S. Army colonel John H. Sherburne proposed the use of observation balloons to be lofted at night to search for Seminole campfires. Secretary of War Joel Poinsett authorized Sherburne to contact Charles Ferson Durant, a balloonist remembered by some historians of flight as "America's first professional aeronaut." However, Sherburne's commanding officer, General W. K. Armistead, allowed no ascensions. In 1846, during the U.S.-Mexican War, John C. Wise, a balloonist from Lancaster, Pennsylvania, volunteered his services for an assault against Veracruz. That key Mexican city was protected from land assault by a formidable fortress and shielded from seaborne attack by dangerous reefs. Wise proposed an attack from the air, using a balloon tethered by five miles of cable to effect aerial bombardment from an altitude of 5,000 feet. The scheme came to nothing, but the War Department returned to John Wise years later, during the Civil War.

By the time of the Civil War, the United States had produced a host of balloonists in addition to Wise and Durant, including Samuel King, James

Allen, William H. Helme, W. D. Bannister, John Steiner, and John La Mountain. O. A. Gager, with Wise, La Mountain, and an unidentified newspaper reporter, made a spectacular flight from St. Louis, Missouri, to Henderson, New York, on July 20, 1859—a distance of 1,100 miles, which they covered in under 20 hours. Of the small legion of balloonists active in America by 1861, the most flamboyant was Thaddeus Sobieski Constantine Lowe, who flew from Cincinnati to Unionville, South Carolina, a thousand miles, on April 19, 1861. By sheer accident, Lowe's exploit was the first balloon ascent of the Civil War.

On the same day that Lowe made his flight, James Allen, a balloonist with four years' experi-

Union army hot air balloon, 1862   *(National Archives)*

ence, and his friend, a dentist named William H. Helme, both members of the 1st Rhode Island Regiment, volunteered their services to the federal government as balloonists. They traveled to Washington, bringing with them a pair of balloons. On June 9, the two aeronauts inflated one of their balloons at a gas main in central Washington. The craft was towed to a farm a mile north of the city, and Allen and Helme made the Union army's first official captive balloon trial ascent. The army was sufficiently impressed to attempt a reconnoitering mission for General Irvin McDowell on the eve of the First Battle of Bull Run. Allen took the larger of his two balloons to Alexandria, Virginia, where he attempted inflation at a coal gas plant. The balloon, aged and in disrepair, split under pressure. Allen successfully inflated his second balloon, but the craft was destroyed when it struck a telegraph pole. Yet the army's interest in ballooning continued, and, on June 12, 1861, Major Hartman Bache, acting chief of the Topographic Engineers, contacted John Wise to request an estimate of the cost of building and operating a small balloon. Early in July, Wise was hired as a military balloonist and commissioned to construct a balloon for $850. Completed on July 21, the army's first balloon was delivered to the capital, where it was inflated, then walked by a ground crew up Pennsylvania Avenue to Georgetown, thence up the C&O Canal, across the Potomac, and to Fairfax Road. There Albert J. Myer, chief signal officer, tethered it to a wagon for the trip to Manassas, where it was to be used to observe the battle now in progress. Unfortunately, Major Myer, anxious to deliver the balloon to the battle site, ordered the wagon driver to whip up the horses—this despite the protests of John Wise. As the balloonist had feared, the gas bag was soon snagged by overhanging branches, which tore gaping holes in the fabric as Wise attempted to free it. Wise repaired his balloon and made observation ascensions on July 24 at Arlington. On July 26, a crew was towing the balloon to Ball's Crossroads. It hit some telegraph wires, which severed the tow ropes, sending the balloon in free flight toward the Confederate lines. Rather than allow the craft to fall into Confederate hands, Union troops were ordered to shoot it down.

Concluding that the problem with balloons was the necessity of inflating them wherever coal gas was available and then having to transport them while inflated, Wise designed a portable hydrogen gas generator. The army declined to build Wise's generator, but it did accept John La Mountain's offer not only of his services as a balloonist but also two balloons and a ready-made portable hydrogen generator. Major General Benjamin F. Butler, headquartered at Fortress Monroe, Virginia, hired La Mountain as a civilian aerial observer on June 5, 1861. His first ascent, at Hampton, Virginia, on July 25, was hampered by heavy winds that prevented his attaining sufficient altitude to observe the enemy. On July 31, however, he rose to 1,400 feet and, commanding a view 30 miles in radius, was able to inform Butler that Confederate strength around Hampton was much weaker than had been thought. This was the first useful balloon reconnaissance mission for the army. On August 3, La Mountain made the first ascension tethered to a waterborne vessel, and, beginning on October 4, he used prevailing winds in a series of untethered, free-flight reconnaissance missions.

On June 18, 1861, La Mountain's fellow balloonist and rival Thaddeus Lowe made the first telegraph transmission from aloft, demonstrating the feasibility of real-time reconnaissance. President Abraham Lincoln personally persuaded the Union army's superannuated commander Winfield Scott to establish a balloon corps. In September, Lowe used the balloon for artillery spotting, transmitting ranging observations by telegraph. Four new balloons were built by November 10, 1861, and, in January 1862, two more were added, giving the army's still-unofficial balloon corps a total of seven. These craft and the men who tended and flew them were, in effect, the first air arm of the U.S. military.

Having amassed his small fleet of aircraft, Lowe set about staffing his balloon corps. With rivalries among the nation's leading aeronauts running high, Lowe could recruit neither Wise nor La Mountain, the men with the greatest experience, but, instead, chose William Paullin, John R. Dickinson, Ebenezer Seaver (almost immediately dismissed over a salary dispute), John Starkweather, John H. Steiner (who resigned after a year of service), Ebenezer Locke Mason, Jr. (who, like Ebenezer Seaver, was dismissed over pay issues), and the experienced balloonist James Allen, who brought along his brother Ezra. All of the early balloonists were civilian employees of the army, who, in turn, hired civilian assistants, but also used the services of enlisted men attached to the balloon corps either permanently or on an as-required basis. Although the army declined to assign Lowe and his balloon corps official status, Lowe dubbed himself variously "Aeronaut," "Chief Aeronaut," and even "Chief of Aeronautics, Army of the Potomac." The balloon corps itself was shuffled from one military jurisdiction to another, originating at the behest of the Topographic Engineers of the Army, with the Quartermaster furnishing supply (however irregularly); after March 31, 1862, the balloon corps became entirely the province of the Quartermaster until May 25, 1862, when it came under the tactical control of Brigadier General Andrew A. Humphreys, chief topographic engineer on General McClellan's staff. On April 7, 1863, control was transferred to the Army Corps of Engineers under the direction of Captain Cyrus B. Comstock, who immediately informed Lowe that his pay was being cut from 10 dollars a day to six. After making a protest, Lowe resigned—though he volunteered to remain in service until battles in progress had been resolved. On May 7, 1863, he left the corps, and command was briefly given to Brigadier General Gouverneur K. Warren. In June, General Joseph Hooker assigned Chief Signal Officer Colonel Albert J. Myer to take over the "balloon department." Myer, no advocate of aerial observation, protested that he had neither the men nor the appropriation to run the department. In the meantime, General Daniel Butterfield summarily declared, without basis, that balloon operations were of no value, and, in 1863, the balloon corps, never really an official military entity, was disbanded.

The U.S. Army neglected aviation from the disbanding of the balloon corps in 1863 until October 1, 1890, when Congress assigned to the Signal Corps the duty of collecting and transmitting information for the army. In 1891, Chief Signal Officer brigadier general Adolphus V. Greely requested appropriations to create a balloon corps. The following year, a balloon "section" was formally established within the Signal Corps. In 1891, Greely had sent Lieutenant William A. Glassford to Europe to study the latest developments in balloon aeronautics. The lieutenant procured from the French a small balloon, the *General Myer,* equipped with a telephone for air-to-ground communication. At Fort Logan, Colorado, Glassford, promoted to captain, used the *General Myer* in an operational balloon section as part of a Signal Corps telegraph train. When the *General Myer* was destroyed in a severe windstorm in 1897, Glassford directed Sergeant William Ivy—who, in civilian life, had earned a reputation as a stunt balloonist/parachutist under the alias of Ivy Baldwin—to build a new one. Ivy and his wife had completed a balloon, made of silk and with a capacity of 14,000 cubic feet, just the year before, and this Ivy now readied for Signal Corps service. It was destined to be the only balloon used in the Spanish-American War. When the United States declared war on Spain on April 25, 1898, Lieutenant Colonel Joseph E. Maxfield of the Signal Corps was ordered to transport Ivy's balloon to Santiago, Cuba. Maxfield was hurriedly assigned a command of 24 enlisted men and three officers detailed from the Signal Corps and from two infantry units. The balloon train arrived in Santiago on June 22, but disembarkation was delayed until June 28. Logistical problems prevented the balloonists from going ashore with their cumbersome portable hydrogen generator and the even more cumbersome stock of iron filings and sulfuric acid from which the hydrogen was produced. They had to use ready-filled hydrogen cylinders, which meant that the balloon could be inflated only once in the field. The balloon reached headquarters on June 29 and was unpacked. The tropical heat had softened the varnish coating on the fabric envelope, which now stuck together and partially disintegrated, causing a number of large tears that had to be sewn and patched.

Equipped with a patched balloon manned by an inexperienced ground crew, Ivy and Maxfield made their first ascension on June 30. Others followed, which confirmed, among other things, the presence of the Spanish fleet in Manila harbor. Enthusiastically positive reports were made to U.S. expedition commander General William R. Shafter. But even more impressive were the observations made on July 1 during the make-or-break Battle of San Juan Hill. Balloon observers were able to discover a trail that not only relieved congestion, enabling the troops to advance much faster, but also allowed the American and Cuban forces to deploy and coordinate two columns against the Spanish, one along the main road. Observers also proved effective in directing and redirecting artillery fire. Some historians believe that the use of the balloon was a determining factor in this hard-fought victory.

Despite the success of balloon reconnaissance in the Spanish-American War, little was done after the war to develop the balloon corps. In 1900, Congress appropriated $18,500 for a balloon house and administration and instruction buildings at Fort Myer, Virginia. Two years later, a balloon detachment consisting of a dozen enlisted men (later expanded to 22) was organized at Fort Myer under the command of Lieutenant A. T. Clifton. Equipment was modest: a German-built kite balloon, three French-built silk balloons, five small cotton signal balloons, five observer baskets, three nets, an inflation hose, steel tubes, sandbags, a compressor unit, and a hydrogen generator. The balloon detachment did very little ballooning until 1906, when the Signal Corps was able to obtain sufficient compressed hydrogen for regular operations. In August 1906, balloon instruction was expanded from Fort Myer, Virginia, to Fort Leavenworth, Kansas, but much of the training was limited to classroom theory because of chronic equipment shortages. In any case, by this time, balloons were being outmoded by dirigibles, steerable (the word "dirigible" was coined from the Latin *dirigere,* meaning "to direct") balloons, powered by engines.

Count Ferdinand von Zeppelin of Germany designed the first practical dirigibles during 1899–1902. In 1907, Brigadier General James Allen, chief signal officer of the army, met an aerial showman named Thomas Scott Baldwin, who had worked with aviation pioneer Glenn Curtiss, who designed a lightweight four-cylinder engine to propel a new dirigible. General Allen approached Baldwin to supervise the design and construction of an experimental dirigible for the army. On February 24, 1908, he produced U.S. Army Dirigible No. 1 with a 20-horsepower water-cooled gasoline engine developed by Glenn Curtiss. Baldwin trained three officer pilots, Lieutenants FRANK P. LAHM, BENJAMIN D. FOULOIS, and THOMAS E. SELFRIDGE. The first flight was made on September 18, 1908, with Lieutenant Foulois as pilot.

Dirigibles were destined to a short life in the army air service, as they were almost immediately eclipsed by the introduction of heavier-than air craft, the airplane. The U.S. Navy would, however, go on to develop uses for these "steerable balloons." Nevertheless, both dirigibles and balloons were important in the birth of military aviation and were the seeds from which an American air force would eventually grow.

Barksdale AFB, Louisiana See AIR FORCE BASES.

Basic Military Training Honor Graduate Ribbon See DECORATIONS AND MEDALS.

basic training

All USAF basic training—also known as basic military training (BMT)—is conducted at Lackland AFB, Texas. In the USAF, basic training is a six-week course, which consists of academic instruction, physical training (PT), and marksmanship. The object of basic training is to teach enlistees how to adjust to military life, to prepare them for military life, and generally to promote pride in being a member of the USAF. In addition, trainees who have enlisted with an aptitude-area guarantee are given orientation and counseling to help them choose a job specialty that is compatible with both USAF needs and their own skills, education, civilian experience, and desires.

From basic training, graduates proceed to one of the AIR EDUCATION AND TRAINING COMMAND (AETC) technical training centers.

Beale AFB, California See AIR FORCE BASES.

Berlin Airlift

The alliance between the Western democracies and the Soviet Union forged during WORLD WAR II rapidly disintegrated with the defeat of the common enemy. Occupied Germany was divided into sectors controlled by the United States, France, Britain, and the Soviet Union. As early as the end of March 1948, the Soviets became wary of the strong alliances being formed among the Western allies to coalesce the German sectors they controlled into a separate capitalist state, West Germany. Accordingly, Soviet forces began detaining troop trains bound for West Berlin—the U.S./French/British-controlled sector of the divided German capital, which was deep inside the Soviet-controlled eastern sector of Germany. On June 7, 1948, the Western nations announced their intention to create West Germany. A little more than two weeks after this announcement, on June 24, Soviet forces blockaded West Berlin, protesting that, given its location, the city could never serve as the capital of West Germany.

Declaring that to give up West Berlin would mean relinquishing all of Germany to the Soviets, President Harry S. Truman called on the newly independent USAF to organize a massive emergency AIRLIFT to keep West Berlin supplied. From June 26, 1948, to September 30, 1949, the USAF made 189,963 flights over Soviet-held territory into West Berlin (U.K. forces made 87,606 flights). The USAF flew in a total of 1,783,572.7 tons of food, coal, and other cargo (the British an additional 541,936.9 tons) as well as 25,263 inbound passengers and 37,486 outbound (the British flew in 34,815 and 164,906 out). The result of this unrelenting and extremely hazardous mission was a logistical and political triumph for the West. On May 12, 1949, the Soviets officially lifted the blockade, and East and West Germany were formally created later that very month. The joint Western action in Berlin became the basis of the NATO alliance.

On June 25, 1948, U.S. Army general Lucius D. Clay telephoned Lieutenant General CURTIS EMERSON LEMAY, commander of UNITED STATES AIR FORCES IN EUROPE (USAFE), with a question: "Curt, can you transport coal by air?" LeMay responded: "Sir, the air force can deliver anything." On June 26, LeMay set into motion the marshaling of transport aircraft not only in Europe but from the Alaskan, Caribbean, and Tactical Air Commands, 39 C-54 Skymasters and other passenger and cargo aircraft, together with some 825 aircrews and support personnel. From Hickam AFB, Hawaii, came more C-54s and another 425 personnel. On June 27,

Brigadier General Joseph Smith was appointed to lead the Berlin Airlift Task Force in what was dubbed Operation Vittles. General Smith's tenure as commander lasted approximately one month, during which time he established the extraordinary goal of flying 65 percent of the available aircraft *every* day, a schedule that allowed barely enough time for maintenance and operations personnel to service the aircraft. Second, Smith ordered each plane to make three round trips to Berlin daily. Third, he established a block system, so that aircraft of the same cruising speeds could travel together. Finally, he created an Air Traffic Control Center at Frankfurt to schedule and coordinate the flights.

On July 23, 1948, MILITARY AIR TRANSPORT SERVICE (MATS) took over airlift operations, and Major General William H. Tunner replaced Brigadier General Smith as commander of the operation. Tunner orchestrated the airlift according to what he called a "steady rhythm, constant as the jungle drums." Aiming to move maximum tonnage to Berlin each and every day, Tunner calculated that there were 1,440 minutes in a day and set an ultimate goal of landing an aircraft every minute. Tunner knew this was impossible at the

Transport airplanes taking part in the Berlin Airlift   *(National Archives)*

time, but, on most days, he achieved landings every three minutes.

Tunner insisted on maximum efficiency. He ordered that no crew member was to leave the site of his airplane at Tempelhof and Gatow airports. When a plane touched down, the operations officer would come to the pilot with any necessary information, as did a weather officer. A third jeep rolled up to the plane with hot coffee, hot dogs, and doughnuts. Tunner even hired motion-study experts to analyze loading and unloading. Soon, 12 men could load 10 tons of bagged coal into a C-54 in six minutes flat, while unloading crews reduced 17-minute tasks to five. Similarly, refueling crews learned techniques to cut refueling times from 33 to eight minutes. Ultimately, aircraft turnaround time, which had been an impressive 60 minutes, was cut to a phenomenal 30 minutes.

The machinelike efficiency of the airlift, sustained for nearly a year, forced the Soviet Union to yield, giving the West its first victory of the cold war.

Blesse, Frederick C. ("Boots") (1921–)
fighter pilot

Blesse flew fighters in the KOREAN WAR and in the VIETNAM WAR, compiling a record of 10 victories, which made him America's sixth-ranking jet ace. For USAF doctrine, he is especially important as the author of an influential essay entitled "No Guts, No Glory," on air superiority jet fighter tactics.

Born in the Panama Canal Zone, Blesse graduated from the U.S. Military Academy at West Point in 1945, too late to fly in WORLD WAR II. In addition to two tours in Korea and 157 sorties flown in the Vietnam War, Blesse won all six trophies in the 1955 Worldwide Gunnery Championship meet, a record yet to be equaled. He retired from the USAF with the rank of major general.

Bolling AFB, Washington, D.C.   See AIR FORCE BASES.

bombing, strategic

Strategic bombing attacks vulnerable aspects of a whole nation with the objective of disrupting the nation's economy, its ability to produce war materiel, and its ability to feed, clothe, and shelter its citizens. Although strategic bombing is not directed exclusively against civilian targets, such targets do become fair game in achieving the desired objective. The idea, however, is not to "punish" the people of an enemy nation, but to destroy that nation's will and ability to make war.

Military aviation planners in the United States began developing strategic doctrine after WORLD WAR I. The Air Corps Tactical School focused on strategic bombing using large bombers, and the U.S. ARMY AIR FORCES carried out strategic bombing operations against Germany and Japan in WORLD WAR II. In the KOREAN WAR, strategic bombing was not applied, but, in the VIETNAM WAR, it was used in a somewhat abridged form.

The doctrine of strategic bombing has been subject to a great deal of controversy, particularly with regard to its application in World War II. Some studies have suggested that the USAAF's costly campaign of strategic bombing had relatively little effect on Germany's ability (or will) to continue the war, whereas other studies suggest that the campaign was indeed instrumental in the Allied victory. Post–World War II USAAF and USAF opinion was that, when the objective is the unconditional surrender of the enemy, only strategic bombing that makes some use of nuclear weapons can guarantee results. In short, the ultimate objective of strategic bombing must be the total annihilation of the enemy—or, at least, the fully credible threat thereof.

See also BOMBING, TACTICAL.

bombing, tactical

For the air arm, tactical operations are conducted against enemy armed forces, in contrast to strategic operations, which may be conducted against the entire society and social infrastructure of the enemy, civilian as well as military. Typically, tactical air operations are carried out in coordination with friendly surface (land or naval) operations.

Tactical bombing is an aspect of attack aviation. It includes carefully targeted bombing of enemy bases, supply points, convoys, and communication. Interdiction can be carried out against the enemy on the battlefield as well as deep within the enemy's interior. (A sustained campaign of interdiction tends to become a campaign of strategic bombing; see BOMBING, STRATEGIC.) In addition to interdiction, tactical bombing may be carried out in direct support of ground attack. Carpet bombing consists of massive aerial bombardment of enemy troops on the battlefront (see CLOSE AIR SUPPORT).

Following WORLD WAR II, which ended in Japan with a nuclear attack, USAF planners emphasized the development of strategic doctrine and weapons at the expense of tactical doctrine and weapons. Yet the conflicts the USAF was called on to fight after World War II, especially the KOREAN WAR and the VIETNAM WAR, required the extensive use of tactical bombing. The USAF improvised, often with considerable success, as in the "Linebacker" operations of the Vietnam War.

Bong, Richard I. (1920–1945) *World War II ace and test pilot*

Bong, who, having won every possible U.S. ARMY AIR FORCES decoration, was awarded the Medal of Honor in December 1944, was America's ace of aces, with 40 combat victories scored during WORLD WAR II.

Born in Poplar, Wisconsin, he flew P-38s with the 35th Fighter Group and then with the 49th Fighter Group. By November 1943, he had racked up 21 victories. After serving for a time on the operations staff of the FIFTH AIR FORCE, Bong flew

Major Richard Bong—the "ace of aces"—is the highest-scoring U.S. ace of any war.   *(U.S. Air Force)*

in New Guinea, where he achieved another seven victories. After taking a course in aerial gunnery back in the United States, Bong returned to the Pacific and scored a dozen victories in 30 sorties.

After December 1944, Bong returned to the United States and was subsequently assigned as a TEST PILOT for early jets. He was killed in August 1945, testing an F-80 near Burbank, California. In 1986, he was inducted posthumously into the National Aviation Hall of Fame, Dayton, Ohio.

brigadier general   See RANKS AND GRADES.

Brooks AFB, Texas   See AIR FORCE BASES.

C

Cannon AFB, New Mexico See AIR FORCE
BASES.

captain See RANKS AND GRADES.

careers

The USAF is a very large organization, which offers opportunities in most of the careers one might find in civilian life and many that are to be found only in the military or in an advanced aerospace organization. Because many USAF activities rely extensively on advanced and complex technology, career opportunities in scientific and technical fields are especially strong.

There are 12 broad USAF occupational groups:

1. Human services;
2. Media and public affairs;
3. Health care;
4. Engineering, science, and technical;
5. Administrative;
6. Service;
7. Vehicle, aircraft, and machinery mechanic;
8. Electronic and electrical equipment repair;
9. Construction;
10. Machine operator and precision work;
11. Transportation and material handling; and
12. Combat specialty

Enlisted Careers

1. **Human Services Occupations**
   Caseworkers and counselors
   Religious program specialists
2. **Media and Public Affairs Occupations**
   Audiovisual and broadcast technicians
   Broadcast journalists and newswriters
   Graphic designers and illustrators
   Interpreters and translators
   Musicians
   Photographic specialists
3. **Health Care Occupations**
   Cardiopulmonary and EEG technicians
   Dental specialists
   Medical laboratory technicians
   Medical record technicians
   Medical service technicians
   Optometric technicians
   Pharmacy technicians
   Physical and occupational therapy specialists
   Radiologic (X-ray) technicians
4. **Engineering, Science, and Technical Occupations**
   Air traffic controllers
   Chemical laboratory technicians
   Communications equipment operators
   Computer programmers
   Emergency management specialists
   Environmental health and safety specialists
   Intelligence specialists

Meteorological specialists
Nondestructive testers
Ordnance specialists
Radar operators
Radio intelligence operators
Space operations specialists
Surveying, mapping, and drafting technicians

5. **Administrative Occupations**
Administrative support specialists
Computer systems specialists
Finance and accounting specialists
Flight operations specialists
Legal specialists and court reporters
Personnel specialists
Postal specialists
Preventive maintenance analysts
Recruiting specialists
Sales and stock specialists
Supply and warehousing specialists
Training specialists and instructors
Transportation specialists

6. **Service Occupations**
Firefighters
Food service specialists
Law enforcement and security specialists
Military police

7. **Vehicle, Aircraft, and Machinery Mechanic Occupations**
Aircraft mechanics
Automotive and heavy equipment mechanic
Divers
Heating and cooling mechanics
Powerhouse mechanics

8. **Electronic and Electrical Equipment Repair Occupations**
Aircraft electricians
Communications equipment repairers
Computer equipment repairers
Electrical products repairers
Electronic instrument repairers
Photographic equipment repairers
Power plant electricians
Precision instrument repairers
Radar equipment repairers
Weapons maintenance technicians

9. **Construction Occupations**
Building electricians
Construction equipment operators
Construction specialists
Plumbers and pipe fitters

10. **Machine Operator and Precision Work Occupations**
Compressed gas technicians
Dental and optical laboratory technicians
Machinists
Power plant operators
Printing specialists
Survival equipment specialists
Water and sewage treatment plant operators
Welders and metal workers

11. **Transportation and Material Handling Occupations**
Air crew members
Aircraft launch and recovery specialists
Cargo specialists
Flight engineers
Petroleum supply specialists
Quartermasters and boat operators
Seamen
Vehicle drivers

12. **Combat Specialty Occupations**
Special operations forces

Officer Careers

1. **Executive, Administrative, and Managerial Occupations**
Communications managers
Emergency management officers
Finance and accounting managers
Food service managers
Health services administrators
International relations officers
Law enforcement and security officers
Management analysts
Personnel managers
Postal directors
Purchasing and contracting managers
Recruiting managers
Store managers

Supply and warehousing managers
Teachers and instructors
Training and education directors
Transportation maintenance managers
Transportation managers

2. **Human Services Occupations**
   Chaplains
   Social workers
3. **Media and Public Affairs Occupations**
   Audiovisual and broadcast directors
   Music directors
   Public information officers
4. **Health Diagnosing and Treating Practitioner Occupations**
   Dentists
   Optometrists
   Physicians and surgeons
   Psychologists
5. **Health Care Occupations**
   Dietitians
   Pharmacists
   Physical and occupational therapists
   Physician assistants
   Registered nurses
   Speech therapists
6. **Engineering, Science, and Technical Occupations**
   Aerospace engineers
   Air traffic control managers
   Chemists
   Civil engineers
   Computer systems officers
   Electrical and electronics engineers
   Environmental health and safety officers
   Industrial engineers
   Intelligence officers
   Lawyers
   Life scientists
   Marine engineers
   Meteorologists
   Nuclear engineers
   Physicists
   Space operations officers
   Surveying and mapping managers

7. **Transportation Occupations**
   Airplane navigators
   Airplane pilots
   Helicopter pilots
8. **Combat Specialty Occupations**
   Missile system officers
   Special operations officers

Carswell AFB   See AIR FORCE BASES.

Castle AFB   See AIR FORCE BASES.

chain of command

As in all United States military service branches, the chain of command is a system designed to resolve problems at the lowest possible level. Each link in the chain represents a level of responsibility, extending from the president (as commander in chief) to the secretary of defense, to the SECRETARY OF THE AIR FORCE, to the CHIEF OF STAFF, USAF, then to the relevant commander of a MAJCOM. From here, depending on the command structure of the MAJCOM, the chain descends each supervisory level, ultimately to the noncommissioned officer level of first sergeant. In the chain of command, each level is responsible for the next lower level and accountable to the next higher level.

Chandler, Charles deForest (1878–1939)
U.S. Army pilot

Chandler was the first commander of the USAF's first direct antecedent organization, the AERONAUTICAL DIVISION, U.S. ARMY SIGNAL CORPS, which was created in 1907.

Chandler was a native of Cleveland, Ohio, and was commissioned in the Signal Corps in 1898. In 1907, when he was placed in command of the Aeronautical Division, Chandler was qualified as a balloon pilot. He gained dirigible qualification two years later and, in 1911, became a qualified airplane pilot. A year later he was awarded the rating of Military Aviator.

Chandler was in charge of the Signal Corps aviation schools at College Park, Maryland, and Augusta, Georgia. In 1913, he commanded the 1st Aero Squadron, based at Texas City, Texas, and he established the U.S. Army balloon school at Fort Omaha, Nebraska. In WORLD WAR I, Chandler replaced FRANK P. LAHM as head of the AEF's Balloon Section. He retired with the rank of colonel in 1920.

Chanute AFB, Illinois   See AIR FORCE BASES.

Charleston AFB, South Carolina   See AIR FORCE BASES.

Chennault, Claire L. (1893–1958) *U.S. Army Air Forces general*

Chennault is best remembered as the irascible, resourceful, daring, and always controversial commander of the AMERICAN VOLUNTEER GROUP, the celebrated Flying Tigers, who flew for the Chinese Air Force in WORLD WAR II. He was later promoted to command of the FOURTEENTH AIR FORCE.

Born in Commerce, Texas, Chennault entered the infantry as a first lieutenant in 1917, then transferred to the Signal Corps to become a pilot in 1919. He was assigned as the commander of a pursuit squadron and, from this point on, became a student of fighter strategy and tactics. After graduating from the Air Corps Tactical School in 1931, Chennault served as an instructor there until 1936.

As an advocate of the strategic importance of fighters, Chennault ran afoul of the pre–World War II "bomber mafia," planners who stressed the bomber as the air weapon par excellence. Discouraged, Chennault retired from the army with the rank of captain in 1937.

In 1937, with China embroiled in a desperate war against Japanese invaders, Mme. Jiang Jieshi (Chiang Kai-shek) recruited Chennault to organize

Claire Chennault on the cover of *Life* magazine, October 8, 1942   *(Life)*

and train the American Volunteer Group, the Flying Tigers, which flew already obsolescent P-40s against technologically superior Japanese fighter aircraft. Chennault chose and trained his AVG pilots so skillfully that, despite their handicaps in numbers and quality of aircraft, between December 1941 (when operations began) and July, when the AVG became the 23rd Fighter Squadron of the U.S. ARMY AIR FORCES, the Flying Tigers shot down 299 Japanese aircraft with a loss of 32 planes and 19 pilots. (Some recent scholars believe these figures are variously inflated.)

Chennault returned to U.S. service in April 1942 with the rank of colonel but was soon promoted to brigadier general, and, in July, became commanding general of the USAAF in China. In

March 1943, he was named to command of the 14AF, which supported the China-Burma-India (CBI) theater operations of army general Joseph Stilwell. Even as a U.S. Army commander, however, Chennault remained a maverick, confounding his superiors by dealing directly with China's Jiang Jieshi rather than through the CHAIN OF COMMAND or even with President Roosevelt. Chennault saw the war through, however, and retired in 1945.

After the war, Chennault remained loyal to Jiang, organizing the Chinese National Relief and the Civil Air Transport to assist in the fight against the communists. The USAF acknowledged Chennault's achievements by promoting him to the honorary grade of lieutenant general just nine days before he succumbed to cancer in 1958.

Cheyenne Mountain Air Force Station

Located in southwest Colorado Springs, Colorado, this installation is an underground command center for monitoring the skies and space for hostile incoming weapons. Built in anticipation that it would be a primary target for a nuclear attack, Cheyenne Mountain is perhaps the most heavily fortified large underground installation in the world. It consists of 15 steel buildings, laid out in a 4.5-acre grid *inside* the mountain, and accessed through a tunnel and 30-ton blast doors. The buildings themselves are suspended on 1,300 47-inch steel springs designed to absorb the shock of a nuclear detonation. Thirty days' supplies and 6 million gallons of water are stored inside the installation. About 1,500 people work inside the mountain, which is operated by NORAD and the U.S. Space Command, a unified command headquartered in nearby Peterson AFB.

As thoroughly secured as Cheyenne Mountain is, military planners acknowledge that it could not withstand a direct hit from one of its own nuclear missiles; therefore, a similar facility at Offutt AFB, Nebraska, would be used as a backup in case of a mission failure at Cheyenne Mountain.

chief   See RANKS AND GRADES.

chief master sergeant   See RANKS AND GRADES.

chief master sergeant of the air force   See RANKS AND GRADES.

Chief of Staff, USAF

Created by the NATIONAL SECURITY ACT OF 1947, the position of Chief of Staff, USAF, is the head of the USAF. The Chief of Staff is a general appointed by the president for a four-year term. He or she is a member of the Joint Chiefs of Staff as well as the Armed Forces Policy Council and is an adviser to the president, the National Security Council, the secretary of defense, and to the SECRETARY OF THE AIR FORCE. Ex-officio, the Chief of Staff presides over the AIR STAFF.

Civil Air Patrol (CAP)

CAP performs three main functions: emergency services, aerospace education, and cadet training. CAP was founded on December 1, 1941, and, during WORLD WAR II, its principal purpose was to allow private pilots and aviation enthusiasts to use their light aircraft and flying skills to aid in civil defense efforts. In 1943, the organization came under the control and direction of the U.S. ARMY AIR FORCES and, on July 1, 1946, became a permanent peacetime institution when Public Law 476 established it as a federally chartered, benevolent civilian corporation. Two years later, in May 1948, Public Law 557 made the organization the official auxiliary of the USAF. Known as the CAP Supply Bill, the 1948 law authorized the SECRETARY OF THE AIR FORCE to assign military and civilian personnel to liaison offices at all levels of CAP.

Today, CAP's emergency services include air and ground search and rescue, disaster relief, and civil defense for natural disasters. CAP members fly approximately 85 percent of the search and rescue mission hours directed by the Air Force Rescue and Coordination Center (AFRCC) at Langley AFB. In 1985, CAP agreed to assist the U.S. Customs Service in its counternarcotics efforts by flying air reconnaissance missions along U.S. boundaries, and, in 1989, similar agreements were made with the Drug Enforcement Administration (DEA) and the U.S. Forest Service.

CAP's aerospace education programs provide its members and the educational community information about aviation and space activities through support of some two hundred education workshops for teachers at approximately 100 colleges and universities around the country. CAP conducts the National Congress on Aviation and Space Education, an annual national convention for aerospace teachers.

The CAP Cadet Program is open to U.S. citizens and legal residents of the United States, its territories, and possessions between the ages of 12 and 21. Cadets progress through achievements that include special activities, aerospace education, leadership programs, moral leadership, and physical fitness and may compete for academic and flying scholarships. On completion of initial training, cadets receive the General Billy Mitchell Award, which entitles them to enter the USAF as an airman first class, should they choose to enlist.

CAP is organized into eight geographic regions composed of 52 WINGS, one for each state, Puerto Rico, and the District of Columbia. Wings are subdivided into groups, squadrons, and, sometimes, flights—approximately 1,700 individual units in all. The organization is headquartered at Maxwell AFB and is staffed by military and civilian personnel. CAP membership consists of approximately 26,000 cadets and more than 35,000 adult volunteers. Members operate more than 3,700 privately owned aircraft and 530 CAP-owned aircraft and more than 950 CAP-owned ground vehicles.

Clark AB   See AIR FORCE BASES.

close air support (CAS)

CAS is the use of air power to attack enemy targets (typically personnel, artillery, tanks, and so on) that are close to friendly ground forces. Typically, the object of CAS is to give friendly ground forces room to maneuver and generally to bolster offensives and counteroffensives. USAF aircraft most frequently used for CAS include the A-10 Thunderbolt II, AC-130H Spectre gunship, and the F-16 Fighting Falcon.

Cochran, Jacqueline (?–1980) *American aviator*

After earning fame as a civilian aviator in the 1930s, Cochran, in 1939, suggested that women be recruited and trained to fly military aircraft. In response, Major General HENRY HARLEY ARNOLD, chief of the U.S. ARMY AIR CORPS, suggested that she recruit women volunteers to serve in Britain's Air Transport Auxiliary, which would give her the experience necessary should the USAAC ever create a women's unit. Cochran recruited 25 American women to serve the ATA and became the chief of these U.S. volunteers.

In October 1942, Arnold instituted training to produce 500 women ferry pilots, principally to fly aircraft from manufacturers to air bases within the continental United States. In June 1943, Cochran was appointed special assistant and director of women pilots for the U.S. ARMY AIR FORCES. This became the WOMEN AIRFORCE SERVICE PILOTS

Jackie Cochran in the cockpit of a Canadair F-86 with Chuck Yeager   *(U.S. Air Force)*

(WASP) on August 5, 1943, but it was deactivated in December 1944.

After the war, Cochran became a lieutenant colonel in the AIR FORCE RESERVE and, in 1953, was the first woman to fly faster than sound. In 1964, she took an F-104 to Mach 2, breaking all speed records for the time. In civilian life, Cochran ran a cosmetics firm and served on the board of directors of Northeast Airlines.

College of Aerospace Doctrine, Research and Education (CADRE)

Headquartered at Maxwell AFB and operating under the aegis of AIR UNIVERSITY (AU), CADRE is charged with assisting in the development of wargaming and the development and analysis of the concepts, doctrine, and strategy of aerospace power, and to educate USAF and joint communities on warfighting at the operational and strategic level through research, wargaming, and military education.

CADRE publishes *Airpower Journal*, the USAF's professional quarterly and primary institutional forum for exchanging ideas about airpower and other matters relating to national defense. CADRE's Public Affairs Center of Excellence conducts public affairs–related research to assist in the development of USAF doctrine. CADRE's wargaming component plans, develops, and conducts war games in support of USAF operational, analytical and educational requirements. The Warfare Studies Institute educates USAF and joint warfighters on issues concerning aerospace warfare, including contingency war planning, joint doctrine air campaign development, information warfare applications, and aerospace power. The CADRE Intelligence Directorate provides intelligence services to the commander and staff organizations of Air University; the commander and staff organizations of the 42nd Air Base Wing, and Air University professional military education (PME) schools and institutes. The Plans and Operations Directorate supports CADRE budget needs and long- and short-range plans, security, and logistics.

colonel   See RANKS AND GRADES.

Columbus AFB, Mississippi   See AIR FORCE BASES.

Combat Control Team (CCT)

The CCT consists of specially trained personnel airdropped to front lines to provide local air traffic control and to advise on all aspects of landing, airdrop, and extraction zone requirements.

First organized by the USAF as discrete units in 1952, the CCTs evolved into the "Blue Berets" of the VIETNAM WAR. In 1968, there were 485 combat controllers in the USAF, deployed by the Airlift Control Center as needed. Personnel on each were divided into three teams, each headed by an officer and consisting of air traffic controllers and radio maintenance specialists. One team was always on alert status, ready with a jeep, radio, and portable navigational aids to deploy by AIRLIFT within 15 minutes.

The CCTs performed varied missions, such as providing air traffic control at remote airstrips, guiding in airlift craft—the C-130s, C-123s, and C-7s—and accompanying army and marine units to provide control for emergency airdrops of ammo and supplies. Combat controllers were required to maintain proficiency in air traffic control procedures, in packing parachutes, in performing radio maintenance, and in use of weapons (M-16 and CAR-15). Their training included jump school, and courses in control tower, combat control, survival (tropical, arctic, and water), amphibious training, High Altitude, Low Opening (HALO) parachute rigging, and radio maintenance. They also attained proficiency in Ground Proximity Extraction System (GPES) airdrop procedures. The informal motto of the CCTs was "first in, last out."

Combat Readiness Medal   See DECORATIONS AND MEDALS.

Comm Squadron

Comm Squadron is an informal term denoting a communications squadron, the unit on a base that is responsible for all communications, including radar, air traffic control, telephone service, and all message centers.

Community College of the Air Force (CCAF)

CCAF is the world's only degree-granting institution of higher learning dedicated exclusively to enlisted people. It offers career-oriented airmen and NCOs the opportunity to earn a job-related, two-year undergraduate degree (Associate in Applied Science) and is open to all active-duty, AIR NATIONAL GUARD, and AIR FORCE RESERVE members.

The college curriculum combines technical and professional military education with off-duty education at civilian institutions. As America's largest community, junior, or technical college, CCAF has awarded more than 125,000 associate in applied science degrees since it first opened in 1972.

Continental Air Command (CONAC)

Activated as a MAJCOM in 1948, CONAC replaced the TACTICAL AIR COMMAND (TAC) and AIR DEFENSE COMMAND (ADC). CONAC also controlled the AIR FORCE RESERVE. Tactical Air Command was reestablished in 1950, during the KOREAN WAR, and Air Defense Command was reactivated as a MAJCOM in 1951. CONAC was relegated to administering the AIR NATIONAL GUARD and the Air Force Reserve. In 1968, CONAC was inactivated.

cruise missile

A small, pilotless jet- or rocket-propelled aircraft with folding wings and fins, a cruise missile may be launched from the ground, from a ship, or dropped from an aircraft. Cruise missiles are typically "smart weapons," guided by highly sophisticated computer programs and navigational systems—incorporating a terrain contour-matching guidance system, an onboard global positioning system (GPS), and an inertial navigation system (INS)—so that they can follow complicated routes to a target. Some cruise missiles are fitted with conventional warheads, some with nuclear devices.

Currently, the USAF cruise inventory includes:

Boeing AGM-86B cruise missile (nuclear warhead) and AGM-86C (conventional warhead) air-launched cruise missile, designed to be dropped by B-52H bombers. The AGM-86B has a range of about 1,500 miles.

McDonnell-Douglas AGM-84D Harpoon, an all-weather, over-the-horizon, antiship missile system. Designed to fly at low altitudes, skimming the sea, the Harpoon uses active radar guidance to reach its target. The missile is designed for launch from B-52H bombers.

D

Davis, Benjamin O., Jr. (1912–2002) *U.S. Air Force general*

The son of the first African-American U.S. Army general, Davis became the first African American to graduate from the U.S. Military Academy at West Point in the 20th century and the first African-American general in the U.S. Air Force.

Benjamin O. Davis, Jr., climbs into an advanced trainer at Tuskegee Army Air Base in 1942. *(Library of Congress)*

Davis enrolled in flight training in 1941 at Tuskegee Army Air Field (see TUSKEGEE AIRMEN) as a member of the segregated unit's first class. He went on to become commander of the 99th Pursuit Squadron, a segregated unit he led into combat in North Africa. Despite discrimination practiced against the unit, the 99th excelled, as did Davis's next command, the 332nd Fighter Group.

Using the war record of the Tuskegee Airmen as evidence, Davis, after the war, worked toward the integration of the USAF. President Harry S. Truman's Executive Order 9981, mandating the integration of the armed forces, was issued in 1948, and the following year, HOYT SANFORD VANDENBERG, chief of the USAF, explicitly ordered full integration of the USAF. In the new integrated USAF, Davis was assigned a number of important commands and staff postings, culminating in an appointment as deputy chief of staff for operations of the UNITED STATES AIR FORCES IN EUROPE (USAFE). He held this post until his retirement in 1970. In civilian life, he served as assistant secretary of transportation (environment, safety, and consumer affairs) in the administration of Richard M. Nixon. Davis succumbed to Alzheimer's disease on July 4, 2002.

Davis-Monthan AFB, Arizona   See AIR FORCE BASES.

decorations and medals

Each U.S. military branch has its own medals and decorations, and the U.S. Air Force is no exception. Although USAF personnel are eligible for many awards from the other services, this entry mostly concerns itself with those awards that originated with the U.S. Air Force.

Aerial Achievement Medal

This decoration was established by the SECRETARY OF THE AIR FORCE on February 3, 1988, and is awarded by the DEPARTMENT OF THE AIR FORCE to U.S. military and civilian personnel for sustained meritorious achievement while participating in aerial flight. The achievements must be accomplished with distinction above and beyond that normally expected of professional airmen. Approval authority is delegated to WING commanders for military personnel and to the secretary of the air force for civilians. MAJCOMs identify the missions and positions that qualify for this award.

Air Force Achievement Medal

This award, authorized by the SECRETARY OF THE AIR FORCE on October 20, 1980, is presented to USAF personnel for outstanding achievement or meritorious service rendered specifically on behalf of the USAF. It may also be awarded for acts of courage lesser than those meriting award of the Air Force Commendation Medal.

Air Force Basic Military Training Instructor Ribbon

The SECRETARY OF THE AIR FORCE established this ribbon on December 7, 1998, to acknowledge military training instructors who display commitment and dedication to the training of USAF personnel. Instructors serving in USAF basic military training and at USAF officer training schools are eligible for the ribbon; however, instructors at technical training schools are ineligible.

Air Force Commendation Medal

Authorized by the SECRETARY OF THE AIR FORCE on March 28, 1958, this medal is awarded to members of any of the armed forces of the United States who, while serving in any capacity with the USAF after March 24, 1958, distinguished themselves by meritorious achievement and service. The degree of merit must be distinctive, though not necessarily unique. Acts of courage that do not involve the voluntary risk of life required for the Airman's Medal may be considered for the AFCM.

Air Force Cross

The decoration was established by Congress, Public Law 88-593, on July 6, 1960, which amended Section 8742 of Title 10, U.S. Code, to change the designation of Distinguished Service Cross to Air Force Cross in cases of awards made under USAF authority. This cross, then, is the USAF version of the Distinguished Service Cross and is awarded for extraordinary heroism, not justifying the award of a Medal of Honor, to any person serving with the USAF while engaged in military operations involving conflict with an opposing foreign force or while serving with friendly foreign forces engaged in conflict against an opposing armed force in which the United States is not a belligerent party.

The first award of the Air Force Cross was a posthumous presentation to Major Rudolf Anderson Jr., for extraordinary heroism in connection with military operations against an armed enemy from October 15, 1962, to October 27, 1962, during the Cuban missile crisis.

Air Force Good Conduct Medal

Authorized by Congress on July 6, 1960, along with other medals for the USAF, the AFGCM was not actually created until June 1, 1963, when the SECRETARY OF THE AIR FORCE established it. It is awarded to USAF enlisted personnel for exemplary conduct during a three-year period of active military service or for a one-year period of service during a time of war. Persons eligible for the award must have had character and efficiency ratings of excellent or higher throughout the qualifying period, including time spent in attendance at service schools, and there must have been no convictions of court-martial during this period.

USAF personnel awarded the Army Good Conduct Medal either before or after June 1, 1963, were permitted to wear both the USAF and army medals.

Air Force Longevity Service Ribbon

DEPARTMENT OF THE AIR FORCE General Order 60, November 25, 1957, authorized this ribbon for award to all USAF members who complete four years of honorable active or reserve military service with any branch of the U.S. armed forces. This ribbon replaces the Federal Service Stripes previously worn on the uniform.

Air Force Organizational Excellence Award

The SECRETARY OF THE AIR FORCE authorized this award on August 26, 1969, to recognize the achievements and accomplishments of USAF organizations and activities. It is awarded to USAF internal organizations that are entities within larger organizations. Such organizations must be unique, unnumbered organizations or activities that perform functions normally conducted by numbered wings, groups, squadrons, and so on.

Air Force Outstanding Unit Award

The Air Force Outstanding Unit Award was authorized by DEPARTMENT OF THE AIR FORCE General Order 1 of January 6, 1954, and is awarded by the SECRETARY OF THE AIR FORCE to numbered units that have distinguished themselves by exceptionally meritorious service or outstanding achievement clearly setting the unit above and apart from similar units. Eligible services include performance of exceptionally meritorious service, accomplishment of a specific outstanding achievement of national or international significance, combat operations against an armed enemy of the United States, or military operations involving conflict with or exposure to hostile actions by an opposing foreign force.

Air Force Overseas Ribbon—Long Tour

The ribbon was authorized by the CHIEF OF STAFF, USAF, on October 12, 1980. Before January 6, 1986, the ribbon was awarded to USAF and AIR FORCE RESERVE members credited with completion of an overseas tour on or after September 1, 1980. USAF and Air Force Reserve members serving as of January 6, 1986, or later are entitled to reflect all USAF overseas tours credited during their career. A service member may wear both the long tour ribbon and the Air Force Overseas Ribbon—Short Tour, if appropriate. The short tour ribbon takes precedence over the long-tour ribbon when both are worn.

Air Force Overseas Ribbon—Short Tour

The ribbon was authorized by the CHIEF OF STAFF, USAF, October 12, 1980. Before January 6, 1986, it was awarded to USAF and AIR FORCE RESERVE members credited with completion of an overseas tour on or after September 1, 1980. USAF and Air Force Reserve members serving as of January 6, 1986, or later are entitled to reflect all USAF overseas tours credited during their careers. A service member may wear both the short tour and the Air Force Overseas Ribbon—Long Tour ribbons, if appropriate. The short tour ribbon takes precedence over the long-tour ribbon.

Air Force Recognition Ribbon

Authorized by the CHIEF OF STAFF, USAF, on October 12, 1980, this ribbon is awarded to individual USAF recipients of special trophies and awards, excluding the Twelve Outstanding Airmen of the Year nominees (see Outstanding Airman Of The Year Ribbon).

Air Force Recruiter Ribbon

On June 21, 2000, the SECRETARY OF THE AIR FORCE established this ribbon to recognize USAF recruiters, both officers and enlisted personnel.

Air Force Training Ribbon

Authorized by the CHIEF OF STAFF, USAF, on October 12, 1980, the ribbon is awarded to USAF service members on completion of initial accession training after August 14, 1974.

Airman's Medal

This decoration, one of a number of USAF awards established by Congress on July 6, 1960, replaces the Soldier's Medal for USAF personnel and is awarded to any member of the armed forces of the United States or of a friendly nation who, while serving in any capacity with the USAF after the date of the award's authorization, shall have distinguished himself or herself by a heroic act, usually at the voluntary risk of his or her life but not involving actual combat.

Air Medal

Established by Executive Order 9158, May 11, 1942, as amended by Executive Order 9242, September 11, 1942, the Air Medal is awarded to military and civilian personnel for single acts of heroism or meritorious achievement while participating in aerial flight. It may be awarded to foreign military personnel in actual combat in support of operations. The magnitude of the achievement is less than that required for the Distinguished Flying Cross, but it must be accomplished with distinction above and beyond that expected of professional airmen.

The Air Medal is not awarded for peacetime sustained operational activities and flights. Approval authority is delegated to MAJCOM for U.S. military personnel and to the SECRETARY OF THE AIR FORCE for civilians and for foreign military personnel. This decoration is the same for all branches of the armed forces, but it is significant to note that the colors of the ribbon—a broad stripe of ultramarine blue in the center flanked on either side by a wide stripe of golden orange, with a narrow stripe of ultramarine blue at the edge—are the original colors of the U.S. ARMY AIR CORPS.

Air Reserves Forces Meritorious Service Medal

Originally established as a ribbon bar by the SECRETARY OF THE AIR FORCE on April 1, 1964, the award was created as a medal by an amendment of May 1, 1973. It is awarded for exemplary behavior, efficiency, and fidelity during a four-year period while serving in an enlisted status in the AIR FORCE RESERVE.

Basic Military Training Honor Graduate Ribbon

Authorized by the CHIEF OF STAFF, USAF, on April 3, 1976, this ribbon is awarded to honor graduates of basic military training (see BASIC TRAINING) who, after July 29, 1976, have demonstrated excellence in all phases of academic and military training. The ribbon is limited to the top 10 percent of the training flight.

Combat Readiness Medal

Authorized by the SECRETARY OF THE AIR FORCE on March 9, 1964, and amended August 28, 1967, the award was originally created as a personal decoration ranking above the commendation medals, lifesaving medals, and the Purple Heart; however, it currently holds the status of an achievement/service medal and is awarded to members of the USAF and AIR FORCE RESERVE (and, after, August 1, 1960, to members of other services) for sustained individual combat or mission readiness or preparedness for direct weapons-system employment. For eligibility, a service member must meet the following criteria: complete an aggregate 24 months of sustained professional performance as a member of USAF combat or mission-ready units subject to combat readiness reporting, or be individually certified as combat or mission ready and have maintained individual readiness the entire period according to a major headquarters, or subject to an individual positional evaluation program according to a higher headquarters standard. "Combat ready" means being professionally and technically qualified in an aircraft crew position in an aircraft that can be used in combat.

Distinguished Flying Cross

This medal is awarded to any officer or enlisted man of the armed forces of the United States who shall have distinguished himself in actual combat in support of operations by "heroism or extraordinary achievement while participating in an aerial flight, subsequent to November 11, 1918." The decoration may also be given for an act performed prior to November 11, 1918, when the individual has been recommended for, but has not received the Medal of Honor, Distinguished Service Cross, Navy Cross, or Distinguished Service Medal.

The first recipient of the Distinguished Flying Cross, authorized by an act of Congress of July 2, 1926 (amended by Executive Order 7786 on January 8, 1938), was Captain Charles A. Lindbergh, U.S. Army Air Corps Reserve, for his solo flight across the Atlantic in 1927. Commander Richard E. Byrd, of the U.S. Navy Air Corps, received the medal on May 9, 1926, for his flight to and from the North Pole. Amelia Earhart received the Distinguished Flying Cross as well—the only instance in which the award was made to a civilian. (An executive order of March 1, 1927, directed that the DFC should not thereafter be conferred on civilians.)

During wartime, members of the armed forces of friendly foreign nations serving with the United States are eligible for the award, which is also given to those who display heroism while working as instructors or students at flying schools.

Medal for Humane Action

This medal was awarded to personnel assigned or attached to and present for duty for at least 120 days during the period of June 26, 1948, to September 30, 1949, inclusive, with any of the units cited in DEPARTMENT OF THE AIR FORCE general orders for participating in the BERLIN AIRLIFT or for direct support of the Berlin Airlift. The Medal for Humane Action may also be awarded to foreign armed forces members and to U.S. and foreign civilians for meritorious participation in the Berlin Airlift. Persons whose lives were lost while participating in the Berlin Airlift, or as a direct result of participating in the Berlin Airlift, may be awarded the Medal for Humane Action without regard to length of service. The medal depicts a C-54 cargo aircraft, the type extensively used in the airlift.

Medal of Honor

Established by Congress on July 6, 1960, as the highest of several awards created specifically for the air force, the Medal of Honor is given in the name of Congress to officers and enlisted members who distinguished themselves by gallantry and intre-

pidity at the risk of their lives, above and beyond the call of duty, in action involving actual combat with an armed enemy of the United States.

The first presentation of the Medal of Honor to a member of the USAF was made by President Lyndon Johnson, on January 19, 1967, to Major Bernard F. Fisher. The Air Force Medal of Honor has been awarded 13 times for actions during the war in Vietnam. Four of these decorations, to Captain Steven L. Bennett, Captain Lance P. Sijan, Captain Hillard A. Wilbanks, and A1C William H. Pitsenbarger, were posthumously awarded. Two were awarded for extraordinary heroism while the recipients were prisoners of war, one to Captain Sijan and the other to Colonel George E. Day, who was the most highly decorated officer in the USAF.

Others who received the medal for their actions in the VIETNAM WAR are Major Merlyn Hans Dethlefsen, Captain James P. Fleming, Lieutenant Colonel Joe M. Jackson, Sergeant John L. Levitow, Lieutenant Colonel Leo K. Thorsness, Captain Gerald O. Young, and Colonel William A. Jones III, who received the medal posthumously.

Four other airmen received the Medal of Honor —before it was created specifically for the USAF— during the KOREAN WAR. Majors George A. Davis Jr., Charles J. Loring Jr., and Louis J. Sebille, and Captain John S. Walmsley Jr., were awarded the medal posthumously. During WORLD WAR II, 35 members of the U.S. ARMY AIR FORCES were presented the nation's top honor for their actions during air missions.

Outstanding Airman of the Year Ribbon

This ribbon is awarded to airmen nominated for competition in the Twelve Outstanding Airmen of the Year Program.

Small Arms Expert Marksmanship Ribbon

This ribbon, authorized by the SECRETARY OF THE AIR FORCE on August 28, 1962, is awarded to USAF members who, after January 1, 1963, qualify as expert in small-arms marksmanship with either the M-16 rifle or issue handgun.

USAF NCO PME Graduate Ribbon

This award, authorized by the SECRETARY OF THE AIR FORCE, August 28, 1962, is presented to graduates of the following certified NCO PME schools: NCO Preparatory Course, Airman Leadership School, NCO Leadership School, NCO Academy, and SRNCO Academy. Graduation from each successive level of PME entitles the member to an oak leaf cluster.

Department of the Air Force

Established by the NATIONAL SECURITY ACT OF 1947, the department provides civilian administrative control over the USAF and reports to the Office of the Secretary of Defense. As originally conceived, the service departments—Department of the Army, Department of the Navy, and Department of the Air Force—wielded a great deal of power relative to the Department of Defense. In 1958, however, the Reorganization Act reduced the authority of the department secretaries and terminated the CHAIN OF COMMAND with the secretary of defense.

Direct Reporting Unit (DRU)   See ORGANIZATION, USAF.

Distinguished Flying Cross   See DECORATIONS AND MEDALS.

division   See ORGANIZATION, USAF.

Doolittle, James Harold ("Jimmy") (1896–1993) *Army Air Forces general, engineer, test pilot*

A U.S. ARMY AIR FORCES officer, Doolittle is best known for his daring and unprecedented aircraft carrier–launched B-25 raid on Tokyo early in WORLD WAR II.

He was born in Alameda, California, and educated at Los Angeles Junior College, then at UCLA.

James H. "Jimmy" Doolittle   *(U.S. Air Force)*

He joined the Army Reserve Corps in October 1917, after the United States entered WORLD WAR I, and was assigned to the Signal Corps, in which he served as a flight instructor through 1919. In 1920, Doolittle was commissioned a first lieutenant in the U.S. ARMY AIR SERVICE and quickly gained national attention by making the first transcontinental flight—in less than 14 hours—on September 4, 1922. The U.S. ARMY AIR CORPS then sent Doolittle to the Massachusetts Institute of Technology for advanced study in aeronautical science. In 1925, Doolittle earned a doctor of science (Sc.D.) degree, then was assigned to a series of military aviation testing stations. He also became an avid air-race competitor and an aerial demonstration pilot during 1925–30. The object of racing and demonstration was to promote military aviation. Perhaps his single most significant achievement during this period came on September 1929, when he demonstrated the potential of instrument flying by making the first-ever blind instrument landing.

In February 1930, Doolittle resigned his commission to become aviation manager for Shell Oil, where he worked on the development of new high-efficiency aviation fuels. He also continued to race, claiming victories in a number of prestigious competitions, including those for the Harmon (1930) and Bendix (1931) trophies. In 1932, he set a world speed record.

As war loomed, Doolittle returned to active duty in July 1940 as a major in the USAAC. In the weeks and months following the Japanese attack on Pearl Harbor (December 7, 1941), U.S. and Allied forces fought a desperate and dispiriting defensive war in the Pacific theater. In an effort to raise American morale—and to force the Japanese to divert a portion of their air forces to defense—Doolittle planned and commanded an extraordinarily hazardous bombing raid against Tokyo, leading 16 B-25 Mitchell bombers from the aircraft carrier *Hornet* on April 18, 1942. The twin-engine medium bombers were not designed to take off from an aircraft carrier, but Doolittle and the other pilots managed to do just that. They also realized that fuel limitations meant that no round trip was possible, and, in any case, the bombers could not land on an aircraft carrier. They planned to carry out the raid, then land in China, hope to evade capture, and find their way back to Allied lines. Although the damage inflicted on Tokyo and industrial targets was slight, the Doolittle raid was a tremendous morale boost, which, as planned, also served to tie down a portion of the Japanese air force for home defense. Perhaps most remarkable of all was the fact that Doolittle and most of his raiders survived the action and returned to U.S. military control.

After the raid Doolittle was promoted to brigadier general (he was later awarded the Medal of Honor) and was sent to England to organize the TWELFTH AIR FORCE in September 1942. With the temporary rank of major general, he commanded 12AF in Operation Torch, the Allied invasion of French North Africa. From March 1943 to January 1944, he commanded strategic air operations in the Mediterranean theater and was promoted to the temporary rank of lieutenant general in March 1944. During January 1944 to May 1945, he commanded the British-based EIGHTH AIR FORCE's bombing operations against Germany.

After V-E Day, Doolittle returned to the Pacific, where his 8AF provided support in the battle for Okinawa (April–July 1945) and carried out some of the massive bombardment of the Japanese home islands. With the conclusion of the war in the Pacific, Doolittle left active duty (remaining in the reserves) in May 1946 and took a senior executive position with Shell Oil. He was, however, frequently asked by the government to serve on scientific, technological, and aeronautical commissions during 1948–57. After retiring from Shell and the AIR FORCE RESERVE in 1959, he continued to work as a consultant in the areas of technology and aeronautics as well as in the field of national security.

Dover AFB, Delaware   See AIR FORCE BASES.

driver
USAF slang for pilot.
    See also JOCK.

Dyess AFB, Texas   See AIR FORCE BASES.

E

Eastern Air Defense Force

A named air force created in 1949 under Continental Air Command (CONAC), the Eastern Air Defense Force had as its purpose the air defense of the United States. Reassigned to the AIR DEFENSE COMMAND (ADC) in 1951, it was inactivated in 1960 when Air Defense Command was reorganized to eliminate the air force level of organization.

Edwards AFB, California   See AIR FORCE BASES.

Eglin AFB, Florida   See AIR FORCE BASES.

Eielson AFB, Alaska   See AIR FORCE BASES.

Eighteenth Air Force (18AF)

A numbered air force established in 1951, the 18AF was originally designated Eighteenth Air Force (Troop Carrier) and was under the TACTICAL AIR COMMAND (TAC). It was the 18AF that transported French paratroops to Vietnam for the momentous Battle of Dien Bien Phu. The 18AF was originally based at Donaldson AFB, South Carolina, then moved to Waco, Texas, in 1957. It was inactivated the following year.

Eighth Air Force (8AF)

The most celebrated numbered air force in the USAF, 8AF was the nucleus of U.S. ARMY AIR FORCES strategic bombing (see BOMBING, STRATEGIC) missions against Germany during WORLD WAR II.

The antecedent organization of 8AF was the VIII Bomber Command, created in January 1942. It moved from the United States to England in the spring and began combat operations in August. It was not until February 1944 that the VIII Bomber Command was redesignated 8AF. The unit flew B-17 and B-24 heavy bombers and had a Fighter Command made up of 15 fighter groups flying F-47s, F-51s, and P-38s. Whereas the strategic bombing role of 8AF fell short of demonstrating that strategic bombing alone could win a war, the Fighter Command achieved air superiority by effectively destroying the German Luftwaffe, downing 9,275 German aircraft.

Half of USAAF casualties during World War II were incurred by 8AF—more than 47,000 casualties, including more than 26,000 killed. Seventeen Medals of Honor were awarded to 8AF personnel during the war, along with 220 Distinguished Service Crosses, 850 Silver Stars, 7,000 Purple Hearts, 46,000 Distinguished Flying Crosses, and 442,000 Air Medals. The 8AF had 261 fighter aces. After the German surrender, 8AF moved to Okinawa in 1945 and, after the war, in 1946, was headquartered at MacDill Field, Florida, where it served as a STRATE-

GIC AIR COMMAND (SAC) unit. Later in the year, 8AF headquarters was moved to Carswell AFB, Texas, and in 1955 to Westover AFB, Massachusetts. In 1970, 8AF was moved to Andersen AFB, Guam, and conducted B-52 and KC-135 operations during the VIETNAM WAR. In 1975, 8AF moved to Barksdale AFB, Louisiana, and absorbed the functions of the SECOND AIR FORCE. During the PERSIAN GULF WAR, 8AF spearheaded the air war campaign with B-52 strikes directly from Barksdale. Current 8AF units include 2nd Bomb Wing, 5th Bomb Wing, 7th Bomb Wing, 28th Bomb Wing, 509th Bomb Wing, 27th Fighter Wing, 67th Information Operations Wing, 70th Intelligence Wing, 65th Air Base Wing, 85th Group, and 3rd Air Support Operations Group.

See also EIGHTH AIR FORCE HISTORICAL SOCIETY.

A USAF E-3B Sentry aircraft is readied for flight. *(U.S. Air Force)*

Eighth Air Force Historical Society

The EIGHTH AIR FORCE, the most celebrated U.S. ARMY AIR FORCES organization of WORLD WAR II, also holds the record for numbers of Americans who served in a single military organization: more than 1 million. Veterans of the organization formed the Eighth Air Force Historical Society on May 15, 1975, to collect, preserve, and publish the history of this distinguished unit. The society publishes *8th AF News* and has some 15,000 members.

electronic warfare (EW)

The origin of electronic warfare (EW) may be traced as far back as WORLD WAR I, when radio was first used on the battlefield and signals were intercepted. By the time of WORLD WAR II, EW came to include radar technology as well as the use of chaff (metal foil strips released from aircraft) to confound enemy radar returns, LORAN navigation systems, and radio proximity fuses (which use radar to trigger bomb detonation). By the end of the VIETNAM WAR era, EW had assumed such importance that an entire class of USAF aircraft was designated "E" for electronic warfare. These aircraft are equipped with cutting-edge radar and

other detection and imaging equipment as well as computers, to enable the tracking of enemy air and ground resources, to coordinate friendly resources, to direct ground, air, and naval attack, and to jam enemy radio communication and radar operation. The role of EW in USAF operations will almost certainly continue to expand in the future.

element   See ORGANIZATION, USAF.

Eleventh Air Force (11AF)

Originally, this numbered air force was a named air force, the Alaskan Air Force, which was activated in January 1942. Within a month, it was redesignated the 11AF.

During WORLD WAR II, 11AF conducted U.S. ARMY AIR FORCES operations in the Aleutian Islands. In 1945, it was again redesignated as the ALASKAN AIR COMMAND, and a new organization was designated 11AF in June 1946. The new unit was assigned primarily to train AIR FORCE RESERVE personnel. Inactivated in 1948, the 11AF was reactivated in 1990 when it replaced the Alaskan Air Command.

Currently, the 11AF is headquartered at Elmendorf AFB, Alaska, and consists of the 3rd Wing, 354th Fighter Wing, 611th Air Operations Group, and 611th Air Support Group.

Ellsworth AFB, South Dakota   See AIR FORCE BASES.

Elmendorf AFB, Alaska   See AIR FORCE BASES.

England AFB, Louisiana   See AIR FORCE BASES.

Executive Order 9877

Issued by President Harry S. Truman on July 26, 1947, this order unified the U.S. Army and U.S. Navy and established a United States Air Force independent of the U.S. Army. The executive order stated the roles and missions of each service, including the USAF, whereas the NATIONAL SECURITY ACT OF 1947, which went into effect on the same day, stated the principles of the unification of the services and the creation of the USAF.

With regard to the USAF mission, Executive Order 9877 specifically addressed provisions for air superiority, strategic operations, tactical operations, airlift operations, air defense, and assistance to the army and navy.

F

Fairchild AFB, Washington   See AIR FORCE
BASES.

Far East Air Forces (FEAF)   See PACIFIC AIR
FORCES.

field operating agency (FOA)   See ORGANI-
ZATION, USAF.

Fifteenth Air Force (15AF)

15AF, a numbered air force, was established in
November 1943 in Tunisia, assigned to the
Mediterranean theater of operations in WORLD
WAR II. In December, it moved to Bari, Italy, and
served primarily as a strategic bombing organization, hitting targets in Italy, southern France, and
the oil refineries at Ploesti, Romania. Major General JAMES HAROLD DOOLITTLE commanded 15AF
from 1943 to 1944.

15AF was inactivated in Italy in September
1945, then reactivated in the United States the following year. Assigned to the STRATEGIC AIR COM-
MAND (SAC) at that time, 15AF was reassigned to
AIR MOBILITY COMMAND (AMC) in 1992 and, in
1993, was moved from March AFB to Travis AFB,
California. Fifteenth Air Force flew bombers in the
KOREAN WAR, then, during the 1960s, added tankers
to its complement of aircraft. Between the VIETNAM

WAR and 1991, 15AF commanded reconnaissance
aircraft and intercontinental ballistic missiles in
addition to tankers, but, on September 1, 1991, it
became exclusively a tanker command. When 15AF
moved to Travis AFB, it merged its tankers with the
AIRLIFT aircraft of the TWENTY-SECOND AIR FORCE,
which left Travis for the AIR FORCE RESERVE at Dobbins AFRB, Georgia. Fifteenth Air Force includes
22nd Air Refueling Wing, 60th Air Mobility Wing,
62nd Airlift Wing, 92nd Air Refueling Wing, 317th
Airlift Group, 319th Air Refueling Wing, 375th Airlift Wing, 615th Air Mobility Operations Group,
715th Air Mobility Operations Group, and the
302nd Airlift Wing, gained from 22AF.

Fifth Air Force (5AF)

Activated in September 1941 as the Philippine
Department Air Force and redesignated the Far
East Air Force in October of that year, the unit
became 5AF in February 1942. Most of the Far East
Air Force's aircraft were destroyed on the ground
when the Japanese attacked the Philippines in
December 1941. The survivors—personnel and aircraft—retreated to Australia and, in January 1942,
the Far East Air Force was sent to Java for combat.
In September 1942, 5AF was reorganized to command all U.S. ARMY AIR FORCES units in Australia
and New Guinea. Under the command of Major
General George Kenney, 5AF used fighters (especially P-38s) to win air superiority in the South

Pacific and also carried out tactical AIRLIFT missions in support of ground offensives in New Guinea. The 5AF was also instrumental in attacks on Japanese naval forces attempting to transport reinforcements to the islands. In August 1944, 5AF played a key role in operations to retake the Philippines. As soon as air fields were available on Okinawa, 5AF moved operations there in order to concentrate on Japanese shipping, the China coast, and Kyushu.

After the surrender of Japan, 5AF took part in the occupation, then moved headquarters to South Korea with the outbreak of war there. The 5AF handled tactical operations during the KOREAN WAR, having flown by the time of the armistice in 1953 more than 625,000 missions, in which 953 North Korean and Chinese aircraft were downed and enough CLOSE AIR SUPPORT had been provided to account for 47 percent of all enemy troop casualties. In Korea, 38 fighter pilots were identified as aces, including Lieutenant Colonel JAMES JABARA, the first U.S. jet ace, and Captain Joseph McConnell, the leading Korean War ace, with 16 confirmed victories.

After the Korean War, 5AF returned to Japan and, during the VIETNAM WAR, operated from there. Since 1990, 5AF has been headquartered at Yakota AB, Japan. It currently includes 18th Wing, 35th Fighter Wing, 374th Airlift Wing, 605th Air Operations Group, 605th Air Operations Squadron, 605th Air Intelligence Squadron, 605th Air Support Squadron, 605th Air Communications Flight, and 20th Operational Weather Squadron.

films, USAF portrayed in

Life in and the exploits of the United States military have long been favorite subjects for the movies, and the USAF and its predecessor organizations have been especially popular because of the glamour, excitement, and danger of combat flight.

The most notable post–WORLD WAR I film was the 1927 *Wings*, directed by William Wellman. The central story, which concerns two American lads who are in love with the same girl and who become World War I pilots, is paper thin, but the aerial combat footage, featuring dogfights, is remarkable for 1927 or, indeed, any era. The movie won the first Academy Award for best picture, and it increased recruitment of U.S. ARMY AIR SERVICE pilots.

WORLD WAR II saw the production of many service-related movies. The best-known films focusing on the U.S. ARMY AIR FORCES include *I Wanted Wings* and *Keep 'Em Flying*, both from 1941, and both focusing on pilot training. Films emphasizing battle action came a bit later in the war. *Flying Tigers* (1942) was a very popular portrayal of the exploits of the AMERICAN VOLUNTEER GROUP in China, and *Thirty Seconds over Tokyo* (1944) told a romanticized version of the daring Doolittle raid against Tokyo (April 18, 1942). Most important from this era was *Air Force*, released in 1943 and directed by the great Howard Hawks. The film is set in the Pacific theater and tells the story of a single B-17 crew. It won a best-picture Academy Award. Perhaps the most effective movie about the USAAF in World War II produced after the war was *Twelve O'Clock High* (1950), which vividly portrays the psychological toll strategic bombing (see BOMBING, STRATEGIC) took on American air crews and their commanders.

The KOREAN WAR occasioned *Sabre Jet* (1953), and the cold war era brought *Strategic Air Command* (1955), which emphasized the sacrifice and the skill of AIR FORCE RESERVE personnel reactivated to meet the needs of the nuclear air arm. The 1960s, heavily influenced by anti-Vietnam War sentiments, produced a spate of films not so much specifically critical of the USAF as of a general "war mentality." *Fail-Safe* (1964) chillingly dramatized the genesis of a thermonuclear accident and the high price of averting World War III. Stanley Kubrick's *Dr. Strangelove, or How I Learned to Stop Worrying and Love the Bomb* (also 1964) exploited the same theme from the perspective of the blackest possible comedy.

Films after the end of the VIETNAM WAR have tended to return to a more celebratory view of the U.S. air arm, although often with a nostalgic historical perspective. The 1990 *Memphis Belle*, for

A movie poster for *Thirty Seconds over Tokyo,* 1944   *(Library of Congress)*

example, evoked the look and feel of the 1940s to tell the story of the first British-based EIGHTH AIR FORCE B-17 crew to complete the 25 missions that entitled the crew members to rotate back to the United States.

First Air Force (1AF)

A numbered air force, 1AF was activated as the Northeast Air District in 1940 before it was redesignated in 1941. Headquarters during WORLD WAR II was Mitchel Field, New York, and the unit functioned as a training organization and, until 1943, also provided air defense for the East Coast. It was moved to Fort Slocum, New York, in 1946 as part of the Air Defense Command, then, in 1948, it was transferred to the CONTINENTAL AIR COMMAND and, in 1949, returned to Mitchel. Inactivated in 1958, it was reactivated in 1966, reassigned to Air Defense Command, and moved to Stewart AFB, New York. At this time, 1AF was responsible for the air defense of the northeastern United States, Greenland, Iceland, and parts of Canada. Inactivated in 1969, 1AF was reactivated in 1986 at Langley AFB, Virginia, and assigned to the TACTICAL AIR COMMAND (TAC). It was now composed of units of the active USAF as well as the AIR NATIONAL GUARD (ANG).

In 1992, 1AF, now headquartered at Tyndall AFB, Florida, became an AIR COMBAT COMMAND

(ACC) organization, and it was the first numbered air force to be made up primarily of ANG personnel. The current mission of 1AF is to plan, conduct, control, coordinate, and ensure the air sovereignty and defense of the United States. The unit primarily operates F-15 and F-16 fighters and consists of the 102nd, 119th, 120th, 125th, 142nd, 144th, 147th, 148th, and 158th Fighter Wings.

first lieutenant   See RANKS AND GRADES.

first sergeant   See RANKS AND GRADES.

flexible response

Flexible response was a cold war doctrine intended to provide the U.S. military, especially the USAF, with credible means to match nonnuclear escalation. The word "flexible" implied the availability of multiple options to use in responding to a crisis. In the volatile climate of the cold war, this was deemed preferable to formulating a handful of hard-and-fast war scenarios.

In practice, flexible response called for the continued European presence of large U.S. conventional forces. These forces would serve as a deterrent to Soviet aggression and would also fight limited wars.

Although flexible response was formulated as an alternative to nuclear war, Secretary of Defense Robert McNamara (in the administration of John F. Kennedy) did not believe that new conventional weapons were needed, and thus the USAF continued to direct most of its resources to developing strategic (nuclear and thermonuclear) weapons. The tactical requirements of the VIETNAM WAR vividly exposed the inadequacies of this development policy, although USAF personnel brilliantly improvised such tactical weapons as AC-47 and AC-130 gunships and the use of B-52s for tactical carpet bombing.

flight (organizational unit)   See ORGANIZATION, USAF.

flight surgeon

A medical officer (M.D.) with special training in aviation medicine, the flight surgeon serves with an aviation unit.

Flying Training Air Force (FLY TAF)

FLY TAF was a named air force established in 1951 and assigned to the Air Training Command (ATC). It trained pilots, navigators, and radar observers. FLY TAF was deactivated in 1958.

folklore

As with many other occupations, the profession of military aviation has developed its own body of occupational folklore involving indoctrination rituals and procedures, rituals and routines to enforce conformity, narrative folklore to share experiences, narrative and other kinds of folklore to reduce anxiety, folklore to cope with authority, and special jargon or folk speech. The folklore of this latter category may be the most important, since a command of the group's folk speech is essential to admission to full membership within the group. Some of the folk speech heard within the USAF is familiar almost exclusively to insiders. A "shit screen," for example, is a fall guy, the person who takes the blame for some foul-up or infraction. "Above my pay grade" is a phrase used to pass responsibility to some higher power: "That decision, George, was made above my pay grade. Sorry." "Brown shoe" is used to describe someone who has been in the service for many years or who takes a rigid position on how standards will be maintained and things done—by the book. (Dress shoes in the old USAAF were brown.) "Check-six" is used by fighter pilots to mean check your tail—the six o'clock position (12 is straight ahead); by figurative extension, the phrase means watch your back and be sure your facts are straight. "Delta Sierra" is the phonetic alphabet version of the initials "DS" and signifies "deep shit"—that is, big trouble. A "fast burner" is a person who is a go-getter, highly capable, and highly respected. A "boot" is a recruit in basic training. A first shirt/first skirt is a male or female first sergeant.

Other elements of military vocabulary have become part of the folk speech of the general population. For example, official military jargon is replete with acronyms. During WORLD WAR II, airmen and other soldiers invented some of their own, the most popular of which was *snafu*—Situation Normal, All Fucked Up. The word, without its obscene connotation and, indeed, without a sense of its even being an acronym, is now in general speech. (Variants on *snafu* never entered general speech and have vanished from military folk speech as well. These include: FUBAR, Fucked Up Beyond All Recognition; TARFU, Things Are Really Fucked Up; and so on.) Almost as popular as *snafu* was *SOS,* which had been adopted in 1908 as the international radiotelegraph Morse Code signal for distress and, some time during World War II, was adopted in the enlisted men's mess as a signal of specifically gustatory distress. A staple of World War II military cuisine was creamed chipped beef on toast, unofficially and universally dubbed Shit On a Shingle: SOS. The utility of this acronym rapidly increased as the expression came to signify any old lies, chores, or routines the U.S. ARMY AIR FORCES dished up day after day: Same Old Shit. In this latter sense, it, too, has entered general folk speech, as have such expressions as *grunt,* which, in the USAF, means an ordinary enlisted person, but, in the general population, means any working stiff; *scut work,* which originated in military folk speech as a label for any disagreeable task (such as cleaning latrines) and is now found outside the military as well; and *down the tubes,* meaning total failure.

Other items of military folk speech have been borrowed *from* general folk speech. In the air arm, for example, *bogey* has long been a term for an unidentified air contact that is assumed to be hostile. The word seems to have come into general use during the early years of jet and electronic air combat—that is, during the KOREAN WAR—and is usually used to describe radar-screen blips interpreted as hostile aircraft, though bogies can also be sighted visually, usually on one's tail (or *six*). The word recalls the bogey or bogey man of fairy tale and nightmare.

Military folk speech also borrows words from general standard English. WORLD WAR I produced the term *dogfight* to describe aerial combat between two or more fighter planes. During the PERSIAN GULF WAR, USAF pilots often used the term *fur ball* to describe the same situation. This latter term aptly evokes the visceral effects of high-speed jet combat, an amalgam of pumping adrenaline, blackout-inducing G-forces, an urge to kill, and ever-churning fear. It is almost certainly descended from pilot slang dating back to the USAAF of World War II, when a close call or frightening situation was referred to as "hairy."

Soldiers in combat are, of course, under great stress, and such emotionally intense circumstances often produce folklore intended to bring luck or explain things that are essentially irrational and terrifying. Thus much military folklore resembles tall tales or miracle narratives and includes stories of near misses, brushes with death, miraculous escapes, and even ghost stories (in the form of the returning spirits of fallen comrades). Widely discussed among military aircrews during World War II were *gremlins,* which were imagined as imps or demons that cause problems with aircraft. To the action of gremlins were attributed mechanical failures and other difficulties that could not be otherwise explained. This was done tongue in cheek, to be sure, yet with an unmistakable edge of earnestness, too. By the middle years of the war, USAAF aircrews even provided descriptions of gremlins, which were depicted as about 20 inches tall and looking like a Jack Rabbit crossed with a bull terrier. Some descriptions clothed the gremlins: "green breeches and red jackets, ornamented with neat ruffles," as well as spats and top hats. Other descriptions depict them more frankly as demons: six inches tall with horns and black leather suction boots. Gremlins were not imagined as primitive beings, but as technically sophisticated saboteurs, who also possessed superhuman strength.

Another subject of aircrew folklore were *foo fighters.* These were strange balls of light and disk-shaped objects that World War II Allied bomber crews reported seeing as they flew missions over

Germany and Japan. The term *foo-fighter* was apparently a pun on the French word *feu* (fire), which appeared in "Smokey Stover," a popular comic strip of the period ("Where there's foo, there's fire," was a frequent Smokey tag line). Foo fighters appeared to dance off the bombers' wingtips, or they kept pace with the aircraft in front and in back. Many explanations for the foo fighters were offered, ranging from static electricity discharges to Japanese and German secret weapons. After a cursory investigation, the EIGHTH AIR FORCE officially (if unconvincingly) dismissed them as "mass hallucination."

Superstitions are common in high-risk, high-anxiety occupations such as combat flying. Many pilots and other aircrew members wore and wear "lucky" scarves, hats, gloves, and items of jewelry. Fighter pilots still typically insist on "mounting" their aircraft as one mounts a horse, always from the left side. "Short timers"—combat aircrew members whose tour of duty is approaching its close—make it a point never to speak of the number of missions remaining, lest misfortune follow.

Foulois, Benjamin D. (1879–1967) *U.S. Army Air Corps general*

The third chief of the U.S. ARMY AIR CORPS, serving from 1931 to 1935, Foulois was an activist on behalf of the creation of an independent air arm.

He was born in Washington, Connecticut, and enlisted in the U.S. Army Engineers in 1898. After serving in the Philippines during the Spanish-American War and afterward, Foulois was commissioned an officer. He left the engineers for the Signal Corps in 1908 and piloted the first dirigible (see BALLOONS AND DIRIGIBLES) purchased by the U.S. government. He taught himself to fly airplanes and, in 1910, was assigned to fly the U.S. Army's first airplane and became the service's first (and, for a time, only) pilot, instructor, and observer. In 1911, he designed the first radio transceiver ever used on an airplane and, with it, became a pioneer in aerial reconnaissance. He was also instrumental in developing early tactical doctrine.

As commander of the 1st Aero Squadron, Foulois served in the PUNITIVE EXPEDITION against Pancho Villa in 1916. The following year he was assigned to Washington as chairman of the Joint Army-Navy Technical Aircraft Committee. With

Benjamin D. Foulois   *(U.S. Air Force)*

America's entry into WORLD WAR I, he was jumped rapidly in rank. A captain in May 1917, he was a brigadier general in July. He was shipped off to France, where he served as chief of the USAAS for the American Expeditionary Force (AEF). Like many officers rapidly promoted during the war, he reverted in rank—to major—after the armistice. Foulois regained his rank as brigadier general in 1927, when he was assigned as assistant to the chief of the USAAC. He became chief in 1931.

In an effort to achieve some degree of independence from the army and establish an air operations identity apart from the navy, Foulois established the GENERAL HEADQUARTERS AIR FORCE. Always pushing to demonstrate the value of air power, he persuaded President Franklin D. Roosevelt to assign to the USAAC the dangerous job of flying the air mail routes. This proved disastrous, and, under congressional pressure over the air mail fiasco and disputes over procurement procedures, Foulois retired from the military in 1935.

Fourteenth Air Force (14AF)

Fourteenth Air Force, which, with the TWENTIETH AIR FORCE, is currently one of two numbered air forces in the AIR FORCE SPACE COMMAND (AFSPC), provides space warfighting forces to U.S. Space Command and is located at Vandenberg AFB, California. The mission of 14AF is to manage space forces to support U.S. Space Command and North American Aerospace Defense Command (NORAD) operational plans and missions.

The organization was first activated in 1943 at Kumming, China, and consisted of the former AMERICAN VOLUNTEER GROUP, the famed "Flying Tigers," plus reinforcing units. The 14AF was a small defensive air force, which (like many Allied military units in the CBI, the China-Burma-India theater) was given low priority and operated mainly to jab at Shanghai and Japanese shipping off the China coast. From 1943 to 1945, 14AF was commanded by CLAIRE L. CHENNAULT, the colorful and irascible commander who had created the American Volunteer Group.

In December 1945, 14AF returned to the United States and was inactivated from January to May 1946. It was assigned to AIR DEFENSE COMMAND (ADC) and then, in 1948, to CONTINENTAL AIR COMMAND (CAC), based at Orlando AFB, Florida. From 1946 to 1960, 14AF supervised AIR FORCE RESERVE and AIR NATIONAL GUARD activities. Inactivated in 1960, it was reactivated in 1966 at Gunter AFB, Alabama, once again as part of the Air Defense Command. When it moved to Colorado Springs in 1968 it was redesignated the Fourteenth Aerospace Force. Moved to Dobbins AFB, Georgia, in 1976, it was returned to its 14AF designation and made a USAFR unit. Fourteenth Air Force finally moved to Vandenberg AFB as part of the AFSPC.

Fourth Air Force (Reserve)

Activated as the Southwest Air District at March Field, California, in 1940, the unit was redesignated Fourth Air Force (4AF), a numbered air force, in 1941 and moved to Hamilton Field, California. The mission of 4AF was to provide air defense for the western continental United States and, until 1943, to train new units. After 1943, the training focus of 4AF rested on replacements for combat units.

After WORLD WAR II, 4AF was assigned in 1946 to AIR DEFENSE COMMAND (ADC) and, in 1948, to CONTINENTAL AIR COMMAND (CAC). It was inactivated in 1960, then reactivated in 1966, again under ADC. Three years later, it was again inactivated, then reactivated in 1976 at McClellan AFB, California, at which time it became an AIR FORCE RESERVE unit. Now located at March AFB, California, 4AF is assigned to AIR MOBILITY COMMAND (AMC) when called to active duty. Units within 4AF include 349th Air Mobility Wing, 433rd Airlift Wing, 434th Air Refueling Wing, 445th Airlift Wing, 446th Airlift Wing, 452nd Air Mobility Wing, 507th Air Refueling Wing, 916th Air Refueling Wing, 927th Air Refueling Wing, 932nd Airlift Wing, and 940th Air Refueling Wing.

Francis E. Warren AFB, Wyoming   See AIR FORCE BASES.

G

general   See RANKS AND GRADES.

General Headquarters Air Force (GHQ Air Force)

Established on March 1, 1935, GHQ Air Force was intended as a means of creating for the U.S. ARMY AIR CORPS a separate mission for reconnaissance and bombardment directly under the U.S. Army chief of staff. In effect, GHQ Air Force was a first step toward creation of an independent air arm. Because GHQ Air Force controlled reconnaissance and bombardment missions only, whereas supply, training, and doctrine remained under control of the chief of the air corps, the organizational scheme had the effect of splitting USAAC functions and soon proved unwieldy. GHQ Air Force was deactivated in 1941, on the eve of United States entry into WORLD WAR II.

General of the Air Force   See RANKS AND GRADES.

George, Harold L. (1893–1986) *Air Force strategist*

George was one of the principal architects of American air power and was a central figure in creating U.S. ARMY AIR FORCES strategic operations, doctrines, and war plans. He radically reconfigured the AIR TRANSPORT COMMAND (ATC) into a force capable of performing tactical and strategic AIRLIFT anywhere in the world, thereby providing the basis from which the MILITARY AIRLIFT COMMAND (MAC) and the AIR MOBILITY COMMAND (AMC) would develop.

A native of Somerville, Massachusetts, George was commissioned a second lieutenant in the AVIATION SECTION, U.S. ARMY SIGNAL CORPS, in 1918. He served during the close of WORLD WAR I as a bomber pilot in the Meuse-Argonne offensive. After the war, George became an ardent disciple of the air power ideas of WILLIAM MITCHELL and was one of the pilots who participated in Mitchell's demonstration bombardment of captured German warships. George carried Mitchell's ideas into his work with the Air Corps Tactical School, where he served as chief of the bombardment section from 1932 to 1934 and as director of air tactics and strategy from 1934 to 1936. A mentor who exercised great influence on the officers who would shape air power strategy and tactics in WORLD WAR II, George was a thoroughgoing advocate of precision daylight bombing as the chief means of conducting strategic operations (see BOMBING, STRATEGIC).

In 1941, George was appointed assistant chief of the AIR STAFF for war plans. In collaboration with other Air Corps Tactical School theorists, George formulated AWPD-1, the bomber-focused plan the USAAF would ultimately employ against Germany.

George was named to head the Ferry Command in 1942, charged with the task of expanding USAAF airlift capabilities to a worldwide scale. When George took command, he had 130 aircraft and 11,000 people. By the end of World War II, he had expanded airlift to the Air Transport Command, with more than 3,000 planes and 300,000 people. The emphasis was on transoceanic operations, so that the reach of the USAAF—and the other services it assisted—became truly and even routinely global.

Goodfellow AFB, Texas   See AIR FORCE BASES.

Grand Forks AFB, North Dakota   See AIR FORCE BASES.

Griffiss AFB, New York   See AIR FORCE BASES.

Grissom AFB, Indiana   See AIR FORCE BASES.

group   See ORGANIZATION, USAF.

H

Hanscom AFB, Massachusetts   See AIR FORCE BASES.

Headquarters Air Force (HAF)

HAF, also called Headquarters Department of the Air Force, and familiarly known as Dash 1, is housed chiefly in the Pentagon and is headed by the SECRETARY OF THE AIR FORCE. Directly reporting to the secretary is a Secretariat, which includes many administrative departments and functions. Also directly responsible to the secretary, but completely separate from the Secretariat, is the AIR STAFF, head by the CHIEF OF STAFF, USAF. Within the Air Staff level are the various field operating agencies (see ORGANIZATION, USAF).

Hickam AFB, Hawaii   See AIR FORCE BASES.

Hill AFB, Utah   See AIR FORCE BASES.

history, overview of USAF

The USAF came into being as an independent service, of equal status with the U.S. Army and U.S. Navy, on September 18, 1947, by virtue of the NATIONAL SECURITY ACT OF 1947; however, its full history may be traced as far back as the Civil War, when, between 1861 and 1863, the Union army made substantial use of tethered BALLOONS for battlefield observation. The army invested $50,000 in a grant to aviation pioneer Samuel P. Langley for development of an airplane during the Spanish-American War in 1898. Langley failed to develop a workable aircraft, and it was not until August 1, 1907—four years after the Wright brothers made their first flight—that President Theodore Roosevelt, an aviation enthusiast, authorized the AERONAUTICAL DIVISION, U.S. ARMY SIGNAL CORPS. A modest organization, the Aeronautical Division was primarily concerned with assessing the capabilities of aircraft for military applications.

On July 18, 1914, the AVIATION SECTION, U.S. ARMY SIGNAL CORPS was formed. This organization brought American military aviation into WORLD WAR I in 1917, but it was unable to manage the necessary expansion of the service. A bigger, more autonomous organization, the U.S. ARMY AIR SERVICE, was established on May 24, 1918. Under this organization, U.S. airmen flew very significant missions during the closing months of World War I. In 1916, the American air arm consisted of 311 men, total. By the end of World War I, the USAAS mustered 195,023 officers and enlisted personnel.

The outstanding individual to emerge during the period of the USAAS was Brigadier General WILLIAM MITCHELL, an abrasive, tireless, and far-seeing advocate of military air power. His demonstration of the effectiveness of aerial bombardment against large naval vessels failed to move the U.S. Army to expand the USAAS, but it did interest the navy in aviation. Although Mitchell's outspoken

Samuel Pierpont Langley and Charles M. Manly (left), chief mechanic on board the houseboat that served to launch Langley's Aerodrome aircraft over the Potomac River near Washington, D.C., in 1903. Even though he was one of the pioneers of flight in America, Langley never saw his dreams fulfilled. He is remembered as one of the most unlucky trail blazers in flight history. *(NASA)*

frustration with his superiors ultimately resulted in his high-profile court martial in 1925, his public agitation did influence the passage of the AIR CORPS ACT OF 1926, which established the U.S. ARMY AIR CORPS on July 2, 1926. With greater autonomy than the USAAS, the USAAC developed aircraft, tactics, strategy, and doctrine, all aimed at establishing the independence of air power in warfighting.

On the eve of the United States' entry into WORLD WAR II, the army recognized the necessity of creating a nearly independent air arm, and, on June 20, 1941, the U.S. ARMY AIR FORCES came into

being. The new service quickly geared up for war, expanding personnel from 23,455 in 1939 to 2,372,292 in 1944. As visionaries like Mitchell had predicted, air power played an extraordinarily important role in the war. It was the USAAF that delivered the first offensive blow against Japan in the form of JAMES HAROLD DOOLITTLE's daring raid on Tokyo on April 18, 1942, and it was USAAF bombers that brought the war to the Germans well before effective Allied offensive action on the ground was possible. While military analysts and historians continue to argue over the effectiveness of strategic bombing (see BOMBING, STRATEGIC) in World War II, it is a fact that two USAAF B-29s brought World War II to an end by delivering nuclear weapons against Japan in August 1945. And the war also made it clear that the time had come to establish an entirely independent air arm, of status equal to that of the navy and the army.

The United States Air Force was born by act of Congress (National Security Act of 1947) on September 18, 1947, and, in a nuclear age, it soon became the principal strategic force of the United States, capable of delivering nuclear—and then thermonuclear—weapons to any target anywhere in the world. While the thrust of USAF development during the Cold War period was in the area of strategic deployment, the first test of the USAF was tactical: the BERLIN AIRLIFT during 1948–49. The success of the airlift marked a major victory against Soviet expansion in Europe, and it served as the impetus for the creation of NATO, in which the USAF would play a major role.

Even as the USAF, through the STRATEGIC AIR COMMAND (SAC), developed as a nuclear deterrent force, the next major challenge was also tactical in nature. The KOREAN WAR (1950–53) called for CLOSE AIR SUPPORT of ground forces, although USAF strategic operations against North Korean irrigation and dam systems were also effective in bringing the communists to the negotiating table.

After Korea and until the escalation of the VIETNAM WAR, the emphasis for the USAF again turned to strategic deterrence, especially after the Soviet Union and, later, Communist China acquired nuclear and thermonuclear weapons. Under General CURTIS EMERSON LeMAY, who led the USAF from 1948 to 1965, the service became the chief American means of maintaining a policy of mutually assured destruction (MAD), in which the existence of massive atomic arsenals in U.S. as well as Soviet hands discouraged both sides from declaring war. During this period, the USAF developed the massive B-52 bomber and an arsenal of ICBM (INTERCONTINENTAL BALLISTIC MISSILE) weapons, as well as important advances in aerial reconnaissance, including the U-2, the SR-71, and an array of military satellites.

The escalation of the Vietnam War beginning in 1965 once again showed the shortsightedness of preparing almost exclusively for strategic warfare at the expense of readiness to fight a limited war on a tactical level. The war drew on USAF ingenuity and the ability to improvise as well as to adapt strategic aircraft (most notably the B-52) to a tactical role. As the PERSIAN GULF WAR demonstrated in 1990–91, the USAF had become a tremendously

flexible service, capable of maintaining strategic deterrence as well as coordinating with ground and sea forces to achieve a rapid tactical victory. In the "war against terrorism," the campaign against terrorist-held Afghanistan that followed the terrorist attacks against the World Trade Center in New York and the Pentagon outside of Washington, D.C., on September 11, 2001, the USAF again played the major role. At the beginning of the 21st century, there could be no doubt that the USAF was the largest and most effective air force in history.

Holloman AFB, New Mexico   See AIR FORCE BASES.

Howard AFB, Panama   See AIR FORCE BASES.

Hurlburt Field, Florida   See AIR FORCE BASES.

I

Incirlik AB, Turkey See AIR FORCE BASES.

insignia, aircraft

Once bright and bold, the insignia on USAF combat aircraft since the VIETNAM WAR has been generally gray or black to reduce rather than enhance visibility. This reflects a recognition of the sophistication of air defense weaponry.

The first insignia on U.S. Army aircraft was carried on planes used in the PUNITIVE EXPEDITION led by General John J. Pershing against Pancho Villa in 1916. Planes were marked with a red star, sometimes enclosed within a solid white circle. This insignia was never made official, however, and, in May 1917, the month after the United States entered WORLD WAR I, the official insignia became a white star within a blue circle, with a solid red disk within the star. Aircraft rudders carried vertical red, white, and blue stripes. In 1918, Brigadier General WILLIAM MITCHELL changed the insignia to a roundel with a white disk inside a larger blue ring, which was in an even larger red ring. The change was made to bring the U.S. insignia into line with the insignia of the other Allies, and, in 1919, with the war over, the 1917 star insignia was adopted once again. The rudder insignia changed in 1927, becoming a vertical blue stripe forward with alternating horizontal red and white stripes aft. This was used until 1940.

During WORLD WAR II, in 1942, the red disk was removed from the center of the white star to avoid possible confusion with the Japanese "rising sun" insignia. Also in 1942, some insignia added a narrow yellow ring outside of the blue field, but this was used on an unofficial basis. In 1943, white rectangles ("wings") were added at the sides of the blue circle to heighten visibility, and a red stripe was run around the entire insignia. This was soon replaced by a blue stripe for the rest of the war.

After the war, in 1947, the red outline was restored to the insignia, which now also included a horizontal red stripe in the middle of the "wing" rectangles. This design endured until the advent of the modern, lower-visibility insignia. The insignia on today's "stealth" aircraft barely contrasts with the prevailing color of the aircraft fuselage and air surfaces.

Inter-American Air Forces Academy (IAAFA)

The mission of the IAAFA is to train and support Latin American air forces, in Spanish, so that they may support United States national interests and the security interests of the hemisphere. Located at Lackland AFB, Texas, IAAFA also seeks to promote "inter-Americanism" and to expose students to the American lifestyle. Staffed by Spanish-speaking USAF instructors, IAAFA provides instruction for both officers and enlisted personnel in over 60 supervisory, specialization, and technical-academic courses including aircraft systems and maintenance, helicopter maintenance, electronics, communications, intelligence, supply, logistics, air base ground defense, security, pilot instrument procedures, computer resources, and information systems management. Training is conducted at three geographically separated locations: Lackland AFB, Kelly AFB, and the U.S. Army's Camp Bullis, outside of San Antonio, Texas.

IAAFA is older than the USAF itself, having been established on March 15, 1943, at the request of the Peruvian minister of aeronautics, General Fernando Melgar. In 1943, the newly established academy trained 11 Peruvian students at Albrook Field, Panama Canal Zone. IAAFA expanded during the 1950s and was officially named "The Inter-American Air Forces Academy" in 1966.

intercontinental ballistic missile (ICBM)

The AIR FORCE SPACE COMMAND (AFSPC) manages and controls the USAF's ICBM program, which is one leg of the so-called triad that makes up the United States' strategic forces. (The other two legs are nuclear-capable manned bombers and the U.S. Navy's fleet of nuclear-missile submarines.)

ICBMs are long-range missiles, in contrast to shorter-range IRBM (INTERMEDIATE-RANGE BALLISTIC MISSILE) weapons. ICBMs consist of a rocket engine, fuel, oxidizer, guidance system, and a nuclear or thermonuclear warhead. The missiles are an outgrowth of the German V-2 rockets of WORLD WAR II. After the war, the USAF conducted research on the Atlas ICBM, and, in 1953, the USAF and the U.S. Army independently (and competitively) developed missiles. At last, in 1957, all ICBM programs, operations, and arsenals were put under the direction of the USAF.

ICBMs currently in the USAF inventory include:

The LGM-30G Minuteman. Built by Boeing, the Minuteman has a range of more than 6,000

The Peacekeeper missile   *(U.S. Air Force)*

miles and can carry nuclear or thermonuclear warheads. The current Minuteman force consists of 500 Minuteman III missiles located at Warren AFB, Wyoming, Malmstrom AFB, Montana, and Minot AFB, North Dakota. If the Start II nuclear limitation treaty is fully implemented, the Minuteman III will become the only land-based ICBM in the triad.

LG-118A Peacekeeper. Built by Boeing and with a range in excess of 6,000 miles, the Peacekeeper was first deployed in 1986. It can deliver 10 independently targeted thermonuclear warheads with great accuracy. Currently, 50 of these $70 million missiles are deployed, but they may be retired if the Start II treaty is fully implemented.

intermediate-range ballistic missile
(IRBM)

Although the USAF inventory includes many types of missiles, the only strategic missile weapons in the AIR FORCE SPACE COMMAND (AFSPC) inventory today are ICBM (INTERCONTINENTAL BALLISTIC MISSILE) weapons. Beginning in the 1950s, however, the USAF inventory also included IRBMs with nuclear warheads. The most important of these were:

Chrysler PGM-19 Jupiter. Developed by the army's Ballistic Missile Agency at the Redstone Arsenal, Alabama, under Dr. Wernher von Braun, the Jupiter was placed under USAF control in 1959. Jupiter was a single-stage, liquid-propellant missile using an all-inertial guidance system to direct it toward the target. Its range was 1,500 miles, and Jupiter squadrons of 15 missiles each were deployed at NATO launch sites in Italy and Turkey in 1961. The Jupiter was withdrawn from military use in 1963.

Douglas PGM-17 Thor. The single-stage Thor entered active military service in September 1958 and was the free world's first operational IRBM. The Thor was assigned to the STRATEGIC AIR COMMAND (SAC) and was also deployed to England early in 1959. The Thor was retired from military service in 1963, although it was modified for space research, either as a single-stage booster or in combination with various types of upper stages for such satellite programs as Tiros, Telstar, Pioneer, and Discoverer.

Jabara, James (1923–1966) *fighter pilot*

USAF pilot James Jabara became America's first jet ace, achieving 15 victories against MiGs during two tours in the KOREAN WAR. A native of Muskogee, Oklahoma, Jabara became an aviation cadet in 1942, during WORLD WAR II, and entered the U.S. ARMY AIR FORCES as a commissioned pilot the following year.

During World War II, Jabara flew with the NINTH AIR FORCE and the EIGHTH AIR FORCE in F-51s, a total of 108 sorties. He was credited with one and a half victories. His first tour in Korea began in 1950 with the 4th Fighter Interceptor Wing of the FIFTH AIR FORCE, flying F-86 jets. Having scored six victories, he returned to the United States in 1951, where he was assigned to USAF headquarters, then, at his request, he served another tour in Korea, scoring nine more victories.

In 1964, as colonel, Jabara commanded the 4540th Combat Crew Training Group at Luke AFB, Arizona, overseeing the training of U.S.-allied foreign pilots in the F-104G. Jabara was killed in an automobile accident.

James Jabara   *(U.S. Air Force)*

Japan Air Defense Force (JADF)

A named air force, the unit was created in 1952 to replace the 314th Air Division and was under the FAR EAST AIR FORCES (FEAF). The JADF was created to defend Japan while the FIFTH AIR FORCE, established as the occupying air force of Japan after WORLD WAR II, was in Korea during the KOREAN WAR. JADF was dissolved in 1954.

jock

USAF slang for pilot; typically applied to fighter pilots—"fighter jocks." See also DRIVER.

Joint Services Survival, Evasion, Resistance, and Escape (SERE) Agency (JSAA)

JSAA is the Department of Defense executive agency for operational evasion and escape matters, for code of conduct and survival, evasion, resistance, and escape (SERE) training, and for the DOD Prisoner of War (POW)/Missing in Action (MIA) program. JSAA headquarters is at Fort Belvoir, Virginia.

Joint Strike Fighter (JSF) Program

The JSF Program (formerly the Joint Advanced Strike Technology (JAST) Program), is a Department of Defense project to define affordable next-generation strike aircraft weapon systems for the USAF, navy, marines, and the forces of our allies. The principal goal of the program is to produce an affordable aircraft that will satisfy the following needs:

USAF: Multirole aircraft (primary-air-to-ground), to replace the F-16 and A-10 and complement the F-22A

U.S. Navy: First-day-of-war, survivable strike fighter aircraft to complement F/A-18E/F

Boeing and Lockheed Martin competed for the Joint Strike Fighter contract. This Lockheed-Martin prototype won the contract. *(Lockheed-Martin photo)*

U.S. Marine Corps STOVL (short takeoff and vertical landing): Aircraft to replace the AV-8B and F/A-18 as the only USMC strike fighter

United Kingdom Royal Navy and Royal Air Force: STOVL aircraft to replace Sea Harriers and GR.7s as a supersonic strike fighter

The JSF program originated in the early 1990s, and the Joint Advanced Strike Technology (JAST) Program was initiated in late 1993. As of the close of 2001, the JSF program was nearing the end of the concept demonstration. It is anticipated that the USAF will be the largest JSF customer, purchasing 1,763 CTOL (conventional takeoff and landing) aircraft. The U.S. Marine Corps is expected to purchase 609 STOVL aircraft, and the U.S. Navy about 480 carrier-launched aircraft. The U.K. Royal Air Force and Royal Navy will purchase 150 of the STOVL variant. Boeing and Lockheed Martin both produced prototypes, but the final contract was awarded to Lockheed Martin in October 2001.

Joint Surveillance Target Attack Radar System (JSTARS)

Joint STARS or JSTARS is a joint USAF/U.S. Army program that provides air and ground commanders with near real-time wide-area surveillance and deep targeting data on both fixed and moving targets, day or night and under all weather conditions. JSTARS can detect, locate, track, and classify targets in enemy territory beyond the Forward Line of Own Troops (FLOT).

The airborne platform for the JSTARS electronics is the E-8, a specially modified C-18 transport (the military version of the Boeing 707-323C). JSTARS was first used extensively in the PERSIAN GULF WAR of 1990–91.

Jones, David C. (1921–   ) *Air Force general*

Chairman of the Joint Chiefs of Staff from 1978 to 1982, Jones was the third USAF officer to hold the position. He had served as chief of staff of the

USAF from 1974 until his appointment as JCS chairman.

A native of Aberdeen, South Dakota, Jones was an aviation cadet and entered the U.S. ARMY AIR FORCES through that program in 1943. During WORLD WAR II, Jones served as a flying instructor, and, in the KOREAN WAR, flew more than 300 combat hours in B-29s. Returned to the United States, he served as operations planner and as aide to General CURTIS EMERSON LEMAY at STRATEGIC AIR COMMAND (SAC) headquarters. In 1960, Jones graduated from the National War College and served on the AIR STAFF. He became commander of the SECOND AIR FORCE in 1969, then commander in chief of UNITED STATES AIR FORCES IN EUROPE (USAFE) in 1971.

Jones was an advocate of the B-1 bomber program and an expanded AWACS program. He initiated and directed important USAF organizational changes, including the reduction in the size of numbered air forces and the creation of Allied Air Forces Central Europe under the auspices of NATO. He strengthened the role of the JCS, and, although he retired in 1982, he continued to work successfully toward that end.

Jungle Jim

The name was applied to the 4400th Combat Crew Training Squadron established at Eglin AFB, Florida, in 1961. The unit's purpose was to train airmen for guerrilla warfare and air commando operations. A Jungle Jim detachment was deployed to South Vietnam in October 1961, ostensibly as part of U.S. military advisory forces to train South Vietnamese personnel. In the VIETNAM WAR, the Jungle Jim detachment was called Farm Gate and flew U.S. aircraft bearing Vietnamese air force markings.

K

Kadena AB, Japan See AIR FORCE BASES.

Keesler AFB, Mississippi See AIR FORCE BASES.

Kelly AFB, Texas See AIR FORCE BASES.

Kenly, William L. (1864–1928) *U.S. Army Air Service director*
The first head of the U.S. ARMY AIR SERVICE, Kenly was born in Baltimore and graduated from West Point in 1889. Originally commissioned in the artillery, he attended San Diego Signal Corps Aviation School shortly before the United States entered WORLD WAR I. Although he shipped out to France as commander of an artillery unit, he was subsequently appointed chief of the USAAS. In November 1917, General BENJAMIN D. FOULOIS relieved him, and, after briefly serving in artillery again, Kenly returned to the United States early in 1918 to head the Division of Military Aeronautics, effectively commanding the USAAS through the end of World War I. Kenly had little effect on the USAAS because funding was drastically reduced with demobilization. He retired in 1919.

Key West Agreement of 1948
Although EXECUTIVE ORDER 9877 of July 26, 1947 clearly specified the roles of the newly created USAF,

a dispute arose among the services, all of which wanted to use air power. Particularly acrimonious was the conflict between the navy and the USAF. The navy rejected the idea of using heavy bombers to fulfill the strategic role and favored the use of carrier-based aircraft. The USAF continued to champion the role of the heavy bomber. Somewhat less acute was the dispute between the army and the USAF. The army saw coastal air defense as its mission, and the army also sought control over ICBM (INTERCONTINENTAL BALLISTIC MISSILE) weapons.

In an effort to resolve the disputes, Secretary of Defense James V. Forrestal convened conferences with the Joint Chiefs of Staff to be held in Key West, Florida, in March 1948. The conferences produced an agreement (historically referred to as the Key West Agreement—although no official document was so titled) that the USAF held prime responsibility for strategic operations and the navy for control of the seas. Air defense was assigned to the USAF, but the army was given the function of organizing, equipping, and training air defense units.

The Key West Agreement did not definitively settle the USAF-army controversy over ICBM and surface-to-air operations. In 1949, control of surface-to-air missiles with up to a 100-mile range was given to the army, whereas the USAF controlled those with ranges exceeding 100 miles. In 1956 the secretary of defense settled the matter of which service would control ICBMs by assigning to the

USAF control over all ballistic missiles with a range in excess of 20 miles.

Kirtland AFB, New Mexico   See AIR FORCE BASES.

Korean War

Background of the War

The Korean War of 1950–53 had its immediate cause in the invasion of South Korea by forces from the communist North. However, Korea had an ancient heritage of internal conflict and, through the centuries, was also often subject to invasion by China or Japan. In 1910, Japan, expanding its empire, annexed Korea without incurring objection from the rest of the world, including the United States. After the December 7, 1941, Japanese attack on Pearl Harbor, however, the United States' declaration of war acknowledged, among many other things, that Japan had made Korea one of its first victims of imperialist aggression, and, from this point on, the fate of Korea became a subject of interest to America. At the 1943 Cairo Conference among China, Great Britain, and the United States, the Allies agreed to include the independence of Korea among the objectives of their joint prosecution of WORLD WAR II. At the Potsdam Conference (July 27–August 2, 1945), Soviet premier Joseph Stalin declared his intention to abide by the Potsdam agreement to establish an international trusteeship for Korea after the defeat of Japan. The sudden surrender of Japan on August 14, 1945, after the atomic bombings of Hiroshima and Nagasaki, made an Allied occupation of Korea unnecessary. Nevertheless, the United States proposed that the Soviets receive Japan's surrender in Korea north of the 38th parallel while the United States accept surrender south of this line. The idea was that this de facto partition would be strictly temporary and would remain in place only until Korea could be restored to a full peacetime footing. The Soviets, however, seized on it to divide Korea and bring the northern portion into the communist sphere. The

38th parallel became a fortified line, and, in September 1947, the United States requested that the United Nations intervene to bring about Korean unification. Over a Soviet objection, the UN decided that a unified government be established for Korea following a general election. Moreover, it was resolved that, after the government had been established, the UN would dispatch a security force to Korea to protect it. Encouraged by the Soviets, the North Korean communists barred the UN commission from holding elections north of the 38th parallel. South of the parallel, the 1948 elections created the Republic of Korea (ROK) under President Syngman Rhee. In response, on May 25, 1948, Soviet-sponsored elections in the north created a Supreme People's Assembly, which purported to represent all of Korea. The People's Democratic Republic of Korea (DRK) was put under the leadership of Kim Il Sung, a Soviet-trained Korean communist.

Having set up a North Korean government, the Soviets pledged to withdraw Red Army troops from the country by January 1, 1949. Although heartened by this announcement, the United States began to train and equip an indigenous Korean security force for the South and provided economic aid. The situation was delicate, because the United States wanted neither to abandon South Korea nor to give the appearance of sponsoring South Korean aggression, which might trigger a new world war. Accordingly, the United States supplied defensive weapons only. President Rhee protested that his nation needed much more, and he even hired as a military adviser CLAIRE L. CHENNAULT, the famed U.S. ARMY AIR FORCES major general, retired, who had commanded China's "Flying Tigers" (see AMERICAN VOLUNTEER GROUP) during WORLD WAR II. Rhee asked Chennault to plan a South Korean air force.

The United States completed its official military withdrawal from Korea on June 29, 1949, leaving behind only a 500-man U.S. Korean Military Advisory Group (KMAG).

War Begins

During May 1950, KMAG reported a military buildup on the northern side of the 38th parallel. At four o'clock on the morning of June 25, 1950, these forces invaded, crossing the 38th parallel and brushing aside the inferior South Korean army. The main invading force headed toward Seoul, the South Korean capital, about 35 miles below the parallel, while smaller forces moved down the center of the Korean peninsula and along the east coast. The North Korean People's Army (NKPA) took Seoul, whereupon President Harry S. Truman ordered General Douglas MacArthur, commander of the U.S. Far East Command, to supply the ROK with equipment and ammunition, because most supplies had been abandoned in the retreat of ROK forces.

USAF elements were the first U.S. military units to respond to the invasion. By the afternoon of June 25, North Korean fighters attacked South Korean and USAF aircraft and facilities at Seoul airfield and Kimpo AB, just south of the capital. On June 26, FAR EAST AIR FORCES (FEAF) fighters provided protective cover while ships evacuated American nationals from Inchon, 20 miles west of Seoul. On June 27, as the communists closed in on Seoul, FEAF transports evacuated more Americans, and FIFTH AIR FORCE fighters, escorting the evacuation transports, shot down three North Korean MiGs— the first aerial victories of the war.

The U.S. delegation to the United Nations secured a Security Council resolution that UN members assist the ROK. Armed with this, President Truman mobilized U.S. air and naval forces. On June 28, FEAF, under the command of Lieutenant General George E. Stratemeyer, began flying interdiction missions between Seoul and the 38th parallel, photo-reconnaissance and weather missions over South Korea, airlift missions from Japan to Korea, and CLOSE AIR SUPPORT missions for the ROK troops. On June 29, the 3rd Bombardment Group made the first American air raid on North Korea, bombing the airfield at Pyongyang, and FEAF Bomber Command followed with sporadic B-29 missions against North Korean targets through July. At last, in August, major B-29 raids were launched against North Korean marshaling yards, railroad bridges, and supply dumps.

U.S. ground forces were committed to war on June 30, 1950. On July 7, the UN established an allied command under President Truman, who named General MacArthur as UN commander in chief. In the meantime, the 5AF, under Major General Earl E. Partridge, established an advanced headquarters in Taegu, South Korea, 140 miles southeast of Seoul, also the location of Eighth Army headquarters. However, during this early period of the war, most FEAF bombers and fighters operated from bases in Japan, which was a major disadvantage in flying short-range F-80 jet aircraft. Nevertheless, USAF pilots worked in concert with carrier-launched naval aircraft to attack enemy airfields, destroying much of the small North Korean air force on the ground. Before the end of July, USAF and navy and marine air units claimed air superiority over North and South Korea.

By August 5, the relentless retreat of UN ground forces had stopped, and FEAF air support, effective ground action, and the unsupportable lengthening of North Korean supply lines ended the communist offensive. The UN troops held a defensive perimeter in the southeastern corner of the peninsula, in a 40- to 60-mile arc about the seaport of Pusan. Holding the Pusan perimeter required careful coordination between ground action and close air support.

UN Forces Take the Offensive

Beginning on September 15, 1950, UN forces assumed the offensive when the U.S. X Corps made a spectacular amphibious assault landing at Inchon, 150 miles north of the battle front. In the south, the U.S. Eighth Army (including U.S., ROK, and British forces) counterattacked on September 16. The 5AF provided close air support, while, far to the north, FEAF bombed Pyongyang, the capital of North Korea, and Wonsan, an east coast port 80 miles north of the 38th parallel.

U.S. Marines retook Kimpo AB on September 17. On the 19th, the first FEAF cargo aircraft landed there. From this point on, the AIRLIFT of supplies, fuel, and troops would be virtually continuous. Air controllers accompanied advancing Eighth Army tank columns to support tank commanders with aerial reconnaissance and to call in close air support. Seoul was recaptured on September 26, and, on September 28, fighter-bombers returned permanently to Taegu. Engineers also rebuilt other airfields, beginning with Pohang, on the east coast 50 miles northeast of Taegu, and, on October 7, USAF flying units returned to Pohang and to other rebuilt airfields at Kimpo and at Suwon, 20 miles south of Seoul. The ability to operate from bases in Korea greatly increased the effectiveness of the limited-range jet fighters.

On October 9, UN forces took the war into North Korea when the Eighth Army crossed the 38th parallel near Kaesong. American and South Korean forces entered Pyongyang on October 19 while FEAF B-29s and B-26s continued to bomb transport lines and military targets in North Korea,

and B-26s, F-51s, and F-80s provided close air support to the advancing ground troops. FEAF also continuously supplied photo reconnaissance, airlift, and air medical evacuation.

On the east coast of Korea in the meantime, ROK forces crossed the 38th parallel on October 1 and captured Wonsan on October 11. On October 26 South Korean forces reached the Yalu River, the border with China, at Chosan, 120 miles north of Pyongyang.

Chinese Intervention

On the night of November 25, 1950, Chinese forces, in great strength, attacked the Eighth Army on its center and right. Two days later, even more

This photo shows the results of dropping a 2,000-pound bomb on the Korean side of a bridge across the Yalu River into Manchuria, on November 15, 1950. *(National Archives)*

powerful Chinese attacks overran units of X Corps on its left flank. By November 28, UN positions were caving in as about 300,000 Chinese troops entered North Korea.

UN troops rapidly withdrew, and even UN air superiority vanished as Soviet-built Chinese MiG-15 jet fighters easily outflew U.S. piston-driven craft. By December 15, UN forces had withdrawn all the way to the 38th parallel and were now establishing a defensive line across the breadth of the Korean peninsula.

5AF provided close air support to cover the withdrawal, and U.S. F-80s did their best against the Chinese MiG-15s. During November, FEAF medium and light bombers, along with U.S. Navy aircraft, attacked bridges over the Yalu River and supply centers along the Korean side of the river —operations severely hampered by orders to avoid violating Chinese air space. Despite the handicap, on November 25, bombers destroyed key bridges, but the communists responded by rapidly erecting pontoon bridges. As winter set in, they also crossed the ice of the frozen Yalu. B-29 raids were effective against North Korean supply dumps, however.

In response to the introduction of Chinese MiG 15s, USAF commanders requested and received rush consignments of the newest and best jet fighters. On December 6, the 27th Fighter-Escort Wing, flying F-84 Thunderjets, arrived at Taegu. On December 15, the 4th Fighter-Interceptor Wing flew its first mission in Korea using the most advanced aircraft, the F-86 Sabre. It was the timely introduction of the Sabres that allowed UN forces to regain and maintain air superiority.

As 1950 came to a close, FEAF flew interdiction and armed reconnaissance missions to slow the advancing Chinese. 5AF pilots killed or wounded some 33,000 enemy troops during December, forcing the Chinese to move only by night. Yet the communist advance continued, and, on January 1, 1951, Chinese forces crossed the 38th parallel. They entered Seoul three days later. On January 15 UN forces halted the Chinese and North Korean armies 50 miles south of the 38th parallel, on a line from

Pyongtaek on the west coast to Samchok on the east coast.

UN Counteroffensive

UN forces began a counteroffensive on January 25, 1951, with the object of wearing down the overextended enemy. On February 10, Kimpo AB was again recaptured, and, when thawing roads made ground transport impossible, the 315th Air Division airdropped supplies to the ground forces. UN forces reoccupied Seoul on March 14. On the 23rd, FEAF airlift forces dropped a reinforced regiment at Munsan, 25 miles north of Seoul.

Up north, between the Chongchon and Yalu rivers, communist forces established an air presence so formidable that 5AF pilots called the region "MiG Alley." By March 10, Sabres were fighting in MiG Alley while also escorting FEAF B-29 attacks against area targets. From April 12 to 23 the FEAF bombers attacked rebuilt airfields on the outskirts of Pyongyang. By this time, Eighth Army ground units had regained the 38th parallel. Between April 17 and 21, with close air support, ground units penetrated beyond the 38th parallel.

Communist Chinese Spring Offensive

On April 22, 1951, Chinese forces began a new offensive with an assault on ROK army positions 40 to 55 miles northeast of Seoul. U.S. Army and marine forces, in concert with British ground troops, stopped the new communist drive by May 1. Two weeks later, however, the Chinese and North Koreans attacked near Taepo, between the east coast and Chunchon, 45 miles northeast of Seoul. The advance was halted by May 20, and, on May 22, UN Command (now under the overall direction of General Matthew Bunker Ridgway, who had replaced General MacArthur—removed by President Truman for insubordination) launched a counterattack. FEAF and navy fliers maintained air superiority during this period by means of aerial combat and continual bombing of North Korean airfields. The 5AF and a U.S. Marine air wing extended airfield attacks on May 9 to include Sinuiju airfield in the northwest corner of Korea.

The attacks were devastating to communist air power in the region.

General Stratemeyer, FEAF commander, suffered a heart attack in May 1951, and Lieutenant General O. P. Weyland took over FEAF. Throughout most of this period, Chinese pilots stayed on the Manchurian side of the Yalu River, but, on May 20, 50 MiGs engaged 36 Sabres in aerial combat. It was during this fight that Captain JAMES JABARA shot down two MiGs, which, added to his four prior kills, made him the first jet ace in aviation history.

FEAF, marine, and navy air forces coordinated carefully to help force the North Koreans and Chinese to restrict their movements and attacks to periods of darkness and bad weather. FEAF also supplemented sealift with airlift during this period. In late May, FEAF began Operation Strangle to interdict the flow of communist supplies south of the 39th parallel, and, in June, the campaign was extended to attacks against railroads.

Negotiations Begin

In July 1951, delegations began cease-fire negotiations at Kaesong, North Korea, on the 38th parallel. During these talks, UN forces continued pushing the communist troops northward, until, by July 8, the front had returned to the 38th parallel.

Negotiations formally began on July 10, 1951, and broke down on August 23, whereupon the UN Command launched an offensive in central Korea. FEAF settled in for a war of attrition and devoted much effort to rebuilding and improving its Korean airfields. Beginning late in July, the Chinese air force conducted an air campaign to challenge UN air superiority. In September they targeted the 5AF, whose pilots, however, shot down 14 MiGs, while suffering 6 losses.

Despite U.S. victories, the Chinese air offensive forced the 5AF to suspend fighter-bomber interdiction in MiG Alley until the winter. During this period, UN air command concentrated on railroad targets outside of MiG Alley and on new North Korean airfields. These raids proved unsuccessful. However, on November 12, 1951, truce negotiations resumed, now at Panmunjom, and UN ground forces ceased offensive action, settling into a war of containment.

Stalemate

While negotiations dragged on, the USAF received more F-86 Sabres to counter the Chinese air force. Beginning in December 1951, members of the 51st and 4th Fighter-Interceptor Wings downed 26 MiGs in two weeks, breaking the back of the Chinese air offensive. For the rest of the winter, MiG pilots generally avoided aerial combat. Despite this, pilots of the 5AF destroyed 127 communist aircraft in aerial combat between January and April 1952. USAF losses were only nine planes. 5AF B-29 raids also continued during this period. However, during the winter of 1951–52, with battle lines static, the need for the close air support mission was greatly diminished. USAF commanders concentrated instead on aerial bombardment of enemy positions alternating on a daily basis with artillery attacks on those same positions. The communist response was to dig in, rendering both aerial and artillery bombardment fairly ineffective.

In an effort to end the stalemate at Panmunjom, UN air commanders resolved to attack targets previously exempted or underexploited. Accordingly, in May 1952 the 5AF shifted from interdiction of transportation to attacks on supply depots and industrial targets. Beginning on June 23, U.S. Navy and 5AF units also made coordinated attacks on the electric power complex at Sui-ho Dam, on the Yalu River near Sinuiju, followed by strikes against the Chosin, Fusen, and Kyosen power plants. On July 11, Pyongyang was bombed by aircraft of the Seventh Fleet, the 1st Marine Air Wing, the 5AF, the British Navy, and the ROK air force. At night, FEAF sent in B-29s. Allied air forces returned to Pyongyang again on August 29 and 30, and, in September, 5AF attacked troop concentrations and barracks in northwest Korea, while FEAF bombed similar targets near Hamhung in northeast Korea.

During the summer of 1952, many F-86Es were upgraded to more powerful and more maneuverable F-86Fs. MiG activity increased during August and September, but U.S. pilots achieved an 8-to-1 ratio of victories to losses.

Despite the pressure of the air campaign, the Panmunjom talks produced nothing, and the war entered its third winter.

Continued Stalemate

While the stalemate continued, USAF Sabre pilots continued to shoot down MiGs, even though they were generally outnumbered and flew aircraft that were still technically inferior to the MiG-15, at least at high altitude. On February l8, 1953, near the Suiho Reservoir on the Yalu River, four F-86Fs attacked 48 MiGs, shot down two, and caused two others to crash while taking evasive action. All four Sabres returned safely to base.

The success of 5AF Sabres was not matched by that of the aging B-29s of FEAF Bomber Command. The big bombers increasingly fell victim to interceptor and antiaircraft artillery attacks at night. Missions were curtailed, although important industrial targets continued to be targeted.

In the spring of 1953, a POW exchange agreement broke the stalemate at Panmunjom, and productive talks continued.

The War Winds Down

During the renewed talks, the communists sought to improve their position with a major assault on June 10 against the ROK II Corps near Kumsong, a small town in central Korea. In combating this offensive, FEAF flew a record-breaking 7,032 sorties, mostly to deliver close air support. When the offensive was renewed, FEAF flew another 12,000 combat sorties, again mostly in close air support.

During the offensives, the 315th Air Division airlifted an Army regiment (3,252 soldiers and 1,770 tons of cargo) from Japan to Korea, and, from June 28 through July 2, airlifters flew almost 4,000 more troops and over 1,200 tons of cargo from Misawa and Tachikawa air bases in Japan to Pusan and Taegu airfields in Korea. These were the last major airlift operations of the Korean conflict. During May, June, and July 1953, Sabre pilots achieved 165 aerial victories with only three losses—a magnificent achievement.

The war ended not in victory or defeat, but with the armistice of July 27, 1953. The number of Chinese and North Korean troops killed is unknown, but estimates range between 1.5 and 2 million, in addition to at least a million civilians killed. South Korean civilian casualties probably equaled those of North Korea. United States losses were 142,091 casualties, including 33,629 deaths and 7,140 captured. USAF losses were fairly light, 1,841 casualties including 379 killed in action, 11 deaths from wounds, and 821 missing in action and presumed dead. In addition, 224 fliers were captured.

UN and U.S. action in the Korean War did succeed in confining communist rule to North Korea, but, beyond this, the conflict ended inconclusively.

Kunsan AB, Republic of Korea See AIR FORCE BASES.

L

Lackland AFB, Texas See AIR FORCE BASES.

Lafayette Escadrille

This celebrated WORLD WAR I unit of American volunteer aviators was originally a French unit staffed by U.S. volunteers and commanded by a French officer and assistant. It was officially designated N. 124 when it flew the Nieuport 28, and, later, S. 124 when it flew the Spad XIII. Its mission was reconnaissance, patrol, and fighter escort.

Lafayette Escadrille was mainly the brainchild of Bostonian Norman Prince, who had volunteered early in the war (1915) to fly for the French. (Prince would die in a night landing accident on October 12, 1916.) He lobbied his commanders to create an all-American flying unit, which was authorized on March 21, 1916. The French wanted to call it the "American Escadrille," but the requirements of U.S. neutrality prompted a name change to "Lafayette Escadrille." The unit was dispatched to the front in April 1916 and operated until February 1918, when it became the 103rd Aero Squadron and was placed fully under U.S. military control.

During the course of its service, the Lafayette Escadrille roster had 38 U.S. pilots, suffered approximately a 30 percent casualty rate (killed in action), and was credited with 37 victories—a middling record, and 17 of those kills were credited to a single pilot, Raoul Lufbery.

Lahm, Frank P. (1877–1963) *U.S. Army pilot*
The first person to earn a pilot's rating in the first USAF antecedent organization, the AERONAUTICAL DIVISION, U.S. ARMY SIGNAL CORPS, Lahm flew BALLOONS as well as airplanes. He was born in Mansfield, Ohio, and graduated from the U.S. Military Academy at West Point in 1901. Eight years later, he soloed in an airplane, having already set an endurance record of one hour, 12 minutes in a flight with Orville Wright. Lahm later flew the Aeronautical Division's first flight cross country.

In WORLD WAR I, Lahm commanded balloon units and served on the General Staff during the major Saint-Mihiel and Meuse-Argonne offensives. In 1926, he was appointed assistant chief of the U.S. ARMY AIR CORPS and organized and trained the Air Corps Training Center. He retired in 1941 as chief of aviation for the First Army.

Lajes Field, Azores, Portugal See AIR FORCE BASES.

Langley AFB, Virginia See AIR FORCE BASES.

Laughlin AFB, Texas See AIR FORCE BASES.

LeMay, Curtis Emerson (1906–1990) *Air Force general and Chief of Staff*

LeMay was born in Columbus, Ohio, and set out to obtain an appointment to West Point. When he was disappointed in this attempt, he enrolled at Ohio State University, leaving that institution in 1928, to join the army after having completed the ROTC program. In September, LeMay became a cadet in the U.S. ARMY AIR CORPS Flying School and earned his wings on October 12 of the following year. He was commissioned a second lieutenant in January 1930 and posted to the 27th Pursuit Squadron, headquartered in Michigan.

Under army sponsorship, LeMay spent several years completing the civil engineering degree he had begun at Ohio State. Awarded that degree in 1932, he was seconded by the army to the Depression-era CCC (Civilian Conservation Corps) public works program, and he flew the air mails when President Franklin D. Roosevelt assigned Army fliers to air mail operations in 1934. After promotion to first lieutenant in June 1935, LeMay attended an over-water navigation school in Hawaii. In 1937, he transferred from pursuit planes to the 305th Bombardment Group at Langley Field, Virginia, and became involved in exercises demonstrating the ability of aircraft to find ships at sea.

Curtis LeMay was one of the first army pilots to fly the new B-17 bomber. He led a flight of them on a goodwill tour to Latin America during 1937–38. After returning from this tour, he attended the Air Corps Tactical School (1938–39) and, in January 1940, was promoted to captain and given command of a squadron in 34th Bomb group. In 1941, he was promoted to major. With the U.S. entry into WORLD WAR II following Pearl Harbor (December 7, 1941), promotion came even faster. By January 1942, LeMay was a lieutenant colonel, and three months later was promoted to colonel. At this point, in April, he assumed command of the 305th Bombardment Group in California and brought that unit to Britain as part of what became the EIGHTH AIR FORCE.

Once in place in Britain, LeMay set about improving precision bombing tactics by the extremely

Curtis LeMay *(U.S. Air Force)*

risky means of abandoning evasive maneuvering over targets and by also introducing careful target studies prior to missions. The combination of these tactics soon doubled the number of bombs placed on target, and, in June 1943, LeMay was assigned to command the 3rd Bombardment Division, which he led on the so-called shuttle raid against Regensburg in August. The following month, LeMay was promoted to temporary brigadier general, followed by promotion to temporary major general in March 1944. He was then sent to China to lead the 20th Bomber Command against the Japanese.

LeMay took command of the 21st Bomber Group on Guam in January 1945. He stunned his air crews by modifying their B-29s to carry more bombs, stripping the aircraft of defensive guns (as well as gun crews and ammunition). LeMay further ordered the aircraft to attack targets not in formation but singly, and at low level. Crews feared a heavy casualty toll, but, remarkably, their survival rate actually improved, and bombing effectiveness was dramatically increased. Under LeMay's command, the 21st annihilated four major Japanese cities—including Tokyo—with incendiary bombs. Indeed, LeMay's fire-bombing raids were far more immediately destructive than the atomic bombing of Hiroshima and Nagasaki.

As the war drew to a conclusion in the Pacific, LeMay was named commander of the TWENTIETH AIR FORCE in July 1945 and then deputy chief of staff for research and development, a post he held through 1947. In that year, he was promoted to temporary lieutenant general in the newly independent USAF and was given command of the UNITED STATES AIR FORCES IN EUROPE (USAFE) on October 1, 1947. LeMay was a key planner in the great BERLIN AIRLIFT of 1948–49, which kept Berlin supplied during the Soviet blockade of the city.

In October 1948, LeMay returned to the United States as head of the newly created STRATEGIC AIR COMMAND (SAC), the USAF unit tasked with waging nuclear and thermonuclear war. Under LeMay, the USAF greatly expanded and entered the jet age with B-47 and B-52 bombers and in-air refueling tankers (KC-135s). By the 1950s, LeMay oversaw the introduction of ICBM (INTERCONTINENTAL BALLISTIC MISSILE) weapons into the USAF inventory of strategic hardware. He was promoted to general in October 1951, becoming the youngest four-star general since Ulysses S. Grant.

In 1957, Curtis LeMay was named vice chief of staff of the air force and became CHIEF OF STAFF, USAF, in 1961. During the 1960s, his hard-nosed conservatism frequently brought him into conflict with the administrations of John F. Kennedy and Lyndon Johnson, and his relations with Secretary of Defense Robert S. McNamara were strained and, at times, bitter. LeMay never mellowed; rather, he became increasingly irascible, and, on February 1, 1965, he retired from the USAF. His political conservatism drove him to become the running mate of segregationist George Wallace in his failed 1968 bid for the presidency. It was an association that, many felt, tarnished LeMay's remarkable career.

An uncompromising commander, LeMay always demanded "maximum effort" from his air crews and from their aircraft. He was also a forward-thinking planner who shaped the modern USAF and established its place as the most strategic of the three services. The modern doctrines of precision bombing and strategic bombing (see BOMBING, STRATEGIC) were largely his work, and it was under his leadership that the USAF was ushered into both the jet age and the nuclear age.

lieutenant colonel   See RANKS AND GRADES.

lieutenant general   See RANKS AND GRADES.

literature, USAF portrayed in

Like movie makers (see FILMS, USAF PORTRAYED IN), novelists have seen the air arm as an exciting subject for fiction. The first notable air service fiction was written by Elliott White Springs, who achieved ace status flying with the U.S. ARMY AIR SERVICE in WORLD WAR I, and who published widely in magazines during the 1920s. During the 1920s and 1930s, popular magazines published a good deal of fiction portraying the air service in World War I. Novel-length fiction did not emerge until after WORLD WAR II, however. Important books include the 1947 *Command Decision,* by William Wister Haines, about the EIGHTH AIR FORCE. The "command decision" in question was whether to bomb a German jet aircraft factory, even though the mission was sure to result in terrible losses among bomber crews. Another Eighth Air Force story was *Twelve O'Clock High* from 1948. Written by Beirne Lay, Jr., and Sy Bartlett, the novel focused on the emotional toll of strategic bombing. Perhaps the most enduring of the immediate postwar air force novels was James Gould Cozzens's 1948 *Guard of Honor,* which concerned relationships among commanders and subordinates, with particular emphasis on racial tensions. The novel was awarded the Pulitzer Prize. The 1959 novel *The War Lover,* by John Hersey, author of the powerful documentary *Hiroshima,* was a best-selling antiwar treatment, again depicting the world of the Eighth Air Force.

The 1950s saw several important KOREAN WAR novels, including *Don't Touch Me* (1951) by MacKinlay Kantor and *MiG Alley* (1959) by Robert Eunson. But the decade also introduced novels speculating about war in the future—thermonuclear war. Peter Bryant's 1958 *Red Alert* was the first significant contribution to this genre, and the next decade saw the chilling *Fail-Safe* (1962), an imagination of a computer glitch that unleashes a thermonuclear catastrophe.

The general antiwar feeling of the 1960s produced several notable novels satirically hostile to the air arm, including Joseph Heller's *Catch-22* (1961), which was subsequently made into a motion picture, and *Dr. Strangelove, or How I Learned to Stop Worrying and Love the Bomb,* which, in 1964, was adapted into novel form *from* the Stanley Kubrick motion picture screenplay. The VIETNAM WAR gave rise to *Sweet Vietnam* (1984), by Richard Parque, and an important semi-documentary series by Cat Branigan, *Wings over Nam, The Wild Weasels, Linebacker,* and *Bird Dog,* all published between 1989 and 1990.

Little Rock AFB, Arkansas   See AIR FORCE BASES.

Los Angeles AFB, California   See AIR FORCE BASES.

Love, Nancy Harkness (1914–1976) *Aviator*
A prominent female aviator in the 1930s, Nancy Harkness Love successfully proposed the use of women as ferry pilots for the U.S. ARMY AIR FORCES and became director of the WOMEN'S AUXILIARY FERRYING SQUADRON (WAFS). Unlike JACQUELINE COCHRAN, whose similar proposal ultimately resulted in the creation of the WOMEN AIRFORCE SERVICE PILOTS (WASP), Love did not advocate training women pilots, but, rather, recruiting already highly qualified female commercial aviators.

Love came to flying early, earning her license at age 16 and working as an activist in the creation of student flying clubs. She earned her transport license at age 18 and her commercial license a year later, in 1933. With her husband, Robert Maclure Love, she operated Inter City Aviation and often personally delivered planes to customers. Love was a TEST PILOT in the later 1930s and was instrumental in the development of tricycle landing gear, which proved essential for medium and heavy bombers.

Love not only directed the WAFS, she personally flew ferrying missions and was the first woman in U.S. military aviation to fly a bomber, a B-25, taking it from the West Coast to the East Coast in record time. She was the recipient of the Air Medal.

Luke AFB, Arizona   See AIR FORCE BASES.

M

MAJCOM   See ORGANIZATION, USAF.

major   See RANKS AND GRADES.

major general   See RANKS AND GRADES.

Malmstrom AFB, Montana   See AIR FORCE BASES.

master sergeant   See RANKS AND GRADES.

Maxwell AFB, Alabama   See AIR FORCE BASES.

Maxwell AFB, Gunter Annex, Alabama
See AIR FORCE BASES.

McChord AFB, Washington   See AIR FORCE BASES.

McClellan AFB, California   See AIR FORCE BASES.

McConnell AFB, Kansas   See AIR FORCE BASES.

McGuire AFB, New Jersey   See AIR FORCE BASES.

Medal for Humane Action   See DECORATIONS AND MEDALS.

Medal of Honor   See DECORATIONS AND MEDALS.

Military Airlift Command (MAC)

MAC was absorbed, with the STRATEGIC AIR COMMAND (SAC), into the AIR MOBILITY COMMAND (AMC) in June 1992. Before this, it was a MAJCOM in its own right, responsible for USAF AIRLIFT operations. MAC was headquartered at Scott AFB, which is now home to the AMC.

MAC's first predecessor organization was the Air Corps Ferrying Command (ACFC), created in May 1941, and the AIR TRANSPORT COMMAND (ATC), activated in July 1942. In 1948, ATC was redesignated the MILITARY AIR TRANSPORT SERVICE (MATS), which, in turn, became MAC in 1966. Up to 1974, MAC was responsible for strategic airlift; in 1974, it was also assigned a tactical airlift role.

Military Air Transport Service (MATS)
MATS was created in June 1948 when the AIR TRANSPORT COMMAND (ATC) was redesignated. The ATC had been created from Air Corps Ferrying Command in July 1942. The greatest test of MATS was the BERLIN AIRLIFT, beginning in 1948. MATS was redesignated the MILITARY AIRLIFT COMMAND (MAC) in 1966. In turn, MAC was absorbed (with the STRATEGIC AIR COMMAND [SAC]) into the AIR MOBILITY COMMAND (AMC) in June 1992.

Minot AFB, North Dakota   See AIR FORCE
BASES.

Misawa AB, Japan   See AIR FORCE BASES.

missiles, strategic
The USAF is an aerospace force, with an arsenal that includes manned aircraft as well as unmanned missiles. Strategic missiles are those designed to carry nuclear and thermonuclear warheads. A missile capable of intercontinental range is an ICBM (INTERCONTINENTAL BALLISTIC MISSILE), while a missile of shorter, but still strategic, range is an IRBM (INTERMEDIATE-RANGE BALLISTIC MISSILE).

Navaho: This early USAF missile project was inspired by the German V-1 and V-2 rockets of WORLD WAR II. The Navaho was to combine the CRUISE MISSILE characteristics of the V-1 with the ballistic missile characteristics of the V-2, principally by adding wings to what was essentially a V-2 body and combining a ramjet with a booster engine. The object was to give a cruise missile intercontinental range.

North American Aviation produced the Navaho prototype, which first flew in 1956—unsuccessfully. After 11 more attempts, the missile did fly in 1957, but the program was cancelled before any Navahos went into production. Had it reached production, the Navaho was intended to achieve a 5,500-mile range carrying a 7,000-pound warhead.

Jupiter: The Jupiter was designed in the 1950s as an IRBM not by the USAF but by the Army Ballistic Missile Agency (ABMA); it was designated SM-78. Late in 1955, Secretary of Defense Charles E. Wilson directed the ABMA to work in conjunction with the U.S. Navy to develop both a land-based and a sea-based version of the Jupiter, but in 1956, Wilson transferred to USAF control all missiles with a range of over 200 miles. In fact, the Jupiter became something of an orphan under USAF control because its development had competed with the USAF-developed Thor. Nevertheless, it would be the Jupiter that became the nation's first IRBM.

Jupiter was built by Chrysler, which began delivery to the USAF in 1957. The first test occurred on April 26 of that year. The missile was retired in 1964.

In addition to its role as a weapon, the Jupiter led to the development of the *Juno I* rocket, which launched America's first satellite into orbit. Approximately 60 feet long, the Jupiter had a range of 1,976 miles.

Thor (SM-75, PGM-17): Development of this IRBM began in November 1955, leading to an intense rivalry between USAF and U.S. Army missile programs. Douglas Aircraft completed design of the missile in July 1956 and delivery began in October. Fuel was liquid oxygen/RP-1 (kerosene), which produced 150,000 pounds of thrust at launch through two Rocketdyne vernier engines. However, the first four test launches, beginning on January 25, 1957, failed. It was 1959 before Thor was declared operational. Thor missiles served until 1965. The 65-foot-long Thor had a range of 1,976 miles.

Atlas: With a range 11,500 miles (Atlas E and F), the Atlas was the first U.S. ICBM. Built by General Dynamics, the missile was operational with the USAF from 1958 to 1965. The first three versions, A, B, and C, were test vehicles only; D, E, and F were the operational models.

The Atlas pioneered a unique, two-booster propulsion system and a super-thin, frameless propellant tank. Fuel was a mixture of RP-1 (kerosene) and liquid oxygen. In addition to its role as a nuclear weapons platform, the Atlas launched the first American astronauts into orbit, beginning with John Glenn.

Titan: In 1955 a decision was made to develop a successor to the Atlas ICBM. The two major improvements desired were a two-stage propulsion system and a self-stabilized light alloy frame that would not need to be pressurized to remain rigid. The missile also used a pure inertial guidance system and was designed to be housed in underground silos exclusively. Built by Martin Marietta, the result was the biggest (98 feet long) ICBM in the USAF inventory, capable of a range of 8,000 miles.

The first test launch was made on February 6, 1959, and the missile became operational at Lowry AFB, Colorado, on April 18, 1962. The Titan I fleet was deactivated by 1966 and replaced by the Titan II. Unlike the Titan I, which was stored in an underground silo but lifted out for launch, the Titan II was launched directly from the silo. It used a new fuel, hydrazine and unsymmetrical dimetheylhydrazine plus nitrogen tetroxide, which significantly increased thrust. The Titan II could deliver a 10-megaton thermonuclear warhead over 9,300 miles.

Skybolt: Designated GAM-87A, the Skybolt was an air-launched ballistic missile, designed to be carried by B-52H bombers. Douglas Aircraft began design in 1959, and the first launch came in 1961. Although the missile was successful, the Skybolt program was cancelled in December 1962 before full production began. The missile had a range of 1,000 miles.

Snark (SM-62): The Snark was designed as a ground-launched intercontinental cruise missile. North American began design in 1946, basing the missile on a German World War II prototype, the A-10, which had never entered production. The first flight came in 1951, but, because of multiple test failures, the Snark did not enter service until 1961. It was retired before the end of the year, 30 having been built. The idea of an intercontinental cruise missile was replaced by reliance on the ICBM for long-range delivery of nuclear weapons.

Snark was subsonic, with a top speed of 524 mph and a range of 6,000 miles.

Minuteman: The Minuteman was the world's first solid-fuel ICBM, and, in its LGM-30G Minuteman III configuration, it remains a key element of the U.S. strategic deterrent forces. The Minuteman was designed by Boeing beginning in the late 1950s, and the first Minuteman I was launched on February 1, 1961. The solid-fuel Minuteman reacts much more quickly than earlier liquid-fuel missiles, making it more survivable in a thermonuclear exchange. At its peak, about 1,000 Minuteman missiles were deployed; today's inventory consists of 500 Minuteman III's located at Warren AFB, Malmstrom AFB, and Minot AFB.

The Minuteman III has three solid-propellant rocket motors and is capable of flying more than 6,000 miles at about 15,000 mph (Mach 23). Ceiling is 700 miles. Production ended in December 1978.

Peacekeeper (MX): Development of this four-stage ICBM began in 1972 and was designated "ICBM Missile-X," or "MX," a name that stuck. The principal purpose of the missile was as a counterforce hard-target weapon: a missile to kill enemy missile silos. A MIRV (multiple independent reentry vehicle) weapon, the MX was designed to carry 10 independently targeted thermonuclear warheads. First flight came in 1983, and, after much controversy over how and where the MX would be based, the missiles were deployed in converted Minuteman silos at Warren AFB in October 1986. By December 1988, all 50 MX missiles in the USAF inventory had been deployed. Range is nearly 7,000 miles at a velocity of 15,000 mph (Mach 23) and a ceiling of 500 miles. Under the terms of the START II arms-reduction treaty, the Peacekeeper missile was slated for retirement, but renegotiation of the weapons-reduction agreement modified this goal to reduction rather than elimination.

AGM-86B Air-Launched Cruise Missile (ALCM): Boeing's ALCM is equipped with a nuclear warhead and can be launched from the B-52 or the

B-1B. Between 1980 and 1986, 1,715 were produced. Speed is 550 mph, range 1,500 miles.

missiles, tactical

Tactical missiles are of relatively short-range—compared with IRBM (INTERMEDIATE-RANGE BALLISTIC MISSILE) and ICBM (INTERCONTINENTAL BALLISTIC MISSILE) weapons—and carry conventional (nonnuclear) warheads or relatively low-yield (tactical) nuclear warheads. Weapons of this type may be launched from aircraft against other aircraft (air-to-air), from aircraft to surface targets (air-to-surface), from the surface to air (surface-to-air), or from the surface to surface (surface-to-surface).

Air Decoy Missile (ADM) and Air-Ground Missiles (AGM)

ADM-20 Quail: This Air Decoy Missile was built by McDonnell, first flew in 1958, and entered service in 1960. Designed to be launched from the B-52, the Quail was intended to decoy enemy radar by mimicking the actions of the B-52. It had no warhead. The missile was retired in 1978.

AGM-12 Bullpup: Martin Marietta's Bullpup entered service in 1959 as an air-to-surface guided missile capable of delivering a conventional or nuclear warhead or a special antipersonnel warhead. During the Vietnam era, it was replaced by the AGM-6 Maverick. Speed was Mach 1.8, range 10 miles.

AGM-28 Hound Dog: This early CRUISE MISSILE was built by North American Aviation and was designed to be launched from a B-52; two Hound Dogs could be carried under the bomber's wings. The Hound Dog's engines were used to assist B-52 takeoff, thereby compensating for its own weight. The missile entered service in 1960 and was retired in 1976. It reached Mach 2.1 and had a 700-mile range.

AGM-45 Shrike: Designed and built by the Naval Weapons Center, the Shrike was an early antiradar or antiradiation missile, designed to passively home in on enemy radar. The AGM-45 was used by the USAF in the VIETNAM WAR, launched from F-105G Wild Weasels. Production stopped in 1978, by which time some 12,000 had been received into the USAF inventory. It is still in use by the USAF and the U.S. Marine Corps. Range is about 25 miles.

AGM-65 Maverick: This air-to-surface missile is extensively used by the USAF and allied air forces. Developed by Hughes Missiles Systems Group in the 1970s (first delivered in 1972), it is expected to be in use well into the 21st century. The "D" version of the missile is especially designed to work with the LANTIRN (Low-Altitude Navigation and Targeting Infrared Night) sight used on the F-16. The "G" version uses infrared and improved flight controls. Both the D and G versions are still in production. Range is about 14 miles.

AGM-69 Short-Range Attack Missile (SRAM): Boeing's air-to-surface SRAM was produced from 1971 to 1975 and acquired in a quantity of about 1,500. Designed to be launched from B-52s and other bombers, the AGM-69 strikes SAM (surface-to-air missile) sites and other ground targets. Speed is Mach 2.5; range from high altitude is 100 miles, from low altitude, 35 miles.

AGM-78 Standard Antiradiation Missile (Standard ARM): Built by General Dynamics, the missile went into production in 1968 and was intended, like the AGM-45 Shrike, as an antiradar or antiradiation air-to-surface missile. The missile was not produced in large numbers and was retired in 1986. Top speed was Mach 2; range was 15 miles.

AGM-84A-1 Harpoon: This antiship missile, made by McDonnell Douglas, was designed for the U.S. Navy, but it was also adopted by the USAF in the mid 1980s. It can be launched from ships, submarines, or aircraft—although the only USAF aircraft equipped to carry it is the B-52. With a high subsonic speed, it has a range of nearly 60 miles.

AGM-88A High-Speed Antiradiation Missile (HARM): This Texas Instruments HARM missile homes in on enemy radar and destroys it. It was first deployed in 1986 against Libya. Top speed is Mach 2, and range is over 10 miles.

AGM-129A Advanced Cruise Missile (ACM): Built by General Dynamics, the AGM-129 was developed from the AGM-109 Tomahawk and is intended to deliver a conventional or tactical nuclear (200-kiloton) warhead. The missile incorporates advanced stealth technology, so that it is virtually impossible to detect by radar or other means. Range is 1,550 miles and propulsion is by a turbofan jet.

AGM-131A Short-Range Attack Missile (SRAM II): The Boeing SRAM II replaces the AGM-69 and is designed to be carried in rotary launchers on B-52, B-1, and B-2 bombers. The ground-attack missile incorporates stealth and a laser inertial guidance system.

AGM-136A Tacit Rainbow: The Northrup Ventura AGM-136A was designed in the early 1980s as a jet-powered drone for finding and destroying enemy ground-based radars. The vehicle was intended for low-cost production, so that it could be used in great numbers—"swarms"—against dense enemy air defense networks. Once launched, the missile traveled to the target area, then "loitered" until it sensed enemy radar transmission. This triggered attack.

The first Tacit Rainbow was test launched on July 30, 1984, but the missile failed to reach production before the program was cancelled for budget reasons in 1991. Speed was subsonic and range was in excess of 50 miles.

AGM-142A Have Nap: The Have Nap is a USAF version of the Israeli-made air-to-surface Popeye guided missile and was acquired in 1988. The missile is guided by television and is launched and guided from the B-52. Range is 50 miles.

Air Interceptor Missiles (AIM)

AIM-4 Falcon and Super Falcon: The Falcon was the world's first air-launched guided (SARH, semiactive radar homing) missile. Built by Hughes, it became operational in 1956 and was launched from F-89 and F-102 aircraft. The Super Falcon improved range and accuracy. The Super Falcon was not retired until 1988. Top speed was Mach 2.5 over a range of seven miles.

AIM-7 Sparrow: The AIM-7 is used by the U.S. Navy, the USAF, and NATO forces. Made by Raytheon, it is radar-guided and, in its earliest version, was developed in the 1950s. The AIM-7M is the latest version and is widely used. Most of its specifications are classified.

AIM-9 Sidewinder: The Sidewinder is the most successful air-to-air missile in the USAF inventory

An F-16C Fight Falcon fires an AIM-9M Sidewinder heat-seeking missile. *(U.S. Air Force)*

and is the most important air-to-air missile ever made. Production has approached 200,000 units, and it is used by all the U.S. services as well as by many foreign countries. It was developed by General Dynamics in the early 1950s, first flew in 1953, and entered USAF service in 1956. It is supersonic and heat seeking. The current version is the AIM-9M, and, despite the age of the basic design, it is expected to serve well into the 21st century. Top speed is in excess of Mach 2, with a range of more than 10 miles.

AIM-120 Advanced Medium-Range Air-to-Air Missile (AMRAAM): Faster, smaller and lighter than the AIM-7 Sidewinder, and with improved capabilities against low-altitude targets, the AIM-120 is intended as a follow-on replacement for the AIM-7. With all-weather, beyond-visual-range capability, the missile can be carried by the F-15, F-16, and F-22 fighters. It uses active radar with an inertial reference unit and micro-computer system, so that, once the missile closes on a target, its active radar guides it to intercept. This gives the pilot the ability to aim and fire several missiles simultaneously at multiple targets. While the missiles guide themselves to their targets, the pilot can perform any necessary evasive maneuvers.

Hughes Aircraft and Raytheon developed the missile, which began production in 1987 and was deployed beginning in 1991. It was used in Operation Southern Watch and in Bosnia. Speed is supersonic.

Air-Intercept Rocket (AIR)

Air-2A Genie: This air-intercept rocket was developed by Douglas Aircraft in 1955 to be launched from the F-106. It was mated with a small nuclear warhead. The rocket can best be described as a semi-guided weapon: the system acquired a target, computed a launch point and flight time, programmed a timer within the missile, alerted the pilot to arm the warhead, then fired the missile at the correct time. The Genie went out of service with the F-106, which was retired in 1988. Speed was Mach 3 and range six miles.

Other Tactical Missiles

BGM-109G Gryphon Ground-Launched Cruise Missile (GLCM): This small cruise missile, built by General Dynamics, carried a 200-kiloton tactical nuclear warhead. It was designed to be launched from a mobile launcher and was capable of great accuracy, flying at low altitudes and high subsonic speeds. The first GLCMs were deployed as part of the NATO defense of Europe beginning in 1983. This deployment was highly controversial and was instrumental in bringing about the Intermediate Nuclear Forces (INF) Treaty between the United States and the USSR—the first nuclear forces reduction in history. Under the terms of the 1988 treaty, all USAF GLCMs were eliminated. Speed was about 500 mph and range 1,500 miles.

GBU-15: Built by Rockwell International, the GBU-15 is a Guided Bomb Unit used to convert an Mk-84 bomb into a guided weapon.

IM-99 BOMARC: Produced in the late 1950s, this "interceptor missile" was the product of design research carried out by Boeing Airplane Company and the University of Michigan's Aeronautical Research Center—hence, the name BOMARC. It was a ground-launched interceptor and figured as an important element in the defense of the continental United States. The missile was retired during the early 1970s. Top speed exceeded Mach 2, ceiling was 80,000 feet, and range over 400 miles—all of which made the BOMARC effective against incoming bombers.

JB-2 Loon: An early step in the USAF cruise missile program, the JB-2 was a copy of the World War II German V-1 buzz bomb and began development, under the U.S. ARMY AIR FORCES, in 1944. Willys-Overland, the jeep manufacturer, was awarded a contract for 50,000 JB-2s, but none reached production before the end of the war. Most of the planned production was cancelled, and those produced were used as target drones (designated KUW-1).

TM-61 Matador and Mace: This air-breathing, turbojet-propelled cruise missile was designed by the Glenn L. Martin Company in 1945, The first flight (unsuccessful) came in 1949, and the missiles were deployed to Europe during 1955–62. The original Matador guidance system was subject to jamming, and the missile had a very limited range of 250 miles. The TM-61B Mace, introduced in 1954, substantially improved the guidance system and greatly extended range to 1,288 miles at high altitude (ceiling, 42,000 feet). Top speed for the Mace was Mach 0.85. The Mace was deployed in Europe from 1959 to 1966 and in Okinawa from 1961 to 1969.

Mitchell, William ("Billy") (1879–1936)

U.S. Army general and military aviation advocate

Mitchell was born, in Nice, France, to John Lendrum Mitchell, who later became U.S. senator from Wisconsin. Young Mitchell was raised in Milwaukee and educated at Racine University and Columbian (later George Washington) University, then enlisted in the 1st Wisconsin Infantry at the outbreak of the Spanish-American War in 1898. He fought in Cuba, rising to lieutenant of volunteers and was subsequently commissioned a lieutenant in the regular army. Assigned to the Signal Corps, he attended the Army Staff College at Fort Leavenworth, Kansas, from 1907 to 1909, then served for a short time on the Mexican border before securing an assignment to the General Staff in 1912. Three years later, Mitchell resigned the coveted staff post to join the AVIATION SECTION, U.S. ARMY SIGNAL CORPS. Enrolling in flight school at Newport News, Virginia, he earned his wings in 1916 and was immediately sent to Europe as an observer. In April 1917, with U.S. entry into WORLD WAR I, Mitchell was appointed air officer of the American Expeditionary Force (AEF) and promoted to lieutenant colonel in June. In May 1918, he became air officer of I Corps with the rank of colonel and was the first U.S. officer to fly over enemy lines.

Mitchell's principal command was large-scale bombing. In September 1918 he led a successful Franco-American bombing mission consisting of 1,500 aircraft—the greatest number of planes ever massed to that time—against the Saint-Mihiel

Billy Mitchell   *(U.S. Air Force)*

salient. The mission demonstrated the utility of air support of ground action. Appointed next to command the combined Franco-American air services for the Meuse-Argonne offensive and promoted to brigadier general, Mitchell led another massive formation against targets behind enemy lines on October 9.

After the armistice, Mitchell was named assistant chief of the U.S. ARMY AIR SERVICE in 1919, and he embarked on an intensely heated and controversial campaign to create a separate and independent air force. Beyond this, Mitchell was also a vocal advocate of unified control of military air power. Even more than his call for an independent air arm, his advocacy of unified control put him at odds with the military establishment. Of a confrontational disposition, Mitchell tweaked navy officials by boasting that the airplane had rendered the battleship obsolete. He purported to demonstrate this by bombing the captured German dreadnought *Ostfriesland* and sinking it in 21 1/2 minutes in 1921. To the credit of the navy, officials responded to the demonstration by conducting further tests, which initiated the navy's development of the aircraft carrier as an offensive weapon.

In the meantime, Mitchell continued a relentless campaign for enlargement of the present USAAS and the eventual creation of an independent air force. Frustrated superiors attempted to discourage and block Mitchell by demoting him to colonel and reducing his command responsibility to an assignment as air officer of the VIII Corps area in San Antonio, Texas (in April 1925). With single-minded dedication, however, he refused to back down. On the contrary, he fanned the flames of controversy by appealing directly to the press.

When the navy dirigible *Shenandoah* crashed in a thunderstorm on September 3, 1925, Mitchell went to the papers with accusations of War and Navy Department "incompetency, criminal negligence, and almost treasonable administration of the National Defense." This "betrayal" proved to be the last straw. Mitchell was court-martialed and, in a highly publicized trial, was convicted of insubordination in December 1925. Sentenced to five years' suspension from duty without pay, Mitchell decided to resign his commission, effective February 1, 1926. A private citizen, he continued to speak out on air power from his Middleburg, Virginia, home.

As an advocate and strategist in the field of military air power, Billy Mitchell was clearly ahead of his time. WORLD WAR II, which Mitchell did not live to see, proved most of his theories true, including his remarkable (and much derided) assessment, made in the 1920s, that the navy's fleet at Pearl Harbor in the Hawaiian Islands was vulnerable to a carrier-launched air attack and that the attack would be made by Japan.

Working against Mitchell was his almost deliberately caustic and provocative manner, and it was not until after his death that his positions were largely vindicated. He was—posthumously—recognized as one of the founding fathers of U.S. air

power in general and the USAF in particular. His memory was honored in World War II when the twin-engine B-25 bomber, one of the ablest aircraft of the conflict, was named for him: the Mitchell bomber.

Moody AFB, Georgia   See AIR FORCE BASES.

Mountain Home AFB, Idaho   See AIR FORCE BASES.

museums, USAF

The principal USAF museum is the UNITED STATES AIR FORCE MUSEUM at Wright-Patterson AFB, the oldest and largest aviation museum in the world, established in 1923 (and given its current name in 1956). More than 300 aircraft are on display at the museum, which is dedicated to the history of flight in general and military aviation in particular.

Other USAF museums include:

- Davis-Monthan AFB Museum, Davis-Monthan AFB, Arizona
- AF Flight Test Center Museum, Edwards AFB, California
- Castle AFB Museum, Castle AFB, California
- 475 Fighter Group Museum, March AFB, California
- Travis AFB Museum, Travis AFB, California
- Air Force Academy Visitors Center, UNITED STATES AIR FORCE ACADEMY, Colorado
- Peterson AFB Museum, Peterson AFB, Colorado
- Air Mobility Command Museum, Dover AFB, Delaware
- USAF Armament Museum, Eglin AFB, Florida
- Museum of Aviation, Warner Robins AFB, Georgia
- Reflections of Freedom Air Park, McConnell AFB, Kansas
- Eighth Air Force Museum, Barksdale AFB, Louisiana

- Sawyer AFB Museum, Sawyer AFB, Michigan
- National Aviation Hall of Fame, Wright-Patterson AFB, Ohio
- Museum of Aerospace Medicine, Brooks AFB, Texas
- Hill AFB Museum, Hill AFB, Utah

In addition to museums administered by the USAF, many aviation museums located throughout the United States are run by civilian organizations or by other military services. Many of these include material relevant to the history and present operations of the USAF.

mustang

Slang term for a noncommissioned officer with prior enlisted service.

N

named air forces **named air forces**   See ORGANIZATION, USAF.

National Security Act of 1947

The National Security Act reorganized the Department of Defense, providing for unification of the armed forces, and created the USAF as an independent service. The law went into effect as Public Law 253, on July 26, 1947, the same day that President Harry S. Truman signed EXECUTIVE ORDER 9877, which addressed the administrative details and missions of the unified armed forces and the newly created USAF. Pursuant to the act, the USAF came into existence on September 18, 1947.

The National Security Act and the executive order provided for a single secretary of defense; the Department of the Army, the Department of the Navy, and the Department of the Air Force; the creation of a National Security Council, a National Security Resources Board, the Joint Chiefs of Staff, a Research and Development Board, a Munitions Board, and the Central Intelligence Agency, in addition to the creation of the USAF.

Nellis AFB, Nevada   See AIR FORCE BASES.

Newark AFB, Ohio   See AIR FORCE BASES.

"New Look" Air Force

The "New Look" was a term applied to all of the armed services pursuant to a reevaluation of the role of the military during the administration of President Dwight David Eisenhower in the 1950s. The "New Look" Air Force emphasized strategic (i.e., nuclear) operations and, as such, fostered development of a strategic bomber (the B-52) and an array of ICBM (INTERCONTINENTAL BALLISTIC MISSILE) weapons. General Nathan F. Twining, fourth CHIEF OF STAFF, USAF, from 1953 to 1957, oversaw the introduction and early development of the New Look.

Nineteenth Air Force (19AF)

Formed in 1955 at Foster AFB, Texas, the 19AF was a subcommand of the TACTICAL AIR COMMAND (TAC). In 1958, 19AF headquarters moved to Seymour Johnson AFB. The unit was inactivated in 1973. 19AF was intended as a mobile task force headquarters for the Composite Strike Force, a special force combining the services for response to crises. In addition, 19AF conducted joint field training with the U.S. Army.

Ninth Air Force (9AF)

This unit was formed during WORLD WAR II, in November 1942, from what had been designated as the Middle East Air Force. The 9AF operated B-17 and B-24 bomber aircraft and P-40 fighter escorts. Later, F-47s and P-38s were added. Until it moved to England late in 1943, the 9AF supported Allied actions in North Africa and then Sicily. The unit played a major role in supporting the Normandy invasion ("D-day") during 1944 and was instrumental in supporting the spectacular breakout and advance of George S. Patton's Third Army. At the time of its inactivation in December 1945, 9AF was the largest tactical air force in the world.

In March 1946, 9AF was reactivated and has since served as a tactical unit. Today the 9AF is part of CENTAF and is headquartered at Shaw AFB, South Carolina. The unit is responsible for six active-duty flying wings and for overseeing the operational readiness of 30 designated units of the AIR NATIONAL GUARD and AIR FORCE RESERVE. The primary mission of today's 9AF is to project decisive air and space power for United States Central Command and America; 9AF has the dual role of serving also as the headquarters for U.S. Central Command Air Forces to conduct U.S. air operations throughout Southwest Asia.

North American Aerospace Defense Command (NORAD)

NORAD—the North American Aerospace Defense Command—is a binational U.S. and Canadian military organization charged with the missions of aerospace warning and aerospace control for North America. The aerospace warning mission includes monitoring artificial objects in space as well as the detection, validation, and warning of attack against North America by aircraft, missiles, or space vehicles. The aerospace control mission includes surveillance and control of the airspace of Canada and the United States.

NORAD is under command of a commander in chief (CINC) appointed by both the president of the United States and the prime minister of Canada. The CINC maintains headquarters at Peterson AFB, Colorado, with a command and control center nearby at Cheyenne Mountain Air Station. It is Cheyenne Mountain that serves as the central collection and coordination facility for a worldwide system of sensors that provide an accurate picture of any aerospace threat. In addition, three subordinate regional headquarters at Elmendorf AFB, Alaska (Alaska NORAD Region, ANR), Canadian Forces Base Winnipeg, Manitoba (Canadian NORAD Region, CANR), and Tyndall AFB, Florida (Continental U.S. NORAD Region, CONR) control air operations within their geographical areas of responsibility.

NORAD provides to the governments of Canada and the United States integrated tactical warning and attack assessment of an aerospace attack on North America. NORAD's aerospace control mission includes detecting and responding to any air-breathing threat to North America. NORAD uses a network of ground-based radars and fighter aircraft to detect, intercept, and engage any air-breathing threat to the continent. NORAD also assists civilian agencies in the detection and monitoring of aircraft suspected of illegal drug trafficking.

NORAD was activated on September 12, 1957, and superceded earlier U.S.-Canadian binational defense and early warning programs known as the Pinetree Line (a network of radar stations), followed in 1957 by the Mid-Canada Line and the DEW Line, or distant early warning system.

Northeast Air Command (NEAC)

NEAC was established as a MAJCOM in 1950 as a means of monitoring and intercepting Soviet transpolar air attacks on the United States. The predecessor organization was the Newfoundland Base Command, which started operations in WORLD WAR II. NEAC worked in cooperation with Canada and Denmark and operated Thule AFB in Greenland. In 1957, NEAC was inactivated, its mission and resources divided between the AIR DEFENSE COMMAND (ADC) and the STRATEGIC AIR COMMAND (SAC).

numbered air forces (NAFS)   See ORGANIZATION, USAF.

O

Offutt AFB, Nebraska   See Air Force bases.

organization, USAF

The Department of the Air Force was created when President Harry S. Truman signed the National Security Act of 1947, which became effective on September 18, 1947, after Chief Justice Fred M. Vinson administered the oath of office to the first secretary of the Air Force, W. Stuart Symington. The National Security Act transferred the functions assigned to the U.S. Army Air Forces' commanding general to the Department of the Air Force over a two-year transfer period. Later, pursuant to the Department of Defense Reorganization Act of 1958, the departments of Army, Navy, and Air Force were eliminated from the chain of operational command, and commanders of unified and specified commands became responsible to the president and the secretary of defense through the Joint Chiefs of Staff.

The mission of the air force is to defend the United States and protect its interests through aerospace power. The Department of the Air Force incorporates all elements of the air force. It is administered by a civilian secretary appointed by the president and is supervised by a military Chief of Staff, USAF. The Secretariat and Air Staff help the secretary and the Chief of Staff direct the air force mission.

The secretary of the Air Force has authority to conduct all affairs of the Department of the Air Force, including training, operations, administration, logistical support and maintenance, and welfare of personnel. The secretary's responsibilities include research and development, as well as any other activity prescribed by the president or the secretary of defense. The secretary of the Air Force exercises authority through civilian assistants and the Chief of Staff but retains immediate supervision of activities that involve vital relationships with Congress, the secretary of defense, other governmental officials, and the public. Principal civilian assistants within the Secretariat are:

- Under Secretary of the Air Force
- Deputy Under Secretary for International Affairs
- Assistant Secretary for Acquisition
- Assistant Secretary for Space
- Assistant Secretary for Manpower, Reserve Affairs, Installations, and Environment
- Assistant Secretary for Financial Management

The Office of the Secretary of the Air Force includes a general counsel, auditor general, inspector general, administrative assistant, public affairs director, legislative liaison director, small and disadvantaged business utilization director, and certain statutory boards and committees.

The Chief of Staff, USAF, is appointed by the president, with the advice and consent of the Senate, from among air force general officers, normally for a four-year term. The Chief of Staff serves as a member of the Joint Chiefs of Staff and the Armed Forces Policy Council. As a member of the Joint Chiefs, the chief serves as a military adviser to the president, the National Security Council, and the secretary of defense, as well as to the secretary of the Air Force. The Chief of Staff presides over the Air Staff, transmits Air Staff plans and recommendations to the secretary of the Air Force, and acts as the secretary's agent in carrying them out. The chief is responsible for the efficiency of the USAF and the preparation of its forces for military operations. The chief supervises the administration of personnel and supervises support of forces as directed by the secretary of defense. In addition, the chief has responsibility for activities assigned to the air force by the secretary of defense.

Other members of the Air Staff include:

- Vice Chief of Staff
- Assistant Vice Chief of Staff
- CHIEF MASTER SERGEANT OF THE AIR FORCE
- Deputy Chief of Staff for Personnel
- Deputy Chief of Staff for Plans and Programs
- Deputy Chief of Staff for Air and Space Operations
- Deputy Chief of Staff for Installations and Logistics
- Air Force Historian
- Chief Scientist
- Chief of the AIR FORCE RESERVE
- Chief of the National Guard Bureau
- U.S. AIR FORCE SCIENTIFIC ADVISORY BOARD
- Judge Advocate General
- Director of Test and Evaluation
- Surgeon General
- Chief of Chaplain Service

Air Force Field Organization

Eight MAJCOMS (major commands), 35 field operating agencies, four direct reporting units, and their subordinate elements constitute the air force field organization. Additionally, there are two reserve components, the AIR FORCE RESERVE, which is also a MAJCOM, and the AIR NATIONAL GUARD.

MAJCOM (Major Command)

MAJCOMs, or major commands, are organizations that group similar functions together and provide a command level intermediate between base-level operations and HEADQUARTERS AIR FORCE (HAF). The MAJCOMs are organized by function and, in overseas areas, by geographical location. They perform either operational or support missions. Since major restructuring in 1991, the USAF currently has eight MAJCOMs, each of which is treated in a separate entry:

- AIR COMBAT COMMAND (ACC)
- AIR MOBILITY COMMAND (AMC)
- AIR FORCE SPACE COMMAND (AFSPC)
- PACIFIC AIR FORCES (PACAF)
- UNITED STATES AIR FORCES IN EUROPE (USAFE)
- AIR EDUCATION AND TRAINING COMMAND (AETC)
- AIR FORCE MATERIEL COMMAND (AFMC)
- AIR FORCE SPECIAL OPERATIONS COMMAND (AFSOC)

In descending order of command, elements of major commands include numbered air forces, wings, groups, squadrons, and flights.

Air Force

Until the air force underwent a major organizational restructuring in 1993, "air forces" were organizational units that equated to an "army" in the U.S. Army. They were subordinate to operational and support commands, but superior to a division. There have been numbered air forces and named air forces—as many as 23 numbered air forces and 13 named air forces. After 1993, only the numbered air forces (NAFs) were retained, and these were restructured for strictly warfighting and operational roles; all support functions were allocated elsewhere. Today, an NAF is typically commanded by a major general or lieutenant general, and its staff (about half the pre-1993 strength) is dedicated to operational planning and employment of forces for several wings within the NAF.

In the U.S. ARMY AIR FORCES, before the air force became an independent service arm (in

1947), the NAFS were the equivalent of today's MAJCOMs.

Named Air Forces
Formerly, air force organizational units consisted of numbered air forces and named air forces. The named air forces have been phased out, and only the numbered air forces continue to be used.

Numbered Air Forces (NAFs)
After restructuring of USAF organization during 1991–93, numbered air forces (NAFs) became strictly operational and warfighting units, without support functions. Two or more wings are typically grouped with auxiliary units to form a NAF, usually commanded by a major general or lieutenant general. There have been 23 numbered air forces.

Wing
The basic unit for generating and employing combat capability is the wing, the air force's principal war-fighting instrument. Composite wings operate more than one kind of aircraft, and they may be configured as self-contained units designated for quick air intervention anywhere in the world. Other wings continue to operate a single aircraft type, ready to join air campaigns anywhere they are needed. Air base and specialized mission wings—such as training, intelligence, and testing—also support the air force mission.

Group
A group is an organizational unit intermediate between a wing and a squadron. Typically, groups are identified with up to three Arabic digits, although a few specialized-mission groups are named for their mission and do not have a number. Groups under a wing carry the number of the wing followed by the group's task—for example, the unit responsible for maintenance functions within the 28th Bomb Wing may be designated the 28th Maintenance Group.

In the U.S. ARMY AIR FORCES, the distinction between group and wing was blurred, and a USAAF group was approximately equivalent to a USAAF wing.

Squadron
The squadron is subordinate to a group and superior to a flight. With the single exception of the USAF Demonstration Squadron (the THUNDERBIRDS), air force squadrons are numbered (using Arabic numerals).

Flight
A flight is an operational flying unit generally consisting of four aircraft. The unit is typically used in fighter operations, in which it is composed of two two-airplane subunits, or elements.

The flight was extensively used as an operational unit during WORLD WAR II (it had been developed by German combat aviators in the 1930s during the Spanish Civil War) and well into the KOREAN WAR. In more recent years, by the late 1980s, faster, more maneuverable fighters called for a more flexible unit than the flight, and today the basic air force combat unit for fighters is the element.

Two alternative senses of *flight* are as a subordinate administrative unit of a squadron and as a term applied to certain units used in parades and ceremonies.

Element
An informal subunit, the element is able to operate by itself and, traditionally, has consisted of half a fighter flight—that is, two aircraft in formation, a

An F-15E pilot checks his wingman   *(U.S. Air Force)*

leader, and a wingman (follower). The element is a tactical team, in which the leader is the attacker and the wingman the defender, who covers the attacker and warns him of any threats. Generally, the senior pilot serves as the element leader, and the less experienced or less qualified pilot as wingman.

Field Operating Agencies and Direct Reporting Units

Field operating agencies and direct reporting units are additional air force organizational subdivisions, which report directly to Headquarters Air Force (HAF). They are assigned a specialized mission, which, in contrast to the mission of a MAJCOM, is restricted in scope. Field operating agencies carry out field activities under the operational control of a HAF functional manager, whereas direct reporting units are not under the operational control of a HAF manager because of a unique mission, legal requirements, or other factors.

The USAF field operating agencies include:

- AIR FORCE AUDIT AGENCY
- AIR FORCE BASE CONVERSION AGENCY
- AIR FORCE CENTER FOR ENVIRONMENTAL EXCELLENCE
- AIR FORCE CIVIL ENGINEER SUPPORT AGENCY
- AIR FORCE COMMUNICATIONS COMMAND
- AIR FORCE COST ANALYSIS AGENCY
- AIR FORCE FLIGHT STANDARDS AGENCY
- AIR FORCE FREQUENCY MANAGEMENT AGENCY
- AIR FORCE HISTORICAL RESEARCH AGENCY
- AIR FORCE HISTORY SUPPORT OFFICE
- AIR FORCE INSPECTION AGENCY
- AIR FORCE LEGAL SERVICES AGENCY
- AIR FORCE LOGISTICS MANAGEMENT AGENCY
- AIR FORCE MANPOWER AND INNOVATION AGENCY

- AIR FORCE MEDICAL OPERATIONS AGENCY
- AIR FORCE MEDICAL SUPPORT AGENCY
- AIR FORCE NATIONAL SECURITY EMERGENCY PREPAREDNESS Office
- AIR FORCE NEWS AGENCY
- AIR FORCE NUCLEAR WEAPONS AND COUNTERPROLIFERATION AGENCY
- AIR FORCE OFFICE OF SPECIAL INVESTIGATIONS
- AIR FORCE OPERATIONS GROUP
- AIR FORCE PENTAGON COMMUNICATIONS AGENCY
- AIR FORCE PERSONNEL CENTER
- AIR FORCE PERSONNEL OPERATIONS AGENCY
- AIR FORCE REAL ESTATE AGENCY
- AIR FORCE REVIEW BOARDS AGENCY
- AIR FORCE SAFETY CENTER
- AIR FORCE SECURITY FORCES CENTER
- AIR FORCE SERVICES AGENCY
- AIR FORCE STUDIES AND ANALYSES AGENCY
- AIR FORCE TECHNICAL APPLICATIONS CENTER
- AIR FORCE WEATHER AGENCY
- AIR INTELLIGENCE AGENCY
- AIR NATIONAL GUARD Readiness Center

Air force direct reporting units include:

- 11th Wing
- AIR FORCE DOCTRINE CENTER
- AIR FORCE OPERATIONAL TEST AND EVALUATION CENTER
- UNITED STATES AIR FORCE ACADEMY

Osan AB, Republic of Korea   See AIR FORCE BASES.

Outstanding Airman of the Year Ribbon
See DECORATIONS AND MEDALS.

P

Pacific Air Forces (PACAF)

PACAF is the chief air component of the U.S. Pacific Command (PACOM), a unified command of U.S. armed forces. The PACAF mission is to plan, conduct, control, and coordinate offensive and defensive air operations in the Pacific and Asian theaters, as well as arctic areas under U.S. control, encompassing Alaska and the west coast of the Americas to the east coast of Africa, and from the Arctic to the Antarctic. It is headquartered at Hickam AFB, Hawaii.

Patrick AFB, Florida   See AIR FORCE BASES.

Persian Gulf War

Background

The origin of the Persian Gulf War may be traced to August 2, 1990, after talks between Iraq and Kuwait failed to resolve a conflict over oil pricing. On that date, Iraq's president, Saddam Hussein, invaded Kuwait, a small, all-but-defenseless country when matched against its neighbor, which had the fifth-largest army in the world.

Operation Desert Shield Commences

On August 2, President George H. W. Bush proclaimed an economic embargo against Iraq, and United Nations Security Council action followed. When Saddam Hussein refused to withdraw from Kuwait, President Bush ordered the commencement of Operation Desert Shield on August 7. The action involved a buildup of U.S. and UN forces in the region that was intended ultimately to liberate Kuwait.

The operation was put under the direction of Headquarters U.S. Central Command (CENTCOM) and was commanded by U.S. Army general H. Norman Schwarzkopf. CENTCOM's immediate mission was to oversee and coordinate U.S. force deployment to the Persian Gulf and to ensure the security of Saudi Arabia as well as other Arab states. Supreme air command was assigned to USAF lieutenant general Charles A. Horner, who established Headquarters Central Command Air Forces (Forward) in Saudi Arabia. Five fighter squadrons, a contingent of AWACS, and part of the 82nd Airborne Division moved into the theater within five days. Twenty-five fighter squadrons flew nonstop to the theater, and, within 35 days, the USAF had deployed a fighter force equal in number to that of the Iraqi air force.

Late in August, President Bush authorized the call-up of reserves for active duty. The AIR FORCE RESERVE and AIR NATIONAL GUARD would play central roles in strategic and tactical AIRLIFT, in fighter and reconnaissance operations, and in flying tanker support.

As U.S. and coalition forces were built up and deployed, President Bush set a deadline of January 15, 1991, for the withdrawal of Iraqi forces from

Kuwait. When that deadline came and went, Operation Desert Shield entered the attack phase as Operation Desert Storm. The Persian Gulf War began.

Air Power Opens Operation Desert Storm

On January 16, 1991, coalition aircraft began the SURGICAL BOMBING of principal Iraqi military targets, including command and communications centers, missile launch sites, radar facilities, airports, and runways. Also targeted were Iraqi ground forces. Using highly advanced guided missile and smart bomb technologies and guided by AWACS and JOINT SURVEILLANCE TARGET ATTACK RADAR SYSTEM (JSTARS) aircraft, the air strikes were massive, but they were targeted precisely against military objectives. During the first 10 days of the war, 10,000 air sorties were flown. Within this brief time period, Iraq's nuclear, biological, and chemical weapons development programs were either destroyed or badly damaged, and its air defenses and offensive air and ballistic missile capability were drastically degraded. By February 25, after continual air attack, the ground war began. Within 100 hours, Kuwait had been liberated, and the Iraqi army was totally and unconditionally defeated.

Key Statistics

Operations Desert Shield and Desert Storm involved more than 55,000 USAF personnel in theater. In addition to executing the combat role, USAF engineers erected more than 5,000 tents, built buildings totaling more than 300,000 square feet, and laid more than 1,600,000 square feet of concrete and asphalt. The USAF deployed to the theater 15 air transportable hospitals with a total 750-bed capacity and one 1,250-bed contingency hospital.

For the first time, the USAF employed cutting-edge space and intelligence assets. Space support included the satellite-based Defense Meteorological Support Program, which accurately predicted weather—critical in Desert Storm, since during the period of the conflict the area experienced the worst weather in 14 years. It also included the Global Positioning System (GPS), essential to accurate navigation to targets. The Defense Satellite Communications System provided secure voice and data communications for more than 100 ground terminals for Desert Shield/Desert Storm commanders.

USAF intelligence systems included the Mission Support System, which provided integrated mission planning support for USAF pilots. This system reduced mission planning from a matter of days to a total of four hours per mission. Another aspect of advanced USAF communication was tactical digital facsimile, which provided the capability to send high-resolution pictures and other data nearly in real time.

From the January 16, 1991, commencement of the offensive until the February 27 cease-fire, the USAF continuously deployed four AWACS aircraft to control more than 3,000 coalition sorties daily. Two JSTARS E-8 aircraft—at the time still in the late testing phase—were also deployed and supported all mission taskings. One of the two aircraft was in the air every day, its mission to track *every* vehicle that moved on the ground, and to identify and target Iraqi Scud missiles and launchers, convoys, trucks, tanks, surface-to-air missile sites, and artillery pieces.

USAF strategic airlift to the Persian Gulf was the largest since WORLD WAR II. By the time of the cease-fire, USAF airlifters had moved 482,000 passengers and 513,000 tons of cargo—the equivalent to repeating the 56-week BERLIN AIRLIFT every six weeks. Within theater, more than 145 C-130 aircraft were deployed to move units to forward bases. The tactical airlift aircraft flew 46,500 sorties and moved more than 209,000 people and 300,000 tons of supplies within the theater. During the 100 hours of the ground campaign, C-130s flew more than 500 sorties a day.

Air refueling operations during Operation Desert Shield and Operation Desert Storm were massive. The USAF deployed 256 KC-135 and 46 KC-10 tankers to the Persian Gulf.

AIR FORCE SPECIAL OPERATIONS COMMAND (AFSOC) units were also deployed to Desert

Air Force F-15 fighters fly over a Kuwait oil field that has been set ablaze by retreating Iraqi troops during the Gulf War, 1991.   *(Hulton/Archive)*

Storm, in which they performed such missions as infiltration, exfiltration, and resupply of Special Operations Forces teams on direct action missions. Also included among Special Operations responsibilities was the rescue of downed crew members, psychological operations broadcasts, the dropping of 15,000-pound "daisy cutter" antipersonnel bombs, and supporting counterterrorist missions.

Combat aircraft deployed during Operation Desert Shield and Desert Storm included 120 F-15C/Ds. Every Iraqi fixed-wing aircraft destroyed in air-to-air combat, including five Soviet-made MiG-29 Fulcrums, were downed by F-15Cs. No coalition aircraft were lost to Iraqi fighters. In addition, 48 F-15E Strike Eagles were deployed to the theater; two were lost in combat. The USAF sent 144 A-10s to the Persian Gulf. These flew 30 percent of the total USAF sorties, but they accounted for more than

half of the confirmed Iraqi equipment losses. In 8,000 sorties, five A-10s were lost in combat.

The F-117 Stealth Fighter flew more than 1,250 sorties, dropping more than 2,000 tons of bombs. These aircraft were assigned to bomb strategic targets in downtown Baghdad. No F-117 was damaged by enemy air defenses.

The venerable B-52 Stratofortress flew 1,624 missions and dropped more than 25,700 tons of ordnance on Kuwait and southern Iraq, hitting airfields, industrial targets, and storage areas—41 percent of all USAF bombs dropped during the conflict.

F-111F aircraft targeted chemical, biological, and nuclear sites, as well as airfields, bunkers, and command, control and communications facilities as well as parts of the integrated air defense system. In more than 4,000 sorties, only one F-111F was damaged by enemy air defenses.

Eighteen EF-111 Ravens were deployed to jam enemy radar. F-4G Wild Weasels—48 in number—flew 2,500 sorties with high-speed antiradar missiles (HARM), which effectively suppressed Iraqi use of radar. The F-16 Fighting Falcon was deployed in great numbers—249 aircraft—and flew in excess of 13,450 sorties, more than any other aircraft in the war.

From D-day to cease-fire, the USAF flew 59 percent of all sorties with 50 percent of the aircraft and had 37 percent of the losses. At the beginning of the conflict, coalition air forces faced Iraqi assets consisting of 750 combat aircraft, 200 support aircraft, Scud surface-to-surface missiles, chemical and biological weapon capability, excellent air defenses, 10 types of surface-to-air missiles, some 9,000 antiaircraft artillery pieces, and untold thousands of small arms. USAF fighters were credited with 36 of the 39 Iraqi fixed-wing aircraft and helicopters downed during Desert Storm. In all, Iraq lost 90 aircraft to coalition air forces; 122 were flown to Iran, making for a total loss of 234 aircraft. Beyond this, of Iraq's 594 hardened aircraft shelters, 375 were damaged or destroyed, and it is believed that 141 additional aircraft were destroyed within these shelters.

Peterson AFB, Colorado   See Air Force Bases.

Pope AFB, North Carolina   See Air Force Bases.

precision bombing   See Surgical Bombing.

Project Blue Book

In the late 1940s, during a rash of public sightings of unidentified flying objects (UFOs), the USAF was tasked with investigating the phenomena. Best known of its investigation programs was Project Blue Book, the successor to three earlier programs, Project Sign, Project Grudge, and Project Twinkle (a suboperation under Project Grudge). From its origin in Project Sign in 1947, until it was officially shut down in 1969, Project Blue Book was the focus of much UFO folklore, controversy, and even conspiracy theory, as UFO enthusiasts saw Project Blue Book as the nucleus of a government effort to cover up information about UFOs and even visitation and contact by extraterrestrials.

Project Blue Book (officially the Aerial Phenomena Group) was formally created in September 1951 and headquartered at Wright-Patterson AFB. A small unit, it employed USAF electronics and radar personnel, as well as civilian science advisers from the Battelle Memorial Institute and Ohio State University, in addition to Dr. J. Allen Hynek, a Northwestern University astronomer and the most highly respected student of UFO phenomena. Intelligence officers at USAF bases throughout the world were ordered to report all sightings to Blue Book, and Blue Book in turn was given the authority to communicate directly with any USAF base or unit without going through the normal Chain of Command.

The public generally regarded as authoritative Project Blue Book's pronouncements on UFOs; the unit dismissed most reports as natural phenomena, weather balloons, conventional aircraft sight-ings, or hoaxes. On March 20, 1966, however, Project Blue Book became the target of intense public and official criticism after its chief adviser, Hynek, dismissed a Michigan mass sighting as the effect of "swamp gas." Gerald R. Ford, at the time a Michigan congressman, called for hearings, which were held by the House Armed Services Committee in April 1966. The hearings concluded that the USAF should review Project Blue Book. In the end, the unit was discredited, and the USAF admitted that its 19 years of investigation had been inadequate. An attempt was made to revitalize Project Blue Book, but a USAF-sponsored commission headed by the distinguished physicist Edward Uhler Condon independently concluded in 1969 that UFOs were "not of significance for scientific study." Taking this as leave to get out of the flying saucer business, the USAF terminated Project Blue Book on December 17, 1969.

Punitive Expedition (1916)

In 1911, Mexico's hated president Porfirio Díaz was deposed, creating a power vacuum that, gradually, Francisco "Pancho" Villa (1877–1923), with some American support, came to fill. In 1915, however, the troops of Álvaro Obregón defeated Villa's forces and installed as Mexico's acting president Villa's bitter enemy, Venustiano Carranza. In a swift about-face, the United States repudiated Villa and recognized the Carranza government. Outraged, Villa launched attacks against Americans in Mexico; then, on March 9, 1916, his forces crossed the border into the United States, raiding the hamlet of Columbus, New Mexico, and killing as many as 17 (history records anywhere from 12 to 17) U.S. citizens. The next day, President Woodrow Wilson ordered Brigadier General John J. Pershing to organize a force to protect the border and to apprehend Villa—dead or alive. Hoping that aerial reconnaissance would be an invaluable asset in a border-country manhunt, Pershing directed the 1st Aero Squadron of the Aviation Section, U.S. Army Signal Corps, to accompany his forces to Columbus.

The 1st Aero Squadron consisted of 11 pilot-officers, 82 enlisted men, one civilian mechanic, a medical officer, and three enlisted medical corpsmen. Equipment consisted of eight Curtiss JN-3 "Jennys," 12 trucks, and an automobile. The first reconnaissance flight from Columbus into Mexico was made on March 16. By April 19, only two of the eight planes were in working condition. The rest had fallen victim to landing accidents and forced landings and had generally succumbed to heat and sand. Overweight and underpowered, the Jennys had trouble climbing in the hot, dry, thin air of the high country (elevation 12,000 feet). On April 20, after four brand-new Curtiss N8s were received at Columbus, the remaining two JN-3s were condemned. After a week of testing, the N8s were likewise condemned on May 9. Between May 1 and May 25, a dozen new Curtiss R-2s arrived. More adequately powered with 160-horsepower engines, the R-2s were declared satisfactory, but, once in the field, they were found to have defective propellers, engine parts, and various construction flaws. Aviation Section mechanics worked heroically on the aircraft from May through July under extremely adverse conditions in a successful effort to keep at least some of the aircraft flying. Near the end of August, 18 new aircraft arrived in Columbus, including 12 Curtiss H-2s and six Curtiss twin-engine craft. The latter planes were declared unsuitable for desert flying and were returned to Fort Sam Houston.

The many mechanical, structural, and logistical problems that beset the 1st Aero Squadron did not make for a promising maiden battle for the Aviation Section. Nevertheless, between March 15 and August, the squadron flew 540 reconnaissance sorties in Mexico for a total of 346 hours of flying time covering 19,533 miles. This aerial reconnaissance was no more successful than Pershing's ground forces in locating and neutralizing Pancho Villa (although Pershing did eliminate a number of Villa's top commanders and inflicted substantial casualties on his forces). The Punitive Expedition was recalled in February 1917.

R

RAF Lakenheath, United Kingdom   See AIR FORCE BASES.

RAF Mildenhall, United Kingdom   See AIR FORCE BASES.

rainbow
Term used for a new airman at basic training before he or she is issued a uniform; that is, he or she still wears multicolored civilian clothing and not the green fatigue uniform. See RANKS AND GRADES.

Ramstein AB, Germany   See AIR FORCE BASES.

Randolph AFB, Texas   See AIR FORCE BASES.

ranks and grades
USAF personnel hold rank and grade either as a commissioned officer, a noncommissioned officer, or an airman.

Commissioned Officers (in descending order)

General of the Air Force
The highest rank in the USAF, ranking above general (grade O-10), but, in practice, very rarely awarded. As of 2002, the late HENRY HARLEY ARNOLD remained the only general ever to have held this rank. It is the equivalent of general of the army.

General
Although applied to all general officers in the USAF, a general is, strictly speaking, a four-star general, ranking below only general of the air force (five stars), a rank seldom awarded, so that, effectively, general is the highest rank in the USAF and equivalent to a naval admiral. The pay grade for general is O-10.

Lieutenant General
In the USAF (and army and marines), a lieutenant general is a commissioned officer (grade O-9) who ranks above a major general (O-8) and below a general (O-10). The insignia is three silver stars, and it is equivalent to a naval or coast guard vice admiral.

Major General
A general officer of grade O-8, who ranks above a brigadier general and below a lieutenant general. The insignia of rank is two silver stars. The equivalent naval rank is rear admiral upper.

Brigadier General
The lowest-ranking general officer in the USAF, the brigadier ranks above a colonel (grade O-6) and below a major general (grade O-8). Insignia is a single star in silver. The equivalent naval rank is rear admiral, lower.

Colonel

This field-grade USAF officer (O-6) ranks below a brigadier general and above a lieutenant colonel. Insignia of rank is a silver eagle.

Lieutenant Colonel

In the USAF (as in the army and marines), a lieutenant colonel is a commissioned officer (grade O-5) who ranks above a major but below a colonel. The equivalent naval rank is commander. Insignia is a silver oak leaf.

Major

An officer of grade O-4, ranking below a lieutenant colonel and above a captain. The insignia is a gold oak leaf, and the naval equivalent is a lieutenant commander.

Captain

In the USAF, as in the army and marines, a captain is a company-grade officer (grade O-3), ranking below a major and above a first lieutenant. This rank is equivalent to a naval or coast guard lieutenant. (In the navy or coast guard, captain is equivalent to a USAF, army, or marine colonel.) The insignia of rank is two silver bars.

First Lieutenant

In the USAF, army, and marines, first lieutenant, grade O-2, ranks above second lieutenant and below captain. Insignia is a single silver bar. The naval and coast guard equivalent is lieutenant (j.g.).

Second Lieutenant

The lowest-ranking commissioned officer in the USAF (grade O-1), the second lieutenant is equivalent to a naval and coast guard ensign. Insignia of rank is a single gold bar.

Noncommissioned USAF Officers (in descending order)

Chief Master Sergeant of the Air Force

Chief master sergeant of the air force is a unique position in the USAF and the highest noncommissioned officer grade (E-9). The CMSgtAF advises the CHIEF OF STAFF, USAF, and the SECRETARY OF THE AIR FORCE on matters concerning the effective utilization, welfare, and progress of the enlisted members of the USAF. Insignia is three chevrons above five inverted chevrons with a USAF device in the middle of the lower chevrons.

Chief Master Sergeant

With first sergeant, chief master sergeant is the highest noncommissioned grade in the USAF (E-9). The insignia is three chevrons above five inverted chevrons.

First Sergeant

In the USAF, a first sergeant is a noncommissioned officer of grade E-8 or grade E-9, ranking above a master sergeant (E-7) and equivalent to a senior master sergeant (also E-8) or a chief master sergeant (E-9). Insignia for the E-8 first sergeant grade is five inverted chevrons below three chevrons, with a diamond device in the center. Insignia for the E-9 grade adds a third chevron above the V (inverted) chevrons, also with a diamond device in the center.

Senior Master Sergeant

A senior noncommissioned officer (grade E-8) ranking above all other enlisted personnel except for chief master sergeant (E-9). Insignia of rank is two chevrons over five inverted chevrons. The USAF senior master sergeant is equivalent to an army or marine master sergeant or first sergeant and to a senior chief petty officer in the navy or coast guard.

Master Sergeant

In the USAF, a master sergeant is a noncommissioned officer of grade E-7, in contrast to this grade in the army and marines, which is E-8. The USAF master sergeant ranks above a technical sergeant (E-6) and below senior master sergeant (E-8) and an E-8 first sergeant (the USAF has E-8 and E-9 first sergeant grades). Insignia of rank is one upright chevron over five chevrons. Equivalent naval noncommissioned grade is senior chief petty officer.

Technical Sergeant

In the USAF, a technical sergeant (grade E-6) ranks below master sergeant (E-7) and above staff sergeant (E-5). Insignia is five stacked V (inverted) chevrons with a star above the middle. A USAF technical sergeant is equivalent to an army and marine staff sergeant and a navy petty officer, first class.

Staff Sergeant
In the USAF, a staff sergeant ranks (E-5) above a sergeant or senior airman (both E-4) and below a technical sergeant (E-6). The USAF staff sergeant is equivalent to the army sergeant (the army staff sergeant is equivalent to a USAF technical sergeant), to the marine sergeant, and to the navy and coast guard petty officer, second class. Insignia is four inverted chevrons with a star above the lowest chevron stripe.

Sergeant/Senior Airman
Promotion to sergeant/senior airman (SrA) depends on vacant positions and is open to airmen first class who meet certain eligibility requirements, including a skill level 5 within their AIR FORCE SPECIALTY CODE (AFSC) classification (or skill level 3, if no skill level 5 exists in the applicable AFSC); 36 months time in service (TIS) and 20 months time in grade (TIG) or 28 months TIG, whichever occurs first; and recommendation by the promotion authority. A special Below-the-Zone Promotion Program also offers an opportunity for early promotion. Grade is E-4. Insignia is three inverted chevron stripes emanating from an encircled star.

Airman (in descending order)

Airman First Class
Promotion to airman first class (A1C) is made on a noncompetitive basis generally after 10 months' time-in-grade as an airman. Grade is E-3. Insignia is two inverted chevrons emanating from an encircled star.

Airman
USAF enlisted recruits begin at the grade of E-1 with the title of Airman basic and are promoted to airman on a noncompetitive basis generally after six months as an airman basic. Insignia is a single chevron stripe emanating from an encircled star. Grade is E-2.

Airman Basic
USAF enlisted recruits begin at the grade of E-1 with the title of airman basic (AB) and are promoted to airman on a noncompetitive basis generally after six months as an airman basic. This rank carries no insignia.

recruiting policies and practices
Like the other services, today's USAF is an all-volunteer organization. More than any other service, its personnel needs call for relatively high to very high degrees of technical training. Accordingly, USAF recruiters look for applicants of substantial aptitude and motivation. In return, the USAF offers extensive education and training, typically in fields that readily transfer to the civilian world. As with any branch of the military service, an emphasis is put on patriotism and service to the nation as well as defense of freedom; however, emphasis is also placed on opportunity for personal development and growth through education, vocational experience, and career development.

The official USAF recruiting website (http://www.airforce.com/index_fr.htm) outlines five "mission" areas to interest potential recruits: humanitarian, health care, flight, aerospace, and scientific research. The image presented is of a professional organization, both committed and cutting edge. Warfighting and combat roles do not receive top billing.

In all of today's armed services, the Internet and mass media advertising have greatly supplemented and extended the reach of the individual recruiter. However, the brunt of the recruitment mission still falls on this highly motivated enlisted person (grade E-5 to E-7), whose job is simultaneously to "sell" prospects on the USAF while also identifying prospects worthy of the service. The recruiter's job is grueling—often 60 to 70 hours per week—and is spent largely in the civilian world rather than within the confines of an air base. No sales person enjoys rejection, and recruiters learn to accept a rejection rate of about 95 percent on a daily basis. The recruiter's performance is evaluated by the number of recruits he brings into the service (typically, each recruiter is expected to bring in three or four per month) and by the performance of those recruits at least through basic training. The special demands of the recruiter's job are recognized by the Air Force Recruiter Ribbon, a decoration authorized on June 21, 2000.

See also AIR FORCE RECRUITING SERVICE.

Reese AFB, Texas   See AIR FORCE BASES.

Rhein-Main AB, Germany   See AIR FORCE BASES.

Rickenbacker, Captain Edward V. (Eddie)
(1890–1973) *ace fighter pilot, airline executive*

One of the most famous American military aviators, Eddie Rickenbacker became the U.S. ace of aces in WORLD WAR I, racking up 26 victories to become the seventh-ranking U.S. ace of all time.

Born Edward Rickenbacher in Columbus, Ohio, he changed the "h" to "k" to anglicize his name, and he also added Vernon as a middle name, because he thought it sounded more distinguished. Before U.S. entry into World War I, Rickenbacker earned fame as a race car driver. He enlisted in the Signal Corps in 1917 and was assigned to France as the personal driver of General John J. Pershing, commander of the American Expeditionary Force (AEF). In this position, he was promoted to sergeant first class.

Rickenbacker persistently agitated for assignment to flight training, and, in October 1917, he was graduated as a pilot and commissioned a first lieutenant. However, Rickenbacker was assigned as an engineering officer, not a combat pilot, at Issoudon, the principal U.S. air training and supply base, under Major CARL A. SPAATZ. Rickenbacker now urgently requested combat duty, but Spaatz did not assign him to the front until March 1918, when he joined the 1st Pursuit Group's 94th Aero Squadron, nicknamed the "Hat-in-the-Ring-Squadron," after its distinctive insignia.

Rickenbacker scored his first victory on April 25 and made ace by May 30. Stricken with a mastoid infection in the summer of 1918, he was out of service for two months. When he returned to the 94th it was as commander. He scored six victories in September and 14 more in October. (Rickenbacker was awarded the Air Force Medal of Honor in 1930 for an action of September 25, 1918, in which he singlehandedly attacked five fighters escorting two observation planes; he shot down one fighter and one observation plane.)

Rickenbacker started an automobile manufacturing company after the war, but, following initial success, the company failed in 1927. Seeking a way out of debt, Rickenbacker returned to auto racing and became president of the Indianapolis Speedway. In 1934, he became general manager of East-

Edward "Eddie" Rickenbacker   *(U.S. Air Force)*

ern Air Lines, which he soon took from the edge of bankruptcy to profitability. In 1938, he was able to purchase Eastern and ran it as president until he was nearly 70.

During WORLD WAR II, Rickenbacker traveled internationally on a morale-boosting tour of U.S. ARMY AIR FORCE units. During one of these trips, the B-17 transporting him ditched in the South Pacific. Thanks in large part to his leadership, Rickenbacker and all but one of the crew survived for 24 days in open rafts. Rickenbacker died of heart failure in 1973 and, at his funeral, was honored by a "missing man" formation flight of USAF F-4s.

Robins AFB, Georgia   See AIR FORCE BASES.

S

Schriever AFB, Colorado   See AIR FORCE BASES.

Scott AFB, Illinois   See AIR FORCE BASES.

Second Air Force
The predecessor unit of 2AF was the Northwest Air District, created in 1940. Early in 1941, it was redesignated 2AF and assigned to air defense and training. During WORLD WAR II, beginning after 1942, 2AF conducted training for heavy and very heavy bombers. Inactivated in March 1946, 2AF was reactivated in June of that year and assigned to AIR DEFENSE COMMAND (ADC). Inactivated again in 1948, it was reactivated the following year and assigned to the STRATEGIC AIR COMMAND (SAC), charged with the mission of training personnel for strategic operations. Headquartered at Barksdale AFB, 2AF was permanently inactivated in 1975.

second lieutenant   See RANKS AND GRADES.

secretary of the Air Force
The NATIONAL SECURITY ACT OF 1947, which, among other things, created the USAF as an independent service, created the position of secretary of the air force. Appointed by the president of the United States, the secretary of the air force serves under the secretary of defense, but also has direct access to the president and to the director of the budget. The secretary of the air force does not direct USAF operations, but manages funding, procurement, and legal plans and programs.

Selfridge, Thomas E. (1882–1908) *army aviator*
Second Lieutenant Thomas E. Selfridge was the first military officer of any nation to make a solo flight. He was also the first person killed in a powered airplane crash.

Born in San Francisco, he graduated from the U.S. Military Academy (West Point) in 1903 and in 1907 was detailed by the army to work with Alexander Graham Bell and Glenn H. Curtiss to design and build aircraft. On May 19, 1908, he flew the "White Wing" aircraft at Hammondsport, New York, thereby becoming the first military officer to solo in an airplane. Selfridge was next sent to Fort Myer, Virginia, as an official observer at the acceptance trials of the Wright Flyer, which was being considered for purchase by the U.S. Army Signal Corps. On a flight of September 17, 1908, with Orville Wright piloting and Selfridge as passenger, the Flyer crashed, seriously injuring Wright and killing Selfridge—the first fatality to result from a powered crash.

Sembach AB, Germany   See Air Force bases.

senior airman   See ranks and grades.

senior master sergeant   See ranks and grades.

separate operating agency (SOA)   See organization, USAF.

service associations

The leading USAF-related service associations include the following:

Air Force Association: See Air Force Association.

Air Force Enlisted Widows: Founded in 1967 by a group of active duty and retired Air Force NCOs to provide a home for the surviving spouses of enlisted USAF personnel.

Air Force Historical Foundation: See Air Force Historical Foundation.

Air Force Sergeants Association: A lobbying and special-interest organization dedicated to the USAF NCO.

Air Force Memorial Foundation: The Air Force Memorial Foundation's goal is to establish a permanent Memorial to recognize the many significant contributions to peace and freedom rendered by the United States Air Force and its predecessors, such as the Army Air Corps.

Airmen Memorial Foundation: The Airmen Memorial Foundation was created in 1983 to solve contemporary problems among all components of the Air Force Enlisted Force through the provision of programs and services, conceived from the enlisted perspective, that no one else provides.

Association of Air Force Missileers: Organization for those who have earned the USAF Missile Badge or the Missile and Space Badge, as well

as others with an interest in past or current USAF missile and space systems.

United States Air Force Academy Association of Graduates: The alumni association for the United States Air Force Academy.

Seventeenth Air Force (17AF)

Established in 1953 as a United States Air Forces in Europe (USAFE) unit, 17AF was first located at Rabat-Sale, French Morocco, then moved to Wheelus AB, Libya, in 1956. In 1959, it relocated to Ramstein AB, Germany, then to Sembach AB, Germany, in 1972. The 17AF controlled USAF tactical operations forces in Germany until it was inactivated on September 30, 1996.

Seventh Air Force (7AF)

The 7AF is one of the four numbered air forces in the Pacific Air Forces (PACAF). It was activated on November 1, 1940, as the Hawaiian Air Force and was ultimately redesignated 7AF on February 5, 1947.

The unit was heavily involved in the Pacific theater during World War II, executing bombing missions against the Gilberts, the Marshalls, the Carolines, the Marianas, Iwo Jima, and Okinawa, all targets across the Central Pacific.

Inactivated in 1949, 7AF was reactivated on March 28, 1966, and was designated a combat command at Ton Son Nhut AB, Republic of Vietnam. From April 1966 until 1973, 7AF assumed responsibility for most USAF operations in Vietnam and (as the 7/13AF) shared responsibility with the Thirteenth Air Force for operations conducted from Thailand. On March 29, 1973, 7AF transferred to Nakhon Phanom Royal Thai AB, Thailand, from which it controlled air assets and operations in Thailand until its second inactivation on June 30, 1975.

In September 1986, 7AF was again reactivated and has served since then as the USAF component to the U.S. and Republic of Korea Combined Forces Command's Air Component Command, a force charged with deterring aggression from

North Korea. The 7AF currently plans, directs, and conducts combined air operations in the Republic of Korea and in the Northwest Pacific in support of PACAF, U.S. Pacific Command, United Nations Command, U.S.-ROK Combined Forces Command, and U.S. Forces Korea. Headquarters consists of about 10,000 USAF personnel located primarily at Osan AB, Kunsan AB, and five other operating bases throughout the Republic of Korea. Aircraft flown include the F-16 Falcon and the A/OA-10 Thunderbolt.

Seymour Johnson AFB, North Carolina
See AIR FORCE BASES.

Shaw AFB, South Carolina   See AIR FORCE BASES.

Shemya AFB, Alaska   See AIR FORCE BASES.

Sheppard AFB, Texas   See AIR FORCE BASES.

Sixteenth Air Force (16AF)
Headquartered at Aviano AB, Italy, 16AF is one of two numbered air forces of the UNITED STATES AIR FORCES IN EUROPE (USAFE). It also functions as the southern air component of the U.S. European Command. The mission of 16AF is to execute aerospace operations through expeditionary force command and control in support of USAFE and NATO. The organization plans and executes combat air operations in southern Europe and portions of the Middle East and northern Africa. It supports about 11,000 USAF and civilian members at two main operating bases, four support bases, and other sites in Spain, France, Germany, Italy, Croatia, Kosovo, Bosnia-Herzegovina, Hungary, Former Yugoslav Republic of Macedonia, Greece, Turkey, and Israel.

Equipment assets of the 16AF include the F-16 Fighting Falcon, with contingency support to the F-15 Eagle, KC-135 Stratotanker, E-3B Sentry (AWACS), U-2 Dragonlady, MC-130P Combat Shadow, HH-60 Pave Hawk, RQ-1A Predator, and a full complement of conventional weapons. 16AF operates two main bases: Aviano AB, Italy, home to the 31st Fighter Wing; and Incirlik AB, Turkey, home to the 39th Wing. In addition, 16AF operates three expeditionary wings: the 31st Air Expeditionary Wing, Aviano AB, Italy; the 39th Air and Space Expeditionary Wing, Incirlik AB, Turkey, and the 16th Air Expeditionary Wing, Aviano. This latter unit operates expeditionary sites at Camp Bondsteel, Kosovo; Camp Able Sentry, the Former Yugoslav Republic of Macedonia; Sarajevo and Tuzla AB, Bosnia-Herzegovina; Taszar AB, Hungary; Zagreb, Croatia; Istres AB, France; and Naval Air Station Sigonella and San Vito Air Station, Italy; in addition to a contingency processing center at Rhein-Main AB, Germany. 16AF also operates support bases in Spain, Italy, Greece, and Turkey.

The predecessor organization to 16AF was the Air Administration, established in Madrid, Spain, in 1954. This unit was redesignated as Headquarters, 16AF. In addition, 16AF operated STRATEGIC AIR COMMAND (SAC) bases in Morocco from 1958 through 1963. In 1966, a year after SAC withdrew its B-47 alert force from Spain, 16AF was reassigned to USAFE.

Sixth Air Force (6AF)
Activated in 1940 as the Panama Canal Air Force and redesignated the Caribbean Air Force in 1941, the unit became the 6AF in 1942 and was charged with the defense of the Panama Canal as well as conducting antisubmarine operations. After WORLD WAR II, in 1946, 6AF was inactivated as a numbered air force and was redesignated Caribbean Air Command, based at Albrook Field, Canal Zone. It is no longer active.

Small Arms Expert Marksmanship Ribbon
See DECORATIONS AND MEDALS.

Soesterberg AB, Netherlands   See AIR
FORCE BASES.

Spaatz, General Carl A. ("Tooey") (1891–
1974) *Army Air Forces general*

The last commanding general of the U.S. ARMY AIR
FORCES, Carl Spaatz was also the first CHIEF OF
STAFF, USAF, and, with General of the Air Force
HENRY HARLEY ARNOLD, is considered one of the
fathers of the independent air arm.

Born in Boyertown, Pennsylvania, Spaatz graduated from the U.S. Military Academy (West Point)
in 1914, took flight training, became a pilot, and
was assigned to the 1st Aero Squadron during the
PUNITIVE EXPEDITION against Pancho Villa. With
U.S. entry into WORLD WAR I in 1917, Spaatz was
sent to France as commander of the 3rd Aviation
Instruction Center at Issoudon. During the last
three weeks of the war, he served in combat and
was credited with two victories in air-to-air
engagements.

Between the wars, Spaatz worked closely with
Brigadier General WILLIAM MITCHELL and commanded the successful 1929 "Question Mark" experiment in-air refueling. On the eve of U.S. entry
into WORLD WAR II, Spaatz was sent abroad, during
the summer of 1940, as an observer of the Battle of
Britain. When the United States entered the war,
Spaatz was named principal combat commander
of the U.S. ARMY AIR FORCES and was primarily
responsible for the massive buildup of the EIGHTH
AIR FORCE. He also served directly under General
Dwight D. Eisenhower as air commander for the
African, Sicilian, and Italian campaigns. Spaatz
then presided over the planning and execution of
air support in Operation Overlord, the "D-day"
invasion of western Europe. It was under Spaatz's
command that the USAAF achieved air superiority
over the Luftwaffe, and it was Spaatz who successfully insisted on targeting the German oil industry
for strategic bombing.

Directly after V-E Day, Spaatz transferred to the
Pacific theater, where he commanded the B-29

W. Stuart Symington, first secretary of the Air Force, and General Carl Spaatz, first Air Force Chief of Staff, at a press
conference announcing the new organizational setup for the Department of the Air Force, 1947.   *(U.S. Air Force)*

strategic bombing campaign against Japan. It was Spaatz who supervised the nuclear raids on Hiroshima and Nagasaki. With the creation of the USAF in 1947, Spaatz became the new air arm's first chief of staff. He retired the following year.

space doctrine

The DEPARTMENT OF THE AIR FORCE is charged with the primary responsibility to organize, train, and equip for prompt and sustained offensive and defensive operations in space. Beginning in 2001, the SECRETARY OF THE AIR FORCE ordered a major "realignment" of headquarters and field commands "to more effectively organize, train, and equip for prompt and sustained space operations." AIR FORCE SPACE COMMAND (AFSPC) was assigned responsibility for space research, development, acquisition, and operations.

As of early 2002, the development of space doctrine is a major ongoing USAF initiative.

Spangdahlem AB, Germany   See AIR FORCE BASES.

Special Experience Identifiers (SEIs)

SEIs identify special experience and training that are not otherwise identified by AIR FORCE SPECIALTY CODES (AFSC). The SEIs are used to identify positions requiring unique experience or training and to track individuals who possess this experience or training.

Special Operations   See AIR FORCE SPECIAL OPERATIONS COMMAND.

Special Weapons Command (SWC)

In the postwar years, nuclear, biological, and chemical weapons were grouped together under the rubric "special weapons," and in 1949 the USAF formed the Special Weapons Command as a MAJCOM charged with supervising units that handled

such weapons. Redesignated Air Force Special Weapons Center in 1952, Special Weapons Command became part of the AIR RESEARCH AND DEVELOPMENT COMMAND (ARDC) and, as such, lost its own status as a MAJCOM. The Special Weapons Center was in turn inactivated in 1954.

squadron   See ORGANIZATION, USAF.

staff sergeant   See RANKS AND GRADES.

stealth aircraft

Stealth is the general term for the science of designing an aircraft (or naval vessel) such that its detectability by visual and electronic means is significantly degraded. Ideally, the aircraft (or vessel) is rendered virtually invisible to the enemy.

In aircraft design, stealth technology combines innovative aerodynamics with the use of radar-absorbent materials and paints, and technologies to mask active emissions (especially acoustical and

The Boeing B-2 Spirit is the USAF's only full-stealth bomber.   *(U.S. Air Force)*

infrared). The most notable USAF stealth aircraft are the F-117 Nighthawk and the B-2 bomber and the emerging YF-22 and YF-23.

Strategic Air Command (SAC)

Until it was absorbed by AIR COMBAT COMMAND (ACC) on June 1, 1992, SAC was the USAF MAJ-COM charged with conducting strategic—that is, nuclear and thermonuclear—operations.

SAC was established on March 21, 1946. It was intended to deter other nations from starting World War III, and, under the leadership of Lieutenant General CURTIS EMERSON LEMAY, pursuant to the nuclear deterrent policy established by President Harry S. Truman, SAC became a mighty deterrent force. During the decade of the 1950s, it added ICBMs (see INTERCONTINENTAL BALLISTIC MISSILES) to complement its force of long-range bombers and became responsible for two-thirds of the "triad" that formed the U.S. nuclear deterrent (the navy's fleet of guided missile submarines was the final third). During this same period, the USAF emphasis on SAC certainly retarded development of tactical assets, and the USAF found itself scrambling to improvise in order to fight conventional wars in Korea and Vietnam (see KOREAN WAR and VIETNAM WAR).

SAC's first long-range bomber was the B-29, which was followed by the hybrid piston-jet B-36 Peacemaker, introduced in 1948, and the B-52 Stratofortress in the mid-1950s. The B-52 became the mainstay of SAC's piloted nuclear deterrent force (see AIRCRAFT, COLD WAR AND AFTER). Added to this were ICBMs, including the Minuteman II and III and the Peacekeeper.

At the time of its absorption into ACC, SAC had two numbered air forces under it, the EIGHTH AIR FORCE (Barksdale AFB, Louisiana) and the FIF-TEENTH AIR FORCE (March AFB, California).

Strategic Defense Initiative (SDI; "Star Wars")

SDI was announced in March 1983 by President Ronald Reagan as a plan for a system to defend against nuclear weapons delivered by ICBM (IN-TERCONTINENTAL BALLISTIC MISSILE). As planned, SDI would constitute an array of space-based vehicles that would destroy incoming missiles in the suborbital phase of attack.

The plan was controversial on three broad fronts. First, the Soviet Union, at the time the world's other great nuclear super power, saw SDI as a violation of the 1972 SALT I Treaty on the Limitation of Anti-Ballistic Missile Systems and therefore an upset to the balance of power. Second, proponents of the policy of mutually assured destruction ("MAD"), who saw the policy as the chief deterrent to nuclear war, criticized SDI as a means of making nuclear war appear as a viable strategic alternative. Third, a great many scientists and others believed SDI was far too complex and expensive to work. These critics dubbed the "futuristic" program "Star Wars," after the popular science fiction movie, and the label was widely adopted by the media.

Indeed, the technical problems involved in SDI were daunting. Multiple incoming missiles, which could be equipped with a variety of decoy devices, had to be detected and intercepted in space. Even those friendly to the project likened this to "shooting a bullet with a bullet." Congress, unpersuaded, refused to grant funding for the full SDI program, although modified and spin-off programs consumed billions of dollars in development.

The collapse of the Soviet Union beginning in 1989 seemed to many to render SDI a moot point—although others pointed out that a Russian arsenal still existed and that other nations had or were developing missiles of intercontinental range. There were, during the early 1990s, accusations and admissions that favorable results of some SDI tests had been faked, and former secretary of defense Caspar Weinberger asserted that while the SDI program had failed to produce practical weapons and had cost a fortune, its very existence forced the Soviet Union to spend itself into bankruptcy. In this sense, SDI might be seen as the most effective weapon of the cold war.

In the administration of George W. Bush, beginning in 2001, SDI was revived, and the USAF resumed development and testing of components of the system. As of 2005, Congress debated ongoing investment in SDI.

support command

A support command provides supplies, services, maintenance, administration, transportation, training, or other similar nonoperational (noncombat) functions.

surgical bombing

Also known as precision bombing, surgical bombing is the extremely accurate bombing of a specific target to destroy that target while reducing the possibility of damaging or destroying nearby buildings or killing civilians. Surgical bombing tactics and techniques were first applied in the VIETNAM WAR and were used most dramatically in the 1986 attacks on Libya, in which F-111s hit Mohammar Qaddafi's principal headquarters without damaging nearby buildings in downtown Tripoli. The use of computer-guided "smart weapons" in the 1991 PERSIAN GULF WAR bought surgical bombing to a new height of development, and the selective bombing of targets in Baghdad during Operation Iraqi Freedom (2003) demonstrated the latest state of the art.

Survival, Evasion, Resistance, and Escape (SERE)

SERE (survival, evasion, resistance, and escape) is an important part of USAF pilot training. It teaches survival skills, as well as tactics to evade and to resist enemy capture, and to escape if captured. In 1991, after the PERSIAN GULF WAR, a sexual assault component was added to SERE training, but it was modified in 1995 following complaints that SERE rape demonstrations were too realistic and, in themselves, approached the level of sexual assault.

In the USAF, SERE training is part of the UNITED STATES AIR FORCE ACADEMY curriculum and is also conducted by the U.S. Air Force Survival School under the 336th Training Group. Elements of the 66th Training Squadron, based at Fairchild AFB, Washington, Eielson AFB, Alaska, and Naval Air Station Pensacola, Florida, is responsible for all training of USAF personnel who specialize in the SERE career field as experts and instructors. SERE course work includes instruction in basic survival, medical, land navigation, evasion, arctic survival, teaching techniques, roughland evacuation, coastal survival, tropics/river survival, and desert survival. Water-survival training includes instruction in signaling rescue aircraft, hazardous marine life, food and water procurement, medical aspects of water survival, personal protection, and life raft immediate-action procedures. SERE experts are also trained in surviving in the four extreme biomes: barren arctic, barren desert, open ocean, and jungle.

USAF SERE training conforms to standards established by an interservice agency, the Joint Services SERE Agency (JSSA).

T

Tactical Air Command (TAC)

Until it was absorbed with STRATEGIC AIR COMMAND (SAC) into AIR COMBAT COMMAND (ACC) on June 1, 1992, TAC was a USAF MAJCOM responsible for coordinating offensive and defensive air operations with land and sea forces.

TAC was created in 1946, activated at Tampa, Florida, then moved to Langley Field (Langley AFB), Virginia, in order to be nearer the headquarters of the other military service branches. TAC trained and equipped air units for tactical operations worldwide. It conducted operations from three numbered air forces, FIRST AIR FORCE (at Langley), NINTH AIR FORCE (at Shaw AFB, South Carolina), and TWELFTH AIR FORCE (at Bergtrom AFB, Texas). Under TAC control were the USAF Tactical Fighter Weapons Center, the 28th Air Division, and the Southern Air Division (at Howard AFB, Panama).

Tactical Air Control Party (TACP)

The TACP is a ground-based CLOSE AIR SUPPORT team tasked with controlling aircraft and providing air liaison to land forces. TACPs first saw duty in the VIETNAM WAR, beginning in 1961 as the USAF's tactical liaison with the U.S. Army. Personnel lived and worked on army posts, wore the green fatigues of the army, and even had army patches on their shoulders. TACPs kept the army commander informed of what air support could do for him and coordinated close air support from the point of view of the troops on the ground. "In a sense," a 1966 *Airman* magazine article put it, "they run the air war in South Vietnam."

At brigade level, the TACP consisted of three USAF officers—ALO (airlift officer), FAC (forward air controller), and TALO (tactical airlift officer)—and three airmen; at battalion level, there were two officers (ALO and FAC) and two airmen.

technical sergeant   See RANKS AND GRADES.

Technical Training Air Force (TECH TAF)

TECH TAF was established as part of the former Air Training Command (ATC) (now AIR EDUCATION AND TRAINING COMMAND) in April 1951 to conduct basic, preofficer, and technical training. It was inactivated in 1958.

Tenth Air Force (10AF)

The 10AF was created to conduct air combat in India and Burma during WORLD WAR II and was built up in India in 1942. With the FOURTEENTH AIR FORCE, the 10AF constituted the major American combat forces in the China-Burma-India (CBI) theater. Both the 10AF and 14AF were disbanded in December 1945, but 10AF was reactivated on May 24, 1946, at Brooks Field (Brooks AFB), Texas, and was assigned to Air Defense Command (see AERO-SPACE DEFENSE COMMAND [ADC]). It moved to Offutt AFB, Nebraska, on July 1, 1948; then to Fort Benjamin Harrison (later, Benjamin Harrison AFB), Indiana, on September 25, 1948. Assigned to CONTINENTAL AIR COMMAND (CAC) on December 1, 1948, 10AF moved to Selfridge AFB, Michigan, on January 16, 1950. The organization was inactivated on September 1, 1960, then reactivated on January 20, 1966, and assigned to Air Defense Command. Based at Richards-Gebaur AFB, Missouri, the unit was again inactivated on December 31, 1969.

In 1976, 10AF was reactivated and assigned to the AIR FORCE RESERVE and AIR NATIONAL GUARD, with headquarters at Bergstrom AFB, Texas. On October 1, 1993, the unit assumed management responsibility for the AFR rescue mission and for AFR B-52 bomber operations at Barksdale AFB, Louisiana. On July 1, 1994, 10AF assumed command and control of all FOURTH AIR FORCE C-130 AIRLIFT, special operations, and weather units, and, in October, took over all TWENTY-SECOND AIR FORCE C-130 units. In 1996, 10AF was functionally transferred to Naval Air Station Fort Worth Joint Reserve Base, Texas, where it now directs activities of some 11,400 reservists located at more than 23 military installations throughout the United States. There are six fighter wings, three geographically dispersed rescue units, one bomber unit, one AWACS (Airborne Warning and Control System) associate unit, one special operations wing, one space group, one Regional Support Group, and more than 120 nonflying units in logistics and support roles. Flying organizations within 10AF include fighter units equipped with the F-16 Fighting Falcons and A-10 Thunderbolt IIs, air rescue units equipped with the HC-130 Hercules tankers and the HH-60 Blackhawk helicopters, a bomber unit equipped with the B-52H Stratofortresses, and a special operations unit equipped with the C-130 Combat Talon/Combat Shadow aircraft.

test pilots

USAF test pilots are highly qualified (1,000+ flying hours) and highly trained pilots who fly new or experimental aircraft to ensure they perform as expected and planned. The USAF maintains the AIR FORCE FLIGHT TEST CENTER (AFFTC) at Edwards AFB, California, which runs the UNITED STATES AIR FORCE TEST PILOT SCHOOL. USAF testing takes place at Edwards and at Nellis AFB, Nevada. Typically, aircraft manufacturers employ civilian test pilots, who may work under the supervision of the USAF for a particular aircraft test.

Third Air Force (3AF)

Headquartered at RAF Mildenhall, United Kingdom, 3AF is one of two numbered air forces in UNITED STATES AIR FORCES IN EUROPE (USAFE), and is responsible for all USAF operations and support activities north of the Alps. Its area of responsibility includes missions and personnel in the United Kingdom, Germany, the Netherlands, Norway, Belgium, Denmark, Luxembourg, and parts of France.

With Allied victory in Europe and the end of WORLD WAR II came the demobilization and withdrawal of all U.S. air units from the United Kingdom. Their absence, however, was short-lived. In 1948, in response to the Berlin blockade, the U.S. deployed long-range B-29 strategic bombers to four East Anglian bases. Third Air Division was activated to receive, support, and operationally control the B-29 units.

The 3AF was activated on May 1, 1951, to oversee tactical air operations in much of Europe during the cold war. Throughout much of the period 3AF controlled strategic and tactical resources, including bombers and missiles, as part of the United States' NATO presence. The unit participated in Operations Desert Shield and Desert Storm before and during the PERSIAN GULF WAR in 1990–91, playing a major support role and deploying half its combat aircraft, several thousand vehicles, and approximately 50,000 tons of munitions to the theater.

In March 1996, the SEVENTEENTH AIR FORCE was inactivated, leaving 3AF with sole responsibility for overseeing all USAF units north of the Alps. This included taking on two main operating bases, Ramstein AB and Spangdahlem AB, both in Germany, and five geographically separated units. Currently, 3AF consists of 25,000 military personnel and more than 200 aircraft, including KC-135s, F-15s, A-10s, F-16s, C-9s, C-20s, C-21s, and C-130Es.

Thirteenth Air Force (13AF)

Called the "Jungle Air Force" because it was a major component of the WORLD WAR II "island hopping" strategy in the Pacific theater and because it was always remotely headquartered during the war, the 13AF was activated at New Caledonia in the Coral Sea on January 13, 1943, and was initially assigned to defend against advancing Japanese forces. Soon, however, it played a key role in the Pacific offensive, traveling northeast from the Solomons to the Admiralty Islands, New Guinea, Morotai, and, finally, the Philippines. Its first postwar headquarters was at Clark Field (Clark AFB), Philippines, established in January 1946. In December 1948, 13AF moved to Kadena AB, Okinawa, then returned to Clark in May 1949.

During the KOREAN WAR, 13AF provided staging areas for Korea-bound units. After the war, its principal role was training and surveillance. With the beginning and escalation of the VIETNAM WAR, 13AF managed staging and logistics. Its combat units and facilities were expanded in Thailand, and, at the height of 13AF involvement in the Vietnam War, the unit consisted of seven combat wings, nine major bases, 11 smaller installations, and more than 31,000 military members.

The 13AF provided aircraft and support before and during the PERSIAN GULF WAR of 1990–91 and is currently responsible to PACIFIC AIR FORCES (PACAF) for planning, executing, and controlling aerospace operations throughout the Southwest Pacific and Indian Ocean areas. The unit is now headquartered at Andersen AFB, Guam. It consists of the 36th Air Base Wing, the 613th Air Communications Squadron (613 ACOMS), the 613th Air Intelligence Flight (613 AIF), the 613th Air Operations Squadron (613 AOS), and the 613th Air Support Squadron (613 ASUS), all at Andersen. In addition, 13AF is responsible for the 497th Combat Training Squadron (497 CTS), Paya Labar, Singapore, and Detachment 1 of the 613th Air Support Squadron (DET1/613 ASUS), Diego Garcia. The unit has never been stationed in the United States.

Thunderbirds

The Thunderbirds constitute the U.S. Air Force Air Demonstration Squadron and perform precision aerial maneuvers demonstrating the capabilities of USAF high-performance aircraft to people throughout the world. The squadron also exhibits the professional qualities the USAF develops in the people who fly, maintain, and support these aircraft. Squadron objectives include:

- Support of USAF recruiting and retention programs
- Reinforcement of public confidence in the USAF
- Public demonstration of the professional competence of USAF members
- Strengthening of USAF morale and esprit de corps
- Support of USAF community and public relations
- Representation of the United States and its armed forces to foreign nations

Thunderbirds squadron is an AIR COMBAT COMMAND (ACC) unit composed of eight pilots (including six demonstration pilots), four support officers, three civilians, and more than 130 enlisted personnel. A Thunderbirds air demonstration combines formation flying with solo routines. For example, the four-aircraft diamond formation demonstrates the training and precision of USAF pilots while the solo aircraft highlight the maximum capabilities of the F-16. Approximately 30 maneuvers are performed in each demonstration during a show that runs about one hour and 15 minutes. The demonstration season lasts from March to November; new members are trained during the winter months. Officers serve a two-year assignment with the squadron, while enlisted personnel serve three to four. More than 280 million people in all 50 states and 57 foreign countries

The U.S. Air Force Demonstration Squadron, the Thunderbirds, flies the F-16C Fighting Falcon.   *(U.S. Air Force)*

have seen the red, white, and blue jets in more than 3,500 aerial demonstrations.

The Thunderbirds were activated on June 1, 1953, as the 3600th Air Demonstration Team at Luke AFB. At this time, the team flew the straight-winged F-84G Thunderjet. Early in 1955 the team transitioned to the swept-winged F-84F Thunderstreak, and, the following year, after moving to its current home at Nellis, the Thunderbirds traded the F-84 for the world's first supersonic fighter, the F-100 Super Sabre. This was the Thunderbird aircraft of choice for the next 13 years, except for a brief interval during which the Republic F-105 Thunderchief was used.

From 1969 to 1973, the Thunderbirds flew the F-4E Phantom, converted in 1974 to the T-38 Talon, the world's first supersonic trainer. Early in 1983, the team reinstituted its traditional role of demonstrating USAF frontline fighter capabilities by adopting the F-16A. The team converted to the F-16C in 1992.

Tinker AFB, Oklahoma   See AIR FORCE BASES.

top three

The top three enlisted ranks or grades in the USAF include master sergeant (e-7), senior master sergeant (e-8), and chief master sergeant (e-9).

Travis AFB, California   See AIR FORCE BASES.

Tuskegee Airmen

Like the other services (except, to a limited degree, the USN), the U.S. ARMY AIR FORCES were racially segregated before and during WORLD WAR II. As an experiment in providing greater opportunity for African Americans in the service, on July 19, 1941, the USAAF initiated a program to train black men—separately from whites—as military pilots. Most of the men selected for admission to the cadet program were college graduates or undergraduates. Others could gain admission by demonstrating academic qualifications on rigorous entrance examinations. The black candidates had to meet the same standards as their white counterparts. In addition to training pilots, the program was open to enlisted personnel for such ground-support functions as aircraft and engine mechanics, armament specialists, radio repairmen, parachute riggers, control tower operators, security police, administrative clerks, and so on.

Primary flight training was conducted by the Division of Aeronautics of Tuskegee Institute, the black vocational school and college founded in Alabama by Booker T. Washington in 1881. After completing primary training at Tuskegee's Moton Field, cadets were sent to Tuskegee Army Air Field to complete flight training and to make the transition to combat aircraft.

The first cadet class began in July 1941 and was completed nine months later in March 1942. Of the 13 cadets who enrolled in the first class, five completed the training, including Captain BENJAMIN O. DAVIS, JR., a West Point graduate, son and namesake of the army's only African-American general officer, and destined to command the all-black 332nd Fighter Group. Between 1942 and

1946, 992 pilots graduated from the Tuskegee program and received commissions and pilot's wings. On other bases, in Texas and New Mexico, African-American navigators, bombardiers, and gunnery crews were trained. Mechanics were trained at Chanute Air Base in Rantoul, Illinois, until adequate training facilities were completed at Tuskegee late in 1942.

The first Tuskegee airmen were trained as fighter pilots and joined the segregated 99th Fighter Squadron, which flew already obsolescent P-40 Warhawks in North Africa, Sicily, and the Italian mainland from April 1943 until July 1944, when they were transferred to the 332nd Fighter Group in the FIFTEENTH AIR FORCE. Under the command of Davis, who had been promoted to colonel, the 332nd Fighter Group originally consisted of the 100th Fighter Squadron, 301st Fighter Squadron, and 302nd Fighter Squadron. These units underwent combat training at Selfridge Air Base, Michigan, from March 1943 until December

Major James A. Ellison returns the salute of Mac Ross of Dayton, Ohio, as he passes down the line during review of the first class of Tuskegee cadets, U.S. Army Air Corps basic and advanced flying school, Tuskegee, Alabama, 1941. *(U.S. Air Force)*

1943, using P-40s and even older P-39 Airacobras. The group, as originally constituted, saw its first overseas combat operations near Naples, Italy, assigned to the TWELFTH AIR FORCE, beginning in February 1944. In April 1944, the 332nd Fighter Group transferred to the Adriatic shore at Ramitelli Air Strip, near Foggia, Italy, and was assigned to the 15th AF to conduct long-range heavy bomber escort missions in the new P-51 Mustangs. In July 1944, the 99th Fighter Squadron was transferred to Ramitelli as the fourth squadron of 332nd, which thereby became the largest fighter escort group in the 15th AF. Incredibly, the group flew all of its escort missions, mostly over central and southern Europe, without losing a single bomber to enemy aircraft.

In September 1943, black pilots also began training to fly twin-engine aircraft, but the war was over before any of these fliers saw combat. Of the 992 Tuskegee graduates, 450 saw combat, completing a total of 15,553 sorties and 1,578 missions, and earning from the Germans the admiring epithet, *Schwartze Vogelmenschen* (Black Birdmen). At first many American bomber crews resented and derided the members of the 332nd; before long, however, these crews took to calling them "The Black Redtail Angels" because of the bold red marking that distinguished the tail assembly of their aircraft and because they earned a reputation, on escort duty, of defending bombers with uncommon skill and determination.

In addition to bomber escort duty, the 332nd attacked rail and road traffic, as well as coast watching surveillance stations. Sixty-six Tuskegee pilots were killed in action and 32 were made prisoners of war. Members of the 332nd were awarded 150 Distinguished Flying Crosses and Legions of Merit as well as the Red Star of Yugoslavia.

Acceptance was not so forthcoming for many of those Tuskegee airmen who remained in training in the United States. In 1945, black officers ordered to stay out of the segregated officer's club at Freeman Field, Indiana, protested what they considered an illegal and immoral order by attempting to enter the club; 103 were arrested and charged with insubordination. Court-martial proceedings were immediately dropped against 100 of the officers and eventually dropped against two others as well. A third, Lieutenant Roger "Bill" Terry, was convicted, a stain that was not removed from his record until 1995 (see AFRICAN AMERICANS IN THE U.S. AIR FORCE).

Tuskegee Army Air Field continued to train African-American airmen after the war, until 1946. African-American women were also accepted for training in some ground-support functions. Although the newly independent USAF planned as early as 1947 to institute racial desegregation, actual integration of African-American personnel into white units did not begin until 1948, after President Harry S. Truman signed Executive Order 9981, barring the military services from racial discrimination.

Twelfth Air Force (12AF)

The 12AF was formed in WORLD WAR II as part of the force being readied for Operation Torch, the U.S. and Allied invasion of North Africa. The unit was activated at Bolling Field (Bolling AFB) on August 20, 1942, and, under the command of General JAMES HAROLD DOOLITTLE, participated in Operation Torch, as planned. Subsequently, 12AF saw extensive action in Sicily, mainland Italy, and southern France. The unit was inactivated after V-E Day, on August 31, 1945, but it was reactivated at March Field (March AFB), California, on May 17, 1946, and became a training command under the TACTICAL AIR COMMAND (TAC). On January 21, 1951, 12AF was installed at Wiesbaden, Germany, assigned to UNITED STATES AIR FORCES IN EUROPE (USAFE), and was the first USAFE unit to be committed to NATO. The unit was relocated to Waco, Texas, on January 1, 1958, returned to TAC, and assigned the mission of training tactical air crews. The 12 AF moved to Bergstrom AFB, Texas, in 1968 and, during the VIETNAM WAR, served as a principal source of tactical fighter, reconnaissance, and AIRLIFT forces.

Today, 12AF furnishes the USAF component of the U.S. Southern Command (USSOUTHCOM), a unified command responsible for Central and

South America, and is referred to, in this role, as U.S. Southern Command Air Forces, or SOUTHAF. One of its principal missions is involvement in interdicting illegal narcotics trafficking.

On July 13, 1993, 12AF headquarters moved from Bergstrom to Davis-Monthan AFB, Arizona, from which the unit oversees the activities of 10 active-duty wings and 21 AIR FORCE RESERVE and AIR NATIONAL GUARD units.

Twentieth Air Force (20AF)

Located at Francis E. Warren AFB, Wyoming, 20AF operates the ICBM (INTERCONTINENTAL BALLISTIC MISSILE) weapons systems of the AIR FORCE SPACE COMMAND (AFSPC). The unit includes three operational space wings with more than 9,500 people and 500 Minuteman II and 50 Peacekeeper missiles broadcast across 45,000 square miles in parts of Colorado, Montana, Nebraska, North Dakota, and Wyoming. Today, these constitute the only on-alert strategic forces of the United States.

Major 20AF units are the 90th Space Wing (at F. E. Warren AFB), the 91st Space Wing (at Minot AFB, North Dakota), and the 341st Space Wing (Malstrom AFB, Montana). The 625th Space Operations Flight at Offutt AFB, Nebraska, verifies missiles targeting, trains airborne launch control crews, and oversees the operation and integrity of communication networks between the missile sites and national command authorities.

The unit was activated in April 1944 for action in the Asian and Pacific theaters of WORLD WAR II. Headquartered in Washington, D.C., until July 1945, when it was moved to Harmon Field, Guam, 20AF moved to Kadena AB, Japan, in 1949. It was inactivated in 1955, until it assumed its current role.

Twenty-first Air Force (21AF)

With headquarters at Mcguire AFB, New Jersey, 21AF is one of two numbered air forces in AIR MOBILITY COMMAND (AMC). The unit commands and assesses the combat readiness of assigned air mobility forces over the Atlantic half of the globe in support of the "Global Reach" mission. This encompasses forces at more than 55 locations in eight countries, and 21AF major units include six active duty wings, two operational flying groups, and two mobility operations/support groups. The unit also serves as liaison to 40 AIR FORCE RESERVE component wings.

The 21AF operates a strategic AIRLIFT force consisting of C-5 Galaxy, C-17 Globemaster III, C-130 Hercules, and the C-141 Starlifter aircraft. It also operates a tanker force consisting of KC-10 Extenders and KC-135 Stratotankers. The 12AF's 89th Airlift Wing, base at Andrews AFB, Maryland, provides presidential airlift (see AIR FORCE ONE) as well as administrative airlift support to other top government officials. Also under 12AF direction is the Andrews-based Malcolm Grow USAF Medical Center.

At Dover AFB, Delaware, the 436th Airlift Wing flies the C-5. The 437th Airlift Wing at Charleston AFB, South Carolina, flies the C-141 and the newly acquired C-17. The 305th Air Mobility Wing (McGuire) flies the C-141 and KC-10 aircraft. The 6th Air Refueling Wing (Macdill AFB, Florida) and the 19th Air Refueling Group (Robins AFB, Georgia) fly KC-135s. The 43rd Airlift Wing (Pope AFB, North Carolina) and the 463rd Airlift Group (Little Rock AFB, Arkansas) fly the C-130.

In Europe, 21AF directs a network of organizations in support of AMC operations throughout Europe, Africa, and South America, including 621st Air Mobility Support Group (Ramstein AB, Germany), and 621st Air Mobility Operations Group (McGuire). Airlift support squadrons are located at Incirlik AB, Turkey; Lajes Field, Azores; Rota Naval Air Station, Spain; Rhein Main AB, Germany; and RAF Mildenhall, England.

The 21AF predecessor units were the 23rd Army Air Forces Ferrying Wing (created in June 1942), which became the North Atlantic Wing of the AIR TRANSPORT COMMAND (ATC) in February 1944. Redesignated the North Atlantic Division in June, it became the Atlantic Division in September 1945 and was moved to Fort Totten, New York. With creation of the USAF in 1947, 21AF was assigned to the AIR TRANSPORT SERVICE (ATS) and moved to Westover Field, Massachusetts. A year later, it was assigned to MILITARY AIR TRANSPORT SERVICE (MATS). After moving to McGuire AFB, New Jersey, in 1955, it was redesignated a named air force in 1958, becoming the EASTERN TRANSPORT AIR FORCE. It became the 21AF in 1966.

On October 1, 2003, the 21AF was redesignated as the Twenty-first Expeditionary Mobility Task Force

Twenty-first Expeditionary Mobility Task Force   See TWENTY-FIRST AIR FORCE.

Twenty-second Air Force (22AF)

The first predecessor organization of the 22AF was Domestic Division, Air Corps Ferrying Command, activated on December 28, 1941, in Washington, D.C., and assigned to Air Corps Ferrying Command. On February 26, 1942, the unit was redesignated as Domestic Wing, Air Corps Ferrying Command and then, on March 9, 1942, as Domestic Wing, Army Air Forces Ferry Command. It became Domestic Wing, Army Air Forces Ferrying Command, on March 31, 1942, and Ferrying Division, AIR TRANSPORT COMMAND (ATC), on June 20, 1942. After WORLD WAR II, on October 10, 1946, the unit moved to Cincinnati, Ohio, and was subsequently redesignated Continental Division, Air Transport Command, then discontinued shortly afterward. It was not until March 29, 1979, that the unit was reactivated, this time consolidated with the Continental Division, MILITARY AIR TRANSPORT SERVICE (MATS), which had been organized at Kelly AFB, Texas, in July 1948.

In 1958, it moved to Travis AFB, California, and, later that year, was redesignated Western Transport Air Force. On January 8, 1966, it became 22AF.

With the termination of the MILITARY AIRLIFT COMMAND (MAC) in 1992, 22AF was assigned to AIR MOBILITY COMMAND (AMC) on June 1. A year later, 22AF was inactivated at Travis and reactivated at Dobbins Air Reserve Base, Georgia, with a change in assignment to the AIR FORCE RESERVE. Today, 22AF is under the peacetime command of Headquarters Air Force Reserve Command at Robins AFB, Georgia, and manages more than 25,000 reservists and has 149 aircraft, including C-141Bs, C-130s, C-17s, C5A/Bs, and KC-10As. Fifteen reserve wings, 24 flying squadrons, and more than 225 support units are spread throughout 14 states, from New York to Mississippi, and from Massachusetts to Minnesota.

In peacetime, the 22AF recruits and trains reservists and maintains subordinate units. In war, the 22AF provides combat-ready airlift and support units and augments personnel requirements of the Air Mobility Command in the United States. In war, 22AF would come under the operational control of the TWENTY-FIRST AIR FORCE (now Twenty-first Mobility Task Force).

Twenty-third Air Force (23AF)

The 23AF was the last numbered air force, organized on February 10, 1983, and activated on March 1, 1983. It was redesignated as a MAJCOM, AIR FORCE SPECIAL OPERATIONS COMMAND (AFSOC), on May 22, 1990.

Tyndall AFB, Florida   See AIR FORCE BASES.

U

uniforms

When the USAF was created as an independent service arm in 1947, a distinctive uniform was contemplated. Although army officers speculated that the "flyboys" would chose something garish, the choice, ultimately, was quite conservative, a new and distinctive blue dress (Class A) uniform (in a shade similar to that worn by the RAF of Great Britain) designed (as General HOYT S. VANDENBERG said) to look like a "military business suit." Some insignia were also designed to be distinct from those of the army. Oxidized silver was used in lieu of army brass, and, for enlisted personnel, the USAF adopted V-type grade insignia (suggesting wings) to replace the army chevron stripes. The uniforms were approved by the secretaries of the army and navy in 1949 and had officially replaced the army-style uniforms by 1951. Fatigue (later called utility) uniforms were identical to those worn by USA personnel, except for the distinctive USAF V-type rank insignia.

Even before it achieved independent status, the air arm introduced uniform elements to distinguish its members. Aviator badges were introduced in 1913, and, after the United States entered WORLD WAR I in 1917, pilots spurned the choke-collar army uniforms for uniforms with open lapels. During this era, however, sticklers for spit-and-polish insisted that flying officers retain the riding boots and spurs worn by cavalry officers. Pilots were willing to wear the boots, but they pointed out that the spurs interfered with operation of rudder pedals and even tore through fuselage fabric. The army never officially relented, but pilots typically shed their spurs for flight.

By 1925, all of the army had adopted open-lapel uniform blouses, which meant that the fliers' uniforms no longer appeared distinctive. Airmen rejected the army's Sam Browne belt and adopted a simple leather belt. Later, when the rest of the army followed suit, the fliers began wearing a cloth belt. The visored cap worn by U.S. ARMY AIR CORPS and U.S. ARMY AIR FORCES officers was much floppier than that worn by regular army officers, and flying clothes—especially the A-2 leather flying jacket— were worn as much as possible even away from the flight line.

In January 1993, the USAF selected a new design for the Class A uniforms of officers and enlisted personnel. While the 1949 uniform had departed from the army look, the 1993 design moved even further from traditional military styling. The new design was uncluttered and shed many military adornments, including outer patch pockets and name tags. The longer cut of the lapels more closely resembled the civilian business suits worn by men as well as women. Even the fabric approached more closely to a high-grade civilian standard. Beginning in 1976, USAF uniform blouses and trousers had been made of 100 percent polyester; the new uniforms were a blend of polyester and wool. The only nod to tradition was a return to the inclusion of a silver star in the center of all enlisted chevrons, a feature that had been removed in the late 1970s.

During the era of the VIETNAM WAR, USAF personnel found themselves increasingly assigned to combat ground duty that required appropriate battle dress. For the most part, army jungle uniforms were used, and it was not until 2003 that the USAF considered adopting its own battle dress uniform (BDU) or utility uniform. Inspired by the distinctive camouflage uniform adopted by the USMC early in the 21st century, the new USAF BDU is made of an advanced wash-and-wear fabric and incorporates a redesigned camouflage pattern that corresponds to the jobs airmen do in most situations that require a utility uniform. The pattern roughly recalls the "tiger-stripe" camouflage patterns the U.S. military used during the Vietnam War, but it incorporates the distinctive Air Force emblem embedded into a gray-green color scheme that promises to provide better camouflage.

Flight suits are, of course, an important aspect of the uniform of any nation's air arm. The World War I Army Air Service flier wore essentially a cavalry dress uniform. At higher altitudes, a long, fur-lined leather coat was added, as was a fur-lined leather helmet with tight-fitting goggles—essential in an open cockpit. WORLD WAR II flying uniforms varied from simple, loose fatigue clothes for warm climates to fleece-lined leather flight jackets, insulated trousers, insulated boots, and leather balaclava-style helmets for high-altitude strategic bombing missions in unheated cabins. Many suits were electrically heated.

The jet age introduced radially redesigned flight suits that were designed to provide warmth as well as protection against blackouts during tight, high-speed turns, which create extraordinary high-G-force stresses on airmen. As early as 1941, Dr. Wilbur Franks, a Canadian researcher, developed an "anti-gravity" flight suit, which inflated strategically placed bladders to prevent blood from pooling in the pilot's extremities during high-G maneuvers. This helped to keep the brain supplied with sufficient blood to prevent loss of consciousness. The anti-gravity, or G-suit, concept was developed

extensively through many generations of flight suits to improve the mechanism as an aid to circulation in high-G environments. In addition to the G-suit, USAF pilots developed a forced-breathing technique called the anti-G straining maneuver. While executing high-G maneuvers, the pilot breathes rapidly, then holds his breath for several seconds while simultaneously tightening leg and stomach muscles. Although effective, the maneuver is quickly tiring. To decrease fatigue, researchers developed a technique called positive pressure breathing, which requires forcing pressurized air into the lungs through the pilot's face mask. The drawback of this technique is the possibility of damage to the lungs through overinflation. To counteract this, researchers introduced the Combat Edge System in the early 1990s. The system combines positive pressure breathing with a counterpressure vest fitted over the flight suit to protect the chest.

As of the early 21st century, the USAF was testing a new Advanced Technology Anti-G Suit, or Atags. The suit surrounds the legs and covers the entire lower body in one air-pumped garment. This more efficient flight suit, used in conjunction with the Combat Edge system, was expected to increase crew high-G endurance by some 350 percent. However, even more advanced research was being conducted with the so-called Libelle suit, under development by Life Support Systems, a Swiss company. This single-piece, full-body suit uses long tubes filled with fluid, not air, to combat high-G acceleration forces.

In addition to mechanisms necessary to counteract high-G forces, the modern USAF flight suit incorporates survival equipment, including a life vest and basic survival gear and an emergency radio and transponder beacon, to aid in air-sea rescue. The suits are fire resistant. Modern flight helmets are designed for comfort, maximum peripheral vision, and injury protection. They incorporate connections for advanced communication devices and for hookup of an oxygen mask. The modern flight suit is thoroughly utilitarian. Insignia and unit patches and emblems may be affixed to the suit by means of Velcro strips; however, it is the usual practice for pilots to remove all such distinguishing patches when flying combat missions, so that an enemy cannot readily identify a pilot's unit, if he is shot down.

United States Air Force Academy

On April 1, 1954, President Dwight D. Eisenhower authorized creation of the United States Air Force Academy, and in the summer of that year, SECRETARY OF THE AIR FORCE Harold Talbott selected a site near Colorado Springs, Colorado, for the academy's permanent residence. The first academy class entered interim facilities at Lowry AFB, Denver, in July 1955 while construction began. Occupancy by the cadet wing began in late August 1958.

The academy offers a four-year program of instruction and experience designed to provide cadets with the knowledge and character essential for leadership, and the motivation to serve as USAF career officers. Each cadet graduates with a bachelor of science degree and a commission as a second lieutenant in the USAF. The academy curriculum provides a general and professional foundation of a career USAF officer. Professionally oriented courses, including human physiology, computer science, economics, military history, astronautics, law, and political science address the special needs of future officers while the core curriculum includes courses in science, engineering, social sciences, and the humanities. About 60 percent of the cadets complete majors in science and engineering; the other 40 percent graduate in the social sciences and humanities.

Most of the academy's nearly 600 faculty members are USAF officers selected primarily from career-officer volunteers who have established outstanding records of performance and dedication. Each has at least a master's degree and more than 35 percent have doctorates. The academy's staff also includes several distinguished civilian professors and associate professors, and officers from other services are members of the faculty as well, as are a small number of officers from allied countries, who teach in the foreign language, history, and political science departments.

The academy's athletic program is designed to improve physical fitness, teach athletic skills, and develop leadership qualities. Cadets take at least three different physical education courses each year. Additionally, an aerospace-oriented military education, training, and leadership program begins with basic cadet training and continues throughout the four years. Seniors are responsible for the leadership of the cadet wing, while juniors and sophomores perform lower-level leadership and instructional tasks.

The academy offers courses in flying, navigation, soaring, and parachuting, building from basic skills to instructor duties. Cadets may fly light aircraft with the cadet aviation club. Those not qualified for flight training must enroll in a basic aviation course. Astronomy and advanced navigation courses also are available. Students bound for pilot training enroll in the pilot indoctrination course and fly the T-3 Firefly.

Cadets are required to complete two training periods per summer. Combat survival training is a required three-week program during cadets' second summer. For the other second-summer training period, cadets have options such as working with young airmen in an operational unit at a USAF installation, airborne training, soaring, or basic free-fall parachute training. During their last two summers, all cadets are offered leadership training as supervisors or instructors in summer programs, such as basic cadet training, survival training, and soaring.

Enrollment in the USAF Academy is by nomination, which may be obtained through a congressional sponsor or by meeting eligibility criteria in other categories of competition established by law. Women entered the academy on June 28, 1976, as members of the class of 1980.

Early in 2003, the academy was rocked by a widespread rape scandal. By March, 23 women—13 former cadets and 10 who were enrolled at the time—brought charges that male cadets had sexually assaulted them, and they accused academy officials of not only failing to investigate the incidents they reported but also actively discouraging such charges of sexual misconduct or rape. When some women nevertheless lodged charges, they suffered retaliation in the form of disciplinary action or unfavorable reports from superiors.

The sexual assault scandal was investigated by the office of the SECRETARY OF THE AIR FORCE and, independently, in January 2004, by the U.S. Senate's Armed Services Committee. Criminal investigations were also conducted, and, as of late 2004, several cadets had been indicted on rape or sexual assault charges; one, Darwin M. Paredesillescas, pleaded guilty to rape on July 26, 2004.

On March 25, 2004, U.S. Air Force secretary James G. Roche and U.S. Air Force Chief of Staff general John P. Jumper announced the transfer to other duties of the academy superintendent, General John R. Dallger, his second-in-command, Brigadier General S. Taco Gilbert III, the vice commandant, Colonel Robert D. Eskridge, and the commandant of cadet training, Colonel Laurie S. Slavec. The academy established a zero-tolerance policy on sexual assault, instituted revised training for academy personnel and cadets, and provided protection for anyone who reports misconduct.

United States Air Force Battlestaff Training School

Under direction of the AIR WARFARE CENTER (AWFC) the Battlestaff Training School develops and conducts command, control, communications, computers, and intelligence exercises. The school is located near Eglin AFB, Florida.

United States Air Force Chaplain Service

The USAF Chaplain Service is headquartered at Maxwell AFB, Alabama, and includes chaplains ordained in the Catholic, Protestant, Orthodox, Jewish, and Islamic faiths. Officer chaplains are assisted by enlisted specialists.

United States Air Force Museum (USAFM)

USAFM is the world's largest and oldest military aviation museum. It was opened in 1923 at McCook Field, Ohio, then moved in 1927 to Wright Field, Ohio. The collection was put in storage during WORLD WAR II, and the museum reopened at Wright-Patterson AFB, Ohio, in 1954.

Its mission is to portray the history and traditions of the USAF through specialized displays and exhibition of historical items, including more than 300 aircraft and missiles. More than 500,000 visitors tour the museum each year.

In addition to the museum itself, the USAF Museum manages the worldwide USAF Museum System (USAFMS) and it is responsible for all USAF historical property.

The USAF Museum is open seven days a week from 9 A.M. to 5 P.M., closed on Thanksgiving Day, Christmas Day, and New Year's Day only. It is located at historic Wright Field, Wright-Patterson AFB, six miles northeast of Dayton, Ohio.

United States Air Force NCO PME Graduate Ribbon   See DECORATIONS AND MEDALS.

United States Air Force School of Aerospace Medicine

Located at Brooks AFB, Texas, the USAF School of Aerospace Medicine is under the direction of the AIR FORCE SPACE COMMAND (AFSPC) and is the center for aeromedical education, training, and consultation in direct support of USAF, Department of Defense, and international aerospace operations. The school provides peacetime and contingency support in hyperbarics, human performance, clinical and dental investigations, environmental health, expeditionary medical support, and aeromedical evacuation. It trains 6,000 students annually, including physicians and nurses as well as other biomedical and biophysiological military and civilian professionals. See AVIATION MEDICINE for historical background and antecedent organizations.

United States Air Forces in Europe (USAFE)

USAFE conducts, controls, and coordinates offensive and defensive air operations in the European theater in an area of responsibility extending from the United Kingdom to Pakistan. USAFE operates as a component of the U.S. European Command, a unified command of the U.S. armed services. USAFE is a MAJCOM under supervision of the CHIEF OF STAFF, USAF, and the USAFE commander also serves as the commander of NATO's Allied Forces.

USAFE is headquartered at Ramstein AB, Germany.

"United States Air Force Song"

Also familiarly known as "Off We Go, Into the Wild Blue Yonder," the "United States Air Force Song" was originally called "The Army Air Corps Song" and was composed in 1939 in response to a $1,000 prize offered by *Liberty* magazine. The composer, Robert Crawford, was a civilian pilot and professional singer (known as "The Flying Baritone"), who, at the behest of the U.S. ARMY AIR CORPS, performed his composition nationally. The song was modified as "The Army Air Forces Song" and as "The United States Air Force Song." The song is copyrighted.

United States Air Forces Southern Command

In 1940, U.S. military aviation in the Panama Canal Zone was expanded, and the Panama Canal Air Force became a MAJCOM. In August 1941, it was redesignated the Caribbean Air Force, then the SIXTH AIR FORCE in 1942. In July 1946, the unit was redesignated Caribbean Air Command and, in July 1963, the U.S. Air Forces Southern Command. Inactivated in 1976, the unit's resources and mission were transferred to the TACTICAL AIR COMMAND (TAC). In turn, TAC created the 830th Air Division to handle the mission of the former Caribbean Air Command. The 830th Air Division was assigned to the TWELFTH AIR FORCE in 1990.

United States Air Force Special Operations School

Reporting directly to AIR FORCE SPECIAL OPERATIONS COMMAND (AFSOC), the Special Operations School educates U.S. military and other personnel

in the mission and functions of special operations in the evolving world threat. As the primary support unit of the USAF component of U.S. Special Operations Command and component of the Joint Special Operations Forces Institute, the school provides joint education to 8,000 students annually.

The school's antecedent organization, the U.S. Air Force Special Air Warfare School, was activated at Hurlburt Field (see Hurlburt AFB) in April 1967 and was redesignated the U.S. Air Force Special Operations School the following year. On June 1, 1987, the school was assigned to U.S. Special Operations Command as an organizational element of TWENTY-THIRD AIR FORCE. Courses offered include:

- Crisis Response Senior Seminar
- Latin America Orientation Courses
- Revolutionary Warfare Course
- Special Operations Liaison Element Staff Officer Course
- Dynamics of International Terrorism
- Responsible Officer's Course/Force Protection II
- Commander's Responsibilities and Awareness Course/Force Protection III
- Introduction to Special Operations
- Middle East Orientation Course
- Russia, Central Europe and Central Asia Orientation Course
- Special Operations in the 21st Century Seminar
- Asian-Pacific Orientation Course
- Joint Special Operations Staff Officer Course
- Sub-Saharan Africa Orientation Course
- Civil-Military Strategy for Internal Development Course
- Joint Special Operations Planning Workshop
- Cross-Cultural Communications Course
- Joint Psychological Operations Course
- Joint Special Operations Intermediate Seminar
- Joint Senior Psychological Operations Course

United States Air Force Test Pilot School

Located at Edwards Air Force Base, California, the United States Air Force Test Pilot School trains air force TEST PILOTS to impart the scientific and engineering knowledge, critical and reasoned judgment, and managerial skills required to test sophisticated modern aircraft. The school also provides training in precision handling of aircraft as well as systematic training in gathering and interpreting flight data.

The origin of the school dates to 1914, when the army set up its first dedicated aeronautical research and development establishment at North Island, San Diego. During WORLD WAR I, this function was transferred to McCook Field at Dayton, Ohio, which included a sophisticated aviation engineering laboratory. During the 1920s, the facilities were again moved, to nearby Wright Field, but most of the nation's basic flight research was shifted to the civilian National Advisory Committee for Aeronautics (NACA). Indeed, during the 1920s and early 1930s, aviation companies contracting with the army were encouraged to conduct their own flight tests and verification. By 1934, the army ceased developing its own aircraft, but established a small Flight Test Section to verify performance of aircraft under contract. The training of these early test pilots was entirely informal until the exigencies of World War II called for greater professionalism among test pilots and engineers. At Wright Field, Colonel Ernest K. Warburton, chief of the field's Flight Section, studied the British example. The Royal Air Force (RAF) had established its Empire Test Pilots' School at Boscombe Down, U.K., and Warburton adopted many of its procedures and standards. Ultimately, this resulted in a Flight Test Training Unit established on September 9, 1944 under the command of Major Ralph C. Hoewing.

The school, established at Ohio's Vandalia Municipal Airport (now the Dayton International Airport), was initially staffed by three or four instructors, who set up a formal three-month long curriculum stressing performance flight test theory and piloting techniques.

In the meantime, Colonel Albert Boyd had become chief of the Flight Test Division. He personally chose a staff of test pilots and assigned them to the Flight Test Division's Accelerated Service Test Section. Those who survived Boyd's scrutiny were given formal classroom training.

After World War II, Boyd's program moved to Muroc Air Force Base, California, and became the Flight Performance School, then, in 1951, the Air Materiel Command Experimental Test Pilot School. At this same time, Muroc was renamed Edwards Air Force Base. Before the year ended, the school was again renamed and became the Air Research and Development Command (ARDC) Experimental Test Pilot School. In 1952, it reverted to the less cumbersome U.S. Air Force Experimental Flight Test Pilot School. The school was very demanding. Not only did candidates have to be outstanding pilots, they had to be capable of excelling in course work that included flight mechanics, differential calculus, and supersonic aerodynamics.

The school emerged as the premier institution of its kind in the world and was renamed the United States Air Force Flight Test Pilot School on June 9, 1955. During the 1950s, its cutting-edge focus came to encompass space projects, including, most famously, work with the X-15 rocket plane. Ultimately, the school became the air force training ground for its astronauts, and on October 12, 1961, the school was redesignated the U.S. Air Force Aerospace Research Pilot School (ARPS). All U.S. military pilots wishing to qualify as astronauts were now sent here. Curriculum was expanded to include thermodynamics, bioastronautics, and Newtonian mechanics and occupied an entire year.

In 1972, the school shifted its focus from space and spaceflight training, once again becoming the United States Air Force Test Pilot School, with an emphasis on advanced classroom training, especially in the use of computers in the testing mission.

United States Central Command Air Forces (CENTAF)

CENTAF—U.S. Central Command Air Forces—is headquartered at Shaw AFB, South Carolina, and is charged with planning for and executing contingency operations ranging from humanitarian airlift to integration of multinational forces into coherent air operations in support of a major theater war. CENTAF is capable of deploying tactical aircraft and carrying out strategic reconnaissance and intelligence collection. CENTAF orchestrates the multinational Operation Southern Watch, through Joint Task Force–Southwest Asia.

CENTAF's tactical mission includes antiarmor capabilities to create a credible deterrence in the Middle East. If this deterrence fails, CENTAF's mission is to gain and maintain air superiority as a first step toward victory in a major theater war.

United States Strategic Air Forces (USSTAF)

USSTAF was established on February 4, 1944, as successor to the U.S. Strategic Air Forces in Europe (USSAFE)—not to be confused with UNITED STATES AIR FORCES IN EUROPE (USAFE)—that had been established in November 1943 to oversee and coordinate operations of the EIGHTH AIR FORCE and the FIFTEENTH AIR FORCE. Headquarters was at Bushey Park, near London. USSTAF was responsible for planning missions, selecting targets, setting the length of combat crew operational tours, and managing the movement of personnel between 8AF and 15AF.

U.S. Army Air Corps (USAAC)

With the U.S. ARMY AIR SERVICE (USAAS) and U.S. ARMY AIR FORCES (USAAF), the USAAC is one of the three major antecedent organizations of the USAF. It was established on July 2, 1926, by the AIR CORPS ACT OF 1926 to improve and expand the nation's air arm, the U.S. Army Air Service, which it replaced. Most significantly, unlike the USAAS, the USAAC had its own assistant secretary of war for air and air sections in the General Staff, together with a five-year plan for expansion. F. Trubee Davison was appointed as assistant secretary, serving until 1932. President Franklin D. Roosevelt never appointed a successor.

As originally established, the USAAC had five agencies: Training Center, for flight training; Technical School; Balloon and Airship School; Tactical School; and Materiel Division (which included an Engineering School, Depots, Procurement Planning Representatives, and Plant Representatives). In 1926, USAAC had 919 officers, 8,725 enlisted men, and 1,254 airplanes. On the eve of WORLD WAR II, it had 23,455 enlisted men, and when the war in Europe began, it rapidly expanded to more than 150,000 men in 1941, when it was replaced by the USAAF. In 1939, the USAAC had an inventory of 2,177 planes, a small number, although most were relatively modern.

In addition to managing men and materiel, USAAC made strides in developing air power strategy and doctrine, and it was as USAAC that the nation's air arm began to expand into a large modern air force capable of fighting a world war. USAAC also took a critical step toward operational independence with the creation in 1935 of GENERAL HEADQUARTERS AIR FORCE (GHQ Air Force), which centralized organization and, by 1939, was transferred from control by the army chief of staff to the chief of the Air Corps.

In June 1941, the USAAC became the USAAF.

U.S. Army Air Forces (USAAF)

With the U.S. ARMY AIR SERVICE (USAAS) and U.S. ARMY AIR CORPS (USAAC), USAAF is one of the three major antecedent organizations of the USAF.

As Nazi aggression increased after the Munich Conference of 1938 and culminated in the outbreak of WORLD WAR II in Europe in September 1939, the U.S. Congress, although generally isolationist, appropriated funds to expand the USAAC in anticipation of U.S. entry into the war. Between 1940 and 1941, USAAC tripled in size, and, seeing in the German *Blitzkrieg* of Europe the tremendous importance of air power, USAAC planners anticipated creating an air arm that would eventually number 2,165,000 men. An organization of this magnitude required a new status. Therefore, on

June 20, 1941, Army Regulation 95-5 created the USAAF, which would take its place alongside the army's three other major divisions: Army Ground Forces, Army Service Forces, and Defense and Theater Commands.

Internally the USAAF was divided into Combat Command, successor to GENERAL HEADQUARTERS AIR FORCE (GHQ Air Force), which would conduct air operations, and the Air Corps (AC), which encompassed two subcommands: Materiel, and Training and Operations. In turn, Training and Operations had four subordinate organizations—Technical Schools, Southwest Training, Gulf Training, and Southeast Training—designed to build a credible air force as quickly as possible.

The six-month-old USAAF had had precious little time for training before the attack on Pearl Harbor, December 7, 1941, thrust the United States into World War II. In its first year, USAAF quintupled to 764,000, and in its second year tripled this number. By 1944, it reached a staggering 2,372,292 —31 percent of U.S. Army strength—which would be the all-time high for the USAAF as well as the USAF. By the middle of 1944, the USAAF inventory boasted 78,757 aircraft, of which 445 were very heavy bombers and 11,720 were heavy bombers.

By 1944, the USAAF was organized into 10 major commands in the continental United States: Training, I Troop Carrier, Air Transport, Materiel, Air Service, and Proving Ground Commands, in addition to the FIRST AIR FORCE, SECOND AIR FORCE, THIRD AIR FORCE, and FOURTH AIR FORCE. There were also eight USAAF agencies: AAF Board, Tactical and Redistribution Centers, Army Airways Communications System and Weather Wings, School of Aviation Medicine, First Motion Picture Unit, and Aeronautical Chart Plant. Overseas organizations used air forces subordinate to theater of operations command.

In Europe, the USAAF conducted STRATEGIC BOMBING against the German aircraft industry, although, by June 1944, much of the USAAF effort was diverted to tactical operations in support of the Allies' Normandy invasion "Operation Overlord." Overlapping with invasion duty was a strategic campaign against the German oil industry,

beginning in May, and then an attack on the German transportation system, beginning early in 1945.

In the Pacific theater, the USAAF began a strategic bombing campaign against Japan from bases in the Marianas beginning in October 1944. By August 1945, bombing combined with a submarine blockade had reduced Japanese production by 75 percent, and the USAAF and the U.S. Navy believed the war against Japan could be ended without a land invasion. The U.S. Army disagreed, but the dropping of atomic bombs on Hiroshima (August 6, 1945) and Nagasaki (August 9, 1945) rendered the argument moot as Japan suddenly surrendered.

Recruiting poster for the Army Air Service *(Library of Congress)*

USAAF forces rapidly demobilized after the war. Only two forces remained outside the continental United States, in occupied Germany and Japan. By May 1947, the USAAF mustered only 303,000 men and 25,000 aircraft. Counterpointed to this, however, was the restructuring of USAAF as an independent air arm, the USAF, which was created on September 18, 1947, pursuant to the NATIONAL SECURITY ACT OF 1947 and EXECUTIVE ORDER 9877.

U.S. Army Air Service (USAAS)

With the U.S. ARMY AIR CORPS (USAAC) and the U.S. ARMY AIR FORCES (USAAF) the USAAS was one of the three major antecedent organizations of the USAF.

On May 21, 1918, by executive order, President Woodrow Wilson transferred military aviation from the U.S. Army Signal Corps and created the USAAS, directly under the secretary of war. As originally conceived, the USAAS consisted of two agencies, the Bureau of Aircraft Production and the Division of Military Aeronautics. On August 27, Wilson assigned a new assistant secretary of war, John D. Ryan, as director of the USAAS. Wilson's wartime actions were confirmed by Congress after the war by the National Defense Act of 1920, which officially made the USAAS an arm under the army.

During WORLD WAR I, the USAAS totalled 190,000 men. By June 1919, this number had been slashed to 27,000. Procurement of aircraft and other equipment stopped, and much was sold as surplus. In 1920, the now-diminutive organization was divided into four principal subsections: Administrative, Information, Training and Operations, and Supply. The USAAS had two wings, divided into seven groups and 27 squadrons, plus 42 companies for lighter-than-air aviation. Flight training, which had been suspended with demobilization, recommenced in January 1920, as did other aircrew, technical, and professional training. Procurement also resumed to a limited degree, but the service remained very small, mustering between 9,000 and 11,600 men during 1920–26. In 1924, the USAAS inventory consisted of 1,364 aircraft, of which only 754 were in commission. A large proportion of the inventory, 457 aircraft, were observation craft—only 78 were fighters and 59 bombers. In addition, the USAAS counted eight attack aircraft. Morale during this period was understandably low, and air power advocates, most notably Major General WILLIAM MITCHELL, vigorously campaigned for more and better aircraft (more fighters and bombers, fewer observation craft) and greater status within the army—or even independence from it. Ultimately, this activity resulted in the AIR CORPS ACT OF 1926, which replaced the USAAS on July 2, 1926, with the USAAC.

V

Vance AFB, Oklahoma   See AIR FORCE BASES.

Vandenberg AFB, California   See AIR FORCE BASES.

Vandenberg, Hoyt Sanford (1899–1954)
U.S. Air Force general and Chief of Staff

One of the principal architects of the USAF, Hoyt Vandenberg was born in Milwaukee, Wisconsin, and graduated from the U.S. Military Academy (West Point) in 1923. After graduation, he attended flying school at Brooks Field (Brooks AFB) and Kelly Field (Kelly AFB), both in Texas. After qualification as a pilot, he was assigned to the 3rd Attack Group in 1924, and, in 1927, he became a flight instructor at the Air Corps Primary Flying School, March Field (March AFB), California. Promoted to 1st lieutenant in August 1928, Vandenberg joined the 6th Pursuit Squadron at Wheeler Field, Hawaii, in May 1929. In November of that year, he was named to command of the squadron, then returned to the mainland in September 1931 as an instructor at Randolph Field (Randolph AFB), Texas.

Vandenberg attended the Air Corps Tactical School, from which he graduated in 1935. From there, he continued on to the Command and General Staff School at Fort Leavenworth, Kansas, graduating in 1936. He returned to the Air Corps Tactical School as an instructor. After graduating from the Army War College in 1939, Vandenberg was assigned to the war plans division of Headquarters, U.S. Army Air Corps, Lieutenant General HENRY HARLEY ARNOLD. Promoted to major in July 1941, lieutenant colonel in November, and colonel on January 27, 1942, Vandenberg became opera-

Hoyt S. Vandenberg   *(U.S. Air Force)*

tions and training officer in the Air Staff, as well as chief of staff of the TWELFTH AIR FORCE under Lieutenant General JAMES H. DOOLITTLE. In this assignment, he played a major role in planning the American air component of the invasion of Operation Torch, the invasion of North Africa, during November 1942. After the success of this mission, Vandenberg was promoted to brigadier general in December.

In March 1943, Vandenberg was named chief of staff of the Northwest Africa Strategic Air Force. With his men, he flew many missions over Tunisia, Sicily, Sardinia, and southern Italy from March through August, when he was recalled to Washington as deputy chief of the Air Staff. In September 1943, Vandenberg was named to a delegation sent to the Soviet Union to arrange bases for shuttle-bombing missions against eastern European targets. After successfully negotiating the use of the bases, he returned to Air Corps Headquarters in Washington, where he formulated plans for the air component of the Normandy ("D-day") invasion.

Vandenberg was promoted to major general in March 1944 and was assigned to General Dwight D. Eisenhower's staff as deputy to Britain's Air Vice-Marshal Sir Trafford Leigh-Mallory, who was commander of the Allied Expeditionary Air Force. After the success of the Normandy invasion, Vandenberg was assigned to command the NINTH AIR FORCE, which provided extensive air support for Lieutenant General Omar N. Bradley's Twelfth Army Group, which swept across Europe. Promoted to lieutenant general in March, Vandenberg returned to Washington after V-E Day and, in July 1945, was named assistant chief of staff for operations for the Army Air Forces. After V-J Day, he became chief of the army general staff's Intelligence Division in January 1946. In June, he was made director of the Central Intelligence Group—precursor to the CIA.

In September 1947, Vandenberg returned to military aviation as vice chief of staff of the newly independent USAF. In July 1948, he succeeded GENERAL CARL A. SPAATZ as Air Force Chief of Staff, a position in which he served during the early years of the cold war. It was Vandenberg who was responsible for planning and directing the execution of the BERLIN AIRLIFT from June 1948 to May 1949. He also directed air operations during the KOREAN WAR, from June 1950 to July 1953. Stricken with cancer, Vandenberg retired from the USAF in June 1953 and died the following year.

Vandenberg brilliantly executed the mission of ground support in WORLD WAR II and, during the cold war, he was an effective champion of the development of the USAF as the nation's chief strategic deterrent force.

Vietnam War

Origins of the War

During the 19th century, France had established colonial hegemony in Laos, Cambodia, and Vietnam. At the beginning of WORLD WAR II, after France capitulated to Germany in 1940, the Japanese allowed French colonial officials nominal authority while actually assuming de facto control of these areas themselves. In 1945, with the liberation of France, the Japanese seized full control, eliminating the French police agencies and other armed authorities that had long kept in check indigenous nationalist groups seeking independence. In Vietnam, the largest and most powerful of these groups was the Viet Minh, which, under the leadership of Ho Chi Minh, launched a guerrilla war against the Japanese forces of occupation and soon took control of the nation's northern regions. In this, Ho Chi Minh was aided by U.S. Office of Strategic Services (OSS) military teams.

After the war in Europe had ended, Allied forces turned their attention to Vietnam (and the rest of Southeast Asia), a theater they had largely neglected during most of the Pacific war. Nationalist Chinese troops moved into the Tonkin provinces of northern Vietnam, and the British, anxious to restore France to the status of a world power in order to help counter the Soviet Union's rapidly expanding postwar sphere of influence, secured southern Vietnam for the reentry of the French, who ruthlessly suppressed all agitation for independence in that region. The French began talks with Ho Chi Minh, now firmly established in the north, but these quickly proved fruitless, and a state of chronic guerrilla conflict developed.

The conflict escalated during 1946, when Nationalist Chinese forces, who had occupied the northern part of the country, were voluntarily replaced there by the French military. Although Nationalist Chinese leader Chiang Kai-shek (Jiang Jieshi) harbored no love for French imperialism, in battling Mao Zedong's communist forces, he feared a communist takeover in Vietnam and preferred French control of the region. In November, fire was exchanged between a French patrol boat and Vietnamese militia in Haiphong harbor. The French retaliated by bombarding Haiphong, killing some 6,000 civilians and prompting Ho Chi Minh to break off all talks with the French, retreat with his government into the hill country of Tonkin, and conduct an all-out guerrilla war against the French.

Many in the United States strongly sympathized with Ho Chi Minh's nationalism. President Harry S. Truman, like President Roosevelt before him, was an anti-imperialist. But he also felt that an independent Vietnam would likely become a communist Vietnam. Still, Truman urged the French to reach a political solution in Vietnam and barred direct export of war materiel to French forces there—though he vacillated to the important extent of refusing to bar arms shipments to France itself, which, of course, was free to transship the materiel to its troops in Vietnam.

U.S. Involvement Begins

The fall of China to communism in 1949, together with the intensification of the cold war in Europe by the end of the decade, including the induction of much of eastern Europe into the Soviet camp, compelled the United States to accept French authority in Vietnam, no matter how distasteful. Moreover, if the newly formed North Atlantic Treaty Organization (NATO) were to succeed as a force against communism in Europe, the full support of France was required. Its military resources drained by the fierce guerrilla warfare in Vietnam, France was hardly in a position to offer the full

degree of support. Finally, on February 7, 1950, the United States recognized Vietnam as it was constituted by the French under their puppet, the former emperor Bao Dai. Within less than two weeks, the French requested U.S. economic and military aid, threatening to abandon the nation to Ho Chi Minh if the aid were not forthcoming. Some $75 million was appropriated immediately. Shortly afterward, on June 25, 1950, communist forces from North Korea invaded South Korea. Truman responded by stepping up aid to the French in Vietnam, sending eight C-47 transports directly to Saigon.

Flown into Vietnam by USAF pilots, these eight aircraft were the first aviation aid the United States furnished in the region. On August 3, 1950, the first contingent of U.S. military advisers—the U.S. Military Assistance Advisory Group (MAAG)—arrived in Saigon. Air assistance operations were at first directed by the air attaché in Saigon, then, on November 8, they came under the direction of the Air Force Section of MAAG–Indochina. At this point, the mission of the American advisers was primarily to supply aircraft and materiel to the French and, secondarily, to work with the French forces to improve their military capabilities. The least important aspect of the mission was to develop indigenous Vietnamese armed forces.

By 1952, the United States was financing one-third of the French military effort in Vietnam, yet it was becoming apparent that the French, though they were enjoying moderate success against the insurgents, were losing heart. It was at this juncture, on January 4, 1953, that the first sizable contingent of USAF personnel (other than those attached to MAAG) was deployed to Vietnam. This group included a substantial complement of enlisted USAF technicians, mainly to handle supply and the maintenance of aircraft. The contingent remained in Vietnam until August 14, 1952, when they were relieved by French forces.

In April 1953, the Viet Minh staged a major offensive in western Tonkin, advancing into Laos and menacing Thailand. The French requested the loan of C-119 transports to AIRLIFT heavy equipment into Laos. President Eisenhower, wary of committing USAF crews to a combat mission, ordered military crews to fly the aircraft to Nha Trang, where nonmilitary contract pilots took them over for the flight to Cat Bi Airfield near Haiphong. Enlisted ground personnel were dispatched to Cat Bi from the 24th Air Depot Wing to carry out maintenance and supply functions, and then accompanied the aircraft north to Gia Lam Airfield near Hanoi. The detachment withdrew in July, after completing their mission.

General Henri-Eugène Navarre, France's new commander in charge of operations in Vietnam, presented a plan to defeat the Viet Minh by luring them into open battle and reducing them to a low level of guerrilla warfare that could be contained by indigenous Vietnamese troops. Additional cargo planes were loaned to the French, and, in the fall of 1953, Navarre began operations on the strategically located plain of Dien Bien Phu in northwest Tonkin, near Laos. French paratroopers fortified an airstrip there beginning on November 20, and, on December 5, the U.S. FAR EAST AIR FORCES (FEAF) flew more C-119 transports to Cat Bi, from which civilian contract pilots or French personnel would fly them into the combat area. Ground personnel from the 483rd Troop Carrier Wing, the 8081st Aerial Resupply Unit, and a provisional maintenance squadron of the Far East Air Logistics Force were stationed at Cat Bi to service the aircraft.

American military officials and the Eisenhower administration were becoming increasingly anxious, however, noting that the Viet Minh were menacing Hanoi and Haiphong—from which Navarre had drawn forces to bolster Dien Bien Phu—and that the Viet Minh were also massing around Dien Bien Phu. President Eisenhower authorized increased military aid—short of committing American personnel to combat—and B-26s and RB-26s were dispatched on loan to the French. However, French air units were seriously undermanned, and the fateful decision was made on January 31, 1954, to dispatch some 300 airmen to service aircraft at Tourane and at the Do Son Airfield near Haiphong. This, the first substantial commitment of U.S. airmen—indeed, of U.S. military personnel—to the war in Vietnam, was highly classified. Addressing the American public, President Eisenhower described the forces he was committing as "some airplane mechanics . . . who would not get touched by combat."

Despite American logistical support, it became apparent day by day that the French situation at Dien Bien Phu was hopeless as the defensive perimeter steadily contracted around the enclave. President Eisenhower contemplated direct U.S. military intervention, principally in the form of air support, but decided not to act in the absence of approval from the British and a demonstration of a French willingness to train and employ indigenous troops and ultimately to grant Vietnam its independence. On April 7, 1954, President Eisenhower presented to the American press a rationale for fighting communism in Vietnam. "You have a row of dominoes set up," he explained, "you knock over the first one, and what will happen to the last one is the certainty it will go over very quickly." Yet American military experts were not sanguine about the prospect of committing U.S. combat forces in the region, concluding that French colonialism had alienated the indigenous people, who lacked the will to fight Ho Chi Minh's forces. Moreover, logistics in Southeast Asia generally were nightmarish, presenting support problems of gargantuan proportions. Finally, it was feared that commencing a war in Vietnam would mean beginning a war with Red China—under the worst conditions imaginable. On May 7, 1954, Diem Bien Phu fell to the forces of Ho Chi Minh. Dien Bien Phu was followed by additional Viet Minh victories, and, in July, at the conference table in Geneva, the French and the Viet Minh agreed to divide Vietnam along the 17th parallel and concluded an armistice.

In accordance with the terms of the armistice, the USAF evacuated its personnel from Vietnam and assisted in the medical evacuation of wounded French troops. Ho Chi Minh felt confident that the reunification plebiscite mandated by the armistice and scheduled for July 1956 would result in a communist victory. The United States, in the meantime, worked with French and South Vietnamese authorities to create a stable government and build an effective South Vietnamese military. The United States also sponsored the creation of the Southeast Asia Treaty Organization (SEATO) as a shield against communist aggression and Washington proposed building up the MAAG staff in Saigon to accommodate its increased advisory role. However, the international commission charged with enforcing the Geneva armistice refused to approve the buildup. When 350 men were authorized as a "Temporary Equipment Recovery Mission," ostensibly assigned to inventory and remove surplus equipment, MAAG appropriated them as logistical advisers, and they became (despite the international commission) the Combat Arms Training and Organization Division of MAAG. With the French now withdrawing, these men formed the nucleus from which U.S. involvement in Vietnam would expand.

When South Vietnam refused to conduct the reunification plebiscite mandated by the Geneva agreement, American officials braced for an anticipated invasion from the north. It failed to materialize, and President Eisenhower decided to commit the United States to a long-term advisory role, intending to accomplish what the French had not—the creation of an effective indigenous Vietnamese military. Nevertheless, North Vietnamese insurgency into the south increased during the closing years of the decade, and, in September 1959, the Vietcong—South Vietnamese communists—commenced guerrilla warfare by ambushing two South Vietnamese army companies in the Plain of Reeds southwest of Saigon. In 1960, the United States expanded its MAAG advisers to 685 men, including Special Forces teams assigned to train Vietnamese rangers. Despite these efforts, relations between the South Vietnamese civil government and disaffected elements of the military became strained to the point of an attempted coup against President Ngo Dinh Diem on November 11, 1960. Compounding this crisis was the situation in Vietnam's neighbor, Laos, the government of which was being challenged by military forces of the pro-communist Pathet Lao.

When President John F. Kennedy took office in January 1961, the number of Vietcong insurgents in South Vietnam had swelled to some 14,000. They waged a combination guerrilla war and campaign of terror and assassination, successfully targeting thousands of civil officials, government workers, and police officers. On April 29, 1961, President Kennedy authorized an additional 100 advisers, the establishment of a combat development and test center in Vietnam, increased economic aid, and other measures. On May 11, Kennedy committed 400 U.S. Special Forces troops to raise and train a force of irregulars in areas controlled by the Vietcong, particularly along the border.

U.S. Air Force Presence

The first USAF personnel to arrive in Vietnam on a permanent duty status were the 67 men assigned to a mobile combat reporting post, essentially a radar installation, which was secretly airlifted to Vietnam during September 26–October 3, 1961. After it was installed at Tan Son Nhut on October 5, 314 additional personnel were eventually assigned to the unit. These officers and airmen created the nucleus of what would become a massive and highly sophisticated tactical air control system. Within a short time, the USAF also assigned photo reconnaissance personnel to the region, and, on October 11, 1961, President Kennedy ordered the first combat detachment to Vietnam. Officially called the 4400 Combat Crew Training Squadron, this elite force of 124 officers and 228 airmen equipped with 16 C-47s, eight B-26s, and eight T-28s was nicknamed Jungle Jim and code named Farm Gate. This was an "air commando" organization, and the officers as well as airmen were chosen for their physical and emotional hardiness, their combat skill, and their sense of adventure.

The first air force contingent soon found themselves at the mercy of an ambiguous sense of mission. They were trained as a combat unit, yet were officially expected only to train Vietnamese forces. Nevertheless, they were briefed for combat. In fact, the group did train Vietnamese crews and performed difficult and frustrating aerial reconnaissance missions. Flying actual combat strikes was another matter, and, on December 26, 1961, word came from the highest level of command that the unit was to conduct combat missions only when the Vietnamese air force could not. Restrictions and mixed signals concerning their mission undermined the morale of Farm Gate. The situation would prove prophetic of the tenor of the entire war.

In October 1961, President Kennedy dispatched General Maxwell Taylor and Walt Rostow to survey the situation in Vietnam and advise him as to whether to continue the U.S. advisory role there or to commit to a direct combat function. Taylor and Rostow advised continuing USAF reconnaissance flights, setting up a tactical air-ground system, which included training functions, and giving Farm Gate a freer hand, but not committing substantial U.S. combat forces. Kennedy's approval of these recommendations on November 3, 1961, marked a shift from a purely advisory role for the United States to what was described as a "limited partnership and working collaboration." The flow of aid and materiel increased dramatically, so that by June 30, 1962, there were 6,419 Americans in South Vietnam. Even as these forces were building, President Kennedy reported to the press and public that no U.S. combat forces were in Vietnam. However, he admitted, the "training units" present there were authorized to return fire if fired upon. From this point through 1968, American involvement in the Vietnam War rapidly escalated.

Escalation, 1962–1964

Beginning in January 1962, the USAF executed an airlift operation dubbed Mule Train, transporting quantities of cargo and personnel into Vietnam. Shortly after this, the USAF launched Operation Ranch Hand, an early experiment in spraying chemical defoliants to reduce cover and concealment available to the Vietcong. On February 2, 1962, a C-123 training for this mission crashed, probably the result of ground fire or sabotage. The

three crewmen killed were the first USAF fatalities in South Vietnam.

By June 1963, 16,652 American military personnel—including 4,790 USAF officers and airmen—were stationed in Vietnam, and Farm Gate, still the nucleus of the USAF presence there, officially became the 1st Air Commando Squadron. At this time, the 33rd and 34th Tactical Groups came into being as well at Tan Son Nhut. The 33rd included the 33rd Air Base Squadron and the 33rd Consolidated Aircraft Maintenance Squadron. The 34th Tactical Group, based at Bien Hoa, likewise included maintenance and support squadrons, all staffed largely by enlisted airmen. Other support units, including Mule Train, were reorganized and enlarged as troop carrier squadrons. Yet, during 1963, Vietcong attacks increased and, in the Mekong Delta, the Vietcong escalated the war from guerrilla engagements to full-scale field operations. By the end of the year, the Vietcong were clearly defeating the forces of South Vietnam, the administration of President Ngo Dinh Diem was rapidly losing support, and friction between the Diem government and the United States was intensifying. On September 2, 1963, President Kennedy declared in a television address to the American public that the Diem government was out of touch with the Vietnamese people and that the war could be won only if it had popular support. The seeds of dissent were also present in the United States, as many objected to America's increasing involvement in a distant war to support an unpopular and repressive regime. On November 1, 1963, elements of the Vietnamese army staged a coup against Diem, who was assassinated the following day. A military junta set up a provisional government, which the United States recognized on November 8. Taking advantage of the confusing situation, the Vietcong stepped up their attacks, and the USAF heightened its response to them.

Gulf of Tonkin Incident, 1964

In the midst of the deteriorating situation in Vietnam, on November 22, 1963, President John F. Kennedy was assassinated, and Vice President

The Vietnam War saw the introduction of the gunship, modified C-47s and C-130s, capable of pouring concentrated fire onto ground positions. Pictured is an AC-130. *(U.S. Air Force)*

Lyndon Johnson took office. General CURTIS LEMAY and the Joint Chiefs of Staff advised the new president to expand the war with quick, decisive action against North Vietnam, including the bombing of Hanoi. Secretary of Defense Robert McNamara favored a more conservative approach, confining operations principally to South Vietnam, but relaxing the rules for air engagement within South Vietnam and thereby expanding the role of USAF personnel working with Vietnamese crews. A short time later, however, when Hanoi responded negatively to American peace feelers, Secretary McNamara called for the formulation of an air strike plan against North Vietnam. Formulated in the summer of 1964, the plan was held in abeyance, but the situation in Vietnam took a dramatic turn on August 7, 1964, when the U.S. Senate passed the so-called Gulf of Tonkin Resolution after the U.S. destroyer *Maddox,* conducting electronic espionage in international waters in the Gulf of Tonkin, was reported fired upon on two separate occasions (the second time in company with the *C.*

Turner Joy) by North Vietnamese torpedo boats. The Senate resolution gave the president almost unlimited authority to expand the war as he saw fit. (It was subsequently discovered that the second attack was a phantom and did not actually occur.)

It was during this period that USAF personnel were successfully improvising the tactical weapons that the hitherto strategically oriented air arm lacked. C-47 and, later, C-130, aircraft were modified as gunships, firing 7.62-mm Gatling guns from side cargo doors. Infrared reconnaissance techniques were also being developed, and defoliation and crop destruction operations were stepped up.

Airmen were increasingly called upon to augment Vietnamese forces to maintain interior security and provide perimeter defense for major air bases. On November 1, 1964, Vietcong forces penetrated the perimeter of the Bien Hoa air base, killing four USAF personnel and wounding 72 in addition to destroying or damaging a number of aircraft and buildings. Although the Joint Chiefs recommended severe reprisals against North Vietnam, President Johnson, on the eve of election, bided his time. Following his victory, however, Johnson authorized a program of restricted air strikes on infiltration targets in Laos (Operation Barrel Roll). When a 300-pound charge exploded in the Brink Hotel, bachelor officers' quarters for U.S. advisers, killing two Americans and injuring 64 others in addition to 43 Vietnamese, the Joint Chiefs again urged immediate reprisals. President Johnson demurred. A few days later, on December 27, Vietcong raided the hamlet of Binh Gia, then, on December 31, surrounded the U.S. 4th Marine Battalion, which had marched to Binh Gia's relief, inflicting heavy casualties. This action, combined with the Brink Hotel explosion, prompted Ambassador Maxwell Taylor, who had earlier argued for restraint, to recommend immediate air action against North Vietnam. Then, on February 7, Vietcong mortar squads and demolition teams attacked U.S. advisory forces and Camp Holloway, headquarters of the U.S. Army 52nd Aviation Battalion, near Pleiku, killing nine Americans and wounding 108. In response, the USAF launched Operation Flaming Dart against a Vietcong military barracks near Dong Hoi. A Vietcong counterstrike came on the tenth against a U.S.-ARVN barracks at Qui Nhon, killing 23 airmen and seven Vietnamese troops. This was followed by a U.S. response the next day. These exchanges marked the beginning of a long offensive escalation.

Rapid Escalation, 1965–1969

The air strikes against North Vietnam soon became known by the code name Rolling Thunder and began on March 2, 1965, continuing through May 11, when they were suspended while the United States sought peace talks. Rolling Thunder resumed on May 18 and continued through 1968. In May 1965, 10,000 USAF personnel were serving in Vietnam. By year's end, that number grew to 21,000 operating from eight major bases. By 1968, 58,000 USAF personnel were stationed "in country."

Aside from combat, the most formidable problems airmen met were logistical. Heavy tropical rainfall during the monsoon season made runway construction extremely difficult, and the dry season brought its own problems as sand under temporary aluminum taxiways and runways caused them to shift, buckle, and dip. By the end of 1966, Air Force "Prime Beef" (BEEF: Base Engineering Emergency Force) construction teams were working feverishly at Tan Son Nhut, Bien Hoa, Da Nang, Nha Trang, Pleiku, and Binh Thuy, building aircraft revetments, barracks, Quonset huts, aprons, guard towers, and adequate plumbing and electrical facilities. "Red Horse" (Rapid Engineering and Heavy Operational Repair Squadron, Engineering) engineering squadrons provided more long-range services.

By 1967, the USAF introduced a host of innovations and refinements in communication, aircraft, and munitions in an effort to find technological solutions to the daunting problems of providing air support to ground forces fighting a guerrilla war along a highly fluid front and often in impenetrable jungle terrain.

Ground commanders made ever greater demands on air support. Air traffic control over Southeast Asia became a major priority. Sorties by STRATEGIC AIR COMMAND (SAC) B-52s—operations collectively code named "Arc Light"—numbered 1,562 in 1965, 5,217 in 1966, and 9,686 in 1967. Total tactical sorties for all USAF aircraft numbered 672,935 in 1967. In one operation alone, Junction City, which targeted the northern part of Tay Ninh Province along the Cambodian border and spanned February 22 to May 14, 1967, 5,002 tactical air sorties delivered to targets 7,430 tons of munitions, and 126 B-52 sorties delivered an additional 537 tons. Airlift sorties for this operation, transporting cargo and personnel, totaled 2,057. Control and coordination was provided both from ground radar sites and from airborne strike control aircraft such as the EC-121. At the height of the air war, Tan Son Nhut AB became the busiest air facility in the world.

Tet Offensive, 1968

The new year, ushering out 1968, in Vietnam began with the massive Tet offensive, in which North Vietnamese forces attacked major cities and military bases from Quang Tri and Khe Sanh near the demilitarized zone (DMZ) in the northern region of South Vietnam to Quang Long near the country's southern tip. Airmen had to defend Tan Son Nhut Air Base. Up north, near the demilitarized zone (DMZ), the U.S. Marine outpost at Khe Sanh was cut off by Vietcong beginning on January 30 and held under heavy siege until mid-March. In defense of Khe Sanh, B-52s and fighter bombers flew over 24,400 sorties, dropping 100,000 tons of ordnance, and airlift operations kept the isolated marines supplied. Weather conditions were so poor, that, for the first time in airlift history, crews dropped supplies under instrument flying conditions.

"Vietnamization" Period, 1969–1972

In January 1969, shortly after taking office, President Richard M. Nixon announced as one of the primary goals of his administration an end to U.S. combat involvement in Southeast Asia. "Vietnamization"—turning the war over to South Vietnamese forces—became a top priority, and the joint SEVENTH AIR FORCE—USAF Advisory Group Ad Hoc Committee was established in South Vietnam to aid in planning, implementing, and expediting the Vietnamization process. USAF officers and airmen trained Vietnamese operational and training crews in security, fire protection, weather, communications, electronics, air traffic control, and civil engineering.

During 1970–72, the Vietnamese air force was greatly expanded and reorganized, and, by 1971, the VNAF was flying more combat sorties than the USAF, which also transferred an increasing number of aircraft to Vietnamese control. By the end of 1971 the VNAF held sole responsibility for direct air support centers at Pleiku, Bien Hoa, and Da Nang. At the end of 1972, the Vietnamese air force had grown to 42,000 officers and enlisted men (with an additional 10,000 in training) and was equipped with 2,000 aircraft of 22 types, making it the fourth largest air force in the world, behind the People's Republic of China, the United States, and the Soviet Union.

Paris Peace Talks

In May 1969, the withdrawal of U.S. Army ground units from Vietnam began in earnest. USAF air support units lingered. In 1972, taking advantage of the reduced American ground presence, communist forces of the National Liberation Front crossed the DMZ and seized a South Vietnamese province. President Nixon ordered the mining of harbors of Haiphong and other North Vietnamese ports, and peace talks between the United States and North Vietnam, which had been conducted sporadically since 1968, broke down entirely in December. Nixon then ordered 11 days of intensive "Christmas bombing" of North Vietnamese cities. This operation was carried out by B-52s out of Anderson AFB on Guam and was dubbed "Linebacker II"—though many who served on the mission referred to it as the "Eleven-Day War."

Linebacker II, conducted from December 18 to December 29, followed Linebacker I, a campaign of B-52 interdiction bombing in North Vietnam during the spring, summer, and fall of 1972. Linebacker I, in turn, had followed the sustained program air interdiction over North Vietnam conducted from 1965 to 1968 and known as Rolling Thunder. The Linebacker II operation was far more concentrated and intensive than the earlier sustained operations and was intended to force the North Vietnamese back to the conference table at Paris. During the 11 days of Linebacker II, the B-52s flew 729 sorties against 34 targets in North Vietnam above the 20th parallel. Linebacker II broke the deadlock of mid-December, and the North Vietnamese resumed negotiations on January 8, 1973. A cease-fire agreement was hammered out by January 28.

This final major USAF mission was a success, but the cease-fire it produced did not bring an end to the fighting. Nevertheless, the United States continued to withdraw from Vietnam. On January 27, Secretary of Defense Melvin Laird announced an end to the military draft, and, on March 29, the last U.S. troops departed the country, leaving behind some 8,500 U.S. civilian "technicians." On June 13, a new cease-fire agreement among the United

States, South Vietnam, North Vietnam, and the Vietcong was drawn up to end cease-fire violations. Nevertheless, from 1973 to 1975, fighting continued. In January 1975, communist forces captured the province of Phuoc Binh, then launched a major offensive in the central highlands during March. South Vietnamese forces withdrew from parts of the northwest and central highlands, and, on March 25, 1975, the old imperial capital of Hue fell. In April, Da Nang and Qui Nhon followed, and, after a fierce battle, the South Vietnamese gave up Kuon Loc on April 22. A day earlier, President Nguyen Van Thieu resigned and was briefly replaced by Tran Van Huong, whom the communists found unacceptable for negotiations. Lieutenant General Duong Van Minh became South Vietnam's last president and surrendered to the forces of North Vietnam on April 30. North and South Vietnam were officially unified under a Communist regime on July 2, 1976. The war was over.

Weighted Airman Promotion System (WAPS)

WAPS is the primary program used to select airmen for promotion to staff sergeant, technical sergeant, and master sergeant. Six weighted factors are used to score candidates for promotion:

1. Specialty Knowledge Test (SKT) for the applicable career field
2. Promotion Fitness Examination (PFE), a test of general USAF knowledge
3. Time in service (TIS) credit
4. Time in grade (TIG) credit
5. Credit for decorations awarded
6. Average numerical score for ratings received on performance reports

Promotion is based on WAPS and USAF vacancies in the applicable grade within the career field specialty.

Western Air Defense Force

Established in 1949 at Hamilton AFB, California, this named air force was assigned to CONTINENTAL AIR COMMAND (CONAC) and was charged with the air defense of the western continental United States. Reassigned to AIR DEFENSE COMMAND in 1951, it was discontinued in 1960.

Whiteman AFB, Missouri   See AIR FORCE BASES.

wing (organizational unit)   See ORGANIZATION, USAF.

Women Airforce Service Pilots (WASP)

Acting on an earlier suggestion by famed aviator JACQUELINE COCHRAN, Lieutenant General HENRY HARLEY ARNOLD, Chief of Staff of the U.S. ARMY AIR FORCES, authorized on October 7, 1942, a training program for 500 women ferry pilots, which became the Women Airforce Service Pilots (WASP) on August 5, 1943. It was the *second* USAAF women's auxiliary force, after the WOMEN'S AUXILIARY FERRYING SQUADRON (WAFS), which had been authorized in September 1942. Whereas the WAFS recruited only pilots with at least 500 flying hours' experience, of which at least 50 hours had to be in aircraft rated at 200 horsepower or more, WASP requirements were much lower. Admission to the first WASP training class, which graduated in November 1942, required 200 hours; the second class (December 1941), 100 hours; the third class (January 1943), 75 hours; and all subsequent classes required only 35 hours' flying time as a prerequisite for enrollment. There was no horsepower requirement at all; however, it should be noted that the USAAF had *no* flying-time prerequisite for male pilot cadets. Originally, only women between the ages of 21 and 35 were enrolled in the WASP. Beginning in August 1943, the age requirement was lowered to 18 $\frac{1}{2}$. In the segregated WORLD WAR II USAAF, only white women were accepted for service.

In August 1943, all women pilots serving with the USAAF became members of WASP, and the WAFS, therefore, ceased to exist. During its period of operation, from 1942 until it was deactivated in December 1944, WASP attracted 25,000 applicants, of whom 1,857 were accepted for training and 1,074 graduated. WASP pilots delivered a very wide range of planes from manufacturers to air base destinations in the continental United States, including training aircraft, transports, attack aircraft, and bombers. In addition to performing ferrying service, WASPs also flight tested some production (not prototype) aircraft, and, in a pinch, made repairs on the aircraft they delivered. Flying military aircraft is always hazardous and is

even more dangerous with new aircraft just off the assembly line; 38 WASP pilots were killed in the line of duty.

Altogether, WASPs flew some 75 million miles, with each pilot averaging 14 flying hours each month. For this, they were paid significantly less than their male counterparts. Whereas a male second lieutenant was paid $291 per month, a first lieutenant $330, and a captain $396, a WASP received $250 per month. Even less equitable were the differences between the compensation provided the male USAAF cadet and the WASP trainee. Male cadets were transported to flight school at no expense, whereas WASPs had to pay their own way. If a male cadet washed out of the program, he was assigned to other duty; a WASP paid her own way home. Men were furnished their

These three female pilots leaving their ship at the four engine school at Lockbourne are members of a group of WASPs who have been trained to ferry the B-17 Flying Fortresses. *(U.S. Air Force)*

room and board, but WASPs generally paid $1.65 a day for food and lodging. Male cadets were automatically furnished with a $10,000 G.I. insurance policy; not only did WASPs receive no insurance from the government, private insurers generally canceled whatever policies they might have carried. The WASP program did, however, contribute to an emergency fund. Uniforms were furnished free to all servicemen, whereas a WASP was required to pay more than $100 for hers. The army furnished full medical care for servicemen, but—at least initially—each WASP was responsible for her own medical care. Even in death, the unequal treatment continued. Fallen servicemen received a military funeral, including a military escort home, and the family of the airman was entitled to display a Gold Star. The government provided $200 for funeral expenses and a pine box for WASPs killed in the line of duty, but no military funeral or escort was provided, and the American flag could not be used on the coffin. Families were not authorized to display a Gold Star.

The WASP program was deactivated in December 1944, and the former WASP pilots were denied all veteran's benefits. Over the years, the women appealed to the U.S. government for recognition as veterans, but it was not until 1978 that Congress acted, at last recognizing those who served as veterans entitled to full benefits.

See also LOVE, NANCY HARKNESS; WOMEN IN THE AIR FORCE.

Women in the Air Force (WAF)

The Women's Army Corps (WAC) was created when President Franklin D. Roosevelt signed a bill on July 1, 1943. By January 1945, 42,181 WAC members served with the U.S. ARMY AIR FORCES, all in noncombat roles. It was not until after WORLD WAR II, when President Harry S. Truman signed the Women's Armed Services Integration Act on June 12, 1948, that women were permitted to join the newly created USAF as members of WAF, the first director of which was Geraldine Pratt May.

WAF members received the same training as male enlisted USAF members. Although women served in most enlisted roles, none performed flying duties, except for flight nurses. In 1958, restrictions were introduced barring women from service in intelligence, information, weather, certain maintenance specialties, and control tower operations. By 1965, almost 70 percent of WAF members served in clerical and administrative roles and 23 percent in medical fields. Women officers also held mainly desk jobs. On November 8, 1967, President Lyndon B. Johnson signed Public Law 90-130, which removed most restrictions for women officers. In June 1976, WAF ceased to exist, and women were fully integrated into the USAF.

Women's Auxiliary Ferrying Squadron (WAFS)

NANCY HARKNESS LOVE was one of two prominent female aviators of the 1930s who proposed the use of women in noncombat flying roles. But whereas JACQUELINE COCHRAN proposed training women as pilots, Love wanted to recruit women who already held commercial pilot's licenses, had 500 hours of flying time logged, and were rated to fly 200 horsepower craft. At first, Major General HENRY HARLEY ARNOLD, chief of the U.S. ARMY AIR FORCES, rejected Love's proposal, but, in September 1942, he approved the creation of a women's ferrying squadron. The WAFS was founded the same month.

Although the WAFS was established as the Second Ferrying Group, New Castle Army Air Base, near Wilmington, Delaware, with Love as its director, the organization was never formally activated as a USAAF squadron and was really a civil auxiliary. By the beginning of 1943, there were only 23 WAFS performing ferry duties, albeit performing them with a high degree of proficiency. Arnold decided to authorize a training school at Avenger Field, Sweetwater, Texas, and the WAFS were merged with the new women pilots. In August 1943, all women pilots serving

Mrs. Betty Gillies was the first woman pilot to be "flight checked" and accepted by the Women's Auxiliary Ferrying Squadron. *(U.S. Air Force)*

with the USAAF became WOMEN AIRFORCE SERVICE PILOTS (WASP).

World War I

Background

World War I began among the nations of Europe at the end of July 1914. Under President Woodrow Wilson, the United States struggled to remain neutral as the war, on its principal front—the western front in France and Belgium—ground on with great destructiveness but little discernible progress. On May 7, 1915, German U-boats torpedoed and sank the British steamer *Lusitania,* with the loss of 1,198 lives, including 124 Americans. More sinkings followed, also with loss of American lives, and evidence of German espionage and sabotage in the United States came to light, most infamously with the Zimmermann Telegram of January 19, 1917, a coded message sent by Germany's foreign secretary, Alfred Zimmermann, to the German ambassador in Mexico, proposing a Mexican-German alliance against the United States through which Mexico might regain territory it had lost in the Mexican-American War of 1846–48. The revelation of the Zimmermann Telegram, on March 1, came only one month after Germany had resumed unrestricted submarine warfare against all Atlantic shipping. On February 3, 1917, the USS *Housatonic* was sunk without warning, and the United States severed diplomatic relations with Germany. On April 2, 1917, President Wilson asked Congress for a declaration of war, which was delivered on April 6, 1917.

Unpreparedness

The United States entered the war at what was a low point for the Allies, who reeled under a series of German offensives and who had just suffered the loss of Russia, which, after the revolutions of 1917, had made a "separate peace" with Germany, thereby releasing massive numbers of German troops, who had been committed to the eastern front, for service on the western front. For the French and English, the prospect of fresh troops from America was a brilliant ray of hope. However, the United States, staunchly isolationist since the end of the Spanish-American War in 1898, was ill prepared to fight in 1917. At the time of the war declaration, the U.S. Army numbered only about 200,000 men.

As modest as the U.S. Army was at the beginning of America's involvement in the war, the AVIATION SECTION, U.S. ARMY SIGNAL CORPS, was downright minuscule, in April 1917 consisting of 131 officers (almost all of them pilots or pilots-in-training) and 1,087 enlisted men. As General John J. Pershing, commander of the American Expeditionary Force (AEF) recorded in his diary, of this number, only 35 could fly and, "with the exception of five or six officers, none of them could have met the requirement of modern battle conditions." The Aviation Section's inventory of airplanes numbered fewer than 250, all of which were so obsolescent that, by European standards, they were fit to serve only as trainers—and primary trainers at that. The mainstay of army aviation at the time of America's entry into the war were Curtiss aircraft, chiefly the famed "Jenny," the JN-3, and the R-2. In terms of the prevailing European state of the art, the Aviation Section had no fighters or bombers.

Congress had turned a blind eye to preparedness during the European phase of the war and had consistently declined to appropriate significant funds for military aviation. Nor did the army formulate plans for building an air force. The small corps of American military pilots available in the spring of 1917 had received personalized rather than standardized flight training and no training at all in combat flying. Brigadier General BENJAMIN FOULOIS and others quickly inspected the Canadian flight training system in April 1917 and, under the direction of Hiram Bingham, a Yale professor now serving in the U.S. Army Signal Corps, inaugurated ground schools for flight cadets at a half-dozen major American universities. For those who made the cut, ground school was followed by primary flight training in the United States, then advanced training overseas.

Changing Role of U.S. Military Aviation

On entering the war, the U.S. Army planned to raise a force of a million men, with aviation playing (in the words of the original mobilization plan) "a relatively insignificant part." But France and Great Britain pressed for a major American air program, and French premier Alexandre Ribot cabled President Wilson on May 26, 1917, proposing a gargantuan U.S. "flying corps" consisting of 4,500 aircraft, 5,000 pilots, and 50,000 mechanics. With unbounded faith in America's industrial might, Ribot proposed the production of no fewer than 16,500 planes during the first six months of 1918. The month before, on April 12, 1917, the newly formed National Advisory Committee for Aeronautics had recommended a program for producing 3,700 aircraft in *all* of 1918, working up to 6,000 in 1919, and 10,000 in 1920. Even these more realistic goals must be regarded as extravagantly

optimistic for a U.S. aircraft industry that had produced fewer than 1,000 aircraft from the Wright brothers' "Flyer" of 1903 through 1916. Early in June 1917, the U.S. Department of War proposed to turn out 22,625 airplanes, 44,000 engines, and the equivalent of another 17,600 airplanes in spare parts—all by the end of 1918. Congress immediately appropriated $640 million for "aeronautics," the greatest sum ever appropriated for a single purpose in U.S. history up to that time. In a single stroke, air power had advanced in American military thinking from a virtual nonpriority to the chief means of winning the war in Europe, and, in August, the Aviation Section finalized a plan for creating 345 combat squadrons (up from the *single* squadron it could field as of April 1917), plus 45 construction companies, 81 supply squadrons, 11 repair squadrons, and 26 BALLOON companies; 263 of the combat squadrons were to be deployed in Europe by June 30, 1918.

The reality was that the United States concentrated on building training aircraft. Pursuit planes and bombers were purchased from the French and manufactured in France from raw materials supplied by the United States. Some 6,000 French-made craft and 8,500 engines were to be delivered by July 1, 1918. American manufacturers did produce about 3,000 De Havilland 4 (DH-4) two-seater reconnaissance bombers, under license from the British firm. Other U.S. firms produced far lesser numbers of the Handley-Page and the Italian Caproni bombers. Only one American design, the twin-engine Martin MB-1 bomber, was developed during World War I, but it did not enter production until after the war. American engineers did make one original and very valuable contribution to World War I aeronautical development, the 8-cylinder and 12-cylinder Liberty engines, but the fact was that the Aviation Section and, subsequently, the U.S. ARMY AIR SERVICE flew exclusively foreign-built or foreign-designed aircraft, except in primary flight training (see AIRCRAFT, WORLD WAR I).

Toul

The Aviation Section and the USAAS flew for only seven months of World War I, from April to

November 1918. Prior to this period, U.S. aero squadrons struggled with strategic, training, and supply issues. However, as early as 1915, Americans had been flying in the European war, both with the French and the British—though it was the American-manned LAFAYETTE ESCADRILLE of France that earned the most enduring fame. In February 1918, the Lafayette Escadrille became the basis of the 103rd Pursuit Squadron, but remained attached to the French army because no other U.S. squadrons were yet ready for action. The 1st Aero Squadron was the first American air unit, under American control, to reach France, arriving on September 3, 1917.

Trained by the French as an observation squadron, the 1st would participate in a concentration of American forces in the Toul sector, the eastern end of the front that extended from the English Channel coast to Switzerland. However, the first American air units actually to reach Toul were the 95th Pursuit Squadron, in February, followed by the 94th on March 5. Both of these units were equipped with French Nieuport fighters, but they lacked the machine guns for them. This notwithstanding, the units began flying patrols, unarmed, on March 15. Nor did the arrival of the machine guns solve all of the American fliers' problems. The pilots of the 95th had never received gunnery training and had to be sent to French gunnery school before they could take to the air in active combat. The pilots of the 94th did have the requisite training and, therefore, as the famed "Hat-in-the-Ring" squadron, became the first American air unit to fight at the front, commencing operations on April 3, 1918. On the following day, the 1st Aero Squadron arrived in Toul. Its pilots flew two-place Spad reconnaissance missions beginning on April 15, the day after two pilots from the 94th—Lieutenants Alan F. Winslow and Douglas Campbell—scored the first two kills for their squadron.

The Toul buildup continued in May with the arrival of two more squadrons, which, with the 1st, formed the 1st Corps Observation Group, operating under French tactical control. In the meantime, the 94th and 95th pursuit squadrons were merged as the 1st Pursuit Group. On June 12, the 96th Bombardment Squadron, equipped with French Bréguets, began bombing raids on railroad yards at Dommary.

Château-Thierry

At the end of June, the 1st Pursuit Group and the 1st Corps Observation Group joined some French units as the First Brigade, under the command of Colonel WILLIAM MITCHELL, at Château-Thierry, which was taking the brunt of the great offensive the Germans had begun in March. The aircraft assigned to the Americans were greatly outclassed by the newest German Fokkers, and the German pilots outmatched the less-experienced Americans. Nevertheless, the First Brigade succeeded in carrying out its primary mission, which was reconnaissance, and even participated with a force of British bombers in a successful assault on the important German supply base at Fère-en-Tardenois.

Saint-Mihiel

Reinforced by fresh American troops, the Allies, in September 1918, launched a major offensive against the infamous "Saint-Mihiel salient," a strong German incursion into the French lines that had endured since the beginning of the war. Mitchell had combat command of what now totalled 49 squadrons of the USAAS, First Army, of which only half were American. Mitchell also commanded more than 40 additional French squadrons of a French aerial division and had secured the cooperation of nine British bombardment squadrons. Mitchell massed his forces—some 1,500 aircraft—in what he correctly called the "largest aggregation of air forces that had ever been engaged in one operation on the Western Front at any time during the entire progress of the war." They opposed approximately 300 German aircraft defending the Saint-Mihiel salient. The assault on the salient began on September 12, 1918, but bad weather kept most of the aircraft grounded until the 14th and 15th. During these two days, Mitchell unleashed some 500 observation and pursuit planes in support of the ground forces while using the balance of his aircraft—about a thousand ships—to strike behind German lines, disrupting communication and supply lines and strafing advancing columns of reinforcements. The air campaign was a success, keeping the Germans on the defensive and forcing them to fight well behind their own lines.

Meuse-Argonne

The offensive against German positions at Meuse-Argonne was launched on September 26, and, while Mitchell had fewer planes to deploy, he had a greater proportion of Americans: U.S. pilots flew 600 out of 800 craft. He used his forces to disrupt the Germans' rear in order to keep them on the defensive and deflect attack from American ground troops. For the first time, Americans were involved in large-scale bombing missions. On October 9, 200 Allied bombers were escorted by 100 pursuit aircraft and 50 three-seater planes in a raid behind the lines on a position where German forces were massing for a counterattack. The bombers were met by heavy fighter resistance, but nevertheless delivered some 30 tons of bombs onto critical targets. This final air campaign of World War I was the greatest Allied air success of the war.

World War II: North African and European theaters

For a brief discussion of the origins of World War II, see WORLD WAR II: PACIFIC AND ASIAN THEATERS.

The December 7, 1941, surprise attack on Pearl Harbor elicited an outcry for immediate vengeance against Japan, but, on December 22, 1941, British prime minister Winston Churchill met in Washington with President Franklin D. Roosevelt to formulate Anglo-American strategy for the war. It was decided to concentrate first on Nazi Germany, while fighting essentially a holding action against the Japanese in the Pacific.

First U.S. Army Air Force Contingents

Despite a military buildup that had begun in anticipation of American entry into the war, the U.S. ARMY AIR FORCES were short of aircraft, personnel,

and supplies. The first contingent of 1,800 personnel departed for Liverpool on April 27, 1942, and the first airplanes, 18 B-17s, began reaching England on July 1. By the end of August, 386 planes (119 B-17s, 164 P-38s, and 103 C-47s) had crossed the North Atlantic.

On July 4, 1942, the 15th Bomb Squadron became the first USAAF unit to go operational. Six 15th Bomb Squadron crews accompanied six British crews on a low-level attack against enemy airfields in Holland. A little more than a month later, on August 17, 1942, the 97th Bomb Group made the first U.S. heavy bomber raid. A dozen B-17s, escorted by RAF Spitfires, attacked the Sotteville railroad yards at Rouen, France, while six B-17s made a diversionary sweep along the French coast. An increasing number of U.S. missions were flown through early October, before the pace slackened as USAAF units prepared for Operation Torch, the Allied invasion of North Africa.

North African Campaign

Largely at the urging of the British, Allied planners decided to make their first offensive move against what Adolf Hitler called "Fortress Europe" via Italy, which Winston Churchill dubbed the "soft underbelly" of Europe. This, it was argued, would relieve some of the pressure on the Russians in the east and allow them to begin to assume the offensive. Once pressure was applied to the Axis forces from the east and south, a major Allied invasion could be launched from the west.

The first step in invading southern Europe would be the defeat of the Germans and Italians in North Africa. But during the spring of 1942, the German Afrika Korps, under the command of the notorious "Desert Fox," Field Marshal Erwin Rommel, had pushed the British back and had advanced across North Africa to El Alamein, deep inside Egypt. The British asked for USAAF assistance. American aircraft attacked Axis airfields and supply, munitions, and fuel dumps, as well as harbors and shipping. These attacks disrupted logistics sufficiently to force the Afrika Korps to retreat west on October 23, 1942. RAF and USAAF units quickly occupied the airfields abandoned by the Axis, and by the end of January 1943, German and Italian forces had been pushed back more than 1,000 miles to the Tunisian frontier.

During this period, on November 8, 1942, with the Afrika Korps in retreat, the Allies invaded French West Africa in Operation Torch. This pinched Axis forces between Allied armies to the east and west. In response, Germany and Italy flew forces into Tunis and Bizerte from Sicily, and over the next six months, these reinforced units battled the Allies on the frontiers of Tunisia.

The USAAF worked in concert with the RAF, hurling fighters, medium bombers, and heavy bombers (the B-17 and B-24) against ports, ship convoys, and supply depots, as well as in CLOSE AIR SUPPORT missions. On April 5, 1943, USAAF fighters concentrated attacks on the German airlift from Italy to Tunisia. By nightfall, the USAAF had shot down 201 enemy airplanes. By early May, combined USAAF and RAF forces had achieved air supremacy. Almost immediately afterward, German resistance on the ground folded, and, on May 10, 1943, the 15th Panzer Division surrendered, bringing an end to the Axis presence in North Africa.

Invasion of Sicily and Italy

Pantelleria and Lampedusa are Italian islands in the Mediterranean Sea between North Africa and Sicily. Pantelleria in particular was very well fortified and had to be taken in order to proceed with the invasion of Sicily from North Africa. Because the topography of Pantelleria made amphibious assault impractical, USAAF aircraft began, on May 18, 1943, almost daily bombardment in concert with naval bombardment. Allied forces began landing on the island on June 11, and, thanks to the air action, met with no resistance.

As Pantelleria surrendered, the USAAF sent B-25s, B-26s, A-20s, and A-36 dive bombers as well as British-made Wellington bombers against Lampedusa. The attack extended over June 11 and 12, and was followed by the dropping of surrender leaflets. Lampedusa was in Allied control by June 13, and

Allied aircraft were based at Pantelleria and Lampedusa to support the invasion of Sicily, which began with a day and night bombing raid on July 10, followed by an airdrop of glider troops and paratroops—the first large-scale Allied airborne operation of the war. This aerial assault was in turn followed by amphibious landings under close air support over the next two months. As Allied forces were built up on the island, German and Italian defenders withdrew.

By mid-July, the Allies had achieved air superiority over Sicily and, on July 19, the USAAF began air operations over mainland Italy with an air raid against Rome. Italian authorities surrendered on September 3, 1943. German occupying forces, however, continued to resist, and, for the Allies, the Italian campaign would be one of the most bitter, frustrating, and costly of the war.

The Ploeşti Raid

Even as the invasion of Sicily was under way, USAAF commanders decided to stage a daring strategic raid against the target identified as supplying some 60 percent of Germany's crude oil: the Ploeşti oil fields of Romania.

The raid was launched on August 1, 1943, using USAAF B-24 Liberators based in Libya. The target was a thousand miles away and was known to be very heavily defended. The bombers hit dense cloud cover over Bulgaria, which broke up the tight formations so important to defending against fighters. Worse, German radar tracked the incoming bombers, and the Ploeşti defense forces were ready for the attack.

The B-24s braved intense antiaircraft fire and fighter sorties, inflicting substantial, but not decisive, damage on Ploeşti. The cost, however, was great. Of the 177 planes and 1,726 men who took off from Libya, 54 planes—with 532 men—were lost.

The Daylight Bombing Campaign

Although the Allied strategy of invasion via the "soft underbelly" of Europe restricted ground action to Italy, air operations from England, by the

A Consolidated B-24F Liberator of the 98th Bomb Group, IX Bomber Command, pulls away from the target in the low-level bombing attack against oil refineries at Ploesti, Romania, on August 1, 1943. *(San Diego Aerospace Museum)*

USAAF and the RAF, continued during the winter of 1942–43. During this period, the primary targets were Nazi submarine pens on the French coast. These proved difficult to penetrate, however, because they were built of heavily reinforced concrete.

USAAF planners advocated daylight precision bombing, whereas RAF commanders considered this too hazardous and favored saturation bombing by night. Thus the two services worked in conjunction: The USAAF units that had begun arriving in England in the spring of 1942 (and that would be officially designated the EIGHTH AIR FORCE in February 1944) conducted daylight raids, while the RAF bombed at night. The problem was that low-level precision bombing by day brought terrible losses from antiaircraft fire. In December 1942, for example, USAAF losses were a staggering 8.8 percent.

The Schweinfurt Raid

For the USAAF, the crisis came during the second week of October 1943. On October 9, 352 bombers flew along the Baltic Sea north of Germany to hit targets in Poland and East Prussia. The massive raid produced devastating results on the ground, but at a loss of 8 percent of the bombers committed. On October 10, Münster was targeted. Of 236 bombers launched, 30 were lost.

With these losses looming in the background, a major raid was launched against the ball-bearing industries at Schweinfurt, Germany. The idea behind strategic bombing (see BOMBING, STRATEGIC) is to attack a nation's very ability to make war, and Allied planners reasoned that, without ball bearings, nothing mechanical could operate. Reduce the supply of ball bearings, and every war industry and instrument of war would suffer.

The raid was launched on October 14, 1943. As soon as the relatively short-range P-47 fighter escorts turned back at the German border to return to England, the bombers were set upon by Luftwaffe fighters. The surviving B-17s dropped their bombs on target, but they were again attacked on the return trip. Of 251 B-17s launched, 60 were shot down and another 138 damaged. Between October 9 and October 14, 148 USAAF heavy bombers had been lost.

It was clear that the Luftwaffe had regained air superiority over Germany, and the USAAF refrained from making deep clear-weather penetrations into Germany for the rest of 1943. Other targets were hit, but USAAF commanders decided to hold off on long-distance raids until P-38 Lightning and P-51 Mustang fighter escorts, capable of long range, arrived in England.

The Air Offensive Resumes

In January 1944, now equipped with long-range escort aircraft, the USAAF was prepared to recommence the strategic bombing of Germany. The first objective was the German aircraft industry. Once that was crippled, the ability to produce interceptors would be greatly reduced, and air superiority over Germany could be regained. Broader strategic targets could be attacked.

Despite USAAF crew and aircraft readiness, bad weather over England delayed major operations until February 20, 1944, when, at last, over 1,000 heavy bombers, with massive fighter escorts, struck a dozen aircraft factories in Germany. Over the next week—February 20–25, known in USAAF lore as the "Big Week"—raids were launched from England and Italy, the USAAF going by day, the RAF by night. By this time, USAAF heavy bombers were equipped with radar for bombing through clouds, and poor weather over the target seldom forced the USAAF to change to a secondary target.

In all, 3,300 bombers flew from England and 500 from Italy. Of the British-based bombers, 137 were lost; 89 of the Italian-based force also failed to return. In human terms, 2,600 U.S. personnel were killed, wounded, or missing as a result of the Big Week, but the raids destroyed 75 percent of the buildings attacked, greatly crippling the German aircraft industry. Moreover, some 600 Luftwaffe planes were shot down in what amounted to the greatest air battle in history.

Raids on Berlin

Berlin was among the first targets chosen after Big Week. Bombing the capital of Germany not only targeted an important industrial site but also one that the Luftwaffe would act to defend at all costs—and the Allies intended that those costs would be high.

The first attack, launched on March 4, 1944, was disappointing, because, due to bad weather, only 29 bombers reached Berlin. On March 6, however, 660 USAAF heavy bombers attacked Berlin and, as expected, were met by massive opposition. Of the 660 bombers flown, 69 were lost, together with 11 fighter escorts; however, USAAF pilots shot down 179 Luftwaffe aircraft—and caused extensive damage to Berlin. On March 8, 462 bombers, heavily escorted by 174 P-51s, bombed the Erkner ball bearing factory. The Luftwaffe, flying to the defense, suffered severe losses.

Preparation for D-day

During the early spring, Italian-based fighters and bombers of the FIFTEENTH AIR FORCE began target-ing shipping, railroads, and highways with the objective of severely compromising the German transportation network to expedite the Allied ground advance on Rome.

While the 15AF tackled this mission, British-based 8AF planes concentrated on V-1 launch sites on the coasts of France and Belgium and also attacked Luftwaffe airfields and coastal defenses. The 8AF then turned to a campaign against the transportation network in northwestern France, hitting railroad yards and bridges there and also in Belgium. The objective was to reduce German ability to reinforce Normandy, the landing site for the planned amphibious invasion of France. The campaign proved highly successful. Prior to D-day, all 12 railroad and 14 highway bridges across the Seine River from Paris to Le Havre had been destroyed.

As D-day drew near, USAAF reconnaissance aircraft flew many sorties to obtain detailed photographs of German beach defenses. Some flights were made as low as 15 feet. Then, in the days immediately preceding the June 6, 1944, landings, 1,083 B-17s and B-24s dropped 3,000 tons of bombs on German defenses. This initial assault was followed by sorties by medium bombers and fighter bombers, which attacked targets further to the rear.

The Shuttle Raids

While strategic bombing was stepped up in western Europe, U.S. commanders persuaded the Soviet Union's Joseph Stalin to allow USAAF heavy bombers to fly "shuttle" missions to Russia in order to bomb eastern Germany and the Balkans without having to fly all the way back to England and Italy. USAAF crews and aircraft were stationed at three airfields near Kiev in the Ukraine.

The first shuttle raid took off from Italy on June 2. On June 6, a raid was launched from the Ukraine against a target in Romania. On June 11, the planes returned to Italy, bombing another Romanian target on the way. More shuttle missions followed through September 13, 1944, by which time the eastern front had advanced so far west that the Soviet bases were no longer needed.

The Normandy Invasion

Not only was air power essential in the preparation for the invasion of France, the invasion itself, on June 6, 1944, began from the air. USAAF C-47s carried paratroops and towed gliders, in the biggest airdrop in history: 17,000 men. Despite heavy antiaircraft fire and poor visibility, most of the transports and gliders reached their landing areas—although many paratroopers and gliders came down well outside their intended drop zones. Some historians believe this accidental scattering of the airborne troops actually contributed to the success of the invasion by confusing the enemy.

Throughout the Normandy landings, USAAF and RAF aircraft flew close air support (the British-based NINTH AIR FORCE was chiefly responsible for tactical action) before returning primarily to the strategic bombing mission. By the autumn of 1944, German oil production, a prime target of the strategic campaign, had been seriously curtailed—but at the cost of 922 bombers and 674 fighters during the summer of 1944.

Battle of Arnhem

USAAF units balanced the demands of the strategic mission with the tactical requirements of supporting the breakout from the Normandy beachheads and the advance across France. By the late summer of 1944, Allied troops had reached the border of Germany and Holland, and it was decided to attempt a breakthrough in southeastern Holland toward the Ruhr, a great German industrial region.

Operation Market Garden began on September 17, 1944, with a paratroop and glider drop behind German lines, with American, British, and Polish soldiers participating in landings at Eindhoven, Nijmegen, and Arnhem. The effectiveness of the German response had been badly underestimated. Powerful counterattacks were launched, especially against the British at Arnhem, and poor weather delayed aerial resupply and reinforcement. On September 23, the British withdrew from Arnhem.

Battle of the Bulge

While the advance in the north had been stopped at Arnhem, elsewhere Allied troops tore across France and into Germany. However, beginning on December 16, 1944, the Allies were met with a new crisis, as the Germans threw everything they had into a massive counteroffensive in the Ardennes, with the object of breaking through the Allied lines to Antwerp.

Withdrawing before the German onslaught, American commanders rushed the 101st Airborne to hold the strategically positioned village of Bastogne, Belgium. The paratroopers did just that, fighting a desperate holding action over Christmas while enveloped by German forces. Extremely adverse weather grounded Allied airpower, but, once the weather lifted, the USAAF (chiefly 9AF) and RAF prevailed against the now greatly outnumbered Luftwaffe. By the end of January 1945, the Allies had reclaimed most of the territory that had been lost in the counteroffensive, and, in February, the Allies approached the Rhine River, crossing at Remagen on March 7.

The Drive through Germany

North of Remagen, more Allied troops crossed the Rhine at Wesel during the night of March 23–24. On the morning of the 24th, the crossing was supported by an aerial invasion of more than 2,800 U.S. and British gliders and paratroop transports. By this point, most of the great strategic targets in Germany had been destroyed, and the USAAF turned to strafing and low-level bombing of targets of opportunity, in addition to providing close air support for the ongoing advance.

Although the Luftwaffe had begun to use its most advanced aircraft, early jet fighters, there were too few available to have much effect. In the final advance through Germany, the Allied air forces enjoyed air supremacy.

Toward V-E Day

During April 1945, Germany was being overrun from the west and the east. The last USAAF mission against an industrial target took place on April

25, with the bombing of the Skoda armament works at Pilsen, Czechoslovakia. After this, much of the USAAF's work consisted of missions of aid and mercy, air dropping food to civilians in northern Italy and the Netherlands, and evacuating liberated prisoners of war.

On May 2, German forces in Italy and southern and western Austria surrendered, and, on May 7, Germany surrendered unconditionally.

While no one would dispute the importance of air power in World War II, many military thinkers and historians have debated the effectiveness of strategic bombing. Certainly, the air war was costly to prosecute. The USAAF lost 27,694 aircraft in the war (from all causes), including 8,314 heavy bombers, 1,623 medium and light bombers, and 8,481 fighters. Personnel casualties totaled 91,105, including 34,362 killed, 13,708 wounded, and 43,035 missing, captured, or interned.

V-E Day meant an end to the war in Europe. The war in the Pacific continued, and many USAAF personnel and airplanes were transferred to the other theater; see WORLD WAR II: PACIFIC AND ASIAN THEATERS.

World War II: Pacific and Asian theaters

For a discussion of the war in North Africa and Europe, see WORLD WAR II: NORTH AFRICAN AND EUROPEAN THEATERS.

Origins of the War

The Treaty of Versailles, which ended WORLD WAR I, was so harshly punitive against Germany that the nation, already reeling economically from the war, was saddled with crippling reparations, humiliatingly compelled to admit guilt for having caused the war, and limited to a skeleton army of 100,000 men. Combined with the great worldwide depression of the 1930s, Germany's economic hardships and collective national disgrace wrought by the terms of the treaty pushed the nation over the brink of desperation. Threatened, too, by the effects of communist revolution in nearby Russia, the German people looked for a leader who prom-

ised not only immediate salvation but also a return to greatness. That man appeared to be Adolf Hitler, who rose through the 1920s and 1930s to become absolute dictator of Germany. He embarked on a program of rearmament and territorial expansion, in which the war-weary democracies of Europe, primarily France and Britain, acquiesced. On March 7, 1936, German armies violated the Treaty of Versailles by occupying the demilitarized Rhineland. The democracies did not respond. On July 11, 1936, Italy, under the fascist dictatorship of Benito Mussolini, agreed with Hitler that Austria should be deemed "a German state," and, on November 1, Italy and Germany concluded the Rome-Berlin Axis, which was followed on November 25 by the German-Japanese Anti-Comintern Pact—an alliance ostensibly against communism, but, in fact, an alliance of general military cooperation. Thus, Germany, Italy, and Japan, all militaristic states at this point in history, became allies in the Rome-Berlin-Tokyo Axis.

On March 13, 1938, having secured the blessing of Mussolini, Hitler invaded Austria and annexed it to Germany. This put Germany in position to make its next move, into Czechoslovakia. British prime minister Neville Chamberlain, seeking to avoid a new world war by a policy of "active appeasement," agreed, in the Munich conference of September 29–30, 1938, to Germany's annexation of the Czechoslovakian Sudetenland. Hitler promised an end to expansion, only to seize the rest of Czechoslovakia by occupying Prague on March 16, 1939. On August 23, 1939, Hitler signed a "Non-Aggression Pact" with his great ideological rival, Soviet premier Joseph Stalin, which gave him leave to invade Poland. That invasion came on September 1, 1939. The democracies could not overlook this act of aggression, and World War II commenced.

In the Pacific, in the meantime, Japan intensified its policy of expansion, which had begun early in the century. In the 1930s, Japan invaded China and annexed Manchuria (calling it Manchukuo). With the formation of the Rome-Berlin-Tokyo Axis, the administration of U.S. president Franklin Roosevelt introduced economic sanctions against

Japan in an effort to curb its expansionism and to pressure it to withdraw from China. FDR saw these sanctions as an alternative to war, but, in fact, Japan took them as a provocation. In the face of a U.S. embargo, Japan could not long continue the war against China. Rather than withdraw from China, the militarists who now controlled the Japanese government decided not only to risk war with the United States but also to move so aggressively throughout the Pacific that America would be overwhelmed into helplessness.

America Enters the War

At 7:55 on Sunday morning, December 7, 1941, a Japanese force of 183 carrier-based aircraft attacked without warning U.S. military and naval facilities at and around Pearl Harbor, Hawaii. The first assault was over in 30 minutes. A second wave of 170 planes launched an hour-long attack. The result was devastating: 2,343 U.S. service personnel killed, 960 missing, and 1,272 wounded; 151 planes were destroyed on the ground, and all eight great battleships at anchor in Pearl Harbor were either sunk or damaged.

While the attack was a tactical triumph for the Japanese, it was a strategic disaster, because it instantly mobilized a hitherto reluctant United States to war. The declaration came on December 8. Germany and Italy, bound by treaty with Japan, declared war on the United States on December 11, and the United States declared against them in turn.

Fall of the Philippines

After Pearl Harbor, the Japanese offensive moved swiftly. The Philippine Islands, at the time a U.S. territory, were attacked from the air on December 8, 1941, and invaded on the 9th. Overwhelmed, U.S. and Filipino forces made a fighting withdrawal to the peninsula of Bataan and to Corregidor Island in Manila Bay. Bataan fell on April 9, 1942; Corregidor, surrounded, held out until May 6, 1942.

U.S. ARMY AIR FORCES aircraft in the Philippines then consisted of only 72 P-40Es, 52 obsolescent P-

35As, and 12 obsolete P-26s. More than half the USAAF force was lost on the ground and in aerial combat. Many USAAF ground personnel were hurriedly transferred to army combat units and were ultimately captured or killed on Bataan or Corregidor. Others withdrew to the southernmost island of Mindanao along with a handful of B-17s. Those bombers that survived the initial attacks were soon withdrawn to Australia, evacuating as many men as they could carry. Many more, however, were left behind. On June 9, the last American and Filipino holdouts surrendered.

Action in Java

Simultaneously with the assault on the Philippines, the Japanese attacked the Netherlands East Indies. The USAAF attempted to assist the Dutch by bombing targets on the Malay Peninsula eastward to the Celebes Islands. The effort was small and inadequate, and, by early March, Java was evacuated. Except for the portion of New Guinea around Port Moresby, the Japanese now occupied territory from the eastern border of India, across the islands of the Southwest Pacific, to the northern doorstep of Australia.

The Doolittle Raid

U.S. military planners understood that, given time, American industrial and military forces would become a formidable and eventually overwhelming presence. However, since December 7, 1941, the United States had suffered one humiliating defeat after another and had fought a desperately defensive war. USAAF Lieutenant Colonel JAMES HAROLD DOOLITTLE and others formulated a morale-boosting offensive action, a bold air raid against Tokyo to be carried out by 16 B-25 Mitchell bombers launched from the aircraft carrier *Hornet*.

The planes were launched on April 18, 1942. Because the flotilla had been sighted by the Japanese, the aircraft took off not 450 to 650 miles from Japan, as planned, but 800 miles out, making it extremely difficult for the pilots to reach friendly airstrips in China after the raid. All 16 bombers did reach the Japanese islands, and they dropped their bombs on oil stores, factory areas, and military installations.

In strictly military terms, the damage inflicted by 16 medium bombers was minor. But it thrilled Americans, and it stunned the Japanese, who were forced to transfer back to the home islands fighter units that otherwise could have been used against the Allies. Incredibly, most of the Doolittle aircrews survived and eventually made their way back to U.S. military control. Doolittle himself went on to higher command.

Coral Sea, Midway, and New Guinea

Seeking to complete its conquest of New Guinea, Japanese invasion forces sailed to Tulagi and Port Moresby, New Guinea, in May 1942. Tulagi fell without opposition, but the larger Japanese force sailing to New Guinea was intercepted on May 7 by naval aircraft launched from *Lexington* and *Yorktown*. The main phase of the Battle of the Coral Sea began on May 8 and was entirely a duel between carrier-launched aircraft. U.S. aircraft damaged the carrier *Shokaku*, but 33 out of 82 of the attacking planes were lost. The Japanese sank the *Lexington*, a destroyer, and a tanker, losing 43 of 69 aircraft in the attack. The Battle of the Coral Sea was thus a Japanese tactical victory, but a strategic defeat; although U.S. losses were heavier, the Japanese advance had been stopped, Port Moresby saved, and the Japanese fleet driven out of the Coral Sea.

The next Japanese objective was Midway Island, which would provide a critical airbase to whichever side held it. Japanese admiral Isoruko Yamamoto sent a diversionary force to the Aleutian Islands, while Admiral Chuichi Nagumo, who had led the Pearl Harbor attack, took a four-carrier strike force followed by an invasion fleet—some 88 ships in all—to Midway. His American opponent, Admiral Chester A. Nimitz, having anticipated such an attack, brought together two task forces east of Midway, designated Number 16 (under Admiral Raymond Spruance) and Number 18 (under Admiral Frank Fletcher). The task forces included the carriers *Enterprise*, *Hornet*, and *Yorktown*, in addition to land-based U.S. Marine and USAAF aircraft

on Midway itself. The Midway-based planes attacked elements of the Japanese fleet on June 3, but inflicted little damage. On June 4, 108 Japanese aircraft struck Midway, destroying 15 of 25 U.S. Marine aircraft. U.S. Navy torpedo bombers twice attacked the Japanese fleet, but without success. A third attack, by Midway-based USAAF B-17 bombers, also failed to damage or sink any of the enemy carriers. A navy torpedo bomber attack, in which 35 of the 41 aircraft engaged were lost, also inflicted little damage, but it did open the way for a massive attack by 54 dive bombers from *Enterprise* and *Yorktown*, which sunk three Japanese aircraft carriers. The fourth Japanese carrier, *Hiryu*, was sunk in a separate attack later in the day—although not before *Hiryu*'s planes had delivered a fatal blow against the *Yorktown*.

Japanese forces began withdrawing on June 5, 1942, and Midway was the hard-fought turning point of the Pacific war. From this point forward, the United States would take a relentlessly offensive posture in the Pacific.

Guadalcanal and the Solomons

After the Midway battle, the Japanese moved into the lower Solomon Islands and, on Guadalcanal, rushed to complete an airfield, which would give them a base from which to attack the lifeline between Hawaii and Australia. USAAF B-17s performed reconnaissance that enabled U.S. Marines to make a surprise landing on Guadalcanal on August 7, 1942. In coordination with the navy and the marines, the USAAF successfully held the island.

Guadalcanal became a base from which U.S. forces conducted offensive operations in the Solomons, the campaign culminating in the November 1, 1943, marine landing on Bougainville.

It was during the Solomons campaign that, acting on intercepted and decoded Japanese radio traffic, P-38 pilots of the THIRTEENTH AIR FORCE intercepted and shot down an airplane transporting Admiral Yamamoto. The loss of Japan's most important naval strategist was a terrible blow to the Imperial Navy.

Aleutian Campaign

During the Midway campaign, as mentioned, the Japanese staged a diversionary strike far to the north, against the Aleutian Islands of Alaska. In June 1942, the enemy bombed Dutch Harbor in the Aleutian chain and landed troops on Kiska and Attu islands. Despite severe weather, the ELEVENTH AIR FORCE operated continuously against the enemy. In a six-month period, 13AF lost 72 planes—nine in combat, the others to the weather.

In May 1943, U.S. forces captured Attu, and on July 10 the USAAF set up a base on this forbidding island from which raids were staged against the Japanese-held Kuriles. When U.S. troops invaded Kiska on August 15, they found the enemy had already evacuated.

Central Pacific Action

From the beginning of the war through the Battle of Midway, the role of the SEVENTH AIR FORCE, based in Hawaii, had been primarily defensive. After Midway, the Japanese made little attempt to advance in this theater. However, by late 1943, 7AF aircraft were being used to soften up islands scheduled for amphibious assault. The 7AF also flew missions to neutralize enemy forces on islands that were being bypassed by Allied forces as part of the "island-hopping" strategy that proved so effective in the Gilberts and Marshalls. The aircrews of 7AF often flew missions against targets more than a thousand miles away, and navigation over vast expanses of ocean became a high-risk proposition.

Gilbert and Marshall Islands

Each island wrested from the Japanese became a potential airbase. B-24s of the 7AF used Ellice Island as a refueling stop en route to bomb Tarawa and Nauru (in the Gilbert group) during April 1943. In November, after aerial bombardment by USAAF B-24s and carrier-based naval aircraft, Tarawa and Makin were invaded by the U.S. Army. Once these islands were secured, USAAF planes were transferred to bases in the Gilberts to support amphibious assaults in the Marshalls, and, by the end of February 1944, those islands were in Allied hands. Among the Marshalls were Kwajalein and Eniwetok, which provided bases from which to attack and invade the Marianas, which, in turn, would furnish bases needed for operations by B-29 Superfortresses. These aircraft, the biggest bombers of the war, had the range to deliver huge bomb loads onto the Japanese home islands.

Triumph in New Guinea

While the campaign was ongoing in the Gilberts and Marshalls, the Thirteenth Air Force, based in New Guinea, flew to the Admiralty Islands to join the 7AF and naval units in neutralizing the Carolines, islands that were slated to be "hopped over." During these operations, General Douglas MacArthur's Southwest Pacific forces advanced west along the northern New Guinea coast. To protect this advance, it was necessary to attack Rabaul, a major Japanese base on New Britain Island. Therefore, in October 1943, 5AF and 13AF bombers pounded New Britain almost daily.

By the summer of 1944, the Allies had completed their advance along the northern New Guinea coast. This left many thousands of Japanese troops behind in the Solomons, on New Guinea, and elsewhere—completely cut off.

Philippines Campaign

General Douglas MacArthur was determined to redeem the famous pledge he had made when, in the face of Japanese invasion, he was forced to flee the Philippines: "I shall return."

Prior to the campaign to retake the Philippines, USAAF bombers hit petroleum facilities in the Netherlands East Indies. Next, Allied forces invaded the Palau Islands and Morotai, acquiring airfields from which targets in the Philippines could be struck, beginning in August 1944.

American forces landed on Leyte on October 20, 1944, and, a week later, 34 P-38s landed there, becoming the first USAAF aircraft in the Philippines since early 1942.

It was, however, during the desperate Battle of Leyte Gulf that Japan unleashed its latest air weapon: the Kamikaze suicide pilots, who transformed their airplanes into human-guided missiles. Nevertheless, by December 31, 1944, USAAF and U.S. Marine pilots shot down more than 356 Japanese planes—with the loss of only 23 U.S. fighters.

U.S. troops landed on Mindoro on December 15, 1944, and on January 9, 1945, Americans invaded Luzon, with USAAF aircraft operating freely, having won air supremacy. Explicitly targeted was Japanese shipping in the South China Sea and enemy forces in Formosa.

The culmination of the Philippine campaign was the recapture of Corregidor. The first U.S. troops were airdropped on February 16, 1945, by USAAF transports. Within two weeks, the Japanese had been defeated and, by June, most of the Philippines had been liberated.

Action in the Marianas

Just prior to the Allied assault on the Philippines, naval forces under Admiral Chester Nimitz in the central Pacific attacked the Marianas beyond Truk and the Carolines to secure bases for B-29s. Saipan was invaded on June 15, 1944, and, within a week, the airfield there had been captured. USAAF fighters moved onto the field to provide air cover for the island and to support amphibious assaults against Guam and Tinian, which were invaded on July 21 and 24. By mid-August, both Guam and Tinian were securely in U.S. hands, and major airbases were built to support the B-29s for operations against the Japanese homeland. The bombers began arriving in October and November.

Operations in China

While U.S. and other Allied forces were largely deployed in the central Pacific and southern Pacific areas, the China-Burma-India (CBI) theater was chronically undermanned and undersupplied. Very early in the war the AMERICAN VOLUNTEER GROUP, the celebrated "Flying Tigers," were the only U.S. presence in the theater—a mere 43 P-40B fighters manned by 84 former military pilots. In its brief career, spanning December 1941 to July 1942, the

Flying Tigers destroyed 296 Japanese aircraft in China and Burma. (Some recent historians believe their number is somewhat inflated.)

The USAAF arrived in the CBI in July 1942. The Flying Tigers were dissolved, and some pilots joined their commander, CLAIRE CHENNAULT in a regular army unit called the China Air Task Force, which evolved into the FOURTEENTH AIR FORCE. The 14AF and its associated ground forces were supplied via "the Hump," the extraordinarily hazardous 500-mile air route from India to China over the Himalayas.

Despite chronic shortages, 14AF pilots destroyed or damaged more than 4,000 Japanese aircraft and sank in excess of 1 million tons of shipping. On land, 14AF planes interdicted rail and road transport.

Burma Operations

For most of the war, Allied operations on the Asian mainland were focused on holding the enemy while the principal offensive effort was directed elsewhere. By the middle of May 1942, the Japanese had taken all of Burma and had cut the Burma Road into China. The TENTH AIR FORCE, equipped with a handful of B-17s and LB-30s (export version of the B-24), was unable to stop the Japanese advance, and, in June, the 10AF's bombers were transferred to Africa to bolster defenses there.

Only as the Allies in CBI gradually received reinforcements did the British Royal Air Force (RAF) and 10AF begin to gain air superiority over the Japanese in Burma. Once this had been achieved, medium bombers and fighter bombers targeted enemy river traffic, bridges, and railroads.

In March 1944, Allied troop carrier units and a USAAF air commando group used gliders and C-47s to land and drop far behind enemy lines some 9,000 British "Chindit" raiders commanded by Major General Orde Wingate. These raiders struck enemy communications and supply routes. USAAF airdrops also sustained the U.S. guerrillas of Brigadier General Frank D. Merrill ("Merrill's Marauders") in a northern Burma campaign that reopened the Burma Road to China by January

1945. The 10AF and RAF also supported the capture of Mandalay in March 1945 and Rangoon in May, driving the remnants of the Japanese forces out of Burma.

Strategic Bombing of the Japanese Homeland

Major General CURTIS EMERSON LEMAY took command of the 21st Bomber Command on January 20, 1945 and, on February 3, conducted a high-altitude incendiary raid against the important industrial city of Kobe. Based on the results of the Kobe raid, LeMay decided to increase the effectiveness of raids against Japanese cities by changing from high-altitude, daylight precision bombing with high-explosive bombs to low-altitude night missions using incendiary bombs. His first major target was Tokyo, which 334 B-29s struck from only 5,000 to 9,000 feet on the night of March 9-10. The raid created firestorms that destroyed almost 16 square miles of the city. Tokyo was the first of many massive raids against the cities and industrial centers of Japan.

Iwo Jima Campaign

Iwo Jima is a sterile volcanic island halfway between Saipan and Japan. Uninviting, it was nevertheless of great strategic importance because it presented an obstacle to B-29 formations flying to Japan, and it was used as a staging area for Japanese strikes against B-29 bases in the Marianas. It also threatened air-sea rescue operations along the B-29 flight routes. If Iwo Jima could be captured, not only would these obstacles be removed, but the island could be used as a crucially important emergency landing field for B-29s and a base from which short-range USAAF fighters could escort the B-29s to Japan.

The campaign to take the island began with weeks of USAAF and naval aerial bombardment as well as shelling. With the island softened up, U.S. Marines landed on February 19, 1945. Despite the long preparation, the Japanese defended the island fanatically through late March. Once secured, Iwo Jima did provide landing facilities that ultimately saved the lives of some 24,000 B-29 crew members, and the island also served as a P-51 base.

Okinawa Campaign

The ongoing B-29 incendiary bombing against Japan was interrupted during April and May 1945 as USAAF B-29s were diverted to attack airfields and aircraft plants and to mine Japanese waters in preparation for the invasion of Okinawa, largest of the Ryukyu Islands. Five days after the U.S. landings on Okinawa (April 1), the Japanese launched a massive aerial counterattack, including more than 350 Kamikaze sorties. In response, on April 8, the USAAF targeted the Kamikaze bases in Japan—to no avail, however, as the Kamikaze attacks approached 1,900 by June 22, resulting in the loss of 25 ships. Nevertheless, early in May, the USAAF moved P-51 fighters onto Okinawa airfields to provide more adequate aerial defense. Deemed secure on July 2, Okinawa became a base for 7AF medium bombers and fighters, close enough to attack the home islands.

Hiroshima and Nagasaki

As devastating as the unremitting incendiary raids against Japan had become, it was apparent that the nation intended to fight to the death. Air power alone seemed unable to achieve victory, and Allied planners prepared for a massive invasion that would dwarf the Normandy landings in Europe and that would cost perhaps a million Allied lives.

Unknown to all but the highest-placed government and military officials, the United States had been developing nuclear weapons since early in the war. Two bombs were ready for use, and, at 8:15 A.M. on August 6, 1945, the B-29 *Enola Gay*, based on Tinian, released a single atomic bomb over the city of Hiroshima, a virgin target. As planned, the weapon detonated at about 2,000 feet, instantly destroying most of the city. Called on to surrender, the Japanese government refused, and, on August 9, another B-29, *Bock's Car*, released an atomic bomb over Nagasaki at 10:58 A.M. The results were similarly devastating.

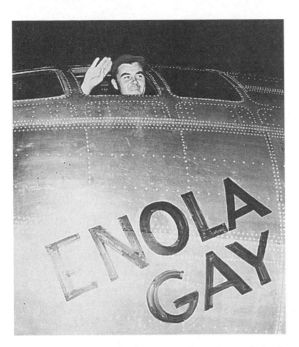

Colonel Paul Tibbetts, pilot, waves from the cockpit of the *Enola Gay* before taking off to drop the first atomic bomb on Hiroshima, Japan.   *(U.S. Air Force)*

On August 10, the Japanese government announced its willingness to accept most of the peace terms set forth by the Allies in the Potsdam Declaration. Negotiations faltered, and conventional bombing was resumed. The last USAAF raid was carried out on August 14, 1945, just before President Truman announced Japan's unconditional surrender. The Pacific War—and, with it, World War II—was over.

Wright-Patterson AFB, Ohio   See AIR FORCE BASES.

Y

Yeager, Charles E. "Chuck" (1923–   )
World War II ace and test pilot

Yeager was the first human being to fly faster than the speed of sound, exceeding Mach 1 in the Bell X-1 aircraft on October 14, 1947.

Born in Myra, West Virginia, Yeager enlisted in the U.S. ARMY AIR FORCES in 1941. He worked as an aircraft mechanic before enrolling in flight training in 1942. Late in 1943, Yeager flew F-51 Mustangs for the 363rd Fighter Squadron, based in England.

Captain Charles E. Yeager is shown here standing in front of the Air Force's Bell-built X-1 supersonic research aircraft.   *(U.S. Air Force)*

Shot down over France in March 1944, he successfully evaded capture and returned to the 363rd. Credited with 13 victories, Yeager ended the war as an ace.

Following WORLD WAR II, in 1945, Yeager became a TEST PILOT at the Fighter Test Branch, Wright Field, Ohio. His performance as a test pilot earned him selection as pilot of the Bell X-1, built expressly to investigate supersonic flight. Yeager was assigned to Edwards AFB, California, and, after flying the X-1 there, he continued to test every new experimental and prototype aircraft in the USAF inventory. In December 1953, he flew an X-1A to Mach 2.44. Although he nearly lost control of the aircraft due to high-speed instability (inertial coupling), his record-breaking achievement earned him the 1953 Harmon Trophy.

Yeager left Edwards in 1954 and was given command of operational units in Europe and California through 1961, when he was named to command the USAF Test Pilot School at Edwards. In 1966, he assumed command of the 405th Fighter Wing, stationed at Clark AB, Philippines, and, between 1966 and 1967, he flew 127 sorties in the VIETNAM WAR. Leaving the 405th in 1967, Yeager was given a number of command assignments and was ultimately named director of the AIR FORCE INSPECTION AND SAFETY CENTER. He served in this post from 1973 to 1975, when he retired.

Yokota AB, Japan   See AIR FORCE BASES.

Z

Zulu, or Zulu time
Greenwich Mean Time; always used in conjunction with 24-hour military time, for example 1300 Zulu. In written communication, "Zulu" is designated as Z, for example: 1300Z.

U.S. Air Force Abbreviations and Acronyms

★ ────────────────────────────────────

AAC Alaskan Air Command

AAFAC Army Air Forces Antisubmarine Command

AB Air Base

ACC Air Combat Command

ADC Aerospace Defense Command

AEDC Arnold Engineering Development Center

AETC Air Education and Training Command

AF Air Force Association

AFAA Air Force Audit Agency

AFAMS Air Force Agency for Modeling and Simulation

AFB Air Force Base

AFBCA Air Force Base Conversion Agency

AFC Air Force Council

AFCAA Air Force Cost Analysis Agency

AFCC Air Force Combat Command; also, Air Force Communications Command

AFCCC Air Force Combat Climatology Center

AFCCCA Air Force Command, Control, Communications, and Computer Agency

AFCEE Air Force Center for Environmental Excellence

AFCERT Air Force Computer Emergency Response Team

AFCESA Air Force Civil Engineer Support Agency

AFCOMS Air Force Commissary Service

AFCQMI Air Force Center for Quality and Management Innovation

AFCSTC Air Force Cost Center

AFDC Air Force Doctrine Center

AFDD Air Force Doctrine Document

AFDTC Air Force Development Test Center

AFESC Air Force Engineering and Services Center

AFFMA Air Force Frequency Management Agency

AFFSA Air Force Flight Standards Agency

AFFTC Air Force Flight Test Center

AFHRA Air Force Historical Research Agency

AFHSO Air Force History Support Office

AFI Air Force Instruction

AFIA Air Force Inspection Agency; also Air Force Intelligence Agency

AFISC Air Force Inspection and Safety Center

AFIT Air Force Institute of Technology

AFIWC Air Force Information Warfare Center

AFLC Air Force Logistics Command

AFLMA Air Force Logistics Management Agency

AFLSC Air Force Legal Services Center

AFMC Air Force Materiel Command

AFMEA Air Force Management Engineering Agency

AFMIA Air Force Manpower and Innovation Agency

AFMOA Air Force Medical Operations Agency

AFMPC Air Force Military and Personnel Center

AFMSA   Air Force Medical Support Agency

AFNEWS   Air Force News Agency

AFNSEP   Air Force National Security Emergency Preparedness

AFOMS   Air Force Office of Medical Support

AFOSI   Air Force Office of Special Investigations

AFPC   Air Force Personnel Center

AFPCA   Air Force Pentagon Communications Agency

AFOSP   Air Force Office of Security Police

AFOG   Air Force Operations Group

AFOSR   Air Force Office of Scientific Research

AFOTEC   Air Force Operational Test and Evaluation Center

AFPC   Air Force Personnel Center

AFPD   Air Force Policy Document

AFPEO   Air Force Program Executive Office

AFPOA   Air Force Personnel Operations Agency

AFR   Air Force Reserve

AFRBA   Air Force Review Boards Agency

AFRC   Air Force Reserve Command

AFREA   Air Force Real Estate Agency

AFRL   Air Force Research Laboratory

AFROTC   Air Force Reserve Officer Training Corps

AFS   Air Force Specialty, or Air Force Station

AFSAA   Air Force Studies and Analyses Agency

AFSAB   Air Force Scientific Advisory Board

AFSC   Air Force Specialty Code; also Air Force Safety Center; also Air Force Systems Command

AFSOC   Air Force Special Operations Command

AFSPA   Air Force Security Police Agency

AFSPACECOM   Air Force Space Command

AFSVA   Air Force Services Agency

AFTAC   Air Force Technical Applications Center

AFWA   Air Force Weather Agency

AIA   Air Intelligence Agency

ALS   Airman Leadership School

AMC   Air Mobility Command

ANG   Air National Guard

ARPC   Air Reserve Personnel Center

AU   Air University

AVG   American Volunteer Group

AWACS   Airborne Warning and Control System

AWC   Air War College

AWFC   Air Warfare Center

AWS   Air Weather Service

BMT   Basic Military Training

C^{3}I   Command, Control, Communications, and Intelligence

C^4   Command, Control, Communications, and Computer Systems

C^{4}I   Command, Control, Communications, and Intelligence

CAP   Civil Air Patrol

CAS   Close Air Support

CCAF   Community College of the Air Force

CCT   Combat Control Team

CENTAF   U.S. Central Command Air Forces

CINC   Commander in Chief

CMSAF   Chief Master Sergeant of the Air Force

COMPUSEC   Computer Security

COMSEC   Communications Security

CONAC   Continental Air Command

CONUS   Continental United States

DOD   Department of Defense

DRU   Direct Reporting Unit

EW   Electronic Warfare

FLY TAF   Flying Training Air Force

FOA   Field Operating Agency

HAF   Headquarters Air Force

IAAFA   Inter-American Air Forces Academy

ICBM   Intercontinental Ballistic Missile

IRBM   Intermediate Range Ballistic Missile

JADF   Japan Air Defense Force

JSF   Joint Strike Fighter

JSTARS   Joint Surveillance Target Attack Radar System

MAJCOM   Major Command

MAC   Military Airlift Command

MATS   Military Air Transport Service

MPF   Military Personnel Flight

MWR   Morale, Welfare, and Recreation

NAF   Numbered Air Force

NCO   Noncommissioned Officer

NCOIC   Noncommissioned Officer in Charge

NORAD   North American Aerospace Defense Command

OJT   On-the-Job Training

OTS [Air Force] Officer Training School
PACAF Pacific Air Forces
PME Professional Military Education
QAF Quality Air Force
SAC Strategic Air Command
SDI Strategic Defense Initiative
SEI Special Experience Identifier
SERE Survival, Evasion, Resistance, and Escape
SOA Separate Operating Agency
SP Security Police
SWC Special Weapons Command
TAC Tactical Air Command
TACP Tactical Air Control Party
TECH TAF Technical Training Air Force

USAAC United States Army Air Corps
USAAF United States Army Air Force
USAAS United States Army Air Service
USAF United States Air Force
USAFE United States Air Forces in Europe
USAFM United States Air Force Museum
USAFSC United States Air Forces Southern Command
USSTAF United States Strategic Air Forces
WAF Women in the Air Force
WAFS Women's Auxiliary Ferrying Squadron
WAPS Weighted Airman Promotion System
WASP Women Airforce Service Pilots